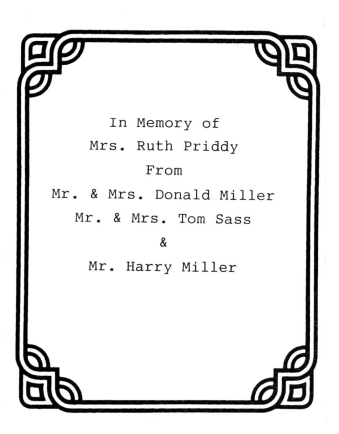

In Memory of
Mrs. Ruth Priddy
From
Mr. & Mrs. Donald Miller
Mr. & Mrs. Tom Sass
&
Mr. Harry Miller

Also available in this series

Timpani and Percussion
Jeremy Montagu

THE YALE MUSICAL INSTRUMENT SERIES

The Flute

Ardal Powell

Yale University Press
New Haven and London

For information about this and other Yale University Press publications, please contact:
U.S. Office: sales.press@yale.edu   yalebooks.com
Europe Office: sales@yaleup.co.uk   www.yaleup.co.uk

ISBN 0-300-09341-1 (hbk)
ISBN 0-300-09498-1 (pbk)

Library of Congress Control Number 2002102865

A catalogue record for this book is available from the British Library

Typeset in Columbus by Northern Phototypesetting Co. Ltd, Bolton, Lancs.
Printed in China through Worldprint

Contents

List of illustrations — *vi*

Preface — *ix*

Acknowledgements — *xi*

Introduction — *1*

1   Shepherds, monks, and soldiers — *7*

2   The flute at war and at home — *27*

3   Consort and solo: the seventeenth century — *49*

4   The early eighteenth century: the 'baroque' flute's golden age — *68*

5   Quantz and the operatic style — *88*

6   The Classical flute — *107*

7   Travelling virtuosi, concert showpieces, and a new mass audience — *127*

8   Flute mania — *144*

9   The Boehm flute — *164*

10   Nineteenth-century eclecticism — *186*

11   The French Flute School — *208*

12   The flute in the age of recording — *225*

13   The flute in the early music revival — *246*

14   The postmodern age — *264*

Abbreviations — *282*

References and notes — *283*

Index — *335*

Illustrations

page

1. Woodcut from a series (Strasbourg, 1578) attributed to Tobias Stimmer showing a woman playing a transverse flute. Print Collection, Miriam and Ira D. Wallach Division of Arts, Prints and Photographs, The New York Public Library, Astor, Lenox, and Tilden Foundations. *3*

2. A shepherd playing the flute in a manuscript of the early eleventh century. Paris: Bibliothèque nationale de France, Greek MS 533, f. 34v. *8*

3. Fiddle, flute and voice: *Der Kanzler*, a miniature from the Manesse manuscript (*c*1340). Heidelberg: Universitätsbibliothek Cod. Pal. Germ. 848, ff. 413v and 423. *9*

4. Two flutists, from a compendium of instruments shown in the *Cantigas de Santa Maria*. Madrid: Patrimonio Nacional, Escorial Library j.b.2, miniature 240. *18*

5. Miniature in the *Petites Heures* of Jean de Berry (*c*1388). Paris: Bibliothèque nationale de France, Lat 18014, f. 48v. *25*

6. Drawing by Urs Graf of four flute-playing comrades, 1523. Basel: Öffentliche Kunstsammlung, Kupferstichkabinett K. 108. *28*

7. Woodcut showing drummer and fifer, 1555. *29*

8. Fifers from the *Triumph of Maximilian I*. *31*

9. Biber's *Battalia à 10* (1673). *33*

10. Virdung's plate of wind instruments (1511), showing shawms, tabor pipe and fife, and a set of recorders. *34*

11. Jambe de Fer's diagram of the scale (1556). *35*

12. Dancers prepare for a torch dance, Flemish Book of Hours, *c*1500. London: British Library MS Add. 24089, f. 19v. *37*

13. Two almost identical images frequently used in Flemish Books of Hours, showing combination of lute and flute or recorder. (a) Flemish Book of Hours, *c*1500, London: British Library MS Add. 24098, f. 22v; (b) Simon Bening (1483–1561), Hennessy Book of Hours, Brussels: Bibliothèque Royale, MS II, 158. *40–41*

14. Version of an image derived from a prototype of *c*1520 showing female flutist, singer, and lutentist. St Petersburg: State Hermitage Museum. *45*

15. Female flute-player of *c*1600 in an allegory of Music. Vienna: Kunsthistorisches Museum, Gemäldegalerie 3080. *50*

16. Flutes and recorders from Praetorius's Theatre of Instruments (1618–19). *51*

17. Johann Sadeler, after Maerten de Vos, *The Magnificat a 5 by Cornelius Verdonck* (1585). *54*

18. *Air de cour* by Henri Le Jeune, an example of music for flute consort from Mersenne's *Harmonie Universelle* (1636). *57*

19. Two kinds of *Flustes d'Allemand*, or *Fluste d'Allemand* and *Fifre*, from Mersenne's *Harmonie Universelle* (1636). *59*

20. Robert Bonnart, *Simphonie du tympanum, du Luth, et de la Flûte d'Allemagne*, 1692. Paris: Bibliothèque nationale de France, Département des Estampes. *64*

21. André Bouys (1656–1740), *De Labarre and Musicians*. London: National Gallery. *69*

22. Michel de Labarre, *Pièces pour la flûte traversière* (1702). *71*

23. Bernard Picart (1673–1733), frontispiece from Hotteterre-le-Romain, *Principes de la Flûte traversière …* (1707). Washington, D.C.: Dayton C. Miller Collection, Music Division, Library of Congress.   *73*

24. Portrait by Jan Kupecký of a flutist believed to be Ferdinand Joseph Lemberger. Nuremberg: Germanisches Nationalmuseum.   *77*

25. Trade card for the London instrument-maker and dealer Thomas Cahusac, *c*1750. Dayton C. Miller Collection.   *87*

26. Carl Heinrich Jacob Fehling (1654–1725), drawing of the stage and orchestra, Dresden Opera House. Dresden: Sächsische Landesbibliothek Kupferstichkabinett.   *89*

27. Plan of the Dresden Opera House under Hasse, 1734–64.   *92*

28. Portrait of Johann Joachim Quantz, *c*1741. Bayreuth: Schloss Ermitage, Bayerische Verwaltung der staatlichen Schlösser, Gärten und Seen.   *96*

29. (a) French and (b) German images of Frederick the Great. Dayton C. Miller Collection.   *102–3*

30. Thomas Gainsborough (1727–88), portrait of gentleman amateur William Wollaston, *c*1759. Ipswich Borough Council Museums and Galleries.   *108*

31. Johann Georg Ziesenis (1716–76), an unofficial view of Karl Theodor von der Pfalz playing the flute (1757). Munich: Bayerisches Nationalmuseum.   *109*

32. Jacob Tromlitz, engraving of his father Johann George Tromlitz (1725–1805). Courtesy Karl Ventzke.   *116*

33. A flute lesson, frontispiece by E. F. Burney (1787). Dayton C. Miller Collection.   *120*

34. The blind virtuoso Friedrich Ludwig Dülon (1769–1826). Courtesy Chairman Frank Parnell.   *128*

35. Charles Nicholson's recommended embouchure and body position (1836). Dayton C. Miller Collection.   *133*

36. The flutist Caspar Fürstenau (1772–1819) and his son and pupil Anton Bernhard (1792–1852). Dayton C. Miller Collection.   *140*

37. Charles Nicholson's ornamented version of *Roslin Castle* (1836). Dayton C. Miller Collection.   *142*

38. H. W. T. Pottgiesser's drawing of his proposed new flute (1825). Courtesy Broekmans & van Poppel B.V.   *144*

39. Eleven fingering patterns, from Anton Bernhard Fürstenau's *Die Kunst des Flötenspiels* (1844). Dayton C. Miller Collection.   *153*

40. Mid-nineteenth-century print by J. W. Childe illustrating 'Major Wheeler' in the Farce of 'New Notions'. Dayton C. Miller Collection.   *157*

41. Flutes by Theobald Boehm, Boehm & Greve, and Boehm & Mendler. Dayton C. Miller Collection.   *165*

42. (a) Boehm's flute of 1831; (b) Gordon's flute, *c*1833; (c) Gordon's flute, *c*1838. Dayton C. Miller Collection.   *168–9*

43. Antoine Sacchetti and Theobald Boehm. Dayton C. Miller Collection.   *181*

44. Mechanism of the 1847 flute's body section.   *182*

45. The Paris Opéra Orchestra, 1868–9, by Edgar Degas. Paris: Musée D'Orsay. Réunion des Musées Nationaux.   *187*

46. John George Brown (1831–1913), *The Music Lesson*. New York: Metropolitan Museum of Art, Gift of Colonel Charles A. Fowler, 1921 (21.115.3). Photograph ©1982 The Metropolitan Museum of Art.   *194*

47. Flutes from a Rudall Carte catalogue, *c*1937. Dayton C. Miller Collection.   *201*

48. Adolphe Hennebains (1862–1914) as Pan. Courtesy Trevor Wye.   *209*

49. Jean-Louis Tulou (1786–1865). Dayton C. Miller Collection.   *213*

50. Paul Taffanel demonstrating his embouchure and body position. Courtesy Claude Dorgeuille.   *217*

51. Jean-Pierre Rampal in an HMV recording studio, *c*1950.   *226*

52. Georges Barrère and William S. Haynes, mid-1930s. Courtesy William S. Haynes Co.   *229*

53. The assembly, padding and finishing department of the William S. Haynes Co.,
    Boston, c1949. Courtesy William S. Haynes Co. 239
54. The Team: principal wind players of the Philharmonia Orchestra, London, c1950.
    Courtesy Gareth Morris. 242
55. César Charles Snoek as a student, with the beginnings of his collection of early
    instruments. Staatliches Institut für Musikforschung, Bildarchiv Preussischer Kulturbesitz. 247
56. Dayton C. Miller's collection of instruments, c1928. Dayton C. Miller Collection. 255
57. A scientific attempt to investigate the 'unsolvable problem' of vibrato.
    Gustav Bosse Verlag. 265
58. Metal flutes the subject of humorous comment, cartoon, 1922. Dayton C. Miller
    Collection. 267
59. Murray flutes, record sleeve, 1974. Courtesy Alexander Murray. 271

Efforts to trace the copyright holders of illustrations 27 and 51 were unsuccessful.

Preface

Since the late Philip Bate wrote his study of the flute a generation ago, a vast body of new knowledge has come to light about the instrument and the people who made it in earlier times, as well as about those who wrote, played, and heard its music. This new information and the fresh perspectives it brings have altered some of our most basic assumptions about the flute, along with all the other instruments.

Perhaps the most powerful new idea in music, one that emerged as more details about musical life in the past became known, is that repertoire, instruments, and playing style are – and always have been – inextricably woven together: that works conceived with a certain set of performing and listening conditions in mind lose much of their intended impact if those conditions alter, as they almost always do with time. As so many of the pieces we play and hear today were composed in ages before our own, this point has led a growing number of people to recognize that we must grasp the ideas and practices of those eras if we are to lay claim to their musical material. The tone, tuning, and character of instruments have changed so much even in the recent past that the special sound and feeling of music that moved our parents' and grandparents' generations is all but lost to us. Thus earlier instruments, so distinct from their modern forms, often hold the key to understanding the particular qualities of pieces they were meant to play. And so the history of musical instruments and performance styles, once the dusty pastime of antiquarians, has now become part of a fascinating inquiry that holds vital importance in today's cultural life.

This volume, a sort of progress report on a part of that inquiry, presents a survey of what is now known about the flute and flute-playing in the past and in the present. It is not an encyclopaedia, and does not set out to extend the boundaries of scholarship any further by contributing new material: in fact information is so copious that I have been at constant pains to find ever more drastic ways of summarizing it. The accelerating pace of discovery in recent decades makes this a dynamic and fast-changing field, so that a single definitive account lies no more within reach now than it ever did, despite all the new facts and insights we possess. But if a survey like this cannot delve deep into detail or answer all the questions it raises, I have tried to make it comprehensive enough to explore the subject in the new light in which our generation now sees it.

The invitation to write a book for this series came with a proposed structure that began with the flute of today and worked backwards, in a logical sense, from there. But I saw two objections to this quite conventional plan. The first is that it would require the reader to know something of the modern flute, whereas I think the instrument's history is far too interesting to exclude all the potential readers who could not pass this test. Secondly, since all artistic endeavour depends – knowingly or not – upon what has gone before, I think the best perspective to take on the flute and flute-playing is a historical one – that is, a view that tries to see events in the light of their own times rather than with indiscriminate hindsight. For these reasons my preferred chronology begins at the beginning and, as far as possible, works towards the present.

This book will be of interest in the first place of course to flutists, flute teachers, and flute students. Since most in the last group are young people, I planned the book to be accessible to the attentive and curious among them, as well as to musicians in general and to academic readers. That is not to say that I have felt it necessary to skip over areas where little is known or to oversimplify complex topics out of a fear that some readers would lack the patience for detailed discussion; on the contrary, I find that areas that demand critical attention always prove the most interesting to explore. But I have not assumed any specialized knowledge of music history, and where necessary have presented brief summaries of certain crucial aspects of musical theory, discussions of terminology, and similar special subjects in sidebars as an aid to non-specialists. Nonetheless, a certain amount of general familiarity with geography, history, and music is expected of all readers, and so younger ones who encounter unfamiliar names of people, places, and things may find it helpful to keep an atlas and a musical dictionary at hand. I hope that any questions that remain will, as one young person put it after reading an early draft, 'provide a spark of curiosity, leaving them wanting to learn more about music in general'.

A guide to works that will help satisfy that curiosity can be found in a separate Bibliographic Essay for each chapter, collected with the notes toward the back of the book. These essays combine acknowledgement of my scholarly debts with a survey of the literature that points out the special merits and qualities of each work – and, where necessary, warns of its faults. Sources of quotations and occasional references that need precise citation are given in notes in the usual way, but in addition I felt it important sometimes to use modern authors' names in the text itself to note contributions to scholarship (and their dates) that have played an especially important part in forming modern views. Readers with advanced knowledge who are particularly interested in this aspect of the book may find it easier to read the Bibliographic Essay for each chapter before reading the chapter itself.

A.P.
Folkers & Powell, Makers of Historical Flutes
Hudson, New York
Ash Wednesday, 2001

Acknowledgements

Working on this book has been a great privilege and learning opportunity for me. I am grateful for three terms' leave supported by grants from Furthermore, the publication programme of the J. M. Kaplan Fund (U.S.A., 1998, 1999, 2000), for Authors' Foundation grants from the Society of Authors (U.K., 1997, 1999), and for additional leave funded by my employer, Folkers & Powell, Makers of Historical Flutes (U.S.A., 2000–01).

The book has benefited in general lines and in countless details from the contributions and criticism of experts and friends so numerous that space forbids my listing them all here. My greatest debt is to Joan Davidson, M. J. Gladstone, Laurie Schafer, and Ann Birckmayer of Furthermore, and Mark LeFanu of the Society of Authors, whose financial support made it possible for me to take time away from making flutes to read and write. Malcolm Gerratt, Kevin Brown, and Robert Baldock of Yale University Press in London have kindly indulged and encouraged my somewhat unorthodox vision for the book, while Polly Fallows improved the accuracy and consistency of its text and references. The staffs of the National Sound Archive at the British Library, the New York Public Library for the Performing Arts, Music Division, and the George Sherman Dickinson Music Library, Vassar College, have been of constant help by locating and supplying documents and other materials for study. Two in particular, David Lasocki, Head of Reference Services at the William and Gayle Cook Music Library, Indiana University, and Robert Sheldon of the Dayton C. Miller Collection, Library of Congress, have repeatedly proved helpful beyond the ordinary course of duty. Susan Nelson has fed me a steady diet of ear-opening samples from her magnificent collection of early recordings of flute-playing, some of which I hope will soon become more widely available in re-issues (http://recordings.flutehistory.com). I am grateful to all these, and once again to my wife and partner, Catherine Folkers, for her patient support and encouragement.

Introduction

Tempora mutantur nos et mutamur in illis.
Times change, and we change with them.

The instrument we call simply 'flute' belongs to a large, diverse, and widely distributed family which includes any hollow object that can produce sound when the player blows air across a hole in its surface, or over an internal edge such as those in whistles and recorders. Musicians all over the world use many kinds of flute: vessel flutes like the ocarina, duct flutes like the recorder, and end-blown types like the *kena* of South America, as well as transverse ones like the *bansuri* of north India or the *di-zi* of China. Despite this variety on the global scale, Europe and the New World have seen a single type come to dominate in the modern era: a long tube held sideways, having a hole (the embouchure) near one end for the player to produce the sound, as well as a number of toneholes to control the pitch. This western instrument, along with the continuous changes in its design, uses, and playing styles, forms the subject of this book.

Though myths of the transverse flute's creation by legendary characters have long figured in its culture (ill. 1), the question of how it had actually developed first aroused general interest less than two hundred years ago. At that time, educated people were still some decades away from the stirring awareness that music, like architecture and the visual arts, had a history of its own. Only a few specialists knew anything about music more than a generation old, and historical musicology, far from being the rigorous academic discipline of today, remained the pursuit of a few dedicated individuals. Most musicians considered the collecting of obsolete musical instruments, if they knew anyone pursued such an eccentric hobby, as of no practical value.

Yet if the Victorians placed little value on art whose time had passed, except for that of classical times, their age, like our own, was obsessed with progress. They saw history as the story of a steady improvement in technology, institutions, artistic taste, and even human nature, 'a process of continuous change from a lower, simpler, or worse to a higher, more complex, or better state: progressive development'.[1] So the first people to write about the flute's history assumed that, to whatever degree instruments and music might have changed over the course of time, the most modern manifestations must be the most advanced, and therefore the best. Rather than study the musical life of earlier times to learn of their forebears' ideas and achievements, the Victorian writers cited it merely to highlight what they saw as the shortcomings of its primitive instruments, the incompetence of its musicians and theorists, and the unsatisfactory nature of its compositions according to current standards (see the essay below on pp. 285–8, 'History and criticism of the flute').

Many of the individuals dedicated and energetic enough to have gained detailed knowledge of the past already knew, of course, that such a simplistic view was inaccurate, and that 'the whole story of art is not a story of progress in technical proficiency, but a story of changing ideas and requirements'[2] – or, as the nineteenth-century collector and musicologist François-Joseph Fétis more aphoristically put it: 'Art does not progress, it transforms itself.'[3] But in the case of music, this more enlightened view remained rare until new conditions in the late twentieth century brought it to wider notice. The rise of radio and the recording industry (chapter 12), the avant-garde movement (chapter 14), the revival of folk music (including the 'Irish' flute), a new interest in ancient non-western traditions such as that of Indian classical music (with its bamboo flute, the *bansuri*), and the blossoming of period-instrument performances of early music (chapter 13) all introduced unfamiliar and challenging repertoires to a musical mainstream that had begun to fossilize. These new styles showed that the western orchestral instrumentarium, as it had taken shape in the late nineteenth and early twentieth centuries, had serious limitations for the performance of some musics other than its own.

That insight provided musicians with an urgent reason to take a deeper interest in the history of their art and its instruments. Interpretations of renaissance, baroque, and classical music multiplied. Many of them attempted to follow contemporary performance instructions and to use period instruments, some of which had never been a regular part of the orchestra. The failures as well as the successes of these experiments soon made clear even to non-expert listeners some of the ways in which instruments, musical style, and performance practice are interconnected. Many people quickly came to see that no musical work can be fully grasped without knowing how it was originally expected to be heard, any more than we can understand instruments (except in the coldest and most theoretical sense) without learning about appropriate methods of playing them in their own special repertoire.

So it is that historical studies have transformed our view of the flute's history along with our musical world over the past forty years. We can at last seek in the history of the flute not what the Victorians did, an abstract line of mechanical development, but rather a story of much greater detail, richness, and human interest: the practical and continual adaptation of a tool to the changing purposes it was meant to serve in changing times.

With this better-informed and clearer perspective, our study of the flute needs a fresh start, free of the preoccupations of the past. First, its chronological span must change. Palaeolithic, Neolithic, Bronze Age, and Iron Age finds in Spain, France, and Britain indicate that people in those times made wind instruments of various types from bone. Though some people have had the confidence to pronounce on the scales these relics produced and the kinds of music they could play, nobody has yet shown that any of the supposed prehistoric wind instruments is a transverse flute, as opposed to the end-blown kind typified by the 9,000-year-old Chinese examples brought to wide notice

Wiewol Minerve gar mißfälle	Although Minerva [Athene] is displeased
Die Pfeif/weil sie den mund verstelt:	with pipes because they distort the mouth,
Soll man sich doch nicht ärgern fon/	one should not pay her heed:
Dann sie red wie ein Weib dar von:	it is just her woman's chatter
Und vil mehr auf Poeten geben	Listen rather to the poets,
Die solche Pfeif gar hoch erheben/	who highly praise this pipe
Weil sie ihn der Natur bestehet	because it holds its own outdoors and also
Und auch zu allen Spilen gehet.	fits into all kinds of ensemble.
Die Zwerchpfeif erstlich Midas macht	The cross-flute was first crudely made
Nur auß Krauchbeinen ungeschlacht:	by Midas from the bones of cranes
Die man darnach macht auß den Roren	Later they were made from reeds;
Heut kan man sie zum schönsten boren.	today they are very finely bored.

Trans. modified from Jan LaRue and Jeanette B. Holland, 'Stimmer's Women Musicians: A Unique Series of Woodcuts', Unity Sherrington and Guy Oldham, eds, *Music Libraries and Instruments: Papers Read at the Joint Congress, 1959, of the International Association of Music Libraries and the Galpin Society* (London: Hinrichsen, 1961), 261–8, 266. The print is one of six, New York Public Library, Bartsch 37–45, Classmark MEOG+.

in *Nature* in 1999.[4] In fact, archaeology to date provides no justification for tracing the history of our transverse flutes back to those periods. Some of the Victorian writers tried to trace the modern flute to classical antiquity, but those efforts too fail to stand up to scrutiny (chapter 1).

On the other hand, the modern transverse flute's pedigree as it is generally given, beginning around 1700, is much too short. It is now clear that it extends at least three times as far back, to the twelfth century of the Christian Era. Though we know little or nothing about the instrument's repertoire, construction, or playing technique in the earlier part of that period, the ideas and mythology associated with it, as well as some of its customary uses, survived to exert a strong influence on later thought and practice. Those early influences are just as important in music as they are in the visual arts, which inherit works that provide a sense of continuity since long before the beginning of recorded history.

This study must also extend its scope beyond that of previous attempts. They asked only rather limited questions about earlier forms of the flute: who developed this or that mechanical 'improvement'? When? How did it 'advance' the mechanism, fingering, and acoustics of the flute? But because today we understand that we cannot sensibly ask questions about the design of musical instruments without also finding out in full and precise detail how the instruments are used to make music, the traditional approach holds little interest beyond an academic one. Our better understanding of the relationship between instruments and music now compels us to ask more practical and more interesting questions about each earlier flute type: What did it sound like? What kinds of people played it, what music did they play, how did they learn, and make a living? Who listened? What did these listeners hear and feel?

Questions like these have led more and more researchers to seek out the instruments themselves, instructions for playing them, and the repertoire they were intended to perform, in order to try to reassemble the practical and aesthetic conditions for earlier music-making. They have searched a wide array of other sources, including pictures of instruments being played, diaries and literary references, instrument makers' catalogues and directories, and archival records such as inventories and payment rolls, for guidance on the circumstances of performance. Editors have returned to original manuscripts and early editions of music in a search for documents that reflect the composer's own ideas about performance, rather than those of some later editor whose tastes and judgements were perhaps quite different. Those who study recent times can consult even more evocative materials: more than a century's worth of recordings, which teach us, among other lessons, how diverse performance styles were in the past, how fast and how radically styles of playing change, and how imperfectly we can rely on words to describe musical performance. While we could never gather enough information from these sources to precisely recreate an actual historic performance – even if we decided such an exercise would be worth the effort – the illuminating details turned up during attempts at reconstruction provide endless insights into the meaning of the music of the past, permitting musicians to produce more coherent, sensitive, and inspired readings of it in the present.

In other respects, this book has a narrower focus than its predecessors. Earlier treatments of the flute made a point of explaining the instrument's acoustics, chiefly in order to demonstrate the frequently tacit proposition that modern flutes were superior to earlier types, rather than merely different from them. But the Boehm flute's struggle for recognition essentially ended a hundred years ago, and a line of argument that made sense while the new instrument still had to prove itself now seems irrelevant.[5] Attempts to explain the flute's acoustics have never seemed very successful in any case: the physics and mathematics of flute design, despite advances made in the twentieth century, still are unable to describe how flutes work without reducing them to implausibly simple sketches, so that one of the leading academic researchers calls the theory of how wind instruments function 'one of the most slippery in all of musical acoustics'.[6] And while modern science may provide some insight into the workings of the comparatively straightforward modern flute, it has so far been unable to shed any useful light at all on the more complex earlier types. For all these reasons, acoustics have found no place in the present volume, except where the history of such knowledge has played a part in the flute's own story.

A full study of the flute's repertoire also lies beyond our scope, though the links among instruments, playing style, and music make this a much more relevant area of interest. Considerations of space, however, allow us to touch only on the most important aspects of composition for the flute and to mention some of the most influential or significant repertoire at key junctures in its history.

The purpose of this volume is not merely to present facts, though of course those are available in greater abundance than ever before to anyone who cares to seek them. What it now seems more important to discover is a sense of where flutists are and where their cultural heritage lies. While today mechanical training has reached unprecedented levels and the flute's repertoire is broader than ever, competition, even for school ensemble positions, has become increasingly ruthless. Live musical performance itself becomes more and more an appendage of the multi-media entertainment industry, which competes for mass attention by appealing to the lowest common denominator: the familiar, the predictable, and the populist. This battlesome world places a higher value on the mechanics of expression, 'tone, [finger] technique, articulation, and intonation', than on what is being expressed, 'the music, the interpretation, and the personality of both music and player'.[7] The pressure to excel in such demanding and inhospitable surroundings conspires to make flute-playing itself a dull, automatic, paint-by-numbers activity rather than a creative one that springs from a warm, human sympathy for the special distinctiveness of real musical expression.

A rich sense of heritage, I feel sure, could do much to enrich the sterile music-making so often heard today from players of historical as well as modern flutes. Most obviously it provides perspective, enlarging our awareness of time from a scale of minutes and our own busy lives to one that stretches over decades and centuries. An expanded time-scale alone can help us understand varied ideas about flute-playing and develop a sense of musical style broad enough to leave space for a vivid appreciation of essential details. But perhaps more important, the very action of investigating the history of flute-playing holds the promise of making us – flutists or listeners – more aware of our musical selves. We encounter facts that challenge our preconceptions: we learn how those preconceptions came about, and eventually we become conscious of our own particularities and earn the ability to transcend them. Nobody can learn of the distinctions earlier flutists made between different instruments, musics, and styles of playing and remain convinced that today's relatively uniform manner of playing is the only correct one that has ever existed, as a surprising number of people still hold. On the other hand, finding a way to put such a diversity of historical information to use in present-day interpretation poses a personal challenge to each musician: everyone has to choose for him- or herself how much to use, and whether to use it out of a genuine conviction that it is musically compelling, or merely because we have been told it is historical or traditional. Accepting this challenge strengthens our understanding by forcing us to adjust our perspectives frequently. Thus we can learn to sense creative possibilities in our own moment that would otherwise remain blocked or hidden. Those creative possibilities, rather than the mere factual information that inspires them, are the rewards that await flutists willing to follow the thread as the flute 'transforms itself' again and again.

Chapter 1

Shepherds, monks, and soldiers

Custom dictates that the story of the modern flute begins around the year 1700, when the instrument's baroque form is supposed to have been invented and its first printed music published. This convenient habit situates us in relatively familiar territory, that of a time only a few generations ago when people read and wrote books we can still make sense of today, played upon instruments built by makers whose names we can learn, and performed music preserved in notation that a little practice enables us to interpret plausibly.

By these standards, the six centuries before the Baroque era seem almost impenetrably remote. First of all, medieval people expressed themselves in Latin and in unfamiliar forms of our vernacular languages. More inconvenient still, they dealt with ideas and symbols in ways that often seem disconcertingly childlike to us sophisticated postmoderns, accustomed as we are to literal veracity and lucid expression. The Middle Ages offers us different, non-factual testimony: making sense of it challenges our interpretive powers and our imaginations.

So let us first consider the limits to our inquiry, and then ask what we can learn within those boundaries. All we know of the medieval flute comes from a handful of images and a few fragments of poetry and other writing, material that can present us at best with 'scarcely more than a damaged mosaic', in the memorable words of Christopher Page (1986). No transverse flutes at all survive from the Middle Ages, so the only practical insight we can gain into what the medieval flute may have sounded like or how it may have been played comes from parallels with traditional cultures in parts of the world most of us will never visit. Only a fraction of medieval music was written down, but even that small collection comes without instructions for instrumentation, still less for performance. None of it indicates that it should be played by a flute, though as we shall see, scattered hints suggest that some of it could have been so performed. We might easily conclude that much of the flute's repertoire was different in nature from the written music we know in that it was improvised or played by ear. And yet the distinction we make between written and orally transmitted music is partly an illusion. In many cases the music in manuscripts had already been known for many years – indeed music that everybody knows does not need writing down, and even pieces that do occur in written form often continued (and continue) to evolve, as we know from folk music.

Even today, a notated composition forms only one ingredient in the recipe for performance. Before a musician can turn a written score into any kind of sound,

2. A shepherd playing the flute, from the sermons of St Gregory of Nazianzus in a manuscript of the early eleventh century. Flutes were most commonly associated with nature and the pastoral life in Byzantine images such as this.

3. (*facing page*) Fiddle, flute, and voice: *Der Kanzler*, a miniature by Meister Rumslaut from the Manesse manuscript (*c*1340) of songs by Johannes Hadlaub. How the instruments and singer may have performed the single line of music together is uncertain.

she must first know how to interpret it, ideally in light of the ideas and practices of its times. In dealing with familiar mainstream repertoire we may take this step only unconsciously. But lack of consciousness is never a good thing in performance or art in general. Fortunately, studying medieval music unconsciously is impossible, since it makes us confront questions we need to ask of all music: what is it for, who is meant to sing or play it, with what instruments or forces, on what occasions, and before what audience? What is it meant to communicate, and how?

This is why the fragmentary and inconsistent evidence in early pictures, poems, and other writings is worth exploring. The first step of our journey into the past is to recognize the strangeness of that place, the otherness of the world before our time, the difference of earlier musicians and listeners from ourselves. We must take nothing on trust, and question everything, our own deepest assumptions most of all. Each piece of testimony needs careful testing before we decide how to interpret it. Even when considering relatively recent times we need to give due regard to where our information comes from and to what extent we can rely on its accuracy. In a landscape like that of medieval Europe, the questions we must ask about what we know and how we know it stand out in sharp relief.

Compared with fiddles or harps, which figure much more often in images and texts, the flute was clearly a rare instrument in the Middle Ages. Or to state it more precisely: flutes only infrequently appear in the musical situations depicted in medieval art – however those might correspond to those in real life. When flutes do appear, they often act as emblems for figures of myth and legend, as well as of nature and the idealized pastoral or spiritual life. Illustrations, then, are just as likely to represent imaginary scenes as they are to record reality. This is especially true when combinations of musical instruments are shown: quite often instrumental groupings serve as emblems or symbols in themselves, and we cannot assume that such ensembles regularly played together.

If it is unwise to take pictures at face value, we may consciously interpret what we see. Most medieval writing and illustration had a religious context: the monasteries, the crucibles of literacy, learning, and art, produced most of the period's books, the majority of which were studies on religious topics or daily psalm books. We would be rash to read illustrations from such sources as though they were diagrams in an encyclopaedia: often the artist may have based a decision as to how to represent an instrument or its playing position on compositional considerations rather than on an effort to show exactly what he saw. Thus the flutist in the Manesse manuscript of *c*1340 (ill. 3), the only one of this period shown holding the flute to his right, mirrors the posture of the fiddler opposite so that both players are pointing their instruments to the centre of the image.

Interpreting written materials presents another problem. Writers rarely referred unambiguously to the transverse flute, since 'flute' was a general term that could include recorders and whistle-like instruments – as *die Flöte* still does in German (see p. 37). We would search in vain for a description of a professional musician as a 'flutist' or 'flute-player', since the role of musicians was far less specialized than today, and performers by most accounts played all sorts of instruments, strings, wind, and percussion. While a jongleur or minstrel might have spent less time than a modern musician studying flute technique, he probably knew more about creating a festive atmosphere and holding the attention of an audience.

The incompleteness of literary and iconographical evidence on the medieval flute presents us with what Christopher Page calls the 'iceberg problem'. Writing of twelfth- and thirteenth-century France, he observes: 'The forms which dominate our view of secular music-making are those which survive, but the view of contemporaries was dominated by material that left relatively little trace'.[1] And Page was writing about the bowed and plucked strings, instruments of high status about which we have much more information than about the lower-caste woodwinds. Medieval woodwind music, even more than that for strings, must have relied largely on traditions of memory and improvisation. Scholarship is silent about such traditions except where they manifest themselves in written evidence, for how else except through writing would we know of extinct traditional practices? Yet because written music made up only a small part of life in the Middle Ages, we cannot focus only on what Howard Mayer Brown

(1989) called 'the fixed and written repertoires of European art music' without our inquiry becoming irrelevant.

Many early pictures of flute-players represent mythical scenes. Myths are by definition unreliable, and some of those about the flute are, to say the least, highly improbable in a factual sense. Greece, India, and Egypt have inherited legends holding that the flute was an invention of the gods – whether Pan or Athene in Greece, Krishna in India, or Osiris in Egypt. Among these only the legend of the Greek shepherd-god Pan has passed into the heritage of western flutists. Shown as a bearded man with the legs, horns and ears of a goat, Pan was an Arcadian cave-dwelling deity who haunted the forests and fields. A god of fertility, he pursued the nymph Syrinx, whom the river-nymphs saved from his unbridled male sexuality by changing her into a reed-bed. On her escape in this way, Pan sighed across the reeds, and their moaning sound inspired him to create the pan-pipes or *syrinx* by binding together reeds of unequal length. Pan's instrument was no transverse flute, but that small detail never stood in the way of an association between flutes of all kinds and the pastoral.

Among the three legendary birthplaces of the flute only India in fact has a transverse instrument. Egypt has an end-blown or oblique variety, the *nay*, which western observers have sometimes mistaken for the transverse kind in images dating both from ancient times and from the Greco-Roman period. Transverse flutes in Indian classical music today are of two kinds: a short instrument of about 30cm called the *menali* or *pulangoil*, used in the southern Carnatic music, and a northern, or Hindustani, instrument about twice as long in its commonest size, called the *bansuri*. The southern instrument has seven or eight fingerholes, and the *bansuri* six or seven. Although we do not know how closely these resemble the instruments of nearly a thousand years ago, their simplicity would support the contention that the Indian flutes have not changed much in that time. We shall see that the proportions and appearance of the flutes in many of the medieval illustrations that do survive, such as the *Cantigas de Santa Maria* (ill. 4), certainly seem reminiscent of the Indian flutes we know today.

Curt Sachs, one of the pioneers of the study of instruments in the early twentieth century, wrote in *The History of Musical Instruments* that the Chinese *chi* was the earliest recorded transverse flute, datable to the ninth century B.C.E., but that it may have derived from a central Asian flute that was even older. The *chi* was principally a ritual instrument, while another sort, called the *di*, originally a military instrument, was later used in opera and other kinds of music. Whether the Chinese and Indian forms are historically connected is not clear. Both are played left-handed, that is, held to the player's left and with the right hand uppermost. That is also the most common orientation in medieval depictions of flute-playing. It is usually assumed that some kind of Indian flute became known in Byzantium around the tenth century, and was thence transmitted to Europe. In support of this theory, Liane Ehlich (1984) notes that many of the medieval flutes are shown with bindings or mounts at the ends, like those of the Indian bamboo instrument, and she concludes her study with the deduction that, like Indian flutes, medieval instruments had a wide bore, thin walls, and a compass of up to three octaves.

Classical antiquity seems to have done without a transverse flute. Neither the ancient Greeks nor quite probably the Romans knew the transverse flute at all. The Greek *aulos* and the Roman *tibia* are not flutes as has sometimes been thought, but rather windcap instruments; that is, they sound by means of a reed enclosed within a cover, like a bagpipe chanter. Post-classical Greek and Etruscan civilizations, on the other hand, may perhaps have known the transverse flute – but the evidence is scanty and ambiguous enough that this must still be considered doubtful. Athanaeus wrote in his *Histories of Poseidonos of Apameia* (135–50 B.C.E.) of the *photinx* – a new Greek word invented, as Raymond Meylan has suggested, to denote the transverse flute:

> They took along donkeys laden with wine and all sorts of provisions, and also *photinges* and *monauloi*, instruments for feasting, and not for war.[2]

And yet we have no description of the actual instrument, so the *photinx* could have been another sort of instrument than a transverse flute.

An Etruscan funeral urn or sarcophagus of the late second or early first century B.C.E. apparently depicts a transverse flute player holding his instrument to the right, with his left shoulder hunched under the blowing end.[3] This carving, however, is the only plausible indication of the transverse flute's existence in the Roman world, whereas evidence for the transversely-held reed instrument the *plagiaulos* is more abundant. It would be rash, then, to pin on this single indication any assertion that the Etruscans possessed a transverse flute.

Images of transverse flutes in Byzantine culture provide our first clues about the instrument just outside the borders of the European world-view. According to Liane Ehlich, tenth- and eleventh-century Byzantine manuscript illustrations provide hundreds of images of flutes, most often held to the player's right. These representations appear to blend the instrument's legendary connotations of nature and the spirit world with reality, such as in a frequently-depicted scene of the birth of Zeus, in which it accompanies dancing alongside drum, lyre, cymbals and voice. The transverse flute is often shown too in the hands of shepherds, as are reed pipes and duct flutes. One such rustic flutist perches on a rock in an early eleventh-century copy of the sermons of St Gregory of Nazianzus (ill. 2), while in the accompanying sermon St Gregory describes the rebirth of nature at Eastertide. The shepherd-flutist's posture is worth noting, as something like it is shown in other pictures: he holds his instrument to the left, turns his head to the right and hunches up his right shoulder to rest the flute on it. In another Greek manuscript the young King David is shown as a shepherd. Surrounded by his herd, he is holding his flute to his right in a more relaxed posture, while an angel in the accompanying poem calls upon him to leave his flocks. Perhaps both these images gain resonance from the myth of Pan. When seventeenth- and eighteenth-century song and opera composers presented shepherds and shepherdesses as idealized individuals endowed with innocence and perfect love, it seems clear they were drawing on a well of mythology that extended back at least to the Byzantine world.

Mythology seems absent from one depiction of a flutist, in a wall painting at Hagia Sophia, Kiev, showing a group of acrobats of the Imperial Byzantine Circus playing flute, trumpets or shawms, lute, psaltery, and cymbals. In such an apparently realistic scene we may regard the instruments as fairly true to life. In that case we should note that the flute looks as though its outer form is conical and that it is blown at the narrow end, a form unlikely to be due to perspective since the concept was unknown at the time.

A small ivory casket dated to the tenth century shows a male figure, naked but for a cloak, holding a transverse flute to his left and resting its stopped end on his right shoulder, which is hunched and rather exaggerated in size.[4] Perhaps the figure represents Pan: the god is often depicted naked with stylized curly hair, pointed ears like those of a sheep or goat, and horns, as in the popular image of Satan that survives today. The Florentine figure lacks the horns, but resembles Pan in other respects. Another ivory casket of the tenth century shows a centaur with fiery wings holding a flute in the same way as the Florentine figure.[5]

Because these images from Byzantine culture are the earliest representations of transverse flute players, the instrument itself is reasonably supposed to have travelled to Europe from the East along with other aspects of Byzantine art. It remains unclear whether shepherds of old really did play transverse flutes among their flocks, or whether the flute simply served to identify them as shepherds to the viewer. In any case shepherds are often shown playing other instruments besides the flute: Italian images of the following few centuries invariably give them bagpipes or reed pipes rather than transverse flutes, which seem to have been unknown beyond the Alps in the Middle Ages. But what matters more is that the *idea* of flute-playing shepherds seems to have been transmitted westward along with the artistic style of the images.

Bridging the gap between the Byzantine images and those of Europe itself is a bronze aquamanile, or water-vessel, of *c*1100, found in eastern Slovakia and now in the National Museum, Budapest. It depicts a centaur beating a drum, and supporting on his back a tiny human figure who plays a short, stout flute to his left. Probably the centaur represents Chiron, who taught Achilles the art of music, among other things. We can hardly doubt that this representation, at least, is not meant to depict a realistic scene, though to judge by later indications the pairing of flute and drum may indeed reflect an actual practice.

The principal instruments for performing art music in the early Middle Ages were the bowed and plucked strings: fiddle, rebec, harp, psaltery, and gittern. The transverse flute appears only occasionally along with other instruments such as portative organ and hurdy-gurdy, and until the fourteenth century, when it appears in France and Spain, seems to have been known only in the Holy Roman Empire, or the lands loosely known as Germany. This is probably the source of the designations *flûte d'Allemagne* and 'German flute' for the transverse instrument.

Most instrumentalists of the Middle Ages, professional minstrels who worked for courts or civic authorities, were illiterate. They learned their trade by apprenticeship and experience rather than from books, yet for information about music in medieval Europe we must rely largely on writings by monks, nuns, and priests, who though they of course had liturgical music of their own were probably only distantly acquainted with profane instrumental music.

Flahute traversaine, fleuthe traversaine, flaüste traversienne, flaüste brehaingne, traversaine, fleute, flatilla, floite, floet.... Did medieval writers and musicians name instruments consistently, or haphazardly?

We would be wrong to assume that because medieval terminology does not fit our expectations it is therefore confused or inexact in itself. Our term 'flute', though it indicates a transverse instrument and excludes recorders and whistles, is valid for the *bansuri*, the baroque flute, the traditional Irish instrument, and the Boehm flute – though not for the piccolo or the fife (for this term, see p. 37). Christopher Page draws a witty parallel between the terminology of instruments and underwear: the modern French *culotte(s)* is equivalent to the English 'shorts', 'tights', 'breeches', and 'knickers', yet French speakers do not feel that *culotte* is an imprecise term. Page also draws to our attention the almost limitless forms of a modern instrument covered by the term 'guitar': acoustic, electric, six-string, twelve-string, with f-holes or rosettes, with flat or curved bellies.[1]

In attempting to separate mentions of transverse flutes from those of recorders, tabor pipes, and other duct flutes, we are asking medieval terminology to make more of this particular distinction than it was accustomed to doing. To interpret references to the 'flute' we first need to distinguish between different languages and periods, but also, less obviously, between usages. A writer like Machaut, enumerating as many instruments as he can think of, will take care to multiply the entries in his list by including both *flaüstes traversiennes* and *flaüstes, dont droit joues quant tu flaüstes.* Yet another writer with a different purpose, such as Konrad of Mengenberg, will classify all reedless woodwinds together as *flatillas*, since discriminating between types would have no significance for him. As Joscelyn Godwin has written:

[Machaut] is writing not as a musician but as a poet, and a medieval epic poet at that, whose object is to fill his listeners' minds with images to the extent that they lose themselves in the story. This poetry loses much of its magic if it is read silently, rather than listened to: on the printed page it seems naïve, the rhymes forced, the whole thing rather overdone. But when read aloud these names are like an incantation, summoning visions of music that never was heard on earth. And in this way it resembles exactly the carved and painted visions of human and celestial musicians whose concerns far transcend the lowly realm of organology.[2]

Long poems in the vernacular (a local language other than Latin) began to appear in this period, containing descriptions of musical performance and perhaps using music as the medium for their performance in public. Harping is heard in the heroes' halls of the ninth- or tenth-century Old English epic poem *Beowulf,* though eleventh-century Old French epic poetry such as the *Song of Roland* (c1080) contained no instruments beyond the trumpets of war and the horn of the hero. Later stories such as those of Arthur and Tristan belong to the genre of courtly Romance, whose heroes, while still warriors, take time to woo women, sing, and play the harp.

In the years between about 1050 and 1200 the troubadours appeared at the courts of Provence together with their most favoured instrument, the fiddle. Like most medieval instrumentalists, the troubadours were professional entertainers, expected to bring a festive atmosphere to noble assemblies, often after meals. But the fact that their performances were designed for a particular purpose other than to satisfy their own creative drive is not to say their art was superficial or slight. Although some of their music survives in written form, their performances, whatever they were like, were events rather than objects, that is to say they were crafted in the moment rather than read from a script. And despite the conjectures of some early twentieth-century writers on the subject, we have no record of their using wind instruments.

Not until the twelfth century do we find the transverse flute in western literature or art, and then it is shown in the hands not of a human figure but, once again, one from pagan mythology. In one of the two earliest representations of transverse flute-playing in western art, we see sirens, with the faces and hands of women but the feet and wings of birds of prey. One of them plays the flute, holding the instrument to her left and tilting her head towards her right shoulder to reach the mouth-hole, while another siren plays the harp and a third sings. In the sermon that the miniature illustrates, the siren's flute is called *tybia*, a word that literally means 'leg bone' but was also the name of a Roman reed pipe. The word is given in German as *swegel*, a Gothic word often used in Germanic lands for all kinds of flute. The original image was found in a manuscript entitled *Hortus Deliciarum*, compiled by the twelfth-century Benedictine Abbess Herrad von Landsberg of Hohenburg Sainte-Odile in Alsace.[6] The work is sometimes referred to as an encyclopaedia, but it is better described as a compendium of sermons and other educational religious writings and images, drawing widely from pagan mythology and the classical authors as well as from Christian teachings. The effect of the sirens' music-making on the ship's crew is meant to remind us of the fate of those who fall prey to the seductions of the world. Although the sirens are not humans and the scene represented is allegorical rather than literal, Herrad's grouping of voice and instruments may well represent something real. Evidently the scene is an update of the Greek myth in which three sirens, whom Odysseus escaped by tying himself to the mast and sealing his crew's ears with wax, lured mariners to shipwreck with the sound of their voices. Herrad certainly intended the combination of voice, flute, and harp to evoke an even more irresistible ideal of musical beauty than that of the unaccompanied voices in the Greek version. In view of the company the flute keeps in other religious illustrations of the period, perhaps the ensemble was even a common one.

Psalters, the books that contained the texts of the psalms chanted in the daily religious office, were the most common books of the Middle Ages: examples with elaborately decorated page borders and initial capitals, often showing scenes and figures from daily life, were commissioned from monastic workshops by rich noble patrons for their personal use. A second twelfth-century Benedictine illustration, in an initial 'B' in the psalter of Wiblingen, a monastery near Ulm, resembles Herrad's in that it shows the flute being played in combination with other instruments, in this case a fiddle and a harp played by King David.[7] Another psalter from the same region, the Würzburg-Ebrach Psalter, contains an illustration of a transverse flute as part of an allegorical grouping in an illuminated initial 'B'.[8] Inside the letter one minstrel is shown playing the flute while others play organ, bells, and hurdy-gurdy, with David enclosed in a decorative loop left of the letter's centre. Fiddle, drum, and horn are banished to the letter's perimeter, along with fabulous beasts that belong to the devil.[9] Gianni Lazzari (1997) notes the presence of a transverse flute in an ensemble with harp, fiddle, and rote, in an illustration in Rudolf von Ems's *Weltchronik* of *c*1255–70.[10] Since the same combination of instruments occurs in Ulrich von Türheim's *Der starke Rennewart* (*c*1300),[11] Lazzari concludes that such an ensemble may actually have existed in Austrian and Bavarian aristocratic circles in the thirteenth century.

We can be reasonably sure that by the late thirteenth century the flute was in use by musicians outside Germany, since it is included in a French literary set-piece, *Cleomadés* (c1285), by Adenet le Roi, listing the musical instruments owned by a famous minstrel.[12] Adenet, himself the chief minstrel at the court of Gui de Damperre, Count of Flanders, was following a not uncommon literary convention by displaying his encyclopaedic knowledge of music in this extensive enumeration: it seems unlikely that even the wealthiest minstrel could have actually owned and played his long list of instruments. In fact the device of cataloguing musical instruments seems not to have belonged to poets alone: Joscelyn Godwin (1977) has suggested that certain ecclesiastical stone carvings and brasses can be considered as idealized 'collections' of instruments intended to catalogue the artist's astonishing knowledge. Although there is no confirmation that most of the instruments named were ever used in the performances of minstrels during and after banquets, the list itself conveys the richness and variety of courtly music-making in general.

Although Adenet's list is not the earliest such instrumentarium, it gives the first unmistakable literary reference to transverse flutes:

La sont trestout si estrument,	Every sort of instrument was there
qui valent un granment d'argent:	that was worth any money:
harpes, rotes, gigues, vïoles,	harps, rotes, fiddles, viols,
leuus, quitaires et citoles,	lutes, gitterns, and citoles,
et tinpanes et micanons,	and dulcimers and half-canons [small psalteries],
rubebes et salterïons	rebecs and psalteries.
Tabours et muses et flajos	Tabors and pipes and whistles
y a assez, grelles et gros,	there were many, small and large,
flahutes d'argent traversaines,	silver [valuable?] transverse flutes,
estives, cornés et douçaines,	hornpipes, cornetts and dulcians,
et d'autres instrumens assés	and so many other instruments
que ne vous ai pas tous nonmés.	that I have not told you all their names.
Se j'ere la, jes venderoie	If I had been there, I would have sold them
et de l'argent me cheviroie,	and come into some money,
car de nul instrument ne sai …[13]	for I do not know [how to play] any instrument …

Of the three references to silver (*l'argent*) in this short passage, two clearly refer to money. Perhaps, then, *flahutes d'argent traversaines* are costly instruments, or those decorated in silver, or perhaps the rarity of the type made them valuable. Or the adjective 'silver' could conceivably refer to their tone. The final possibility, and surely the remotest, is that the tubes themselves were made of silver. Even a tube having walls no thicker than bamboo would have been desperately heavy as well as extremely expensive.

In the late thirteenth century solmization, or the naming of notes with syllables, seems to have entered instrumental playing, and the gamut, or scale, became the

Modes are the arrangement of tones and semitones in a scale that give tonal character to melodies. To play all the three major and three minor modes commonly used in medieval music, an instrument would have to be able to play semitones between every pair of degrees. But each mode has no more than two semitones. Thus it is possible to transpose any melody to lie well on an instrument even without using sharpened or flattened notes. Semitones lie between pairs of notes in bold.

Major modes

Mixolydian, like the major scale with natural 7th
GABCDEFG
Ionian, like the major scale
CDEFGABC
Lydian, with a sharp 4th
FGABCDEF

Minor modes

Dorian, like the ascending melodic minor scale with a natural 7th
DEFGABCD
Aeolian, like the natural minor
ABCDEFGA
Phrygian, not like any modern scale
EFGABCDE

Major modes with Ionian and Lydian transposed to start on G:

Mixolydian:	GABCDEFG
Ionian:	GABCDEF♯G
Lydian:	GABC♯DEF♯G

Minor modes with Aeolian and Phrygian transposed to start on D:

Dorian:	DEFGABCD
Aeolian:	DEFGAB♭CD
Phrygian:	DE♭FGAB♭CD

Source: Hendrik van der Werf, *The Chansons of the Troubadours and Trouvères* (Utrecht: A. Oosthoek's Uitgaversmaatschappij, 1972), 53–9.

basis of musical education. This did not necessarily indicate that reading notation provided the foundation for performance or even that musicians ever needed to use written music. All it meant was that a system for easily determining the positions of the semitones in the scale came into common use. Of the six note-names, ut, re, mi, fa, sol, la, the most important to know were mi, which had a semitone above, and fa, which had a semitone below, since on an instrument with only a few semitones available, the position of mi and fa determined what note a melody needed to begin on to make it lie correctly. Incidentally, the medieval system of solmization closely parallels that still practised by Indian musicians, in which the names of the notes do not indicate their absolute pitch, only their relationship to one another. This raises a question as to whether medieval instrumentalists transposed music to fit on their instruments. That would seem like an obvious solution to us, but then so is shifting hand position on the neck of a stringed instrument – a technique not mentioned in Jerome of Moravia's instructions for the *rubeba* or rebec (probably Paris, *c*1280), which hold that once the fourth finger has been used to produce the ninth note on the higher string, no higher notes can be played. If what we would call transposition was practised, it might have worked as shown above in the text panel, 'Medieval modes'. On the other hand, perhaps an activity like this is too straightforward and instinctive to deserve the name of 'transposition'.

4. Two flutists, from a compendium of instruments shown in the *Cantigas de Santa Maria* (late thirteenth or early fourteenth century). The players' posture and eye contact, similar to those of players in many of the manuscript's other miniatures, may indicate that they are tuning their instruments together.

None of the depictions of flutists mentioned so far contain any hint as to what sort of music they played. But a late thirteenth or early fourteenth-century illustration that appears to link instrumental performance with a particular vocal repertoire is found in a Spanish collection of monophonic sacred songs in the Galician language made by, or at the direction of, King Alfonso X the Wise, King of Castile and León (1221–84). The illustrations in the *Cantigas de Santa Maria* depict altogether more than forty different instruments, a far richer and more varied instrumentarium than French or Italian sources of the same period. Scholars do not unanimously agree that the miniatures show the *Cantigas* themselves being performed: for one thing the variety of instruments shown is so great that it is difficult to believe they all played the same kind of music. In any case, nine years after Alfonso's death his son employed 27 salaried musicians at court, including a Jew, and 13 Arabs or Moors, of whom two were women. One of the miniatures shows two seated flutists (ill. 4).

The players' hands are shown wrapped around the instruments, as though the fingerholes were large ones like those of the north Indian bamboo flute, which is played with the middle joint of the fingers rather than with their tips. Yet the players' left hands probably do not indicate the positions of the holes, as they are too near the middle of the flute to be acoustically workable unless a vent hole on the player's side of the tube provides its effective end point. Although both instruments are about the same length and are held to the player's left, the picture indicates several obvious differences between them. One flute is of a darker material and somewhat thicker than the other, which clearly shows bands that may represent ornamental wrapping or turning, or possibly even material to strengthen a joint between two sections.

The *Cantigas* flute-players stand apart from other surviving medieval depictions because of their close ties to Arabic and European musical cultures. Alfonso the Wise's courts at Toledo and Seville evidently provided a two-way exchange of musical traditions between Muslim and Christian, Moor and European. The Arab musical culture that flourished during the Muslim occupation of Spain still survives in the form of the Andalusian court ensembles in Algeria, Tunisia, and Morocco. Exiles from Spain between the tenth and twelfth centuries carried these traditions from Seville, Córdoba, and Valencia to Tunis, Tlemcan, and Fez, along with later emigrations in the fifteenth century from Granada to Fez and Tetuán. Today's musicians striving to bring medieval European secular monody to life use the traditional forms of instrument technology and playing techniques in North Africa as a living example. Indeed the idea of using living traditions to supplement written historical information is not a new one: in 1555 Pierre Belon du Mans wrote:

> Those who wish to find out something about the music of ancient instruments will find better material for their enquiries in the instruments found in Greece and Turkey than in what has been written about them.[14]

At the same time the music of the *Cantigas* contains borrowings from well-known troubadour-style sources beyond the Pyrenees. More than a hundred of the songs refer to France, Italy, England, and other foreign countries. Thus the *Cantigas* illustrations seem to provide authority for instrumental practice in the whole of Europe.

A somewhat later source from France shows flutes in an altogether different role. A manuscript of the *Roman d'Alexandre*, illustrated by Jehan de Grise in 1339–44, contains marginal drawings and miniatures that show soldiers and sentries playing the instruments on high battlements, most often alongside large bells, drums, bagpipes, and trumpets.[15] These pictures, together with references in the great German saga, the *Niebelungenlied* (c1300), comparing the sound of the flute to the trombone and trumpet, indicate that a military form of the flute, or at least a military use for it, existed in the early fourteenth century, in both France and Germany.

Another fourteenth-century miniature is found in Jeanne d'Evreux's *Book of Hours*, a personalized prayer book with lavish hand-painted decoration, illustrated by Jean Pucelle in c1325.[16] The effect of Pucelle's whimsical and fantastic decoration is, as Emanuel Winternitz noted (1988), 'almost sacrilegious', as well as typical of northern European artists from Flanders, France, and England. A surprising number of the creatures are playing musical instruments. 'Surprising, that is,' comments Winternitz, 'to the spectator who is not familiar with the teeming, colourful musical life of the Middle Ages, and especially with the number and variety of musical instruments as compared with the standardised specimens which make up our modern symphony orchestra.'[17]

French and Flemish miniatures and border decorations of the fourteenth century often borrow from the style of German models. Howard Mayer Brown and Jane Bowers (1979, 1989) suggest either that the artists were copying German pictures, or that the instrument itself travelled westwards. Though Germanic and French lands knew the transverse flute by the thirteenth century, Brown has noted that the transverse flute is never shown in Italian art of the fourteenth: not a single example appears in his comprehensive index of Trecento pictures with musical subject-matter.[18] If the pictures are credible evidence, then, the flute was still quite unknown beyond the Alps at this period. Even a late fifteenth-century writer from Ferrara is quoted by Sachs in his *Real-Lexikon* as being unfamiliar with transverse flutes, which are described as 'Falauti alemani che si sonano a mezo el flauto, et non in testa, come si fanno li nostri' (German flutes that are blown at the middle of the flute and not on the top as ours are).

Though written information about instrumental performance in the Middle Ages is scarce, it does turn up in some of the most surprising places. Konrad of Mengenberg's *Yconomia*, a manual on household management written between 1328 and 1352, has recently been brought to light by Christopher Page.[19] The work contains a chapter on 'servants who entertain', as opposed to those with administrative duties, or professional minstrels whom he calls *ioculatores*. These domestic musicians lived quite differently from those travelling individuals who, though they may have come in useful as messengers, mediators, and spies, had no legal rights and were excluded from society and the moral code in village and town. Konrad classifies musician-servants in an institutionalized hierarchy. He identifies three groups: singers, instrumentalists, and imitators of birdsong. He subdivides instrumentalists into string or wind players, and wind players into *macrofistulus* and *microfistulus*, that is, players of larger or smaller pipes. The *macrofistulus* plays the loud brass or reed instruments of the trumpet and shawm families, which 'sound well together according to due proportions in fourths, fifths and octaves just as the character of the melody requires'. Of the *microfistulus* Konrad writes:

> The microfistulus is the one who makes music on a smaller pipe. And I call those pipes 'smaller', named 'flutes' [*flatillas*], because they give a sound with little blowing of the breath of the mouth, but the noise is weak and feeble. Whence they sometimes play together with fiddles.

Konrad leaves it unclear why 'weak and feeble' instruments should necessarily play with fiddles, and his words do not necessarily refer to the transverse flute in any case, but his testimony to this instrumental combination is amplified by another piece of evidence so as to constitute one of the very few indications we have as to how the flute was used. We can see the fiddle and the transverse flute together in illustrations in the Manesse manuscript, produced in the monastery of Ötenbach near Zurich in about 1340, about the same time as Konrad was writing (ill. 3). The miniatures are found in a manuscript containing 54 songs by the *Minnesänger* (a German equivalent of a troubadour) Johannes Hadlaub, which of course suggests that the music itself might have been performed by the instruments in the illustrations. The question of whether or not the monophonic songs of the Provençal troubadours were ever accompanied by instruments has been much discussed, with a consensus emerging that they never were. Yet the Manesse manuscript seems to tell a different story concerning the Germanic *Minnesänger* repertoire. Still, the music in the Manesse manuscript is monophonic, that is, it consists of only one line of written music. Thus the function of the instruments remains unclear: perhaps they doubled the vocal line, or played drones, or perhaps the instrumentalists wove parts improvised on the spot around the written line of music. A practice known as 'fifthing' or 'sights', as described in English manuals on vocal discant from the thirteenth to fifteenth centuries, allowed the singer to create a new part using both parallel and contrary motion and all the consonant intervals against the main part: the unison, third, fifth, sixth, and octave. Or perhaps other parts were improvised in a freer manner like that of folk singers and players in many cultures today. If the Manesse illustrations are a trustworthy guide, flutes were not standardized in size and pitch even within the same period and in the same place: the fiddler in each of two illustrations that show flute and fiddle together holds his instrument on his right shoulder and bows with his right arm, but the two flute players have instruments different in appearance, one held to the left and the other to the right. But as we saw towards the beginning of this chapter, the artist may have had his own reasons for showing the flute pointed to the right.

In chapter 49 of his treatise, Konrad gives an interesting explanation for the action of various instruments on the human spirit, in which the flute's effect reminds us of the Pan legend and of its association with human as well as spiritual love. Not surprisingly, he assigns a warlike character to trumpets, shawms, and drums, which are used 'in the first attack of battle to terrify the enemy and encourage allies'. He tells us that the harp and other plucked instruments 'incline human minds to the mildness of piety', while fiddles, formerly used for dance music, have in recent times been displaced by louder instruments:

> Fiddles inspire joy in minds, and they are therefore more appropriate to the dances of women .... Indeed, in modern times the shawms and loud trumpets generally banish the sober fiddles from the feasts, and the young girls dance eagerly to the loud noise, like hinds, shaking their buttocks womanishly and rudely.

Turning to the flute, Konrad's remarks put a Christian gloss on the instrument's traditional association with erotic love and the spiritual world:

> Flutes arouse or inflame amorous spirits, and to an extent move them to the sweetness of devotion. Organs, therefore, on account of their variety and multitude [of flutes], are fittingly allotted a place in churches where divine services are celebrated.

Konrad's treatise is addressed to wealthy householders, whom he encourages to engage in music as dilettantes, or amateurs. In this he follows Aristotle, who argued in the *Poetics* that Zeus did not play an instrument, and that anyone who does so professionally is vulgar, 'behaving in a way in which a man would not behave unless he were drunk or jesting':

> All ability exercised for gain is beggarly, and of maidservant's condition, because to practise it is to play the beggar. But the begging artist perverts precious arts, making a handmaid of the mistress and a slave of the freewoman. For which reason young paupers who sweat at their instruments can expect dubious praise .... The rich should exercise the young in these skills – but temperately – as a measure of their cultivation.

Thus for Konrad the distinction between amateur and professional music-making had less to do with skill or training than with whether or not it was done for payment. We should take careful note of this, since a similar view remained current in the following six centuries, and we misjudge the important role of amateur flutists if we assume that their standards of performance were always and uniformly lower than those of professionals. Konrad's view also helps us understand why professional musicians lacked social status until the cult of romantic genius elevated the most famous to a higher plane in the early nineteenth century.

At about the time Konrad wrote, the composer and poet Guillaume de Machaut provided interesting lists of instruments in several of his writings.[20] In *Le Remède de Fortune* (before 1357, and perhaps before 1342), he describes a feast followed by music, played with instruments including

Tymbre, la flaüste brehaingne,	The tambourine, Bohemian flute,
Et le grant cornet d'Alemaingne,	And the large German cornett,
Flajos de saus, fistule, pipe,	Whistles of willow, fistula, (reed?)-pipe,
Muse d'Aussay, trompe petite ...[21]	Alsatian (reed) pipe, small trumpet...

Joscelyn Godwin (1977) translates *flaüste brehaingne* as 'Bohemian flute', on the theory that the *flaüteurs de Behaigne* Machaut mentioned in his poem *Le jugement du Roi de Behaigne* (written for his patron King John of Bohemia) were playing an instrument that had particular associations with central Europe, where Bohemia is situated. Godwin points out in support of this interpretation that in a parallel passage in *La Prise d'Alexandrie* (c1369), which is set in Prague during a visit Pierre de Lusignan made to the emperor, Charles I of Luxembourg in 1364, Machaut gives a similar list of instruments to that in the *Remède*.[22] In the second list the transverse flute is present but the Bohemian one absent, suggesting that both terms refer to the same instrument. Machaut's later list includes both *flaüstes traversiennes* and *flaüstes, dont droit joues quant tu flaüstes*, that is, 'flutes you blow straight [i.e. vertically] when you play them' – a distinction he probably made simply so as to add one more to his impressive list of instruments. If Godwin's interpretation of *flaüste brehaingne* is correct, the use of that name for the transverse flute in the fourteenth century suggests that people at that time believed the transverse flute to have travelled westward to France, that is, from Germanic lands.

Machaut's pupil Eustache Deschamps (c1346–c1406) gave another list of instruments containing both *flaustes* and *traversaines* in a lament on the death of his teacher in 1377. In another *ballade*, which enumerates the instruments that had fallen into neglect while a craze for the trumpet flourished, Deschamps mentions the *vielle fleuthe traversaine* (old transverse flute), here grouped with *maint doulz instrument* (many a soft instrument) such as gittern, rebec, harp, psaltery, and douçaine. Yet in what seems like a perverse about-face fifteen years later, Deschamps classifies the *fleutes* with the loud instruments in a treatise on the art of reciting and composing songs.[23] Since, as Jane Bowers has pointed out, transverse flutes appear in Machaut's *Prise d'Alexandrie* in a list with drums, and since Jehan de Grise's drawings for the *Roman d'Alexandre* show them in company with loud outdoor instruments, it seems clear that late fourteenth-century France knew the flute both as a military instrument and as an indoor one of more peaceable character. Whether the same type of instrument fulfilled both roles is unclear; in any case, the term 'fife' had apparently not yet come into existence to signify a military instrument as opposed to a domestic one (see p. 37).

Concerning the relationship between poetry and song, Deschamps wrote in his manual on composing these forms that they could be performed independently, that is, that vocal music could be sung without words or recited without the music. But Page emphasizes that Deschamps gave us no authority for the playing of songs on instruments, even if the untexted parts with their leaps, short melodic fragments, and spun-out ornamented passages often seem 'unvocal' to us.[24] Page has also argued that instruments were not mixed with voices in the performance of late medieval French songs. Accounts of performances in fifteenth-century France mention noble amateurs singing alone or in groups of courtiers, but instruments, played by minstrels, are mentioned only in connection with dancing or ceremonial. True, courtiers themselves sometimes play instrumental settings of songs on bowed or plucked stringed instruments – but not while singing.

The first of many art works to associate the flute with royalty, and a far cry from shepherds and sentries, is a Flemish monumental brass in Schwerin cathedral, commemorating two bishops who died in 1314 and 1375.[25] This highly intricate work 4.5 metres long contains an elaborate border representing a tree of Jesse, all of whose descendants are playing instruments. The flute appears in a prominent position on the lower border, alongside the trumpet, harp, and psaltery. Kings play all four of these instruments, while others are played by angels or grotesque figures.

Jane Bowers has observed that transverse flutes appear rather frequently in the hands of angels in illuminated manuscripts made in Bourges and Paris around the turn of the fifteenth century. In an essay on these fifteenth-century angel concerts Emanuel Winternitz noted that progress in the study of anatomy and perspective had ushered in a new way of seeing the universe, in which humankind rather than God stood at the centre. Angels looked rather like people, and the ceremonial of heaven increasingly came to reflect that of earth, allowing us a more realistic glimpse of events and instruments as the artists saw them. In the *Petites Heures* of Jean de Berry (c1388, ill. 5), a Coronation of the Virgin is surrounded by a large band of angelic musicians playing stringed and percussion instruments, portative organ, bagpipes, and two transverse flutes. A human flute player, along with harp, timpani, lute, fiddle, and portative organ, decorates a border in an Annunciation scene in the *Belles Heures* of Jean de Berry (1408–13), illuminated by the Limbourg brothers. Angels playing the same set of instruments appear in the frontispiece to the Limbourgs' *Bible moralisée* (c1411) for Philippe de Hardi. Once more the same group of instruments is repeated in a Virgin and Child in a Book of Hours (c1417–18) for the Anjou family, attributed to the Rohan Master and Workshop. Whether the instruments held some symbolic significance is not clear, but it seems that this grouping represents a combination that actually existed in the real world.

Turning to the flute itself, individual instruments evidently differed greatly from one another, so that the sole defining feature of the European medieval flute we can point to with full certainty is that it was held sideways, most commonly to the player's left. Liane Ehlich's conclusion as to the flute's wide bore and thin walls seems well justified, and if it is also true that medieval flutes had a large compass, then military instruments could have used the highest part of their range to make them audible outdoors and over long distances, and thus need not necessarily have been constructed differently from instruments for playing art music. A standard tuning for the flute surely did not exist any more than it did for other instruments: Jerome of Moravia gave three different tunings for the fiddle, and the harpist-heroes of the Romances are nearly always said to tune their instruments before they play. This does not mean that they made small adjustments to a standardized scale, but rather that they set a different mode, or sequence of tones and semitones, appropriate to the song: in the *Tristan en prose*, quoted by Page, the hero even takes a harp that has just been played by someone else and re-tunes it 'in his way and after his fashion'. Another time Tristan tunes the harp differently for each of two songs. So it is difficult to imagine that all flutes played the same notes, or used the same fingerings.

With theoretical sources so utterly lacking, and despite the lack of evidence for transposition already mentioned, the simplest conclusion is that medieval flutists played music wherever it lay best on their instruments. In other words, the player

5. One of the 182 miniatures in the *Petites Heures* of Jean de Berry (*c*1388), by Jean Le Noir and his school. Transverse flutes appear rather commonly in similar bands of angel-musicians in illuminated manuscripts made in Bourges and Paris around the turn of the fifteenth century.

would know where the semitones were on the particular instrument at hand, and be able to pick the appropriate starting note for any melody so that it would fit the pattern of tones and semitones the instrument could manage.

But medieval tuning was more of an art than merely placing the semitones correctly. Because the tuning theory of that period relied largely on Pythagoras, modern performers of medieval music have often taken Pythagorean tuning, in which fourths and fifths are pure, as a standard scale. In some repertoires, however, the commonest consonant intervals in the music are thirds and sixths, which are too wide in Pythagorean tuning, though certainly drones at the fifth work well when they are perfectly pure. Still – and this point should be borne in mind for music at least up to the mid-nineteenth century – melody instruments are not required to conform to the strictures of temperaments devised for fixed-pitch instruments like keyboards, because their intonation is somewhat flexible. Jacques de Liège may have been referring to either Pythagorean tuning or meantone when he wrote that instrumentalists divided the whole tone into unequal parts.[26] In either case, as Christopher Page writes: 'Since Gothic musicians regarded the semitone as the "condiment" of music it is unlikely that they would have been careless with such delicate spices', that is, they would have been careful to play large and small semitones in their proper places and not mix them up.

Whatever medieval flute-playing sounded like, we may be quite sure it was different from ours. Art music in particular may have used a wider range of techniques than are allowed in proper modern flute-playing. Did players start and end sounds with their tongue? Or could finger articulations and even glissandos between notes be effective? Traditional techniques for playing Indian flutes use the middle joint of the three fingers on the right hand, rather than the pads, to cover the holes. This is a logical way of covering large, widely-spaced holes – indeed, on instruments as large as those in the *Cantigas* illustration, it is the only feasible way. And while Indian flute technique allows for almost as much flexibility in pitch, tone, and articulation as the human voice, Indian flutists manage to play much better in tune at all times than their western counterparts. The possibilities for re-creating medieval music with such techniques seem endless, but remain largely unexplored.

Chapter 2

The flute at war and at home

To judge from the rarity of early fifteenth-century pictures and literary references, the flute seems to have fallen into disuse for about fifty years after the time of the angel band paintings of c1400.[1] Jane Bowers has found a number of tantalizing references to *flahutes* and *fleutes* in contemporary documents – reports of celebrations and banquets, and even an order to an instrument-maker – but the imprecision of the terminology makes it impossible to be sure whether these refer to duct flutes or the transverse kind (see p. 14). But if the story of the flute seems frustratingly vague for much of the fifteenth century, a remarkable change thrust transverse flutes into prominence in all parts of Europe during its last decades.

At the battles of Grandson and Morat in Burgundy in 1476, Swiss infantry squadrons won famous victories against the Burgundian cavalry of Duke Charles the Bold, using a rigidly disciplined and porcupine-like formation of pikes, halberds, swords, crossbows, and firearms that was all but impregnable in defence as well as highly mobile in attack.[2] Witnesses reported that the Swiss troops stepped precisely in time, almost like some deadly corps de ballet, to the beat of a fife and drum in the centre of each formation. Word of these new techniques of conducting warfare on foot swept the continent in the late fifteenth century. Six thousand Swiss mercenaries had entered the pay of Louis XI of France by 1481.

After another twenty years over two thirds of the continent's infantry had adopted the pike and aspects of Swiss technique, along with the flute and drum signals integral to their use.[3] First German and French, then Spanish and Italian forces copied the Swiss tactics. Though the German *Landsknechte* (country lads) adopted a characteristic drum beat that cut the brisk tempo of the Swiss *Eidgenossen* (sworn comrades) in half, and despite the mutual hatred between the two groups, the Germans grasped the Swiss idea most firmly, so that both corps found their services as mercenaries much in demand in the political and religious unrest spreading throughout Europe. Thus the use of flutes and drums became a permanent part of European infantry culture.

According to Luca Verzulli (1999) the flute was already a common folk instrument in the Swiss cantons in the sixteenth century, as it still is today. The flute may have been the most natural exponent for a role in the Swiss soldiery's feared and imitated infantry drill, for the city of Basel had engaged fifers as early as 1374. Evidently because the Swiss instruments and playing style were not well known elsewhere, other national armies learning the new techniques employed Swiss fifers and drummers at first. Two drummers and *ung sonneur de fluste* (a flute-player) who were specifically,

6. Urs Graf (1485–1527), a soldier himself, made this pen-and-ink drawing of four flute-playing comrades, two *Eidgenossen* and two *Landsknechte*, in 1523. Finger positions are quite consistent, showing the fifth finger of both left and right hands tucked under the instrument, even on the unwieldy bass flute (see also ill. 7).

though perhaps loosely, identified as Germans performed at the wedding festivities of Charles VIII and Anne of Brittany in 1491, while drums, fifes, and trumpets announced the entry of the food at a French banquet in 1489.[4] By 1494 the French *Ecurie*, or military provisioning department, was making payments to *tambourins suisses*, probably the fife and drum corps of Swiss mercenary troops who accompanied

Charles VIII on his Italian campaigns. A little more than a decade later, by 1516, the French king had established his own fife and drum corps, the *phiffres et tabourins*, though again its musicians came largely from Switzerland and Germany. Its five fifers and three drumslades may have been those reported to have played in 1520 at the Field of the Cloth of Gold, the famous summit meeting between Henry VIII of England and François I of France. By that time fifes and drums had already filled Europe from south to north: a Swedish altarpiece by Lars Snickare in St Värmdö Church, Uppland, depicting the battle of Stiklastad (1514), shows a drummer and a fifer in a cockaded hat playing as the battle rages in the foreground. Such was the reputation of the Swiss mercenaries that in 1505 Pope Julius II founded his own Guard of Swiss pikemen at the Vatican. From 1548, when two drummers (*tamburi*) and two fifes appeared in the rolls of the Papal Swiss Guard, until 1814, when bugles replaced fifes as they had most other European military establishments, flutes and drums provided music on all ceremonial occasions, a practice that has recently been revived in the still extant corps.[5]

7. Anonymous woodcut from a German manual of military law and science of 1555. Like several other compositions of the same general type, this image shows the drummer from the front, and the fifer from the back, where his fife case is hanging. This has spaces for four instruments, of which one is long, at least two medium, and one may be shorter. The style is naturalistic, showing the men in a convincingly relaxed posture and in detail down to the cut of their hair and the drape of their tunics, while the flute and drum have similar proportions to those in the pictures already mentioned. The black dot shown on the batter head of many contemporary military drums looks like the *syaji* of Indian *tabla* drums, which helps the drum produce a tunable tone.

Italian sources of the mid-fifteenth century provide the earliest documentary references to fifes or military flutes. A 1463 inventory of the possessions of the Florentine magnate Piero di Cosimo de' Medici (1416–69) listed 'Four Flemish fifes (*zufoli fiamminghi*), three of our [i.e. Italian] fifes (*zufoli nostrali*), three fifes decorated with silver', along with an organ, a double harp, and a lute also described as Flemish. Another inventory, that of Piero's son Lorenzo 'Il Magnifico' de' Medici (1449–92), contained 'a set of fifes for the use of fifers with black and white ferrules (*uno giocho di zufoli a uso di pifferi cholle ghiere nere e bianche*), five fifes in all', 'three fifes with silver ferrules (*zufoli con ghiere d'argento*) in a case garnished with silver, 8 florins', and 'a set of large fifes in a case (*uno giocho di zufoli grossi*), 12 florins'.[6]

Though the flute and drum ensembles in sixteenth-century paintings and woodcuts appear to be far from uniform, the characteristic Swiss configuration consistently shown in numerous depictions consisted of a flute two to three feet long and a drum $c2\frac{1}{2}$ feet in diameter and about the same depth, with a snare on the lower head, played with heavy beaters and a vigorous stroke (ill. 7). Some illustrations depict military flutes that, like some modern fifes, were provided with seven or eight fingerholes. Thus, if the illustrations are at all reliable, the military flutes of the early sixteenth century were quite different from the instruments later described in written sources for playing consort music, or notated ensemble compositions, as well as from the smaller instruments we recognize as the fife of Colonial times.

The first fifer whose name we know appears in a woodcut by Hans Burgkmair of Augsburg (1473–1531), part of the extraordinarily rich and detailed set of prints entitled *Triumph of Maximilian I* (1526). The Holy Roman Emperor Maximilian (1459–1519) personally designed the *Triumph* as a monument to his own glory, employing the best artists of his day to attract attention to his brilliant life and achievements.

Scholars have long recognized Maximilian's *Triumph* as an important source of evidence about many aspects of sixteenth-century life, including musical instruments. What has not been noted before is the prominence of Anthony of Dornstätt, apparently the Emperor's personal fifer, who with his instruments hanging in a case at his belt leads the mounted group of fifers and drummers at the head of the procession, in the third of 137 plates (ill. 8). According to the instructions for the execution of the *Triumph* that Maximilian dictated to his secretary in 1512, a verse was to be inscribed in the banner Anthony carried:

I, Anthony of Dornstätt, have played my fife
For Maximilian, great in strife,
In many lands on countless journeys,
In battles fierce and knightly tourneys,
At grave times or in holiday,
And so in this Triumph with honour I play.[7]

In place of the long, narrow military flutes shown in this and other German woodcuts of the early sixteenth century, Thoinot Arbeau described a quite different kind of fife in his French dancing manual *Orchesographie* (1589):

8. Fifers led by Anthony of Dornstätt. All three players appear to be using instruments with eight fingerholes, four for each hand. The nearest fifer is covering holes 123 and 567, with holes 4 and 8 clearly visible beneath his raised fingers. The middle fifer is fingering 12 567, with fingers 348 raised and a hole visible beneath 8. The farthest from the viewer is fingering 124 57, with holes 6 and 8 visible.

What we call the fife is a little transverse flute with six holes, used by the Germans and Swiss, and, as the bore is very narrow, only the thickness of a pistol bullet, it has a shrill note [i.e. pitch or tone]… players of the said drum and fife are known by the name of their instrument, and we say of two soldiers that one is the drummer and the other the fifer of some captain …. Those who play them improvise to please themselves and it suffices for them to keep time with the sound of the drum.[8]

Such differences aside, the details Arbeau gave about the music of the fifes leave no doubt that its nature was quite different from consort music. He described a characteristic Swiss playing style, in which fifers using a special hard articulation played together with large side drums, and although he wrote that the fife music was improvised on the spot, he did provide examples of the kind of figurations it played. Despite the unwritten nature of the fife-playing tradition, Arbeau tells us more about the manner of playing the fife in these few words and in a musical example than all the early instrumental tutors convey. He provides an example of a fife tune set in both duple and triple metre, describing the tonguing as follows:

> You must remember that there are two ways of playing the flute, one by sucking [spitting?], and the other by rolling the tongue. In the first case the player's tongue goes té, té, té, or teré, teré, teré, and in the second relé, relé, relé. I warn you of this because the example I wish to set down for you should be played té, té, and not rolled .... Because the sound of té, té, is shriller and harsher, consequently more warlike than the roll.[9]

Another of Luca Verzulli's articles (1999) presents examples of descriptive battle pieces, many containing imitations of the military flute style, and some written as late as the eighteenth century. One such piece we could add to Verzulli's collection occurs in a *Sonata Representativa* by Heinrich Ignaz Franz Biber (1644–1704) for violin and continuo. After movements imitating the nightingale, cuckoo, frog, cock and hen, quail, and cat, the violin plays a 'Musquetir Mars', or musketeer's march, over a drum-like rhythm in the continuo (see also ill. 9).[10]

If fifers specialized in improvising in a particular way on a special kind of instrument, the fifer-soldiers may well have played consort music too, if only in off-duty moments, using flutes having proportions much more like those we find described in writing and represented by surviving examples from a later period. The consort of flutes shown in a drawing of flute-playing soldiers by Urs Graf (1485–1527) consists of a bass, two tenors, and a discant, apparently with no more than six holes (ill. 6). Graf, a soldier himself, had an acute eye for the men's relaxed but alert posture, as well as for precise distinctions in their insignia, headgear, and weapons.

While Maximilian's *Triumph* showed fifes in a rare ceremonial appearance on horseback, the playing of fifes had surely spread beyond the infantry by the late sixteenth century. English regiments of the line and Guards commonly used ensembles consisting of drums and fifes, sometimes adding trumpets, with the artillery using similar groupings to those found in the infantry, and only cavalry forces employing the nobler sound of trumpets and kettledrums. In 1557 Henry VIII's artillery captain general at the siege of St Quentin had two trumpets, a drum, and a fife, the master of ordnance had a drum and fife, while the captain general of infantry had six 'wyfflers', one drum, and one fife.[11] Still, because of the military flute-playing style's unwritten nature, we can only catch such occasional echoes of it as we have already discussed. But fortunately a new source of information emerged during the sixteenth century to provide more concrete details about how flutes were played in other situations.

People in western Europe had been playing transverse flutes for half a millennium before anything about how to do so was written down. Though the earliest instruction books on musical instruments drew no distinction between the fife, with its shrill, improvised music, and the flute, with the same kind of four-part repertoire as other wind instruments, they explicitly linked the flute with the Swiss military tradition. Yet clearly the goals of the early writers of books on instruments were quite different from those of military flutists. Books of hours dating from around 1500 show

9. Heinrich Ignaz Franz Biber's *Battalia à 10* (1673), a piece for strings and continuo reminiscent of the famous *Capriccio Stravagante* of Carlo Farina (*c*1604–39), contains a section entitled 'Der Mars', or march. A violin plays pseudo-improvised fife music in a range from E_2 to E_3, over the rhythmic accompaniment of a double bass with a piece of paper placed between its strings to imitate a snare drum.

the flute as well as other instruments in the hands of clerics and bourgeois, but the Reformation, growing hand in hand with the new printing industry, placed great importance on the dissemination of musical knowledge beyond these elite circles to the common people. The Reformers believed that everyone should read the Bible and sing hymns in their own language, as a break with the tradition in which the scriptures were read aloud in church by a priest, the choir sang in Latin, and the organ provided instrumental music. To bring these changes about, the Reformers needed to make verbal and musical literacy commonplace skills, if not universal ones, for the first time in history.

The earliest printed treatise on musical instruments, *Musica getutscht*, by the priest Sebastian Virdung (*c*1465–*p*1511), appeared in a richly illustrated edition of 1511 in Basel, where presumably the Swiss fife was not unfamiliar. Virdung wrote in the contemporary vernacular for an unsophisticated readership who, without needing to read musical notation, could learn to play instruments from tablature, a diagrammatic representation of how to place the fingers.

Virdung uses the term *Flöten* to refer to recorders, reserving the word *Zwerchpfeiff* for the military fife and making no specific mention of the transverse flute in consorts, or indeed in any other non-military use. He shows a single transverse flute in a

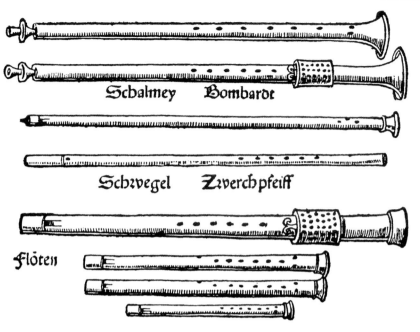

10. Virdung's plate of wind instruments (1511) shows shawms (*Schalmey* and *Bombardt*), tabor pipe and fife (*Schwegel* and *Zwerchpfeiff*), and a set of recorders (*Flöten*).

grouping of other woodwinds including shawms, tabor pipe, and recorders, describing its use during a discussion of drums. Unfortunately, Virdung tells us nothing of the drums that were played with fifes. We can only fill in the missing information from the woodcuts already mentioned.

A second and more revealing German-language treatise on instrumental music, *Musica instrumentalis deudsch*, was published at Wittenberg by Martin Agricola (*c*1486–1556) in 1529, and in a revised edition of 1545. Agricola, a Lutheran music teacher from Saxony, wrote to serve essentially the same educational and religious goals as his predecessor, and copied many of Virdung's woodcut illustrations. Although he referred to *Schweitzerpfeiffen* (Swiss fifes) as well as *Querfeiffen* or *Querpfeiffen* (transverse fifes/flutes), Agricola was clearly not really describing military flutes at all, but rather a quite different type of instrument for playing four-part consorts.

In place of Virdung's solitary fife, Agricola shows a set of transverse flutes in four sizes. Altus and tenor sizes are depicted as being slightly different lengths, but the illustration may be incorrect, since only one fingering chart is given for both types (lowest note A re), along with one for Discantus (lowest note E mi) and one for Bassus (D re). Agricola's modern editor, William E. Hettrick, as well as Howard Mayer Brown (1986), have stated that all these sizes are meant to sound an octave and a fourth higher than written. This is perhaps only another way of saying what Agricola himself revealed in his revised edition of 1545, that the fingering chart showing a D-A-E consort is really for a G-D-A consort transposing the notated music up a fifth – the flutes sounded an octave higher than written in any case. Because the ability to read

Interpreting renaissance music requires the player, or more commonly, all the players of a four-part consort, to make certain decisions about what pitch the notated music will sound at, and consequently what sizes of instruments to use, for each composition.

The notes are grouped into three patterns of six, each containing the same arrangement of tones and semitones with the same names: ut, re, mi, fa, sol, la, though of course these do not connote absolute pitches. These patterns can be overlapped seven times, beginning a fifth apart on F, C, and G, to cover a range of twenty notes, from G an octave and a fourth below our middle C, to E an octave and a third above it.

The semitone in each hexachord falls between mi and fa. The hexachord beginning on C, called the 'natural' hexachord, contains C, D, E, F, G, and A. The next contains G, A, B, C, D, and E, with mi-fa between B and C. This is called the 'hard' hexachord because in medieval notation the B was designated as a square or 'hard' b, while B flat was notated as b – the round or 'soft' B. The 'soft' hexachord begins on F and contains F, G, A, Bb, C, and D. The name for B tells us whether it is flat or natural. In the soft hexachord, the note is fa, a semitone above mi as fa always is. In the natural hexachord it does not appear, and in the hard hexachord it is mi, a semitone below fa as mi always is. Thus *B fa* and *B mi* stand a semitone apart, and a separate designation for Bb is not strictly necessary. *B fa* is the only 'flat' in the hexachord system, and sharps do not exist except in the artificial concept of *musica ficta*.

Jambe de Fer provides a fingering chart for the flute that gives precedence to the soft, or flat, hexachord. In describing his fingering chart, he tells us that

> Playing in flats [*le Jeu de b mol*] is marked right on the table, because it is the most pleasant, easy, and natural way. ...

The basic scale he gives, if we transpose it for a D tenor flute as he intended, has an F natural (a minor third), a B natural (a major sixth), and a C natural (a natural seventh) – all the characteristics of the Dorian mode. Other notes playable on the flute are listed in a separate column as 'feints', or artificial notes.

Moien E			La ✳	Mi
D		La b	Sol ✳	Re
C		Sol b	Fa ✳	Vt
B		Fa b	Mi ✳	Nature, dicte ne tre par ou'urs.
Haut A	La	Mi b	Re ✳	
G	Sol	Re b	Vt ✳	
Bas F	Fa	Vt b	♮ quarré dit ♮ dur.	

Nature dicte neutre par aucuns. | b mol dit b rond.

De ces six voix reiterables en la Game, tant que l'on veut infiniement trois sont pour monter, qui sont v T, R E, M I, & trois à descendre, qui sont F A, S O L, L A.

11. Jambe de Fer's diagram of the scale (1556) looks like a puzzle to modern eyes, but is quite simply and economically arranged. On the left are three clefs, from the bottom up: an F clef on the middle line (F3), labelled *Bas* or 'low'; a G2 clef, labelled 'high'; and a C3 clef designated 'medium'. These are, simply enough, the predecessors of our bass, treble, and alto clefs. The clefs have no direct association with the note names to their right.

In the next column to the right appear the names of the notes, F, G, A, B, C, D, and E, then come the three hexachords: the natural, split between the second and fifth column, and labelled *Nature* (Natural); the flat (*b mol*), with flat signs alongside the names ut, re, mi, fa, sol, la; and the hard (*b quarré*), with sharp signs alongside the note-names.

Jambe de Fer's table shows that each of the letter-named notes can have more than one syllable associated with it, depending on where it occurs. D in the natural hexachord is called *D re*, and stands a whole tone above *C ut. D sol*, a fifth above ut in the hard hexachord, has a quite different function, as does *D la*, the sixth note in the soft or flat hexachord.

The name for B tells us whether it is flat or natural. In the soft hexachord, the note is *B fa*, and in the hard hexachord, *B mi*.

different clefs made transposing at sight so much easier (see p. 53), Agricola recommended that the instrumentalist should forget about tablature and instead learn to read music notation.

Each of the three sizes of flute in Agricola's 1529 edition has a range of three full octaves, so that a consort of flutes (sounding an octave higher than the written notes) can cover a range from D below the bass stave as far as E3 above the treble. The range of Agricola's 1545 fingering tables, in contrast, is more restricted: two octaves and a note, plus an extra three notes for the discant. After moving on to other matters, Agricola interrupts himself to return to the 'Swiss' flutes and give another set of fingering charts, this time 'regular' ones, now pitched a fifth below those of the 1529 edition and a fourth below the first chart of 1545. Now, for the first time, Agricola provides us with a chart that shows the actual untransposed pitches the flutes play, so that we can see that G, D, and A are really the lowest sounding notes of each flute. This chart gives ranges of two octaves and a fifth (bass), two octaves and a fifth (tenor-alto), and two octaves and a sixth (discant).

Agricola refers to playing the flute 'in the Swiss manner' without, unfortunately, defining precisely what that means. He insists that a technique that sounds very much like breath vibrato is an integral part not just of Swiss flute playing but of all wind-playing:

> [I]f you want to master the fundamentals and basics, then learn to play with quivering breath [*mit zitterndem Winde*], for it graces the music very much on all wind instruments that one plays.[12]

Nancy Hadden amplifies Agricola's statement by referring to other testimony that vibrato of the breath and the fingers were considered not only by flutists but by other instrumentalists and singers as 'fundamental elements of sound and expression'. The sixteenth-century Italian writers Hadden cites applied the *tremolo* with careful attention to the appropriate emotional content of the music, appealing, as so many later writers did, to good taste and discretion in its employment.[13]

Agricola gives us interesting hints on the subject of tonguing, again not specifically that of the Swiss fife tradition but as a general rule applied to all wind instruments. He instructs the student to tongue each note distinctly, and explains that the type of finger articulation used on bagpipes – heard today in some folk flute-playing – is inappropriate for wind instruments on which tonguing is possible. Long notes such as minims use the syllable *de*, while shorter note values can be tongued with *de*, or with a compound tonguing, *di ri di ri de*, having *di* as the stressed syllable. Fusas, or quavers, use only the compound tonguing, which Hettrick dubs 'double-tonguing', though that term, when used by later writers, is actually reserved for a quite different method of articulating quick passages. The flutter-tongue (*flitterzunge*) *tellellellellellellellel/le*, a method of tonguing which 'some people employ in playing divisions', a form of florid ornamentation, is evidently intended for playing of the greatest rapidity.

Agricola's tonguing syllables seem rather unsophisticated if we compare them with another detailed set of instructions that appeared in a work printed in Venice at about

It is difficult to be sure whether any physical distinction between the 'fife' and the 'flute' existed in the sixteenth century, when military flutes became so prevalent. The first written works on how to play wind instruments make it clear that the military flute known in sixteenth-century German-speaking lands was played in a special style associated with the Swiss. The term 'fife' itself occurs in a description of an occasion in 1489 in which drums, fifes, and trumpets (*tambourins, fifres et trompettes*) played together at a French feast. The question of exactly what the difference may have been between flutes and fifes is complicated by the fact that the instruments shown in sixteenth-century military images are far from uniform in length and number of fingerholes.

The English word *fife* itself evidently comes directly from the German *Pfeife*, or pipe, whence also the French *fifre*, the Italian *fiffaro* or *phiffaro* (sometimes spelled *piffaro*, which usually referred to the shawm), and the Spanish *pifano*. Welch (*Six Lectures*, 232) gives variant English spellings of the word such as fyfe, fieft, fiphe, phyfe, phife, and piphe, suggesting that the words fife and pipe are etymological cognates. In English as well as other European languages, however, *pipe* has a rather different history as a general term for wind

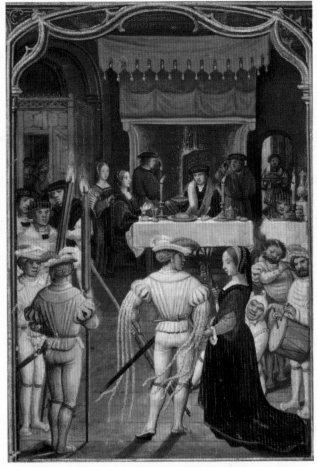

12. White-clad dancers and musicians prepare for a torch dance, from a Flemish Book of Hours, *c*1500.

instruments, which indicates that *fife* is a back-formation from the German rather than just another form of *pipe*. The late Latin *pipa* gave rise to the Italian *piva*, the Italian and Spanish *pipa*, and the French *pipe*. In 1023 Wulfstan wrote of 'Hearpe and pipe', and before 1100 another English source gave 'pipe odde hwistle' (*Oxford English Dictionary*, s.v. 'pipe', p. 893, col. 2).

The English chronicler Holinshed gives an account of a mask, or masked dance, of 1510 in which King Henry VIII participated, which began when 'there came in a drum and fife apparelled in white damaske & gréene bonnets, and hosen of the same sute. Then certain gentlemen followed with torches, apparelled in blue damaske.' On a similar occasion in 1530, Henry VIII unexpectedly visited Cardinal Wolsey 'in a maske with a dozen maskers all in garments like shéepheards … having sixtéene torch bearers, besides their drums … with such a noise of drums and flutes as seldome has béene heard the like'. Yet even in 1591, when William Byrd included a battle piece for virginals with an imitation of fife and drum music (*My Ladye Nevells Booke*) he labelled the section 'The flute and the droome'. Hence it seems that *flute* and *fife* could be interchangeable terms. Since any clear distinction between 'flute' and 'fife' is lacking, we use the terms interchangeably here.

the same time, Sylvestro Ganassi's *Fontegara* (1535).[14] Though intended for the recorder, Ganassi's rules for tonguing closely resemble those other Venetian authors laid down for cornett, trumpet, and other instruments, and can profitably be applied to the transverse flute. *Fontegara*'s principal purpose is to teach rapid, lavish divisions, or embellishments of the written notes. Like other treatises on this topic, several of which were published in Italy during the sixteenth century, *Fontegara* makes no distinction between vocal and instrumental embellishment, nor yet among different instruments. Ganassi distinguishes a hard articulation, with *teke*, and soft one with *lere*, and a medium one with *tere*, each form having a direct first syllable and a reversed second one. Though Ganassi did not use the concept of 'double-tonguing', *teke* is almost indistinguishable in practice from the double-tongue used on the modern flute, even if the case is less clear with *lere* and *tere*.

Agricola gives a useful and important indication of how a set of wind instruments should be tuned, and confirms Virdung's testimony, the earliest such indication, that wind instruments were made by specialist makers, advising his pupils to buy instruments as a set, 'for the others are generally out of tune'. He also gives valuable information about intonation. In discussing the placement of frets on the lute fingerboard, he complains about the out-of-tune, narrow fifths of 'the majority' of lutenists who play in equal temperament:

> The fact that the majority of the brotherhood of lutenists and fiddlers make all of the frets the same [distance] from each other is truly a telling indication of their great inexperience – of the fact that they have no knowledge of the science that noble Music proclaims. Thus they too go astray, for they understand nothing at all about how the division of the whole-tone is accomplished. They also do not know that a fret that produces a minor semitone should stand somewhat farther [back] from the following [higher] fret, for the closest fret [i.e. the one for the lower pitch of the minor semitone, placed at the back of the first fret in question] takes precedence. Thus the major semitone is indeed somewhat larger that the minor semitone, for the major has five commas and the minor only four, as the monochord displays.[15]

We will encounter remarkably similar instructions in eighteenth-century writings on the flute by Quantz, Telemann, Tromlitz, and others (see p. 83).

Italy, where the flute had perhaps been a novelty a century earlier, put the instrument to the same military uses as the rest of Europe in the sixteenth century as the wars of 1494–1529 brought troops from France and Spain to the Italian states. A print in the Uffizi Gallery in Florence shows the triumphal entry of Charles V into Bologna in 1529 for his coronation as Holy Roman Emperor, at the head of a procession that includes fifers and drummers among the pikemen and harquebusiers.[16] A roll of members of the Pope's Swiss Guard at the Vatican included two drummers and two fifes (*pifferi*) in 1548, and when the mathematician, medic, and statistical theoretician Girolamo Cardano described wind instruments in his manuscript *De Musica* (1574), he was aware of no transverse flute other than the military fifes (*fifolae*), which had a range of only nine tones.

By the end of this period of unrest and troop movements, four-part transverse flute consorts had appeared in Italy, for as early as 1529 one such ensemble played at a dinner Ercole d'Este gave for his father Alfonso I, Duke of Ferrara. At this time such a consort may still have seemed exotic and unfamiliar at the court, for the writer of a document of the following year requesting a case of German, or transverse, flutes found it necessary to explain the difference between these and the more familiar Italian flutes, or recorders:

> I would like them to bring me a case or a set of German flutes that are played in the middle of the flute and not from the head, as ours are; but make sure they come to me in good condition and that they have all the notes [or perhaps, sizes] necessary.[17]

A few decades later in 1559, transverse flutes had apparently found favour in Venice, where a contract identified three musicians as *pifferi del Doge* along with two instrument makers, one of whom was Jacopo da Basan, or Jacomo Bassano, a member of a famous family of musicians and instrument makers. In the same contract tenor flutes, or *phiffari tenori*, were priced at two lire each, bass flutes at three.[18]

While all the terms *pifferi*, *fifolae*, *traverse*, and *flauti d'Alemagna* were used interchangeably for all sorts of flutes and flutists, the instrument was appearing more and more frequently in mid-sixteenth-century Italy in a masque-like theatrical entertainment, not only in whole consorts but also in mixed ensembles with other instruments. At the wedding of Cosimo de' Medici in 1539, three sea monsters played *traverse* in an *intermedio*, or musico-dramatic interlude in a play, by Francesco Corteccia. When Henry II married Catherine de' Medici in 1548, instruments variously designated *flauti d'Alamagna* and *flauti traversi* were played. Howard Mayer Brown has noted that transverse flutes appeared in the *intermedi* as often as cornetts, and that among wind instruments only the trombone was used more.[19]

We learn more about the kind of transverse flute employed in four-part consort music from two books published in Lyon in the mid-sixteenth century, testimony to the instrument's popularity as a recreational instrument in that cosmopolitan city's literary golden age. One, Simon Gorlier's *Tablature de flûte d'Allemand* (1558), apparently a method for converting music notation to a tablature for the flute, is lost. But the earlier of the two, Philibert Jambe de Fer's *L'Epitome musicale de Tons, Sons et Accords, des Voix humaines, Fleustes d'Alleman, Fleustes a Neuf trous* [i.e. recorder], *Violes, et Violons* (1556), a comprehensive introduction to musical theory and practice, gave the transverse flute pride of place.

Though Jambe de Fer intended his book to instruct amateurs, as Virdung and Agricola had done, the conditions in Lyon were altogether different from those in Basel and Wittenberg. Apart from the city's proximity to Italy and the draw of its commercial fairs, Lyon stands out because amateur music-making featured prominently in its culture, at least before the upheaval of the religious wars of 1562–98. The transverse flute and the recorder were the favourite instruments among amateurs in a city Frank Dobbins describes as 'the literary capital of sixteenth-century France'. The city's population of liberal, enlightened free spirits such as Rabelais –

13. Two almost identical images of a type frequently used in Flemish Books of Hours, *c*1500. A group of men and women in a boat, with May-branches, often near a bridge. Here the instrumental combination of lute and flute or recorder may be accompanying a female singer, and perhaps the man steering the boat is also singing. The pairing of these illustrations serves to remind us that much of what painters represented was idealized rather than strictly realistic. The architecture, the costumes, the stonework, the position of the branches, even the ripples in the river are derived from a common model. (a) Flemish Book of Hours, *c*1500 (b) (*facing page*) Simon Bening (1483–1561), Hennessy Book of Hours.

whose character Gargantua (1535) played the *flûte allemande* – indulged in poetry, music, and theatre. The copying and printing of music in sixteenth-century Lyon provides insight into the repertoire of amateur flutists not only in that city, but far afield, since Lyonnais music found wide distribution via the trade fairs. Popular songs were customarily adapted to instrumental use, and anthologies of this kind by the publisher de Villiers contained music by Claudin, Gombert, Janequin, and Arcadelt, as well as pieces of Spanish, Italian, and even Hungarian origin.

Grand spectacles staged during the frequent visits of the French court to Lyon, as well as figures such as its Archbishop, Ippolito II d'Este, show the city's culture to have been steeped in Italian influence, as well as in the transverse flute. During the reception of Henry II and his wife Catherine de' Medici in September 1548 the King's Swiss Guard brought its own corps of fifes and drums, and extra fifers were hired to lead processions of guilds and columns of infantry though the city. Descriptions of

the theatrical events featured on such occasions record performances at which transverse flutes appeared in consort with stringed instruments. For example, on the evening following the processions of 1548 a grand theatrical presentation entertained the court, with *intermedi* depicting mythical and allegorical figures between the acts of the play. In the first, Dawn appeared in a chariot, combing her long golden hair and singing a *canzona* (literally, 'song', but actually a type of instrumental music) to the accompaniment of two spinets and four transverse flutes (*flauti d'Alamagna*). In a second *intermedio*, four viols and four transverse flutes (*quatro violini da gamba & [...] quatro flauti d'Allamagna*) played a *sonata*. Then the four flutes appeared again, with two spinets and four bass viols, to accompany Night in a closing *canzona*.[20]

Drawn like many others to the opportunities Lyon presented, Jambe de Fer, a Burgundian musician and professional gambler, made his home there from 1553 to 1564. His instructions provide a few further details about flute-playing. Like Agricola, he encourages his readers to tongue each note, observing that people who do not use their tongues when speaking sound as though they are drunk, and that poor tonguing can likewise make flute-playing sound inarticulate:

> Further I point out that for those people who have no tongue, this way of playing is forbidden as [it is] in speaking, for, with each note that you pronounce, the tongue must be guide, and so in this regard you who take pleasure in this kind of playing [i.e. the forbidden kind], keep your tongues from mildew, that is to say, drink often.[21]

Jambe de Fer's fingering chart for the tenor flute is unfortunately missing from the only extant copy of his treatise. His chart for the bass flute, with a range of nineteen notes, gives precedence to the soft, or flat, hexachord (see p. 35). In describing his fingering chart, he tells us that '[p]laying in flats [*le Jeu de b mol*] is marked right on the table, because it is the most pleasant, easy, and natural way'. 'Feints', or notes that lie outside the flat hexachord, are less successful in the lower notes, apparently because the feinted notes, though they are acceptable in the higher part of the range, sound most uneven in tone in the lowest octave:

> As for the embouchure of this said German flute, it is quite difficult to give good and sufficient explanation of it, in any case I will tell you my opinion in a few short words, so that you will not accuse me of laziness. One must have the skill and the courage to place the said flute right in the middle of the lower lip, blowing softly and moderately, increasing in strength little by little in ascending, and in going lower one must gradually moderate it according to the disposition of the music without being afraid to purse the lips.[22]

More light is shed on who Jambe de Fer's readers were and where they obtained their instruments by Frank Dobbins (1989), who lists an increasing number of instrument makers and dealers in Lyon over the course of the sixteenth century and suggests that the expanding trade fairs boosted sales and production. Dobbins observes that most of the professional musicians mentioned in archival references played outdoor instruments for ceremonial occasions, but that the business of makers and traders was instead aimed at the probably much larger amateur market. When Jambe de Fer observes of the violin that 'few people play it, apart from those who earn their livelihood by it', he is clearly drawing a class distinction between professional musicians and their social superiors, the amateurs who play the flute, recorder, and viol.

At least two of the eight flute-makers listed in the Lyon archives were members of the Rafi family (also spelled Raffin, Raphin, Rapin, and Ruffin), from which survive four recorders and seven transverse flutes. In 1512 Michaud Raffin (?–?) was documented as 'fleustier', reappearing in 1523 as 'faiseur de fleustes', or flute and recorder maker, as such the first in recorded history. In this capacity he was apparently followed by his son Claude (*fl p* 1515). Contemporary poetic references to their work confirm that the Rafi flutes were well known, and suggest that the family made other instruments as well, including a *double chalumeau* (double shawm or reed pipe) and *musette* (bagpipe) – though because these references are in poetry rather than archival records, as well as because the instruments mentioned are so stereotypically those of the ancient shepherds, we should perhaps not place too much credence in this testimony. Other flute-makers named in Lyon records were Jacques Pillon (1503) and Mathurin de la Not or de la Nou (*fl* perhaps 1523–55) who executed a 1542 contract with a French merchant for *ung jeu de flustes unyes, façon d'allement*, a set of flutes in the German or transverse style.[23] Both these individuals were also listed as players, along with Toussaint Fabre (1530), Pierre Fantin (1548), Ludovic (1521), and Michaud Raffin again (1506–24).

That the Rafi flutes were not intended solely for amateurs is indicated by the presence of one in an inventory of the possessions of the musician Guillaume Masnet.[24] Other indications that transverse flutes in general were not the exclusive province of amateurs include a record of 1569 in which professional musicians in Paris were hired to play them in ensembles with bagpipes or trombones. Professional musicians in Italy too included the transverse flute in their instrumentarium: Giovanni Pietro Rizeffo sought employment with the Duke of Parma in 1546 for a company of six musicians, all of whom could play trumpet, trombone, shawm, cornett, cornemuse, recorder, flute, and violin, improvise from a vocal part, and sing.[25] The Doge of Venice's three *pifferi* contracted with Jacomo Bassano and his son Santo in 1559 to supply flutes along with cornetts, crumhorns, recorders, and shawms.[26]

By the mid-sixteenth century flute consorts such as those the Rafis built had evidently found a special and indeed perhaps a dominant place in many European courts, quite apart from the military and ceremonial functions flutes of other kinds fulfilled in nearby circles. Various court inventories between 1547 and 1613 list no fewer than 597 transverse flutes, compared with 404 recorders, 505 cornetts, and 288 viols. An inventory of 1547 indicates that Henry VIII of England possessed 77 transverse flutes, including examples in lacquered ivory and in glass, while Maria of Hungary (1555) owned more than 50, and Philip II of Spain (1598) 54. These figures are dwarfed by the Baden-Württemberg court at Stuttgart (1589), which owned no fewer than 220 transverse flutes, as against 48 recorders, 113 cornetts, and 39 viols. Though many or all of these examples probably fell into the three categories of G bass, D tenor/alto, and A discant, it seems that establishments that could afford so many instruments kept several sets of differently tuned flutes on hand to play music in a wide range of modes, as well as at the different pitches used for church and chamber music. The Stuttgart inventory supplies the useful additional detail that most of the flutes were at choir pitch, the same as the mute cornetts but a tone lower than the ordinary cornetts, with the exception of two sets of tenor and bass transverse flutes tuned one tone lower than choir pitch. This is the first of several indications, borne out by surviving examples, that entire sets of flutes were made to play at different pitches a whole tone apart.

Despite the presence of so many flutes in the inventories of so many courts, the playing of whole flute consorts was apparently considered something typically French during much of the sixteenth century. François de Scepeaux, Sieur de Vielleville and

Marshal of France, remarked after an evening of chamber music at Metz in 1554 that the transverse flute 'is quite wrongly called German flute: for the French make better and more musical use of it than any other nation; and it is never played in four parts in Germany as it usually is in France'.[27] Indeed, prominent positions as flutists even outside France's borders were held by Frenchmen. Henry VIII of England built up a transverse flute consort, consisting of musicians who could double on cornetts, to supplement the trombone consort he inherited from his father Henry VII and the ready-made ensembles of recorders and viols/violins he engaged from the Continent. The younger Henry began by importing two French flute-players around 1530, another in 1539, and a fourth by 1547, and added a French rebec player who doubled on flute by the same date, making a total of five members. After Henry's death the flute consort gained another member and remained at that strength until 1630, at which date David Lasocki has identified its members as Jerome, Clement, and Andrea Lanier and Henry and Alfonso Ferrabosco, members of families that made important contributions to English music.[28]

At around the same time as it became so popular at Europe's royal courts, we learn from its iconography that the flute had also come into favour as a chamber instrument with bourgeois and noble amateur musicians of both sexes in Italy, France, and the Netherlands. In Jan Cornelis Vermeyen's painting *The Parable of the Prodigal Son* (c1540), a woman plays the flute while another plays the lute and a man between them points to the flutist's part-book on the table in front of them.[29] The same grouping of figures occurs in Willem van Aelst's (1625/6–83) *The Concert*, except that here the man is beating time and possibly singing.[30] In an Italian painting, *Open Air Concert* by the Flemish painter Ludovico Pozzoserrato (Lodewijck Toeput, 1550–1604), men playing lute, viola da braccio, flute, and perhaps singing, are shown in a group with women singing and playing the virginals.[31] In French art too, the instrument is frequently seen in the hands of women – Jane Bowers lists an impressive tally of pictures showing ensembles including a female flutist, often joined by a lutenist or mixed ensemble. The most famous of these is a later image derived from a prototype attributed to the Master of the Female Half-lengths, thought to have been active in Paris around 1520 (ill. 14). Paintings by Tintoretto (1518–94) and others indicate that in Italy and the Netherlands too, the flute was a not uncommon instrument for ladies to play, at least in allegorical settings. The instrument's mythical origins are referred to in a fine German engraving of the goddess Minerva by Tobias Stimmer (ill. 1).

The second and third decades of the sixteenth century provide the earliest printed examples of the kind of music the four-part flute consorts played. The first surviving collection of this repertoire to mention transverse flutes as suitable exponents has the extraordinarily descriptive title *In this booklet you wll find 75 pretty songs with discant, alto, bass, and tenor parts for joyful singing. Also some that can be artfully played on recorders, flutes, and other musical instruments.*[32] Other collections, mainly of dance music and popular songs, and intended for unspecified instrumental combinations, were published by Jacques Moderne in Lyon, and Pierre Phalèse and Tielman Susato in the Low Countries.

14. One of several versions of an image derived from a prototype of *c*1520 attributed to the Master of the Female Half-lengths, thought to have been active in Paris. The flutist, singer, and lutenist are performing Claudin de Sermisy's chanson 'Jouissance vous donneray'. Copies of the painting survive in Vienna, St Petersburg, Meiningen, and Rohrau. In some the flutist plays the superius part, in others the tenor.

The most famous flute consort music of this period was presented in two collections containing instrumental settings of a total of 58 *Chansons* (1533) published in Paris by Pierre Attaingnant. These four-part songs by Claudin de Sermisy, Janequin, Josquin des Pres, Gombert, Heurteur, Passereau and others, are described as suitable for *fleuste dallemant* or *fleuste a neuf trous*, or for both. Those most suitable for transverse flutes are marked with a letter A, are in flat modes, and have wide ranges, as high as F or G in the superius part. Those pieces for recorders, marked with a B, are in modes with a natural B such as G Mixolydian or Hypoaeolian. Chansons suitable for consorts of either instrument are marked AB. The ranges of the AB pieces are smaller, allowing them to be played on flutes at their written pitch on a G-D-D-D consort. In two exceptional AB pieces, 'Voyant souffrir' and 'Allons ung peu', the bass parts descend one note below the range of the bass flute: the solution here seems to be to transpose up a fifth and play the top part on a discant flute (in A) such as the one Agricola, and later Praetorius, described.

Outside France, mixed consorts as well as all-flute ones appear to have been common. In *Frische teutsche Liedlein* (Nuremberg, 1539) the publisher Georg Forster presented music for unspecified instruments by Senfl, Wolff, Forster himself, and others: a contemporary user has written manuscript indications of instrumentation in a copy of the fourth edition (1552), frequently designating the tenor part for *Zwerch pfeif.*

Mixed consorts including flutes first appeared in sacred compositions as well as in domestic settings in Germany. The Bavarian court in Munich under Orlando di Lasso's direction began using stringed instruments in church music as early as 1563. Lasso's ensemble clearly used all sorts of instruments and voices, as a famous painting by Hans Mielich of *c*1565–70 shows, though of course it is unlikely so many musicians played all at once.[33] Instrumentation is not specified in the scores, but the German composer and theorist Michael Praetorius gave Lasso's motets 'In convertendo', 'Quo properas', and 'Laudate' of 1565 as examples of music for a whole consort of transverse flutes in 1619.[34] Whole consorts, as well as mixed ensembles including flutes, also appeared at the wedding of Wilhelm V to Renata of Lorraine (1568) in dance music and vocal works.[35]

The idea of grouping instruments into choirs of contrasting sonority was soon taken up in Venice by musicians who had worked in Munich. Andrea Gabrieli's first published motet collection, which appeared there in 1565, was for *tum viva voce, tum omnis generis instrumentis* (voices or instruments of all kinds). It was not until Giovanni Gabrieli's *Sacrae Simphoniae* appeared in 1597 that specific instruments were suggested, and indeed Praetorius gives a 'Beati Omnes' from this collection as another example of music for flute ensemble. That was already fifteen years after a proposal was made to lower the pitch of Cremona cathedral's organ by a semitone, specifically to enable it to play with instruments in such compositions.

These few sixteenth-century published musical items aside, written sources and iconography give few indications as to what music was played on these instruments and what it sounded like. But with the Renaissance we encounter the first period in history that has left us specimens of flutes that are still playable. We can have no hope of understanding the instructions for playing without being familiar with the instruments they were meant for, just as the instruments remain a mystery until re-united with the instructions, the theory, and the music.

So although the task presents many difficulties, we must try to make sense of the surviving instruments. Our own expectations present the first obstacle. Since the 1970s, cheap and simple-looking 'renaissance' flutes, widely available in Europe and the U.S., have influenced our perceptions of the early flute's musical capabilities.

Almost without exception, these modern folk designs play a D major scale rather than the true renaissance flute's Dorian scale, and so in tuning, tone, and conception exemplify sixteenth-century playing qualities only remotely, if at all. Access to the surviving sixteenth-century flutes is restricted because of their age and fragility, so that only a very few people have studied these objects carefully, and fewer still have made accurate replicas and learned to play them according to contemporary instructions. We rely heavily, therefore, on the educated opinion of these few individuals to form an idea of the renaissance flute's playing qualities.

The next task is to determine which of the more than fifty quasi-cylindrical flutes we know today, mostly found in museums and mostly in Italy, were actually made in the sixteenth century or the early seventeenth, and which are spurious. Fortunately two painstaking researchers, Filadelfio Puglisi and Philippe Allain-Dupré, have made much recent progress on the question, but as Puglisi remarked in a 1988 article, establishing the authenticity of rare museum specimens remains 'a most troublesome problem'.

By far the largest number, about twenty instruments, are signed only with an unknown maker's mark or none at all. Some, such as the group of three at the Vleeshuis Museum in Antwerp, show signs of being nineteenth-century attempts at copying old instruments. Other groups of specimens come with an impeccable provenance to establish their authenticity. The collections in Verona are especially well served by documentation: the five tenor flutes and four basses in the Accademia Filarmonica have been in that institution's collection since around 1570–1600. Inventories of the Biblioteca Capitolare taken in 1640 and 1659 listed twenty-two flutes (*pifari*), mostly still present, as having been bequeathed to the library in 1631.

As early as the fifteenth century artisans occasionally signed their work, and in later generations trademarks were often licensed by guilds or municipal authorities to protect them from unauthorized use. Frank P. Bär (1995) has made the illuminating remark that the Rafis were among the first makers to sign their work with their own name, an innovation that clearly contributed to their fame at a time when most other craftsmen signed with a more cryptic symbol.[36] The Verona flutes carry the trade-marks of at least five different workshops: a crowned eagle, a mark like a rabbit's foot, the letters AA, a trefoil, and two different stamps containing the name Rafi. We still do not know who used the crowned eagle stamp, but new research has taught us a great deal about the meaning of the other signs.

In a recent study of the Bassano family of musicians and woodwind makers of Venice and London, David Lasocki argued that the 'rabbit's foot' mark found on no fewer than 121 sixteenth-century woodwind instruments actually represented silkworm moths, which figured in the Bassano coat-of-arms. A still more recent essay by Maggie Lyndon-Jones dates what are now generally believed to be Bassano flutes in Brussels and Verona to *c*1559–1608 and one in Vienna to before 1596.[37]

The mark A or AA likewise belonged to a dynasty of instrument makers, in this case the two interrelated families of Schnitzers in Nuremberg active over the course of five generations. Some are documented as transverse flute makers: Mathes Schnitzer (*c*1500–53) supplied *Zwerchpfeifen* and cornetts to the Nuremberg council in 1538. Hans Schnitzer I the Elder (*c*1486–1565) was described in a document as *Flötenmacher*, suggesting he specialized in recorders rather than the shawms for which the family was also well known, and in 1566 Hans Schnitzer II (c1530–1601) supplied a case of *Zwerchpfeifen*. In any case, it is not clear that the surviving instruments are representative of their work: while Puglisi finds the Verona examples have been altered, Allain-Dupré believes their present state is the result of crude original workmanship.[38]

The flutes stamped with a trefoil mark can only tentatively be ascribed to Hans Rauch von Schrattenbach in Bavaria. Three makers of this name, perhaps successive generations, are recorded, one as dying in 1526, and another as being a *Pfeifenmacher*, probably not specifically a maker of fifes but simply woodwinds in general, in 1595. Most surviving instruments are stamped with a double trefoil, its stalk turning to the right. But the mark of the Verona flutes, a single trefoil with its stem to the left, does not allow a secure attribution.

Of the signed flutes in Verona and elsewhere, instruments by the Rafi family are the most numerous. Most carry Claude Rafi's mark and are D flutes, the tenor/alto size of the consort, with a smaller group of basses, and no discants. The most common pitch, according to Puglisi's study, is A=410, with a smaller group at A=435. Puglisi notes that tenor flutes at about A=410 make up about half the total number. The Verona collections indicate that sixteenth-century musicians could and did obtain instruments from makers far afield. Many of the surviving renaissance flutes are today preserved in European cities that, as Puglisi has pointed out, are situated on long-established trading routes, notably along the chain of cities linking Venice and Germany via Milan and the Alps.

Subtle differences between these types in construction and playing qualities aside, nearly all the extant instruments follow the rule that renaissance flutes generally work best in flat modes. One possible exception, a flute signed with a maker's mark of a caret with a cross below, was discovered in 1871 among the effects of a Dutch polar expedition that became trapped by ice on the island of Nova Zembla in 1596. The Nova Zembla flute, now in the Rijksmuseum in Amsterdam, differs from the period's consort flutes in several significant respects. Its walls are much thinner, and its toneholes larger, so that it can easily play F$\sharp$ as well as F$\natural$ and B$\natural$ as well as B$\flat$, and its tone is brighter overall. Chapter 3 will recount the emergence of a kind of repertoire quite different from that of the consort flutes, a repertoire which instruments like the Nova Zembla flute may perhaps have been suited to play.

Chapter 3

Consort and solo: the seventeenth century

By the late sixteenth century the flute consort's heyday had passed. Though Anthony Holborne and others in England still published pieces for homogenous consorts of strings or winds after 1600, works in more varied scorings began to include a single flute at around the same time. Thomas Morley's *First Book of Consort Lessons* (1599 and 1611) and Philip Rosseter's *Consort Lessons* (1609) contained songs and dances for a mixed ensemble of treble viol, lute, cittern, bandora, and bass viol, with a D flute on the tenor part, playing an octave higher than written. Michael Praetorius described a similar group of instruments in 1619 as a '*chorus instrumentalum* [choir of instruments] as in an English Consort': 'a loud harpsichord, two or three lutes, a theorbo, bandora, cittern, bass viol, recorder or transverse flute, muted trombone, viola bastarda, and a small discant fiddle',[1] or, in a different specification for music of another sort, 'theorboes, lutes, harpsichord (or spinet or virginal), cittern, and five viols or other fiddles, with a transverse flute or recorder and even a bassoon or dulcian tuned together'.[2] Whether this sort of grouping was really exclusively English, however, seems open to doubt. In Vienna Pietro Melij's *Balletto detto L'Ardito gracioso* (1615) was scored for harpsichord, three sizes of lute, theorbo-guitar, double harp, bass viol, violin (first treble part), and flute (second treble part), while similar instrumental groupings used in the Florentine *intermedi* may well have travelled to England with Italian musicians such as the Bassanos.[3] In any case English troupes of actor-musicians were travelling to the Continent by the early seventeenth century, and England had even begun to export players of wind instruments, in contrast to their wholesale importation a century earlier under Henry VIII. The traffic now evidently flowed both ways: after serving with another English cornettist at the court of Duke Charles III of Lorraine in *c*1604, John Adson returned to his native land, received an appointment in the prestigious London Waits in 1614, and on 4 November 1633 succeeded Henry Lanier in the royal flutes and cornetts.[4]

Musicians in Germany too maintained strong ties with Italy. German composers, Schein, Schütz, and Praetorius, specified transverse flutes for their most notable roles of the early seventeenth century in 'sacred concertos' or 'sacred symphonies', a form Monteverdi and others cultivated in Venice. One of Johann Sebastian Bach's predecessors as *Kantor* (Music Director) of the Thomaskirche in Leipzig, Johann Hermann Schein (1586–1630), composed seven ensemble works that specified a transverse flute (designated by the Italian name *traversa*), always assigned to the second voice, below a cornett or violin on the upper part. With a single exception

15. A female flute player *c*1600 in an allegory of Music, attrib. Dirck de Quade van Ravesteyn.

such compositions are in the hypodorian mode, or the key of G minor. Heinrich Schütz (1585–1672), Kapellmeister (Music Director) at the Saxon court in Dresden for nearly half a century, wrote for the flute only in the highest part of its range in *Jauchzet dem Herrn* (1619) and in *Anima mea liquefacta est* (Venice, 1629). In the latter work he designated the instrument as *fiffaro*, but he called it *traversa* in the four other works in which he specified a transverse flute.

Michael Praetorius (1571–1621), author of important theoretical writings as well as of music specifying transverse flutes, held a post at Wolfenbüttel while developing connections with several other courts including Dresden, where he became acquainted with Schütz. His sacred ensemble works typically employed choirs of contrasting instrumental colour. Most frequently in his collection *Polyhymnia Caduceatrix et Panegyrica* (1619) he left the instrumentation open to numerous alternatives and substitutions, within strictly specified limits of appropriateness. In his musical encyclopaedia *Syntagma Musicum* (1619) he specified certain pieces by other composers as playable on transverse flutes, despite the absence of instrumentation in their scores. In most cases Praetorius designated one of several four-part choirs in a polychoral composition as suitable for flutes, as in his *Erhalt uns, Herr, bei deinem Wort*, in which he specified a choir of *fiffari*, or violins, or mute cornetts, with the bass taken by a bassoon or voice, and in *Jesaia dem Propheten*, where a choir of *fiffari* again had its lowest part performed by voice or bassoon. Thus in 'whole' flute consorts only the three upper parts were to be played on (tenor) flutes, while the bass was to be taken by an instrument (or voice) of more penetrating tone than the bass flute. In other compositions, Praetorius also specified mixed choirs that combined flutes with other instruments such as violins and cornetts. In one choir of *Herr Christ, der einig Gottes Sohn* he specified, as we have already seen, a so-called English Consort, with a flute on the third voice from the top, notated in the tenor clef.

The most important German musician of the early seventeenth century, Praetorius not only wrote over a thousand musical compositions but also provided valuable details of the practicalities of music-making. His three-volume *Syntagma Musicum* aimed to accumulate all the significant musical knowledge of his time. The 'Theatre of Instruments', an appendix to the second volume, published in Wolfenbüttel in

16. Flutes and recorders, from Praetorius's Theatre of Instruments (1618–19). 1: Recorders, whole consort. 2: *Doltzflöt* in G. 3: Transverse flutes, whole consort. 4: Swiss fife. 5: Tabor pipes, bass and discant. 6: Tabor, to be used with the tabor pipes.

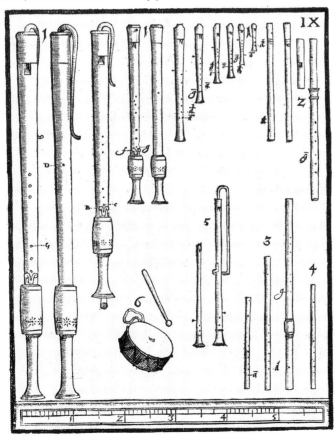

1618–19, described and illustrated all the instruments in detail. It distinguished between consort flutes and military fifes, and provided information about a third kind of transverse flute, the *Doltzflöt*, related to the recorder, of which we have no other information.

> The *Querpfeiffen* (*Traversa* or *Fiffaro* in Italian) have six holes in front, none behind: they naturally produce 15 pitches or notes, and four more falsetto notes [that is, notes that skilled players are able to produce] besides, and thus 19 notes, just like a cornett.

> This is the same situation as with the *Doltzflöten* (which are otherwise called *Querflöten*) except that these are tuned and played like a recorder.

> Here belongs also the Swiss fife (*Schweitzerpfeiff*), otherwise called Military fife (*Feldpfeiff*). This has its own special fingering, which is not at all the same [*ganz nicht überein kommet*] as the *Querflöte*, and is only used with soldier-drums.

Praetorius mentions that the *Schweitzer Pfeiff* (ill. 16, bottom right corner, identified by the number 4) is the same length as the English tabor pipe, a fact apparent from the plate, where its length matches that of the pipe in D, the shorter of the two at number 5.

The *Doltzflöt* (top right corner, indicated by a 2 that resembles the letter Z) is something of a puzzle: David Z. Crookes suggests that we interpret it as a type of recorder with a flute headjoint, an instrument of which the earliest extant examples date from the eighteenth century. There are apparently two sizes, in G and D, but the pitch of the large *Doltzflöt* is given as G1 – the same as that of a recorder half its length.

The consort of ordinary transverse flutes (number 3) contains a G bass, a D tenor/alto, and a discant in A1. However, Praetorius's remarks reveal that the bass and discant were relatively rarely used in his day, and that when he refers to the flute without qualification he means the tenor/alto flute. Philippe Allain-Dupré notes that in Praetorius's chart of woodwind instruments, drawn precisely to a scale of Brunswick feet, the measurements of the transverse flutes indicate that they were tuned two tones lower than the recorders and one tone below the mute cornetts. Praetorius specified the pitches used in different ensembles and countries: thus in some places a chamber pitch a whole tone higher than choir pitch was used, and in England and the Netherlands another pitch a minor third lower than chamber pitch, at which harpsichords and flutes sounded better – but this pitch was not used for large ensembles. From the 1589 Stuttgart court inventory, it appears that curved cornetts there were at chamber pitch (about A=460), while mute cornetts and flutes were at choir pitch (A=410). Thus chamber-pitched flutes were probably exceptional, a conclusion borne out by the pitches of the majority of surviving seventeenth-century flutes, which were meant to sound at least a whole tone lower than recorders and cornetts.

'Even today,' writes Anne Smith (1992), 'the subject of the renaissance flute and transposition always seems to involve mental acrobatics.' Part of this difficulty may be due to the obligatory transposition much vocal and consort music of the sixteenth and early seventeenth centuries implies in its notation. For singers especially, written notes represented interval relationships rather than fixed pitches. The position of the clef and the presence or absence of a flat (the only key-signature in existence) dictated where the semitones fell in the scale. Schütz's *Psalmen Davids* op. 5 (1628 R/1661) contains 158 psalms of which 30 are written in high clefs and over 100 come with explicit instructions for transposing a fourth or a fifth, as do many of Praetorius's polychoral pieces. Transpositions in most of the period's repertoire, however, must be deduced from the clefs alone.

Chiavi naturali (low or natural clefs) and *chiavette* (high or transposed clefs) were terms first used by eighteenth-century theorists to describe the two most commonly used sets of clefs, each with its own variants, in the four-part music of the previous two centuries. In the natural system the cantus part would be notated in C1 (i.e. C clef on the first line), the alto in C2 or C3, the tenor in C3, and the bass in F4. Violins and transverse flutes might have to transpose pieces in these clefs up a fourth to make them fit the instruments' range.

In some modes, however, the range of the parts, whether for voices or instruments, would run off the stave if the natural clefs were used. Rather than draw ledger lines, scribes or printers would write the parts in transposed clefs. For example, to prevent music in the Hypodorian or Second mode lying below the staves, as it would if written in natural clefs, the piece would be transposed a fourth higher and written in high clefs (G2, C2, C3, and F3, C4, or C3). Then whole consorts of voices, recorders, or viols would transpose these pieces back down to their original pitches, while flutes, cornetts, and violins would play them at the written pitch.

In practice, flutes could play in both kinds of clefs, but the transposed-clef settings placed the music best in the flutes' ranges. A third clef combination *in contrabasso*, using C2, C3, F4, and F5, was used only for special mournful pieces or for consorts of tenor and bass viole da gamba.

Since early seventeenth-century ensemble music rarely specifies instrumentation precisely, anyone today wishing to play such music on flutes of the period, or to understand how this was done, needs to make certain decisions as to what pieces are suitable. These are the same decisions that faced seventeenth-century musicians, and consequently Praetorius's discussion of how to tell if a piece is suitable for flutes is one of the most interesting and helpful parts of his testimony for us. Praetorius's instructions amplify Jambe de Fer's observation that the flat hexachord is most suitable for the flute. As well as indicating pieces in flat modes as suitable for flute consort, he notes that some natural modes are also available. Pieces in Aeolian or Hypoaeolian mode can be played by transposing down a tone and adding a flat key-signature (i.e. from A minor to G minor):

For although transverse flutes are sometimes used in Cantu H duro [i.e. in the hard hexachord], it does not quite work in all Modes or Tones; which is why it is customary to play in the tenth mode Hypoaeolian a tone lower on transverse flutes. And there is nothing more suitable to it than Dorian, Hypodorian, and Hypoaeolian *in secundo inferiore* [a tone lower].[5]

17. Johann Sadeler (Antwerp, c1570–1629) after Maerten de Vos (1532–1603), *The Magnificat a 5 by Cornelius Verdonck* (1585). The music is in five parts rather than the four shown: the tenor part is marked 'Canon in diapason', indicating that a second voice begins singing or playing when the first tenor reaches the fourth note. The cornett plays the *superius*, the viola da gamba on the left plays the *tenor*, the flute plays the *altus*, and the viola da gamba on the right plays the *bassus*. The *canon in diapason* is sung by the soprano (the Blessed Virgin Mary), or perhaps by the angel holding the music on the left (see Gianni Lazzari, 'Il Magnificat di Cornelius Verdoncks nel repertorio del flauto traverso', *SIFTS* 2.2 (September 1997), 12–22).

Praetorius suggests using three tenor flutes to play the upper three parts, tenor, altus, and cantus, with a bassoon, shawm, trombone, or tenor violin on the bassus when the part's tessitura would place it in the weak lower range of the bass flute. He mentions three vocal works by other composers as suitable music for three flutes and bass, all of them in *cantus mollis* (flat modes): Claudio Merulo's *Cantate Domino* and *Magnum hereditatis mysterium*, Giovanni Gabrieli's *Beati omnes*, and Hans Leo Hassler's *Venite exultemus*. To achieve a good balance in the top three parts, he writes, it is important that the tenor part not lie too low, because the flute's low register is softer than the upper range, where the cantus and altus parts will lie. Again none of the works Praetorius indicates is given any instrumental specification by its composer. In fact the only Venetian composer of the period who did call specifically for transverse flutes, Claudio Monteverdi, gave a pair of instruments designated *fifara* or *pifara* a cameo role in the 'Quia respexit' of his *Vespers* of 1610, and again, as an alternative to recorder, in 1619 in *A Quest'olmo*, a concerted work in six parts. Like Schütz he wrote for the flute only in the highest part of its range.

Into a musical scene now permeated by mixed consorts of viols, violins, recorders, flutes, cornetts, trombones, and plucked and keyboard instruments, a totally new kind of instrumental music emerged in Italy at the end of the sixteenth century: the solo sonata. The new music, following the example of a progressive style of dramatic singing that emphasized the expression of character, placed one instrument in a dominant position and made the *continuo*, a harmonic accompaniment improvised from a specially annotated bass line, subservient to the soloist's emotional message.

An increasing number of musicians began to publish compositions of this type, for sale not only to other professional performers, but also to a growing market of merchant-class people with the leisure and income to develop their talents as amateur musicians. Such a market could never have become established without the efforts to increase musical literacy through the printing press we saw in Chapter 2. Solo instrumental pieces first appeared in print in Italy, specifically in the commercial Republic of Venice, where a vigorous printing industry had flourished in the absence of political and ecclesiastical censorship. With the high cost of producing printed music by means of movable type, and before the growth of a distribution network, it was imperative on composers, who underwrote publication with their own money or that of a patron, to sell as many copies of each composition as they could locally. Therefore they usually specified not that the music should be played on cornett, violin, transverse flute (*traversa*), or viola bastarda, but rather that it was suitable for any and all of these instruments, and others besides. As the introduction to Giovanni Bassano's *Ricercate, Passagi et Cadentie* (1585) explained, the publication of such pieces was intended to train the player in the exercise of divisions. Evidently some editions were intended to teach instrumental execution as well, since one of the few collections to specifically indicate the flute gave basic instructions for playing it. Book 3 of Aurelio Virgiliano's *Il Dolcimelo* (c1600), a collection of *Ricercate* for cornett, violin, transverse flute, or other instruments, contains a fingering chart for a D flute with a range of two and a half octaves. Virgiliano mentions that the flute can transpose a fourth higher, and a fourth or a fifth lower, though the pieces he specifies for flute, violin, or cornett, notated in a C1 clef, suit only the flute's range while requiring the other two instruments to transpose up a fourth.[6] Ludovico Zacconi's *Prattica di musica* (1592) gave a smaller range of two octaves, but if the notes were fewer their intonation could be more nuanced, since players were advised to shade or leak certain toneholes to help play in tune. Francesco Rognoni's singing and instrumental manual *Selva de varii passaggi* (1620), on the other hand, gave the *fifola* a range of only 18 notes.

Italian music in the seventeenth century, as so frequently afterwards, exerted a powerful influence on the rest of Europe. Yet even the Italians still associated the transverse flute with Germany and the Germans at that time. The Roman Vincenzo Giustiniani (1564–1637) thought it worthy of notice that two gentlemen of his acquaintance played such an exotic instrument:

Playing the Fife or Transverse Flute (*Pifero o sia Traversa*) in the German manner, yet with elements of musical counterpoint and with grace and precision, is not something known to many in Italy. In Rome Signor Giulio Cesare d'Orvieto used to play it, and at present it is also played by a prominent gentleman, who among the many virtues and distinguished responsibilities he possesses in great abundance, also plays this instrument to the amazement of those who listen.[7]

Indeed, flutes for consort music seem to have been hard to come by in Italy. At Mantua in 1607, Giovanni Gabrieli's help was sought regarding the acquisition of transverse flutes in Venice, to which the composer replied that 'they cost the maker dearly to make, and are difficult to sell'.[8] Two Italian institutions, however, managed to acquire sets of flutes for their instrument collections. An inventory of the Accademia Filarmonica in Verona (1628) contained three cased sets of *fifferi*, two containing six and the third twenty-six, as well as nine separate instruments of which three were described as unmatched and old (*3 fifferi diversi vecchi*).[9] In 1631 the same city's Biblioteca Capitolare inherited two cases containing five *pifari* and one holding ten, along with two boxwood basses in disrepair (*Due pifari grandi di busso mal all'ordine*).[10] Incidentally, the survival of these inventories alongside the collections to which they all but certainly refer shows that the term *pifaro* could refer to a transverse flute as well as a shawm.

A catalogue published in Latin in 1664 and in Italian two years later detailed the magnificent collection of pictures, art works, natural curiosities, and musical instruments, including four dozen recorders and flutes, belonging to the Milanese physician and priest Manfredo Settala (1600–80).[11] Settala owned four sets of *Helveticae fistulae* (Swiss pipes), described in the Italian as *traverse, ò vogliamo dire Piffari all'Inglese* (transverse flutes, or rather English [i.e. transalpine] fifes), all signed by a maker Frank P. Bär (1995) has identified as Claude Rafi of Lyon.[12] Besides several consorts of recorders, Settala possessed a set of flutes at choir pitch, another set in exotic wood with two-piece basses, a third pitched a tone lower with all the sizes in two pieces, and a fourth a tone higher.[13]

Another document of 1 October 1640 lists musical instruments lent out from a collection held by the Medici court:

> To Vincenzo Bacherelli: two medium transverse flutes (*traverse mezzane*), one large transverse flute, one small transverse flute. To Pacol Gradi: three transverse flutes, one for consorts (*una di concerto*), one small one a fourth higher (*a quarta alta*), and one with two white ferrules.... Six transverse flutes made by the hand of *Il Contadino* [The Peasant] are granted to Vettorio Baldani for personal use.... A large consort transverse flute....[14]

In these listings we can recognize that Vincenzo was borrowing a consort of bass, two tenor/altos, and a discant, and that Vettorio had the loan of a six-flute set like those mentioned in the Verona inventory. However, among the instruments lent to Pacol Gradi was a transverse flute we have not encountered before: a *traversa a quarta alta* (transverse flute a fourth higher), thus with a lowest note of G rather than the usual D.

A more definite indication of such an instrument's existence, together with a repertoire appropriate for it, comes in the preface to Jacob van Eyck's three-part collection of diminution-variations on popular tunes, *Der Fluyten Lust-hof* (The Flute's pleasure-garden, Amsterdam, 1644–9). Though van Eyck's pieces were primarily intended for a small recorder in C as opposed to the apparently more usual discant instrument in G, his publisher tried to broaden his market by suggesting as an alternative a high transverse flute in G, promising to give further information about playing the instrument in the collection's third instalment, which unfortunately either never appeared or has not survived. Certainly Dutch iconography from the golden age of its oil painters presents many examples of small transverse flutes being played: some of these may be military instruments, but the van Eyck publication suggests that a G treble flute was in use in the Netherlands as a solo instrument as well. Thiemo Wind (1995) has noted that van Eyck's divisions represent an old-fashioned style, and warned against assuming too much similarity between Dutch and Italian practices of the time.[15] Nonetheless, it is tempting to speculate that the small transverse flute *a quarta alta* that Pacol Gradi borrowed might have been employed in Italy for playing solo division music in the same way as in the North. Another speculative link might be made between van Eyck's music and an instrument about the function of which little is known: the Nova Zembla flute (see p. 48). This instrument differs from the consort flutes not only in its more brilliant and less colourful tone, but in allowing a D major scale to be played more easily while still favouring the $F_{\natural}$, $C_{\natural}$, and $B_{\flat}$ of the Dorian scale.

Another instrument in G appears in Marin Mersenne's *Harmonie Universelle* (French and Latin editions, 1636), a giant compendium of all learning, ancient and modern, on the subject of music. Its author, a major figure in seventeenth-century scholarship, confirmed Praetorius's indications that flutes were made at *ton de chapelle,* or consort pitch, for playing in ensembles, and that a different instrument such as trombone or serpent was often used to play the bass. As an example of consort music for flutes, Mersenne printed an *Air de cour,* a secular song performed for the king and his courtiers, by Henri Le Jeune, in the unusual mode of C-Ionian (C major), introducing an F$^\sharp$ in a G major cadence in the upper voice (ill. 18). The piece is written in transposed clefs or *chiavette* (see p. 53), which indicates that it is meant to be played at written pitch on a normal (G-D-D-D) consort of flutes.

18. *Air de cour* by Henri Le Jeune, an example of music for flute consort from Mersenne's *Harmonie Universelle* (1636).

Despite his efforts and his erudition, however, and as he himself admitted, Mersenne did not understand the construction and playing of wind instruments well enough to explain them, and inconsistencies, together with possible editing or typographical errors, in his chapter on the flute make matters worse. A thorough explanation of Mersenne's text on flutes awaits the attention of a courageous and patient researcher, but in the meantime we must note some of the problems it presents.

The chapter contains three fingering charts in all, for what are probably intended to be three different types of flute. The first begins with a C clef that changes to a G clef in the second octave, and indicates the fingering with open or closed circles. Two other charts have G clefs and fingerings indicated by lines. The first chart, for a G instrument with a range of nineteen notes, is labelled 'German flute' in the French text, but 'Swiss fife' in the Latin. Mersenne compounds this ambiguity by specifying that the chart with circles is for a particular flute he describes in the text as 'one of the best flutes in the world' – but that it can also serve for the fife. Mersenne's manuscript annotations in his own copy of the *Harmonie Universelle*, preserved at the library of the Museum of Arts and Crafts in Paris, suggest that he was himself unsure about the distinction, if any existed, between flutes and fifes. The annotations include a sketch labelled *Pfifre ou flute traversiere*, its sounding length marked off into 27 equal divisions, with toneholes at 5, 7, 9, 11, 13, and 15 units from the lower end. In the text itself Mersenne writes that the Swiss fife and the kind of flute in the first diagram are quite similar: 'the fife … differs from the German flute only in that it sounds louder (*plus fort*), its sounds are much more vigorous and brilliant, and that it is shorter and narrower'. Yet the fingerings of the first chart actually differ very significantly from those in the second and third. Raymond Meylan (1974) noted that the first chart, for a G instrument, assigns to D and E in the second octave (equivalent to A and B on a D flute) the same fingerings as in the octave below.[16] On ordinary flutes of the sixteenth and seventeenth centuries those fingerings are far too flat to be usable, but in the earliest fingering chart for a conical-bored flute, the one Jacques Hotteterre published in 1707 (chapter 4), these notes are assigned the same fingering in both octaves, so that A and B in the first octave simply overblow to the second, as in Mersenne's first chart. Meylan interprets this congruence to indicate that the G instrument may have had a conical bore, as opposed to the more usual cylindrical one. If he is correct, conical-bored flutes may have been made half a century before the fully-developed 'baroque' flute appeared in *c*1700.

Be that as it may, Mersenne's text presents still more challenges with a set of measurements taken from the instrument he describes as 'one of the best flutes in the world'. The text makes quite clear that the fingering chart for *this* flute is the *first* chart, the one for a flute in G, with its fingerings indicated by circles. Yet the instrument's total length is given as one and five-sixths feet, which unmistakably indicates an instrument in D. On the other hand, the distances given between the toneholes are, as Trevor Robinson noted in 1973, much too small to be practicable on a D flute.[17] In any case, two crucial pieces of data are missing: the distance between the embouchure hole and the first tonehole, and the distance between toneholes 4 and 5. Though with ingenuity those dimensions can be guessed within reasonable limits, Robinson's reconstruction used what seems an unacceptable degree of latitude to interpret the measurements that were given, and no more convincing attempt has yet been published.

This conflicting information makes it difficult to determine whether the bore of 'one of the best flutes in the world' was cylindrical as Mersenne stated, or whether Meylan's conjecture is the more plausible possibility. If the bore of his flute contracted towards the foot and flared out again so that the ends of the tube were of the same diameter, as baroque flute bores typically did, Mersenne could easily have been mistaken on this point. On the other hand if the toneholes of the G flute or fife were much larger than those indicated by the dimensions, it could have overblown its one- and two-fingered notes at the octave even if its bore was cylindrical.

Another French writer's distinction between the German flute and the fife shows that for him too the differences were of size and usage rather than of construction and fingering. Pierre Trichet (1586/7–1644), whose manuscript treatise on musical instruments of about 1640 was never published, considered the question from a historical perspective:

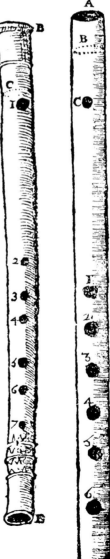

> Glareanus, in the commentary he made on the *Ars Poetica* of Horace, thought the fife [*fifre*] should be placed in the class of German flutes [*flustes d'aleman*]. What made him think this way is the small difference that exists between these two types of instrument. But if he had properly considered that the fife is more hoarse and shorter than any of these flutes he would in my opinion have been dissuaded of this point of view. ...
>
> It is certainly true that at present the fife is hugely popular [in war to rouse the soldiers in combat] [...], not only among the Swiss and the Germans but also among several other nations which use them in their military exercises, accompanying it with the drum [*tambour*], although the former are used in the same way and the latter in another according to the various traditions and the various fingerings [*tablatures*] that are customary.

Whatever instruments the military fifers played, Claude Menestrier wrote thirty years after Trichet that both *flutes traversieres* and *fifres* were suitable for the 'warlike harmony' of public spectacles, while recorders were more suited to gentler music.[18]

19. Two kinds of *Flustes d'Allemand*, or *Fluste d'Allemand* and *Fifre*, from Mersenne's *Harmonie Universelle* (1636).

Fifers, in any case, were neither ordinary musicians nor common soldiers, but members of a select and specialized group within the army. A document of 1621 mentioned that the English army had only forty each of drummers and fifers at that date. Besides their musical duties, fifers, many of whom may even now have been foreigners, were apparently expected to act as interpreters and as drill instructors. In return they received pay of 1s. a day, fourpence more than a private soldier's 8d.[19]

French allegorical iconography of the early seventeenth century continued to show transverse flutes in the hands of angels, in ensembles with voice and lute, and with other more obviously 'angelic' instruments such as harp, organ, trumpet, and cymbals, as well as in representations of the muses. Documentary evidence in French sources, on the other hand, rarely includes mention of flutes in the first half of the century, and the instrument seems to have remained in decline in that country. In 1656, Mathieu Lallemant (i.e. 'the German') lost the position he had held as the only *joueur de flûte de la chambre*, to be replaced by a theorbist, 'because this instrument [whether recorder or flute is not clear] is not used any more these days in chamber music and because the theorbo is more important there'.[20] Yet the flute's status was soon to change once again.

The official musical life of the Sun King's court from the 1660s on was intensely ordered and regulated by patents and royal decrees, extensively rehearsed, and held under the strict control of the violinist, dancer, composer, and impresario Jean-Baptiste Lully (1632–87). The instruments of the formal court music were those played in the various bands of the royal establishment, whose posts were usually held by members of the same family for generations at a stretch, like those of other servants down to the gardeners. These included the violins of the *Vingt-quatre violons du Roi*, founded by Louis XIII; the *Grande Bande* and the *Petits Violons*; the *Musique de la Chapelle Royale*; the winds and brass of the *Grande Ecurie*, whose sections included such antique titles as *cromornes et trompettes marines* and *musettes et hautbois de Poitou*; and the *Musique de Chambre*.

At the same time music of a more impromptu and private nature also held a place in the court's private recreation. Providing respite from the court's intense lifestyle, such intimate musical performances occasionally took place in the private chambers of Louis XIV and the most prominent of his courtiers at palaces such as Fontainebleau, Versailles, and Sceaux. Accounts of these private concerts exist not only in court documents but also in the diaries kept by numerous denizens of the royal circle keen to record every event in the whirl of its life, from which fortune or politics might at any moment eject them with nothing except their memories.[21] Evenings of *appartement* with the King and his closest companions often consisted of card games, sometimes for staggeringly high stakes, and other diversions such as music and dancing of a less formal kind than was usual at the huge court balls. A few favourite musicians were often summoned to play at impromptu parties organized on a whim for only a handful of invited personages. The performances took place in the chambers of courtiers such as the Duchess of Burgundy or Madame de Maintenon, the largest of which were the King's mistress's apartments at Fontainebleau, only a few hundred square feet in area.[22] The most favoured instruments at such events were those best suited to the execution of intimate nuances of expression: the theorbo, the harpsichord, the viola da gamba, and the transverse flute.

Flutists often named among the performers included Philbert or Philibert Rebillé (*fl* 1667–1717), René Pignon Descoteaux (1645–*p*1732), and later Jacques Hotteterre and Michel de Labarre (1680–1743) (see chapter 4), together with their accompanists de Viseé (theorbo), Forqueray (viola da gamba), Buterne, and Couperin (harpsichord). A report of about 1730 by the celebrated eighteenth-century flutist and composer Michel de Labarre described the high status the King bestowed on the first two named flutists:

> It was Philbert who first played [the transverse flute] in France, and then at almost the same time Descoteaux. The King as well as the whole court, whom this instrument pleased infinitely, added two posts to the four *musettes de Poitou* and gave them to Philbert and Descoteaux and they told me several times that the King wished heartily when he gave them to them that the six musettes [bagpipes] could be metamorphosed into transverse flutes, so that at least they would be useful, instead of which the musettes were suitable only for the dancing of peasants. ...[23]

According to accounts quoted by Jane Bowers, it was in 1667 that Philbert first appeared in the records as *Joueur de flutte ordinaire du Cabinet* (flute-player in ordinary to the chamber) and René Pignon Descoteaux was listed as playing in place of his father François *avecq les musettes* – though the term *flutte* could still refer to the recorder and the records do not specify whether or not the two musicians played transverse flutes at that time.

The names of Philbert and Descoteaux, both of whom were famous for their singing as well as their transverse flute playing, became synonymous with the instrument's sad, tender, and languishing character in the last decades of the seventeenth century. Their personal fame clearly did much to promote the flute's reputation at a time when other instruments, such as those of the oboe, violin, lute, and keyboard families, provided musicians with the only realistic prospects of employment. The poet Alexandre Lainez (*c*1650–1710) contributed to Philbert's fame in a poem he wrote for the express purpose of 'immortalizing' him:

Cherchez-vous des plaisirs, allez trouver Philbert;	If you seek pleasure, go and find Philbert;
Sa voix, des doux chants de Lambert,	His voice, in the sweet songs of Lambert,
Passe au bruit éclatant d'un tonnerre qui gronde:	Alters to the violent noise of a rolling thunder:
Sa Flute seule est un Concert.	His flute alone is an ensemble.
La fleur naît sous ses mains dans un affreux désert,	The flower is born under his hand in a frightful desert,
Et la langue féconde	And his fruitful tongue
Imite, en badinant, tous les Peuples du Monde.	Imitates, in jest, all the peoples of the world.
Si dans un vaste Pavillon	If in a great pavilion
Il sonne le tocsin, ou fait un carillon,	He sounds the alarm bell, or plays a chime,
En battant un pöele a frire;	By striking a frying pan;
Le Héros immortel, que nous révérons tous,	The immortal Hero, whom we all revere,
Devient un homme comme nous,	Becomes a man like us,
Il éclate de rire.	He bursts out laughing.
Cherchez-vous des plaisirs, allez trouver Philbert;	If you seek pleasure, go and find Philbert;
Sa Flute seule est un Concert.[24]	His flute alone is an ensemble.

At court, the flutists enjoyed royal favour and were often summoned to impromptu performances both indoors and out:

> [Philbert] played the German flute perfectly. He was a friend of Descoteaux, famous for playing the same instrument. Louis XIV took genuine pleasure in hearing these two individuals interpret melodious songs on their flutes, and often had them come to do so in his apartments and in the groves of Versailles.[25]

An obituary notice for Descoteaux in 1728 gives further details, including the flutists' repertoire:

> He had great talents for music in general, with an admirable taste for singing and for instruments, above all the transverse flute, from which he drew an admirable tone, at a time when that instrument was hardly known at all in France. He was one of the first to make it fashionable. He scarcely played anything but little delicate airs [*petits airs tendres*], but with charming taste and neatness.[26]

The 'songs of Lambert' mentioned in Lainiez's poem are examples of the flute's 'sad, languishing' repertoire.[27] These appeared in a collection of about sixty *Airs* with instrumental *ritournelles* in 1689, and in a monthly series of 'serious airs' and 'drinking songs' (1695–1724) edited by Christophe Ballard, who published another set of *Brunettes ou petits airs tendres* in three volumes (1703–11). The fashion for playing *airs* and *brunettes* on the flute continued throughout the first half of the eighteenth century as other composers published collections, among them Jacques Martin Hotteterre (c1721), Michel Pignolet de Montéclair (c1721–33), and Michel Blavet (1744–*p*50).

These simple pieces were made exquisitely expressive by the addition of ornaments or graces to shape their inflexion and, on plucked instruments with limited control of attack and decay, to add light and shade. Bénigne de Bacilly devoted a chapter of his treatise on the performance of *Airs de cour* (1679) to the manner of ornamenting them, in an old-fashioned style that predated the simpler, more codified ornaments called *agréments* of Lully's style.[28] Bacilly's remarks make clear that such ornamentation called for a flexible tempo, and 'sometimes even mutilating the meter, in order to make them more expressive and to give room for ornamentation'.[29]

Articulation and phrasing were also key techniques for the French manner of expression. Patricia M. Ranum has shown that closely reading and strictly interpreting the rules given by authorities such as Etienne Loulié and, later, Jacques Hotteterre, reveals a highly distinctive character in the phrasings of seventeenth-century French song. Ranum argues that the modern 'Euro-approach' to baroque articulation practised by most original-instrument performers today eliminates this distinction, flattening the features of the music's unique character.

Some of the airs the flute played at the French court took the form of dances. John Playford's *The English Dancing Master* (1651) had contributed to a vogue for French and Scottish music in London in the 1680s, while at about the same time the recreation of Louis XIV's court featured similar country dances, altered to conform to the court's taste by the introduction of characteristic steps. At the French court the dramatic *ballet de cour* made dancing into an activity for spectators, and dance scenes from Lully's operas appeared separately as instrumental pieces. At the same time German composers used some of the stylized musical features of the court dances in instrumental suites that began to establish a standard formula: a stately *allemande*, a rhythmically complex *courante*, a slow and expressive *sarabande*, and a lively *gigue*. The French dance suites published later typically included these as well as lighter and shorter pieces: *gavottes*, *passepieds*, and *bourrées*.

Though by the late seventeenth century a revival in the flute's fortunes was clearly under way, we have almost no direct evidence about the instruments of this period, in France or elsewhere. Composers still wrote for the flute principally in the Hypodorian mode or the key of G minor, the same tonality favoured by Schein, Praetorius, and others. But the French *Airs de cour* and the flute parts in music with strings and continuo now used the range from D1 to D3, in contrast to the higher range (typically D2-G3) the German and Italian composers had exploited. This difference suggests that some new type of flute with a stronger first octave had come into existence.

Four extant instruments may represent this early phase of the baroque flute, in France and elsewhere, but the difficulty of dating them precisely prevents us from drawing many useful insights. A two-piece flute in D at a pitch of about A=450 having a more tapered and ornamented exterior profile than most consort flutes but a similar cylindrical bore and keyless construction (Vienna: Kunsthistorisches Museum) is signed by a maker named Lissieu about whom little is known. Pierre Borjon de Scellery referred to him as an instrument-maker of Lyon in his *Traité de la Musette* (1672), so the Vienna instrument probably dates from the third quarter of the seventeenth century. An instrument, perhaps a military flute, with similar characteristics (Nuremberg: Germanisches Nationalmuseum) may come from Augsburg or northern Italy.[30]

What are probably the earliest surviving examples of flutes having conical bores, three-piece construction, and a key for E♭, are an anonymous D flute (A=395) (I–Assisi: Biblioteca Comunale) and a C flute (A=410; or possibly a D flute at about A=360) by Richard Haka (Amsterdam, before 1646–1705; NL-Utrecht: Stichting Ehrenfeld). The reasons for assigning an early date to the Assisi instrument have been laid out by Vincenzo De Gregorio (1984), and the death of Richard Haka in 1705 provides the latest possible date for the Utrecht flute.[31]

These two instruments exhibit significant technical differences from later flutes, as well as, more obviously, from earlier ones. The Haka flute's bore taper, that is, the difference between the smallest point of its bore and the largest point, expressed as a percentage of the maximum bore diameter, is slightly less than 10 per cent, while the Assisi flute is almost twice as tapered, at 18 per cent. However, these bores are significantly less conical than those of surviving three-piece instruments we think of as 'baroque' flutes, such as those by Bressan (21 per cent), Hotteterre (26 per cent), and Naust (29 per cent).[32] The two instruments only began to attract the attention of researchers and instrument-makers in the 1990s, and have yet to be taken up by players, so that while experts agree that they represent an intermediate form of the baroque flute, it is still too early to give a fuller evaluation of their significance, or their playing qualities in the music of their times.

20. Robert Bonnart, *Simphonie du tympanum, du Luth, et de la Flûte d'Allemagne* (Instrumental ensemble of dulcimer, lute, and German flute, 1692).

Un Consert est charmant lors qu'il est bien d'accord,	An ensemble is charming when it's well in tune,
Et qu'on sçait justement suivre sa tablature;	And when you know how to follow your tablature [or: fingering chart] correctly;
Mail il est bien plus doux, ou je me trompe fort,	But it is much more sweet, unless I'm quite mistaken,
Quand l'Amour prend plaisir de battre la mesure.	When Love takes pleasure in beating time.

Two engravings of the 1690s by Robert and Nicolas Bonnart show flutists in a fashionable setting that associates flutes with feelings of charm and love. One engraving, in which the flute itself appears cylindrical with ornamental turning, shows the instrument in an ensemble with tympanum (dulcimer) and lute (ill. 20).[33]

An association with love also accompanied what was probably the debut of the newly designed baroque flute at the French court. A *ritornello* in the key of G minor for two *flutes d'Allemagne* and continuo appeared in Lully's opera-ballet *Le Triomphe de l'Amour* (1681), in which transverse flutes, specified as an alternative to violas, provided the upper part in an ensemble with lower-voiced recorders in a *Prelude pour l'amour*. Payroll records from 1680–1 list the flutists Descoteaux, Hotteterre, and four members of the Piesche family as participants in rehearsals and performances of the opera. After this the flute began to appear more regularly at court in other ensemble compositions for church, opera, and chamber. French composers of the 1690s continued to score for the instrument in its traditional mode or tonality, but in ensembles that set a pair of them, often playing in thirds or sixths, against a body of strings and continuo instruments. Marc Antoine Charpentier's *Magnificat in G* (late 1680s) contains parts for two flutes, often *soli* and in G minor, and the same composer wrote for flutes in an ensemble with five string parts in his *Médée* (1694). Jane Bowers has identified a wide variety in Charpentier's later scoring for transverse flutes, including the use of larger sizes in the undated *Messe pour plusieurs instruments au lieu des orgues*, as well as solos in Tenebrae lessons probably composed *c*1698–1704.[34] André Campra's *Hesione* (1700) contained two G minor passages for transverse flutes, whereas his *Arethuse* (1701) scored for them in major keys.[35] In Campra's opera *Tancrède* (1702), an aria in C minor is scored for recorders on the upper part, with *tailles de violons et flûtes allemandes* (violas and [tenor] transverse flutes), in a range from F to C two octaves above, but Marco Brolli (1996–7) argues for its performance an octave higher on ordinary transverse flutes.[36] Two foreign musicians who spent time in Paris absorbing Lully's style employed flutes in different ways in their later theatre productions elsewhere: Agostino Steffani's Italian opera *Alarico il Baltha* (Munich, 1687) contained parts for two *piffari*, while a pastoral piece in another love-related opera entitled *Erindo oder die unsträfliche Liebe* (The blameless love; Braunschweig-Wolfenbüttel, 1691, published 1694) by Johann Sigismund Kusser (1660–1727) featured an obbligato *Flauto Tedesco* or German flute in an astonishing F minor aria with voice and continuo.[37]

By the 1690s new chamber ensemble configurations in France included the flute alongside violins and other instruments as well as the earlier favourites, theorbo and viola da gamba. A *Sonate* of *c*1686 attributed to Charpentier specified two German flutes, two 'treble violins', a bass viol, a five-string bass violin (a cello tuned in B♭), a harpsichord, and a theorbo.[38] At a performance in 1701, Philbert and Descoteaux joined the harpsichordist François Couperin, the theorbist Robert de Visée, the violinists Jean-Fery Rebel and Antoine Fave, and a little girl whose activities were not specified.[39] Marin Marais's collection of suites *Pieces en trio pour les flutes, violon, & dessus de viole* (1692) did not specifically call for the transverse flute as distinct from the recorder, but an engraving on the publication's title page showed what may be the earliest representation of the flute in a more advanced stage of development than the Haka and Assisi flutes typify, though the instrument's decorative turning is not quite of the distinctive Hotteterre type (see chapter 4). Another collection of trios, by Labarre (1694), suggests that the instrument's popularity was on the increase, in that the publication was dedicated to a Mlle G.L.C., most likely a female amateur musician.[40]

For some reason (to be explored but not resolved in this essay), we are powerfully drawn to the subject of beginnings. We yearn to know about origins, and we readily construct myths when we do not have data (or we suppress data in favour of legend when a truth strikes us as too commonplace)....
[W]e have origin myths and stories for the beginning of hunting, of language, of art, of kindness, of war, of boxing, bowties, and brassieres.[1]

Stephen Jay Gould might well have added the modern flute to this list of origin myths in his essay (1989) on the 'creation' of American baseball. Since the mid-twentieth century – no earlier – the claim that a member of the Hotteterre family invented the baroque flute has entered the lore of the flute, providing a convenient, though largely imaginary, starting point for the modern French-derived school of flute-playing (see chapters 11 and 12). The claim first surfaced in the 1930s and has been advanced with increasing frequency and confidence since that time, despite the lack of any real evidence to support it.[2] Modern writers commonly claim that Jacques Hotteterre invented the baroque flute in about 1660, though he was only born in 1664, or that his grandfather Jean invented the instrument and then published a tutor for it 47 years later, after he had been dead for 15 years.[3]

Recent historical research has provided a more factual view of developments in woodwinds in France, or at least at the French court. In a 1988 article that upset theories about the baroque oboe's origin, Bruce Haynes suggested that that instrument, also previously believed to have been invented at the French court around 1660, and also by members of the Hotteterre family, seemed in fact to have developed gradually over the course of several decades.[4] Rebecca Harris-Warrick, in an enthusiastic response, made plain how easily misreadings and misinterpretations of documentary evidence had taken root and led to the discredited earlier view.[5] The oboe's history is relevant to our discussion because the only roughly contemporary document to give direct evidence about the flute's revival in France, Michel de Labarre's memoir of c1730 (see p. 61), discussed both instruments together. His testimony was as follows:

[Lully's] rise [1653–73] caused the downfall of all the old instruments except the *hautbois,* thanks to the Filidors and Hotteterres, who spoiled so much wood and played so much music that they finally succeeded in rendering it suitable for ensemble music. From that time the musette was left to shepherds, [while] violins, recorders, theorboes, and viols took their place, *for the transverse flute did not come until later* [car la flute traverssiere n'est venue qu'apres].[6]

Labarre's recollection provides the sum total of direct evidence we have at present: that the new French-style oboe reached fruition before the flute, which, in his ambiguous phrase, was introduced or developed separately.

The baroque flute also came to notice in London, where a woodwind maker originally from the Lyon region was noted as a maker of transverse flutes and other woodwinds as early as c1691–5.[41] Pierre Jaillard Bressan (1663–1731), active in England as an oboist and instrument maker from c1688, is survived by only one complete three-section flute, at the London pitch of A=408. Its bore taper, at 21 per cent, is the shallowest among surviving three-section flutes except the Assisi and Haka instruments. Nonetheless, even in the last decade of the seventeenth century the flute seems still to have been by no means a common instrument in France. A directory of Paris for the year 1692 listed few 'masters of playing and making woodwind instruments, *flûtes*, flageolets, oboes, bassoons, musettes, etc.': Colin Hotteterre, Jean Hotteterre, Fillebert, DesCosteaux, Filidor, Du Mont, Rousselet, Dupuis, le Breton et Froment, Héron, Du Buc, and Roset.[42] Little is known of the maker named Dumont, though two of his transverse flutes survive, one a *flûte d'amour*, with a lowest note of B♭, at A=392. Pierre Naust (*c*1660–1709) appears to have become proprietor of Etienne Fremont's workshop on that master's death in *c*1692. Of the surviving flutes with Naust's stamp, one is at the same unusual pitch as the Haka instrument, while three others are D flutes pitched at around A=395. Jean Jacques Rippert (*fl* 1696–1716) was noted in 1696 as an already long-established master-wind instrument maker and maker of *flûtes*. Surviving flutes by Rippert, who together with Jean Hotteterre the younger was listed in 1701 as one of the most skilled woodwind makers of Paris, will be discussed in chapter 4.

Numerous members of the Hotteterre family held posts as court musicians over several generations, as well as conducting business as instrument makers in the city of Paris. Martin Hotteterre (*fl* 1678–1712), who inherited the position of his father Jean as *hautbois et musette du roy dans sa grande Ecurie* in 1659, was working with his father and his brother Jean *fils aîné* (eldest son) at a workshop in the palace precincts by 1673. Martin inherited his father's business as well as his trademark, the sign of an anchor, and on the strength of an inventory of his workshop in 1711 – the only such document of any member of the family specifically to mention transverse flutes as opposed to *flûtes* in general – Tula Giannini (1993) has proposed that Martin specialized in making the type of instrument that is now so famous as the 'Hotteterre flute'.[43]

One surviving original of this type marked with the anchor stamp and the name HOTTETERRE (A-Graz: Landesmuseum Johanneum) may be the work of Martin Hotteterre or of his son and successor Jacques, while other instruments with similar maker's marks held by museums in Berlin and St Petersburg and previously thought to have been by Hotteterre have recently been re-evaluated as nineteenth-century replicas.[44] All misconceptions aside, the Graz Hotteterre flute is considered the classic type of early French baroque flute: its small bore and moderate taper (26 per cent) set it apart both from the early phase instruments (Haka and Assisi) and from the more conical three-piece flutes developed during the following century, when the flute's repertoire and popularity reached their highest point yet.

Chapter 4

The early eighteenth century: the 'baroque' flute's golden age

If we compare a flute of *c*1700 with one of a hundred years earlier, all its essential sound-producing mechanisms have changed. The cylindrical bore of the earlier instrument has become wider at one end than the other; the new instrument is built in several sections, instead of in one piece; its embouchure and fingerholes have altered their shapes and sizes, and are made in tube walls of increased thickness; and the new instrument has a key for the player's right fifth finger, controlling a seventh hole added to the six of the sixteenth-century flute. These alterations in the design of flutes came as their primary function, along with that of the other woodwind instruments, gradually shifted from playing a part in an ensemble of equals to performing the new, more individualistic solo music. The changes affected not only the construction of instruments but also the skills of the musicians who played them. These continued to include amateurs as well as professionals, and the new type of flute gained much of its popularity in the upper strata of northern European society at the expense of instruments already fashionable: the recorder, viol, and lute. Amateur music received a boost from changes in the way people bought and sold musical commodities such as performances, lessons, instruments, and music, just as the flute moved into position as the favourite melody instrument.

The handful of court musicians who had specialized as flutists in seventeenth-century France had inhabited a closed world of private performances not so very different except perhaps in quality from those in which amateurs participated. Professional flutists began to be heard in larger and more public spaces once the German states and free cities, their economies recovering after the Thirty Years' War, began to import Italian opera productions at least as lavish as those of France in the previous generation. The changing requirements of their work encouraged wind-players who had formerly doubled on several instruments to concentrate on a single one, as J. J. Quantz's early career illustrates (see chapter 5). The new status of the top flutists as virtuosi gave them an opportunity of appearing before a paying audience in public concerts, this time alongside players of the violin, oboe, recorder, and keyboard. Their repertoire presented novel forms such as solos (sonatas or suites for flute and basso continuo) and concertos (compositions that typically contrasted one or more featured instruments with an accompanying or *ripieno* group), borrowing ideas and material from genres as diverse as Italian opera and central European folk music.

Public concerts developed first in England, where the perennial financial troubles

21. André Bouys (1656–1740), *De Labarre and Musicians*. John Huskinson has argued that the picture dates from 1707 or shortly thereafter since the music shown is de Labarre's *Troisième livre de trios* published in that year. He identifies the standing flutist as the composer, and the viol player as Marin Marais. Doubt remains as to the identity of the two seated flutists, who may be brothers from the Philidor, Pièche, or Hotteterre families, and of the man standing in the background. See also Bate, *The Flute*, 89, and Mary Oleskiewicz, 'The Hole Truth and Nothing But the Truth: The Resolution of a Problem in Flute Iconography', *EM* 29 (2001), 56–9.

of Charles II (1660–85), followed by the disbanding of the Catholic King James II's court musical establishment under the Protestant William and Mary (1688), obliged many of the foreign-born court musicians to create their own employment in 'act tunes', overtures, and intermission music for the theatre, as well as at music clubs. Reports of these performances made no mention of transverse flutes before an aria entitled 'Hither turn thee, gentle swain' for 'Flute D. Almagne' from John Eccles's masque *The Judgement of Paris* (London, 1701) was published, and probably heard on the London stage in the following year.[1] The most probable explanation for the new instrument's sudden appearance in London is that a player or a maker from the Continent had introduced it to the professional scene, just as James Paisible and three French colleagues had brought the baroque recorder from France in 1673.[2] Evidence that baroque flutes were being made in London twenty years after the baroque recorder arrived comes from James Talbot's manuscript (compiled by 1695–1701), which described one by the transplanted southern French maker Bressan.[3] Paisible and the oboist François La Riche were to have supplied a flute fingering chart for Talbot's manuscript, but its stave unfortunately remains empty. In any case, the fact that Bressan was making baroque flutes by about 1700 or even earlier does not necessarily indicate that professional musicians were playing them: in fact French wind players engaged in London as opera musicians in 1711 were still bringing over oboes by Colin Hotteterre and bassoons by Rippert of Paris, tuned to the London theatres' pitch.[4]

Paisible, La Riche, and others came to London during the prosperous years after the Restoration, when the city became one of the most inviting destinations for European musicians, a position it held for another two centuries. Besides the steady and growing market for instrumental performance, teaching, and music publishing, the taste of the English upper classes for music-theatrical spectacle created a demand for professional musicians that could only be filled by players who had gained experience in that line of work in Germany, Italy, and France. Thus professional players of the baroque flute in London were mostly foreigners whose main instrument was the oboe. One such was John Loeillet (1680–1730), who had arrived from his native Flanders by 1705. By November 1707 he had become first oboe of the Queen's Theatre, and was noted as an excellent harpsichordist and recorderist as well as transverse flutist. His compositions, including solos, trio sonatas, and suites for harpsichord, recorder, oboe, flute, and violin, found a ready market in four collections published by the London firm of Walsh and Hare.

John Banister, a violinist in Charles II's band, had announced what are usually identified as the first public concerts beginning on 30 December 1672 at his house. However, it was not until 12 February 1706, five years after Eccles's *Judgement of Paris*, that Peter La Tour, a member of the royal oboe band who David Lasocki (1983) suggests may have learned the flute from Loeillet, gave the first performance on the 'German flute' to be announced in newspapers.[5] Another concert of 26 March 1707 featured new pieces by William Corbett (1669–1748), probably his *Six Sonatas with an Overture and Aires in four parts for a Trumpet, Violin's and Hautboys, Flute de Allmain, Bassoons or Harpsichord*,[6] and an aria for transverse flute obbligato, 'Cares on a Crown', presumably written for Loeillet, was heard at the Drury Lane theatre on 1 April 1707 in *Thomyris, Queen of Scythia*, an opera adapted by Johan Jakob Heidegger from works by Alessandro Scarlatti, Bononcini, and Steffani.

In Germany, where as noted in chapter 3, Kusser had included a flute obbligato in his opera *Erindo* (1691), the instrument seems to have remained absent from the theatre until Reinhard Keiser (1674–1739), noted for his imaginative use of instruments, scored for it in his opera *Heraclius* (Hamburg, 1712).

22. Michel de Labarre, *Pièces pour la flûte traversière* (1702), the first published solo music for the baroque flute.

While Campra, Charpentier, and other French composers continued to score for it in theatrical and sacred music, the flute entered an entirely new phase as a solo instrument in the more private settings that continued to prevail at court. The first published collection of flute pieces in the new style, appearing two years ahead of the earliest French works for violin and continuo, was Michel de Labarre's *Pièces pour la flûte traversière avec la basse-continue* (Pieces for transverse flute and basso continuo, 1702; ill. 22).

While professional musicians were accustomed to playing their own works from manuscript, and to copying out by hand works they admired, printed music offered amateur players access to a repertoire that they need never have heard the composer, or anyone else, play. At first such publications seem to have been printed at the composer's expense, and sold through commercial outlets as well as by authors themselves. In London and Amsterdam, on the other hand, John Walsh the Elder put the small-scale publication of sheet music on a more commercial basis in 1695, to be followed by Estienne Roger the next year. The two firms began a race to publish the latest and most fashionable music, quite often without the composer's permission or even his knowledge.

By his early twenties Labarre had already become one of the foremost flutists of France. Explaining in his preface his unprecedented decision to print his compositions, he observed that the music was quite different from the sighing, tender airs of Philbert and Descoteaux:

> The pieces are for the most part of a character so special and so different from the idea that people have had until now of what suits the transverse flute, that I decided not to let them see the light except by playing them myself; but the entreaties of those who heard me play them and the errors which crept into the versions of those who copied them down finally made me determine to have them printed; and since these pieces are the first for this kind of flute to appear, I think it necessary to give some information to those who might wish to play them.

Labarre intended his pieces, like those Marais had published for the viol, to stimulate a rise in flute-playing standards. He included instructions for executing slurs and ornaments, as well as for fingering and for choosing accompanying instruments:

> And so I have risked including in these pieces some of the beauties and the challenges that this instrument is capable of, so as to persuade those who wish to play them to practise enough to succeed.

Despite the novel quality of his music, Labarre's own playing seems to have owed much to the affecting quality Philbert and Descoteaux had projected. One observer recalled thirty years after his death:

> The famous de Labarre had, it is said, the marvellous talent of touching [his hearers], which is a gift of nature such that any kind of art [i.e. artificiality] will never achieve.[7]

In the early eighteenth century as ever after, students valued personal contact with a famous teacher more than any written instructions. Jacques Martin Hotteterre (1674–1763) was among the most highly sought-after teachers by the amateurs of the fashionable world, who included women, and held rank as high as the Duke of Orléans. By 1708, according to the title page of his *Pièces pour la flûte traversière*, Hotteterre was *flûte de la Chambre du Roy* (flutist of the King's chamber), and in 1717 he inherited, conditional on payment of a huge fee, René Pignon Descoteaux's position as *Joüeur de fluste de la musique de chambre*.

In 1707 Hotteterre committed his ideas to writing when he published the first method book for the new flute, his *Principes de la Flûte traversière, ou flûte d'Allemagne; de la flûte à bec, ou flûte douce; et du haut-bois* (Principles of the transverse flute, or German flute; of the recorder, or soft flute; and of the oboe), supplied with an elegant frontispiece by the top engraver Picart (ill. 23). Though intended for beginning players of the transverse flute, the tutor addresses those with some knowledge of music, and gives important indications about Hotteterre's priorities as a performer. He prescribes different pitches for flat and sharp enharmonic tones (see p. 83), though he writes that 'a number of people do not make this distinction at all'. Tonguing, limited to the two syllables *Tu* and *Ru*, is passed over relatively briefly.[8] Hotteterre gives much

23. Bernard Picart (1673–1733), frontispiece from [Jacques] Hotteterre-le-Romain, *Principes de la Flûte traversière ou flûte d'Allemagne; de la flute à bec, ou flute douce; et du haut-bois* (Paris: Ballard, 1707).

more extensive particulars for the performance of the ornaments or *agréments* – trills, *ports-de voix, accents, flattements* and *battements* – so integral to the music of this period, and recommends the *Symphonies du feu Mr. Gaultier de Marseille; divisées par suites de tons* (Paris: Ballard, 1707, written before Gautier's death in 1697) for the practice of more advanced flutists.

On 25 October 1715 the German diarist Johann Friedrich A. von Uffenbach visited Hotteterre's house, where the teacher, 'rather pompous and full of airs and graces', showed him

> many fine *flutes traverses* that he makes himself and claims offer particular advantages. Afterward he brought his musical works, of which he has published five quite successfully, one of which, the method for the *flute traverse*, he sells for two livres. ...[9]

Uffenbach visited another Parisian woodwind-maker, Jean Jacques Rippert, 'a crusty, queer fellow' who never had an instrument ready on time. Manners aside, Rippert's contact with musicians far afield may have given him an unusually cosmopolitan outlook: he produced the first book of French *Sonatas* (as opposed to suites or other French forms) to be published in Paris (1722).[10] Like the unaccompanied flute duos, *Sonates pour deux flûtes traversières sans basse* (1736), by another prominent instrument-maker, Thomas Lot (1708–87), this suggests that some if not all makers could play the flute to at least a reasonably proficient standard themselves.

On the other hand, whether Jacques Hotteterre actually made instruments himself, as Uffenbach reported, now seems to be in doubt. A recently-discovered posthumous inventory of his father Martin's workshop taken in 1711 contained ten transverse flutes along with recorders of various sizes, musettes, oboes, and bassoons.[11] Yet no flutes or flute music at all appear in a similar document listing Jacques's possessions on his marriage in 1728, or in another on his death in 1763.[12] A boxwood and ivory three-section flute that recently came to light, however, is stamped HOTTETERRE with a hitherto unknown monogram of the letters LR below.[13] One plausible explanation of the monogram is that it stands for 'le Romain', an appellation that, though its significance is unclear, began to appear in Jacques's publications between 1705 and 1707. As a fashionable teacher of aristocratic amateurs with a reputation that his method book can only have enhanced, Jacques was well placed to sell instruments whether he made them himself or employed others to do so.

In any case, Uffenbach and other amateurs had plenty of further options for purchasing flutes. Besides Rippert's workshop, others active in early eighteenth-century France included those of Charles Bizey (c1685–1752), Chevalier (*fl* 1680–1715),[14] Louis Cornet (c1678–1745), Antoine Delerablé (1686–1734), Dumont (*fl* 1692), Jean Nicolas Leclerc (*d* 1752), and Pierre Naust (*fl* 1692–1734)[15] in Paris, [Jean-Baptiste] Fortier (Rouen: *fl* c1708), and Panon (Toulouse: ?). Early baroque flutes were also made in London by Thomas Stanesby Junior (1692–1754; *fl* c1713–50) as well as by Bressan, and in Germany by Jacob Denner (Nuremberg: 1681–1735), Johann Heinrich Eichentopf (Leipzig: 1678–1769), Johann Poerschmann (Leipzig: 1680–1757), Johann Schell (Nuremberg: 1660–1732), Johannes Scherer Junior (Butzbach: 1664–1722), and Georg Walch (Berchtesgaden: 1690–1764). In the Low Countries there were Abraham van Aardenberg (1672–1717), Jan Barend Beuker (1691–c1750), Willem Beukers Senior (c1669–1750), Thomas Coenraet Boekhout (1666–1715), Philip Borkens (1693–c1765), Jan Juriaenszoon van Heerde (1638–91), and Engelbert Terton (1676–1752) in Amsterdam, Frederick Eerens (Utrecht and Den Bosch: 1694–1750), and Johann Hyacinth Rottenburgh (Brussels: 1672–1756). Switzerland had a specialist transverse flute maker in Christian Schlegel (Basel: c1667–1746), and Italy in Johannes Maria Anciuti (Milan: c1690–1740).

The flutes all these workshops produced were made principally of boxwood, ebony or ivory, in three sections, having a more or less conical bore and a single key for D♯/E♭. The instrument's acoustics were by no means standardized: each maker developed a personal concept of tone and intonation, and devised original technical means of achieving his ideas. The bore taper could be as steep as 29 per cent or as shallow as 21 per cent, while maximum bore diameters differed by up to 1½ mm.

Hence the surviving instruments have great differences from one another in timbre, intonation, range, and flexibility of tone.

The pitch of early baroque flutes ranged from about A=395 to A=408. Bruce Haynes (1995) has identified two pitch levels in France: *ton de l'Opéra* (A=c390), the pitch in Lully's Academy, at which theatre and opera music was performed; and *ton de Chambre* or *ton de Chapelle* (A=c400–405), the pitch at court in Versailles, and of the organ in the king's chapel.[16] Bach's predecessor as *Thomaskantor* introduced a similar low chamber pitch at Leipzig in 1702, and from about 1715 attempts were made to establish a German standard pitch of A=c410, which Quantz referred to as the German A chamber pitch.[17] In England a standard pitch of about A=408 was used at the Opera. The differences in pitch were to have consequences in flute construction from about 1720 (p. 80).

Because most musical performances other than opera in Paris still took place in private, early eighteenth-century concerts involving transverse flutes have left few traces. Joachim Christoph Nemeitz, a German visitor who wrote before 1718 of his experiences, described concerts by the best masters at the homes of the Duke of Aumont, the wealthy Treasurer Crozat, Hotteterre's pupil the Duke of Orléans, and others. Amateurs played at other, less-frequented domestic concerts. Nemeitz recalled the flute as the most popular melody instrument, confirming Hotteterre's description of it as 'one of the most pleasant and one of the most fashionable':[18]

> The instruments people were most devoted to in Paris at that time were the harpsichord and the transverse, or German, flute. The French today play these instruments with unequalled refinement.[19]

As well as appearing at indoor concerts, flutes were often depicted in engravings and paintings of open-air outings, sometimes with guitar. In fact an entirely new class of composition, the *fête galante*, had to be created at the Royal Academy of Painting and Sculpture to accommodate the work of Antoine Watteau, who specialized in this genre.[20]

Intimate concerts became more frequent in the life of the court, and grand musical-theatrical spectacles correspondingly less so, after a series of military defeats for France, deaths and poisonings among the nobility, and Madame de Maintenon's increased pressure on the king to turn to religion. Sunday afternoon concerts in 1714–15 were played before the king by a small group of musicians for whom François Couperin created the music, his *Concerts Royaux* (Royal ensemble pieces). The flutist was probably Pierre Danican Philidor (1681–1731), *flûtiste de chambre* and *hautbois et flûte ordinaire de la chapelle et chambre du roy*. Couperin envisaged some pieces he published for harpsichord as suitable for other instruments: the bird-imitation, 'Le Rossignol-en-amour' (The nightingale in love), from his third book (1722), is marked that it 'cannot be more successful than on the transverse flute when it is well played'.

Hotteterre's *L'Art de Preluder* of 1719 provides a rare document of a spontaneous musical form suited to intimate or even solitary performance. In contrast to the written Prelude, or opening movement, of a suite, the Prelude Hotteterre describes was made up on the spot, announcing a key before modulating into others and then returning to the main tonality. Though by their very nature improvised preludes were never announced and hardly ever remarked upon in writing, the form appears to have existed well into the nineteenth century, outside France as well as within it.[21]

Hotteterre's work contains a chapter on transposing, to enable unison playing with singers in airs of the old, pre-Lullian style. French music of the early eighteenth century for treble instruments, including the flute, was customarily notated in the French violin clef:

> The clef usually employed for instruments that play the treble is that of G re sol. It has two positions, one on the 1st line and the other on the second. It is the former position that is most usual in French ensemble pieces, and it is the most convenient for flutes and oboes in that it spreads out the range rather evenly, and one is not forced to draw many lines above the five normal ones as is the custom in some foreign countries [i.e. everywhere but France] where this clef is used only on the second line. ...[22]

A G1 clef can be read as though it were a bass (F4) clef, an octave higher. Hotteterre gives instructions for transposing into all keys by imagining G, C, and F clefs in different positions on the stave. Such transpositions enable the flutist 'to play tunes in the correct key, and in unison with the voice'.

Printed music for the flute took longer to appear in Germany owing to an economic climate entirely different from those of London, Amsterdam, and Paris. When it did arrive it was quite unlike the French repertoire, though full of references to French and Italian styles. In 1715 Georg Philipp Telemann (1681–1767), then employed as director of city music in Frankfurt, began publishing his own compositions, which included some of the earliest German works to specify the transverse flute. His *Six Trio* (1718) included one 'à *Violon, Flûte traverse et Basse chiffré*' (for violin, transverse flute and figured bass, Trio 3), probably the first music for the baroque flute published in Germany, which included much writing influenced by Italian music, especially that in a style derived from the violin's idiom. Telemann's *Kleine Cammer-Music* (1716) gave a list of suitable instruments including the *Flûte traverse*. Though the publication was dedicated to four professional oboists, its title page indicated that it was aimed at the growing number of amateur players of instruments including the flute:

> Little Chamber-Music, consisting of VI Suites, arranged and composed for the violin, *Flûte traverse*, as well as keyboard, but especially the oboe, in a light and singing manner, suitable as much for the practice of a beginner as for performance by a virtuoso, by Georg Philipp Telemann.[23]

The first solos specifically for transverse flute to be printed in Germany appeared in Johann Mattheson's *Der brauchbare Virtuoso* (Hamburg, 1720; composed 1717), at about the same time as Walsh published opera arrangements and Johann Christian Schickhardt's sonatas for the instrument in London.[24] Mattheson's style features constant semiquaver or quaver motion, arpeggiated passage-work, and other traits

24. Portrait of a flutist believed to be the imperial court musician Ferdinand Joseph Lemberger by the Bohemian artist Jan Kupecký (between 1709 and 1725).

derived from the Italian violin style; in his *Das neu-eröffnete Orchestre* the composer indicated that all such passage-work was to be tongued individually rather than slurred, though Heinrich Döbbler, the experienced professional flutist to whom he dedicated the publication, might well have added some slurs by way of discretionary ornamentation.[25] Giuliano Furlanetto (1998) has suggested that Johann Martin Blochwitz's *Sechtzig Arien* (Freiburg: Christoph Matthäi, n.d.), for violin or oboe 'but especially for *flute traversiere*', was published as a rejoinder to Mattheson.[26] Blochwitz, a colleague of Quantz at Dresden, addressed his short preface to the amateur 'reader with a taste for music', in contrast to Mattheson's extremely prolix one to the 'skilful virtuoso'. Yet he set his compositions in a wide range of keys, including C major and minor, D major and minor, E♭ major, E minor, F major, F♯ minor, G major and minor, A major and minor, B♭ major, and B minor, instead of Mattheson's easier D, G, and A major, and E, B, and D minor. Blochwitz designed his phrasing to be *Practicabel*, 'so that nobody should have reason to wish for a second pair of lungs', and to be 'good on the ear, so that mere amateurs of *Musique* should be pleased not with crickets [i.e. leaping figures], but with *cantabile* ideas'. The sixty arias typify the composite idiom of the Dresden court, including references to Italian *arioso*, solemn French overture, English dances, the severe German style, and the folk dance of central Europe.

Another picture of the varied repertoire of a German flutist around the same time is given by an unpublished collection of 54 instrumental solos, the largest proportion of which are specifically for flute.[27] The Brussels manuscript, compiled in c1724, contains solos by Johann Heinrich Freytag (one of Johann Sebastian Bach's two flutists at Cöthen), Blochwitz, August Reinhard Stricker (Bach's predecessor at Cöthen), Christoph Förster, Johann Sigismund Weiss, Schickhardt, Loeillet, and Quantz, as well as better-known composers such as Telemann and Handel.

Nearly all the music written for virtuosi by virtuosi remained in manuscript copies like the Brussels manuscript. None of Johann Sebastian Bach's flute solos was published before the nineteenth century, but the Dresden flutists Buffardin, Quantz, Blochwitz, and Christian Friedrich Friese had an opportunity to meet the composer when he visited their city in the autumn of 1717, and in view of Bach's later friendship with Buffardin, this may have been the occasion on which the two met.[28] Bach's A minor *Solo* without bass BWV 1013 (known since its rediscovery in 1917 as the *Partita*), the style of which partakes both of Mattheson's unbroken passage-work and of Blochwitz's English dances, may date from as early as the end of 1717, though a case has also been made for 1724.[29] An early version of Brandenburg Concerto V from 1719 seems to be Bach's first extant ensemble composition involving the flute, which joins the violin and harpsichord in a *concertino* group set against a *ripieno* string orchestra. As such, it is the first appearance of the flute, as well as the harpsichord, as a concerto instrument.

Thus the flute emerged with its own repertoire in Germany that combined ideas from a wide range of influences into a 'mixed style' of composition. For German as well as English composers for the flute, the principal inspiration came from the virtuosity and improvisation of Italian vocal and violin music rather than the precious French flute style. The performance manner of German players was probably a similar mixture. Telemann was perhaps the first to use the term 'mixed taste' in 1718, not to refer to a class of composition but to describe the playing of the Frankfurt banker Heinrich Bartels:

> He has such an exact knowledge of French and Italian music that he performs both as a singer and on various instruments, especially the violin, in either style on its own, or in a style mixed from both of them.[30]

Handel arrived in London for the first time in 1710 to promote Italian opera, having already composed a piece that belongs among the baroque flute's earliest solo works, a D major sonata of around 1706–7 (HWV 378), misattributed to [Johann Sigismund] Weiss in its source, the German Brussels manuscript just mentioned.[31] The second of Handel's four extant solos for the transverse flute was originally written in F for the oboe, but appeared in G for *traversa* in two printed versions. The sonata in B minor was marked *Traversa Solo* in two prints by Walsh dating from around 1732, but a version in D minor for recorder had been composed about twenty years earlier. Handel prepared the autograph of the *Sonata a Travers. e Basso* in E minor (known as opus 1 no. 1b) in about 1727–8, recycling parts of his earliest flute sonata of *c*1706–7, altering material from a violin sonata to avoid E3 and F3, and incorporating phrases from other works including a recorder sonata.

Fifteen of Handel's London operas between 1721 and 1738 included transverse flute parts, which could have been played by oboe doublers such as Loeillet, Francesco Barsanti (after 1714), and Giuseppe Sammartini (after 1729), the last of whom Quantz had noted in Milan in 1726 as an exception to the low standard of woodwind playing in the opera orchestra there.[32] Handel and his operas also attracted specialist flutists to London. Carl Friedrich Weidemann (*d* 1782), a German flutist who featured in engravings by Hogarth and may have been a member of London's musical/homosexual underworld, first played in Handel's opera orchestra in 1725, and Quantz reported John Festing to have been one of the flutists at the opera during his visit two years later.[33] Handel later wrote 'Sweet bird' for solo flute and soprano in the oratorio *L'allegro, il penseroso ed il moderato* (London, 1740), 'in which the technical demands and style of solo writing are not far removed from those of a flute concerto complete with cadenza'.[34]

Festing left a large fortune of £8000 on his death in 1772, having appeared as a transverse flute soloist (as in a concert at the Lincoln's Inn Fields theatre on 12 March 1729) and earned his living principally as a teacher as well as playing at the opera. But a connection with the opera was not a precondition of an active concert career for a flutist. From 1714 onwards, John Baptist Granom was noted as a performer on the German flute and trumpet, and the diarist John Bryom wrote appreciatively of his transverse flute-playing at Bressan's house on 3 April 1724, noting that he was 'the only man for it … he played most sweetly'. According to an anecdote by the music historian Sir John Hawkins, the woodwind-maker Thomas Stanesby stated in 1736 that 'besides Dr Pepusch he had never met with but one person who could solfa by the hexachords, namely Mr John Grano[m]'. However, despite this skill, and in contrast to Festing's success, Granom was committed to Marshalsea prison for debt in May 1728, the same year in which Walsh & Hare advertised his *Solos for a German Flute, a Hoboy or Violin with a Thorough Bass for the Harpsichord or Bass Violin.*

The wind players of Italy, in contrast to its string players, seem to have found better fortune across the Alps than in their native land, since relatively few indications have yet been found of the use of flutes there in the early eighteenth century. Three transverse flutes appeared in the orchestra in an engraving of the Royal Theatre in Turin (Antoine Aveline, 1722), and Antonio Vivaldi first employed transverse flutes in his opera *Orlando Furioso* (1727),[35] two years before his six flute concertos op. 10 appeared in Amsterdam and a year before Ignazio Sieber joined Vivaldi at the Ospedale della Pietà to teach the flute at the school. Among the earliest surviving

Italian flutes are those of Anciuti (Milan). As early as the 1720s a dozen Italian composers published flute solos in London, as well as in Amsterdam, where interest in the flute was stong enough to justify a Dutch translation of Hotteterre's flute tutor in 1729. The plethora of instrument-makers who supplied flutes in a strong mercantile economy of the Netherlands, where professional and amateur musicians mixed in *collegia musica*, has already been noted (p. 74).

By about 1720 flutes in four sections instead of the usual three began to be made, dividing the body between the two hands. The upper part of this divided middle section could be supplied in a series of different lengths to enable the flute to be played at more than one pitch. The first written mention of these alternative middle joints or *corps de rechange* appears in a document of 30 December 1721 from the Naust workshop in Paris.[36]

The surviving instruments generally thought to have been among the early four-joint flutes were built to match fairly precisely the different pitch standards in use. This forms a contrast to later instruments, which were usually supplied with a set of middle joints evenly spaced between a high and a low extreme, as Quantz put it, 'each differing from one another by no more than a comma, or the ninth part of a whole tone'.[37] One example of the earlier type is provided by a boxwood example by Jacob Denner.[38] The instrument, which came to light in 1991 in its original fitted case (p. 262), is supplied with middle joints at pitches variously reported as A=402, 412, and 422, or A=392, 410, and 415, depending on the blowing technique and expectations of the player. These levels permit the flute to play at the commonest low and high chamber pitches (A=392–400 and A=410–15). A fourth interchangeable joint transforms the Denner flute into an instrument with a lowest note of C at the low chamber pitch (i.e. a transposing instrument 'in Bb', in contrast to the normal flute 'in C' with a lowest note of D).

This lowest configuration corresponds to a type of instrument of which little is known, but of which the Haka flute (chapter 3), and one from Naust's workshop (F–Paris: Musée de la Musique) provide two further examples. Perhaps such instruments were meant for playing oboe parts, an especially desirable capability at a time when flute music was scarce.[39] On the other hand Marco Brolli (1996–7) has pointed to an *arioso* which seems to have been written specifically for the instrument in Handel's *Riccardo primo* (London, 1725; Act III, scene 2), scored for *traversa bassa*, strings, and soprano. While the string and voice parts are notated in F minor, the flute part is in G minor.

In a museum not far from Dresden survives a boxwood flute attributed to Quantz, pitched about a major third below the German A-chamber pitch.[40] Quantz mentioned this type, the *flute d'amour*, in a brief and incomplete list of other sizes:

> Besides the usual flute traversiere, there are various other less usual kinds, both larger and smaller in size, there are low fourth-flutes, *flutes d'amour*, little fourth-flutes, &c.[41]

Though extant flutes by makers in many European countries were supplied with sets of middle joints one of which transformed an ordinary flute in D into a *flute d'amour*, a study by Peter Thalheimer (1983) turned up little repertoire intended for this or any of the other lower flutes. He noted a unique concerto in B♭ major for a *flauto d'amore* in A♭, which Johann Melchior Molter (1696–1765) composed some time after 1742. Works for an instrument in A were more common, the largest body being ten by Christoph Graupner (1683–1760): nine cantatas composed in 1730, and a concerto of 1730–6 in G major for *flauto d'amore, oboe d'amore, viola d'amore*, strings, bassoon, and continuo.

Quantz made no mention of still other extant lower-pitched flutes: basses, a fifth or an octave below the D flute. Of the latter kind, mid-eighteenth-century instruments by Bizey, Thomas Lot, and Christophe Delusse (1758–89) survive, as well as by Caleb Gedney (London, c1760), Beuker, and Anciuti (dated 1739). Again many more of these instruments exist than seems justified by the extent of their repertoire, and quite what they were used for remains uncertain. The indication in Diderot and d'Alembert's *Encyclopédie* that 'this instrument provides the *bass* in flute ensembles', such as those of Boismortier and Corrette, perhaps, serves as the only firm indication.

Quantz apparently was not aware of the piccolo either, though it had first been employed by Destouches and Lalande in the ballet *Les Elements* (c1721), and featured in Rameau's opera-ballets *Les Indes Galantes* (1735), *Pigmalion* (1748), and *Acanthe et Céphise* (1751). Corrette's method of c1740 mentioned that these 'little transverse flutes at the octave … have a charming effect in *Tambourins* and in concertos written expressly for the flute'.[42] Third-flutes in F (the same pitch as the treble recorder) also survive, but again Quantz omitted to mention this size, whose repertoire, possibly including flute band and military music, seems slim. Some of the concertos for *flauto traverso* in Vivaldi's op. 10 provide effective vehicles for a third-flute.

Flute-makers in Germany and England attempted in the 1720s to extend the flute's range a whole tone lower than usual by mechanical means rather than by transposition, perhaps to enable it to match the range of the Haka/Naust/Denner type noted above or to play more oboe music. On 3 April 1725 a visitor to the workshop of Pierre Jaillard Bressan (1663–1730) in London was shown what was almost certainly a flute with a footjoint whose range extended to C.[43] A dispute between London instrument-makers John Mason, Caleb Gedney, and Charles Schuchart in the columns of the *Daily Advertiser* in August–September 1756 revealed that Stanesby Junior and John Just Schuchart had also made flutes with a C-foot in the 1720s, and that J.J. Schuchart had known of similar instruments in Germany at that time. C. Schuchart's reference to the C-foot in Germany is confirmed by an illustration in Joseph Christoph Friedrich Bernhard Caspar Majer's instrumental treatise of 1732, and a mention by Quantz.[44] A sole surviving such instrument from this period, by Jacob Denner, with a low C but no C♯, resides in the Germanisches Nationalmuseum in Nuremberg; a second one disappeared from the Berlin museum during World War 2. Another German, the Leipzig virtuoso, writer, and flute-maker Johann George Tromlitz (1725–1805), tried to revive the C-foot in the 1750s and 60s. He gave up the idea, he explained, as the extension did not become popular in Germany owing to its detrimental effect on the flute's tone.[45] Only a handful of pieces may possibly have been conceived for a flute that could play a low C. One such is a trio for two transverse flutes and bass attributed in its surviving manuscript to Fortunato Keller

(1686–1757), but identical with a piece published as Quantz's trio sonata op. 3 no. 5.[46] The manuscript of Bach's *Solo* BWV 1013 contains a C2 in its last movement (bar 50, second beat) that seems to have been adjusted up an octave (*cf* bar 48, second beat). A manuscript entitled *G. Moll Sonata al Cembalo obligato e Flauto traverso composta da Giov. Seb. Bach* contains the harpsichord part of the B minor sonata BWV 1030 transposed down a third.[47] The flute part, absent from the manuscript, could be played in that key without alteration only on a flute that could play a low C.

The decline of court music may have played a part in the rise of public concerts in Paris, as it appears to have done in London. In 1725 the French court flutist Anne Danican Philidor (1681–1728), listed as a member of several court musical ensembles during the eighteenth century's early years, founded the Concert spirituel, a highly successful series of public subscription concerts to provide music during religious fasts when performances at the Académie Royale de Musique, the Paris opera, were suspended. These concerts showcased a new generation of instrumentalist-composers, who made their living in most cases without court appointments, by giving lessons to wealthy students and by providing music for aristocratic and bourgeois patrons. The new stars favoured the sonata over the suite as the principal form of composition, and introduced to French audiences a new, Italian- and German-influenced style of solo music for the flute.

Michel Blavet (1700–68) was by all accounts the most brilliant French flute virtuoso in the first half of the eighteenth century. The son of a turner, he taught himself to play almost all instruments, specializing in flute, which he played left-handed, and bassoon. On Passion Wednesday 1726 he made his debut at the newly-formed Concert spirituel, where he and Lucas (first name and dates unknown) each played a concerto. Numerous enthusiastic reports of Blavet's effect on his audience indicate that the 'exciting, exact, and brilliant' style of his playing made the flute even more popular in France, where the instrument had previously been played only in a languorous manner.[48]

One of his contemporaries specified Blavet's superlative technical command and his abilities in all kinds of music:

> The most precise embouchure, the best swelling and diminishing of tone [*les sons les mieux filés*], a liveliness that had something prodigious, an equal success in the tender, in the voluptuous, and in the most difficult passages: that sums up M. *Blavet*.[49]

His intonation excited particular comment. The remarks of one critic in 1757 suggest that the music he performed at public concerts was quite different from the pieces he published, which were set only in the easiest keys:

> You will also agree if you are sincere that it is very difficult to play in tune on this instrument. I would even have thought it impossible for someone who had practised for a very long time if the inimitable Blavet had not proved the contrary to me, hearing him play difficult pieces chosen in sharp and flat keys, which he plays to the complete satisfaction of the most scrupulous ear.[50]

Since the late nineteenth century and particularly since about 1970, most flutists have come to think of tuning as a match between their instrument's 'scale' and the theoretical system of equal temperament (see chapter 14 and p. 148). In earlier times, however, playing in tune denoted the practical matter of fitting in with other instruments or voices in an exact, or 'just', manner of intonation. The basis of just intonation and the fundamental building block of all tuning systems is the pure interval, that is, two notes that sound together without 'beats' jarring their tone.

The difference between the equally-tempered chords we hear in modern music and the justly-intoned ones sought by earlier ensembles was described by the nineteenth-century acoustician Hermann Helmholtz as 'so marked that every one, whether he is musically cultivated or not, observes it at once': the equally-tempered ones are 'rough, dull, trembling, restless' while the pure ones 'possess a full and as it were saturated harmoniousness; they flow on, with a full stream, calm and smooth, without tremor or beat'.[1]

To achieve these pure intervals in all keys, Quantz and his contemporaries divided the whole tone into nine equal parts, grouped into a large or diatonic semitone of five commas (about 111 cents) and a small or chromatic one of four commas (about 89 cents). The two sizes of semitone meant that enharmonic pairs of notes, such as F♯ and G♭, had different pitches about 22 cents apart, with the flatted note higher in pitch than the sharped one on the line or space below.

A discrepancy of 22 cents in the tuning of an interval makes it unbearably out of tune by any standard, despite which the nineteenth-century Paris Conservatoire took the official position that the difference between enharmonic pairs was imperceptible. Quantz's flute, by tuning the note produced by the key to a pure E♭, and adding a new key for D♯, made it possible without adjusting the embouchure to play a pure third to B, as well as a third from E♭ to G that would otherwise be excessively wide and a fifth from E♭ to B♭ that would be too narrow. Quantz achieved the other enharmonic distinctions by providing each note of the pair with a separate fingering, some of which Hotteterre had already given. As usual, theory lagged behind practice, and Telemann attempted to codify what was clearly a common practice of playing in tune in his *Neues musikalisches System* only in the early 1740s, referring approvingly to the Quantz flute when his essay was published in 1767:

That D♯ and E♭ constitute two different tones is also the case with violins, where D♯ is taken with the fourth finger and E♭ with the little finger; likewise, transverse flutes have two special keys.[2]

As Tromlitz and other writers on the flute confirmed, these enharmonic distinctions continued to be made by violinists and other instrumentalists, as they no doubt also were by singers, at least as late as 1800, by which time intonation practice was changing (chapters 6, 8).

We may note that, with the exception of F♯, one-keyed flutes produce sharps that are less in tune (i.e. farther from just intonation and closer to their equal temperament values) than flats. This may help explain why early flutes sounded better in flat keys related to the Dorian mode, and why music in keys that had sharps in the key-signature remained rare until Germans, including Quantz, addressed the problems of playing in the sharp keys.

Blavet held important posts in French music throughout his career. As a musician in the *Chambre du Roi* he received a stipend of 1200–1400 livres, plus 200–300 in bonuses. When his pay was docked for making only six appearances at the *Musique de la Reine* in 1738 (the year in which he probably turned down a post with Crown Prince Frederick of Prussia that was eventually accepted by Quantz), his basic salary was 1500 livres. As first flute at the Academy of Music he received 700–800 livres plus 500 in bonuses. Eight concerts for the Dauphine in 1753 earned him 120 livres, and a similar number of rehearsals at Fontainebleau netted another 396.[51] The terms of his contract with Philidor for appearances at the Concert spirituel are not known, but surely brought him payments just as munificent. In addition to his activities as a performer, Blavet held a royal publishing licence and may have acted as selling agent in Paris for Telemann's publications, such as the twelve copies of the *Musique de table* for which he subscribed.[52] He may also have conducted a sideline reselling flutes from the workshop of Pierre Naust.

Other flutist-composers who appeared at the Concert spirituel included Jacques-Christophe Naudot (*d* 1762), who is first heard of in 1719 as *Maître de musique* in a marriage document. A Madame Paris de Montmartel who commissioned a book of trios appears to have been a pupil.[53] His first flute compositions were published in 1726. Jean-Daniel Braun *le cadet*, *ordinaire de la musique* of the Duke of Epernon, and his elder brother were Germans who settled in Paris, where both appeared in concerts. The flutist Lucas appeared at the Concert spirituel in 1726 and 1736, and was noted for accompanying the voice. The poet Denesle dedicated his *Syrinx, ou l'origine de la flûte, pöeme à Messieurs Naudot, Blavet, Lucas* (Paris: Merigot, 1739) to the three flutists. Others who appeared were Pierre Evrart Taillart *l'aîné* (*d* 1782) and *le cadet*, Benoît Guillemant, and in 1735 a female flutist presumably related to the Taillart brothers, but identified only as *la demoiselle Taillart*. Virtuosi visiting from abroad also performed: Pierre-Gabriel Buffardin, flutist in the Dresden Hofkapelle from 1715 to 1749, appeared as soloist several times in 1726 and again in 1737. In 1739 Graeff or Greff, a German, played and took part in trios with Blavet and the cellist l'Abbé.[54]

Further new compositions of the 1720s came in publications by Joseph Bodin de Boismortier (1689–1755) and Michel Corrette (1709–95), men independent of court patronage who as far as we know did not play the flute themselves. Both wrote method books which Bowers interprets as suggesting 'that easy financial gains could be expected from any publication related to the flute'. The first entire book of sonatas for flute and bass by a French composer was published by the woodwind maker Rippert in 1722.[55] Boismortier adopted the sonata terminology for two books of duets in 1724, as well as for solos (flute and continuo) and trio sonatas for two flutes and continuo. Between 1726 and 1729 Rippert was followed by Michel Blavet, Jean Daniel Braun, André Chéron, Michel Corrette, J. Handoville, Jean Marie Leclair, Jacques Loeillet, Jacques Christophe Naudot, Quentin *le jeune*, and J. Rebour. When the French publisher Boivin published an unauthorized collection of pieces by Quantz in 1729, he described them as 'Italian sonatas … very appropriate for forming taste and the hand of those who want to succeed in the difficulties that are now common on this instrument'.[56]

French composers adopted the concerto in the late 1720s.[57] The first pieces by a French composer for any instrument to receive this title were works for five flutes Boismortier printed in 1727, and further works for three and four flutes which he and Corrette published in the few years afterwards. Vivaldi's op. 10 concertos were published in Amsterdam by Le Cène in *c*1729–30. Corrette's works included a concerto for solo flute, the first of that kind to appear in France, predating the earliest French violin concertos by several years. Naudot followed with a set of six solo flute concertos in the mid-1730s, and Jean Daniel Braun produced two sets, now lost, that appeared before 1742. An unpublished concerto by Buffardin may have been written in the late 1730s, and Blavet's concerto probably dates from the early 1740s.

Jean Philippe Rameau's *Pieces de clavecin en concerts* (Pieces for harpsichord ensemble, 1741) gave the flute, or violin, a new role accompanying the keyboard, in an ensemble that included bass viol or another violin. Boismortier's op. 91 used a similar combination. As in many of his opera scores, in which the orchestration seems to prefigure the classical style, Rameau here anticipated a role for the flute that was to become common later in the century.

Though the flute had of necessity found a new and more powerful voice for its appearance in public concerts, the instrument's tradition of playing vocal airs in a style now over a century old continued at least until the middle of the eighteenth century. Accompanying a singer remained one of the favourite ways to use the flute, in airs published with the text underlay that gave them their old-fashioned declamatory and rhetorical character. The Preface to Montéclair's *Brunetes anciènes et modernes apropriées à la flûte traversière* (Paris: Boivin, c1725) referred to the enduring emotional impact of such pieces:

> It is important to practise transposing, for nothing is as touching as hearing these little tunes [sung] by a beautiful voice accompanied in unison by a transverse flute. Nobody will doubt what I am saying if, like me, they have heard Mme Perichon sing accompanied by M Bernier, officer of the King, who so worthily fills the chair at the opera of the illustrious M de Labarre who has retired from it to the public's great regret. I cannot express the pleasure I felt at Boulogne on hearing this little ensemble which touched me more than any clever artificial music has ever done.[58]

More frequently printed collections of such pieces now mixed in tunes from Italian and French opera, such as the 'Airs d'Handel' and excerpts from Rameau's ballet-operas in Blavet's three *Recueils de Pieces, petits Airs, Brunettes*. Probably more popular among English amateur flutists than any of Handel's pieces composed with the flute in mind were settings for one or two flutes of his tunes from operas and oratorios, including *Acis and Galatea*, *The musick for the Royal Fireworks*, and even *Messaah*.[59] Peter Prelleur's *The Newest method for Learners of the German Flute* (1731) filled its pages with Handelian music examples – not movements from solo sonatas, but rather 'Favourite Airs' taken from the operas, which it seems Walsh and others could not print fast enough to satisfy the demand.

With the appearance of the one-keyed flute a distinction between flute and fife was first explicitly made. Fifes remained in use in the German army: Hanß Friedrich von Fleming, writing in 1726, noted that he had seen twelve of them (*Querpfeifen*) and sixteen drums march four abreast in Dresden, and by the age of *Lilliburlero* and *Yankee Doodle* such groupings had become standard.[60] At the Hanoverian accession to the English throne in 1714 fifes once again appeared with drums, having last held a prominent place at the coronation of James II in 1685, but now in a new form with a key like that of the flute. In 1747 the Duke of Cumberland, the Commander-in-Chief of the British Army in Flanders and the younger son of George II, ordered a fife and drum in camp at Maastricht, and the nineteenth Yorkshire Regiment, the Green Howards, became the first marching regiment to re-adopt the fife. George II reviewed an Artillery parade in 1753 that included a fife major and five fifers as well as a drum major and ten drummers. The *Feldpfeifer* of the German armies had fallen into low esteem by the early eighteenth century while a new class of *Hautboisten* often moonlighted as string or wind players in town bands, like their colleagues at court. One such was a brother of J. S. Bach's, Johann Jakob Bach (1682–1722), a *Hautboist* in the service of the Swedish guard from 1704 to 1712. While a prisoner of war in Constantinople in 1713, Johann Jakob seized the opportunity to add another string to his bow by taking flute lessons with Buffardin, who happened to be visiting the city.

Court music, public concerts, military and town band employment all provided scope for professional flutists in Germany by the second quarter of the eighteenth century. The teaching of amateurs, though it has left little or no trace, must also have fallen into their purview. Telemann resumed publishing his works, mostly of an educational nature or otherwise designed for amateurs, after moving to Hamburg as director of music for its five principal churches and director of the city's opera.[61] Compositions for flute included *Der harmonische Gottes-Dienst* (Harmonic divine service, 1725), a set of seventy-two solo cantatas with obbligati for violin, oboe, flute, or recorder, and a collection of flute duets (1727). In 1728 he published the *Sonate Metodiche* for violin or flute and continuo, the slow movements of which, provided with both plain and ornamented versions, are excellent sources for learning about this essential yet still neglected aspect of baroque music performance. The *III Triette Methodici* (1731), followed by the *Continuation des Sonates Méthodiques* (1732), dedicated to two wealthy Hamburg amateurs, the brothers Burmester, continued this instructional vein. Telemann dedicated *XII Solos* (1734) for violin or *Traversière* to three Burmester brothers.

After 1723 Telemann expanded his idea of instrumental collections as encyclopaedias, generally presenting twelve rather than six pieces, selected for greatest possible diversity of genre, key, and national style. This class of publication included the *Fantaisies* for unaccompanied flute (1732 or 33), which embraced genres as different as Italian *capriccio* and French *ouverture*. His *Der getreue Music-meister* (The trusty music-teacher), a bi-weekly music journal dedicated to the amateur musicians of Hamburg that ran from 1728 to 1729, carried instrumental and vocal music by various composers for all vocal ranges and popular instruments, in all national styles and genres. It included a four-movement *Sinfonie à Flûte traverse seul, à la Françoise* (flute and continuo) in the French manner but with the overall form of an Italian sonata. The French newspaper *Mercure de France* noted in June 1745 that Blavet played quartets by Telemann on four occasions at the Concert spirituel with Forqueray, the Italian violinist Marellam, and the cellist l'Abbé. These may have been the same quartets Telemann wrote on his visit to Paris of 1737–8, which were played at that time by Blavet, Forqueray, Guignon, Edouard, and the composer himself.[62] A C major sonata for flute, recorder, and continuo long believed to have been by Quantz, and a favourite with twentieth-century players because of its unusual instrumentation, is a recent but controversial addition to the long tally of Telemann's ensemble pieces.[63]

Wilhelm Friedemann Bach, living in Dresden as an organist, became friends with Buffardin and composed his six challenging flute duets between 1733 and 1746, by

25. Trade card for the London instrument-maker and dealer Thomas Cahusac, c1750. Besides building recorders and flutes, Cahusac, like most other woodwind-makers of the day in London, ran a music shop that supplied printed music and all sorts of musical equipment. The text reads as follows:

Thos. Cahusac, Flute Maker, at the [sign of] Two Flutes and Violin Opposite to St Clement's Church in ye Strand, London. Makes & Sells all Sorts of Musical Instruments Vizt. German Flutes, in Ivory, or Fine Wood, plain in ye neatest manner; or Curiously adorn'd with Gold, Silver, or Ivory, necessary to preserve them, approv'd of by ye best Masters. Also English Flutes [i.e. recorders], Hautboys [oboes], Bass Violins, Bass Viols, Violins, French Horns, Trumpets[,] Harpsichords, Spinnets, & all sorts of Wind Instruments. Also variety of ye newest Musick, for all sorts of Instruments now in Use, with Books of Instruction. Ruled Books & Paper, Songs, Reeds, Wire for Harpsichords, & ye best Roman Strings Wholesale and Retail. N.B. All sorts of Instruments neatly Mended and Carefully put in Order.

which time the flute was well established as an instrument for virtuosi and amateurs. Two of this period's books on practical music-making offered more than mere regurgitations of Hotteterre: Majer's *Museum Musicum* (1732) and Eisel's *Musicus Autodidaktikos* (1738). Majer gives only a short summary of the flute, but his fingering chart records the brief vogue enjoyed by attempts to extend its range to low C (see above).

Flutes of the 1730s and 1740s, now routinely made with a set of *corps de rechange*, were just as diverse as earlier types. The workshop of Thomas Lot (1708–86), successor to Naust, supplied large numbers of flutes to an extensive market including many of the noble houses of Europe. Flutes by the Scherer workshop of Butzbach, a town that specialized in the production of ivory objects, became popular with wealthy amateurs perhaps just as much for their conspicuously luxurious appearance as for their musical properties.[64] In Germany, France, England, and the Netherlands, the flute was enjoying a golden age.

Chapter 5

Quantz and the operatic style

Johann Joachim Quantz (1697–1773) deserves a chapter of his own not merely because he authored the golden age's most detailed manual on musical performance of the eighteenth century, his *Versuch einer Anweisung die Flöte traversiere zu spielen* (Essay of a method for playing the flute traversiere, 1752), or because he held the prestigious post of flute teacher to Frederick the Great of Prussia. To be sure, his *Essay* has long provided a treasure trove of information on eighteenth-century performance practice, and its English translation by Edward R. Reilly (1958, published 1966) may fairly be said to have provided the one tool without which the current phase of the early music revival (chapter 13) could never have begun. But as well as writing the *Essay*, Quantz built instruments to his own special design, and performed and composed a repertoire for them that includes lively, challenging, and even moving pieces. Quantz's threefold activities, as a composer-performer, an instrument maker, and a writer, place him at the heart of this book, as a persuasive example of its theme that the flute, its music, and its performance technique are all bound tightly together in a vital but fragile relationship.

The neglect that quickly befell Quantz's music and his instruments illustrates just how brittle this bond often is. Within two decades of his death a Berlin contemporary noted:

> The low tuning of Quantz is no longer used; departed with it are Quantz's flutes, Quantz's concertos, and the true art of playing them, without which they suffer indescribably. Now [1792] there are perhaps no more than three people in Berlin who still know the way to play them.[1]

Quantz's *Essay* too became the target of criticism due to alterations in performance practice in the decades after it appeared in 1752. Only twenty years later the English music critic Charles Burney found Quantz's treatment of *appoggiaturas* incorrect and old-fashioned, his instructions for bowing stringed instruments monotonous, and his use of dynamics too restricted to single notes at the expense of whole passages. In another signal that the emphatic, rhetorical style of the early eighteenth century had shifted to a smoother, more linear sense of melody, the Berlin theorist Johann Friedrich Reichardt (1776) warned against the frequent detaching of the bow Quantz advocated. The classical flutists Ribock and Tromlitz (chapter 6) thought Quantz's flutes behind the times. In the same way the reputation of Quantz's compositions suffered from Burney's

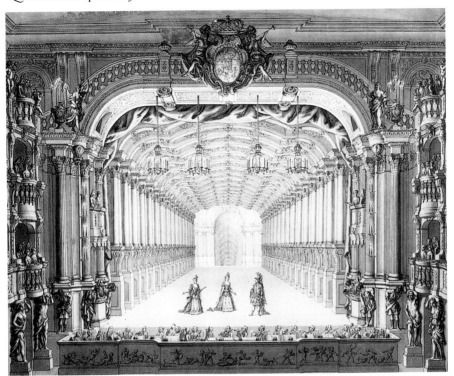

26. Carl Heinrich Jacob Fehling (1654–1725), quill, brush, and india ink drawing of the stage and orchestra in the Dresden Opera House on the Zwinger. The scene is from Antonio Lotti's *Teofane*, performed in September 1719 on the occasion of the wedding of the Saxon prince with the archduchess Maria Josepha, and the first opera Quantz heard.

accusation that they were outdated and unimaginative. Since Burney was writing while Haydn was active in London he was certainly correct to say that musical style had moved on – but today we would no longer share his conclusion that compositions that had become unfashionable could no longer contain anything worth hearing.

Commentators in the late eighteenth and nineteenth centuries, then, despite their relative closeness to Quantz's own time, lacked a perspective that enabled them to see his work accurately and as a whole, and took an unjustly negative, even dismissive, attitude toward his musical spirit. Not until Edward R. Reilly drew attention to Quantz's life and writings did the tide begin to turn. Studies of Quantz's compositions, many of which have been preserved in Dresden and Berlin but overlooked because of disdainful references by earlier writers, took great strides at the end of the twentieth century when Horst Augsbach published a thematic catalogue of the works (1984 and 1997). In 1998 Mary Oleskiewicz produced a doctoral dissertation arguing that details of Quantz's formative years in Dresden, his flutes, and his manner of playing them held important practical lessons for understanding his whole musical ethos. Thanks to these and other scholars, we are in a new position to re-evaluate Quantz's work in light of 'the vital relationships that exist [between] pitch, the characteristics of a performer's instrument, the style of a composition, and the manner in which it is played'.[2]

Quantz's autobiography, published in 1762 in response to criticism of his *Essay*, gives a rare account of the education and employment of one of Europe's first specialist flutists. Despite an unpromising start, he rose to a position of unprecedented eminence for a wind player largely through his own efforts. After the death of his father, a blacksmith, he moved to Merseburg at the age of ten to live and train with his uncle, the town musician Justus Quantz. Such an apprenticeship provided one of three paths to instrumental training open at the time, of which the two others were schools such as Leipzig's Thomasschule, which provided mostly vocal training, and private instruction.[3] Though his uncle died after only a few months, Quantz continued as an apprentice to Johann Adolf Fleischhack, who inherited Justus's post. Besides his principal instrument, the violin, Quantz studied oboe, trumpet, cornett, trombone, horn, recorder, bassoon, cello, viola da gamba, and double bass, and took harpsichord and composition lessons with Johann Friedrich Kiesewetter (d 1715). Completing his apprenticeship at the age of sixteen, Quantz remained in Merseburg as a journeyman musician for two years, specializing in oboe, violin, and trumpet.

Town musicians held a reasonably secure position at the time. They had to pass certain tests – legitimate non-Jewish birth, and a clean criminal record – but even a foreigner like the Frenchman Roger Morell could hold the position of town musician in Wismar in 1694, though 'his knowledge of music, in the French manner, was quite different from the German music here'.[4] Rising from a town band to an aristocratic household was considered risky, since courts would lay off musicians, the least essential of servants, at the slightest sign of financial difficulty. Thus according to a commentator who wrote in 1719, many court musicians would have been happy to join a town band, where jobs were more secure, if only they could be paid as well as at court. Town musicians had recourse to legal complaint, and used it to exclude unlicensed performers, but 'beer-fiddlers', students, military musicians, instrument makers, travelling virtuosi, and dancing masters chipped away at these legal rights, until eventually the French Revolution encouraged authorities to allow complete freedom to exercise trades, including music.

Quantz, however, aspired higher than the Merseburg town band. Dresden in the first decades of the eighteenth century attracted the best composers and musicians in Europe, including Bach, Handel, Vivaldi, and Telemann. Its Hofkapelle (court musical establishment) under Elector Friedrich August I (Augustus II of Poland) and II (III) was widely known as the best instrumental ensemble in Europe, endowed with a vast repertory by old and new composers in antique and fashionable styles. The court provided excellent performing spaces and instruments, and musicians could obtain permission to travel to study their art. Here woodwind players first began to specialize in a single instrument and the flute first took its place as a virtuoso's vehicle in mixed ensembles.

Quantz travelled to Dresden to look for work in 1714. His first step was to accept a position as assistant to a town musician in nearby Pirna, where he came to know the director of the Dresden town band, Gottfried Heine (d 1738), who sometimes employed him as an extra at weddings. At Pirna Quantz learned the concertos of Antonio Vivaldi (1678–1741), which he later described as 'a then completely new species of musical pieces'. After returning to Merseburg he received an offer from

Heine to join the Dresden town band in 1716. The suspension of music owing to an official mourning period permitted Quantz to travel to Vienna in the following year and study counterpoint with Fux's pupil Jan Dismas Zelenka (1678–1745).

Returning to Dresden a year later, Quantz was accepted after an audition on the oboe to fill a position in the newly-formed Kleine Kammermusik, known as the 'Polish Band', an ensemble of twelve musicians who accompanied the King-Elector on visits to Warsaw. The ensemble's flutist, Christian Friedrich Friese, allowed Quantz to play first flute, which the ambitious twenty-one-year-old saw as a more promising means to advancement than the oboe since there was hardly any competition. A year after his entry into the Polish Band as an oboist, Quantz took a series of lessons on the flute from Buffardin, the principal flutist of the Hofkapelle. His four-month course, from about March to June 1719, began his intensive study of the flute.

Though Quantz wrote in his autobiography that solo music for the flute was rare when he took it up, transverse flutes seem to have held a featured position in Dresden concerted music from an early date. When Friedrich August I visited Vienna in 1696 he engaged a band of *Hautboisten* (woodwind players) to join the Instrumentisten and Churfürstliche Kammermusik (Instrumentalists and Electoral chamber music ensemble). Six men were listed as playing *Flutti*, four of them Frenchmen, and another, who doubled on *Fagott*, Italian. While it is not clear what kind of *Flutti* the *Flautenisten* played, the term *Flautenist* continued to appear in the rolls of musicians alongside the better-paid players of *Hautbois* and *Flute allemande* until 1720.

Specialists clearly designated as transverse flutists joined the court's French-style *Orchestra* at its inception in 1709, playing alongside the court *Hautboisten* in performances of French theatrical and orchestral music, including pieces by Dresden composers as well opera overtures and suites by Lully. The court employed two players of *Flute allemande* and four of *Hautbois*, as well as strings and a large continuo group of theorboes, organs, *bassons*, cellos, and contrabass. The flutists were Jean Baptiste D'Ucé, at the highest pay scale of 400 Thalers, and Le Conte senior (whose son played *basson*), at the lowest woodwind level of 250 Thalers. Charles and Jean Baptiste Henrion, listed before 1709 as flutists, were now named as *Hautbois*. D'Ucé was dismissed in 1714 and replaced by Pierre Gabriel Buffardin, at a starting salary of 500 Thalers, raised in 1720 to 800 and in 1741 to 1000. Buffardin remained one of the Hofkapelle's most valued members until 1749 and also held the rank of *Kammermusicus*.

Woodwind doubling seems to have disappeared at Dresden and specialization to have become the norm between 1717 and 1719, when Italian opera and opera singers arrived with the composers Johann David Heinichen (1683–1729) and Antonio Lotti (c1667–1740) of Venice.[5] From this point French influences in the Dresden orchestra, such as the Lullian discipline of orchestral playing imposed by concertmaster Jean-Baptiste Volumier, began to wane. The lavish performance of Lotti's *Teofane* on 13 September 1719 in the brand-new Dresden opera house was the first opera Quantz had ever heard, and he wrote in his autobiography of the strong impression it made on him. The stellar cast of singers attracted Handel to Dresden to recruit for his London productions, and the orchestra depicted in contemporary engravings shows a complement of forty-four musicians, ten more than the normal strength for that year

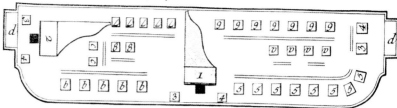

Fig 1.   *Distribution de l'Orchestre de l'Opéra de Dresde,*
Dirigé par le S.ᵣ Hasse.

Renvois des Chiffres.

1. *Clavecin du Maître de Chapelle.*   7. *Hautbois, de même.*

2. *Clavecin d'accompagnement.*   8. *Flutes, de même.*

3. *Violoncelles.*   a. *Tailles, de même.*

4. *Contre-basses.*   b. *Bassons.*

5. *Premiers Violons.*   c. *Cors de Chasse.*

6. *Seconds Violons, ayant le dos tourné vers*   d. *Une Tribune de chaque côté pour le*
   le Théâtre.   *balles et Trompettes.*

27. Plan of the Dresden Opera House under Hasse, 1734–64. (1) Director's harpsichord; (2) Accompanist's harpsichord; (3) Cellos; (4) Double basses; (5) First violins; (6) Second violins, backs towards stage; (7) Oboes, ditto; (8) Flutes, ditto; (a) Violas, ditto; (b) Bassoons; (c) Horns; (d) Balcony on either side for timpani and trumpets. Frank Harrison and Joan Rimmer, *European Musical Instruments* (London: Studio Vista, 1964), pl. 153. Rousseau, *Dictionaire de musique* (Paris, 1768).

(ill. 26).[6] Two flutes appear in the centre of the orchestra box, facing the director, Lotti, who is seated at the harpsichord. The score includes a brilliant, leaping virtuoso flute solo in Act 3, as well as arias featuring obbligato horns, oboes, bassoon, trumpet, and timpani. A pair of flutes played a nightingale song in a bird *arioso* sung by the alto castrato Senesino (Ottone), 'Rosignoli, che celebrate' (Act 2): after a duet in parallel thirds, the first flute takes on the role of soloist, with trills and repeated arpeggiated or leaping figures, often in rapid exchange between the two parts.[7]

Vocal and instrumental performances in the Hofkirche (royal chapel), and in some operas staged outside the Dresden opera house, employed smaller forces than those that appeared in *Teofane*. Extant performance parts indicate that from about 1725 the orchestra comprised pairs of flutes, oboes, and bassoons, four or six violins, one or two violas, two cellos and contrabass, and harpsichord or organ.[8] Concerted works for church and theatre by Dresden composers gave the flute a special role in a varied and challenging repertoire that included pieces in some of the instrument's most difficult tonalities. Heinichen, Zelenka, and later Hasse often reserved flutes for special effects or for concerto-like virtuoso display while the band of oboes and strings provided the normal orchestral voice.

Heinichen wrote difficult and substantial parts for flutes beginning in 1717, often blending them in unison with oboes, a departure from Zelenka's habit of separating and contrasting the two colours.[9] But perhaps the most notable feature of the Dresden opera repertoire, from the flutist's point of view, was its frequent use of flat tonalities: Heinichen, for example, wrote E♭ major arias for flute in 1719, 1724, 1726, and 1728. In her survey of the repertoire Mary Oleskiewicz observes that 'one might contrast Heinichen's early, regular use of [key signatures having] multiple flats and sharps for the flute with that of his contemporary acquaintance in Leipzig, J. S. Bach, who at this time was rarely so tonally adventurous with flutes in his cantatas'.[10] Perhaps some practical reason lay behind the frequent use of flat keys at the opera: works written for performance in Venice had vocal ranges noticeably lower than the European average because of the high pitch that prevailed there (a pitch known as *corista Veneto* of A=440 as opposed to the commoner northern European opera pitch of A=*c*390, a whole tone lower).[11] It is tempting to speculate that when Venetian singers performed their roles in Dresden, they preferred to sing them at the accustomed level while the orchestra parts were written in a higher key to match. Much of Heinichen's early writing for the flute that called for brilliant playing and good intonation was clearly written especially for Buffardin. His *Magnificat* in E♭ dates from May 1724, before Quantz had joined the Hofkapelle and before he had added the second key to his instrument that made playing in that tonality more comfortable. A brilliant instrumental *concertino* in B minor in Heinichen's *Missa 5* in D major of 1726 (while Quantz was away) was scored for *Flauto concertato*, oboes, strings, with long stretches of concerto-style passage work.[12]

Because these concerted works with voices dominated Dresden's musical environment, the Italian vocal style figures prominently in the solos Quantz and others wrote for the flute. The same style informed Handel's music, much cultivated among Dresden musicians: indeed, Quantz himself made copies of several Handel sonatas, which he might have played on violin, oboe, or flute.[13] In the early flute sonata by Handel HWV 378 of *c*1707, the third movement is an operatic recitative, marked *Adagio*. Similar movements appear in a Berlin manuscript of twenty sonatas in a great variety of genres that seem to be among Quantz's earliest for the flute.[14] These are set not only in the usual keys of D major, D, A, E, B, and G minor, but also the remoter E♭ major, C minor, F major and minor, and B♭ major, though Quantz may have considered some of these too difficult for dilettantes since his published flute pieces did not venture beyond the easiest tonalities. Similarly, Handel's trio sonata HWV 386b (*c*1717–19) exists in several manuscript copies of a version in C minor in the Hofkapelle archive in Dresden, whereas the version Walsh published in a scoring for flute, violin, and continuo as op. 2 no. 1b was transposed to the more flute-friendly key of B minor.[15]

In 1722 Quantz travelled to Prague to take part in Johann Joseph Fux's opera *Costanza e fortezza* with a magnificent cast, chorus, and staging at the coronation of the Holy Roman Emperor Charles VI. Two years later he managed to obtain permission to join the party of Count von Lagnasco, the new Polish minister to Rome. Quantz's trip to Italy turned into a three-year Grand Tour, funded by his employer, that would take him to France, England, and the Netherlands as well as Italy. There he studied counterpoint under Francesco Gasparini (1668–1727) and encountered all the important Italian composers of the period. In Naples he met Johann Adolf Hasse

(1699–1783), who later scored for him and Buffardin in Dresden, and through him Alessandro Scarlatti (1660–1725), who famously complained of the bad intonation of wind players – though his comment is often mistakenly quoted with sole reference to the flute. He kept illustrious company in Naples, performing by invitation with the famous castrato Farinelli (Carlo Broschi, 1705–82), the contralto Vittoria Tesi (1700–75), Hasse, and the cellist Franciscello (Franceso Alborea, 1691–1739). Evidently accustomed to the highest standards in Dresden, Quantz, like Scarlatti, found good woodwind players rare in Italy. His own playing attracted rapturous notice for its novelty as well as its quality. When he performed in the Tuscan city of Pistoia on 22 November 1725 with the German oboist Ludwig Erdmann and the local violinist Jacopo Morelli, one resident commented on the unfamiliarity of the transverse flute in terms another Italian commentator had used two and a half centuries earlier (p. 39):

> It is an instrument which has not been heard up to now in Pistoia and it has a voice like that of a recorder, except that they hold it in the mouth sideways, not pointing forward as they hold the recorder, and this gentleman is from Saxony and really he played marvellously well, such as we have never heard before.[16]

After remaining in Italy for almost two years, Quantz travelled to Paris in August 1726 for a stay of seven months. Though he admired the playing style of many individual instrumentalists, including Jacques Christophe Naudot and Michel Blavet, he found French opera performance weak and its repertoire old-fashioned. Perhaps with Scarlatti's criticism of wind players reinforcing his own experience of playing in the company of excellent musicians at Dresden and elsewhere, he had a key for D$^\sharp$ added to his flute, for reasons he explains in the *Essay* (III, 8–11; see also p. 83). Quantz received instructions to return to Dresden in 1727, but instead paid a short visit to England from 20 March to 1 June of that year. In contrast to Paris, he found Italian opera thriving under Handel's direction.

On his return to Dresden in 1727 Quantz entered the main Saxon *Kapelle*, now with a salary of 250 Thalers as well as his stipend of 216 Thalers, displacing Blochwitz from the second flute chair next to Buffardin, and free from duties as an oboist. He concentrated hard on composition, trying to make use of the material he had gathered on his travels. Meanwhile the music the orchestra played continued to place high demands on the flute section. Oleskiewicz has noted that 'a marked increase in Zelenka's use of transverse flutes coincides closely with Quantz's return to Dresden and entry into the Hofkapelle in 1728'.[17] Zelenka used the instrument in a mixture of solo, orchestral, and *colla parte* writing, in which a voice part, usually the soprano in choral fugues, is doubled. Death, lamentation, and pastoral themes often provided the impetus for flute obbligati for Dresden compositions by Zelenka, Hasse, and Bach (in the 'Benedictus' of the *B minor Mass*), while Zelenka employed keys as far from the flute's easiest as E major and C minor, the latter linked with fugal technique and chromaticism. Heinichen's works for the ensemble included an F$^\sharp$ minor aria of 1729 for two flutes.[18]

Hasse, Quantz's friend from his Italian sojourn, joined him in Dresden in 1731, when a performance of his opera *Cleofide*, including a two-flute obbligato aria in B♭, attracted J. S. Bach to the city. Hasse's compositions involving the flute employed tonalities even more extreme than Zelenka's, sometimes making them double oboes or violins in unison or at the octave – an especially difficult feat at a time when woodwinds were played essentially without vibrato.[19] While Zelenka used the flute as a special colour to be introduced at particular moments, Hasse's operas employed a pair of flutes in the normal orchestral sound, often in unison with the violins or *colla parte* with the soloist in arias. Hasse also frequently assigned the flute to play solo obbligato with voice in both opera and oratorio. Though the flute parts generally retained their vocal character and made little use of the highest register (above E3), Hasse's *Asteria* (1737, 'Non vi dolga o piagge amene', Act 3) called for a *tirade* marked *fortissimo* up to F3, often a problematic note for baroque flutes.[20]

In marked contrast to the music Quantz and his colleagues played and composed among themselves, the pieces he released to the public were relatively simple and pedagogical in intention. His first authorized publication, *Sei Sonata, Opera Prima* (Dresden, 1734), avoided difficult keys and emphasized his focus on articulation by notating this aspect of performance. The limited range of the collection (up to E3) on the other hand was not a concession to amateur abilities but quite normal for Dresden composers.[21]

The difficult keys of the music the Dresden flutists were expected to play gives a quite new aspect to Quantz's interest in improving his flute's intonation. Yet while he reported the bare fact that he added the D♯ key to his instrument in Paris in 1726, he left us to speculate how he conceived or executed the idea, as well as how he learned to make flutes, an activity he only began, according to his autobiography, thirteen years later in 1739. Second-hand testimony on the matter comes from his chronicler Nicolai:

> Already in Dresden Quantz had made many observations on the true tuning of the notes of the flute. He knew how difficult it is to play in tune on this instrument. He sought to remedy this defect [and] had his flutes turned [on a lathe] with great care from the best wood, then himself very carefully measured off the tuning, and bored [i.e. drilled] the holes of the flute himself.[22]

Tula Giannini (1993) has observed that when Quantz became friendly with Blavet in Paris, the Frenchman seems to have been buying flutes in quantity from the workshop of Pierre Naust, directed at that time by Antoine Delerablé, whose son was in service as a musician at the Dresden court.[23] The ultimate design and execution of Quantz's flutes does indeed owe much to the work of some early eighteenth-century Parisian makers, but we can only guess about any exchange of ideas that might have taken place. However, second-hand testimony does link the same Dresden/Paris circles with two new devices aimed at making the flute's intonation more precise when altering its pitch by means of *corps de rechange*, since Antoine Mahaut (c1759) attributed the invention of these supplementary gadgets to Buffardin.[24] They were the screw-cork, to make fine adjustments to position of the cork stopper in the headjoint relative to the embouchure hole, and the index or *Register* footjoint, which featured a telescoping tube to make it longer or shorter. Mahaut addressed his method to

28. Portrait of Johann Joachim Quantz, attrib. Friedrich Gerhard, painted at Schloss Ermitage, Bayreuth in *c*1741.

amateurs and provided no separate fingerings for sharps and flats, but he made his own concern for intonation clear when he wrote:

> This last point [a very precise ear], which is very essential, is most often lacking. ... One rarely hears an orchestra whose flutes are in tune[:] the player incorrectly casts the blame on the instrument, while he ought to blame only his ear, which he has not trained enough.[25]

Quantz adopted the screw-cork in his own flutes, but not the index foot, the use of which he described as follows:

> The purpose is supposed to be to make the foot a little shorter for each shorter middle piece, so that with the help of six middle pieces [*corps de rechange*] the flute

might be made a whole tone higher or lower. … But since shortening the foot makes only the D higher, while the following notes, D♯, E, F, G, &c., remain for the most part unchanged and do not rise with the D in the proper proportion, it follows that the flute does indeed become a whole note higher, but also that it becomes completely out of tune, except [when it is used] with the first [i.e. the longest] piece.[26]

To make small adjustments in the instrument's overall pitch, Quantz built a tuning slide in the headjoint of his flutes, to be extended a little more than half a centimetre in its normal position. Quantz's principled opposition to the practice of supplying flutes with a set of middle joints did not prevent him making such instruments himself, but the wear on surviving Quantz flutes unmistakably indicates that only the longest middle joint, for the lowest pitch, received regular use. That pitch was equal to or even somewhat below the opera pitch (A=c390) established by Lully.[27] While Quantz felt this pitch was 'the most advantageous for the transverse flute, the oboe, the bassoon, and some other instruments', he considered the German A chamber pitch of about A=410 the most convenient for general ensemble use by strings and winds. He even ventured the opinion that a prevalent high pitch in Italy, which favoured the strings but made the woodwinds sound unpleasant, might be the reason why wind instruments were so little played there.[28]

Mary Oleskiewicz's study of Quantz's formative years as a flutist has vividly illustrated how closely his ideals of flute tone were bound to the Italian vocal style and to the influence of the particular singers he heard in Dresden. Bearing this background in mind puts Quantz's often-quoted description of the flute's tone quality in a new light:

> In general the most pleasing tone quality (*sonus*) on the flute is that which more nearly resembles a *Contraalt* [a high tenor or a female alto] than a soprano, or which is similar to the range of singers that is called the chest voice. One must strive as much as possible to acquire the tone quality of those flute players who can draw a bright, cutting, thick, round, masculine, but also pleasing sound from the instrument.[29]

Quantz designed the proportions of the flutes he built to aid in the production of such a tone. As one Berlin adherent of his instruments wrote for a French readership shortly after Quantz's death:

> Quantz's flutes are longer, of wider bore, and thicker in the wood than ordinary flutes. Consequently they have a tone of more weight, lustiness, and sonority, but a more limited compass.[30]

The bore of his flutes, as well as being larger than any other, tapered more sharply than that of other contemporary instruments, around 35 per cent compared with about 30 per cent, and their embouchure holes, unlike the round one shown in the *Essay*, were elliptical rather than circular. Both these features, as well as the flutes' characteristic tonehole undercutting, contributed to a strong and penetrating tone, especially in the low register. In the chapter on the embouchure in his *Essay*, Quantz described a firm and steady manner of blowing these flutes to achieve his ideal sound:

> The action of the chest can also be of considerable help with the flute's tone. This must not be rough, that is, trembling [*zitternd*], but relaxed. If one did the opposite the tone would become too noisy [*rauschend*].[31]

Reilly's translation gives the last word as 'loud'. And yet Quantz's flutes already produced a tone more powerful than most. It is difficult to imagine his sound as having been in any sense small, for in a reply to his amateur critic Moldenit in 1758 (p. 101), he ridiculed the Danish amateur's predilection for softness of tone:

> From this softness arises the great delicacy of his playing. How would it sound, however, in a large room? *Of course, amateurs do not play in public.*[32]

In May 1728 Augustus II of Poland visited King Frederick William I of Prussia in his capital at Berlin along with a group of his best musicians, including Pisendel, Weiss, Buffardin, and Quantz. Thereafter Quantz was allowed to visit the Prussian court twice a year to give flute lessons to Frederick William's son, the Crown Prince Frederick, who began to form his own musical ensemble in 1730 against opposition from his father so ferocious that he had to submit to a period of imprisonment. Though Quantz had promised Frederick to enter his service, he was either unable or unwilling to gain his release from Dresden, where by now his salary had been raised to 800 Thalers. In 1731, in the meantime, Quantz took on another noble pupil: Frederick, soon to become Margrave of Bayreuth, husband of Frederick's sister, Princess Wilhelmine.

Most biographers of Michel Blavet report that he visited Crown Prince Frederick at Rheinsberg, probably in 1738, and was offered a permanent post, which he declined.[33] Two years later, once Frederick had become King of Prussia, he was able to offer Quantz terms of employment that proved more attractive: 2000 Thalers a year for life, plus extra payments for compositions and flutes, and performance obligations limited to the Royal Chamber Ensemble, excluding duties in the opera orchestra. The generosity of this offer is easier to grasp if we compare the pay of a few other court employees in 1742–3: Quantz's basic stipend, excluding extras, put him at the same level as the Director of Music, Carl Heinrich Graun, and Field Marshal Graf von Schwerin. The best-paid singer, Signora Gasparini, was paid 1700 Thalers, and Frederick's personal physician received 1332. Quantz received double the remuneration of senior court officials, four times as much as the King's *valet de chambre*, and seven times as much as the King's accompanist, Carl Philipp Emanuel Bach.[34]

C. P. E. Bach, appointed Frederick the Great's keyboardist in 1740, had composed eight sonatas for flute and continuo between 1735 and the time Quantz arrived in 1741. These eight sonatas, as Mary Oleskiewicz has observed, contain relatively few of the *empfindsam* ('sensitive') characteristics normally associated with his style. In Quantz's pieces, however, as well as in sonatas and *trii* Emanuel Bach composed in

1746–55 and in concertos he wrote around 1750, the *empfindsamer Stil* clearly appears.[35] Quantz brought characteristics of the new style from Dresden when he officially entered Frederick's service in December 1741. The focus of his musical activities throughout his tenure was Frederick's private chamber concert, a two-hour event in which the King played his flute, scheduled for 7 pm each evening on which no grander entertainment was planned. The repertoire at these events seems to have consisted entirely of pieces by Quantz and by Frederick himself: sonatas, trios, and concertos accompanied by single strings and continuo, often with C. P. E. Bach at the keyboard. By Quantz's death his catalogue included 153 flute sonatas and 296 concertos. During his lifetime the Berlin court's taste remained centred in the ideals of the *galant* idiom that arose in the second quarter of the eighteenth century. Frederick's musical taste and the establishment he formed were directly influenced by those of the Saxon court, which, ironically, he destroyed in 1757–8 along with the city of Dresden in the Seven Years' War (1756–63). After that event, Frederick's interest in music weakened, and in Reilly's words 'he did little more than perpetuate the pattern he had already created'. By the time C. P. E. Bach fled to Hamburg in 1767, the musical styles of Berlin had – as Burney observed – become conservative and old-fashioned while the rest of Europe moved on.

Though the study of musical style in the flute's repertoire lies outside our scope in this book, the ways in which instruments meet the demands of changing styles falls very much within it. Quantz's and Frederick's Berlin repertoire for the flute, long overlooked as dull and monotonous on the strength of a few unrepresentative pieces, is ready for re-evaluation. But several works already among the best-known eighteenth-century compositions for the flute illustrate how understanding the character of the Quantz flute, particularly its pitch and intonation, can affect the way we feel about music composed for Potsdam. J. S. Bach's E major sonata BWV 1035, dating from the year of Quantz's arrival at the earliest, is connected on the authority of its two nineteenth-century sources with the King's valet and duet partner Michael Gabriel Fredersdorf (1708–58). This passionately expressive, soloistic piece, set in a challenging tonal scheme that ventured as far afield as G♯ minor, is related to a type of sonata Quantz had begun composing late in his Dresden years, and was clearly intended as a compliment to the skill, taste, and special instruments of the Potsdam flutists.[36] The *Musical Offering* trio-sonata (1747) is another piece Bach clearly wrote with the Quantz flute, as well as the Berlin taste and performance practice, in mind.[37] He set the piece in the difficult but effective key of C minor, a favourite of Zelenka, Quantz, and others for writing in fugal style, and made liberal use of difficult trills in its second movement.[38] The dramatic use of *forte* and *piano* in the sonata's third movement recalls the frequent and extreme dynamic indications in Quantz's later Berlin sonatas. The presence at Potsdam of *pianofortes* by Silbermann, and Quantz's involvement in acquiring such instruments for the court, suggests another flattering reason for Bach to have written in this style and indicates how such dynamics were likely executed by the whole ensemble. A *pianoforte* now in the Neues Palais at Potsdam, fitted with a transposing keyboard, even has the marks of wear on its hammers to indicate that it was played mostly at the lower pitch (A=390 or thereabouts) at which Quantz's flutes were built. The mournful *Affekt*, or emotional style, of the trio-sonata also featured quite commonly in Berlin compositions, as did flat keys such as C minor. Reichardt reported that Frederick was especially gifted at rendering sad, slow movements, often bringing his audience to tears, and Frederick wrote to his sister Wilhelmine of Quantz's similar abilities in the *pathétique* affect. In sum, Bach's pieces for the Berlin court clearly resulted from his detailed knowledge of conditions there and his skill at putting them to the highest musical use. As Mary Oleskiewicz has written:

> Contrary to what has becom[e] the received wisdom about Bach's *Musical Offering* and its performance, musical and organological evidence confirms the extraordinary appropriateness of Bach's trio-sonata [for the court's taste] while offering new insights into the performance of the work.[39]

In contrast to the comparatively superficial flute tutors that had hitherto addressed amateurs, Quantz designed his *Essay* 'to train a skilled and intelligent musician, and not just a mechanical flute-player'. Only fifty pages of the original 334 are devoted to flute-playing: thus the *Essay* is less a method for the flute than a compendium covering musical taste and execution on all sorts of instruments. This broad scope, rather than any particular information about flute-playing, is what made it one of the most widely-known instrumental methods of the eighteenth century.

Quantz clearly meant the word 'mechanical' to be taken literally, and frowned upon playing that had this quality. Anachronistic though the concept of a robot flute-player may seem, Jacques de Vaucanson, who had exhibited a mechanical duck, 'eating, drinking, macerating the Food, and voiding Excrements – pluming her Wings, picking her Feathers, and performing several Operations in Imitation of a living Duck' to great applause in the salons of Paris, published accounts in French (1738), English (1742 and 1752), and German (1747 and 1748) of an automaton flute-player he had constructed a short time before the *Essay* appeared. Quantz contrasted Vaucanson's achievement, which evidently left him cold, with his book's goal: 'I must try not only to educate [the student's] lips, tongue, and fingers, but must also try to form his taste, and sharpen his discernment.'

Naturally Quantz wrote the tutor for the two-keyed flute he used, and since he was addressing the aspiring professional he gave separate fingerings for the commonest enharmonic sharps and flats. The *Essay* likewise embodied a highly developed musical taste as it was formed by his experiences in Dresden, in particular his view that the heroic male voice was the basis for an ideal flute tone. Like other contemporary authors who dealt with tempo, Quantz indicated that the freedom of choice allowed performers was small, but the range of tempi and the use of rubato was much greater than is considered tasteful today.[40] The work contains far too many of such general points to permit a full treatment here. His instructions on tonguing, however, which referred directly to the flute and were by far the most sophisticated to date, deserve a brief discussion.

Quantz used a soft and a hard syllable *ti* and *tiri*, *di* and *diri*, for single-tonguing, and *did'll* for double-tonguing, a technique he was the first to mention, notwithstanding the claims made on Agricola's behalf (p. 36). Criticism of this system from a former pupil prompted Quantz to provide further particulars of his own tonguing technique, and how it differed from those used by Blavet and Buffardin. His adversary, Joachim von Moldenit, was a peculiar character whose activities illustrate that dilettantes could buy access to the best teaching, even if they were not always able to make much use of it. Quantz had met the financially independent Dane in Paris in 1726, and introduced him to Blavet, who gave him flute lessons. Moldenit afterward travelled to Dresden, where he studied with Buffardin and then Quantz. According to Quantz, Moldenit helped with copy-editing the *Essay* on visits to Berlin, but took offence on being told he lacked the natural aptitude to become an excellent flutist. To say that they quarrelled would be an understatement, for as Quantz characterized Moldenit's claims: 'Many things are manifest lies, to use the mildest possible expression.'[41]

In May 1758 Moldenit, who had published a set of pieces that greatly exceeded the range of the flute and claimed to have invented a method of articulating with the lower lip rather than the tongue, published a direct attack on Quantz's method of articulation. This prompted a point-by-point refutation in November, in which Quantz defended his choice of tonguing syllables, noting that 'other syllables such as *bibi, pipi, mimi, nini, kiki,* etc., would be useless for this function'.[42] He also emphasized a point that some later commentators have missed in the *Essay* itself: that *tiri* and *diri* are not double-tonguing:

> On page 15 Mr von Moldenit says that Buffardin and Blavet made little [use] of tongue work. They use tonguing with *ti* and *tiri* and with *di* and *diri* just as much as I do. They do not, it is true, use the double tongue [*did'll*]; but do they play as many quick notes, or play them as distinctly as someone who uses the double tongue correctly? Anyone who has heard both can answer this question for me.

When challenged to play his own compositions, Moldenit was observed to hum into the flute to produce the notes below its range, but could produce only the feeblest excuses for not attempting the extreme high register. This prompted Quantz to provide fingerings for $B\flat3$ to E4, a range even the lowest extreme of which found no musical application for almost two centuries to come.[43]

The principal musical supplements to the *Essay* are provided in Quantz's compositions, lamentably few of which have ever been published. The preface to his six duets op. 2, which discusses the usefulness of duets in training good students, suggests that he intended these works in particular as a musical accessory to the *Essay*.[44] A manuscript entitled *Solfeggi Pour la Flute Traversiere avec l'enseignement, Par Monsr. Quantz* came to light in 1958 in the Royal Library in Copenhagen. A kind of practice notebook, it contains extracts from flute repertoire of the day annotated with detailed instructions for performance. The work's modern editors, Winfried Michel and Hermien Teske, assign it an improbably early date of 1728–42, but the Quantz specialist Horst Augsbach argues in his index of Quantz's works that the manuscript is not in Quantz's own hand but rather stems from the circle of his pupil Augustin Neuff, a member of the Berlin Court ensemble from 1751 to 1792, assigning it a date after Quantz's death somewhere in the period 1775–82. The Telemann scholar and

29. A French image of
Frederick the Great (*facing
page*) is much less flattering
than the German (*right*): (a)
*Friedrich der Große im
Stadtschloss* (Frederick the Great
in his Palace of State) (b)
(*facing page*) *Rex Tibicen* (Royal
flutist)

baroque flutist Steven Zohn, in an article of 1997, opines that much of the material
dates from the 1740s and 50s, and that 'most if not all, of its contents originated with
the composer'. Zohn notes that 'Telemann is the best represented composer in the
Solfeggi, with several dozen excerpts from his duets and trios'.

Besides providing many examples of Quantz's tonguing principles, the manuscript
represents a prime source for the study of rhythmic inequality in the late baroque
period. As Claire Fontijn has noted (1995), the *Solfeggi* contain more than fifty
indications of note lengths marked *ungleich* or *unegal* (unequal) in passages from the
works of German composers such as W. F. Bach, Telemann, Blochwitz, Wolff, and
others. The remark made by François Couperin in *L'Art de toucher le clavecin* (The art
of playing the harpsichord, Paris, 2/1717) that French musicians played paired quavers
unequally while the Italians played them equally has led to a perception today that
such inequality was not practised outside France – though John Byrt (1998) has
pointed out that in Italian music a similar inequality was applied at the level of
semiquavers. In any case one of the principal sources of information about the Lullian
style, the late seventeenth-century writings and compositions of the German Georg
Muffat, illustrates the influence of that style outside France, while instrumental works
by Muffat, Telemann, and others show how German musicians perceived and
absorbed the French style. Even Johann George Tromlitz, writing in 1792, taught that
pairs of notes should preserve a feeling of unequal stress, if not of unequal length.

Another Copenhagen manuscript presents short pieces for beginners (*Anfangsstücke*), caprices, and fantasies by Quantz and Blochwitz.[45] The pieces by Quantz are written in a virtuosic style that uses the entire range of the instrument up to A3, while those by Blochwitz recall J. S. Bach's writing for the flute in the *Solo* BWV 1013.

Finally, our brief survey of Quantz's contributions to the flute and flute-playing must try to evaluate the influence he exerted on later generations. The group of students he attracted to Berlin in the 1750s made up the first real 'school' of flute-playing that can be identified anywhere in Europe. Among these pupils and their own students, we first encounter the urge musicians often feel to place themselves in a tradition of playing. Later generations of players in Berlin retained the vivid sense of their heritage throughout the nineteenth century (chapters 10, 12): though perhaps the school's founder would hardly have recognized their instruments and musical style, even German flutists of the early twentieth century traced their lineage back to him much as the French did to Blavet and Devienne, the nineteenth-century English to Nicholson, or modern Americans to Taffanel through Barrère. Thus the Berlin school presents our first opportunity briefly to explore the general question of how such traditions begin and how myths of succession take root among instrumentalists. A full exploration could occupy a book by itself: here, and in a discussion of the French

Flute School (chapter 11), space permits us only to raise the question, not to settle it.

Eighteenth-century flutists seldom identified themselves as pupils of another: in general only people of rank, such as Frederick the Great and the Margrave of Bayreuth, were ever named as the pupils of a particular teacher.[46] Though Quantz studied with Buffardin, his pupillage lasted only four months and his own teaching and practice far surpassed Buffardin's. Quantz's personal fame derived not from his teacher but from his own activities, including his association with the most famous, or notorious, monarch of Europe. Yet it is perhaps only because of this fame that Quantz's pupils began to classify themselves as such. Johann Joseph Friedrich Lindner (*b* 1730) is one of the few Quantz pupils known by name. His uncle, the Dresden concertmaster Pisendel, sent him to study with Quantz in Berlin, where from about 1750 to 1789 he was a member of the Royal Kapelle, and was praised in 1786 as 'the best pupil of the late Quantz' for his charm and polish, his embouchure, and his beautiful tone.[47] Georg Gotthelf Liebeskind was also sent to Quantz in Berlin, this time by another Quantz pupil, the Margrave of Bayreuth, who dispatched him for three years in 1750. Georg Wilhelm Kodowski (*b* 1735), also probably from Bayreuth, entered the Berlin Kapelle in 1754 after studies with Quantz. A nineteenth-century writer named him Quantz's favourite pupil and stated that he had made several successful concert tours.[48] Another player accorded the title of 'Quantz's best pupil' was Augustin Neuff of Graz, who entered the Berlin Kapelle with Kodowski in 1754, and remained at his post until his death in 1792. The commentator in this case was the blind virtuoso Friedrich Ludwig Dülon (chapter 7), whose father, Louis Dülon (1741–*c*98), had himself studied with Neuff. Dülon called Neuff 'the eighth wonder of the world', but though he wrote particularly of his 'thoroughly pure and secure' intonation, he was disappointed with his tone:

> The hissing of the air, which is only perceptible with me when my embouchure is in very bad form, could be heard with him all the time. He had this fault in common with all Quantz's pupils, and everyone who heard the teacher himself says that he was not quite free of it either.[49]

The succession continued into the next generation when Lindner taught Johann Friedrich Aschenbrenner (*b* 1728) 'according to the method of the famous Quantz', as well as Christian Gottlob Krause (1747–1829), whom Frederick the Great frequently called to Potsdam after Quantz's death to play solos. Krause in turn passed on the tradition to the following generation (chapter 10), and eventually to Georg Müller (chapters 12, 13), whose fascination with the music of Frederick the Great's court led him to research eighteenth-century flute makers, to perform on instruments from the king's collection, and to trace a 'genealogy' of Berlin flutists back to Quantz.

What exactly was 'Quantz's method', and what did later generations of the Berlin school inherit from its founder? Edward R. Reilly (1997) has pointed to the link between Quantz's musical goals and his special flutes:

> Although it is tempting to see the history of instruments in terms of mechanical 'improvements' in their manufacture [i.e. design] – and there has been a strong tendency to link these developments with technological progress – Quantz's flutes

suggest that at times musical ideals and goals may be much more influential, and may guide the shaping of instruments more specifically and concretely than is often realized.[50]

Indeed, the two-keyed flute seems to have remained an identifying trait of Quantz's school into the 1780s and perhaps the 90s. The younger Dülon was one prominent exponent of this instrument, though we know this only because he related that once when performing on a two-keyed flute by Kirst, his E♭ key had malfunctioned and he had had to use the D♯ key instead.[51] The instrument also remained in use by certain noble amateurs: Dülon gave lessons in about 1780 to a sister of the Duke of Mecklenburg-Strelitz, who played a flute made by Quantz.[52] The article on the flute in the 1777 Supplement to Diderot and D'Alembert's *Encyclopédie* suggests that the two-keyed flute may have been known in France, since the writer described and illustrated a Quantz flute, which he clearly knew and played himself. But on closer consideration the article's influence in France was probably negligible. It was signed by F. D. Castilon, a member of the Berlin Akademie and apparently the son of Jean François Salvemini de Castilon (1709–91), whom Frederick the Great had brought to Berlin as mathematics teacher.[53] In fact beyond circles touched by the Berlin Enlightenment the two-keyed flute was not taken up by commercial instrument-makers and never came into general use either among professionals or amateurs. Besides the extant Quantz flutes, we know of two-keyed instruments only by the virtuoso Johann George Tromlitz (Leipzig), the instrument-maker F. G. A. Kirst (Potsdam), and an anonymous maker (now uncatalogued in the Musikhistoriska Museet, Stockholm). Only two later methods for flute, both published in Leipzig, covered the two-keyed instrument: Johann Samuel Petri's tutor of 1782, and Tromlitz's more extensive one of 1791 (chapter 6).[54]

Even after it had passed from musical use, however, the two-keyed flute was not forgotten. Frederick the Great's habit of giving away his flutes to his generals ensured that they would become treasured heirlooms, and with the rise of German nationalism under Prussian leadership and control in the 1860s and 70s, these personal relics of the king and of Prussia's glorious military past attracted particular attention.[55] A report in the *Daily Telegraph* of 21 February 1931 dramatized the passionate feeling that surrounded Frederick's flutes in another period of rising German nationalism and military build-up that led to World War 2. One of the flutes came up for auction among the effects of Schloss Glienecke, near Potsdam, but even German Republicans, according to the newspaper, 'felt that an historical souvenir of this kind should not run the risk of being lost to Germany'.

As the turn of the instrument to be put up drew near an officer, who, it afterwards appeared, was acting for the ex-Crown Prince, declared in agitated tones that Potsdam would never allow the flute to leave the country, and that if it were taken across the frontier a legion would be formed to bring it back from wherever it might be.

To this Prince Friedrich Leopold, the younger, who represented his father, replied that perhaps the sale might have been avoided if, in 1918, the people who were now so excited had defended the House of Hohenzollern as they now defended the flute.[56]

A rumoured offer of £4000 from the Metropolitan Opera of New York increased the likelihood that the patriotic legion would have had to sail the Atlantic to retrieve the heirloom. Accordingly the flute was withdrawn from the sale, and is now kept in Burg Hohenzollern at Hechingen, as one of ten Quantz flutes still extant in Germany, the U.S., and Japan.

If a mere souvenir, a totem, or a relic could arouse such strong feelings in the Prussian nationalists of the 1860s and the 1930s, we can see how later generations of Berlin flutists may have felt that they inherited something at least equally substantial and meaningful from Quantz. And yet, as we shall see in chapters 10 and 12, players in Quantz's line of succession were among the least attached to conventional forms of the instrument, and among the first in Germany to accept the revolutionary Boehm flute, even while their countrymen resisted it to preserve a sound concept they considered more traditional. It would seem that a general sense of common heritage, ideals, and goals, more than an identity of instrument or superficial features of performance, enabled players with various priorities to interpret that heritage in different ways.

Chapter 6

The Classical flute

Even with the mass of detail Quantz provided about his own style and with the instruments and music he left behind, it is difficult to gain a vivid sense of how his playing would strike us today, except that we would surely find it unfamiliar. And the uniformly positive comments Blavet's contemporaries made about his playing tell us no more, in the end, than that his playing struck them as brilliant and exceptionally well in tune. What hinders us in grasping the distinctiveness of these and other players of the baroque period is the lack of a contrast among the remarks of commentators with varying points of view.

By about 1740, however, new musical ideas and new modes of performance had come into play. The flute, having established itself as a solo instrument, was becoming the principal wind instrument for virtuosi, who were spending more of their time travelling, so that audiences in various parts of Europe could for the first time regularly hear flutists from other places, each with an individual style of composition and performance (see chapter 7). As listeners focused on novelties and differences in the playing they heard, a more revealing tone and perspective began to inform their comments. This helps us perceive a new bravura style in solo performance, along with an altered role for the flute in the orchestra and in new types of ensemble composition, as well as a connection between these changed musical demands and innovations in the construction of flutes.

The shift in styles of flute-playing, though international in its reach, was perhaps most clearly perceived in France, where the instrument had possessed a special voice of its own a generation earlier. By the 1720s the brilliant Italianate music Blavet, Buffardin, Lucas, Naudot, and others brought to the Concert spirituel (see chapter 4) had already begun to eclipse the older French style. After two more decades the high rate of flute composition by French composers had declined while solos and trios by Germans and Italians increased.[1] Corrette's tutor of c1740 contained instructions for transposing and tricks for making arpeggiated passages in Italian-style violin music fit the compass of the flute, while French writers began to bemoan the difficult technical feats now demanded of the flute and the loss of its simple singing character.[2] One such in 1739 traced the new style to violinistic Italian music for the instrument, longing for a return to the earlier manner of the *Airs de cour*.

30. Thomas Gainsborough (1727–88), portrait of the gentleman amateur William Wollaston (1730–97), painted *c*1759. The sections of the flute are aligned so that the embouchure hole is turned inward, in the normal way for English flutes of the period. Flute instruction books continued to specify a similar alignment well into the nineteenth century.

The flute's true character … has vanished, and is no longer known…. The great musical innovators find nothing too difficult or too fast; everything is possible to them. Instead of the harmonious liaison that ought to be in their melodies, there is a dry leanness, brought about by the striking of intervals whereby they strive to stammer out three or four parts on this limited instrument … the first and second upper parts, the tenor, and the bass, are only heard in hiccups, all melodies truncated and aborted, which give birth to nothing but disorder and confusion; in playing everything, they play nothing…. Do you know what the Remora of these famous Athletes is?[3] It is to play *L'autre jour ma Cloris*, or any other simple Brunette, as the famous *Labarre* played it. That musician knew better than any other the proper limits of the instrument, which are the tender and the pastoral; and was content to play a single part, wisely husbanded by natural, pleasant, and charming sounds; but such prudence is a joke today, for it is so true that everything bends before the taste of the times and of fashion.[4]

Not all flutists conformed to fashion, however. One of the Classical period's most successful was Johann Baptist Wendling (1723–97), of whom the German critic Christian Friedrich Daniel Schubart (1739–91) recorded:

> His playing is clear and beautiful, and the notes at the bottom and top equally full and penetrating. He is prouder of producing the fine and moving than the difficult, fast, surprising.

Wendling, flutist at the Mannheim court from about 1752 and teacher to Karl Theodor, the Elector Palatine (ill. 31), was heard frequently at the Concert spirituel in 1751–80, as well as in London (1771), Vienna (1776), and Prague. Mozart, who travelled to Paris with him on one occasion, is said to have paid tribute to his ability in a remark he made to the flutist's brother:

31. Johann Georg Ziesenis (1716–76), an unofficial view of Karl Theodor von der Pfalz playing the flute in his chamber (1757).

Well, you know it's different with your brother. In the first place he's not just a tootler, and then you don't have to worry all the time with him, when you know there's a note coming, that it's going to be much too flat or too sharp – look, it's always right, he has his heart and his ears and the tip of his tongue in the right place and doesn't think his job ends with just blowing and making forks [i.e. fingering], and then he knows what *Adagio* means too.[5]

Mozart thought Wendling's skill in playing slow movements worthy of notice because the *Adagio* style had fallen from favour in Germany by the late eighteenth century: C. P. E. Bach's *Hamburger* sonata (1785) contained no slow movement at all, and by 1791 J. G. Tromlitz could observe that 'splendid *Adagios* in the Italian style' had 'almost completely disappeared from modern instrumental music'. On the other hand in England, Pietro Grassi Florio (*d* 1795), formerly a flutist in the Dresden orchestra, became renowned for his *Adagio* playing, in which, like Frederick the Great, 'he seldom failed to draw tears from his audience'.[6] The *Adagio* style in fact was to remain the touchstone of English taste in flute-playing for several generations to come (chapters 7, 8).

England's already considerable attraction to musicians such as Florio increased as the elite's taste moved towards larger-scale instrumental music and away from opera and oratorio. Italian symphonies in the early Classical style became wildly popular at public concerts in London that numbered well over five thousand during the second half of the eighteenth century.[7]

As yet, only a select few could attend such performances. Subscribers to series that featured the latest foreign music and the most prestigious soloists were buying social cachet as well as displaying their wealth. Fashions in music, as well as in architecture and design, contained a strong political component: English taste rejected everything to do with the Stuart monarchs, Catholicism, and the Baroque in favour of the supposedly ancient rules of reason, order, and 'correct' discrimination that characterized the Classical style.[8] Rich, educated landowners and the Whig merchant class cultivated instrumental music at home not merely as a pastime, but as a way to develop the artistic taste they needed as a passport to social acceptability. As they saw it, this taste was both a moral and a spiritual gift. Luke Heron wrote of it in almost Romantic terms in his *Treatise on the German Flute* (1771):

Elegance in musical performance, like gracefulness in action or motion, may be improved, but cannot be given. In action, it is the native grandeur or nobility of the mind, beaming forth and throwing a glory, round us. In music, it is the language of the soul, addressing itself to the passions; or rather, it is the sensibility of the soul describing, and as it were painting, itself to us in sound.[9]

In England as in the rest of Europe, the flute was almost exclusively the province of men. Women performed on fashionable ladies' instruments such as harpsichord, piano, or English guittar in the early 1760s, and later on the harp. Performing in public on male instruments, as Marianne Davies did on the flute at this time, was a highly radical act.[10] Miss Davies further tested the boundaries of respectability by advertising her services (1763) as a teacher of '[Glass] Armonica, German Flute, &c.', along with female teachers of viola da gamba and violin.[11]

In increasing numbers that crested after about 1775, male members of the well-to-do mercantile and professional classes began taking up the flute, following the lead of King George III, as well as members of the peerage such as Willoughby Bertie, fourth Earl of Abingdon, an 'excellent performer' and composer. In 1774 twenty-six flutists founded the Gentlemen's Concerts in Manchester, where the instrument was so overwhelmingly popular that members had to take turns to play.[12] Amateur flutists could buy instruments, tutors, and music at a growing number of music shops in the fashionable streets of London and other centres.[13]

THE KEYED FLUTE

During the 1750s, at about the time of the controversy in the London *Daily Advertiser* over extensions of the flute's range to low C (see p. 81), a few English instrument-makers began to build some instruments with new keys for F, B♭, and G♯, as well as a lower extension of the range to C♯ and C. Each new hole, drilled between two existing fingerholes, was sealed by a simple lever having an airtight pad at one end, a touchpiece with a spring attached at the other, and an axle in the middle to fix it to the flute body. To use the key, the player would finger the next lowest note while opening the key. This simple principle lay behind nearly all the keywork the flute subsequently accumulated, and some of the fingering patterns thus introduced survive in the modern flute, even though its keywork operates on quite different lines.

Despite the assertions to be found in modern writings, the new keys did not make playing easier, faster, or more agile, nor did they make the flutes better in tune. Rather their purpose, as contemporary writers explained it, was to provide an alternative to the flute's more veiled notes at the bottom of the first octave, permitting a more cutting and penetrating tone in that part of the flute's range that carries the least well in large performance spaces or in ensembles with strings. The new keyed flutes gave each of the semitones of the octave except C its own tonehole for the first time. Nevertheless, tutors such as those of Gunn (1793) and Tromlitz (1800) continued to specify many fingerings that did not employ the keys. These old fingerings occurred particularly in the second octave where the keys were, by contemporary standards, unnecessary, as well as in combinations of notes where using a key would have complicated fingering.

A flute with the new keywork marked SCHUCHART SENIOR, probably made by John Just Schuchart in 1753–8, seems to be the type's earliest extant example.[1] A few years later two editions of the anonymous 1s 6d tutor (see p. 112) first illustrated such an instrument. Jonathan Fentum's edition of about 1765 described it as 'Florio and Tacet's new invented German Flute with all the Keys', while Thomas Cahusac's edition specified the role of the two players more precisely by identifying the instrument as 'a new invented German Flute with additional Keys, made by T. Cahusac, such as play'd on by the two celebrated Masters, Tacet and Florio'. In Fentum's inexact wording lies the origin of the persistent myth that Florio or Tacet invented the keyed flute.

In about 1770 Thomas Collier and John Hale began to produce keyed flutes under the trade name FLORIO as well as identical models that carried Collier's own mark. This may explain why Florio's name, now representing a competitor in the flute market, had been erased from the printing plates in subsequent editions of the anonymous tutor, leaving Tacet's alone.[2] The sixpenny fingering charts extracted from these tutors and sold separately in England and on the Continent propagated the notion that the keyed flutes had been 'invented by Mr Tacet'. Hence the still more widespread myth of Tacet's sole paternity of the innovation.

continued overleaf

Richard Potter (1726–1806) was building keyed flutes in his London workshop by 1776, for in that year he began producing date-stamped instruments of which at least sixteen are still extant. In 1785 he filed a patent for a quite different type of keyed flute, with a graduated tuning slide in the headjoint and keys that sealed with pewter plugs rather than leather pads. His patent could not, of course, extend protection to all keyed flutes, since these had already been available in London for thirty years.

On the Continent Tacet's name had already become linked with English flutes, and now it became associated by mistake with the pewter-plug keys of Potter's patent. In a pamphlet of 1791 J. G. Tromlitz referred to the pewter plugs of which an English correspondent had informed him, as though Tacet rather than Potter had been their inventor. The error spread quickly as Johann Friedrich Boie of Göttingen advertised flutes in 1794 as made 'after the masterpieces of *Grenser* in Dresden and *Potter* in London', with the pewter plugs he described as a 'very little known invention of the Englishman *Tacett*'.

Caleb Gedney (1729–69), a pupil of Stanesby Junior, joined the group of mythical inventors in the twentieth century. One of the very rare extant flutes by Gedney, a keyed specimen dated 1769 (U.S.–Boston: Museum of Fine Arts), was once in the collection of Max Champion of England and thus well known to instrument historians, including Philip Bate (see Bate, *The Flute*, 97). Though the tutor of *c*1765 establishes that Cahusac had been making keyed flutes at the same time or a few years earlier, it was Gedney's name that ended up in the history books willy-nilly because a single specimen dated four years later had chanced to make itself known.

*c*1753–8	SCHUCHART SENIOR flute with keys for F, B♭, G♯, C♯, and C.
1765	Anonymous tutor for 'a new invented German Flute with additional Keys, made by T. Cahusac, such as play'd on by the two celebrated Masters, Tacet and Florio'.
*c*1780	Florio's name erased from the printing plates of new editions of the anonymous tutor; the keyed flute claimed as 'invented by Mr Tacet'.
1785	Potter's Patent flute introduces pewter plugs
1791	Tromlitz mistakenly attributes pewter plugs to Tacet, citing an English correspondent.
1794	J. F. Boie refers to pewter-plug keys as Tacet's invention.

The flute method books these shops sold to the swelling ranks of English dilettantes continued to rely on basic instructions taken piecemeal from Hotteterre's, of which an English version had been printed by 1729. The same text, after reappearing in Prelleur's *Modern Musick-Master* (*c*1730), was republished at least thirty times over the next four decades in a series of cheap (1s 6d) and elementary anonymous tutors distributed by London music sellers and instrument dealers. Two editions (*c*1765) of this anonymous tutor provide the earliest illustrations of flutes with added keys for B♭, G♯, and F, and an extension to low C. The tutors indicate that Florio and Joseph Tacet (*d* 1795), both veterans of the Concert spirituel who had arrived in London around 1760, had already been performing there on keyed flutes. Nonetheless, the new instrument gained acceptance slowly. In 1771 Luke Heron mentioned that '[t]here are some lately made flutes which have a number of additional keys; these form the sharp and flat notes by means of these keys'. But he did not cite this as a particular advantage, and he estimated that they were 'not very many'.

The new keywork may have been slow to catch on because it was only one of several notable features of Classical flutes all designed to help players produce a new kind of sound. The flutes August Grenser (1720–1807) built in his Dresden workshop, one of Europe's most famous in the mid- to late eighteenth century, were slimmer and lighter than baroque models, tuned to favour sharp keys and voiced with a less full but more penetrating tone. Their toneholes and embouchure holes were smaller and undercut in shapes that could be produced only by special tooling, in contrast to those of instruments by Bizey, Bressan, Denner, and Lot in which the interior walls of the holes were shaped by hand in a somewhat less consistent way. Their bores were narrower and tapered more steeply, to about the same degree as Quantz employed (see p. 97). Though Quantz's embouchure hole was elliptical, that of Grenser and the other early Classical makers remained round for many decades until oval embouchures became standard after c1800. Pioneered by Quantz, flutes with more tapered bores and elliptical embouchures encouraged a stronger style of playing in the first octave to overcome the inherent weakness of that part of the range.

Grenser established his workshop in 1744 and obtained an appointment to the Saxon court in 1753. From that date until the late 1780s his shop produced one-keyed flutes of a standard pattern, having a set of seven middle joints evenly spaced in pitch, a screw-cork, and an index foot. Meanwhile the London instrument makers, whose flutes already featured thick walls and a strong voicing, took steps to strengthen their instruments' low registers. Besides introducing extremely steep bore tapers (around 43 per cent), J. J. Schuchart and Thomas Cahusac (see p. 111), followed by others including Thomas Collier (from 1767) and Caleb Gedney (an example dated 1769), began to build keyed flutes, probably alongside their usual one-keyed models.

Lewis Christian Austin Granom, nephew of the trumpeter and flutist J. B. Granom (chapter 4) and listed as a London flute teacher in 1763, heartily disapproved of the new keyed flutes, blaming their introduction on unnamed 'Foreigners', probably Florio and Tacet. He disliked not only the instruments themselves, but also the music and performance style of those who played them:

> Most of the Performers on the German Flute seem, at present, to have mistaken the nature of that Instrument, by attempting difficulties, which it is not possible for it to admit of, and, if it were, the Tone of the Flute must infallibly be lost.... But as this Innovation has only been introduced by some Foreigners much about the same time when the multiplicity of Keys were revived I shall not Lay the blame on my Country Men, but shall only make some Remarks thereon. Who ever attempts to play a piece of Music on the above Instrument wherein the Tone (which is the most delightful next to the human Voice) is to suffer, may be Justly pronounced no Judge of it; and whoever does not articulate distinctly every Note of an Allegro, or quick movement, but Slurs and slobbers them over, cannot be looked upon as a Player.[14]

The last objection highlights an important distinction Englishmen made between their own manner and that of the 'immoral' Catholic Italians, a distinction most clearly seen in English Protestant church music where florid writing had been banished and each syllable assigned a single note. In fact slurrings may have characterized Italianate instrumental playing in general, as the remarks of another censorious critic suggest: in 1783 the German amateur flutist J. J. H. Ribock castigated the Tuscan court virtuoso Niccolò Dôthel, whose published studies contain many notated slurs, for playing without using his tongue, as well as for his monotonous style, his manner of breathing, and his use of *tempo rubato*.[15]

Granom's complaints, echoing the French remarks of 1739 quoted earlier, also signal an increase in the technical demands of music published by London's virtuoso instrumentalists after the mid-eighteenth century. By now each instrument had begun to develop a characteristic style of writing all its own: broken tenths for the flute, long *messa di voce* notes (swelling and diminishing in tone) for the oboe, string-crossing patterns for violin, high melodies for the cello. Pianists took up an expressive and bravura manner, quite distinct from that of the harpsichord, that even brought out the differences between German and English pianos, while a separate Classical style evolved for the harp. Some instrumentalists made a special point of particular effects: Andrew Ashe advertised that he would play double notes on the flute, the violinist Charles Weichsell performed a solo 'with the Harmonic Stops', and the oboist Johann Christian Fischer showed off his ability to swell a very long note from *pianissimo* to *fortissimo* and back again.[16]

English and continental players alike figured among those who introduced flute-playing to the American colonies in the mid-eighteenth century. Several teachers of the 'German flute' advertised in Philadelphia in 1749 and 1763, one specifying that he would attend young ladies at their houses, while Ernest Barnard, George D'Eissenberg, and John Stadler played it in concerts. Giovanni Gualdo, an Italian wine merchant and composer who had published music in London in 1765, moved to Philadelphia four years later and put on his first concert 'after the Italian method', including a flute concerto of his own composition. Instruments were imported from Europe by Peter Goelet (1773) and John Jacob Astor (1789) of New York. Around 1775 concert activity in Boston and Philadelphia petered out owing to the Revolutionary War, but a concert of 27 April 1782 in British-occupied New York presented quartets and quintets with flute by J. C. Bach, Johann Baptist Vanhall, and Carlo Giuseppe Toeschi.[17]

The distinctive sound of fife and drum bands provided what had now become traditional music for marching and signalling in the German army, and in a revived form in the British. It was first heard in the American colonies in the Seven Years' War (1756–63), and at the time of the Lexington Alarm (1775) many of the Colonial regiments included one or two fifers and drummers per company.[18] A British army regulation of 1803 integrated the hitherto informal military music into the army proper, though bandsmen were to be 'soldiers first, bandsmen second'. As yet, England could provide no military musical training and the first regiment to take advantage of the regulation, the Coldstream Guards, imported a band of ten foreign musicians, mostly Germans.

German military musicians often obtained their training as Quantz had, in a town band, then took positions in military wind bands subsidized or even maintained by donations from officers, who used their musicians to provide dance music and other entertainment. *Hautboisten* were expected to manage several woodwind instruments: at the beginning of 1763, the Hessian Regiment of Life Dragoons advertised in a Kassel newspaper for one who could play oboe, transverse flute, and clarinet.[19] These instruments belonged to a modern mixed ensemble more sophisticated than the traditional fife corps and the French-style military oboe band. From *c*1730 a Saxon form of the new wind grouping dominated, using pairs of oboes, horns, and bassoons, but it expanded to include clarinets about thirty years later, and later still flutes.[20] Wind serenades and orchestral scorings by Mozart, Beethoven, and others drew on these military uses of woodwinds, often treating the section as a discrete *Harmonie* ensemble playing chordally and contrasting with the strings.

Music for wind band, free of narrow social significance and lacking the associations string ensembles and orchestras had with military or aristocratic life, gave it a special position at this time of social and political revolution.[21] Of the many possible combinations of wind instruments, the quintet of flute, oboe, clarinet, horn, and bassoon eventually developed into a common ensemble for chamber music. Towards the end of the eighteenth century the regular instruments of the military band, clarinet, oboe, horn, trumpet, and bassoon, were joined by a new group: flute, piccolo, basset horn, serpent, contrabassoon, and more rarely trombone.[22] Music for the concert room by Spohr and others showed the influence of the exotic Janissary bands of the Turkish army, which included one or more fifes in unison or octaves, five or more shawms of different sizes, drums, cymbals, and triangles.

The flute had built up a large repertoire of solo music by the mid-eighteenth century, enabling musicians, especially in Austria and Germany where music publishing was not yet as commercialized as in northwest Europe, to augment their incomes by selling manuscript copies and acting as commission agents to solicit subscriptions for published works.[23] The Leipzig firm of Johann Gottlob Immanuel Breitkopf (1745) copied manuscripts on a large scale as well as reviving the printing of music from movable type. Catalogues of manuscripts that could be copied to order between 1762 and 1784 listed many older flute compositions, including fifty-two manuscript solos by Quantz.

During the 1790s the quantity of printed music increased by leaps and bounds. Franz Anton Hoffmeister (1754–1812) played a pre-eminent role in the vigorous flute-music industry of the time. After founding a publishing house in 1784, he and a partner opened the Bureau de Musique, later to become C. F. Peters of Leipzig, in 1800. Quartets and duets for flute were among Hoffmeister's earliest compositions, which also included solos and concertos, published by his own firm as well as by others in Paris and London. Arrangements provided another lucrative trade. Mozart's *Magic Flute* and other operas, Haydn's symphonies for Salomon's London concerts and others, and similar popular works of the day appeared all over Europe in printed arrangements for flute duet, flute quartet, and other domestic ensembles.

With an increasingly brilliant style making solo sonatas too difficult for the dilettantes who were now taking up flute-playing in such large numbers, new and less strenuous forms of chamber composition appeared. In 1778 Mozart published a set of violin and piano duos (K. 301–6) four of which, K. 301, 303, 305, and 306, he originally conceived for flute and piano.[24] Here the instruments participate equally, in contrast to solos with continuo, or to accompanied keyboard sonatas in which the parts for flute or violin and cello are optional. Other new chamber forms of the

32. Jacob Tromlitz, engraving of his father
Johann George Tromlitz (1725–1805). The
flutist is pointing to the index foot or *Register*
he claimed to have invented.

Classical era include Beethoven's G major trio for piano, flute, and bassoon WoO 37
(1787/90), for the von Westerholt-Gysenberg family.[25] His *Serenade* in D major for
flute, violin, and viola op. 25 (published 1802, probably composed 1795–6), with a
flute part that uses the instrument's extreme high register, appeared in a version of
1803 as op. 41, the two string voices worked out into a full pianoforte, part.[26] That
piece, as well as the B♭ major sonata for flute and pianoforte, may have arisen out of
Beethoven's friendship with the professional flutist Anton Reicha (1770–1836), a
colleague during his time as a viola player in the Bonn court orchestra.[27] Reicha
himself achieved great success in Paris in about 1817 with twenty-four compositions
that raised the woodwind quintet's status there. These were performed by an ensemble
that included the flutist Joseph Guillou and the oboist Gustav Vogt, professors at the
Paris Conservatoire.[28]

After the symphony, the Classical era's most popular instrumental form was the
solo concerto. Through Wendling Mozart obtained a commission on 9 December
1777 from Ferdinand Dejean, a surgeon in the Dutch East India Company, for 'three
little, easy, short concertos and a few quartets on the flute [i.e. pieces for string quartet
with the first violin replaced by a flute]'.[29] Mozart's supposed characterization of the
flute as 'an instrument *I can't stand*', which has passed into the mythology of the flute,
came in a frustrated letter to his father while trying to finish the pieces.[30] As Andrew
Porter (1980) has observed, his words have been translated far too easily as dislike of
the flute itself, but could equally well refer to his distaste for the tedium of a large
commission that required him to write many pieces for the same instrument.[31] The
passage may also have been an excuse for dragging out the commission so that he
could stay in Mannheim with his new love, Aloysia Weber.[32] On the other hand, he

seems only twice to have written solo compositions for a professional flutist to play: a *Symphonie Concertante* (K. 297, in E♭ major) for flute, oboe, horn, and bassoon for Wendling and friends to perform in Paris,[33] and the G major flute concerto K. 313 (285c) he composed for the violinist Castel to play on the name-day of his sister Nannerl Mozart, 25 July 1777.[34] In the end Mozart sent Dejean two flute concertos: the G major one of July, with the *Andante* in C, K. 315 (285e), perhaps as an alternative middle movement, and the concerto in D, K. 314 (285d), an arrangement of his friend Ramm's 'war horse' oboe concerto K. 314 (285d) (Salzburg, 1777), which had already been heard in public five times. In the year following the Dejean commission, Mozart composed the concerto in C major for flute and harp, K. 299 (297c), for the 'incomparable' amateur flutist Adrien-Louis Bonnières de Souastre, Comte de Guines, and his talented daughter. The Count had served as ambassador in London until 1776, and evidently returned with a new keyed flute, since his part descends to low C.[35]

That Dejean and de Guines commissioned new concertos from Mozart illustrates that even amateurs now hungered for this formerly exclusive genre. All over Europe a flood of flute concertos filled the collections of professionals, amateurs, and courts alike. Karl Stamitz and other Mannheim composers wrote numerous examples, presumably for Wendling. The Thurn und Taxis court in Regensburg, one of the most musically active in Bavaria from 1748 to 1806, employed an Italian flutist, Florante

---

(ABINGDON'S) HANOVER SQUARE GRAND CONCERT, 1784: THIRD CONCERT (3 MARCH 1784)

8 p.m.
By subscription: 6 guineas for 12 concerts.
Source: *Public Advertiser* 3 March 1784, review in *PA* 5 March 1784, cited in McVeigh, *Concert Life in London*, 243.

1 Mozart	Overture		
	Quartet (horn)	Pieltain [P. J.]	
	Song	Sga Dorcetti	'Ah se in ciel'
	Sonata (piano)	Clementi	
Sarti	Song	Miss Cantelo	'Un amanti sventurato'
Graf	Concerto grosso (flute, violin, viola)	Decamp, Cramer, Blake	
2 Haydn	Symphony (new)		
	Song	Harrison	'Calma lisinga'
Stamitz	Concerto (oboe, bassoon)	Ramm, Schwarz	
Rauzzini	Duet	Harrison, Miss Cantelo	
	Lesson (harp)	Mme Clery	
	Full piece		

The length and variety of this programme were usual for its time at public concerts in London, Paris, and Vienna. It began with an overture, featured a new symphony, and contained several vocal arias, as well as concertos featuring several prominent instrumentalists for the sake of variety. Entire programmes dominated by a single star performer were unknown.

Agostinelli (*c*1741–1809), after about 1774,[36] and assembled a music library second only to Frederick the Great's, with about 3000 manuscripts including 154 flute concertos by 51 composers, as well as a thousand symphonies.[37] A pair of French flutists, Niccolò Dôthel (*b* 1721 Nicholas D'Hotel), the son of an *Hautboist*, and Carlo Antonio Campioni (*b* 1720 Charles Antoine Campion), son of a court cook, entered service at the Grand Duke of Tuscany's court in 1737.[38] Dôthel, who founded a Florentine school of flute-playing, produced a vast body of compositions for flute, partly lost, that held top place in the collection at Esterháza, where Haydn's employer Duke Paul Anton was an enthusiastic flutist, with 24 flute concertos, 43 soli and sonatas, 44 duets, 84 trio-sonatas, besides quartets and studies.

As well as appearing in innovative instrumental combinations of various kinds, the flute altered its role in the orchestra as composers began to include it more regularly in the wind section of the Classical symphony, often providing a layer of sound on top of the ensemble, as it had in Rameau's scorings, rather than blending with other instruments or adding a separate colour as it had for Hasse. C. P. E. Bach originally composed two Berlin symphonies of 1755 for strings, but later reworked them to include pairs of flutes and horns (H 649, in F) or flutes, bassoons, and horns (H652, in D). He added flutes and horns to another symphony of 1758, perhaps in 1762 (H655, in F). His first symphonies originally conceived for an orchestra that included flutes were a set he composed in 1775–6 and published in Leipzig in 1780 (H663–6). Their flute parts contained exposed soli sections in thirds and sixths, often using triplet figures, and with a range up to E♭. Haydn's earlier symphonies typically used a single flute in a soloistic role in G or D major: an arpeggio passage ending in F minor and a diminished seventh on B♮ in Symphony no. 41 (1769–70) is unusual, part of the piece's *Sturm und Drang* or 'storm and stress' affect.[39] Mozart, who had previously used a pair of oboists doubling on flutes, adopted a similar scoring after his move to Vienna in 1781, when his piano concertos, symphonies, and arias typically called for one flute and two oboes. His works for the theatre more typically used pairs of flutes and oboes, a difference Neal Zaslaw (1991) has put down to the larger sizes of orchestras and venues for such works.[40]

Haydn, Mozart, and Beethoven, in contrast to Gluck, that other innovator in orchestration, hardly ever used the flute's low register. But orchestral writing from the late 1780s onwards made increasing demands on the flute's abilities at the opposite extreme of its range, distinctly beyond the upper limit of Quantz's vocal ideal for the flute's sound. The piccolo became a fixture of the orchestra only around 1800, when it appeared in military contexts such as the march at the end of Beethoven's Fifth Symphony (1807–8). Yet Anton Reicha, in a work on composition of *c*1816–18, still considered the piccolo a martial instrument, and still did not use its modern name: before Georg Kastner used the term in an instrumentation manual of 1837 it was usually designated by the term Corrette had used in *c*1740, *Petite flûte à l'octave*.[41]

Mozart's scorings in E♭ major for solo flute, such as those in the *Symphonie Concertante* for Wendling, the Symphony K. 182 (Salzburg 1773), and the Symphony K. 543 (1788), may have been difficult for the one-keyed flute on account of their tonality, as Catherine Smith has suggested,[42] but that difficulty, or the challenge presented by fast chromatic writing, was actually no greater than in Dresden opera parts of forty years earlier, and it would certainly be a mistake to assume that the parts require the use of keyed flutes. The high range was another matter, and once composers had learned to write parts for the flute that lay entirely above the treble stave the upper limits continued to rise. Mozart's operas, produced in Munich, Vienna, and Prague in 1781–91, frequently scored for the flute in the third octave as high as G3 (chapter 8). Here a keyed flute can be of some help because it provides numerous alternative fingerings for the third octave.

Haydn's symphonies for London, in which the Irish flutist Andrew Ashe (c1759–1841) played, have been noted as innovative in their use of the high register, and indeed Salomon's provision of a specialist flutist at his concerts signalled the unusual nature of the series. More commonly, however, flute parts in the London symphonies were played by doublers, as in ten concert series from 1752 to 1800 in which flutes, if they were used at all, must have been played by oboists who switched instruments for the slow movements. Ashe (see chapter 7) began using a keyed flute by Richard Potter in 1774 at the age of about fifteen, if an oft-repeated anecdote is correct.[43] He arrived in London in time for Salomon to announce that his second concert of the 1792 season, on 24 February, would contain a 'Concerto, German Flute, Mr. Ashe (Being his first appearance in London)'.[44] His arrival displaced Salomon's current principal flutist, Johann Georg Graeff, who two weeks later was still playing on a one-keyed flute with a D-foot, according to a newspaper report:

> Graeff executed a Flute Concerto with a very powerful tone and rapidity of finger. It was noticed that he played upon a Flute not of the new construction; it had no greater compass than D below.[45]

Besides Salomon's concerts, a pair of flutes appeared at the Professional Concert series in 1787 and 1793. Again an orchestra larger than usual mustered for Haydn's 1795 symphonies, in part due to the size of the King's Theatre concert room. On these occasions the Opera Concert employed doubled pairs of woodwinds: four each of flutes, oboes, clarinets, and bassoons, with brass and timpani. These forces balanced a string section disposed 10-10-6-5-4 rather than the Professional Concert's more modest 6-6-4-3-3. In *The Creation* (1798) Haydn scored tellingly for three flutes using their old association with pastoral bliss. The scene in the opening number of Part Three of his oratorio depicts morning in Paradise: 'From the celestial vaults/pure harmony descends/on ravished earth.' The orchestra parts indicate that the third flute was played by an oboist.[46]

A quarter of a century elapsed between the appearance of keyed flutes in London in 1755–60 and the first reports of their presence on the Continent. Those indications suggest that while continental makers had not yet begun to make the new type, specimens from English workshops had spread far and wide. In 1781 the Leipzig flutist J. G. Tromlitz, who had been building flutes for about thirty years, published the first of a series of announcements of new models inspired by English instruments. At first he offered a flute with the only keys he thought necessary, for B♭ and G♯, as well as a C-foot.[47] Dr Johann Justus Heinrich Ribock, an amateur flutist who published

33. A flute lesson, frontispiece by E. F. Burney to *Dr Arnold's New Instructions for the German-flute*
(1787).

Observations on the Flute in 1782 including the first German fingering chart for a five-keyed flute, knew Tromlitz and used his keyed flutes, but was aware of no others except those by English makers. He had played one- or two-keyed flutes by Quantz, Kirst, Grenser, and Lot.

By the time of another announcement three years later Tromlitz had overcome his reluctance to add keys to the flute, and had developed the first model on which every semitone was supplied with its own tonehole. His flute of 1785 combined a closed C2 key for the left thumb of his own invention, and a duplicate F key invented by Dülon the elder in 1783, with the basic English configuration of thirty years before, retaining on the footjoint Quantz's D♯/E♭, combination rather than extending the range down to C as the English makers did. By 1796 he had further refined this 7-keyed flute by adding a duplicate B♭ key for the right forefinger.

Despite his leadership in developing keyed flutes in Germany, the method book Tromlitz published in the same period, his *Ausführlicher und gründlicher Unterricht* (Detailed and thorough method, 1791), gave the aspiring virtuoso instructions for playing the two-keyed flute rather than the more advanced type.[48] The most complete set of instructions on flute-playing to date, the method bestowed special care upon intonation, including much fuller instructions than Quantz had given for the use of D♯ and E♭ keys. Tromlitz published further instructions for playing his keyed flutes a decade later, in 1800, by which time he held that a keyed flute was the only acceptable instrument for a professional player.[49] In the keyed flute method he made clear that he intended the instrument to be played with enharmonic distinctions: he tuned the keys to the flat (higher) of the pair so that the sharps could be obtained by closing further toneholes to lower their pitch. Though he allowed the possibility that the notes produced by the keys might be tuned to be usable as both flat and sharp with the same fingering, his ideal was clearly to preserve the theoretical basis of eighteenth-century woodwind intonation, not to move it towards equal temperament as would first be suggested a generation or more after his death. The seven extant instruments with his mark have an exceptionally narrow bore with a 36.5 per cent overall taper, giving a strong tone evenly balanced between a resonant low register and a full high range. In the most advanced of various key-configurations from one to seven, these flutes indicate that Tromlitz's work on facilitating tone and intonation eventually achieved a high degree of success.[50]

However, Tromlitz could produce only a limited number of his innovative instruments in his one-man workshop, while the musical instrument trade dealt in larger quantities. In 1785 English keyed flutes won wide notice when Richard Potter

GUILDS AND CAPITALISTS

Even lacking precise records of Richard Potter's business organization and dealings, we can clearly distinguish a significant shift in his station from artisan to capitalist in about 1785. He turned to patent protection after serving as Master (1782) of the Company of Turners, the guild that regulated woodwind-making in London just as similar organizations did with more or less stringency in most other European cities.

The craft guilds had reached the height of their effectiveness in the fifteenth and sixteenth centuries as mechanisms to protect workmen, employers, and customers against incompetence, dishonesty, and foreign competition. Yet in the late seventeenth and early eighteenth centuries the London guild did not prevent continental woodwind makers Pierre Jaillard Bressan (Lyon region of France), Thomas Cahusac Senior (perhaps a Huguenot from southwest France), and John Just Schuchart (Germany) from moving to the city and setting up shop. Even those woodwind makers who were of English birth came from outside the city: Thomas Stanesby Senior from Derbyshire (1682), Potter from Surrey (c1745), and William Milhouse from Nottinghamshire (1787).

A maker was still able to use guild rules to enforce his right to conduct business in Paris in 1752, when Gilles Lot won a judgement against Charles Bizey, Thomas Lot, Paul Villars, Denis Vincent and Jacques de Lusse. These master instrument-makers had conspired to prevent him being admitted to the guild, despite his qualifications of apprenticeship with his cousin Thomas Lot and with Bizey, and of marriage to the daughter of Jean Nicolas Leclerc, whose business he intended to operate.[1]

On the other hand, by the time the woodwind maker Thomas Stanesby Junior served as Master of the Turners' Company of London in 1739–40, market mechanisms had become dominant enough in England that the guilds' traditional power to regulate trade had largely disappeared. Roland Champness (1966), historian of the Turners' Company, has pinpointed the years around 1787 as the time when '[m]ost of the [London] companies appear finally to have abandoned all pretence to any effective control of their trades'.[2]

At just the same time in France, the Revolution introduced the free right to exercise a trade, a measure adopted soon thereafter in other countries in an effort to defuse socially disruptive ideas. Mandatory guild membership, long the only path to employment as a woodwind maker but now no longer enforceable, was eventually abolished everywhere.[3] Some later associations of woodwind makers retained the name 'guild', but in general they functioned more like the newer trade unions.

brought to market the first flute manufactured under patent protection, a mass-produced item having keys fitted with pewter plugs in place of leather pads, and a metal-lined headjoint with a graduated tuning slide. Besides its mechanical novelties, the Potter patent flute had a narrower bore and a brighter sound than the other keyed flutes being made in London. A tutor by Dr Samuel Arnold newly written for the Potter flute followed hard on the heels of the patent in 1787 (ill. 33). Fingering charts in subsequent anonymous tutors used the same printing plate as the anonymous editions of twenty years earlier (see p. 111), but now the names of both Tacet and Florio had been erased so that the tutors could specify the latest instrument. The chart, now more than twenty years old, carried a new heading: 'A Description of Potter's new invented Patent German Flute, With a Complete Scale or Gamut explaining the use of all the Additional Keys'. The publishers frequently took the opportunity to mention that they sold 'Potter's new Invented German Flutes and all other sorts Wholesale & Retail'. Thus by the beginning of the nineteenth century the patent flute had made Potter's name synonymous throughout Europe with all that was newest and most progressive in English flute-making.

Rampant Anglophilia in Vienna enabled Potter's and other English flutes to gain swift entry there and to make an impact on Viennese flute design that lasted throughout the nineteenth century. Mathias Rockobaur (*fl* 1764–77), who supplied woodwinds to Haydn's orchestra at Esterháza, made flutes of an ordinary early classical type similar to Potter's one-keyed instruments, while the few extant Viennese flutes of the 1780s and later, by Kaspar Tauber (1758–1831), Franz Harrach (1750–1831), and Friedrich Hammig (*fl* 1791–1823), show the strong and more direct influence of Cahusac's and Potter's keyed flutes. A notice Hammig placed in the *Wiener Zeitung* in 1791 announced that he made flutes in the English and German styles, the 'English' ones with headjoint tuning slides and pewter-plug keys. Another newspaper announcement in Berlin a few years later made a similar distinction: in 1794 J. F. Boie of Göttingen offered 'improved flutes, which he makes after the masterpieces of *Grenser* in Dresden and *Potter* in London'.[51] His 'English' flutes had a metal-lined tuning slide and index foot like those of the Potter patent flute, while his extant 'German'-style instruments display a general resemblance to the Grenser keyed flutes made in the 1790s, though with their own strongly individual tone and intonation.

Keyed flutes in the Potter style evidently reached even across the Alps. A pamphlet by Giovanni Battista Orazi (Rome, 1797) described a keyed flute essentially like the patent flute, but with a range down to G below the treble stave and with an extraordinary fingering system that permitted quarter tones and glissandi as high as G♯4.[52] Unlike later Viennese flutes that provided an extended low range on a doubled-back section of the flute's tube, Orazi's design specified a straight continuation.

The 'German'-style instruments Harrach and Boie advertised were based on a new and distinctively German style of keyed flute developed in the Grenser workshop in Dresden. August Grenser at first offered keyed flutes simply by adding keys for B♭, G♯, and F to his usual one-keyed flute design that had been in production since 1744, rather than by modifying all its sound-producing parameters as Tromlitz had done.

His earliest extant keyed flute is such a one dated 1789 (U.S.-Washington: DCM 949); he delivered an instrument matching the same description to the Mecklenburg-Schwerin court at Ludwigslust in 1796.[53] Similarly, many German instruments of the late eighteenth century survive to show that one-keyed flutes were often retro-fitted with additional keys. In about 1786, however, when Heinrich Grenser began to work as a qualified journeyman, his uncle's shop introduced a new flute model, bringing the style up to date with a more fashionable outer profile, a higher pitch centre, an oval embouchure hole, and a more current tone. For about a decade, the new-style flute, which could be made in ebony or boxwood with any or all of the keys for B♭, G♯, F, D♯, C♯, and C, was manufactured alongside a slightly modified version of the old one-keyed flute design, still usually in boxwood. By now not only did makers in other cities imitate Grenser products, but Johann Georg Otto (1762–1821) from the nearby Vogtland region, where woodwind makers were in the habit of marking their flutes DRESDEN to disguise their down-market provenance, made at least one flute stamped with August Grenser's name, his trademark of a crossed swords device, and a date (U.S.-Vermillion: Shrine to Music 3574).[54] In Leipzig Tromlitz complained that his own signature, the initials I*G*T on the footjoint, was being forged on instruments of poor quality, while in London similar attempts were made to pass off inferior instruments as the work of Potter and other successful makers.

Friedrich Ludwig Dülon (chapter 7) encountered a keyed flute for the first time in 1783, shortly after Tromlitz announced the first German-made keyed flutes. But the details Dülon provided in his autobiography (1808) show him to have been far less concerned than we are with the technical details of flutes and flute-playing. Instead an encounter with C. P. E. Bach later in the same year suggests that improvisation and fantasy provided the key to these two musicians' view of themselves as creative geniuses. The day after his arrival in Hamburg, Dülon visited Bach's house and played the unaccompanied *Solo* in A minor of 1747 (H562), which had been published in 1763. Bach's comments revealed that he had written the piece for Frederick the Great, and thus for performance on a Quantz flute, but left no doubt that he preferred Dülon's interpretation: 'It is really strange; the one for whom I wrote this piece couldn't play it; the one for whom I did not write it, can.'[55]

In a recent article on the encounter between Bach and Dülon, Leta E. Miller noted that according to his own report Dülon played a prelude before each movement.[56] While we can have no idea of the musical content of Dülon's preludes, and these improvised flourishes for the flute had received little notice since Hotteterre discussed them in 1719 (chapter 4), music in an improvisational style was clearly still cultivated in the late eighteenth century in Italy and France as well as in Germany. Twelve brilliant *Caprices* displaying a quite remarkable fantasy and virtuosity figure in [Christophe] Delusse's *L'Art de la flûte traversiere* [1761], a strikingly original work which records a more advanced level of flute-playing than that most tutors to date had indicated. Delusse gave the earliest prescriptions for harmonics, quarter tones, and tremolo, although as a 1764 letter from Buffardin to the *Mercure de France* claimed, he may not have been the first to practise all of them.[57] A manuscript collection of unaccompanied *Caprici per il traverso* by Wenceslao Zimmerman (?–?), its title page marked with the warning '*Non fa per tutti*' (Not for everyone!), is similar in style to the Quantz *Capricci* as well as to those of Filipo Ruge (c1725–c1770). Zimmerman's pieces progress through all twenty-four keys except D♭, G♭, C♭ major and C♯, G♯, and E♯ minor, indicating them in the antique manner (e.g. *Alamire 3a Maggiore*). Their range extends up to A3, and some have transposing clef indications so that they can be played in two keys a semitone apart, such as B major and B♭ major. Dôthel's *Studi* (c1778) use all the keys without exception, ascending chromatically, but strictly preserving the enharmonic distinctions between tonalities. Christian Karl Hartmann (1750–1804), Joseph Tacet, and Amand Vanderhagen (1753–1822) made later contributions in the Prelude, Caprice, or Study genre, while French tutors of the Classical era by Mathieu Péraut and François Devienne both presented sonatas with preludes before each of their three movements.[58] Further indications that preluding remained common into the nineteenth century appear in chapters 8 and 10.

Another opportunity for fantasy and caprice came in cadenzas and lead-ins, spontaneous events that punctuated every movement of the period's numerous flute concertos. Twenty of the seventy manuscripts Janet Becker examined in the Thurn und Taxis library contain written-out cadenzas in at least one movement.[59] The methods of Quantz and Tromlitz each treat the composition of cadenzas at some length, agreeing that the events themselves should be short and surprising.

In France the flute's golden age appears to have been followed by a deep decline, so that the keyed flute and the bravura performance style made only a small impact. English flutes occasionally made their way to Paris, as we learn from newspaper announcements,[60] but when an inventory of the houses of 113 dispossessed aristocrats was taken in 1794 after the French Revolution, only a solitary boxwood Potter flute was found among a few old-fashioned woodwinds alongside numerous more current Érard fortepianos, harps, violins, and guitars.[61]

One of the many accomplishments of the French Revolution was the foundation of the Paris Conservatoire, which took shape during the 1790s as a school for military band musicians and became the most influential musical institution of the mid-nineteenth to the mid-twentieth centuries (chapter 11). Wind music for the masses and patriotic hymn-singing came to the fore as the school evolved into the nationalist, and especially anti-German, Institut National de Musique, and finally in 1795 into the Conservatoire. The institution's military-style regime introduced a new method of teaching, treating students as identical units who would learn a standard curriculum by following a set programme of technical drill. On its foundation the Conservatoire employed five professors of flute, one of them doubling on oboe, along with nineteen of clarinet and twelve of bassoon. Similar academies were established in several Italian cities in the early years of the nineteenth century to train band musicians, but none offered a flute class, though the most important posts for flutists there, as in France, were those of the theatre orchestras.

François Devienne's *Nouvelle Méthode* of 1794, which became the best-selling flute method in the France and Germany of the 1790s on account of its association with the new Conservatoire, followed the path of institutionalized revolution in its conspicuously dogmatic style. Devienne criticized the new English keyed flutes, though he recognized that the keys had come to stay, and allowed his students that had French-made flutes to use them. He displaced the Anglo-Saxon double tongue (*tid'll*) with a French version (*dougue*), introducing the form still used by modern flutists. Following the method of Amand Vanderhagen (c1788), Devienne prescribed the practice of the *messa di voce* or *son filé* to develop tone (chapter 11), and censured fashions in flute-playing of which he disapproved, including the use of a cutting tone in the low register.

This was one of the chief claims to fame of J. G. Tromlitz, the foremost German advocate both of the keyed flute and the sound it produced. Accounts of Tromlitz's playing stressed his powerful tone and perfect intonation, qualities largely due to the flutes he made and played on. He described his own ideal tone as bright, metallic, firm, well-focused, strong, and brilliant, the low register played with a little extra strength. His obituary in the *AmZ* described his own playing in similar terms:

> As a virtuoso he was distinguished by perfection, but still more by complete purity [of intonation] and security of tone, as by precision in performance. He was also one of the first, and in respect of the influence he had, the foremost, to introduce the now usual bravura- and concerto-style way of playing the flute, and especially the strong, cutting tone best suited to it, and frequent, skilful use of the double-tongue. ...[62]

Ernst Ludwig Gerber, a performing colleague of Tromlitz's, described his tone as 'strong and cutting' in his *Lexicon*, or biographical dictionary, adding that 'his tone was ... more the ringing tone of a trumpet than the soft sound of a flute', and that his concertos with the *Grosses Konzert* were delivered with 'as much fire as perfection'. An anonymous reviewer of one of Tromlitz's books recalled that 'he melted the tone of the flute and oboe into one another'.

Other German sources suggest that the strong low register Tromlitz exhibited and Devienne disliked may have been characteristic of German taste, not just of Tromlitz's – which in light of the contemporary Franco-German antipathy would help explain why a French flutist would find it objectionable. On hearing the blind flutist Josef Winter play on 16 March 1778, Dülon described his tone as that of an angel, citing his strong and manly low register with a pleasant and well-in-tune high range. Some people evidently took the strong low register to extremes, however, since Dülon wrote of the amateur flutist Ribock:

> So as far as his tone was concerned, he really was not bad; nonetheless Ribock took a particular pride in blasting out the low D and E♭, with such monstrous force that it might have made one's ears ring. However this was confined to these two notes; with the others he did not go about things so relentlessly. But where now was that beautiful proportion, in particular that evenness of tone so pleasing to every unspoiled ear? For one may easily see how badly the E, which is in and of itself a weak note on the flute, stood out against it. Yet he set great store by this blaring or (as he calls it in his booklet) this brilliant manner of blowing, because he remarks that the windows sometimes rattled with it, so that he was occasionally

tempted to check that it had not caused the flute to crack etc. So as to his manner of playing it will of course now be evident to all connoisseurs that this was beneath all criticism.[63]

Listeners described Dülon's own sound rather differently. Though a report of his playing in Oldenburg, near Bremen, in 1784 called his tone 'pure, full, and strong', on a visit to London two years later he 'produced sounds … which were enchantingly sweet and new' from his flute, probably a keyed flute by Tromlitz or Grenser. He apparently used the same instrument in 1791 in Vienna, where he played at Schickaneder's Theater auf der Wieden in April, and may have inspired the character of Tamino in Schickaneder and Mozart's opera *Die Zauberflöte* (The Magic Flute).[64]

By the last decade of the eighteenth century, the stronger tone professional flutists cultivated had become widespread, a fact we can gauge at least partly by complaints from players of the old school, including Devienne. John Gunn summed up the points of contention in England in his original and perceptive *Art of Playing the German-Flute* (*c*1793):

> Two opinions seem chiefly to prevail on the method in which this instrument ought to be played: the first is, that an equal fullness of tone ought to be aimed at throughout; and this, when acquired, is thought to be the greatest excellence of which the instrument is capable. The favourers of this opinion have on their side, the example and practice of every public performer. The other opinion is in direct opposition to this: those who adopt it being chiefly pupils of nature, and speak from their own conviction and feelings, without any great deference to authority, say, that this kind of tone is contrary to the very nature of a Flute; the character of which, from its affinity to the female voice, is softness, grace, and tender expression, and can by no means be the bold and warlike expression of those full and loud tones, which seem to emulate the notes of the trumpet; they therefore contend that a soft tone is always to be preferred.

The question would not soon be settled.

Chapter 7

Travelling virtuosi, concert showpieces, and a new mass audience

The instrumental virtuoso of the late eighteenth century was less likely than before to reside at court, wear livery, and wait on the pleasure of his royal or noble master. More typically he spent at least part of his life travelling from one city to another, presenting his own works, pieces written specially for him, and an occasional concerto that was already well-known. Travelling allowed flutists not only to play more concerts and earn more fees, but to make useful or stimulating contacts, learn of new musical ideas, and perhaps find a publisher for new compositions. When Prince Carl Alexander von Thurn und Taxis shortsightedly abolished the usual system of payments to musicians visiting Regensburg and restricted their welcome to a short period in summer, he not only denied visiting virtuosi an excellent location to play, but also limited the exposure of his own court musicians to new styles of music and performance.[1]

For almost a century now, opera singers had operated under a star system whereby those most in demand could command huge sums of money and fill houses in Europe's largest cities, moving from one place to another as new productions called for their services. Opportunities for instrumentalists, by contrast, remained few. Perhaps the instrumental performance series with the highest profile was in Paris, where the Concert spirituel still attracted players in search of success and independence, including not only French flutists such as Blavet, Buffardin, Lucas, Naudot, and Taillart but also foreigners like Tacet (1751), Florio (1753), and Wendling (1751–2).[2]

Germany, with its decentralized geography and smaller cities, provided numerous opportunities that kept the virtuoso on the road more than in other countries. Groups of music-lovers in each place provided an audience of merchants, doctors, lawyers, and shopkeepers – a less exclusive group than the socially stratified people of London and Paris – who now felt in a position to pay for the entertainment that formerly had belonged only to the rich and powerful. As public concert spaces such as inns, churches, and theatres gradually became the most important venues for instrumental music in place of the private chambers of the aristocracy, new commercial and artistic realities began to affect musicians. Now the paymaster was the many-headed public, rather than a single royal institution or a powerful individual. The new audience demanded the variety afforded by a succession of fresh performers from other places, at the same time as it sought the cachet conferred by the most fashionable. It had to be numerous enough to guarantee a fee that would encourage musicians to travel, and this larger audience in turn affected the choice and design of performance spaces, the music to be played in them, and finally, the construction of instruments themselves.

34. The blind virtuoso Friedrich Ludwig
Dülon (1769–1826), perhaps the first
travelling flutist to be thought of as a
'great artist'.

Under these conditions, each audience developed a taste of its own. The playing
of visiting flutists became the subject of commentary in newspapers, magazines, and
diaries, often prompting revealing comments on performance style, repertoire, and
instrument. At the same time the latest flute methods, now often addressed to aspiring
professionals as well as to amateurs, began to focus more and more precisely on a
selected kind of flute and manner of playing, sometimes pointing out differing styles
as incorrect or improper. Thus the increase in travel first made people in Germany,
France, England, and even the remoter European countries aware of the distinct
national playing styles that would dominate the world of the flute for more than a
hundred years to come.

The largest population centres provided the most promising concert venues, but
assembling an audience was far from easy. As early as 1723, G. P. Telemann wrote to
J. F. A. von Uffenbach of the difficulty of filling a house for a concert:

Ten times to one concerts fail and the artist, who thought he was going to make
money, has paid the event's costs but has earned nothing but an empty purse.
'What about the trumpeting in the newspaper?' O you good Virtuoso, don't you
see that that is just a distress call to gather music-lovers? [...] The Virtuoso
calculates: 100,000 inhabitants, rich, well-to-do, given to entertainment and luxury
– of course the house will be full! risks it, and plays – to mostly empty benches.[3]

J. G. Tromlitz presented an equally pessimistic view of an instrumentalist's life a
generation or more later:

Just consider how wretchedly the greater part of those who turn their hand to music, whether Virtuosi or not, must make shift for themselves. The Virtuoso … must do exceptionally well, and must have a great deal of luck if he wants to give the impression of prosperity on tour – I say the impression of prosperity, for if in one place he earns something, the same amount gets spent there, or in another place where he earns nothing. And so time slips by until he grows old and good for nothing, and leaves the world in miserable circumstances.[4]

Tromlitz evidently spoke from experience, for his obituary reported that he toured widely and successfully as far afield as Russia. Still, the life of a travelling flutist occurred largely below the radar of written record, and the only one of Tromlitz's journeys of which a first-hand report has come to light is one he made in 1773 with the keyboardist Johann Wilhelm Hässler (1747–1822) to Göttingen and Kassel.[5] Tromlitz, who from 1754 to 1776 held the post of solo flutist in Leipzig's Grosses Konzert, a forerunner of the Gewandhaus orchestra, found that even a steady appointment provided insufficient means for a musician's living:

If he is appointed to a court orchestra, he will be very lucky to get a salary that he can live from comfortably. Most [orchestral players] still get very little, although there are often many able ones among them who deserve a better fate. To say nothing of those – often excellent people too – who go the rounds without regular employment, have no livelihood, and deserve appointments a thousand times more than those who have them.[6]

One flutist who became famous entirely from touring was Friedrich Ludwig Dülon (1769–1826; ill. 34). Blinded by incompetent treatment of an eye infection at the age of six weeks, Dülon was unable to sight-read music and so was prevented from holding an ordinary permanent post. Instead he developed phenomenal powers of memory and improvisation, dictating his compositions in finished form to a scribe. After flute studies with another blind flutist, Josef Winter, and with his father Louis Dülon, himself a student of Quantz's pupil Augustin Neuff, Dülon made his debut at the age of twelve in 1779, and began touring two years later. In his autobiography (1808) he gave details of his travels up to 1787, which took him to, among other places: Potsdam, where he met Neuff; Lüchow, where he met Ribock; Göttingen, where he met J. S. Bach's biographer Dr Johann Nikolaus Forkel; Hamburg, where he played for Carl Philipp Emanuel Bach; Leipzig, where he played duets with Tromlitz; Berlin, where he met the composer Johann Philipp Kirnberger and the critic Johann Friedrich Reichardt; London, where he performed at court as well as at public concerts; and Vienna, where he gave a concert in 1791 at the Theater auf der Wieden, at which Mozart staged *Die Zauberflöte*.

Dülon also made a highly successful journey to Russia, where he spent about two years in St Petersburg, a destination that attracted Tromlitz and many other German and Italian flutists of later generations. A tour would often pass through the Baltic cities in the autumn, arriving at the Russian capital in time to settle in for the winter. Dülon followed the customary route, playing at Königsberg on the way in 1792, and arrived in the following spring, to be engaged immediately by Grand Duke Alexander Pavlovitch at the high salary of 1000 roubles. Christian Carl Hartmann, who had previously worked in Paris, gave a concert in St Petersburg on 5 October 1786, having performed on his way at Hamburg in the same year C. P. E. Bach wrote his *Hamburger Sonate*. He supplemented his income by introducing a new flute model, perhaps a keyed flute by Tromlitz or an English maker: a notice in St Petersburg's German-language gazette announced that he carried with him flutes for sale, 'made according to his taste, and far superior to ordinary flutes'. Others, having made such a long journey, found attractions that disinclined them to return home: Heinrich Soussmann (1796–1848) visited the city in c1814, serving there for at least sixteen years as first flutist in the Grand Opera and the Chapel Royal, later as musical director at the Royal Theatre. His touring, reversing the usual direction, brought him from Russia to Breslau and Berlin in 1837.

Dülon's autobiography makes clear that without the help of friends in the destination city, it was almost impossible to organize successful concerts on tour. Any time people gathered in large numbers for fairs, celebrations, and feast days, the promoters of concerts, plays, and dances – to say nothing of conjurors, acrobats, and jugglers – strove to win a share of the audience.[7] He described the conditions in cities and inns, emphasizing the many ways in which a travelling musician, especially a blind one, was dependent on others. His autobiography also gives rare details of the instruments he used: his early familiarity with flutes by F. G. A. Kirst (Potsdam) made him prefer those instruments to others he played at various times in his career, by Tölke (Braunschweig), Grenser, Ribock, and Tromlitz.

Another peripatetic flutist of the late eighteenth century was Andrew Ashe, who was adopted by a nobleman as a boy, studied the violin with an Italian teacher in Minorca, and travelled widely with his patron before meeting the flutist Vanhamme in The Hague in 1774. After persuading Vanhamme to sell his instrument, a keyed flute by Richard Potter, he essentially taught himself to play it, though he took some lessons with Wendling, who thought the instrument a bad one. In 1778–9 he won the post of first flute at the Brussels opera from Vanhamme in a public audition, returning in 1782 to Dublin, where he became a popular performer at the Rotunda concerts. A decade later he moved to London, to hold multiple appointments as soloist and orchestral player including performances in Haydn's London symphonies of 1792 (chapter 6).

Even as London's top flutist Ashe was obliged to travel. The nature of a virtuoso's life required him to be noticed by as many people as possible, especially in compositions he wrote himself to display his particular talents. In this sense, the functions of composer and performer remained united in the same person, as they had been for much of the eighteenth century. Yet as Romantic thought penetrated life and music, especially in Germany, the idea that the performer had a separate and special role as a gifted interpreter of works by equally talented composers became more widespread. This concept was hardly entirely novel, since Philbert and Descoteaux had been noted for their moving interpretations of a 'traditional' repertoire of intimate, introverted music. But when public concerts began to present travelling virtuosi to a wider audience, the performer's interpretation, distinguished both by its brilliance and by its 'moving' qualities, became the subject of regular comment. During the rise of the travelling virtuoso, in the climate of the Romantic movement, the idea that a flutist could hold the status of a 'great artist' emerged.

Dülon's blindness, his youth and good looks, and the appearance of a remarkably similar fictional flutist, Julius, in the Romantic writer Jean Paul's novel *Hesperus* (1796) made him the earliest candidate for the title among flutists. Indeed, his instrument itself seemed to possess magically charming properties of the kind Mozart emphasized in *Die Zauberflöte*.[8] Two reviews of Dülon's performance illustrate this new idea. A report of a concert in Weimar on 2 September 1805 mentioned several technical aspects of his playing: the evenness of his tone and the judicious care with which he employed *tempo rubato*, dynamics, staccato, and the double-tongue. Then the reviewer moved on to the emotional impact of his playing:

> He also worked powerfully on our feelings with artistic sorcery by melting and interweaving one note [or: tone quality] into the next. The closing or nightingale-trill he fittingly introduced in the very tasteful cadenza in the Krommer concerto [in G major], which he correctly interpreted not in the normal way but playing the secondary note [F♯] with the right hand second finger [to produce an extremely small semitone], which remained clear, constantly waxing and waning, to a *morendo*, exceeded all possibility that the divinely spirited breath of the artist could achieve a still greater duration and strength.[9]

A review of a concert in Halle on 7 March 1806 took the technical report as read and launched directly into a eulogy of the artist's moving effect on his hearers:

> Of Dülon's playing itself, I shall write nothing; many newspapers have already exhausted themselves in words to give an impression of the excellence of his playing. But music is not a language, and feelings cannot be expressed in words. Who then has the power to describe the delicate transitions from the soft expressions of tender emotions to the powerful performance of high and strong feelings? – Who would comprehend the heavenly spirit that the great artist breathes into a melting Adagio? Who can express in words the sometimes slow, sometimes quick raising and lowering, the melting together and re-dissolving notes [or: tone qualities], and the whole combined and made complete from these? – No, all this must be heard and felt. Here the power of speech is beyond its bounds.[10]

Dülon's telling use of a special fingering in the first report provides the same example of the super-sharpened leading note or 'sensitive note' August Eberhard Müller had mentioned in the *AmZ* of 1798, when he wrote that 'most flutists' fingered F♯ to sound especially high in pitch when using it as a major seventh in G major.[11] Again the same scale degree provided the example in Berbiguier's *Nouvelle Méthode* (1818), in which the author explained that different musical contexts required the note to be played at different pitches: 'F♯ as the leading note of the key of G is necessarily sharper than the same F♯ taken as a third in D major.' Thomas Lindsay's *Elements* (1828) gave the fullest exposition of these 'augmented fingerings' and of their effect in semitone trills, turns and triplets, and in *legato* passages, where 'the DIMINISHED SEMITONE often imparts … a degree of pathos, and always a smoothness and delicacy of manner, which it would be impracticable to give by any other means'.[12] Lindsay assigned special sharp fingerings to 'any passing note placed a semitone below an integral note of the chord … when it is preceded and followed by this integral note'.[13] Though in France tutors by Devienne and by Hugot and Wunderlich (1804) made no mention of these special fingerings, the *Méthode* (1835) of Jean-Louis Tulou (1786–1865), which succeeded Hugot and Wunderlich as the official Conservatoire text in about 1845, included several pages of fingerings for super-sharpened leading notes, as well as charts and exercises illustrating simplified fingerings for difficult passages. The new ideal of the 'sensitive note' stood in direct contrast to instructions by Quantz and Tromlitz in the previous century, in which the size of the diatonic semitone had made leading notes stand a large (five-comma) semitone below their resolutions. The romantic flute once again played two sizes of semitone, but now the diatonic was smaller than the chromatic, and the new super-sharpened leading tone was required not only at cadences but in any melodic context in which the note was felt to lead upward.

A method for the violin by Bartolomeo Campagnoli (c1797) was the first to describe a similar system of intonation for that instrument.[14] Campagnoli's tutor, like many others of the late eighteenth and early nineteenth centuries, contained a growing arsenal of special effects in violin-playing – harmonics, pizzicato, bow effects, vibrato (used as an occasional special ornament) and other instrument-specific tricks – that contributed to the showmanship component of solo instrumental playing. Such acrobatics, though frowned on by more classical writers on violin-playing such as Ludwig Spohr (1832), were practised to the highest extreme by Nicolò Paganini (1782–1840), whose trademarks included the use of harmonics in double stopping, the use of all four fingers on the fingerboard simultaneously, and even playing entire pieces on a single string. Paganini's sickly disposition initially confined him to Italy, where from 1809 he followed a career as a 'free artist', until he made triumphant visits to Vienna (1828), Paris (1831), and London (1831). His performances must indeed have been astounding: on one occasion, 300 people were treated in hospital after a concert for 'over-enchantment'.

The new virtuoso performance style and the large size of audiences and performance spaces led to changes in violin and bow construction around the beginning of the nineteenth century. Violin-makers began refitting older instruments with higher bridges, more angled necks, and heavier internal bracing to support a greater string tension that produced a more brilliant tone. Bows by François Tourte and John Dodd produced a stronger sound and more undifferentiated changes of direction, and allowed more exploitation of the dazzling 'thrown' bow-strokes.[15] To compete for public attention in such a climate, flutists were obliged to cultivate similarly impressive volume of tone and special effects, but chose examples more suited to the capabilities and strengths the flute had already demonstrated. The typical style of writing they adopted in brilliant variations and fantasies – wide leaps delineating several polyphonic voices at once – referred back to the Italianate German

35. Charles Nicholson's recommended embouchure and body position, as illustrated in his flute tutors (1836).

flute music of the early eighteenth century, and to the caprices of composers in Dresden and Florence. Indeed, the final study in Hugot and Wunderlich's Conservatoire method of 1804 was a *Gigue dite Saxone* in the Dresden style, and in a key we now recognize as typically Dresdenesque, C minor. Other effects particularly suited to the flute included harmonics, the glide (which Tromlitz had noted as overworked in 1791), and the vibration, 'a peculiar vibrato in sustained tones, something like a fine tremolo [trill] in singing'.[16]

The last of these was among the special effects of Charles Nicholson (1795–1837). Arriving in London from his native Liverpool in the second decade of the nineteenth century, Nicholson soon earned posts at the Drury Lane Theatre, the Italian Opera, and the Philharmonic Society Concerts, where he appeared regularly as a soloist from 1816 to 1836, though the society's by-laws banned 'instrumental solos, concertos, duettos, and concertantes, for less than three principal instruments'.[17] Despite this regulation the taste for solo concertos was on the rise, so that in 1820 the *Quarterly Musical Magazine* observed that England enjoyed great excellence in its instrumental virtuosi, and that 'London never enjoyed such a galaxy of concerto players'.[18]

Though Nicholson seems not to have felt the need to travel abroad, his movements within Britain give the impression, in David Eagle's phrase (1977), of 'one who must hustle to make a living'.[19] In 1825, for example, his schedule included appearances at the Philharmonic Concerts, at the Italian Opera, at dozens of private and benefit events, at festivals in mid-September in York, late September in Norwich, and early October in Derby. He augmented his income with fees from numerous private students, from the Royal Academy of Music, where he was appointed professor in 1822, from the publication of tutors, and from the licensing of his name in the manufacture of instruments.[20] Nicholson was a one-man flute industry.

According to a report of 1828, Nicholson was 'famed for performing slow national melodies in a highly interesting and expressive manner'.[21] But the most noted characteristic of his playing was his tone, which, as Theobald Boehm wrote after visiting London as a travelling virtuoso in 1829, was so powerful that no continental player could match it. In a tutor of 1836 Nicholson described his manner of producing the sound he was famous for:

> Strength of tone, in the lower part of the instrument, depends on strength of pressure on the lip; for however hard you blow, unless there is a resisting power, your exertions will prove abortive. ... The under lip is made firm by the pressure of the flute, and the upper one by its powerful bearing upon the under one; in this state an embouchure is forced, and the breath ought to enter the mouth-hole in a vertical line to produce the lower notes with fullness and precision.[22]

Yet he was careful to warn against coarseness:

> Quality and purity of tone should be the primary consideration of the pupil, and not loudness of sound, which is too frequently heard, and which may be termed *roaring* on the flute. ... The tone ought to be as reedy as possible, as much like that of the hautboy as you can get it, but embodying the round mellowness of the clarionet. This can only be done by pressure. ...[23]

Nicholson's large tone was due in part to the instrument he played. He began his career in London with a flute by George Astor, 'the favorite [*sic*] maker for my father, who devoted much time and pains in the successful improvement of the instrument by enlarging the holes, &c'.[24] He specified the advantages of these large toneholes: 1) they made the flute more powerful and still capable of delicacy, 2) they allowed mostly unchanged fingerings in the third octave, 3) they made glides, or glissandi, more effectively, and 4) 'vibrations', ornaments produced by the finger, were clearer because of the flute's better tone. His defence of his instruments against criticism shows that they were quite loud enough for the orchestra of the day, and indeed that orchestral playing required refinement and softness more than constant strength: 'It is absurd to call this merely an orchestra flute, when it is well known that for this department of the instrument, the utmost delicacy is required.'[25]

Other London flute-makers also had their champions among the virtuosi. Carl Saust (*b* 1773) favoured flutes by Monzani, Ashe preferred Milhouse, and eventually Nicholson licensed the manufacture of large-holed flutes to Clementi & Co. These instruments, contrary to modern misconceptions of them as useless beyond the keys of D and G major, were actually built to favour flat keys: Nicholson's own pieces often used tonalities such as C minor, A♭ major, and E♭ major, the last of which William Nelson James called 'perhaps, the best in tune, as the flute is manufactured to be perfect in that *key*'.[26]

James, though not a well-known performer himself, also travelled widely in his efforts to earn a living as a flute teacher, publisher, and magazine editor. In January 1825 he took lessons from Nicholson, but left London without paying for them.[27] Ten months later he wrote to Nicholson from Edinburgh that gambling losses and other misfortunes he had suffered in the meantime in Paris had almost ruined him. Having acquired certificates of proficiency from Berbiguier and Tulou, however, he wrote to ask Nicholson for another:

> I only arrived here last week, and think as there is no player of eminence here, a better opening could not have presented itself. … It is my purpose to teach your music from the beginning, and to recommend your flutes to those gentlemen who are not already in possession of one of them.[28]

Nicholson did not reply, but in the following year James published *A Word or Two on the Flute*, a prolix and opinionated history of the flute together with notices of the 'Performers of the Present Day' that mixed flattery with impertinent criticism. James framed his notice of Nicholson in particularly offensive language, censuring his use of the double-tongue, his excessive embellishment, and his compositions, which 'would have been better for his fame had they never been written'.[29] In response Nicholson published a pamphlet addressing 'the self-satisfied pretender, the self-made professor, the great self-constituted arbiter of public taste; in short, the self-bedubbed Mr W. N. JAMES … "Flute Manufacturer! And Teacher of the Flute!! Author of a Word or two on the Flute!!! Translator of Berbigiér's [*sic*] Method!!!! Editor of the Flutists' Magazine!!!!! And Compiler of the London Catalogue of Music!!!!!!"'[30] The response, according to one contemporary, occasioned 'a violent quarrel … which had proceeded so far that arrangements were made for a hostile meeting [i.e. a duel]; fortunately this never took place, or the lion might have perished by the puncture of an asp.'[31]

The high demand for flutes occasioned by an increasing number of amateurs in England had given rise by *c*1800 to a secondary industry of manufacturing cheap instruments, some of them purporting to be the work of famous firms. A magazine article of 1827 reported how a needy workman could quickly make a flute 'without tone, without intonation, "sans everything" in short, but external appearances to recommend it'.[32] James exploited the opportunity provided by the high prices of established makers to go into business for himself. He advertised flutes for 6–8 guineas, as opposed to the 10–14 guineas the three largest firms charged for flutes with six or eight keys.[33] In 1829 he advertised 'James's Improved Flutes ... which Mr Tulon [*sic*] has pronounced the best English Flutes he ever performed on, and ... far superior to Monzani's'.[34] Tulou protested in response that he had never used any English flute *except* Monzani's, to which James's retorted by describing their meeting, when Tulou had played one of James's flutes, 'preluding on this flute for upwards of a quarter of an hour'.[35]

So the prelude evidently continued its almost invisible life in England as well as in France and Germany. Nicholson was evidently a practitioner: his *Complete Preceptor, for the German Flute* (1816) contained *a complete set of preludes, cadences, &c.*, while *Nicholson's Preceptive Lessons* (1821) included Preludes, Capriccios, and English airs with embellishments and variations. In another jab at Nicholson, James observed that the Dutch virtuoso Louis Drouët (1792–1873) was a superior performer, in part, because he played 'no disagreeable preludes'.[36] However, if Nicholson continued the age-old practice, he was not alone. Thomas Lindsay's *Elements of Flute Playing* (London, 1828) gave preludes, ornamented airs, and a long cadenza for an *Andante* by Benoît Tranquille Berbiguier, while Berbiguier himself published a work that contained nothing but preludes in *c*1830. Virtuoso exercises, studies, and preludes of the later nineteenth century, particularly by Italian flutists, grew from and developed similar forms.

Another quasi-improvised form that English players viewed as a test of skill and taste which foreigners, particularly Frenchmen, usually failed was the *Adagio* air, ornamented with embroideries and special effects (ill. 37). *Alexander's Complete Preceptor for the Flute* (1821) indicates how diverse the playing even of English virtuosi could be in this respect. In his tutor, which supplied eighty examples of alternative fingerings, as well as exercises in harmonics and transposition, Alexander provided specimens of the styles of embellishment of Ashe, Weidner, and Nicholson: Ashe's sample contains three extremely florid cadenzas in only sixteen bars of music. The ornamenting of *Adagios*, however, was considered the province of virtuosi, who were meant to reach beyond the merely correct performance a dilettante might attain, striving for the fine and beautiful.[37] In 1816 Nicholson wrote: 'A mistaken idea has long prevailed with regard to slow Airs or Adagios, – namely "that Melody is greatly improved by the introduction of a variety of Embellishments".'[38] Berbiguier was more emphatic:

One must scrupulously guard against adding a single note. ... It is proper only for virtuosi, furnished with extraordinary resources, to permit themselves what are vulgarly called Embroideries, and furthermore those who use them the least, in our opinion, are the most skilful.[39]

In 1827 Drouët noted that the classical composers were to be treated with special reverence with respect to ornamentation:

Embellishments of this kind ... must never be applied to music by Haydn, Mozart, Beethoven, and other composers of similar standing. In compositions e.g. in the finale of a symphony, a theme is repeated several times; but each time it appears in a new aspect through alterations in harmony.[40]

Drouët, who had come to Paris from his native Amsterdam in about 1814 aged 22, rivalled Tulou as France's prime flutist for two seasons. Tulou (chapter 11) had already become principal at the Opéra Italien at the age of eighteen (1802), and succeeded Wunderlich at the Opéra a year before Drouët's arrival. It was in playing the solo flute part in Lebrun's opera *Le Rossignol* (The Nightingale) in 1816 that Tulou was generally judged to have vanquished Drouët in the contest between them.

When Tulou first visited England in 1817, however, his playing, though its refinement was noted, won only faint praise. He met another cold reception at two Philharmonic Concerts on an unsuccessful second visit to London in 1821.[41] The unenthusiastic English reaction was explained by the *Quarterly Musical Magazine*:

> The reputation which Tulou had obtained in his own country was rather injurious to his success in this. The expectation which it raised in a public already accustomed to the brilliancy and clear articulation of Drouët, and the masculine power and expression of Nicholson, was not easily satisfied, and Tulou, although a very elegant and finished performer, was treated with an indifference which his talents by no means deserved.[42]

As the magazine noted, Drouët, perhaps the most peripatetic flutist in the age of travelling virtuosi, had already made a strong impression in London as well as in Paris. He had played at the age of seven at the Conservatoire, where he studied composition under Etienne Nicolas Méhul and Reicha. In about 1807 he was appointed flute soloist to the King of the Netherlands and presented with a crystal flute (chapter 8). Napoleon, the king's brother, invited him to Paris in 1811 and gave him a similar appointment and gift. During the time of his rivalry with Tulou in about 1814–16, Drouët visited England, and in the following years made a brief venture into the flute manufacturing business with Cornelius Ward (c1796–1872), a former foreman at Tebaldo Monzani's workshop. John Quincy Adams, an amateur flutist and sixth President of the United States (1825–9), heard Drouët perform at Covent Garden on 29 March 1816 in an extraordinary programme including Handel's *Messiah* and *Acis and Galatea*, an Italian aria by Mozart, and numerous works by various modern composers. He played a flute concerto that, as Adams recorded, 'surpassed everything that I had ever heard upon that instrument'.[43] The professional musician W. T. Parke gave more details in reporting a Covent Garden concert on 16 February 1818, when Drouët 'displayed uncommon rapidity of tongue but was not equally impressive in adagio playing, which is the test of excellence'.[44] A writer in 1836 looked back on his popularity as a passing fad, but one that had left a permanent imprint on flute-playing:

> Drouët's playing was a mere display of antics and harlequinades, which excited the wonder of the ignorant, but could never gratify the ear of a musician. Yet they became quite the rage, and there are few performers whose style has not been more or less vitiated by them.[45]

The brilliance and sparkle of Drouët's playing was enhanced by the instrument he used, according to an observer who wrote in 1823. But again the contrast was drawn with Nicholson, who had played at Drury Lane within ten days of Drouët a few years earlier.[46] Here the unfortunate foreigner is deemed to have failed the test of *Adagio* playing without even having attempted it:

> It could not escape the attention of an intelligent observer, that his embouchure, as well as the bore of his flute, was exceedingly small, for the purpose of giving great brilliancy to the upper notes, on the display of which he manifestly rested the principal attraction of his performance. This construction of the instrument, however, totally destroyed all its lower rich, mellow tones, and deprived the performer of those contrasts which are so important in bringing back the attention to the very excellences which he was ambitious to display. ... By the manner in which he executed his passages, one would be inclined to think that he had originally practised on a one-keyed flute, for in slow execution the defects of his fingering were very perceptible. His amazing facility in rapid passages concealed these defects, but we are fully persuaded that had he performed an adagio in a flat key, the imperfections would have been manifest to the most cursory observer.[47]

A report of Drouët's playing at Berlin in 1820 contrasted it with that of the local players, and of Germany's leading flutist, Anton Bernhard Fürstenau (1792–1852). Quite absent from the Berlin report is the Romantic eulogy with which reporters from Halle and Weimar had earlier greeted Dülon's playing, despite the similarity of their styles:

> The manner in which he played resembled that of the blind Dülon who was heard here earlier, and one could therefore call it old-fashioned.... The style of his flute-playing comes closest to that of the younger Fürstenau, though Hr. Drouët seems to possess more ability in the tongue.[48]

The equivocal praise of the critics notwithstanding, Drouët toured Europe thereafter with great success, lingering in Naples for three years as director of Royal Opera, visiting Paris at Mendelssohn's invitation in 1828, and appearing in London in double star billing with the composer in the following year (see p. 139). Other triumphs came in Paris and London (1832), London again, for command performances before Queen Victoria and Prince Albert (1841), New York (1854), and Frankfurt (1860).

The player named in the Berlin report of Drouët's playing was another travelling virtuoso, Anton Bernhard Fürstenau (chapter 10). Also like Drouët, Fürstenau was a personal friend of a famous German composer: Carl Maria von Weber, director of the Dresden Hofkapelle that he joined as first flutist in 1820. Fürstenau began lessons with his father, Caspar Fürstenau, at the age of six, before the two undertook their first concert tour together to Copenhagen when the boy was eleven. Two years later, in 1805, father and son travelled to St Petersburg, and, according to Rockstro, 'made

Wednesday evening, 24 June 1829.
Leader of the Band: Mr F. Cramer, Conductor: Sir George Smart.
Source: Rockstro, *Treatise*, §900. Note: Drouët's name was used in the concert announcement probably because it was for his benefit, that is, he would retain the major share of its profits after expenses had been paid.

Part I

New Overture to Shakespeare's 'Midsummer Night's Dream' (British premiere), conducted by the composer		F. Mendelssohn
Recitative and Air (German words)	Madame Drouët	C. M. von Weber
New Concerto, Flute (British premiere)	M. Drouët	Drouët
Aria	Signor Begrez	Rossini
Concerto, Pianoforte	Mr F. Mendelssohn	Beethoven
Duetto from *Ricciardo e Zoraide*	Mademoiselle Blasis and Signor Begrez	Rossini
Variations on Air by C. M. von Weber, Flute	M. Drouët	Drouët

Part II

Quartetto, 'The Huntsmen's Chorus'	the Four Brothers Herrmann	Weber
Scena from *Der Freischütz* (German words)	Madame Drouët	Weber
'God Save the King' (newly arranged by Drouët), Flute	M. Drouët	Drouët
Air, 'The Pledge of Truth' (by particular desire)	Miss Carnaby	T. Welsh
Aria	Mademoiselle Blasis	Pacini
Finale (Instrumental)		Haydn

long journeys almost every year', on one of which (Prague, 1815) they met Weber.[49] After a short period as an orchestral player at Frankfurt in 1817, Fürstenau toured with his father again in 1818–19. Following Caspar's death and Anton's move to Dresden, the younger Fürstenau undertook tours to Denmark (1823), Bavaria (1824), Paris and London (1826, where he performed with Weber), and Vienna and Prague (1828). Rockstro reported his 'but indifferent success' in London, quoting periodicals with the by now familiar accusation that Fürstenau's tone was 'thin and meagre' compared to Nicholson's, though 'in execution he was scarcely inferior to any performer who had previously appeared; his expression, likewise, was of a high character, tender, soothing and appropriate; his articulation perfect and finely softened, and his feelings those of the true musician'.[50] (Fürstenau's choice of instrument is discussed in chapter 8.)

The repertoire of the travelling virtuosi is easy to characterize as slight and ephemeral, but that is to overlook its considerable interest as a document of its times and even, in the best cases, as music. The fantasias and caprices of Quantz, Zimmerman, and other eighteenth-century composers had made fantasy seem like an end in itself, while passage-work in concertos often seemed as though it was put there just to display the

36. The flutist Caspar Fürstenau (1772–1819) and his son and pupil Anton Bernhard (1792–1852), himself the father and teacher of Moritz Fürstenau (1824–89).

skill of the player. The 'Grand Solo' or 'Fantasy' form beloved of the touring flutists, in contrast, worked out an individual treatment of a well-known melody or a quotation from a famous opera or orchestral work, the familiar basic material lending the bravura style an instant attractiveness. Such pieces document the enduring popularity of the tunes they elaborated on – indeed even in the twentieth century Marcel Moyse promoted the interpretation of century-old opera themes as a way of developing an expressive and flexible tone on the flute.

The flute compositions the travelling virtuosi performed, whether reductions, variations, potpourris, or fantasies, were published in the first place for amateurs, a market, as Vera Funk has observed (1999), that has been researched only sparsely.[51] While the instrument-specific nature of much of the writing makes it seem featureless or uninteresting on the modern flute, the refinement in handling the original themes and the instrumental treatments themselves often perfectly match the nuances of contemporary instruments. Cheap musical publications, following the lead of literature for 'the people at large', greatly expanded the market for such compositions. One series (10s 6d) claimed that until it appeared, 'the exorbitant sums demanded for engraved music amounted to a prohibition of its free circulation among the middle classes'.[52]

Accompaniments were provided by guitar, harp, another flute, or pianoforte. The combination of flute and keyboard was not at first a standard one, however: the *Quarterly Musical Magazine* noted in 1820 that '[t]he continual association of the flute with the piano-forte seems to announce the introduction, if not of a novel combination, at least of a much more frequent connection between two instruments, that have seldom till late, been much brought together'.[53] In two-flute compositions or arrangements, mostly in the keys of G and D, the melody appeared in the upper part, sometimes switching to the second flute part. The combination of flute and guitar provided the medium for some of the most successful pieces, such as Anton Diabelli's *Potpourri aus Beethovens beliebtesten Werken* (Mixture of tunes from Beethoven's most popular works, 1817).

The variation form depended for its interest on the artful development of simple themes – and the simpler the better, as the theme ideally had no influence whatever on the character of the variations. Treatments of the old Venetian or Neapolitan song *Carnival of Venice* were produced by many artists including Demersseman and Giulio Briccialdi (1818–81), as well as in a version for two flutes by Franz (1821–83) and Karl (1825–1900) Doppler. Eleven versions remained in the catalogue of the Italian publisher Ricordi in 1911.[54] One of the finest examples of the genre was Franz Schubert's set of variations on his own song, *Trockne Blumen* (op. post. 160, D802). Friedrich Kuhlau (1786–1832), a Copenhagen court composer, published several sets for flute and piano, including variations on *The Last Rose of Summer* op. 105.[55] Anton Bernhard Fürstenau wrote an Introduction and Variations on Weber's *Euryanthe* op. 53 (1824), as well as fantasias for flute and piano on themes from Weber's *Oberon* and a treatment of a work by Weber's successor in Dresden, *Nocturne avec variations sur un thème favori de l'opéra Libella par Reissiger* op. 78. Nicholson published *Introduction and Six Variations on the Fall of Paris* with piano *ad lib*, containing a second stave with an easier version of the flute part 'more adapted to requirements of a lower rank'.

National Airs, a favourite of Nicholson's and a perennial of the flute's repertoire until the twentieth century, were generally indiscriminately labelled 'Scotch' irrespective of their actual origin. Beethoven made arrangements for piano trio of Irish, Welsh, Scottish, and other folksongs for the Scottish publisher George Thomson between 1809 and 1820,[56] but many more compositions based on National Airs took the free fantasia form. Tulou and his pupil Jules August Demersseman (1833–66) were prolific composers of fantasias described as 'concertant' or 'brillant', which could develop a theme more freely than variations tied to the formal design of their theme. Original compositions and reworkings both occurred in another type of composition, the *Pièce de salon*, which, though easier to play, had the same focus on intense, sentimental expression. Karl Joachim Andersen (1837–1909) of Copenhagen, a founding member of the Berlin Philharmonic Orchestra, exemplified the style in his programmatic *Salon pièce. Au bord de la mer* op. 9.

The technical demands of works by Theobald Boehm (1794–1881) for the most part exceeded amateur abilities, not least because he designed them purposely for the

37. Charles Nicholson's ornamented version of *Roslin Castle* (1836) contains many of the traits of his style. The piece is set in F minor, a typical flat tonality, while its notated ornaments include glides, vibrations, trills, turns, appoggiaturas, octave slurs, harmonics, sensitive note fingerings, veiled tones, alternative fingerings, and dynamics from *ppp* to *ff*.

Boehm flute (chapter 9), which was rare at the time. Boehm wrote especially challenging bravura pieces such as *Variations brillantes sur l'air allemand 'Du, du liegst mir am herzen'* op. 22, and the *Souvenir des Alpes* opp. 27–32, specifically to showcase his new flute on tour. He published works for amateurs in a quite different style to develop correct performance style and good taste, including arrangements of Schubert *Lieder* (Munich, 1871) and a transformation of the *Largo* in A♭ from Beethoven's piano concerto op. 15, into an *Adagio* in C major for flute and piano, in the amateur *Journal pour la Flûte*.

Boehm's experiences as a travelling virtuoso played a large part in his new designs for the flute (chapter 9). By about 1820 he had established himself in Munich as a flutist with a royal appointment and salary, a career he maintained alongside the running of his father's jewellery business after the latter's death. He composed his first concerto (in G major, dedicated to A. B. Fürstenau and published in 1822), and premiered it in his fourth series of subscription concerts, on 2 December 1820. Boehm's first concert tour (1821–2), to Vienna by way of Augsburg, Nuremberg, Leipzig, Dresden, and Prague, brought him sufficient notice that he felt able to give up working as a goldsmith and pursue a performing career. In 1823–4 he toured with the violinist Bernard Molique to Berlin and Hanover, and in the following winter season to Switzerland. Reviews of their performances, quoted at length in Boehm's biography, stress the tenderness, charm, and soulfulness rather than the brilliance of his playing. In the winter of 1826 he played in Zurich and made a tour of small Swiss towns. Two years later he travelled to Vienna on business for his new flute-manufacturing workshop, heard Paganini, and persuaded the famous violinist to visit Munich the following year, overcoming the star's reluctance by guaranteeing him sold-out houses. Boehm performed in Vienna again himself, and toured Austria and Upper Italy on a route home that took him through Trieste, Padua, and Venice. Boehm struck out to Paris and London for the first time in January 1831. He made a good impression in London, and his flute, an elegant eight-keyed instrument built in his Munich workshop, attracted the notice of the prominent manufacturers Rudall & Rose, who built Nicholson flutes among other types. But the response of London critics was predictable, and one wrote of Boehm's playing, '[a]s to volume of tone our Nicholson stands unsurpassed'. Boehm's subsequent travels, related in chapter 9, had less to do with his career as a performer than with the promotion of his new flutes and with his efforts to learn English methods of producing iron and steel so as to introduce new techniques in Bavaria.

With the fading of popular enthusiasm for the flute and the growing importance of symphony orchestras in the late nineteenth century (chapter 10), a new generation of flutists arose for whom holding a permanent orchestral post became more attractive than a stressful nomadic living. Nonetheless, Adolf Terschak (1832–1901) and many others still made guest appearances abroad as well as occasional tours, either as soloists or, continuing the long association of flute and voice, with singers. A. B. Fürstenau's son Moritz (1824–89) toured with Jenny Lind in 1855, while Nellie Melba later travelled the world with an array of flutists from various traditions, from Albert Fransella and John Amadio to Philippe Gaubert and Marcel Moyse. But the late-Victorian decline of the travelling virtuoso permitted early twentieth-century stars of the flute, such as Moyse and Jean-Pierre Rampal, to believe they were presenting the flute as a solo instrument for the first time. In reality it was only the first time in living memory.

Chapter 8

Flute mania

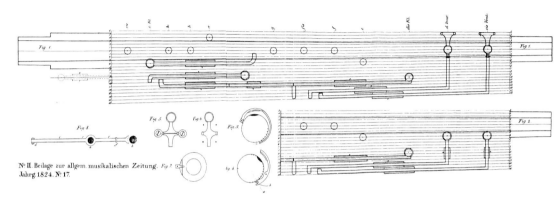

38. H. W. T. Pottgiesser's proposed new flute, a drawing he published in the *AmZ* (1825).

The swelling size and power of European population centres and industry at the beginning of the nineteenth century spurred the most energetic activities yet in musical performance, instrument manufacture, and publication. Travelling flute virtuosi now competed with other instrumentalists for public attention, and with each other for the adulation of flute-playing dilettantes, numerous enough since the last decades of the eighteenth century to support a blossoming industry of flute-related activities. Flutes permeated masculine leisure, doubling as walking sticks, swordsticks, or even (in England) umbrellas. Northwest Europe was in the grip of flute mania.

Now a new interest arose in reforming the instrument itself, not so much among makers as amateur and professional flutists. Some of these men concerned themselves with abstract principles of rationalizing and mechanizing its design, while others made incremental innovations to meet the challenges posed by an increasingly brilliant style of solo performance. Many communicated their ideas for the first time in public documents such as newspapers, magazines, and patent applications. Thus, in contrast to earlier periods of major change in the instrument's design, we have a relatively full first-hand account of the ideas that motivated them, and of how changes in performance made themselves felt in the instrument's capabilities.

First, however, we must dispose of a modern fallacy which claims that the keyed flutes of the period were too defective to give an adequate account of the period's music, and not loud enough for the orchestras of their time. One writer holds that '[b]igger orchestras demanded greater volume and projection … composers became more adventurous in their use of key signatures … [and t]he defects of cross-fingering on the woodwind became increasingly obvious. And so flute makers added more holes and designed the requisite mechanism to control them.'[1] None of these claims has any basis in the historical record. In reality, the demands of orchestral flute-writing played little if any role in the development of new designs until *c*1850 (chapter 10): orchestras remained relatively small until that time, and their flutists seem to have prized *piano* playing and tonal flexibility in contrast to the brilliant *forte* considered appropriate for solo performance. On the whole early nineteenth-century flute music used tonalities less challenging than before, and the perceived difficulty of the keyed flute's fingering, not the tonal unevenness of the already obsolete one-keyed flute, spurred early efforts at redesign.

The single aspect of orchestral scoring that did excite comment around 1800 was the increasing use of the high register and an associated loss of tonal variety. A. André described the changes in 1798 in the first volume of the *Allgemeine musikalische Zeitung* (General Musical Times), the periodical that became Germany's most important forum for the exchange of musical ideas:

> There was a time when the flute was not only called the softest of all the instruments, but it really was; when it was proverbial and the ideal with which everything soft-toned was compared. Now this is changed. The most modern composers usually write for this instrument so that it has to shriek or rather whistle piercingly in the high register; and Virtuosi love this sharp, cutting tone so much that they play everything in it – even their Solos and Adagios. Is this good? I am quite aware that a single flute piping in the high register, which as far as I know *Mozart* first introduced, or at least used most frequently, has an excellent effect in certain circumstances – as for example in the Overture to his *Don Giovanni* – but why do Gentlemen now write everything in this way? Why do Virtuosi now teach their pupils no other tone than this acute one? Why do Virtuosi now deliver everything in this piercing tone? – I know too what the Gentlemen reply: the instrument itself demands it, one cannot play in tune otherwise; with a soft tone the low register is too flat compared with the middle and high, and the high compared with the former, too sharp.[2]

André's complaint set off a lively discussion on the fingering and tone of the keyed flute, but this did not include any suggestion that the instrument was inadequate for its own repertoire, as twentieth-century writers first suggested. At about the same time J. G. Tromlitz proposed an experimental design for a chromatic flute that, unlike the eight-keyed flute he built and described in his tutor of 1800, had only one key and played with a revised fingering system. However, this experiment was not motivated by any defects he could find in the keyed flute, which he still thought perfectly appropriate for professional use. His purpose as he described it, far from extending the instrument's capabilities, was merely to duplicate them while simplifying its fingering. As he introduced his description of the design:

> Since many people get into difficulties with the numerous keys, I thought of building a flute without keys … on which one would be able to do just the same

as can be done on a flute with several keys. … Now that I am old I really do not want to make any further experiments with it, therefore I shall put down here the whole design[;] perhaps someone or other will be served by it.[3]

Tromlitz's experimental flute, with only a single key for D♯/E♭, could play a chromatic (non-enharmonic) scale using none of the forked fingerings that produced notes of more veiled tone-quality on the one-keyed flute. This essentially 'keyless' flute, the earliest of several such designs over the next half century, was also the first to re-position the right-hand toneholes so that the fingering normally used for F♯ produced F natural. William Close proposed another radical keyless flute on quite different lines in a paper of 1801 describing a flute that could 'transpose the key of an air on the German flute without any material alteration in the mode of fingering'. He concluded:

Our small wind instruments have many imperfections, but are the objects of so little direct importance to society, that we do not expect much celerity in their improvement.[4]

Only two years later, however, the doctor and amateur flutist Heinrich Wilhelm Theodor Pottgiesser (1766–1829) took up Tromlitz's challenge in a long anonymous essay in the *AmZ* with ideas for a sweeping redesign of the flute. He aimed 'to further the study of flute construction, to awaken a spirit of inventiveness for this beautiful instrument, and to weaken the belief that the keyed flute is already perfect'.[5] His critique of modern instruments chose Tromlitz's own keyed flutes as the most fully-developed type, citing their unequal intonation (which, as we have seen, Tromlitz considered an advantage), their retention of some one-keyed flute fingerings, and the difficulty of playing a flute on which some fingers had to do double duty on a key as well as a tonehole. Pottgiesser posed basic questions about acoustical matters traditionally the province of instrument-makers: the location of toneholes, the length of the tube, the number and size of holes, the design of the embouchure hole, the placement of the cork, and the thickness of the tube. His essay was far-reaching enough to reflect on the inherent problems of a cylindrical bore, and he had evidently gone to the trouble of building an experimental 'keyless' flute according to Tromlitz's description. He proposed in its place another one-keyed flute that played a chromatic scale with 'equal intonation' – that is, without enharmonic distinctions. However, the essay received little or no attention until he revised his plan twenty years afterwards.

Though Pottgiesser made no specific reference to the demands modern music placed on the flute, and though Tromlitz's proposal for an equal-tempered flute had preceded his own, his proposal of 1803 did promote an ideal of evenness that had not been mentioned before. This quality was cited as a desirable attribute of the voice, the model for all instruments, for the first time only once the emphatic, 'speaking' method of delivery of the eighteenth century had given way to a new mellifluous and sustained style in instrumental playing. In the same way that uniform tone became the focus of technique where differentiation had previously been the key, so did 'equal' intonation. Whereas Quantz's tuning brought out the contrasts in harmony and melody, the 'sensitive' leading notes smoothed over their disturbing quality and softened the harshness of the seventh chord. Pottgiesser's suggestion for an equal-tempered flute thus grew from the general musical spirit of his time, even if the concept only produced notable innovations two decades later.

Hugot and Wunderlich's flute method, adopted at the Paris Conservatoire in 1804 (chapter 11), indicated that the French four-keyed flute had finally become the institution's official instrument in that year. But if the institution accepted Anglo-Saxon changes in flute design only tardily, it was swift to recognize innovations by a Frenchman. In 1806 Claude Laurent (*d* 1848), a clock-maker from Langres, won a silver medal for a crystal flute at the industrial exposition in Paris, the first time an instrument-maker had ever taken part in a trade exhibition. In the same year Laurent filed a patent for his crystal flutes.[6] The specification emphasized the material's dimensional stability and impermeability to moisture, and noted that the saddles that carried the keywork were attached to the flute body with screws. According to an announcement in a German journal in 1806, a commission including Paris Conservatoire officials Gossec, Méhul, Cherubini, Ozi, and Wunderlich had examined the flute.[7] The commission found the flutes less sensitive to temperature-related pitch changes than instrument of wood or ivory, easier to play, and livelier in tone, and noted that their keywork was better made than that on other makers' instruments. Their main disadvantage was their heaviness.

Laurent's flutes were widely noted owing to their exotic appearance, as well as for their musical attributes. The Parisian flutist Dubois gave a concert on a crystal flute in Amsterdam in 1808, and the amateur flutist Johann George Bürkly (1793–1851) of Zurich was noted as using one in 1824.[8] On appointing the fifteen-year-old Louis Drouët as his court flutist, Louis Bonaparte, King of the Netherlands, presented him a crystal flute by Laurent (NL-Amsterdam: Rijksmuseum), and Drouët acquired another on a similar appointment to the French Emperor Napoleon.[9] Drouët may have been using a crystal flute when John Quincy Adams heard him play at Covent Garden in 1816 (p. 137), while James Madison, himself President of the United States at the time (he was fourth President, from 1809 to 1817), received a four-keyed crystal flute by Laurent as a gift from the maker (DCM 378).[10] Demand evidently remained strong for some decades: by 1847 Laurent's workshop employed five workmen and had an annual turnover of 30,000 francs, five times the sum Parisian makers Godfroy and Lot paid Boehm for a licence to manufacture his silver cylinder flute in the same year (p. 183).[11]

In the year of Laurent's patent, Jean Daniel Holtzapffel (1770–1843) filed another for a one-keyed chromatic flute.[12] Holtzapffel's flute replaced the three additional keys of the usual French instruments with open holes, for the left thumb, the left fifth finger, and the right thumb. The two left-hand holes simply replaced the B♭ and G♯ keys, but the right thumb controlled a new hole between toneholes 4 and 5, rather than between 5 and 6 as on the keyed flute and on Tromlitz's experimental model. F natural was played by fingering an E and opening the thumbhole, while the normal F♯ fingering with the thumbhole open gave F♯.

Other patents enhanced pitch flexibility by mechanical means. Richard Potter's son William Henry filed a patent in 1808 for a flute-key mechanism with a sideways

Equal temperament, the system now universally used to tune keyboard and MIDI instruments, was devised in the Renaissance but not widely accepted among instrument builders and musicians until the mid-nineteenth century. The system divides the octave into twelve equal parts, two to a whole tone. Its theory allows for no smaller interval than the semitone, though acousticians now divide this unit into 100 cents (for quarter tones on the flute, see p. 123). Despite the elegant theoretical simplicity of equal temperament, it met resistance in practice because it contained no pure intervals except the unison and the octave, its thirds being particularly out of tune. The resulting faultiness of its triads made it inappropriate as long as harmony and the basso continuo dominated musical thought and practice (see p. 146): an English authority explicitly referred to this in 1759 when he called equal temperament 'that inharmonious system of 12 hemitones' producing a 'harmony extremely coarse and disagreeable'.[1]

Since new styles of composition in the Classical era increasingly emphasized melody rather than harmony, however, the intonation practices of singers and instrumentalists began to change (chapter 6). In a shift that deserves much closer study than it has yet received, musicians began to intone notes in certain melodic positions at pitches above their true values, and to play sharps higher in pitch than flats, reversing the earlier practice.

Intonation practice appears to have changed rather rapidly in France and Germany, but considerably later and more slowly in England. Alexander J. Ellis noted that while equal temperament had become firmly established in England by the time he wrote in 1885 as a tuning system for organs and pianos, it had only become a 'trade usage' among piano tuners fairly recently in 1846, and among organ builders about a decade later.[2] Yet Hector Berlioz, writing of the Wheatstone English Concertina of 1844 in which the enharmonic distinctions between D♯/E♭, and G♯/A♭, made flats higher than sharps in the old manner, noted that this was now 'entirely at odds with the practice of musicians'.[3] Here he was no doubt referring at least in part to the *notes sensibles* or super-sharpened leading notes described in chapters 6 and 7.

The idea that flutes could be tuned in equal temperament was first proposed, not surprisingly, by a keyboard player. In 1758 the organist Georg Andreas Sorge presented an extremely technical but flawed argument based on keyboard tuning to contend that Quantz's system of tuning for the flute was incorrect. Instead he advocated that the flute adopt the tempering used on keyboard instruments.[4] The earliest such proposal by a flutist came when J. G. Tromlitz described an experimental 'keyless' flute with equal-sized semitones in 1800 (p. 146), though the keyed flutes he made himself in the ordinary course of events were designed to preserve the traditional enharmonic distinctions and to play with just intonation (p. 81).

Later experimenters disagreed about how to apply equal temperament to an instrument that, like others which sustain a pure tone, magnifies the defects of any tuning system that permits impure intervals. In a reply to H. W. T. Pottgiesser's essay of 1824, Karl Grenser held that his own keyed flute (by Heinrich Grenser) allowed him to play better in tune than the type Pottgiesser proposed. Grenser thought a maker might well tune a flute with equal temperament as a reference, but a musician could only play it in tune by deviating from such an imperfect system:

Many of these faults [of intonation in Pottgiesser's flute] are the result of applying the notes according to the monochord. The flute must, like the fortepiano, be tuned to equal temperament. Then if a skilled flutist here or there, where it has a good effect; e.g. wants to make a leading note a little higher, or the seventh in a dominant chord a little lower etc., then he has to either find fingerings to bring this about or manage by rolling the mouth-hole in or out and strengthening and weakening the wind.[5]

Throughout his reply Grenser designated notes by their dual enharmonic functions, implying that the flats should still be played higher than the sharps and employ what he called the 'purely tuned intonation that will satisfy every trained ear'.[6]

Yet although flutists seemed to agree that playing strictly in equal temperament was impractical, the matter of what deviations to make remained far from settled. In a letter of 1843 to *The Musical World*, the flute-maker John Pask objected to the intonation of Boehm's ring-key flute (whether because it was unable to make the old enharmonic distinctions or because it could not play 'sensitive' notes is not clear):

> Mr C[linton,] among the many qualities he attaches to the Boehm flute, states, that perfection of tune is attained. How can this possibly be, when the same fingering must be used for the sharps as well as the flats? The effect such an instrument (with this imperfection) would produce, when played with stringed instruments, can easily be conceived.[7]

More specifically, according to Count A. D. de Pontécoulant, Tulou had raised the objection before the Conservatoire commission of 1838 that Boehm's ring-key flute had no separate fingerings for the high leading tones or *notes sensibles*.[8] An instrument designed by W. J. Monzani and manufactured by William Henry Potter addressed the same defect in the eight-keyed flute by employing split keys to allow sharps and flats to be played with different pitches – in this case, the sharps higher than the flats.[9]

In 1846 Richard Carte cited the equal-tempered tuning of Boehm's ring-key flute as a point in its favour but, like Grenser, held that flutes tuned in equal temperament could not be so played, in that the flutist had to deviate from the equal-tempered scale in order to play in tune:

> The Organ, the Pianoforte, &c., are tuned according to what is termed the 'Equal Temperament', which is the nearest approach to *perfect* intonation that can be obtained upon instruments the sounds of which are fixed. The Flute should be tuned according to the same principle. For this purpose its holes are required to be placed at equal distances, merely allowing for the increase (as already explained) in the diameter of the tube. It may also be observed that the notes of the organ and pianoforte are *absolutely* fixed, whilst those of the Flute are capable of slight modifications of pitch by the action of the lips, by which the Performer is enabled to obtain *perfect* intonation.[10]

Even Boehm's fingering and trill charts of 1847 included separate enharmonic fingerings, with the comment: 'The irregular fingerings may be used not only for facilitating certain passages, but also they may be made valuable in many cases for enharmonic differences, such as between F♯ and G♭.'[11]

Thus while the equal temperament was a practical necessity for keyboards with only twelve notes to the octave, and while for musical reasons it became expedient for the tuning of flutes by the mid-nineteenth century, even its most strenuous advocates intended it to provide only an approximate framework from which flutists still had to deviate in order to avoid out-of-tuneness.[12] After another generation, however, some melody instrumentalists and singers had lost sight of this distinction. By 1890, R. S. Rockstro had come to see the keyboard itself as providing universally correct pitches for all the notes, and equal temperament as conferring 'the blessings of the truly philosophical temperament' in place of the 'appalling multitude of notes' in the just scale.[13] In listing the most important points of excellence in flute-playing, Rockstro specified 'Perfect intonation, according to equal temperament' as the third.[14]

motion to permit the 'glide', in which two adjacent notes were joined by a glissando, still much in fashion in England but abhorred by Tromlitz nearly two decades earlier as a 'monstrosity' unless used rarely.[13] Johann Nepomuk Capeller proposed another innovation to allow the pitch of the entire flute to be raised and lowered. His invention, with a movable mouth-hole and tuning slides between each joint, included additional keys to improve certain trills. The royal Saxon instrument-maker Heinrich Grenser, who had disparaged Tromlitz's keyed flutes in the *AmZ* in 1800, swiftly replied to the report of Capeller's flute that Carl Maria von Weber had published, insisting that the keyed flute as he built it was perfectly satisfactory and needed no tinkering. Capeller retorted that Grenser had not even seen the flute, nor yet read a full description of it.[14]

In 1813 the *AmZ*'s correspondent in Vienna reported that the flutist Georg Bayr had announced a new instrument with an extended lower range that, like Orazi's of 1797, could play the violin's lowest notes, B, B♭, A, A♭, and G, without detriment to ease of response or intonation of high A, B♭, and B.[15] Stephan Koch Senior (1772–1828) patented and manufactured similar instruments, apparently using a design by an inventor named Langer.[16] These typically Viennese flutes by Koch, Johann Joseph Ziegler (1795–1858), and their successors were widely used and imitated in central Europe throughout the nineteenth century. In the Frankfurt area makers such as Philip Otto Euler (1760–1834) copied Koch's designs, and in the Lombard and Venetian regions of northern Italy the type was favoured by Giuseppe Rabboni (1800–56), first flutist of the La Scala orchestra and the Milan conservatory's first professor of flute (1830).[17] An edition of Drouët's *Méthode* published in Antwerp in 1827 contained a page of music for flutes descending to B and G, and in 1834 Laurent built a crystal flute in five sections with a range to low G, the weight of which must have made it difficult to play for more than a short time.

Bayr's other claim to fame was the ability to play several notes at once, which aroused such skepticism that he took the trouble to publish a multiphonics manual.[18] But he and the Viennese flute are important for their connections with much of the most innovative music of the early nineteenth century, including that of Beethoven, whose symphonies place greater demands on the flutists' control in the highest register than those of Haydn and Mozart.

Viennese-type flutes have been traced in early performances of many works by Beethoven, Schubert, Weber, Kuhlau, and others. According to Amy Sue Hamilton (1984), who has made a thorough study of nineteenth-century symphonic flute parts and the instruments that played them, no permanent first-rate orchestra existed in Vienna until the 1840s, and some early performances of Beethoven's works were unsatisfactory or too difficult for the wind players engaged.[19] Though the theatre orchestras held few if any rehearsals of instrumental music, they were the most cohesive and permanent ensembles available and gave regular employment to professional wind players. The premiere of Beethoven's First Symphony took place in 1800 at the Hofburgtheater, where the flutist Karl Keller (1784–1855) usually played.[20] Its flute part remains almost entirely within the compass G1–G3, avoiding notes above A3. The Theater an der Wien orchestra premiered Beethoven's *Fidelio*, Fifth and Sixth Symphonies, and several piano concertos. Bayr played in the orchestra in 1800–10 when not touring, and on settling in Vienna in 1810 he became a 'fairly permanent' member.[21] The Sixth Symphony, the 'Pastoral' (1808), contains effective imitative passages for clarinet (cuckoo) and oboe (quail), with the flute making an appearance as the nightingale. The piccolo, which appears in the Storm section, is also used in the Fifth and Ninth Symphonies, the *Egmont* overture, and elsewhere. Flute parts in E♭ and D♭ in the *Eroica* (1803) and the Fourth Symphony (1806) indicate that Beethoven did not consider it necessary to avoid keys considered difficult for the flute. In the *Eroica's* fourth movement, which contains a brilliant solo in D major, the flute is asked to play *piano* up to A3, and *pianissimo* up to G. The flute part of the Eighth Symphony (1812) occasionally reaches B♭3, but in one passage B3s are repeatedly dropped an octave.[22] From 1809 to 1817 Raphael Dressler was first flute of the Kärntnertor Theatre orchestra, before eventually settling in England for fourteen years where he was bandmaster for the tenth Hussars from 1826 to 1834. His post was filled by Johann Sedlatzek (*b* 1789), who also later moved to England and continued to play his Viennese flute there.[23] The Kärntnertor orchestra premiered the Ninth Symphony in 1824, with Sedlatzek playing a flute with a range to low G.[24] In the last movement an unusual low-register passage for doubled flutes scored them with single clarinet, bassoon, and trombone, three-part violas, and a *piano* entrance by the choir.[25]

Another effective low-register passage for flutes by Viennese makers or their Saxon imitators occurred in Weber's *Der Freischütz* (Berlin, 1821, where August Schröck (1779–1854) and Heinrich Soussmann (1796–1848) premiered it),[26] using sustained chords in the low register to create an eerie mood in the Wolf's Glen scene.[27] Weber used flutes to evoke a fairy effect in *Oberon*, scoring many prominent passages and melodies, paired with voice, clarinet, and cello.

Early domestic performances of many of Schubert's works involved Viennese flutes and flutists. At private house performances of the Fifth and Sixth Symphonies in 1818, Michael Zwerger, usually a horn player, was engaged to play the flute. Later Ferdinand Bogner began to be hired to play private concerts of Schubert's works; the variations on *Trockne Blumen* (1824) were written for Bogner, professor of flute at the Vienna conservatory.[28] Those of Schubert's orchestral works that received full-scale public performance were first heard in Leipzig, where the Gewandhaus orchestra premiered many symphonic works during Grenser's tenure, including the Great C major Symphony (1825), which Mendelssohn directed in 1839. As in Beethoven's works, the extreme upper register, above A3, is generally avoided.[29] Schubert's Fourth Symphony (1816), however, which the orchestra premiered in 1849,[30] does not avoid B♭3, and a diminuendo to *ppp* at the end of its second movement includes B♭3 and ends on A♭3 on top of a woodwind chord. The Eighth Symphony (1822), performed in 1865 when Wilhelm Haake (1804–75) was first flutist, uses the flute's middle and low registers more prominently and integrates the instrument more into the wind texture: when the flute is scored in the upper register it is given support from other woodwind instruments so that it seems less exposed.[31] Robert Schumann exploited the flute's low register in his Second Symphony (1845–6), premiered in Leipzig in 1846.[32]

Though many of Friedrich Kuhlau's works used the entire range of the Viennese flute, he dedicated some pieces to players of other types of instrument, such as his Trio for three flutes op. 90 (1826) for Benoît-Tranquille Berbiguier (1782–1838), his six solo Divertimenti op. 68 for P. N. Petersen (1761–1830), and his three Duets op. 39 (1821/2) for Fürstenau.[33] Kuhlau, who had fled to Copenhagen when Napoleon invaded his home city of Hamburg in 1810, met Beethoven on a visit to Vienna in 1816–17. Because he was a prolific composer for the flute, it is often alleged Kuhlau played the instrument: in reality he did not, but produced many excellent flute compositions including quartets for flutes to supplement his income as a pianist. His understanding of how to write for the instrument is explained by the fact that a flutist in the Royal Orchestra advised him.[34]

Music for small mixed ensembles by composers from Berlin, Leipzig, and Paris as well as Vienna in the 1780s and following decades often included a flute: Spohr's *Quintet, Septet,* and *Nonet,* Friedrich Kalkbrenner's *Quintet* op. 81, Hummel's *Grand Military Septet* op. 114, and Reicha's quintets provide some examples. Carl Czerny's *Fantasia concertante* op. 256 for piano, flute, and cello (early 1830s) freely modulates through keys such as D♭, G, E♭, E major and C minor, testing the player's control in high and low registers. Quartets for Viennese and French flutes by Berbiguier, Kummer, Gabrielsky, Kuhlau and others show that the instrument was favoured in the private salons and parlours of middle-class houses as well as in the concert hall.

The Viennese flute also exerted an influence on instrument-makers in other German-speaking lands. When Anton Bernhard Fürstenau, the most influential German player and teacher of the period, wrote his *Flöten-Schule* (1826), he favoured flutes by Koch of Vienna and by Wilhelm Liebel (1793–1871) of Dresden. Fürstenau, a later occupant of Buffardin's chair at Dresden, used a Koch flute to perform Carl Maria von Weber's *Adagio* from his Trio in G minor op. 63 for flute, cello and pianoforte (1819) with the composer and the cellist Juste Jean Frederic Dotzauer.[35] Later, however, his preference altered: by the time of his *Die Kunst des Flötenspiels* (Art of Flute-playing, 1844) he played a boxwood Liebel flute, and withdrew his endorsement of Viennese instruments because he found their tone too thin. He thought French instruments too narrow in the bore, making them weak in the low register, though easy at the top, and found them out of tune except in the keys of D and G. He also criticized the intonation of English flutes, especially in sharp keys, but did note that London players preferred the flat tonalities.

Alongside his preference for Liebel's flutes, Fürstenau's two method books give precious insights into the ideals and playing techniques of an influential German flutist of the early nineteenth century. In his first tutor, one of the earliest to discuss breathing, he instructed the student not to inhale too deeply, but by 1844 he prescribed filling the lungs as much as possible, and practising scales with the *messa di voce* and piano accompaniment. Contrary to Quantz and Tromlitz, he directed the flute to be assembled with the mouth-hole turned out, claiming that otherwise it produced a feeble sound and poor intonation. He rejected the double tongue as monotonous (quite the opposite criticism to the French, who held that it was not sufficiently even), though his father Caspar Fürstenau had used the technique. The largest section of the work, however, was devoted to fingering, which Fürstenau described as the second most important feature of flute-playing after tone. His method of extending the flute's expressive range was to provide a choice of fingerings for each note. Nine alternatives are given for C; ten for C♯; 124 cases in all, followed by

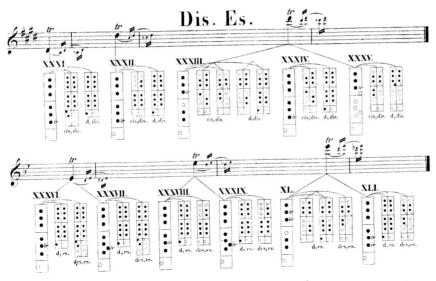

39. Eleven fingering patterns for combinations of notes based on D♯/E♭, in three octaves, from Anton Bernhard Fürstenau's *Die Kunst des Flötenspiels* (1844), 56. Each fingering is identified by number: besides the sixty-one shown in this table, eleven further fingerings are referred to in the remarks that fill the remainder of the page.

extensive examples for use in various combinations of notes (ill. 39). Under the heading of ornaments appear: the *Bebung*, a vibrato made with either the lungs or the chin and used at moments of high emotion; a version of the *flattement*, or finger vibrato, also used on very high, long, dramatic notes; and the glide, which can be used over quite large intervals and combined with trills for the most brilliant violinistic effect.

Though his instrument and sound were quite different, some of the same effects appeared in the music of Charles Nicholson (chapter 7), whose style of playing remained the main influence on amateur flutists in London until his death in 1837, and afterwards when his place as the city's leading player was taken by the Spanish flutist and clarinettist José Maria del Carmen Ribas (1796–1861).[36] Commentators often mentioned Nicholson's use of the instrument's entire range, his abundant 'slurs', or glides, and other ornaments and embellishment, though these aspects of his highly individual style frequently attracted the charge of poor taste, or 'ear-tickling'. But a more expansive view of the period's flute-playing was given in Thomas Lindsay's *Elements* (1828), an informed and literate discussion in the tradition of Heron and Gunn. Far from promoting a single form of that controversial technique, double tonguing, Lindsay presented a critical study of all the methods so far advocated, quoting from Berbiguier, Drouët, Devienne, Hugot and Wunderlich, Gunn, Nicholson and Monzani. He also gave the most complete exposition hitherto of 'augmented fingerings' for leading notes and when they were to be used.

Another common criticism of Nicholson was his limited repertoire. William Annand complained in 1843 that good flute compositions had been crowded out by the lower-quality music Nicholson and others had encouraged:

I particularly allude to the bagatelles called Flutonicons, Scrap-books, Magazines, Bees, Pocket Companions, &c. I do not wish to injure any one; but writing for a class of society which supports me, in justice to its members and myself, I must deprecate the purchase of rubbish; it is in the first place a sad waste of money which the amateur afterwards repents of; its performance is more serious, as it is a shocking waste of time and breath also.[37]

Nevertheless, Nicholson's music did not entirely exclude other styles from the concert room: London audiences could hear professional chamber music of high quality by Viennese and other continental composers, as at the Philharmonic Society concert in April 1817 when Spohr's *Nonet* op. 31 received its London premiere with the flutist Ireland performing.[38]

By about 1820 Paris and Vienna stood out as exceptions to the generalization that the whole of Europe had accepted some kind of flute with eight or nine keys, and C1 as the lowest note: most of the most attractive and enduring flute music from about 1800 to 1890 was written for one of the commonest types: English, German, Parisian, or Viennese. Yet however satisfied players may have felt with the particular flute model each favoured, efforts to devise mechanical and even scientific improvements in the instrument gathered momentum during the 1820s, after the Napoleonic Wars.

This period's new interest in the flute's acoustics grew from seeds planted during the Enlightenment. Johann Heinrich Lambert, a member of Frederick the Great's circle of rationalist scholars, made the first attempts to formulate scientific laws of tube acoustics and to apply them to the flute in 1777.[39] Lambert's paper used minute observation and mathematics to deduce natural laws from practical experiment, the technique that had proved so successful in astronomy and physics. He gave a critical survey of previous work on acoustics by Euler (1725) and Bernoulli (1762), and tried to quantify the behaviour of his own flute, which produced a pitch of A=415.25, in contrast with Bernoulli's standard of A=392. His paper reported on basic experiments and calculations with tubes, studied the effects of the location of the cork stopper, and gave precise details of lip placement (half the embouchure hole should be covered) so as to arrive at a mathematical constant for the end correction, or acoustic resistance, of the embouchure hole. Using his own flute as an example, he discussed the relationship of tonehole size to bore diameter, and the effect of undercutting the toneholes.

Another learned writer focused less narrowly on the quantitative aspects of the flute and flute-playing than on what he might have called its 'natural philosophy'. An 'Essay on the acoustics of the German flute: A contribution to a philosophical theory of flute-playing' appeared in 1806 from the pen of Johann Heinrich Liebeskind, a senior Bavarian judge and the son of Quantz's pupil G. G. Liebeskind. The essay indicates how aware flutists, at least in Germany, had become of differing ideas about the instrument and its playing styles in various countries.[40] Liebeskind followed up with a 'Philosophical-practical essay on the nature and tone-play of the German flute' in 1807–8 and 1810.[41]

If Liebeskind's essays were somewhat abstract, another by Gottfried Weber in 1816–17 devoted itself entirely to the practical acoustics of wind instruments, not just woodwinds.[42] Weber's article did not cite earlier work or focus narrowly on current instrument designs, but attempted to work from first principles. He asserted that end correction caused small toneholes to make instruments behave like stopped tubes, not open ones, and suggested that the experimental positions of toneholes could be found only when the holes were given a diameter as large as that of the tube itself, so that end correction was reduced to zero. Weber noted the problem with all the woodwinds that they required more toneholes than the player had fingers, and suggested solving this by making them work like the trombone, avoiding use of the first harmonic, so that a chromatic scale could be played with only six holes.

In 1822 P. N. Petersen devised a lever for the left hand to open a hole that could raise and lower the pitch by an eighth of a tone while making a *crescendo* or *decrescendo*. Two years later, in 1824, Pottgiesser followed up his largely ignored essay of 1803 to propose another radically new design for the flute.[43] Having recently taken up the instrument again after a lapse of twenty years, he noted that it had acquired more keys, was more elegantly made, had a greater compass and more power in the low register, but that it had made little progress towards the equality of intonation (*gleiche Intonation*) he sought. He found that certain notes remained unsatisfactory in tone, and that keys to improve others were not usable in all combinations of notes. He gave details of a new flute with eight equal-sized toneholes and six keys, and proposed several innovative key mechanisms including ring-keys and crescent touchpieces (ill. 38).

Pottgiesser deposited a specimen of his proposed flute at the *AmZ*'s office in Leipzig, enabling Karl Grenser, first flute of the Gewandhaus orchestra, to evaluate it and write a report for the magazine in June 1824. Grenser considered Pottgiesser's criticisms of the keyed flute to be without merit, and countered with a list of flute-makers in many parts of Europe who could supply good flutes: Grenser & Wiesner in Dresden, Griesling & Schlott in Berlin, Bauer in Prague, Koch in Vienna, Boehm in Munich, Felchlin in Berne, Sax in Brussels, Holtzapffel in Paris, Metzler in London, Maybrick in Liverpool, and Skousboe in Copenhagen. Grenser explained the techniques he used on his own H. Grenser flute to obviate some of the problems Pottgiesser mentioned: for instance, he overcame a slight inherent weakness in the tone of the first- and second-octave E by opening the D$^\sharp$/E$\flat$ key and blowing the note flatter. (For Grenser's ideas on the most practical tuning, see p. 152).

The flute's bore remained a matter for discussion in the 1820s as well as its mechanism, as the report of Drouët's playing quoted on p. 138 and Fürstenau's comments on Koch and Liebel flutes remind us. In 1823, the London woodwind maker William Bainbridge provided another view on the subject, highlighting the difference between orchestral and solo flutes:

> There are various opinions with regard to the width in the bore of German flutes. I lately had an opportunity of hearing a very fine player (a professor and teacher) perform on a wide one, which he had been accustomed to: the tone was certainly rich and full. His opinion was, that the wide-bored flute was more calculated for a large orchestra; but that the narrower was much sweeter in a room, and required considerably less exertion to play on it. I observed, when in Paris, that flutes with a narrow bore were preferred by good players.[44]

The orchestral flutist Karl Grenser, on the other hand, criticized the bore of English flutes as unduly large in 1828, tracing the deficient response and clarity of their upper register to this cause.[45] He felt that though a wide bore produced a large sound, this was not easily altered, and so such a flute was not suited to 'artistic' playing, a style that placed great emphasis on the quality of tonal flexibility (*Modulationsfähigkeit*) that remained the most important criterion for German flute-playing throughout the nineteenth century. Grenser thought English taste disfigured by tasteless stylistic mannerisms and superficial music. He particularly disliked Nicholson's portamento and finger vibrato, and felt his loud sound pushed the flute beyond its limits. Grenser claimed he could produce a full tone on his small-holed eight-keyed flute, and that holes any larger hampered the alteration of tone colour he so valued.

If Nicholson, whose *piano* playing in his solos was noted as well as his *forte*, reserved the 'utmost delicacy' for his orchestral work, Grenser's emphasis on tonal flexibility probably owed much to the small size of the Gewandhaus orchestra of his day. Amy Sue Hamilton summarizes the relative size of wind and string sections in early nineteenth-century orchestras, noting that Nicholson's Philharmonic orchestra (1836) employed 52 players in the string section alone, while Grenser's Gewandhaus orchestra (1832) had only 35 players in total, the same forces as in 1800. Hamilton suggests that '[t]hese numbers alone could well be a deciding factor in explaining the difference between Carl Grenser's concept of flute tone and the ideas of Charles Nicholson'.[46]

France remained in political turmoil during the decades after the Revolution, and its flutists neither participated in the published discussions about mechanical and scientific developments in flute-making, nor considered imitating instruments or styles cultivated by the victors of Waterloo. Though the Conservatoire's official flute had only four keys, French professionals of the 1820s seem to have played instruments that had additional keys for C2 and long F, though rarely if ever a C-foot until the following decade.[47] Giannini's account (1993) indicates that the attention of leading French makers and players was concentrated less on devising improvements in the flute than on intrigues and business rivalries, using official sanction by institutions such as the Conservatoire and the Opéra to exclude competition. Joseph Guillou (1787–1853), for instance, who used a flute by Godfroy, refused to teach pupils who played instruments by Bellisent (*fl* 1819–42), according to a complaint that maker made to the Conservatoire's administration in 1825. Guillou's response indicates both that he played a six-keyed flute and that he had received a 'professor's' discount of 50 francs on its price of 300 francs in 1821.[48] A change in standard pitch at the Opéra in 1825 prompted that institution to supply its players with new flutes and piccolos purchased from Godfroy.

The spirit of mechanical innovation that had found expression in the *AmZ* came to Paris in 1826 when Captain James Carel Gerhard Gordon (1791–1838), a pupil of Tulou's who had lived in the city as an officer in Charles X's Swiss Guard since 1814, first designed a flute based on an open-key system in collaboration with Auguste Buffet *jeune* (1789–p1885), instrument-maker to his regiment. Precise details of this

40. The mid-nineteenth-century controversy over different types of flute in England attracted some degree of popular notoriety, as this print by J. W. Childe illustrates. The caption reads: Mr Hill (the admired American Comedian) as 'Major Wheeler' in the Farce of 'New Notions'. 'I once made an invention on a flute,–you could blow as many tunes as you liked *intew* it,–wax up the holes, & let 'em out when you wanted 'em.'

instrument are lacking, but it appears to have made use of crescent touchpieces more advanced than Pottgiesser's that could transmit key motion to holes beyond the reach of the fingers, allowing a hole beneath the finger as well as another key some distance away to be opened or closed at the same time.

The mention of Gordon and his open-key flute brings us to the events detailed in chapter 9 that led to the development of Theobald Boehm's conical-bored ring-key flute of 1832, a major revision of the instrument's acoustics and mechanism. Boehm's flute located toneholes of the largest practical size in their ideal acoustical positions, many of which lay beyond the reach of the fingers, employing an open-key system operated by interlinked parallel rod-axles to close holes too large for the unaided finger. After developing an early prototype in the workshops of Gerock & Wolf in London in 1831, Boehm modified its fingering and mechanism further in 1832 and began to manufacture the new flute in his own workshop in Munich. The ring-key flute began to win acceptance when its inventor presented it to the French Academy of Sciences at a meeting in May 1837, and appointed Paul Hippolyte Camus his agent to promote it in Paris. In the same year two French workshops, headed by Buffet and by Godfroy and Lot, developed versions of the ring-key flute modified to make its construction more robust and its tone and fingering more like those of the current French flutes.

Only a few French players took up the ring-key flute in the 1830s, but they were among the country's most prominent. Camus and Louis Dorus championed the instrument and wrote tutors for it (1838), while Victor Coche made early attempts to win official recognition for the flute and credit for himself. In 1839 Dorus played Berlioz's *Roméo et Juliette* on a ring-key Boehm-system flute by Godfroy and Lot,[49] and the ring-key flute was introduced at the Brussels Conservatoire by directive in 1842. Jean François Joseph Lahou (*b* 1798), the institution's founding professor of flute and himself a graduate of the Paris Conservatoire, resigned rather than teach the new instrument, and his pupil Jules Antoine Demeurs (1814–47) succeeded him after a period of private study under Dorus in Paris.[50]

Despite the enthusiasm these few influential advocates showed for the ring-key flute in Paris and Brussels, the leading flutists in Europe and America who had tried Boehm's invention felt that it had lost as much as it had gained. According to Fürstenau, writing in 1838, the notes of Boehm's flute were beautifully even, the arpeggios were well in tune, and the tone spoke easily and with uncommon strength. But that very evenness, he concluded, destroyed the flute's character. Fürstenau advocated a middle path between an excessively strong tone and one that was too weak, one 'that can be used in all nuances, and still conveys the characteristic charm of the flute, the sweet longing, the dying fall, the yearning and loveliness that speaks from its sounds, as well as a full, powerful, masculine sound'.[51] Like most accomplished players, he preferred his own familiar instrument:

> Our flutes at present have certainly reached a high level of perfection and the very covered tones that are shunned on Mr Boehm's flute give our present one uncommon charm and opportunity for expression and the rousing of different emotions. ...'[52]

The most influential French flutist felt the same way about the flute's tone. Jean-Louis Tulou, professor at the Paris Conservatoire from 1826 to 1856, prized the flute's 'touching and sensitive' sound (*le son pathétique et sentimental*):

> The flute requires a mellow voice when playing piano, a vibrant and sonorous tone when playing forte. That of Gordon [i.e. Boehm] on the other hand had a thin tone lacking in depth which very much resembled that of an oboe.[53]

Tulou's opposition to the ring-key flute, particularly in the face of an attempt by his teaching assistant, Victor Coche, to institute a class in it at the Conservatoire, was perhaps all the stronger owing to his interests as a flute manufacturer (chapter 11). He set up in business in 1828 and began to supply instruments to the Conservatoire in 1831, the year in which he entered a partnership with Jacques Nonon that lasted until 1853, when Giannini suggests that Nonon became interested in making conical Boehm flutes.

Tulou was keen to develop an improved flute himself, if not before the ring-key flute's advent in 1837 then certainly afterwards. His 'perfected flute' (*flûte perfectionnée*), devised during the 1840s, used rod-axles and needle springs like those of the Boehm mechanism, but retained the acoustical proportions, and thus the character, of the ordinary French flute.[54] 'I am concerned above all', he wrote, 'to scrupulously conserve the natural tone of the flute, as well as the simplicity of its fingering.'[55] His method, first published in 1835, was used at the Conservatoire from about 1845, after which many more editions appeared. By this time, he wrote, nearly all players had tried the Boehm flute and returned to their own instruments, preferring, as he put it, 'charm' to 'astonishment'. The tutor instructed the headjoint to be turned in so that its outside edge lined up with the centre of the fingerholes, and the lower lip covered a quarter or more of the embouchure, though not as much as half or three-quarters, which, he wrote, made the sound uneven, feeble in the low register, and out of tune. He increased Hugot and Wunderlich's three classes of articulation to four, and added several pages of special fingerings for super-sharpened leading notes, as well as charts and exercises illustrating simplified fingerings for difficult passages.

Visits to London by Camus, Dorus, and others after 1837 quickly stimulated an interest in the ring-key flute there. In *c*1839 Cornelius Ward and William Card made premature attempts to build the flute, followed more successfully in 1842–3 by Rudall & Rose in collaboration with Boehm's former workshop partner, Greve. John Clinton (1810–64), Professor of Flute at the Royal Academy of Music, became the first prominent English flutist to take up the ring-key flute in 1841, amid a controversy further detailed in chapter 9. After early manufacturing efforts in New York by James D. Larrabee (*d c*1847) and W. J. Davis (*fl* 1839–43), and after the leading New York player Philip Ernst had adopted the ring-key flute, Alfred G. Badger (1815–92) became the first American maker to produce the instrument successfully in 1845. Other French makers also produced versions of the ring-key flute, including Laurent, who in 1844 made a green fluted crystal example (DCM 11).

The ring-key flute made almost no headway in Germany except among Boehm's pupils, including Moritz Fürstenau, Karl Krüger, and Hans Haindl, perhaps in part because the livelihood of German professional flutists of the 1830s and 40s already relied on orchestral work, in contrast to England and America where the more usual solo performance made the new flute's brilliance and evenness more desirable.[56] Though the first Boehm flutes appeared alongside older models in orchestras in Berlin and Vienna in the 1870s (chapter 10), German orchestral playing successfully preserved its traditional character to the almost total exclusion of the Boehm flute, considered excessively brilliant and monotonous, until the era of recording.

* patented or privileged invention[1]
† design or feature known to have reached commercial production at or about the date noted

1800	J. G. Tromlitz	one-keyed chromatic flute
1802	William Close	transposing diatonic flute
1803	H. W. T. Pottgiesser	one-keyed chromatic flute
1806	Claude Laurent*†	crystal flutes, keys on posts[2]
	J. D. Holtzapffel*†	one-keyed chromatic flute[3]
1807	Tebaldo Monzani*	rings and caps to preserve the tubes and keys[4]
1808	W. H. Potter*	glide keys
	Charles Townley*	telescoping bore, mouthpiece, extra key
	Rev. Frederick Nolan*	ring-key
1810	Thomas Scott*	'additional notes produced without the use of keys'[5]
	Malcolm MacGregor*	improved keys for bass flutes[6]
	George Miller*	cylindrical brass fife and flute
1811	J. N. Capeller	movable mouthpiece, various trill keys
1812	Monzani*†	cork-lapped tenons, metal tenons, one-piece lower body, 'nob' on either side of the embouchure hole
1813	Georg Bayr	Viennese flute to low G[7]
1814	James Wood*	telescopic metal tenons
1815	Capeller	a flute playable with one hand[8]
1820	Stephan Koch Senior*†	Viennese flute to low G
c1820	Charles Nicholson Senior († by others)	large-holed flute, widely imitated
1822	P. N. Petersen	mechanism to adjust pitch for dynamic changes[9]
1824	Pottgiesser	ring- and crescent-key flute with (mostly) equal-sized toneholes
1826	J. C. G. Gordon/A. Buffet	open-key flute, exact nature unknown
1828	G. Weber	left thumb key for C2 (first built by Tromlitz, 1785)
c1830	Boehm and Greve†	rod-axles
1831	Boehm († by Gerock & Wolf)	proto-ring-key flute
1832	Boehm†	ring-key flute, Boehm system
	Rudall & Rose*	tuning-slide and cork-screw mechanism[10]
c1834	Gordon	'Diatonic' flute (illus. in his *Tablature*)

The quest for a one-keyed chromatic flute continued to occupy inventive minds in England, where in 1841 Abel Siccama invented one but failed to interest Rudall & Rose in manufacturing it. Over the next few years a shadowy figure named Dr Burghley developed various designs based on a keyless system (several specimens in DCM). In 1845 Siccama patented his less radical 'Diatonic' flute, which preserved the old fingering while 'closing the A natural and the lower E note each with a key, by which those holes may be enlarged to correspond with the other holes', as Boehm's 1831 Gerock & Wolf flute had done.[57] The Siccama flute was subsequently manufactured by Rudall Carte, Mahillon, Boosey & Co., and others, and taken up by prominent soloists Joseph Richardson (1814–62) and Robert Sydney Pratten (1824–68).[58]

Boehm's metal cylinder flute of 1847 (chapter 9) carried forward the ideas he had introduced in 1832, but the metal flute's altered tone aroused even more deep-seated resistance than that of the ring-key flute. Even after the cylinder flute appeared some artists remained faithful to the conical bore: Camille Saint-Saëns's *Romance* op.7 (1871) and Carl Reinecke's *Undine* (1883) were dedicated to A. de Vroye (1835–90), a student

1837	Godfroy and Lot†	ring-key flute after Boehm 1832
1838	Buffet*†	another ring-key flute after Boehm 1832, with Coche's D#2 trill key, needle springs, and clutches probably developed in 1837
c1838	Gordon	another flute (illus. in Coche *Examen critique* per Mme Gordon)
1839	Louis Dorus († by Godfroy & Lot, Buffet, then many others)	open/closed G# key for Boehm 1832 flute
	Cornelius Ward†	ring-key flute after Boehm 1832[11]
c1839	William Card (1788–1861)†	ring-key flute after Boehm 1832[12]
c1840	J.-L. Tulou/J. Nonon†	*flûte perfectionnée*, official flute of Paris Conservatoire
1840	Benedikt Pentenrieder (1809–49)*†	crescent- and ring-key flute[13]
1841	Abel Siccama	one-keyed chromatic flute[14]
1842	Siccama	an eight-keyed flute
	Ward*†	seven kinds of patent flute; needle springs, 'terminator'
	Siccama (*1845) †	'Diatonic' flute with old-system fingering, key-cups for A and E
1842–3	Rudall & Rose†	ring-key flute after Boehm 1832, under Greve's direction
1844	James D. Larrabee†	ring-key flute after Boehm 1832
1845	W. J. Monzani/Henry Potter†	split-key 'chromatic' flute
c1845	Dr Burghley	various keyless flutes
1847	Boehm*†	cylinder flute, Boehm system
1848	John Clinton*†	'Equisonant' flute combining Boehm-/old-system fingering
1849	Giulio Briccialdi († by Rudall & Rose, Pask, Egidio Forni)	various designs with cylindrical and conical bores, old fingering[15]
	Briccialdi († by Rudall & Rose, then many others)	'Briccialdi' B♭ lever
1850	Richard Carte*†	revisions in fingering system, including 'open D': all fingers off now gives D, not C#; otherwise old-system or Boehm-system fingerings can be used
1851	Rudall, Rose, Carte & Co.†	Carte's 1851 system: cylinder flute with fingering system of 1850
1852	R. S. Rockstro	conical, open-G# Boehm-system flute with Coche's D#2 trill key
	R. S. Pratten†	the first of several different 'Perfected' flutes

of Coche, who continued to play one.[59] The cylinder flute became the official instrument at the Paris Conservatoire when Dorus succeeded Tulou as professor of flute in 1860 (chapter 11).

The composer Hector Berlioz (1803–69), an accomplished flutist himself, noted the special qualities the (old) flute could bring to an orchestra in his instrumentation treatise of 1844:

> If one wishes for example to confer the expression of despair upon a sad melody at the same time as meekness and resignation, the weak middle register of the flute, particularly in C# minor and D minor, will surely give the right tint. Listening to the pantomime-like melodic passage that comes in the Elysium scene in [Gluck's] *Orpheus*, one is immediately convinced that only a flute could be suited to this melody. Even the tenderest tones of the clarinet could not be moderated to the weak, softened, veiled sound of the F in the middle register and the B♭ in the first octave, which give the flute in this key (D minor) where they frequently occur such

an expression of sadness. Furthermore Gluck's melody is invented in such a way that the flute can follow every unsettled impulse of this eternal pain that still carries the traces of mortal suffering.

Despite this appreciation for the old flute's character, Berlioz became the first French composer to promote the Boehm flute after serving on the jury that examined the metal cylinder flute of 1847 at the Great Exhibition (London, 1851). In France, where professors and graduates of the Conservatoire routinely filled the most important orchestral posts, the official acceptance of the cylinder flute at the institute in 1860 made it certain to be used in the most prestigious ensembles after that date. Yet a treatise on the history of instrumentation by H. Lavoix (Paris, 1878) still promoted the old flute.[60]

While Germany remained content with the keyed flute and France was satisfied with the cylinder flute of 1847 as modified by Parisian makers to suit their taste, the spirit of inventiveness remained alive in England after 1850 as makers and players created hybrids of the two types, mainly with a view to preserving the old flute's fingering rather than its tone.

John Clinton, though he had hoped to manufacture the 1847 flute in England under licence from Boehm, found he disliked the metal tube and cylindrical bore, and judged the new mechanism too complicated. By about 1850 he had come to view the altered fingering of the Boehm flutes as an insurmountable obstacle to universal acceptance:

> An object to be sought for in every instrument, is one established system of fingering; but so long as these cross purposes [different systems in use by different professors] are carried out, so long must we expect a want of harmony and unity among those who have made the study of this instrument their profession, and consequently a disinclination amongst amateurs to learn it.[61]

In support of his contention, Clinton quoted Boehm's remark that '[t]he first model I made at my friend Mr Wolf's, in 1831, proves that I wanted to preserve as many notes in the old way of fingering as seemed feasible.'[62] In his *Treatise upon the Mechanism and General Principles of the Flute* of 1852 Clinton advocated a new flute, the result of his own experiments, patented in 1848, and manufactured by Henry Potter (1848–54). He concluded that 'no other system than the shut-keyed can ever ultimately succeed, while any attempt to improve the open-keyed, must end in disappointment and failure'.[63] At the Great Exhibition of 1851 in London (the same event at which Boehm's cylinder flute won the Council Medal for 'important scientific improvements'), his instrument earned praise for its fingering, tone, and cheapness, 'the mechanism being so simple, that its price does not exceed that of the old 8-keyed flute'. Three years later Clinton described his 'Equisonant Flute', now manufactured by the firm of Clinton and Co., as 'a Flute, which, possessing all the essential qualities of tone and tune, has not departed from the established fingering'.

Clinton insisted that wood was preferable to metal, even in flutes made for use by the British army in India:

> To meet the wishes of those who prefer a metal flute, we manufacture such to order; but it would lead to error to suppose that we approve of such material – the tone which a metal flute yields being uncertain, harsh, and hollow in quality, and the *pitch* constantly and *suddenly* changing to the extent of nearly a semitone; while from wood we can ensure vocality, richness, softness, or fullness, at pleasure, and a reedy pliability, such as cannot be elicited from any other material.[64]

In 1862, despite these objections, he patented a silver cylindrical flute which won the exhibition medal for 'flutes on a modification and improvement of the system of Boehm' at the World Exhibition in London of the same year.

Robert Sydney Pratten, a noted performer on the Siccama flute, likewise applied the eight-keyed fingering to the cylinder bore. In 1852 he introduced the first of several 'Perfected' flutes, initially with a cylindrical bore and later with Rockstro's scale and conical bore, all with key cups to cover large toneholes and old-system fingering (the instruments today's Irish traditional flutists call 'Pratten's Perfected' are ordinary open-holed eight-keyed flutes, a type also marketed under Pratten's name). Boosey & Co. began to build some models in 1856.

Richard Carte (1808–91) joined the London firm of Rudall & Rose in 1852, and devised a succession of modified Boehm-system cylinder flutes: the 'Council & Prize model' (1851/2), the 'Boehm's Parabola, Carte's Mechanism' of 1862, and finally 'Carte's 1867' model, which became the second most widely used flute in England and the British Empire until well after the Second World War. It was made in both wood and metal, with open G♯ and open D, and could be played with either old-system or Boehm-system fingerings. Adam Carse, who wrote at a time when some British flutists still played Carte's 1867 flute, called it the 'only important and lasting modification of Boehm's flute'.[65]

Chapter 9

The Boehm flute

We can fix no distinct moment of origin for the flutes we have considered in previous chapters – medieval flutes, various kinds for military and consort use, the one-keyed instrument, and flutes with several keys – despite recent efforts to assign credit for some of these types to selected individuals. In contrast, the modern flute's invention can be traced to one man, since few more brilliant or controversial innovations in the design of any musical instrument can ever have been made than those Theobald Boehm devised for the flute in 1832 and 1847. Yet for mechanical, musical, and economic reasons the construction of Boehm-system flutes has been changing ever since, so that the instruments of today differ in significant ways not only from those Boehm and his contemporaries built and played, but even from those made only a generation ago. Therefore we should investigate in some detail the genesis of Boehm's designs, along with those changes that came as his flutes were gradually adopted and adapted by others.[1]

A man of exceptionally industrious nature, Theobald Boehm exemplified the character of his times in which ingenuity and industrial process magnified or even supplanted human skill and strength in many areas of life. The son of a Munich goldsmith, he acquired his manual dexterity in his youth, developing his knowledge of mechanics as a young man by studying the building of musical boxes in Switzerland. After beginning in his childhood to teach himself to play a one-keyed flute by Proser (London, *fl c*1777–95; now DCM 152), Boehm built himself a copy of a four-keyed instrument by August Grenser in 1810, before taking his first lessons with Johann Nepomuk Capeller, flutist of the Bavarian court orchestra. His teacher, who was already interested in devising improvements in the flute, designed a new model for which, according to Boehm's biographer, it was the young pupil who devised the mechanism.

After completing his studies with Capeller Boehm gained a place in the orchestra of the Isartor Theatre in Munich, a post from which he advanced in 1818, at the age of 24, to a royal court appointment. At this stage, the success of a concert tour (chapter 7) encouraged him to give up his goldsmith's business so as to support himself as a musician instead. His interest in instrument-making evidently continued, as he seems to have collaborated with one of the two Munich instrument-makers named Schöffl on the design and manufacture of some instruments in this period.[2] Though at the time Boehm himself held no legal right to conduct business as an instrument-builder, the flutist Karl August Grenser identified him as already one of the most renowned makers of his time in 1824.[3]

Five years later, having 'acquired flutes at great expense from almost all the famous masters and found not one without significant faults', Boehm established his own flute-making workshop. Without a background as an instrument-maker, the law required him to establish some novelty or invention to justify the award of a royal licence. Accordingly he applied on 8–10 May 1829 to make flutes in his own particular way, referring to his prior experience as goldsmith and flutist, and citing six characteristics of the flutes which, despite their unaltered acoustics, key system, and fingering, he was already calling 'improved':

1. Purity of intonation
2. Evenness of tone
3. Facility of operation
4. Secure speaking of the highest as well as the lowest notes
5. Beautiful profile
6. Thoroughly neat and robust workmanship.

41. Flutes by Theobald Boehm, Boehm & Greve, and Boehm & Mendler (DCM). (*left to right*) (1) DCM 657, by Boehm & Greve, *c*1828–32. (2) DCM 974, by Boehm, 1832–47. (3) DCM 652, no. 1 of two brass flutes by Boehm, 1847. (4) DCM 653, cylinder flute no. 21 by Boehm, 1848. (5) DCM 875, by Boehm, 1847–62. (6) DCM 161, by Boehm & Mendler, 1877 (Macauley flute).

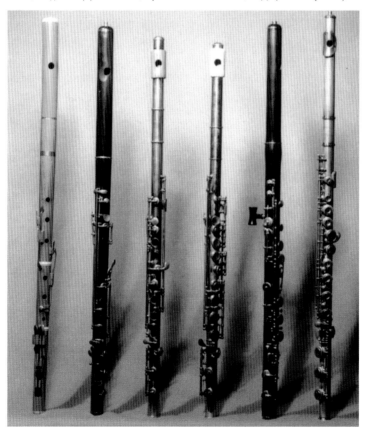

Rodolphe Greve (1806–62), who in 1829 had moved from Mannheim to Munich after training as an instrument-maker with his father Andreas Greve (1770–1840), became Boehm's chief workman and partner in 1830, forming a team with Boehm's brother Jacob (1805–71) that grew with the addition of several other workmen early in 1832.[4] Boehm devised an apparatus for accurately setting the pillars that carried the flute's keywork, and experimented with rod-axles, which, unlike the simple lever axles in common use at the time, carried the motion of the touchpiece along a pivoted tube running along the length of the flute to a key-cover on a remote part of the body. The workshop produced eight-keyed flutes which Dayton C. Miller described as of 'perfect' workmanship, suspending most keys on pillars in the usual way but using rod-axles with right-hand levers for B♭ and C2.

A generation after the addition of keys to the flute in England in the mid-eighteenth century (chapter 6), Germans had now carried inquiry into the construction of flutes to its most intensive stage. As early as 1781 Tromlitz had used detailed announcements of his innovative instruments in the musical and general periodicals as the most effective method of spreading the word. When others who had been experimenting with flute design began to publish their ideas in some of the same media (chapter 8), a more or less public discussion ensued, linking workmen, players, and thoughtful individuals who in the ordinary course of life might never have met to discuss their common interest. A description of Capeller's flute by Carl Maria von Weber had formed a thread in this series of publications.

However, not all those working on flute designs published accounts of their work, and Captain J. C. G. Gordon was one who left only scanty documentation. Gordon first designed a flute based on an open-key system in 1826 in collaboration with Auguste Buffet *jeune* (*b* 1789) (chapter 8), but nothing is known of this early effort. After the devastating loss of his position as an officer in Charles X's Swiss Guards in the Revolution of 1830, when his regiment was massacred by a Parisian mob, it occurred to Gordon that devising a better flute might provide a livelihood for himself and his wife. While visiting London in the following year he commissioned the workshops of Rudall & Rose and of Cornelius Ward to make flutes to other designs. Yet the exact nature of Gordon's flutes at this period too remains obscure, despite many attempts to investigate it. By all accounts, Gordon's flutes made use of an idea H. W. T. Pottgiesser had suggested two years before of employing crescent-shaped touchpieces on certain open-standing keys. The Rev. Frederick Nolan had patented a ring-key device in November 1808, and Pottgiesser had suggested another rudimentary ring-key in 1824,[5] but Gordon's crescent touchpieces provided the first practical means of opening or closing a hole beneath the finger at the same time as another key some distance away. This allowed holes to be placed in their ideal acoustical positions: regarding the tonehole positions in Gordon's 1831 flute Ward wrote that 'the apertures were placed consistently with the proper length of tube required for each fundamental note in the chromatic gamut',[6] a contention generally supported by two engravings of Gordon's flutes published during the 1830s, but contradicted by a remark Boehm made in 1847.

While Gordon was working with the London flute-makers, Boehm combined his first concert tour to venture beyond Germany, Switzerland, and Northern Italy with a business trip to England. In partnership with his friend Karl Franz Emil von Schafhäutl (1803–90), Boehm had undertaken the improvement of the Bavarian steel industry, and made the journey to Britain, the leading producer of iron and steel, to learn more about industrial methods there. No doubt he also had in mind the promotion of his flute business: the firm of Boehm and Greve was thriving, having already sold 65 instruments, 21 of them outside Bavaria.

In London, where his performances on an eight-keyed flute from his own workshop received encouraging notice, Boehm met Gordon and became familiar with his flute. He evaluated the instrument dismissively in his essay of sixteen years later, after he had been accused of pilfering Gordon's ideas:

> He also had on his flute a number of keys and levers, some of which were ingeniously devised; but they were much too complicated, and of no use, as it lacked throughout a correct acoustical basis.

Through the good offices of George Rudall (1781–1871) Boehm met Charles Nicholson, the power of whose tone – due in part to the large-holed flutes he played and marketed – was a legend in his own time (chapter 7). Boehm evaluated his own performance in comparison to Nicholson's in an oft-quoted passage from a letter of 1871 to his English friend W. S. Broadwood:

> I did as well as any continental flautist could have done in London in 1831, but I could not match Nicholson in power of tone, wherefore I set to work to remodel my flute. Had I not heard him, probably the Boehm flute would never have been made.[7]

Before he left London Boehm had already built an instrument to a new design in the workshop of Gerock & Wolf, where he also developed overstrung pianos that the American piano manufacturers Steinway and Chickering brought to fruition a quarter century later. The London firm rushed to market with the new design, which it promoted in a pamphlet on 'Boehm's Newly-invented Patent Flute' (ill. 42a).[8]

Boehm's model of 1831 made dramatic advances in mechanics and changes in fingering. The new design introduced the concept of the ring-key to flute construction: in his essay *On the Construction of Flutes* he wrote of 'adopting' the device rather than 'inventing' it. Probably Buffet *jeune* already knew of it from the clarinet: some years before, in 1826, at about the time he was working with Gordon, he had seen a clarinet with a ring-key which another Parisian maker, Lefèvre, had made for the clarinettist Blève of Le Havre.[9] The ring-key, surrounding the tonehole like *Brille* or spectacles, transmitted the motion of a finger onto keys beyond its reach in a more effective manner than Gordon's crescent touchpieces.

Boehm employed these ring-keys to bring about the change in fingering for F and F♯ that Pottgiesser had suggested in 1803: he assigned the right-hand index finger to play F and the third finger of the right hand to play F♯, achieving the change by giving F♮ a new hole of its own. He placed the toneholes for the left-hand third finger (A) and the right index finger (G) out of the fingers' reach and covered them with

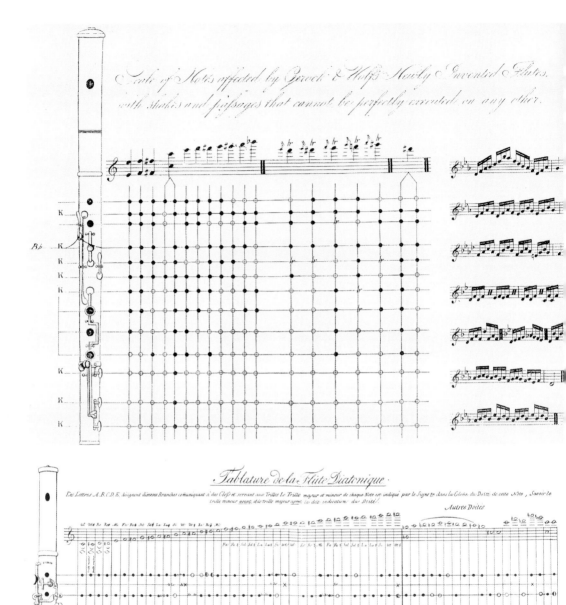

(c)

42. (a) Boehm's flute of 1831 from Gerock & Wolf's prospectus (c1831); (b) Gordon's flute c1833 from Gordon's *Tablature* (1834); (c) Gordon's flute c1838 from Coche's *Examen critique* (1838).

Precise details of Gordon's work before Boehm devised his London flute of 1831 (ill. 42a) are unknown. Gordon published the first illustration of his flute (ill. 42b) only in his prospectus of 1834, after he had further developed it in Boehm's workshop. That prospectus, of which no copy survives, was reproduced by Welch (facing p. 102). Its picture of the c1833 flute was reprinted in John Clinton's tutor of 1846 and in the German version of Boehm's *Essay* of 1847. Ill. 42c appears to derive from a drawing Mme Gordon sent Coche with a letter of 20 May 1838 (Welch, *History*, 127–9). Horizontal lines at each tonehole and key touch probably indicate that the drawing once formed part of a fingering chart, as in the other two cases in this figure.

Philip Bate (*The Flute*, p. 239) and Nancy Toff (*Development*, 50–1) incorrectly stated that ill. 42c had appeared in 1833 rather than five years later. Toff (ibid.) mistakenly wrote that ill 42b had first been published in 1846, twelve years after its actual appearance, and that it represented a Gordon flute of c1831, that is, before he had visited Boehm's workshop.

open-standing keys, while the keys for G♯ and D♯ both stood open rather than closed. Despite these similarities to the instrument Gordon depicted in his prospectus of 1834, the lack of a clear chronology does not permit us to trace whether or not Gordon's 1831 model had any practical influence on Boehm's new flute of that date, or vice versa.[10]

Boehm returned to Bavaria to follow up the 1831 flute's advances in a new model he built in his Munich shop in the following year. On 25 January 1832 he petitioned the King, without success, for a subsidy of 1000 florins from the Fund for Bavarian Industry, citing the expenses of his travels and experiments in London, and the purchase of materials from England, as having used up his means. He held out the prospect that his new flute 'opened up a happy prospect of a lucrative livelihood for me as the tirelessly active head of a household of a wife and seven children'.

The new mechanism of Boehm's 1832 flute used ring-keys operated by interlinked parallel rod-axles, made to a design of his own which the Boehm and Greve keyed flutes had employed in a simpler form for some years. It carried over the fingering for F and F♯ and the open key for G from the design of the previous year. But instead of leaving the left hand so that it could cover the open toneholes towards the top of the tube, Boehm shifted its position downward by a semitone so that the fourth finger could once again reach its lowest tonehole, for A, and the A key of the 1831 system could be dispensed with. Now the tonehole for B♭, formerly located under the tube, was given a new position in line with the other toneholes, and assigned the left-hand middle finger instead of the closed-standing thumb key that had traditionally played that note. This freed the thumb to fulfil the principal function it had had in Tromlitz's 1785 flute of governing a nearby tonehole for C, rather than having the right index finger do duty from a remote position. A separate key for C♯ governed its own hole, now placed too high up the tube for the left index finger to reach. To help steady the instrument now that the left thumb was occupied with the C key, Boehm added a T-shaped crutch to rest in the player's hand between the thumb and index finger.

For the first time, all the flute's keys with the exception of the D♯ key and special trill keys stood open in their default positions, while in practice the D♯ key was always held open except to play D and the notes below it in the first octave. Thus in the 1832 flute every note was now produced by its own tonehole which, when opened, had no closed holes below it on the tube, so that all the artificial fingerings in the flute's chromatic scale had been eliminated. To increase the contribution the open keys made to a powerful tone, Boehm made the toneholes as large as feasible, following Nicholson's example as well as Weber's observation that only the largest holes with the lowest end-correction factor could be placed in their acoustically ideal positions.

Boehm and Greve's workshop began to manufacture the new instrument, using cocus or grenadilla wood, in the course of 1832. Boehm himself inaugurated it at performances in Munich on 1 November 1832 and 25 April 1833, a review of which contained the first published reports of the new flute.[11] Also in 1833, Boehm's pupil Eduard Heindl (1837–96) performed a Kuhlau *Fantasie* on the ring-key flute. A prospectus describing the new instrument, with charts for fingerings and trills, was published in the autumn of 1834. Boehm, though now much occupied with his work in the Bavarian steel industry, found time to demonstrate the new flute in Paris and London in 1833–4. Though he remained in London for a year he found acceptance slow and had sold only one instrument there by 1835.

Gordon, meanwhile, was still determined to develop a viable flute of his own. Boehm lent him his Munich workshop and his foreman Greve to conduct further experiments in early 1833 while he himself again travelled to Paris and London. In July Gordon sent out descriptions of his latest model in a pamphlet entitled *Tablature of the Diatonic Flute Manufactured in the Workshops of Boehm*, of which, though Welch reproduced it in 1896, no original is known to survive (ill. 42b).[12] Still, his flute did not meet with the success he hoped for, and he retired to Lausanne where he continued his work until mental breakdown struck in 1836. Gordon is thought to have died in 1838.

Boehm's revolutionary flute of 1832 won its first champions beyond his immediate circle in Paris. Three men, Paul Hippolyte Camus (*b* 1796), Vincent Joseph Steenkiste *alias* Louis Dorus (1812–96), and Victor Jean Baptiste Coche (1806–81), played important roles in the Boehm flute's acceptance in France during the crucial year of 1837. Nonetheless, Boehm himself won its first official notice in France by presenting it in person. While visiting Paris in the spring, he showed one of his ring-key flutes to the acoustician Félix Savart (1791–1841), who had been elected to the Institute of France's Academy of Sciences in 1827 after a decade's work on electrodynamics and acoustics. Savart arranged for the flute to be examined by the Academy at a meeting of 8 May 1837. On that occasion Boehm read a short description of the flute, and a commission consisting of Savart, another scientist, and two musicians from the Academy of Fine Arts, was appointed to give a formal judgement. On leaving Paris Boehm appointed Camus to represent him before the commission when it met. Tula Giannini (1993) surmises that Boehm chose Camus to represent him in preference to Dorus because the latter had already altered aspects of the original design,[13] but the suggestion that Dorus even possessed a ring-key flute in the spring of 1837, despite Schafhäutl's assertion (see below), is far from certain, and it seems more probable that Camus was its only advocate until the Academy took notice of Boehm.

THE RING-KEY FLUTE IN PARIS

Which prominent Parisian flutist first took up Boehm's ring-key flute? Claims have been made by, or on behalf of, three men: Paul Hippolyte Camus (*b* 1796), Vincent Joseph van Steenkiste *alias* Louis Dorus (1812–96), and Victor Coche (1806–81).

According to Boehm's own testimony, he first showed his flute to Aristide Farrenc (1794–1865), Camus, and Laurent, 'manufacturers of flutes', on a visit to Paris in 1833.[1] Farrenc confirmed this in an article of 1838 in which he contested Coche's claim to have been the ring-key flute's first advocate. At the same time he noted that Camus had devoted himself to the new flute only on a subsequent visit by Boehm four years later, when for the first time the inventor was able to lend an instrument to interested players:

> In March 1837 M. Boehm came to Paris for the 3rd time with his new flute.[2] Until then he had brought only one flute, the one he played on, but this time he had several with him. M. Camus asked to borrow one, and the same day he declared that he would not play any other flute than Boehm's; he kept his word. ... When M. Camus adopted the Boehm flute there was as yet only one instrument of this type in Paris, even in France, thus it was indeed M. Camus who first played this flute, and it was he who *first propagated it.*[3]

Camus put the date of his conversion two months later in his own account, which otherwise confirms Farrenc's.[4]

Schafhäutl claimed that the twenty-two-year-old Dorus had switched to the ring-key flute immediately on hearing Boehm play one in Paris as early as 1834, while the inconsistently reliable musical biographer François-Joseph Fétis (1784–1871) put the date even earlier, at 1833.[5] However, Dorus could not have taken up the ring-key flute unless he had bought a flute from Boehm, at that early date the only possible supplier of such an instrument, and no evidence of such a purchase exists. Dorus must have come by a ring-key flute by 1838, when he appeared as one of three advocates for it before a Conservatoire commission, but by that time two firms in Paris had developed versions of the Boehm & Greve instrument Camus had shown them during 1837 (see p. 172). Dorus adapted his method of *c*1840 to Godfroy and Lot's flute, which appeared late in that year.

The third claimant, Victor Coche (1806–81), as the narrative illustrates, tied his fortunes to Buffet's version of the ring-keyed flute, which he claimed to have first played in public in about 1838.[6]

Since it appears that neither of the French makers who developed the ring-key flutes Dorus and Coche played had any opportunity to study Boehm's model before Camus presented them with it during 1837, Farrenc's claim that Camus took up the Boehm flute when 'there was as yet only one instrument of this type in Paris' remains standing as the most plausible.

That situation changed when Boehm left one or more of the 'several' instruments he had brought to Paris in the hands of Camus for the Academy to study. During the course of 1837 Camus, acting as Boehm's agent, delivered a ring-key flute to Buffet.[14] Welch, whose information came directly from Buffet, described the nature of Camus's mission as follows:

> He had, it seems, been commissioned by Boehm not only to act as an intermediary in procuring flutes from Boehm's factory for purchasers in France, but also to enter into arrangements for the manufacture of the new instrument in Paris. Buffet became acquainted with the flute thus brought to Paris [or more probably, retained there on Boehm's departure] by Camus; indeed, according to Buffet's statement, it was placed in his hands by Camus himself.

Welch concluded that Camus and Buffet failed to devise a satisfactory business arrangement, and so Camus transmitted the model to another Parisian flute-maker, Vincent Hypolite Godfroy, then working in a partnership with Louis Lot established four years earlier under the trade name of Godfroy's father, Clair Godfroy *aîné*.[15] Godfroy and Lot lost no time in producing the first French commercial model of a ring-key flute. A notice of 21 October 1837 in the *Courrier français* indicates that they had produced a Boehm flute by that date, making them the ring-key flute's first manufacturers outside Boehm's own workshop. The Godfroy firm's public announcement signalled that the new instrument had a commercial potential that they were prepared to realize.

On the authority of his acquaintance with Buffet, Welch credited that maker with various modifications to the mechanism of Camus's ring-key flute, which, if he was correct, were made during the course of 1837 around the time Lot and Godfroy were developing their version. Buffet reportedly used needle springs in place of the traditional flat springs, repositioned all the rod-axles on the side of the tube facing the player rather than distributing them on both sides, and developed clutches and sleeves that allowed a single rod to transmit the motion of several independent cups and rings. Despite Welch's testimony, two contemporary illustrations of Buffet's flute show mechanism on both sides of the tube.[16] But whoever was responsible for the mechanical innovations, the French makers modified Boehm's instruments to make them not only more mechanically robust and easier to manufacture, but also more marketable. Boehm's open G♯ forced players who might have been ready to take up the ring-key flute to make a troublesome change in fingering. All the keys on the 'ordinary' flute operated as closed-standing levers: the fingers did not touch them except to open the holes beneath them. The open G♯, on the contrary, functioned as an open-standing key in the manner of Tromlitz's C2 key. It required the player to keep the key closed with the left-hand fifth finger, except to play a G♯, when it was allowed to return to its default open position. Though this action made the fifth finger behave in a way more consistent with the other fingers, flutists of the time were already accustomed to give it a contrary motion, and so the change was an awkward one.

Consequently Louis Dorus, working with Godfroy and Lot, devised a mechanism that retained the traditional function of the G♯ key as a closed-standing lever, at the same time as allowing it to remain open when idle. The Dorus G♯ key added a ring-key to the tonehole for A, governed by the left-hand fourth finger. This ring-key engaged the open-standing G♯ key by means of a clutch, causing it to close when the ring-key was depressed, that is, when a G was sounded. To play G♯, the key was applied in the accustomed way, re-opening the tonehole placed between A and G. Victor Coche collaborated with Buffet, whose design adopted the Dorus G♯ mechanism, to add a D♯ trill-key and a ring-key for the left-hand third finger to play a B♭, with the same fingering used on the 'long' B♭ key of the ordinary flute.

Tula Giannini has made the insightful observation that the alterations Godfroy effected on Boehm's design made it from a musical standpoint more like the instruments French flutists knew:

> Godfroy's flute differed from Boehm's in that its dimensions were modified to produce a sound that was a compromise between that of Boehm's instrument and that of Godfroy's ordinary flute of the 1830s. He accomplished this by giving the bore a steeper angle of decline [i.e. a more pronounced taper] and reducing the size of the embouchure, the tone holes, and the thickness of the body on average by a millimetre. In addition, he eliminated Boehm's crutch and rectangular creviced embouchure, replaced the open G♯ key with the Dorus G♯, and further refined the keywork. The overall effect was a Boehm flute which retained some characteristic features of the ordinary French flute.[17]

By the autumn of 1837 the two French versions of the Boehm flute were ready with their respective advocates to compete for acceptance. Following Godfroy's announcement of 21 October, Coche wrote Boehm a secret letter on 6 November in which he tried to gain the advantage for Buffet by persuading Boehm to take legal action against Godfroy to prevent his making Boehm flutes in Paris, and to appoint Coche his agent in Paris. Two days later Coche, inflating his title as Tulou's teaching assistant to 'Professor at the Conservatoire', wrote directly to the French Minister of the Interior and the Fine Arts to request a hearing for the Boehm flute before the Musical Division of the Commission of Fine Arts:

> Having examined a new flute invented by M. Theobald Boehm, a German maker, I have recognized that this instrument, built on an entirely new system, affords extremely valuable advantages and that its propagation should be considered a most important step forward for art. This thought prompts me to petition of your benevolence the favour of having this flute heard before the Fine Arts Commission, Musical Division, so as to put it in a position to appreciate the advantages which I have just mentioned. ...[18]

Boehm responded with a letter, dated Christmas Day 1837, to the Secretary of the Academy, M. Quatremère de Quincy, in which he notified him that his application of May, with Camus as his deputy, should take precedence over Coche's separate approach to the Minister. Camus likewise wrote to the Academy to remind it of his pending candidacy. But Coche's intrigues apparently ensured that Boehm's flute as he conceived it never received the commission's attention. Instead, on 24 March 1838, Coche presented the Music Committee of the Academy of Fine Arts of the Institute of France with the flute he and Buffet had devised. A new panel, consisting of the original two musicians with the addition of four more including the Conservatoire's Director, Luigi Cherubini, considered 'flutes on the Boehm system by M. Coche', as well as a method book Coche had written for the new instrument. Coche had carefully primed the commission with a paper entitled *Examen critique de la Flute Ordinaire comparée à la Flute de Böhm* (Critical examination of the ordinary flute compared with the Boehm flute), in which he claimed that Gordon had invented the new instrument but that Boehm had stolen the credit, emphasizing in the end his own modifications. Clearly Coche designed these manoeuvres to bring Boehm into disrepute and gain the commercial advantage over Godfroy and Dorus for Buffet and himself.

Coche pursued this claim in promotional literature for a partnership he formed with Buffet, to build flutes 'invented by Gordon, modified by Boehm, and perfected by Coche'. In the *Examen critique* Coche had described the new flute as the 'Boehm flute', while in his *Méthode* of the same year it was called 'the new system flute', or the 'flute of Gordon modified by Boehm'. On 19 April 1838 Camus wrote to Boehm (in an unsigned letter) to inform him that, despite his efforts to secure recognition for him as the inventor of the ring-key flute, 'as regards the Institute, the mischief is done' by Coche's campaign of disinformation.

In pursuit of the advantage thus gained, Louis Auguste Buffet submitted a patent application on 10 October 1838 for the 'new flute' he had developed in collaboration with Coche. In the following year, Buffet and Godfroy each presented their 'new flute' to the jury of the Paris Exhibition, but the instruments were not judged on that occasion owing to their novelty.

Coche's efforts to deprive Boehm of the credit for inventing the new flute set off a dispute that took until the end of the nineteenth century to die down. Hector Berlioz took Coche's part in the *Constitutionnel* of 18 August 1839 when he depicted him as an insurgent against the orthodoxy of the old flute maintained by the tenured professor Tulou. The controversy spread to England when a voluminous correspondence from amateur and professional flutists filled the columns of *The Musical World* in 1843. Cornelius Ward's pamphlet *The Flute Explained* (1844) espoused Gordon's side, while Boehm's case was taken up by John Clinton, Professor at the Royal Academy of Music, in his *Theoretical and Practical Essay* (1843) and *Practical Instruction Book* (1846), as well as by Richard Carte in *A Complete Course of Instructions for the Boehm Flute* (1845, with extracts printed separately in the following year). In 1890 Richard Shepherd Rockstro revived the Boehm-Gordon dispute in his heavily prejudiced account of the events of the 1830s, to which Christopher Welch responded with magisterial thoroughness six years later.

Victor Coche achieved his objective with the Academy of Fine Arts commission when it produced a report that parroted his *Examen critique* and accorded him high praise for his and Buffet's work on the flute. He followed up this success by requesting a meeting of the Conservatoire's Committee on Teaching to consider setting up a special class in the Boehm flute. The Committee, consisting of professors of composition, voice, and instruments other than the flute, most of whom had also served on the Academy's panel, met on 30 December with the institute's President, Luigi Cherubini, in the chair. But owing to the Conservatoire's more formal structure, this Committee could not as easily be swayed. The meeting of 30 December 1839 adjourned for a week so that the panel could summon Tulou, whose standing as Professor of Flute rendered his opinion indispensable. Tulou's commercial interests, as official supplier of flutes to the Conservatoire and author of its official teaching method, made his hostility to any new idea that had not first won his patronage a foregone conclusion. According to Giannini's transcription of the minutes of the meeting, he presented detailed opposition to the Boehm flute:

> He cites quite a number of passages that are much more difficult to execute on the new flute than the old, and he adds that the sounds in general of the Boehm instrument are far from having a quality as agreeable as that of the flute taught at the Conservatoire.[19]

Count A. D. de Pontécoulant reported Tulou's specific objections to the 1832 flute's tone in an account of the Committee's proceedings published in *La France Musicale*:

> [Tulou] said that one must first acknowledge that the flute is a pastoral instrument, with which one must seek more to please than to astonish; that one must express only sentiments that are sweet, tender, expressive, passionate, and not those by which one would want to paint anger or tempest. It requires, therefore, above all, a beautiful quality of sound, or, to say it in a better way, a beautiful voice, a voice that approaches as much as possible the human voice.[20]

Tulou further objected that the flute's mechanism remained a work in progress, since Coche, Camus, and Dorus played on instruments modified differently. Consequently the Committee decided to meet again and hear what these performers, as well as others who had tried and given up the Boehm flute, had to say.

A week later two flutists named Connix and Robert Frisch (*b* c1804) testified that the Boehm flute was out of tune, defective in tone, and mechanically unsound, considerations that had led Connix to give it up after only a fortnight's trial. Dorus and Coche, though they played flutes with slightly different embouchures and mechanisms, spoke in favour of the Boehm flute and demonstrated its potential. Dorus also played an 'old' flute for the sake of comparison, upon which the Committee observed that the old flute was 'more in tune and more agreeable'. Nevertheless, Camus had not yet been heard from, so the Committee adjourned once again.

Four days later, with Camus still absent, Tulou, Connix, and Frisch played passages Coche claimed were 'impossible to execute well' on the old flute. Their brilliant demonstration, combined with Tulou's well-timed announcement that he was working on a 'perfected' flute based on the old system, persuaded the committee that the old flute was perfectly adequate and indeed superior to the Boehm flute in some respects, and it voted unanimously against authorizing the new Boehm flute class. Coche, having lost the battle, also forfeited his position as Tulou's assistant at the

Conservatoire in the following year when the senior professor effectively prevented any of his subordinate's students proceeding to their diplomas.

Giannini interprets Camus's failure to participate in the Conservatoire test as a sign that, as a representative of the original Boehm flute with the open G♯, he had dropped out of the contest. Coche's loss of his position at the Conservatoire doubtless lessened his ability to promote the Buffet version, leaving Godfroy and Lot for the time being as the Boehm flute's foremost manufacturer. Still, Coche remained along with Camus and Dorus a champion of the ring-key flute: his method had appeared in August 1839, two months after Camus's, and he claimed in his *Mémoire* of 1859 that he had been the first to use the new flute successfully in a dramatic orchestra in his position as solo flute at the Théâtre de la Renaissance. Dorus continued to display his superb artistry on a ring-key flute by Godfroy and Lot. Certainly the approval of this prominent soloist, a member of the Opéra orchestra and of the Société des Concerts du Conservatoire, had an important influence in 1838, and his support was to be even more crucial a quarter century later when he succeeded Tulou as Professor at the Conservatoire and made the cylinder flute the official instrument of that powerful institution in 1860 (chapter 11). Dorus's reputation and his method for the Boehm flute of c1840 so raised the ring-key flute's standing that Boehm named him as the man responsible for its success in France and dedicated the French translation of his 1847 essay to him rather than to Camus.

The events of 1837–8 suddenly ended a five-year period during which acceptance of the ring-key flute had been stalled. With the steel industry making heavy demands on his time from 1833 onwards, Boehm had been unable to continue any personal involvement in his Munich workshop, and in 1839, once the French ring-key flutes appeared to have gained the ascendant over his own, he sold the business to Greve for 600 florins, about the value of four and a half flutes. But first it was necessary to renew the establishment's operating licence, which was about to expire, and without which Greve would have no right to make instruments in Munich. In a petition of 7 May 1839 to extend the licence, Boehm noted the enterprise's limited scope:

I founded my flute business less for profit than to promote a good business and for the sake of honour, to make instruments in the Fatherland that have twice been awarded silver medals at our industrial exhibitions, designated the most perfect by the Institute of France, and hitherto copied by the foremost London, Paris, and Vienna instrument-makers only with difficulty and shortcomings.

However, this perfection of my instruments was achieved initially by means of researches that cost me dearly in time and money, and still the prices were not raised in proportion, so as to ensure their publicly beneficial domestic distribution as well as a market abroad, distant transport and high import taxes notwithstanding.

Furthermore, a larger expansion of this business is not really possible due to the great difficulty of finding suitable workers and checking their work carefully, and therefore the pure profit of it is only very small. ...[21]

1831	In London Boehm's Gerock & Wolf flute appears; Gordon has flutes built by Rudall & Rose and by Cornelius Ward.
1832	Boehm develops his ring-key flute in Munich; demonstrates it in Munich, London, and Paris.
1833	Boehm to Paris and London; shows flute to Camus and others.
	Gordon to Munich; in July publishes a prospectus showing his flute.
1836	Gordon's mental breakdown.
1837	May: Boehm presents his flute to the acoustician Savart and the Institute of France's Academy of Sciences. He commissions Camus as his deputy.
	October: Godfroy and Lot produce a Boehm flute in Paris.
	November: Coche reports this to Boehm, asking him to suppress the Godfroy and Lot flute and make Coche his agent. Coche writes to Minister of the Interior.
1838	Coche publishes *Examen critique*. Music Committee of the Royal Academy of Fine Arts considers Coche-Buffet-Boehm flute, parroting Coche's pamphlet in its report, but ignores Boehm's application pending from the previous year.
1839	Buffet and Coche patent their new flute, which appears alongside Godfroy's at the Paris Exhibition. A Conservatoire Committee meets at Coche's request to consider Boehm flutes by Godfroy and Buffet, but rejects both. Coche is frozen out of the Conservatoire by Tulou.
1842	The ring-key flute is adopted at the Brussels Conservatoire.
1843	John Clinton, Professor at the Royal Academy of Music, London, publishes *Theoretical and Practical Essay* on the Boehm flute. Series of letters in *The Musical World* on the Boehm-Gordon controversy.
	Rudall & Rose begin production of the 1832 flute in London under the supervision of Greve.
1844	Cornelius Ward takes Gordon's side in *The Flute Explained*.
1847	Boehm's cylinder flute; production licensed to Godfroy and Lot in Paris, and, after Clinton declines, to Rudall & Rose in London.
1859	Tulou retires; Coche's *Mémoire* asserts his right to be reinstated at the Conservatoire.
1860	Dorus appointed Professor at the Conservatoire, the Boehm flute is adopted, and Louis Lot becomes official supplier.
1890	Rockstro's *Treatise* prejudiced against Boehm.
1896	Welch's *History of the Boehm Flute*, 3rd edition, rebuts Rockstro.

The silver medals Boehm referred to were awarded at industrial exhibitions of 1834 and 1835 in Munich, for instruments Greve made after Boehm had ceased working on the flutes himself. Greve continued to win prizes for his instruments, under the trademark Boehm & Greve, in the Industrial Exhibition of 1840 at Nuremberg and the General German Industrial Exhibition of the Hessian Trade Association in 1842.

By the time Boehm made his fifth visit to England in 1839, his ring-key flute had won some attention there. According to a letter of 7 November 1843 to *The Musical World* from Cornelius Ward, Ignazio Folz[22] was performing in London at that time on a Boehm-system flute Ward had been building since 1839, and the performer and teacher William Card (1788–1861), Nicholson's successor at the Antient Concerts,[23] had promoted the ring-key flute unsuccessfully. Ward's letter intimated that French advocates were also making an effort to advance various ring-key flutes in England, in that 'we had Camus and Dorus endeavouring to introduce it to "English players", by both public and private performances'. Camus reportedly 'caused some sensation' by performing Boehm's music on a Godfroy flute with a Dorus G♯ key.[24]

The first significant conversion in England came when John Clinton, Professor of Flute at the Royal Academy of Music, took up the Boehm flute in 1841. Clinton explained his advocacy of the ring-key flute in his tutors of 1843 and 1846. He singled out for praise, besides its more obvious attributes, the instrument's potential for the English technique of 'Harmonics', providing a table of fingerings as well as musical examples by Cherubini, Rossini, Kuhlau, Nicholson, and Drouët. Clinton explained:

> I do not mean it to be inferred that a thorough knowledge of [the harmonic fingerings] is indispensable, but I offer them, as additional resources, hitherto unknown on the old flute, as an amusing study, and as a means to heighten the effect of Flute music generally, consequently to elevate the character of the Instrument, and as an inducement to the Studious and Talented Flautist, to explore still further, the vast resources offered in Boehm's system.[25]

Clinton's enthusiasm was not enough, however, to bring the new flute widespread acceptance in England. It had to make its way against the priorities and expectations of both amateur and professional flutists, as the series of letters in *The Musical World* for 1843 illustrates. Despite such opposition, Richard Carte (1808–91), a pupil of George Rudall's, invited Boehm's successor Rodolphe Greve to London in 1842 or 1843 to instruct the Rudall & Rose company's workmen in the manufacture of Boehm flutes. Though this has been called the first licensing of the ring-key flute outside Bavaria, the question of whether the inventor authorized or even approved the idea is in fact uncertain, as his business association with Greve had ended several years before. In any event Carte and Rudall had joined Clinton in taking up the ring-key flute by 1843 and its viability in England seemed assured for the time being. Greve returned to Munich in the middle of that year and was granted his own licence as an instrument-maker as well as citizen's rights.[26] Another Boehm flute came on the London market about two years later, when Thomas Prowse, who had vigorously defended his Nicholson-model flute in *The Musical World*, began to manufacture it under the direction of Camus.[27]

Despite his own preoccupation with the steel industry, Boehm's ideas about the flute continued to find applications in the other woodwinds. In 1839, Hyacinthe Eléonore Klosé, Professor of Clarinet at the Paris Conservatoire, exhibited a Boehm-system clarinet he had developed with Buffet *jeune*. The holes of Klosé's instrument were generally larger and more rationally spaced than previously, and the mechanism employed Boehm's ring-keys. Klosé's method for this instrument appeared in 1843, the same year Buffet and Klosé patented the system. According to Macgillivray (1961) the new clarinet was soon adopted in France, but not in England, where in the provinces and the army bands the Boehm clarinet was a rarity as late as 1925.[28] In 1844 Buffet also produced a Boehm oboe, with the assistance of Pedro Joachim Raymond Soler (1810–50) and some acoustical advice from Boehm himself. Macgillivray wrote that it 'had little success save where loudness was the prime consideration'.

The ring-key flute took a few years longer to reach the United States. In about 1844 a Mr Brix visited New York City from South America, bringing with him a ring-key flute he had acquired in Europe.[29] After first seeing the flute at a musical party the flutist John A. Kyle, by his own account, called on the visitor, borrowed the instrument, and took it to the workshop of James D. Larrabee (*d c*1847), who made a copy. Larrabee exhibited his ring-key flute at the Seventeenth Annual American Institute Fair in New York in 1844, winning a silver medal for the 'best Boehm system flute'.[30] In a slightly different account given by the flute-maker Alfred G. Badger in 1853 neither Kyle's name nor Larrabee's appears:

> About the time of my commencement, the first Boehm Flute made it appearance in this country. It was in the possession of a gentleman tourist. Mr W. J. Davis, an eminent Flute professor of New York, examined the peculiarities of its construction, at once perceived its merits, and predicted that its ultimate destiny would be its general adoption. He immediately engaged in its manufacture, but the undertaking proved far from profitable. He found an abundance of opposing interests. The manufacturers of the old Flute did not see the way clear from the profitable investment of their labor and capital in the new. It wanted a mechanical ability they did not possess. Professors of the Flute found they must unlearn their bad habits, and consequently discouraged its adoption.... Philip Ernst, of this city [i.e. New York], a Professor of the Flute, of high standing, and thirty years' experience, was the next to adopt the Boehm Flute. His position was more commanding, and his influence among amateurs great. Many followed in his wake, and it was through the assurances of his patronage, and of its ultimate success, that I commenced the manufacture of the *Boehm Flute*.[31]

Precisely how Davis engaged in the ring-key flute's manufacture remains unclear; Susan Berdahl (1985) has suggested a possible relationship with Theobald P. Monzani (*fl* 1835–66), on the strength of David Ehrlich's assertion that Monzani made a Boehm flute as early as 1843.[32] Berdahl also identifies William Rönnberg (1803–*c*1889) as a maker of conical Boehm flutes in New York at a possibly early date, though the first evidence of this appears to be an entry in an exhibition of 1857.[33] In any case, when Badger (1815–92) set up his flute-manufacturing business in New York in 1845, he became the first American maker to produce ring-key flutes in the regular course of business. He based his instruments rather closely on Boehm's design, employing cocus wood, a double thumbhole, and vaulted arms with adjusting screws, but a Dorus G$^\sharp$ rather than Boehm's open G$^\sharp$ key. Seven of these instruments survive. When Boehm later developed the cylinder flute Badger made his own version as no U.S. patent protected the invention.

Badger made strenuous efforts to promote the Boehm flute. He entered instruments at numerous exhibitions in New York, Massachusetts, London, and Paris, beginning with the American Institute of the City of New York Exhibition of 1846, where he won a silver medal. He used paid advertising, letters to editors, broadsides, testimonials, and personal approaches to professionals to heighten public awareness of the new flute. His *Illustrated History of the Flute* (1853, 1854, 1861, and 1875), the first such work to appear in the United States, borrowed heavily from Carte's history (1851) to argue for the advantages of the Boehm system.

Philip Ernst (1792–1868) became, according to Badger's account, the second leading New York player to take up the ring-key flute. Ernst, a German immigrant, held high standing in New York, having served as flutist to Charles X in Paris and as Nicholson's successor at the Italian Opera in London before taking up a position with the New York Philharmonic.

Meanwhile Boehm's activities in the iron works brought him health problems and financial losses, so that from 1845 he returned to his former profession as court musician and flute teacher. John Clinton visited him in Munich during 4–19 August 1845, at a time when Boehm had begun a study of acoustics under the guidance of his friend Schafhäutl and was ready to enter into a frank discussion with his guest of how the ring-key flute might be improved.[34] Another visitor in August was Moritz Fürstenau, whom Boehm's pupil Hans Haindl had won over to the ring-key flute, and who remained in Munich to study it from 13 August to 11 November.

In his own account of his work in 1847, Boehm wrote:

> I was never able to understand why, of all wind instruments with tone-holes and conical bore, the flute alone should be blown at the wider end: it seems much more natural, that with a rising pitch and shorter length of air-column, the diameter should become smaller … I finally called science to my aid and gave two years to the study of the principles of acoustics under the excellent guidance of Herr Professor Dr von Schafhäutl. After making many experiments, as precise as possible, I finished a flute in the latter part of 1847, founded on scientific principles. …

Indeed, Boehm's studies with Schafhäutl led him to revise the most fundamental aspects of the flute's design. His new instrument featured a cylindrical bore with a so-called 'parabolic' headjoint, a tube of metal instead of wood, toneholes of the maximum possible size closed by padded keys, and a mechanism that built on the innovations of his 1832 pattern.

As early as 1810 the London instrument-maker George Miller had patented a two-jointed fife in brass with a cylindrical bore for use in hot climates, but for thirty-five years no other maker had taken up the idea of a metal tube. Noting that cylindrical wood tubes he made to conduct experiments were unstable, Boehm replaced them with hard drawn brass. This experience convinced him that, as he put it, 'the molecules of the flute tube shall be set into vibration at the same time as the air column', and he determined that a lighter tube, such as one of drawn silver having a mass less that half that of the thinnest possible wood one, required less expenditure of energy to sound. In 1846 he began to experiment with flutes of brass, silver, and German silver (an imprecise term for various alloys of nickel, copper, zinc, and even brass and bronze), noting that the hardest, German silver, gave a 'clear but shrill tone'.

Though his acoustical studies enabled Boehm to calculate the positions of the toneholes, they did not remove the need to determine the length of the tube, its

43. Antoine Sacchetti (*left*) and Theobald Boehm.

diameter, and the size of the toneholes by experiment. In the end Boehm settled on an internal diameter of 19mm for the tube; he preferred 20mm for the richness and volume of tone in the first two octaves, but found that a slightly narrower bore helped the high register to be played softly. Likewise the bore of the headjoint appears to have been arrived at empirically rather than by calculation. Though his acoustical studies did provide a method for calculating the relative positions of the toneholes on the tube, the method he actually used, according to the account he gave in *On the Construction of Flutes*, was still based on experiment as much as on theory. 'For an exact examination of [the first three notes of the second octave], as well as the tuning proportions in general,' he explained, 'I made a model flute with movable tone holes, by which I was able to tune all the notes higher or lower at pleasure.' This perforated brass tube with rotating and sliding collars is preserved in the Dayton C. Miller collection (DCM 471).

Now that Boehm had returned to work on the flute and was contemplating the production of a new model, he had occasion to contest the continued use of his name by the workshop he had sold to his erstwhile foreman Greve.[35] On 21 January 1846 he obtained an injunction from the Munich magistrate against Greve's use of the name 'Boehm' under a penalty of 10 florins. Greve responded in a written protest of 9 March that Boehm was neither an instrument-maker himself nor proprietor of a

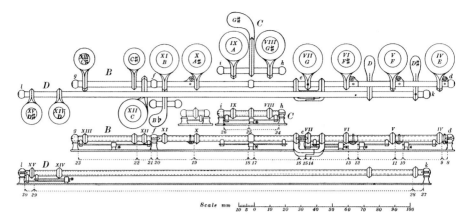

44. Mechanism of the 1847 flute's body section. Dayton C. Miller, trans. and ed., *The Flute and Flute-playing in Acoustical, Technical, and Artistic Aspects by Theobald Boehm* (Cleveland: Author, 1922 R/1963), Fig. 20, between pp. 77 and 78.

business that made instruments, but a Court Musician, that from the beginning Greve and not Boehm had actually made the instruments, and that Boehm had contributed only his name, the right to use which in the instrument business he had duly sold to Greve. Nevertheless, as a result of this dispute, Greve's workshop changed its mark in March 1846 from *Boehm & Greve à Munich* to *Rodol. Greve à Munich*. Munich directories of 1850 and 1852 noted that Greve's shop, still making ring-key flutes, was 'known as the Th. Boehm and Greve establishment'. The fact that Boehm did not mention Greve in any of his publications or letters suggests he bore his former partner a grudge over the matter, though the two continued to live on adjacent floors of the same building.

A Royal Bavarian trade licence for 'a new kind of flute in acoustical proportions and materials' of 13 April 1847 provided Boehm with the legal basis to open a new flute business to produce cylinder flutes, while his injunction against Greve made it possible to use his own name in the firm's trademark, *Th. Boehm in München*, which he used from 1847 to 1861. In the following year he retired on pension as a musician, citing his failing eyesight, to devote himself to making flutes.

Although Boehm judged at first that the toneholes should decrease in size from the bottom to the top of the flute, he found the manufacturing difficulties of this outweighed the advantages and established a standard size for the holes. This size was too large for any hole to be covered by a finger: all were now sealed with padded cups like those he had devised for the G and A holes of the 1832 flute. The pads were of a quite new type, thinner and more rigid than those used on other wind instruments, and held in place by a washer and a screw which engaged in a nut soldered to the inside of the cup. To couple the padded cups to the mechanism Boehm adopted Buffet's solutions of rod-axles, needle springs, and clutches.

On 20 June 1847 Boehm entered the first two silver closed-keyed cylinder flutes in his ledger, and at the end of the month he took them on a journey to London and Paris. Two years earlier he had agreed with Clinton to try to resolve the perceived defects of ring-key flute's fingering and tone, and that if he succeeded in satisfying him, Clinton 'was to have the sole right of his improvements in the Instrument for England'. Boehm accordingly proceeded to London to offer his English champion a licence to manufacture the 1847 flute. Yet the new design disappointed Clinton:

> A most careful and impartial trial fully convinced me, that, as a whole, he was as far as ever from removing the defects, or of perfecting the Instrument; and feeling that I could not adopt it with pleasure or satisfaction, nor conscientiously recommend it to my Pupils, I was (most reluctantly, I confess) compelled to decline it.[36]

In the meantime Boehm travelled to Paris, where on 27 July 1847 he obtained a French patent covering the principle of a cylindrical bore and a parabolic head.[37] Two weeks later, on 14 August, he sold the exclusive French rights under that patent to Godfroy and Lot for 6000 francs, the value of about fourteen silver flutes. He had already sold the partners his second cylinder flute a month previously, evidently so that they could begin preparing a production model of their own.[38] Boehm's passport records that he left Paris two days after the sale. The French makers re-interpreted Boehm's design for the cylinder flute as they had the ring-key instrument. To streamline manufacture, they arranged the toneholes in a straight line, and they perforated some of the cups of the closed keys in the manner of the ring-keys to allow increased venting.

With Clinton out of the picture, the firm of Rudall & Rose, which had made at least 240 ring-key flutes between 1843 and 1847, now presented itself as candidate for the rights to the cylinder flute in Britain. On 2 September 1847 George Rudall wrote to Boehm to ask him to send one of his new flutes with toneholes of the size he thought best. Rudall's letter reveals both that the firm already possessed a silver flute by Boehm – evidently the one Clinton had rejected – and that by September at least one of Godfroy and Lot's silver flutes had already reached England. Rudall, however, apparently thought the French modifications no improvement:

> The French seem to be going from your original Intention, and their Instruments are not usual [i.e. similar] to your silver flute in our possession. There is not the slightest doubt as to the vast superiority of your metal flute over every other … I have been playing upon one of Godfroy's which is not a first rate Instrument; and I shall not rest satisfied until I possess one from the Inventor.[39]

Four days later John Mitchell Rose filed a British patent on behalf of the company, 'being partly a communication from a foreigner residing abroad', for Boehm's metal tube, cylindrical bore, and parabolic headjoint. The company continued to experiment with hole sizes, bore, and fingering: between 1849 and 1851 it built flutes to at least ten different designs based on the Boehm cylinder flute.

On his return to Munich in September 1847 Boehm set to the production of cylinder flutes of his own, assisted at various times by his sons Wilhelm and Theobald. The workshop began with two ring-keyed cylinder flutes of gilded brass with silver mechanisms, one of them for Giulio Briccialdi of Rome (who visited Munich from 11

June until 18 November 1848), and a silver ring-keyed cylinder flute for Sir Charles Douglas of London. Nonetheless, all was not plain sailing. Instruments from Boehm's Munich workshop cost twice as much as other flutes, and German flutists found their mechanism fragile and frequently in need of repair. In 1853 the workshop sold only two instruments, and by the following year Boehm had produced a more robust French-style silver flute 'after Godfroy', which however failed to satisfy him. On 18 March 1854 he patented an 'improved key-mechanism for wind instruments' with the aim of eliminating its most fragile components and simplifying its regulation, but eventually settled on the French manner of mounting the keys on the player's side of the instrument. In 1848 Boehm's workshop made the first flute (no. 20) with a gold lip-plate, and from 1854 on he began to make cylinder flutes in wood as well as metal, sometimes combining wood headjoints with metal bodies. As to the special qualities of the silver instruments, he later wrote that the 'unsurpassed brilliancy and sonorousness' of his silver flutes very often led players to overblow, 'causing the tone to become hard and shrill; hence its advantages are fully realized only through a very good embouchure and diligent tone practice'. He estimated that not one player in twenty had the feeling for a good tone on a silver flute or the patience to develop it, and for the rest he recommended instruments of wood, of which the first two, nos 83 and 84, were delivered to Philip Ernst in New York in November 1854. In 1848 Godfroy and Lot also began to make cylinder flutes in wood, perhaps at the suggestion of Dorus.[40] In 1855 the firm made only five silver flutes to sixty-seven wood ones, but silver flutes became more popular among leading players in Paris after 1860 (chapter 11).[41]

Boehm's cylinder flute won distinction at several international exhibitions of the 1850s. After entering it at Leipzig in 1850 and winning a silver medal, the inventor visited England again in 1851 and presented the new flute at the Great Exhibition, winning first prize and a gold medal. In 1854 at Munich and in 1855 at Paris the cylinder flute again won silver and gold medals respectively, the latter in recognition of 'important scientific improvements to the flute and the successful application of these principles to other wind instruments', namely the Boehm oboe and bassoon. Only the Boehm flutes and clarinets, however, made any headway with professional musicians.

Boehm's workshop ledger precisely details the instruments he made, an average of ten a year between 1847 and 1861. From 1847 to 1858, a total of 130 cylinder flutes were sold, 15 with ring-keys. The vast majority, 76 flutes, remained in German-speaking countries, Poland, and Russia, while 23 were made for English players. America accounted for eight flutes, the low countries seven, and Italy five. Of the eleven sold in the rest of the world, not a single one went to France.

Philip Bate made a study of the early 1847 pattern flutes from Boehm's workshop which Dayton C. Miller had collected. He found that though in the earliest examples the 1832 mechanism was simply applied to a cylindrical tube with larger toneholes, Boehm continued for some time to experiment with covered keys, open rings, and various mechanical variations.

Different methods of playing B♭ in particular continued to occupy Boehm's inventiveness. He originally provided a single open-standing key for C, as in Tromlitz's flute of 1785, assigning B♭ to the right forefinger as in the Tromlitz 1796 system, but dispensing with the thumb B♭ key Tromlitz provided as a duplicate. But since certain note patterns require some other way of playing B♭ than the 'long' or right-hand B♭ provides, Boehm returned to the concept of a C/B♭ for the left thumb. After several experiments (1832, 1849, and 1854) he settled on a version he first supplied on cylinder flute no. 24, built in February 1849 for a Mr Damiani of Liverpool. In this slightly counter-intuitive arrangement, the B♭ touchpiece lies higher on the tube than the C key, which is kept closed by the left thumb. Rolling or shifting the thumb sideways onto the touchpiece keeps the C key closed at the same time as closing the B♮ hole, thus producing B♭. Rockstro ascribed the invention of this key to his friend Dr Burghley, and its first application to Giulio Briccialdi (1818–81) in May or June 1849, and consequently Boehm's 1849 B♭ key is now universally known by Briccialdi's name.

Boehm also devised a closed G♯ arrangement of his own that Philip Bate thought superior to the Dorus G♯ because it did not depend on the relative force of two opposing springs. In Boehm's version, which he built in 1877 on a flute for General Daniel Macauley (DCM 161; ill. 41(6)), the G♯ cover was held closed by a spring while its lever was split into two sections to reverse its effect. To counteract the flattening effect of the closed G♯ key, Boehm placed the A hole 1.2mm above its normal position.

To find the theoretical tonehole positions for a flute built to play at any of the pitch standards then current (he used A=435), Boehm devised a geometrical diagram he called the *Schema*, which he submitted *hors de concours* to the 1862 London exhibition at which he served on the jury for musical instruments, though he did not attend in person. The *Schema* was later submitted to the Paris exposition of 1867, but because its matter was scientific rather than artistic, the jury declined to consider it. It was criticized by the organ-builder Aristide Cavaillé-Coll, who later retracted his objections.[42] The Bavarian Polytechnic Society first published the diagram in its *Kunst und Gewerbeblatt* (October 1866).

In about 1854, when he was around sixty years of age, Boehm produced an alto flute in G. He exhibited it at the Munich Regional Industry Exhibition of the same year and sold the first such instrument in January 1858. Also in 1854, Carl Mendler (1833–1914), a watchmaker, joined Boehm's Munich operation, becoming foreman in 1862 and a partner five years later. Two of Boehm's pupils trained under him as makers: Emil Rittershausen (1852–1927), who established his own firm in 1876, and Thomas Mollenhauer (1840–1914), a member of an instrument-making family, who made a conical-bore piccolo to Boehm's specifications in 1864.

The revolutionary nature of the Boehm flute caused or intensified sharp divisions among flutists, composers, and conductors not merely over the fingering and mechanism of the instrument but over its tone and very character. These controversies raged for more than a hundred years, in terms and with outcomes that form the topics of later chapters.

Chapter 10

Nineteenth-century eclecticism

Wind bands on military lines provided by far the commonest instrumental ensembles throughout Europe and America after *c*1850, and hence the most widespread employment and educational opportunities for flutists. These bands displaced various military flute ensembles that had developed earlier in the century. In early nineteenth-century Northern Ireland the Ulster Orange Order and youth organizations for boys had formed unison flute bands consisting of sixteen or more six-keyed conical flutes in A♭ (called B♭ flutes), with drums, triangle, and cymbals.[1] A polyphonic 'Corps of Drums and Flutes' first appeared in mid-nineteenth-century England: two piccolos, eight flutes in B♭ playing in three groups, two F flutes, drums, and triangle. Around 1848 the bugle or trumpet replaced the drum as a signal instrument in the British army, though a fife and drum band remained at Woolwich, home of the Royal Military Academy and the Royal Arsenal, until 1856, and Scots and Irish regiments received permission to have fifes and a fife major again in 1881 and 1922. But all these ensembles dwindled in importance, remaining only as showpieces after 1918 except in Ulster, while the mixed wind band, built on B♭ and E♭ clarinets, brass, and percussion, emerged as the official ensemble within European armies after *c*1850. In England the Royal Military School of Music, its first class at Kneller Hall (1857) staffed by foreigners, went on to train generations of instrumentalists and bandmasters at a time when civilian music teaching institutions such as the Royal Academy of Music remained hobbled by politics and disorganization. Countless civilian wind bands patterned on this military type played marches, religious music, and opera arrangements, often outdoors or in bandstands, not only in the major cities but in all parts of Europe and America. The playwright and music critic George Bernard Shaw contended that instrument-makers focused their attention on this large market, to the detriment of orchestral instruments:

> [T]he great bulk of the instrument business lies with military bands, and with the innumerable bands on the military model which exist throughout the country … which compete as eagerly for prizes as rival football teams do, and which spend considerable sums out of those prizes in perfecting their instrumental equipment.[2]

As Shaw noted, many band musicians were unpaid enthusiasts. In fact an ensemble of any kind rarely if ever provided a musician's entire livelihood, as an American advertisement of 1888 indicated by seeking '[a] good flute-player who is a first-class

45. The Paris Opéra Orchestra, 1868–9, by Edgar Degas. The bassoonist is Désiré Dihau, and the flutist probably Henri Altès (1826–99), Paul Taffanel's predecessor as Professor of Flute at the Conservatoire.

shoemaker by trade. Must be sober and reliable.'[3] Bands at resorts often provided seasonal jobs for orchestral players from the cities, while Dan Godfrey's Municipal Orchestra (1893) at Bournemouth subsisted by doubling as seaside band and symphony orchestra. Charles Hallé managed to attract the flutist Jean Firmin Brossa (1839–1915; Conservatoire 1865) to Manchester (1870) by employing him concurrently in the Liverpool Philharmonic, the Reid Concerts in Scotland, the Bristol Festival, and in a winter season spread all over Britain.[4] Engagements in other types of bands at music-halls and, later, cinemas, figured in many flutists' work lives until mechanical reproduction displaced live performance in most popular entertainment.

Even in Paris, where orchestras provided steady work including more rehearsal than was usual elsewhere, the leading flutists made a living by holding posts in multiple ensembles and by teaching.[5]

The variety of work required flutists to develop a wide range of skills. Gerald Jackson, later flutist in Sir Henry Wood's Queen's Hall orchestra, described the functioning of the cinema bands that employed thousands of musicians (London alone had 550 cinemas, 45 theatres and numerous suburban music halls) before the Talkies put more than 60 per cent of them permanently out of work. The ensemble, consisting of between four and fifty players, rarely played music composed specially for the film. Instead, the musicians read from a library of ready-made pieces in appropriate styles labelled with designations such as 'neutral light', 'neutral serious', 'dramatic *agitato*', and 'pastoral', changing mood on a signal from the conductor.[6]

Though bands were the commonest ensembles, symphony orchestras had become the most prestigious by the late nineteenth century, when these expressions of the affluence and civic pride of their middle-class audiences had emerged as the central institution of public musical life. As baton conducting, rehearsals, and higher standards became common, many of today's great symphony orchestras and much of their standard repertoire took shape. But though orchestras of all western nations comprised a similar group of strings, woodwinds, brass, percussion, and harp, their notions of woodwind sound and playing style frequently differed along with the instruments their flutists used. Some of the era's famous conductors held strong opinions on these matters and went to great lengths to employ particular flutists who shared or responded to their tastes.

Those tastes covered a wide spectrum during a time of major changes in orchestral sound. By about twenty years after *c*1830 the volume and power of the orchestral string section had grown considerably so that the winds, now regularly including a full complement of brass, no longer overpowered the strings. Yet despite a tendency to double up woodwind posts so that several players shared the work, woodwind forces remained unchanged even as string sections grew as large as forty to fifty players.[7] Consequently in 1853 Heinrich Friedrich Meyer (1814–97) of Hannover began to build a new type of twelve-keyed flute with a range to low B and a metal-lined ivory or wood head with a tuning slide. Meyer modelled his work on the Austrian and German flutes (by Koch, Liebel, and Ziegler) most favoured by German orchestral players, but altered the bore, tonehole size and placement, as well as the size and form of the mouth-hole, and sometimes inserted metal bushings into the toneholes, all with the aim of producing a greater volume of sound and facilitating the extreme high and low registers.[8] Other German and Austrian workshops soon followed suit, flutes by Ziegler adding trill keys and often extending the range down to B♭, A, or G in the traditional Viennese manner. Other German makers produced Meyer-pattern flutes for domestic and overseas markets, exporting cheap instruments labelled *nach Meyer* (after Meyer; see ill. 46) to the United States well into the twentieth century, while the instrument factories headed by Teodoro Bonaventura Rampone (1809–71) and his sons supplied the Italian market. The Meyer flute met the needs of ensemble flutists in Germany, Austria, Italy, Scandinavia, Russia, and even the U.S. well enough that it remained in use in some orchestras until *c*1930 and still later in bands.

* patented invention[1]

All designs and features noted reached commercial production at or about the date indicated. Only those of musical significance after 1900 are noted.

1852–77	R. S. Rockstro (some mfg by J. M. Rose)	various conical and cylinder flutes with modified acoustics and mechanism[2]
1853	H. F. Meyer	modified keyed flute, 12 keys
c1860	William Card	old-system conical flute with F mechanism
	Briccialdi/Forni	Briccialdi-system [conical] flute[3]
1866	Carte*	Carte 1867 System, a modified Carte 1851
c1867	Louis Lot	modified silver cylinder flute
1868	Theodore Berteling*	adjustable regulating screws and other devices
1869	Briccialdi*	Briccialdi metal cylinder flute[4]
1870	John R. Radcliff (mfg by Rudall Carte)	Radcliff model, a simplified Carte 1851 with closed G$\sharp$ and split E
1877	Rockstro (mfg by Rudall Carte)	'Rockstro System', modified Boehm-system cylinder flute
1879	Agostino Rampone*	double-walled metal conical old-system flutes and piccolos[5]
1880	Berteling	improvements to old-system flute[6]
1885	Schwedler & Kruspe	Schwedler & Kruspe model 1885
1888	Carlo T. Giorgi (1856–1956) *(1897)	keyless vertical flute
1889–95	Djalma Juillot* (1895, 1901)	Borne-Juillot System: modified Boehm system with split E mechanism and other, mutually incompatible, innovations
1895	Schwedler & Kruspe*	Schwedler & Kruspe Model 1895[7]
1898	Schwedler & Kruspe*	Reform flute, Schwedler & Kruspe system[8]
	George W. Haynes (1866–1947)	drawn toneholes (independently developed and patented by William S. Haynes in 1914)
1902	J. Thibouville-Lamy & Cie*	supplementary keys for Boehm cylinder flute
1904	Otto Mönnig*	'reform'-embouchure, with raised front wall[9]
1907	Rudall Carte & Co.	Guards' Model, an 1867 flute with closed G$\sharp$
1914	Nicholas Alberti (b 1877?)	transposing C or D$\flat$ flute
c1921	Moritz Max Mönnig*	'full tone head',[10] other modifications to Reform flute

Flutists in Paris, some of whom had been playing their French-modified Boehm flutes in orchestral positions for twenty years, apparently also felt the need of louder instruments by the late 1860s. At the Paris exhibition of 1867 Louis Lot presented a new design alongside his older model, having a thicker tube, larger toneholes and a bigger, more square embouchure, as well as a sturdier mechanism with the modern 'independent' closed G$\sharp$ key replacing the Dorus G$\sharp$.[9] (This device later led to the development of a supplementary mechanism to restore the correct fingering for E3: John R. Radcliff used such a 'split E' in his model of 1870, and Djalma Juillot devised another solution with Paul Taffanel in 1895.)

Besides increasing his flutes' volume of tone, Lot's new embouchure hole affected their pitch and blowing technique, and thus their sound quality. In 1868 Boehm wrote that he was unaccustomed to Lot's relatively small embouchure holes, still modelled on those of conical five- or six-keyed flutes by his early nineteenth-century predecessors:

> The size of the mouth-hole, as well as that of the finger-holes, also materially influences the volume of tone. For a large full tone a large mouth-hole is necessary. I could never play properly with small oval mouth-holes.[10]

Thus he recognized that allowances had to be made for the different embouchure technique of various players when he built instruments for them:

> The difference caused by embouchure (viz., method of blowing) is so considerable that in many cases it amounts to more than a quarter, in some even to half a tone; therefore, in making a flute to any given pitch, it is not enough for me to know the number of vibrations; I must also have some knowledge of the player's embouchure. For instance, I have never yet met with a flautist who played as sharp as myself on the same flute, excepting Tulou, who was celebrated for the largeness of his tone. Dorus would have played a quarter of a tone flatter on the same flute.[11]

Despite indications that French and German orchestral players needed instruments with more volume, German orchestral flutists after c1850 continued to cite the Boehm flute's loudness as a defect, and the traditional flute's dynamic capacity and tonal flexibility (*Modulationsfähigkeit*) as ideal, just as A. B. Fürstenau had in 1838. Most found the ring-key flute, just as much as the cylinder flute, too assertive, monotonous, and emotionally cold for their work. Thus until the era of recording, the sound of the conical wooden Meyer or Ziegler flute remained by and large entrenched in the ears of German and Austrian conductors, composers, and flutists as the only acceptable orchestral flute tone.

The matter had at least as much to do with musical appropriateness as with dogma, since many German flutists felt ambivalent about the Boehm flute. Even Fürstenau held a not entirely negative view, for he sent his son Moritz (1824–99) to Munich to study the ring-key flute with Boehm in 1846 and wrote of his satisfaction with the youngster's success.[12] In fact Boehm, who disliked the Wagnerian long-line vocal style and preferred the more differentiated Italian singing manner, shared Fürstenau's musical taste even if they favoured different instruments.[13] Boehm often underlaid words to *Adagio* movements as an aid to proper phrasing, just as Hotteterre had done, and noted that the flutist should express his feelings as clearly as if he were actually singing a text. He made clear that he felt this more important than volume of tone in a letter to his friend W. S. Broadwood in 1871:

> All Nicholson's immediate successors had, more or less, a powerful tone, but they made a trumpet of the flute. Their tone was loud enough, but *loudness* alone is not what is wanted for *singing*. I always prefer quality to quantity.[14]

Boehm's sophistication notwithstanding, some other Germans still perceived his flute as too loud and too trumpet-like for use in an orchestra. Richard Wagner, much of whose experience was in Munich, the one German city where the Boehm flute dominated, warned in 1869 that orchestral flutists were no longer capable of playing quietly:

[*Piano*] can quite easily be required from the strings, but by contrast [is] quite difficult from the winds, particularly the woodwinds. A softly sustained *piano* is hardly obtainable from them any more, particularly from the flutists, who have transformed their formerly so soft instruments into mighty shawms.[15]

In 1852 Wagner and the Bavarian Court orchestra instructed Moritz Fürstenau, as a condition of his succeeding to the post of first flute, to abandon the Boehm flute and return to his traditional instrument. Indeed, the flutist seems to have done so quite willingly, for in a review of Wilhelm Barge's *Praktische Flötenschule* (Leipzig, 1880), which was critical of the Boehm flute, he concurred with Barge's opinion that it was unsuitable for orchestral use:

I entirely admire the ingenious invention of Master Boehm, but must call into question whether it can be recommended for those orchestras that keep to the distinct tone colours of the woodwind instruments ... for with few exceptions the old flute is still chiefly played in the greater German orchestras.[16]

For Fürstenau, as for Maximilian Schwedler sixty years later, the choice was dictated not by ease of technique or smoothness of tone, but by emotional impact:

Even if the artist who uses the Boehm flute (cylindrical bore) may have an easier time playing in many respects, the player who uses a good conical flute has to my mind more means in his hands to move the hearts of his listeners.[17]

In the 1880s Wagner persuaded another Munich principal flutist, Boehm's pupil Rudolf Tillmetz (1847–1915), to revert to the ring-key flute after playing the cylinder flute for almost twenty years. In his 33 years of experience as an orchestral player and soloist, Tillmetz wrote,

I eventually had to convince myself from my own experience that the various objections on the part of informed authorities were to a great extent justified. When I participated in the *Parsifal* performances of 1882 in Bayreuth as an orchestral player I noticed that Richard Wagner showed no sympathy for the cylindrical flute. Specifically, he gave it the name 'cannon'.

I therefore decided, urged still further by the Royal General Music Director Hermann Levi, to change over to the conical ring-key flute, which I did not regret. ... [18]

Writing as late as 1890, Tillmetz insisted that 'the true elegiac flute tone is lost because of the cylindrical bore' of the 1847 flute, and that the metal instrument sounded too much like a trumpet. In 1882 he ordered a ring-key flute from Julius Max Bürger (*fl* 1881–1904), while Emil Rittershausen (1852–1927), Joseph Poeschl (1866–1947) and Julius Heinrich Zimmermann (1851–1922) offered conical flutes from 1875 until 1920.[19] Tillmetz's ring-key flute 'school' continued with Joseph Lindbauer (*b* 1869), Heinrich Scherrer (*b* 1865), and Gustave Kaleve (1884–1976).

As the orchestra became more important in the late nineteenth century, solo flute-playing no longer enjoyed the popularity the travelling virtuosi had given it (chapter 7). The Dutch periodical *Caecilia* noted this as early as 1853:

> After a century as the fashionable and favourite instrument of connoisseurs and novices, the flute has for perhaps twenty years not only almost completely fallen out of fashion, but is even generally spoken of with a sort of scorn.[20]

London's Philharmonic concerts in the twenty-five years after 1821 featured twenty-one flute solos, but in the following fifty years only one.[21] Contemporary observers had their own theories as to the decline's causes. W. N. James opined in 1846 that the flute was 'fast sinking, and giving way to the new instrument, the concertina'.[22] But however much the flute's popularity may have lessened among amateurs, virtuoso flutists such as Albert Fransella (Boehm flute), Eli Hudson (Carte 1867), and the Australian John Lemmone (Radcliff) continued to find a ready audience at least in England into the age of recording (chapter 12). The repertoire preserved on early recordings rarely consisted of pieces with enduring musical merit. But probably it does not accurately represent what professional flutists played in concert. The music Edward De Jong (1837–1920) performed from 1858 to 1909, for example, covered far more varied and interesting ground, including performances of Hummel's *Septet* op. 74 (1858), Fürstenau's *Fantaisie on Bellini's 'Norma'* (1859), Spohr's *Nonet* (1875), Handel Sonatas (1872, 1882), Nicholson's *Recollections of Ireland* (1871), and Saint-Saëns's *Tarentelle* (1888) and *Romance* op. 37 (1879, 1891). In later years, De Jong performed Andersen pieces (1889–90), Bach's *Musical Offering* trio-sonata (1909), and Beethoven's *Serenade* (1908), among other works. During his career he played pieces by thirty-nine composers including himself, Briccialdi, Boehm, Chaminade, Molique, Richardson, and Kuhlau, as well as flute bird-obbligatos by Benedict, Bishop and the like.[23]

Studies and exercises for flutes of many types indicate that players of each of them achieved a high technical level. In Italy flute soloists poured their energy into challenging and imaginative studies which provided models and ideas for later works by Taffanel, Gaubert, Moyse and others. Many of the Italian virtuoso studies were dedicated to amateur flutists, who clearly played to an extremely high standard. The Neapolitan Emanuele Krakamp's Boehm flute method (1847) and that of the Roman Vincenzo de Michelis (1874) catered to professional pedagogy, while elementary tutors such as those of the Florentines Ciardi (*c*1860), Galli (1870), and Pieroni (1880) were addressed to beginning flutists and band musicians.[24] The brilliant Milanese Ziegler flutist Giuseppe Rabboni (1800–56), a successful travelling virtuoso as well as principal flutist at La Scala and professor at the Conservatory (1830), translated and expanded Berbiguier's method, adding a volume of exercises, studies, and sonatas, as well as transcribing *50 studi brillanti* from the violin works of Rode and Kreutzer. Cesare Ciardi (1818–77), Camillo Romanino (1840–1912), and Vincenzo De Michelis (1825–91) produced *Preludi* and *Capricci* in the form of cadenzas, with imitations of Paganini's *Capricci* in a flute idiom.[25] Further works by Giulio Briccialdi (1818–81), Joseph Fahrbach (n.d.), Giuseppe Gariboldi (1882) and Filippo Franceschini (1841–1918) were followed by Leonardo De Lorenzo (1875–1962) in his *Nove grande studi* (1903) and *L'Indispensible* (1912). De Lorenzo's exercises, each group of which is dedicated to one of the great flutists of the time, demand the highest virtuosity.[26]

Joachim Andersen (1847–1909), Ernesto Koehler (1849–1907), Wilhelm Popp (1828–1903), and Adolf Terschak (1832–1901) wrote methods or studies for the Meyer flute. Siegfried Karg-Elert (1877–1933) composed studies and other pieces for Karl Bartuzat, who played with him in a military band during World War I. Bartuzat was shown holding a Reform flute (see p. 198) in a photograph of 1906, but had switched to the Boehm flute immediately before or during the war.[27]

Until De Lorenzo emigrated to America in the following century, this high level of virtuosity was not as evident in the New World, where simple keyed flute tutors published throughout the nineteenth century provided basic instruction for playing marches, Celtic and operatic tunes, and dance music, sometimes marked with directions for the steps. The fife had become almost a totem of the Revolutionary war, so that when the Militia Act of 1792 raised local detachments, the demand for instruments increased. Early American fife-makers operated in Boston, Hartford, and Albany, while woodwind firms that grew from English traditions made and sold flutes in New York, Albany, and Litchfield, Conn. after *c*1820.

Efforts by Philip Ernst and Alfred G. Badger to promote the Boehm flute in New York helped bring the instrument into nearly universal use by that city's amateurs and symphony players, almost all immigrants, from *c*1850. Drouët first tried a Boehm flute while visiting New York in 1854, when he praised the instrument and wrote a set of studies for it, dedicated to Ernst and published by subscription from fifty-eight Boehm flutists, all but four of them Ernst's pupils.[28] Two of Boehm's students who held distinguished positions in America helped spread the Boehm flute early. Eduard Heindl emigrated in 1864, bringing with him Boehm's cylinder flute no. 19 (DCM 99), in silver with both silver and wood headjoints, open G$\sharp$, and a B-foot, though as first flutist of the Boston Symphony from its foundation in 1881 he preferred to use a wooden Boehm & Mendler flute. Heindl obtained more orders from the U.S. for Boehm than he could fill, from customers who refused to accept a Lot flute as a substitute.[29] Carl Wehner (1838–1912), a third-generation flutist, was offered positions in the New York Philharmonic and Metropolitan Opera orchestras by the German-born Theodore Thomas after seventeen years as the Boehm flute's principal exponent in Russia, where he played under Berlioz, Brahms, Liszt, Tchaikovsky, Verdi, and Wagner. He commonly used his *c*1878 wooden Boehm & Mendler flute (DCM 157) in preference to two earlier silver ones. Eugene Wiener (1847–1903), another Boehm pupil, played with Wehner in the New York Philharmonic and Thomas orchestras, while Boehm's American pupil, James S. Wilkins (*d* 1909), took up a position in Philadelphia.

46. John George Brown (1831–1913), *The Music Lesson*. The flute is a typical *nach Meyer* instrument with an ivory head, probably imported to America from Germany.

The Boehm flute became the principal type offered by American flute-makers during the 1870s. Badger based his early cylinder flutes closely on French models, while his apprentices, including William R. Meinell (*fl* 1860s–1903), and the next generation's William S. Haynes, copied Boehm & Mendler instruments. In *c*1850 Badger introduced ebonite, a mixture of india-rubber and sulphur on which Thomas Goodyear was awarded a widely infringed patent in 1844, retaining exclusive U.S. rights until the 1880s. He began making silver flutes in the mid-1860s, a decade after foreign silver instruments had appeared. Badger and others made tube extensions to low B♭ beginning in the 1860s, but these disappeared from advertising after *c*1900.

William G. Schulze (1856–c1907) built keyed flutes, as well as Boehm and Siccama flutes, but the latter type disappeared by the end of the 1850s. John Clinton produced a Boehm flute method at Badger's invitation in c1860, while Badger's own method of 1861 was adapted to ring-key, eight-keyed, and Siccama flutes. By 1875, however, Badger had discontinued his other lines, as Meinell had in the previous year, and made only Boehm flutes. Theodore Berteling (1821/2–90), on the other hand, continued to offer keyed flutes, and even patented improvements in 1880.[30] The New York dealer Carl Fischer, as well as the Sears Roebuck and Montgomery Ward catalogues, offered old-system flutes as late as 1930, and the six-keyed piccolo lasted even longer. Though the Boehm flute dominated the East Coast orchestras, the Chicago Symphony's principal flutist on its founding by Theodore Thomas in 1891 was Vigo Andersen (1852–95), brother of Joachim and like him a proponent of the old-system flute.[31]

For reasons already examined, German orchestral flutists in general were slow to accept the Boehm flute, but in Berlin, in spite of the strong traditional sentiment among flutists who traced their ideal of a sweet, subtly coloured flute sound to Quantz (chapter 5), it became established in the 1870s. The French Boehm flutist Baptiste Sauvlet served from 1873 to 1876 as principal flute of Benjamin Bilse's Concert Orchestra.[32] He was followed by Ferdinand Seffern (1839–80), the orchestra's first German Boehm flutist, and Charles Molé (1857–1905; Conservatoire 1874). In 1882 the brilliantly trained Meiningen orchestra under Hans von Bülow visited Berlin and made a tremendous impression on Bilse's musicians, 53 of whom left the band to found the Berlin Philharmonic, with the Danish Meyer flutist Karl Joachim Andersen (1847–1909) as principal flute.[33] Molé moved to the Opéra comique until he was engaged by the Boston Symphony in 1887, and later to St Louis and New York.[34]

Despite Molé's displacement by a Meyer flutist, his playing inspired Emil Prill (1867–1940), a pupil of Heinrich Gantenberg (1823–1910) and of Andersen, to take up the Boehm flute in 1882. This sparked a crisis with Gantenberg, who blocked his graduation from the Hochschule until its director, Joseph Joachim, intervened. According to Giannini (1984) Prill ordered four cylinder flutes from Louis Lot in 1890–2: one of wood with a D-foot, and three of metal, all with closed G♯ keys.[35] After three years as solo flutist in the Hamburg Philharmonie (1889–91) he succeeded Gantenberg as solo flute in the Berlin Royal Orchestra, where he remained until 1928. On the question of vibrato, which became a divisive issue after c1905, Prill was vehemently opposed, though his recordings betray traces of it, and as late as 1927 he thought the silver cylinder flute unsuited to orchestral work:

> The silver flute may be strongly recommended to pupils and amateurs, because it responds so easily, whereas it is less suited to orchestral playing owing to the extremely clear metallic tone which forms too shrill a contrast to the rest of the woodwind instruments.[36]

During his tenure from 1903 to 1934 (professor from 1906) Prill taught over three hundred Boehm flute pupils at the Berlin Hochschule, which first admitted women in

1876. He was a frequent soloist (1891–1928) in the Opera house concerts, and appeared as such, or with the wind chamber ensemble he founded, in over a hundred German cities.[37] He published a Boehm flute method and a *Guide to Flute Literature* (1899) that listed all available music for flute, including opera fantasias, variations, and the like, as well as newly edited works by the old masters. Georg Müller (1882–1956) became Gantenberg's last pupil in 1901 and switched to Prill and the Boehm flute a few years later.

Vienna's flute-playing retained its characteristic local instruments as played by Bayr, Bogner, and many flutists of the Vienna Philharmonic until the 1880s and later. However, one of that orchestra's founding flutists (1842), Franz Zierer, also a soloist and teacher at the Vienna Conservatory until 1863, continued to play an old-fashioned six-keyed flute with a D-foot.[38] Touring virtuosi brought unfamiliar instruments and playing styles, as R. S. Pratten did in 1847 with a well-received solo recital on a Siccama flute.[39] Franz Doppler served as principal flute of the Vienna Philharmonic from 1858 to 1879, as well as Kapellmeister at the Hoftheater from 1864 and a teacher at the Vienna Conservatory. In 1879 his pupil Roman Kukala succeeded him as principal flute of the Vienna Philharmonic, and in 1883 at the Conservatory, where he introduced the Boehm flute.[40] To follow Kukala at the Court Opera Mahler engaged the Dutchmen Ary van Leeuwen (1875–1953) and Jacques van Lier, who brought the first silver Boehm flutes to Vienna (1903–20).[41] Van Leeuwen had studied with his countryman and fellow Boehm flutist Albert Fransella (1865–1935) as well as with Andersen. From 1889 to 1903 van Leeuwen was principal of various orchestras in Europe and the U.S., including the Folk Theatre of Amsterdam, the Berlin Philharmonic (1897–1901), the Philadelphia Orchestra (1901–2), and an orchestra in Warsaw (1902–3). While in Vienna, he became a professor at the Conservatory and founded a wind chamber music society modelled on Taffanel's in Paris.[42]

In contrast to the eclectic spirit of other cities, Dresden's flute-playing tradition placed supreme value on its heritage, not only in instrument and playing style but also in its pioneering revival of early repertoire, which took place significantly earlier than the better-known one in Paris (chapters 11, 13). In 1843 Wagner became director of the Hoftheater orchestra, which under Weber's disciplined baton (a new way of conducting at that time of violinist-directors) had enjoyed a high reputation for excellence. Moritz Fürstenau, appointed first flute in 1852 on condition that he give up the Boehm flute, taught thirty-three students at the Dresden Conservatory in 1858–89, the same number as graduated from the Paris Conservatoire in those years. Early works figured prominently in the repertoire: Mozart's Andante (1876), sonatas by Handel and Bach (1879–83), and Mozart's concertos in G and D (1884, 1886; first used as examination pieces at the Paris Conservatoire only in 1918). Paul Taffanel seems to have discovered the pieces at around the same time, or perhaps a little later, and when he played the Mozart G major concerto with the Leipzig Gewandhaus orchestra under Carl Reinecke on 13 February 1890, the Leipzig press reviewed his playing 'quite favourably'. After 1890 a distinct shift in repertoire took place with the appearance of works by a more diverse array of composers including, Ciardi, Demersseman, Doppler, A. B. Fürstenau, Heinemeyer, and Tulou.[43]

Tonkünstler-Verein First Performances of Flute Music, 1854–1929.
Source: John R. Bailey, 'Towards a History of the Dresden Flute Tradition, 1850 to the Present', paper read at the NFA National Convention, Boston, 21 August 1993.

† World premiere
* Dresden premiere

1856–7	Brandenburg 4, Hummel Septet, Reicha E♭, Quintet, Beethoven Serenade
1857–8	Bach B Minor Suite
1858–9	Spohr Quintet
1859–60	Bach B Minor Sonata
1860	Brandenburg 2
1861	Kuhlau Flute Quartet, Bach Trio Sonata
1862–3	Bach Triple Concerto, Spohr Nonet, Haffner Serenade
1864	Brandenburg 4, Reicha Quintet, op. 91, no. 9
1868	Handel A Minor Sonata, Bach E♭, Sonata, Onslow Quintet, Bach E Minor Sonata, C. P. E. Bach Trio, Handel G Major Sonata
1870	Doppler *Bird of the Forest*, Bach B Minor Sonata, Handel B Minor Sonata
1872	Bach E Major Sonata, Musical Offering, Mozart Clarinet Concerto*
1873	Hummel Septet, Onslow Nonet, Bach E♭, Sonata, Handel C Major Sonata, Spohr Quintet
1874	Mozart A Major Quartet (Fritsche), Handel B Minor Sonata (Fürstenau)
1877	Quantz G Major Concerto* (Fürstenau), Bach C Major Sonata (Zizold), Handel A Minor (Fürstenau)
1878	*Siegfried-Idylle**
1879	Schubert *Trockne Blumen* (Meinel), Handel F Major (Plunder), Dvořák Serenade (* with two flutes added [Plunder, Fritsche] with Dvořák's permission)
1882	Mozart Flute and Harp Concerto* (A. Bauer), Strauss Serenade, op. 7 (not indicated as premiere, but supposedly written for this group)
1883	Reinecke *Undine* Sonata (Plunder)
1898	Mozart D Major Quartet* (P. Bauer)
1901	Taffanel Quintet* (Wunderlich)
1902	Klughardt Quintet† (Wunderlich, dedicated to TV)
1905	Reinecke Sextett, op. 271* (P. Bauer), Reger Trio, op. 77a (Wunderlich)
1906	Gounod *Petite Symphonie** (1879) (Wunderlich)
1907	Saint-Saëns Caprice* (Wunderlich)
1908	Weber Trio (P. Bauer)
1912	Schubert *Trockne Blumen* (Wunderlich)
1915	Mozart D Major Quartet, Bach B Minor Sonata (Wunderlich)
1917	Blumer Serenade and Theme and Variations for Quintet† (Peschek)
1919	Blumer Suite for flute and piano† (Amans)
1920	Bach Solo *Partita* (Amans, with piano accompaniment)
1922	Blumer Sextett, piano and winds* (Amans), Debussy Sonata* (Bräunling)

Leipzig too remained a deeply conservative force in German flute-playing throughout the nineteenth century. Wilhelm Haake (1804–75), a student of A. B. Fürstenau's, joined the Gewandhaus orchestra in 1821 and succeeded Karl Grenser as solo flutist in 1855–66. Though Grenser had been nominal flute professor at the Leipzig Conservatory when Mendelssohn founded the institution in 1843, orchestral instruments were not yet part of the curriculum. Edward de Jong, after studies at the Cologne Conservatory beginning in 1850, moved to Leipzig to study privately with Haake and deputize for him, before taking up a position in Manchester.[44] Wilhelm Barge, primarily self-taught, succeeded Haake in 1866, and became the first practising flute teacher at the Leipzig Conservatory in 1882.[45] His nine-volume set of orchestral excerpts shows the growing trend in Germany for the specific training of orchestral flutists. Barge and two Gewandhaus colleagues used Meyer flutes, and his flute method (1880) voiced many objections to the Boehm system.

According to Maximilian Schwedler (1853–1940) a vacancy announcement for the Gewandhaus orchestra's solo flute post in 1881 invited only players who did not play the Boehm flute. Schwedler sailed through the audition, performing two Bach *Adagios* and the solo passage from the Scherzo in Mendelssohn's *Midsummer Night's Dream*, whose 265 notes he played in one breath. He succeeded Barge as principal flute in 1895.[46] Schwedler supported the use of vibrato with great fervour, as opposed to the Berlin school of Emil Prill. He insisted on keeping the chest expanded 'like a soldier's' and performing with distinct emotional affects, such as melancholy, playful, or serene.[47]

From 1885 to 1898 Schwedler devised several modifications of the Meyer flute to improve its mechanism, response, and intonation while preserving the flute's traditional sound, culminating in the Schwedler-Kruspe Reform flute of 1898. The firm of C. Kruspe of Erfurt built the first flute to Schwedler's specifications, the 'Schwedler & Kruspe model 1885'.[48] Following an improved version of 1895, the 'Reform flute' (DCM 62) appeared in 1898, with improved intonation and a new automatic mechanism to eliminate the F key as a vent for the eighteen to twenty notes that had formerly required it, as well as further trill keys. Some time around 1921 Schwedler and Kruspe ended their collaboration, and subsequent Reform flutes were made exclusively by Moritz Max Mönnig (1875–1949) in Leipzig. Mönnig introduced a longer cylindrical metal headjoint, called a 'full tone head'. The body was still usually made in wood, though one extant instrument, DCM 1026 (*c*1925), is made entirely of metal. DCM 1548 is a fully developed Mönnig Reform flute of *c*1930. Many German and Russian makers including Wilhelm Hermann Heckel (1879–1953), Liebel's successor Heinrich Franz Eduard Pinder (1857–1913), Theodor Poppe (*fl c*1880–1930), M. Pupo Pupeschi (1859–1932), and Julius Heinrich Zimmerman (*fl* 1875–1929) copied Reform mechanisms, modifying and adding features.

Otto Mönnig patented a flute head with a raised strike wall, or blowing edge, in 1904, which he rather confusingly named the 'Reform' embouchure. In fact it had no connection to the Reform flute and Schwedler was violently opposed to it.[49] Nonetheless, by 1912 the Boehm flute maker Conrad Mollenhauer (1876–1943) could claim that at least 80 per cent of all German flutists used this embouchure, and even as late as 1960, despite a campaign against it by Gustav Scheck, an early German convert to French-style flutes and flute-playing, the 'Reform' head was still 'overwhelmingly popular' in Germany.[50]

The impetus for Schwedler-Kruspe flutes and the 'Reform' embouchure seems to have come from increasingly extreme use of the flute's high and low registers by Brahms, Tchaikovsky, Richard Strauss, and others. Brahms's symphonies required the utmost control at the upper extreme, as well featuring the dark low register, though generally his flute parts were not meant to stand out individually so much as to blend in to the orchestral texture or emerge unobtrusively from it.[51] Players of both Boehm and Meyer flutes had to correct high-register intonation flaws in order to play these parts, and Hamilton (1984) concludes that the Reform flute, while addressing these problems and allowing its users 'to play in tune and at very soft dynamic levels in the extreme upper register', could also play louder in the low register than the Boehm cylinder flute.[52] On the other hand Erich List, a pupil of Schwedler at the Leipzig Conservatory (1921–6) and later his successor in the Gewandhaus orchestra, noted in an interview with John Bailey that high-register passages were especially difficult on the Reform flute because of the amount of air required.[53] In any case, Schwedler's flutes seem largely to have achieved their goals, since they remained popular with German orchestral players and conductors, including Brahms and Arthur Nikisch, from 1885 to 1910. In 1886 Brahms, who had learned the flute in order to play Kuhlau's flute sonatas, wrote to Schwedler praising the 'especially full-bodied, beautiful and powerful tone' of his newly-developed flute, as well as his playing of it, in one of his compositions performed at Leipzig.[54] Compositions written for the Reform flute include Carl Reinecke's Concerto op. 283 (*c*1908), dedicated to Schwedler, who gave the first performance of Saint-Saëns's *Tarentelle* for flute, clarinet, and orchestra (1893), and played Bach's Brandenburg concerto no. 4 on Reform flutes in 1901 with Barge's pupil Oskar Fischer (*b* 1870).

The period's most demanding composer, Richard Strauss, who worked with widely different ensembles and heard all kinds of playing including Tillmetz's on the ring-key flute (Munich, 1886–9), favoured the Boehm flute, though many of his pieces were probably premiered with Meyer or Schwedler models. Strauss typically scored for three flutes, often adding a piccolo, and gave all the parts what Fitzgibbon (1929) called 'finger-twisting passages of enormous difficulty'.[55] Schwedler vehemently complained about Strauss's use of D4, E♭4 and E4, which he thought 'an absurdity and an unreasonable demand on the player and the instrument', more suited for the piccolo and the *Terzflöte* (flute in F) than the concert flute.

Gustav Mahler's use of the highest register was more cautious than Strauss's. Though he worked with Schwedler as Kapellmeister at Leipzig from 1891 to 1897, Mahler also had experience with Boehm flutists such as Popp, Prill, and Tieftrunk at Hamburg, and as Kapellmeister for the Vienna Court opera in 1897 he appointed the Boehm flutist Ary van Leeuwen.

Boehm flutes and other cylindrical models became more common as flute-making reached a new stage of industrialization in the mid-nineteenth century, spurred by exposure at public exhibitions and greater international competition for market share. If playing and listening to flute solos was no longer a mania among recreational musicians, demand for instruments was still growing, particularly for use in bands, as the number of players expanded along with the middle and industrial working classes. Groups of small workshops in La Couture-Boussey in the Eure region of Normandy, in the Saxon Vogtland centred on Markneukirchen, and in the city of London supplied this market, often now carrying out piece-work for larger capitalist organizations, some of which consolidated operations into factory-like systems. Guilds had enforced regulations less strictly after the French Revolution as supply and demand became the market's regulating factor. In 1894 journeymen in England's musical instrument trades recognized the new structure of their working lives when they formed an industrial trade union, the Military and Orchestral Musical Instrument Makers' Trade Society.[56]

New roads and railways enabled Vogtland instrument-makers, who did not make Boehm flutes, to supply woodwinds and brass as far afield as Bethlehem, Pa., for distribution in the Eastern U.S. as well as to South America, where French instruments had previously monopolized the market. The two dozen masters who built woodwinds in the region in 1800 had increased by 1876 to a total of 119 masters and labourers.[57] J. Friedrich Paulus and Wilhelm August Mönnig (1834–94) specialized in flutes of the *nach Meyer* type: the cheapest cost one third of a Thaler, while the most expensive, with ivory headjoints and silver mounts and keywork, cost 60 Thalers. The region produced 8000 flutes per annum in the lowest price range, 3000 in the medium range of 1–2 Thalers, and 6000 at 2–160 Thalers, for a total annual production of 70,000 Thalers. Piccolos were sold by the dozen at between 1 and 48 Thalers. Owing to the Vogtland's reputation for cheap work, the best and finest instruments were often marked with false indications of origin.[58]

Rudall Carte of London commanded a worldwide market for its modern flutes while England continued to attract foreign musicians, many of whom played old-system instruments. Johann Sedlaztek continued to perform on his extended-range Viennese flute,[59] and Robert Frisch, after taking part in the Conservatoire test of the ring-key flute (chapter 9), travelled to England in 1838 as solo flutist in Johann Strauss's orchestra and became 'a great attraction, especially to the flute-players' at the first promenade concerts of conductor-entrpreneurs Eliason, Musard, and Jullien.[60] According to Rockstro, 'Frisch played on an old-fashioned flute of German make…. In 1840 he began to practise on a flute, made on the new system, by Buffet of Paris', but gave up because of the fingering. The Transylvanian Meyer flutist Adolf Terschak (1832–1901) led the life of a travelling virtuoso to the extreme, visiting Arabia, Astrachan, Siberia, Korea, China, Japan, and Iceland, with a tour of Central Asia in 1897, besides the more usual European and Russian cities. On a visit to London in 1878 'his attempts to tune with the orchestra at the Crystal Palace so signally failed that he left in disgust',[61] an apparently rare case in which the period's variety of instruments caused any practical difficulty. Other foreigners arrived in England as Boehm flutists. The Paris-trained Swiss Boehm flutist Jean Firmin Brossa came to play in the Hallé Orchestra of Manchester and the Liverpool Philharmonic.[62] Queen Victoria's Consort, Prince Albert, took lessons, probably on the Boehm flute, from Benjamin Wells (1826–99), a pupil of Richardson and Clinton. At the Philharmonic Concert in 1839 Wells performed on Siccama's model, but he represented the Boehm flute at the Great Exhibition of 1851.[63] Wells, Professor at the Royal Academy of Music

47. Until World War 2 Rudall Carte's catalogues continued to list flutes of silver, cocus, ebonite, and gold with every one of the commonest fingering systems.

From a catalogue of *c*1937, pp. 4–6. Reading upward: (1) Old-system cocuswood flute; (2) Silver Radcliff model (closed G♯); (3) Boehm-system model (open or closed G♯) in cocuswood; and (4) in silver; (5) Rockstro model (open G♯) in ebonite; (6) Carte 1867 system (open G♯) in silver; (7) Guards' model in cocuswood (closed G♯); (8) Eight-keyed or 'Concert' flute, in cocuswood or ebonite. These last could be supplied 'with either Conical or Cylindrical Bore with Parabolic Head Joint'; all other models had a cylindrical bore and parabolic head. Piccolos, alto flutes, and flutes in E♭ and F were also listed.

from 1855 to 1867, was succeeded there and in the Queen's band (1860) by the Danish Boehm flutist Oluf Svendsen (1832–88), who had studied with Niels Petersen in Copenhagen and Matthieu André Reichert (1830–*c*70) at the Brussels conservatory, migrating in 1855 to England to play for Jullien at his Covent Garden promenade concerts. Svendsen became principal at the Crystal Palace, and played at the Royal Italian Opera (1862–72) and at the Philharmonic Society (1861–85).[64]

German and French Boehm flutes of wood and silver were used side by side in American orchestras, where older keyed flutes also occasionally appeared in the early years. The founding Boston Symphony flutists Heindl (who served for fourteen years) and Paul Fox (twenty-seven years) used wooden Boehm & Mendler flutes, while a third, Wilhelm Rietzel, played an old-system flute by Albrecht of New York.[65] In 1887 Charles Molé brought the first silver Louis Lot B-foot flute (no. 4358, 1887) to the Boston orchestra when he succeeded Heindl as principal, after working under Walter Damrosch in St Louis and New York. Except for Arthur Brooke, who served for twenty-seven years, all the orchestra's flutists after Molé were French Conservatoire graduates, mostly with Louis Lot flutes. These included André Maquarre (1875–*c*1936; Conservatoire 1893 under Altès; BSO 1898–1918; he played a Bonneville), Daniel Maquarre (*b* 1881; Conservatoire 1896 under Taffanel; BSO 1903–4, also in New York and Philadelphia), and Georges Laurent (1886–1964; Conservatoire 1905), also a Taffanel student and for two years solo flutist of the Société des Concerts du Conservatoire (BSO 1918–51 under Rabaud, Monteux, Koussevitsky, and Munch). It appears Wilhelm Gericke reinstated American wooden flutes for the 1905 season, but silver returned the following year.[66]

In 1886 Eduard Heindl persuaded the jewellers George Winfield Haynes (1866–1947) and his brother William Sherman Haynes (1864–1939) to move from Providence, Rhode Island to Boston, where George set up a flute-making and repair shop. Two years later Eustache Strasser, flute professor at the New England Conservatory, joined the Haynes brothers in a partnership that copied Boehm & Mendler and Louis Lot flutes played by Boston professionals, counting Heindl and Molé among its first customers. William S. Haynes left the company in June 1894 to become superintendent of the new Boehm flute manufacturing branch of another company, John C. Haynes and Co. (unrelated to his own family). In this post over the following six years, William Haynes made German silver, silver-plated, and wooden flutes under the Bay State trademark, while the company also imported all grades of instrument, from boxwood eight-keyed to handmade Boehm flutes, by companies including Rudall Carte and Buffet. In 1900 William S. Haynes left J. C. Haynes to establish his own company. His reputation had grown through the recommendation of Carl Wehner, first flute of the Metropolitan Opera, one of several prominent players who had bought a Bay State instrument he had made. By 1901 a Bay State catalogue claimed that the Boston Symphony flutists all used its instruments.

Haynes, trained as a jeweller but self-taught as a flute-maker, devised several innovative production methods. He made silver parts by drop forging, and while seeking a solder that would allow him to build flutes of aluminium, invented a method of extruding the toneholes from the metal of the tube by the same method as a kettle spout. Applying the principle to silver flutes, Haynes employed thicker tubing, using 0.018 inch tube for flutes with drawn holes as opposed to 0.013 inch for soldered. Though he obtained patents in Britain and Germany (1913) and the U.S. (1914), it later transpired that his brother George, now working in California, had already devised the same technique independently in the 1890s. Thus the patent protection became invalid and the process could be adopted by makers of all metal woodwinds.

William Haynes built a silver Louis Lot copy for Maquarre and others in *c*1906, and developed a new model with a modified scale for A=440, A=442, and A=444 in 1911–12.[67] When the new silver flute appeared in 1913, it made little headway against the wooden flute, and only two were sold. But Haynes's silver flute had grown to half his production in 1914–15, and to 75 per cent in 1916. By 1918 he had ceased building wooden flutes except for special orders.

Two other companies played a part in the increasingly important Boston flute industry, which eclipsed that of New York by *c*1900. In 1901 Harry Bettoney bought a controlling interest in the Boston flute factory of Edward H. Wurlitzer (*d* 1911), a descendant of a Saxon flute-making family. After modernizing its operation, the firm, and its successor Cundy-Bettoney (1907), made Bettoney-Wurlitzer flutes, and became the largest woodwind producer and publisher of woodwind music in America. The H. & A. Selmer company originated (1904) as the U.S. importer of clarinets by Henri Selmer & Cie (1885) of France. George Bundy (*d* 1951) managed its New York store (1909), and became president of the company when Alexandre Selmer returned to France in 1918.

These two eastern firms marketed principally to students and band musicians, as did the midwestern C. G. Conn Company. In 1877 Charles Gerard Conn (1844–1931) established a factory for brass instruments in Elkhart, Ind., with eighty-four employees. By 1879 the 'Conn Wonder' line had appeared, going on to win awards at the Chicago World's Fair of 1893 for instruments including Conn Wonder Metal Flutes and piccolos. From about 1893 to 1896 Conn built the 'Conn H. F. Meyer System Metal Wonder Concert Flute', a patented double-tube instrument (earlier patented in Italy by Rampone in 1879), with a construction he also applied to Boehm-system flutes and piccolos. Conn's instruments were priced at half the cost of New York flutes and targeted at amateurs, bandsmen, and eventually the school band market. In 1898 Conn's Boehm flutes cost $50–100, the better class of European flutes $150–400, and Haynes's high-quality flutes $165.[68] Much of the company's advertising touted the advantages of the Boehm system over the much cheaper imported Meyer flute. By 1899 the U.S. Army and Navy had purchased over 100 Conn flutes and piccolos, partly due to a reorganization of military bands Conn had sponsored as a U.S. congressman. As the brass band era waned Conn began to promote the woodwind. He sent to Europe for craftsmen in 1905: two Frenchmen, three Englishmen, and two Germans. The Conn company sold instruments on approval and accepted payment by instalment, and in 1898 published Henry Clay Wysham's *The Evolution of the Boehm Flute* to promote its new Boehm flutes.[69] Wysham later regretted his fulsome praise for the Conn Wonder flute, having become disillusioned with its performance.

Rudall & Rose had made a gold-plated ring-key flute before 1850,[70] an idea Conn took up when it offered inexpensive gold-plated instruments from about 1892 to 1915. Hi Henry's sixty-piece minstrel band and Sousa's band each owned complete sets of Conn gold-plated instruments, and a gold-plated Conn Wonder Boehm flute was presented to the English flutist E. Stanley Redfern (1866–1921) when he performed with Dan Godfrey's band before President McKinley at the White House.

Despite such vigorous efforts at production and promotion, wooden instruments remained prevalent in America until after World War 1. In the late 1880s metal flutes fell out of favour so that from about 1890 to 1912 wood flutes were used almost exclusively.[71]

The combination of a wood or ebonite head on a silver body, as in Heindl's Boehm flute, became popular in America largely through the efforts of the midwestern flutist-entrepreneur Charles T. Howe. Badger had started making wood heads for silver flutes in *c*1876, but Howe publicized the combination vigorously in *All About the Flute* (ten editions, 1898–1911), in which he advertised a model of his own together with courses of lessons by correspondence. Conn's Howe Model of *c*1900 (a wood or ebonite head on a metal body) was one of several named for famous players. Badger offered his P. Ernst's Approved Model, a conical ring-key flute (before 1858), and the Lax Model (1887), a thinned-head ebonite open-G♯ flute. Later Haynes and others introduced the Barrère Model, the Medicus Special Model, and the Hullinger Model, which had a split E.

Almost every U.S. flute-maker also offered C and D♭ piccolos, with both conical and cylindrical bores, in wood and silver. Haynes built his first silver cylinder piccolo in *c*1916, added a conical silver piccolo in 1926, and eliminated the cylinder piccolo in *c*1950. Bands used conical piccolos in D♭ (lowest note E♭) and A♭ (B♭), in wood or silver. Sousa, following Jullien's practice, assigned two transposing C flutes to E♭ clarinet parts, but from about 1890 to about 1920 bands used E♭ flutes for this purpose. Berteling and John C. Haynes offered these instruments from the mid-1880s, and William S. Haynes built twenty-eight between 1902 and 1910. Scores by Sousa and others expressly called for D♭ flute, so that flutists could easily play in the multiple flat keys favoured by B♭ and E♭ brass and clarinet players. By *c*1918 many musicians owned a C flute for orchestra and a D♭ for band work. But with the change of pitch standard to A=440, which took place first in America, players could play band parts on an orchestral flute by transposing the semitone, and demand for D♭ flutes decreased.[72]

In 1858 Carl Wehner bought one of Boehm's alto flutes in G, a type the flutist-poet Sidney Lanier (1842–81) and Wysham played, and Badger advertised, during a brief period around 1870. George Haynes built an alto in 1915 for the Metropolitan Opera, another for Barrère and the Damrosch orchestra in 1917, and two more in 1918 as pieces requiring it, such as Holst's *Planets*, Ravel's *Daphnis et Chloé*, and Atterberg's *Ocean Symphony* entered the repertoire. The instrument became popular around 1920 when famous players began to arrange music for it. Other flutes with lower voices remained rare. Frank Badollet (1870–1934) of the U.S. Marine Band possessed a B♭ tenor flute by Haynes, but this type was better known in England. In 1874 Lanier convinced Badger to make a flute to low G, though only letters to his wife describing the project in September 1874 remain.[73] The octave bass, a vertical flute with a double U-shaped head, was invented in 1910 by Abelardo Albisi (Geneva and La Scala) and made by Vanotti of Milan.

The tone of Boehm flutes, particularly those made in metal, remained a topic of negative comment in England even for some time after they had displaced older models, as in France and America, from virtually every prominent ensemble. In 1895 Henry Wood invited Albert Fransella, founding solo flutist of the Concertgebouw orchestra in 1888 before becoming London's top flutist, to appear as soloist in the first Queen's Hall Promenade Concert. In the previous year, George Bernard Shaw had praised Fransella's recent performance of a Mozart concerto, but supposed that the composer would have declared his Boehm flute 'quite a new instrument'.

> He would, no doubt, have been delighted with the accurate intonation and the fascinating peculiarity and beauty of the lower octave; but I think he would have repudiated the higher notes as having absolutely no flute quality at all…. These harmonica-like sounds got on my nerves after a while; and I am not at all sure that I should not have enjoyed Mr Fransella's skill and taste more if he had played a fantasia by Kuhlau or some other eighteenth-century master on an old-fashioned flute…. Mind, I do not object to the existence of these practically new instruments; but I wish they had not usurped the old names; and I still call for the artist-craftsman to give us once more a flute that is a flute, and a trumpet that is a trumpet. When he has done that he may adapt the inventions of Gordon [i.e. Boehm], Sax, and the rest to his masterpieces as much as he pleases; for naturally I do not want the old defects back….The intonation of the wind is quite bad enough still, without our turning back to the methods of the old days when it was still worse.[74]

Despite Shaw's criticism of the tone Fransella produced on his instrument, all the leading English flutists by now used Boehm-system or hybrid flutes. Carte's 1851 flute and his more successful version of 1867 had made the cylinder flute playable for the eight-keyed flutist, and in 1870 John R. Radcliff (1842–1917) invented the model that bore his name, a simplified Carte 1851 system with a closed G♯ and an early split E mechanism. In designs that were less widely used, William Card (1788–1861) developed an essentially old-system conical flute with an F mechanism, and between 1852 and 1877 R. S. Rockstro made various mechanical and acoustical modifications to conical and cylinder flutes, culminating in a model that Rudall Carte began to manufacture in 1877. Meanwhile the Nicholson-style keyed flute had fallen from favour. Rudall Carte's production of eight-keyed flutes declined from about 3000 in the thirty-five years before 1870 to about 900 in the thirty-five years after that date. While in the 1830s–40s Rudall & Rose's eight-keyed flutes had been the most expensive, half a century later the type had become comparatively cheap.[75]

Though many of the Boehm and hybrid models were offered in silver, wood remained a favoured material for flute bodies well into the twentieth century in most of Europe and America. Ebonite was used in England and America, particularly as a useful replacement for wood in the tropical colonies. Metal-bodied flutes began to increase their predominance in France in the late 1880s (chapter 11).[76] Rudall, Rose, & Carte displayed a gold flute at the London Exhibition of 1862, and had built others by 1869, the year in which Louis Lot made his only instrument in this material for Jean Rémusat, a flute later owned by Jean-Pierre Rampal.[77] The *Musical Times* referred in March 1896 to a new gold flute by Rudall Carte, which Fransella played in a concert of 7 February at the Queen's Hall. 'The middle and lower registers of the instrument certainly possess a fine tone, somewhat suggestive of a saxophone', a reviewer wrote, before concluding that the flute would have to be heard in an orchestra before it could be judged properly. Fransella paid £123.10s for the flute, which was in 18-karat gold with engraved silver keywork, but he later found a better use for this large sum and reverted to his flute of wood or silver.[78] Also in 1896 Henry Jaeger, solo flutist of the U.S. Marine Band, commissioned an 18-karat gold flute from the J. C. Haynes Co. of Boston.[79] After being impressed with a gold flute on a visit to Rudall Carte in the same year, Dayton C. Miller built himself a one-piece 22-karat instrument (DCM 8) over a three-year period ending in 1904. In that year the Berlin dilettante Adolph Goldberg (c1852–1925) gave Prill a gold flute by Rittershausen, which Prill's pupil Georg Müller contended he played for thirty years but which Müller's pupil Nikolaus Delius claimed he made little use of, preferring his wooden Boehm flute. In any case, Prill seems to have been the first flutist known as 'the man with the golden flute' (*Der Meister mit der goldenen Flöte*), and several newspaper pieces for his sixtieth and seventieth birthdays in 1927 and 1937 reported folk legends that the instrument had been the gift of Kaiser Wilhelm II, the Tsar of Russia, or some other famous prince.[80]

One Russian commentator aptly summed up the emancipated spirit that characterized flute-playing in most of the western hemisphere at the end of World War 1: 'we live in an eclectic time, using the best from all flute systems and types of flutes'.[81] The American scientist and flute-collector Dayton C. Miller (1866–1941) perhaps embodied this eclectic spirit most clearly. Miller played his father's Civil War fife as a boy, graduating later to an H. F. Meyer flute and piccolo. In 1886 he ordered his first Boehm flute from William R. Meinell, a silver instrument with a wood head, and ten years later he ordered three Rudall Carte flutes with various Rockstro features. After studying astronomy at Princeton (Ph.D., 1890), he joined the faculty of the Case School of Applied Science in Cleveland, and became head of the physics department in 1893. In 1901 Miller built a silver E♭ flute (DCM 8), followed by his gold flute, which took 1800 hours of work. He published a translation of Boehm's *Flute and Flute-Playing* (1871, trans. 1908 R/1922), and spent much of his spare time and money building four collections, of flutes, books and music, art works, and miscellaneous items, with the primary purpose of 'illustrating the history of the art and science of the music of the European flute'. His will of 22 June 1939, two years before his death, bequeathed the Dayton C. Miller collection to the Library of Congress in Washington, D.C.

Flutists and flute-makers alike worked in a 'melting-pot' atmosphere. While individual playing styles could still be a subject for comment before World War 1, the market for instruments and flute-playing skills at the highest levels had effectively become international, the only barriers being those that prevented foreign players holding permanent positions in France and women holding them anywhere but in all-female ensembles. Their technical advantages were gradually making modern flutes prevalent in orchestral work, and even many German flutists had overcome earlier doubts about the Boehm flute. Indeed, by the end of the nineteenth century the player's personal sound-ideal seems to have determined the quality of tone a flutist produced almost as much as his choice of instrument. Though flutes of only one particular type were allowed in orchestras in Dresden, Leipzig, and Paris, in other places different kinds – Meyer flutes, French and German Boehm flutes of wood and metal, hybrid, and Reform flutes – could be played side by side within the same section. If this state of affairs seems hard for us to credit, it is because we have become accustomed to a relatively unvaried instrument and performing style in all parts of the developed world. We owe our reduced spectrum of variety to two influences that became dominant in the early twentieth century: the French Flute School (chapter 11) and the recording industry (chapter 12).

Chapter 11

The French Flute School

The notion of the 'French Flute School' usually refers to a style of teaching and playing the instrument that originated with Claude-Paul Taffanel (1844–1908) and his pupils at the Paris Conservatoire around the turn of the twentieth century. In a second, less strict sense, the term also refers to a French-influenced style of flute-playing that became dominant in Europe and America as Conservatoire-trained players filled orchestral and teaching posts and as the recording industry carried their sound and style to all corners of the developed world (chapter 12). In that looser sense, we can easily list the style's main attributes: the use of the French-style silver flute (chapters 9, 12), a preoccupation with tone, a standard repertoire, and a set of teaching materials in which the Taffanel-Gaubert method and the tone development exercises of Marcel Moyse (1889–1984; Conservatoire 1906) hold a central place. But today more precise definitions than this of the earlier school's distinctive playing technique and style remain elusive, particularly since changes in tone, repertoire, pedagogy, and even in the instrument itself blurred its distinguishing features as the second style became influential and continued to evolve.

Early recordings provide one clue to help us distinguish the playing style of Taffanel's school itself from the French-influenced International style that later emerged from it. These make clear that although native players such as Geoffrey Gilbert (1914–89) in England, Gustav Scheck (1901–84) in Germany, and William Kincaid (1895–1967) in America adopted the metal flutes, light tone, and vibrato typical of the French flutists (chapter 14), their playing never became fully 'French'. Moyse thought the French style 'an assimilable language … because the English assimilated it'.[1] Others, however, considered its essential Frenchness untranslatable:

> It is often remarked that though 'French schools' of flute-playing exist in several countries, they never quite sound the same as the French players.... As no one can diagnose the difference, the essential ingredient is probably one of personality rather than of method.[2]

Most agree that by the 1970s the French School of the flute, in the strict meaning of the term, had disappeared. Moyse told a masterclass around that time that new styles of music and their associated playing techniques were responsible for its eclipse:

48. Adolphe Hennebains (1862–1914) as Pan.

Seventy-five years ago there was a French School, [but] it's disappeared now.... If you want to play Berio, that's your business. If you want to play the flute backwards, you can do that too.[3]

Claude Dorgeuille agreed that the French School had disappeared during Moyse's lifetime, arguing in a 1983 book on the subject that the persistent reference to Taffanel's authority was out of place by that date. Dorgeuille held that the School, for him typified by René le Roy's playing, had survived in name only:

Over the years, the French Flute School has assumed all the characteristics of myth or legend, and fallen prey to all kinds of mistaken assumptions.... The 'Conservatoire Tradition', which usually features large in histories of music, is just an illusion. Most often it merely provides an authoritative point of focus for something created elsewhere.[4]

Yet the idea of a French School persisted, particularly in connection with Moyse's phenomenal popularity as a teacher in the 1960s and 70s (chapter 14). Trevor Wye, one of his most clear-sighted British devotees, agreed that 'Moyse owed remarkably little to the past'.[5] But Michel Debost, one of his successors as professor at the Paris Conservatoire, perceptively noted that the famous instructor relied on the concept of a 'lost' tradition for an authority beyond himself. This, combined with Moyse's intense personality, allowed him to issue judgements from which there could be no appeal:

> Moyse claimed tradition as a validation of his own opinion. What he perceived of Taffanel and what he conveys to us of Taffanel's tradition is Moyse's interpretation. What Moyse told us was great because it's reconstructed by him, but what is fact, I'm not sure.[6]

If we have an imprecise view of what exactly constituted the French Flute School and of how it came to an end as a distinct style, its beginnings are equally unclear. Trevor Wye's fluid grasp of the French heritage (1993) allowed him to make the apparently self-contradictory statements – on one and the same page – that Moyse felt part of a 'French School tradition reaching as far back as Tulou', and that 'Taffanel was the founder of the French School; there is no doubt about that'.[7] In the period since the school became dominant, however, efforts have been made to provide it with a distinctively French history of its own. The current version of the flute's creation myth traces it back to the presumed invention of the baroque instrument by French musicians in the seventeenth century (see p. 66).[8] This theory, first tentatively stated by Philip Bate in 1969 and commonly advanced since that time as though it were historical fact, replaced an equally uncertain story first propagated by German romantic writers that the baroque flute had been invented by J. C. Denner of Nuremberg.[9] Thus the early Conservatoire professors Hugot and Wunderlich held that 'the transverse flute … was perfected by the Germans, from whom we get the majority of the modern wind instruments'.[10] The search for the Taffanel school's obscure roots may explain why Jane Bowers entitled her fascinating and thoroughly-researched dissertation of 1988 'The French Flute School from 1700 to 1760', even though only Quantz's circle in Berlin might qualify as an embryonic 'school' during the final years of that period (see chapter 5). Bowers's dissertation amply documented styles of music and performance in flux during a period when musical ideas from Italy and Germany mixed with French, and when no single musical personality dominated Parisian flute-playing. In reality France could develop a uniform school of shared, or at least centrally-imposed, taste, instrument, and method only once the Paris Conservatoire had been established.

The Conservatoire evolved as a military musical academy in the wake of the French Revolution. In 1790 François Devienne (1759–1803), already successful in Paris as a soloist and theatre player on bassoon and flute, took up duties as a bandsman in the Garde Nationale that included teaching music to the children of the new republic's soldiers. Two years later when the band organized a formal music school, the Ecole Gratuite de la Garde Nationale, Devienne was joined on the staff by Antoine Hugot (1761–1803), his colleague at the Concert spirituel and another successful operatic flutist. That school became the Institut National de Musique the next year with Devienne as one of nine administrators, and finally in 1795 the Conservatoire National de Musique, in which Devienne remained an administrator and professor of flute alongside Hugot and Jacques Schnietzhoeffer, who also taught oboe. Two more professors, Nicolas Duverger and Johann Georg Wunderlich (1775–1819), were added in November 1795 to teach a second class made up of the youngest players.

The new institute undertook a political and nationalistic purpose in a vastly altered musical climate in which most musical forms except the socially unpretentious comic opera had been swept away by the Revolution. As well as instructing their students in instrumental playing, the professors' duties included teaching patriotic songs to the people, especially children, for performance at national festivals.[11] Students, chosen in equal numbers from each region and both sexes, progressed through three basic stages, each examined by inspectors. The first stage involved *solfège* or basic musicianship, the next singing and instrumental instruction, and the third theory, history of music, and performing skills. Lessons and practice took place at fixed hours in a rotating ten-day schedule – the revolutionaries decimalized even the calendar, though they left twelve semitones in the musical scale.[12] Along with uniform teaching, the institute's centrally-planned organization adopted approved textbooks written by its professors.

As the first flute instruction manual devised according to the Conservatoire's new pedagogical plan, Devienne's *Nouvelle Méthode théorique et pratique pour la flûte* (New theoretical and practical method for the flute, 1794) earned immediate and enduring fame. Comparison with Louis Adam's much more thorough and advanced Conservatoire piano method (1804–5), with Baillot, Rode and Kreutzer's for violin (1803), and with Baillot's *L'Art du Violon* (1834), suggests that it provided the foundation for Conservatoire methods in general by building on the concept of a 'progressive' method, already an established approach to teaching by the 1790s. Delusse's *L'Art de la flûte traversière* (1761) had first introduced exercises in progressive order, beginning with elementary long tones, while John Gunn's *Art of Playing the German-Flute* (c1793) discussed the 'Method and proper Objects of Practice', noting that practising scales and long notes methodically would bring about more rapid progress than playing easy tunes. The studies at the end of Gunn's volume contained the essential idea of method – harmonic and melodic permutation of simple figures – on which all subsequent disciplines were based. Devienne combined these new ideas with a theme introduced in a flute tutor by Amand Vanderhagen, a clarinettist. Vanderhagen's method (c1788) had stressed tone development through the practice of long notes with the *messa di voce* or *son filé*, and Adagio movements.

Devienne's conservative position on tone, already noted (chapter 6), had a parallel in his treatment of articulation. He rejected Hotteterre's *turu* as an ineffectual method of double-tonguing – as indeed it was, being intended for a quite different purpose (p. 62) – and was similarly dismissive of a new syllable, *dougue*, which he was the first to mention. Naturally as a French-speaker he found the Anglo-Saxon *tid'll* and its variant forms unpronounceable and unworthy of notice. Though Devienne allowed his students to use four-keyed flutes, he 'heartily disapproved' of the C-foot and continued to use a one-keyed instrument himself. His extreme conservatism was apparent to the German jurist and amateur flutist Johann Heinrich Liebeskind, who noted in 1806 that the first German edition of Devienne's tutor 'even appears to be fifty years older than it is'.[13]

Nonetheless, Devienne's tutor was widely marketed from the first, soon appearing in a bilingual French and German edition in Hamburg (c.1812) as well as in thirty other editions (1807–1950). Within a few decades its contents had been revised and altered so much that they retained little of the original material; indeed the publication's fame, as represented by Devienne's name on the title-page, outlived much of that material's usefulness by more than a century and a half.[14] What the later French tutors retained from the first edition, whether or not they were marketed under Devienne's name, were its organization, its idea of method, and a concern with tone that, given later changes in musical style, grew to dominate all other aspects of music.[15]

The Conservatoire's first two flute professors met uncannily similar ends in 1803, Devienne when he became insane and died at the age of 43, and Hugot when he too went mad, stabbed himself, and jumped from a fourth-storey window while working on an official Conservatoire method to replace Devienne's. That work was completed by Wunderlich and published in 1804. A bilingual French and German edition edited by A. E. Müller appeared in 1807, followed by twelve others in Paris, Leipzig, Hamburg, Berlin, Mainz, Munich, and Florence over the next hundred years.

In preference to the one-keyed ('ordinary') instrument Devienne had clung to, the Hugot-Wunderlich method considered the four-keyed flute necessary for evenness and intonation, especially of trills, and for 'brilliant' execution. It rejected Quantz's D$\sharp$ key, since the institution had officially decreed the difference between enharmonic tones to be 'negligible', indicating for the first time that the Conservatoire flutists were adapting to equal-tempered tunings and becoming more concerned with melody than harmony (see p. 83). Tone was to be improved by the assiduous practice of *sons filés*, nuances, scales in intervals, triplets, arpeggios, exercises for the equality of fingers, studies, and three classes of articulation. The lower lip should cover one-sixth of the embouchure, and the whole force of tone should be reserved for the low register. As well as elaborating and modifying Devienne's themes, the 1804 tutor introduced what became one of the school's token terms, when the Conservatoire authorities were quoted in a fanciful explanation of the flute's acoustics:

> The formation of the sound is the result of the displacement of the column of air that it contains; this displacement is brought about by the introduction of the player's breath into the body of the instrument....[16]

Flutists later adapted the idea of a 'column of air' to describe the concept of a connected body of wind flowing from the player's lungs into the flute, or of a 'support' for the flute's sound (see also p. 268 for Frans Vester's use of the term).

Benoît Tranquille Berbiguier (1782–1838), a left-handed Conservatoire pupil of Wunderlich, took a more progressive attitude to tone, the use of the keys, and intonation.[17] His *Nouvelle Méthode* (1818), a tutor for the public rather than for the children trained at the Conservatoire, took respectful issue with Devienne on the usefulness of the keys, as well as on the double tongue and the strong low tones,

49. Jean-Louis Tulou (1786–1865), lithograph, Roger & Cie.

effects he accepted did not sound well on the one-keyed flute Devienne preferred. His studies for finger equality in all tonalities introduced the keys in a progressive manner, exercising each one individually and in combination with others. He noted that 'F♯ as the leading note of the key of G is necessarily sharper than the same F♯ taken as a third in D major', the earliest indication that French flutists used super-sharpened leading notes (p. 131).

In 1829 Jean-Louis Tulou (1786–1865; ill. 49) was elected Professor at the Conservatoire, having been passed over ten years previously for Joseph Guillou. Tulou dominated flute-playing in Paris during the 1830s and 40s not only because of his supremely excellent playing and his Conservatoire post, but because he used his connections to further his business as an instrument-maker. He began manufacturing flutes in 1828, and three years later formed a partnership with the flute-maker Jacques Nonon (1802–*p*1867). The two set up a workshop and a domicile in the following year, by which time the company had begun to supply instruments to the Conservatoire. The firm employed six workers and four out-workers by 1839, earning an annual gross income of 45,000 francs, and maintained the connection with the institute until Tulou's retirement in 1856.

Tulou's concern with preserving the true tone of the flute has already been noted as the reason he gave for his staunch resistance to Boehm's ring-key flute on its Conservatoire trial in 1838 (chapter 9). His own response to that innovation, a design he called the *flûte perfectionnée* (perfected flute), was shown in an 1853 edition of his flute method (1835, 1842, and later) as having keys on rod-axles and pillars for C♯, C, B♭, G♯, F♯, F, E♭, and low C♯ and C. Though it used a conical bore and a traditional fingering system, its main innovation was a key that allowed F♯ to be played as an equal-tempered or even a super-sharpened leading note, a capability that had clearly become a definite requirement for flutists everywhere by now. To that end Tulou's method prescribed and gave extensive examples of two kinds of fingerings, simple and compound. The second kind was to be used for *notes sensibles*, a classification that applied not only to the subtonic of the scale, but to almost every other note whenever it occurred between two others a semitone higher. On Tulou's five-keyed flutes and *flûtes perfectionnées*, these fingerings made all melodic semitones as much as 30 cents smaller than the 100-cent equal-tempered semitone. This style of intonation survives to the present day in Conservatoire-style violin-playing and its Russian, Central European, and American offshoots.

Operas by Rossini, Donizetti, Meyerbeer, Auber, and Halévy remained the chief musical form in Paris during the mid-nineteenth century, while virtuoso showpieces provided the flute's most frequent opportunities in solo and chamber music (chapter 8). Tulou maintained a tight grip on the repertoire for his class: from 1832 to 1860 every single solo set at the annual Prize Competition was one of his own compositions.[18] French flutists who favoured the Boehm flute, led by Camus, Dorus, and Coche, were obliged by the professor's conservatism to cultivate the instrument without the Conservatoire's official recognition during his tenure, though as Claude Dorgeuille (1983) noted, the method books they devised for the new instrument in the 1830s retained the traditional framework of earlier efforts.

A new period of interest in the classics had begun in Paris in 1828 when François-Antoine Habeneck performed Beethoven's 'Eroica' Symphony with his Conservatoire students' orchestra after a long and intensive period of study. This focus on the enduring value of music, as opposed to the novelty of the more popular opera, contributed to the growing presence of concert orchestras on the musical scene, as well as to a renewed interest in chamber music. Nearly twenty years after Reicha's woodwind quintets had found favour in Paris, Louis Dorus, now the Boehm cylinder flute's leading French exponent, formed the Société de Musique Classique (c1847) together with a group of leading Parisian musicians, aiming to promote classical chamber music and to encourage French composers to write new works.[19] Dorus played Hummel's *Trio* in B♭, op. 2a/1 (flute, cello, and piano; London, 1792) in 1848 at the society's third concert, in a programme that included pieces by Haydn, Mozart, and Beethoven. Music by Beethoven, Boehm, Haydn, Mozart, Spontini, Rossini, and Weber featured on three Conservatoire programmes in which Dorus played solos in 1850, 1852, and 1854.

Thus when Dorus succeeded Tulou as professor of flute in 1860, the Conservatoire's flute class received an overdue infusion of new energy and old repertoire along with a new official instrument, the Boehm flute. Examination tests broadened to include pieces by Lindpaintner, Reissiger, Boehm, and Briccialdi, besides Tulou and Altès. In the same year Claude-Paul Taffanel, a pupil of Dorus since 1858, won his *Premier Prix*. Taffanel continued his flute lessons at the Conservatoire while earning diplomas in harmony (1862) and fugue (1865), which qualified him as a composer and conductor as well as a performer.

Tulou's retirement provided an opening for a new supplier of flutes to the Conservatoire as well as a new professor, and in 1860 Louis Lot, successor to the firm that had first manufactured the Boehm flute of 1847 in France under licence from its inventor, began to furnish the institute with the Boehm cylinder flute its new professor had made popular. Dorus's personal preference for wood flutes was now overwhelmed by a surging demand for silver. Having produced only five metal flutes to sixty-seven wooden ones in 1855, Lot sold silver instruments, some with gold lip-plates, to Altès, Donjon, Dorus, Gariboldi, Taffanel, and a number of other players prominent in Paris, in 1859–60. Olaf Svendsen, W. S. Broadwood, R. S. Rockstro, and Jean Firmin Brossa of England purchased silver flutes in 1862–3.[20] According to Welch (1883), Parisian orchestral players brought about the compulsory adoption of the silver Boehm flute in state-subsidized orchestras as well as in the Conservatoire,[21] and so, although Lot's production of wooden flutes did not significantly decline until an overall decrease in production set in (1889), his silver flute became a defining characteristic of Parisian flute-playing in about 1860. In that year flutes of silver and nickel silver accounted for half Lot's production, and after holding steady until 1870 the proportion of metal flutes increased to about 60 per cent by 1876.

Almost as soon as the silver flute became established, however, Lot altered the design of his instruments, apparently to make them louder (chapter 10). Probably the players just listed were supplied the earlier model, which the jury at the Paris exhibition of 1867 judged had 'a preferable quality of sound' to the new one, but this early type soon ceased production. Lot's new flute continued to evolve at the hand of his successors, H. D. Villette (*fl* 1875–82), Debonneetbeau de Coutelier (*fl* 1882–9), Emile Barat (*fl* 1889–1904), Ernest Chambille (*fl* 1882–1922), Gabrielle Pauline Chambille (*fl* 1922–8), and Martial Lefèvre (*fl* 1928–39), before the trademark passed to the Strasser-Marigaux company in 1951. Lot's former employees, including Louis Léon Joseph Lebret (1862–*p*1928) and J. Daufresne (*fl p*1880–*p*1914), as well as Godfroy workers such as Auguste Bonneville (*fl* 1876–*p*1950) and Claude Rive (*fl* 1877–*p*1895), founded their own companies which helped supplement the production of high-quality French metal flutes in the early twentieth century. By far the most prolific firm, as well as the most innovative, was that established by Amédée Auguste Couesnon (1882), who patented a flute with a square-sectioned bore in 1895.[22] By 1911 the Couesnon company employed a thousand workers at its eight factories, producing brass instruments, saxophones, and flutes, some under the trade names of defunct workshops such as those of Isidor Lot, Triébert, and Tulou, in numbers that by 1925 had totalled over two million. Couesnon was only the largest of numerous French firms that competed strenuously in the international musical instrument trade of the late nineteenth and early twentieth centuries.

With Lot's silver Boehm cylinder flute officially established at the Conservatoire, Joseph-Henri Altès (1826–99) succeeded Dorus as professor in 1869. In the following year the Franco-Prussian war ended in a humiliating defeat for France that culminated in a siege of Paris by the Prussian army. On their surrender regular French forces brutally suppressed the defiant Commune, or provisional government, and put to death 17,000 Parisian civilians to enforce capitulation.

Not surprisingly under these circumstances, interest in German music, including the classical repertoire, suffered a sharp decline. After 1871, when the Conservatoire examination was cancelled owing to the crisis, works by German composers vanished from the list of pieces set for the annual flute competition.[23] The examinations in 1869–93 contained only two solos of Demersseman (1887 and 1891) to break the monotony of Altès and Tulou.

The chief contribution Altès made to the Conservatoire flute school, apart from his numerous compositions for the instrument, was his *Grand Method* (1880, 1906 R/1956), which he based on Baillot's violin method of 1834 rather than directly on the earlier flute tutors. In a discussion of intonation Altès described the semitone as 'the smallest interval appreciable to the ear', and, following Hugot and Wunderlich, considered the difference between a chromatic and a diatonic semitone too small to be heard. But if his pen remained solid on this point of dogma, his ear directed him otherwise, for one of his tutor's most important sections covered alternative fingerings to aid in 'perfect intonation', recalling Tulou's prescriptions for 'sensitive' fingerings but without making the earlier professor's systematic and expressive distinctions in intonation.

Altès's long tenure came to an end when Paul Taffanel succeeded him in 1893, after a thirty-year performing career in the leading Paris orchestras. Taffanel restructured the traditional masterclass format to give students individual attention, replacing much of the nineteenth-century repertoire that his pupil Louis Fleury (1878–1928; Conservatoire 1900) called 'idle twittering' with the music of the previous century, the eighteenth.

The important changes Taffanel brought to the Conservatoire flute class grew from currents in the musical world at large, so that his playing style, teaching methods, and ideas about music are best understood with reference to those of his forebears and contemporaries. Taffanel became interested in early repertoire, as well as in encouraging new composition by Frenchmen, along with other leading Parisian musicians of the late nineteenth century. While the Franco-Prussian war brought about a rejection of German repertoire, it evoked a new national awareness in France, so that in 1871, immediately following the war's disastrous end and the establishment of the Third Republic, Taffanel joined the composers Fauré, Franck, Massenet, Saint-Saëns, and others in founding the Société Nationale de Musique Française to encourage the work of French composers. In the same year lectures on aesthetics and music history began at the Conservatoire, though voice students had already been studying the history of opera since 1848.[24] The focus on French music and the interest in early repertoire came together in projects such as Saint-Saëns's edition of Rameau's complete works (1895–1913).[25] In 1879 Taffanel brought renewed attention to the woodwind quintet, neglected after Guillou's ensemble disbanded in c1830, with his

50. Paul Taffanel demonstrating his embouchure and body position.

Société de Musique de Chambre pour Instruments à Vent, a group that also owed something to Dorus and the Société de Musique Classique of thirty years earlier. Taffanel's travels, which included solo appearances with orchestras in Leipzig (1890) and Basel (1891),[26] doubtless exposed him to the interest in baroque music already evident outside France. During the 1880s he even took part in 'historic' concerts, playing his Boehm flute alongside antique instruments such as viola da gamba and harpsichord in performances of baroque music (chapter 13).

The efforts of Saint-Saëns and his colleagues to encourage French composers began in the 1890s to bear fruit in one of the richest, if not the most prolific, outpourings of music ever composed for the flute. Claude Debussy, resentful of the Wagner craze among French musicians, joined the chorus of nationalist criticism, writing in praise of Rameau and the French tradition he felt had been perverted by German influence. His *Prélude à l'après-midi d'un faune* announced an entirely new musical personality for the flute – dreamy, sensitive, subtle – when the orchestral tone poem received its first performance on 22 December 1894 with Georges Barrère (1876–1944; Conservatoire 1895) playing its haunting solo flute theme. (While the conductor wrote half a century later that '[t]he audience was captivated, the triumph was complete',[27] Barrère recalled thirty years after the event that 'all kinds of cat calls' greeted the performance.[28]) Other orchestral works including *Pelléas et Mélisande* (1902)

9 p.m.

Tickets: orchestra 18 and 25 fr., balcony 12 fr.

Source: Handbill, DCM.

Françoise Kempf, harp, and Jan Merry, flute.

1. Sonata in e minor (flute and harp)   Blavet (1700–68)
   Adagio–Allemande–Rondo–Tambourin et
   Gigue ·
2. *Bourée* (harp)   Bach
   Danseuse à la fontaine d'Ain-Draham   M. Tournier
3. *Impromptu caprice*   G. Pierné
4. Three *Pièces de Clavecin* (harp and flute)   [François] Couperin [arr. Louis] Fleury
   L'Angille–La Couperinette–Les Tricoleuses
   Barcarola et Scherzo (flute and harp)   Alfredo Casella
5. Sonata in F major (flute and harp)   Benedetto Marcello (1686–1739)
   Adagio–Allegro–Largo–Adagio
6. Suite for unaccompanied flute (for Jan Merry)   Georges Migot (premiere)
7. *Prélude Incantatoire–Pastorale–Conclusion*   Marthe Bracquemond (premiere)
   On a Sonnet of Ronsard (harp and flute; for
   F. K and J. M.)
8. *Gypsy Song* (harp and flute)   Manuel Infante

Early twentieth-century Parisian composers and musicians bestowed special attention on the pairing of flute and harp (compare the domestic associations of this ensemble in Fig. 10.2). New music of a wild or meditative pastoral nature was written specially for flute and harp, which also often played arrangements of baroque works. In general, French flute recitals of this period, whether accompanied by harp or piano, almost invariably began with a Bach sonata and included recent works such as those by Debussy, Honneger, Huë, or Roussel, as well as contemporary pieces written for the performer.

and *La Mer* (1903–5) made highly distinctive use of the flute section, while *Syrinx* (1912) and the Sonata for flute, viola, and harp (1915) enriched the solo and chamber music repertoire with further revolutionary new works. Maurice Ravel's compositions featuring the flute in new roles included a suite for orchestra, *Daphnis et Chloé* (1912), and an *Introduction et allegro* for harp, flute, clarinet, and string quartet (1905). Cécile Chaminade's *Concertino*, op. 107, a light salon work for flute and orchestra commissioned as an examination piece for the Conservatoire in 1902, was taken up by Léopold Lafleurance and Hennebains. The flow of new French works for the flute continued after World War 1 when Arthur Honegger's *Danse de la chèvre* (Goat's dance, 1926), Jean Rivier's *Oiseaux tendres* (Sweet birds, 1935), and Bohuslav Martinů's *Sonate en trio* (1943) were written for René le Roy, Jacques Ibert wrote his Flute Concerto (1934) for Marcel Moyse, and Francis Poulenc wrote his Sonata (1957) for Jean-Pierre Rampal.

    The new French repertoire of the late nineteenth and early twentieth centuries emerged hand in hand with an entirely fresh notion of what made music expressive: here, as in earlier French music for the flute, a particular tone quality, playing style, and emotional sensibility, all entirely French in character, were intimately linked. These new concepts brought about a deliberate rejection of earlier repertoire and playing style, which naturally were seen as lacking the new quality of emotional depth. Georges Barrère colourfully summed up the Taffanel school's scorn (or at least his own) for the 'pompous variations and the ancient acrobatics' in the repertoire of the previous generation:

> These monstrosities, as we regard them today, are dead beyond revival. Written as a rule by flautists, and remarkably well adapted to the instrument, their intrinsic poverty excludes all but a legacy of superannuated interest. To play persistently a repertoire of this character, to call up the lifeless skeletons of a past, alike sterile and baroque [i.e. contrived], is effectually to coerce public sentiment to the conviction that the flute is scarcely to be regarded as a musical instrument.[29]

In accordance with the demands of its new style of music, the flute's expressiveness now derived solely from its quality of tone, the aspect Taffanel's school cultivated most assiduously. As the Taffanel-Gaubert method announced the new creed: 'It is with the tone that the player conveys the music to the listener.'[30] Louis Fleury confirmed his teacher's priorities:

> We place at the head of the list of a flutist's preoccupations the search for a good sound… do not forget that volume is not important, quality of tone is what really counts.…All practising of technique that neglects the quality of sound is deadly.[31]

The axiom that tone quality was more important than loudness need not indicate that Taffanel's sound was a particularly soft one. His low register was often described as 'powerful and brassy', 'ample', or 'full'. Parisian audiences of the period expected the flute, along with all the woodwinds, to play assertively: when the Berlin Philharmonic performed in Paris under Hans von Bülow (1830–94), who demanded 'a flute tone from the flute and not that of an oboe or clarinet', the press and the public criticized the tone of the wind instruments as too small.[32]

On the other hand Fleury's contemporary Barrère recalled in 1921 that '[q]uality as well as quantity of tone and fine technique were only a small part of [Taffanel's] splendid characteristics as a flute-player'. Fleury elaborated on this theme:

> Elegance, flexibility, and sensitivity were the hallmarks of Taffanel's artistry, and his phenomenal virtuosity was made as inconspicuous as possible. He hated affectation, believing that the text of the music should be respected absolutely, and beneath the supple fluency of his playing there was a rigorous adherence to accuracy of pulse and rhythm.[33]

Rigorous adherence, that is, by the standards of the time; for as rhythmic interpretation became more strictly literal in the twentieth century, recordings of the period's flutists came to seem relatively free and informal. Another aspect of the French players' style soon to change was the use of vibrato, which according to the Taffanel and Gaubert *Méthode* the school opposed, particularly in the classics:

Vibrato distorts the natural character of the instrument and spoils the interpretation, fatiguing quickly a sensitive ear. It is a serious error and shows unpardonable lack of taste to use these vulgar methods to interpret the great composers.[34]

Yet according to Fleury, Taffanel himself employed 'a light, almost imperceptible vibrato'.[35] Moyse reported of another Taffanel pupil, Adolphe Hennebains:

When he spoke to us of notes with vibrato or expression, he told us with a mysterious air that these notes, forte or piano, seemed to come from within himself. One had the impression that they came directly from the heart or soul.[36]

A more prosaic examination of how vibrato crept into French flute-playing suggests that violinists gradually accustomed the musicians' ears to a concept of expressiveness previously considered 'vulgar'. Joseph Joachim, a protégé of Mendelssohn and a friend of Brahms with a technique so old-fashioned that he still played with his chin on the left side of the tail-piece in 1854,[37] advised students fifty years later to '[b]reak yourself of the habit of an overdone Vibrato … [which] reminds one of the lamentations of old women. Only use Vibrato when you wish to lay particular stress on a note, which your feeling will suggest.'[38] But at the same time, after Eugène Ysaÿe had encouraged a trend towards a freer use of vibrato, Fritz Kreisler and Jascha Heifetz introduced its continuous use on the violin, and it was later adopted in viola and cello playing.

According to Robert Philip's study of early recordings (1992), 'vibrato as an enhancer of tone [on wind instruments], as opposed to an ornament, was unknown until its development by flautists of the Paris Conservatoire at the very end of the [nineteenth] century'.[39] He notes that the effect was generally extremely delicate and unobtrusive, used as occasional effect or ornament, whereas the celebrated trill of the Italian soprano Adelina Patti (1843–1919) was no wider than the uniform continuous vibrato of many late-twentieth-century singers.[40] Jochen Gärtner's study of the technique (1974) confirms that, despite frequent protestations, all French flutists of the early twentieth century used a clearly audible vibrato.[41]

The key to the apparent paradox posed by the use of vibrato by players who so vociferously condemned it is found in the distinction the Taffanel school drew between what it called 'vibrato' and what Hennebains, in the passage just quoted, identified as 'expression', a gentle enlivening of the flute's tone that became perceptible only when compared with the entirely straight tone British and German players used at the time. The key attribute of this manner of 'expression' was its natural or unstudied quality. Beginning with an article of 1949, Moyse frequently betrayed annoyance with the increasing tendency of students, particularly Americans, to ask him about the physiological aspects of the technique.[42]

Taffanel's status as the founder of the modern French flute school rests as much on his own reputation as one of the world's finest flutists as on subsequent efforts by some of his pupils to codify his teachings. His successor as Conservatoire professor, however, was not among those who sought to give his teacher's principles a particular

The Paris Conservatoire dominated musical education in France, and in much of the developed world, from about 1860 to 1950. Rather than receiving individual tuition, instrumentalists were taught in a class, to which entrance was by competition. Students played in public examinations called *Concours* (competitions), which included a set piece and accompanied sight-reading, and were awarded grades designated First Prize (*Premier prix*), Second Prize, and First or Second Certificate of Merit (*Accessit*). A student graduated on attaining a First Prize, or earlier if satisfied with a lower grade.

Devienne	1795–1803	Moyse	1932–40
Schnietzhoefer	1795–?	Crunelle	1941–69
Hugot	1795–1803	Crunelle and Moyse	1946–48
Duverger	1795–?	Crunelle and Cortet	
Wunderlich	1803–19	(deputy)	1949–50
Guillou	1819–29	Rampal	1969–81
Tulou	1829–59	Debost	1981–90
Dorus	1860–68		(on leave 1989–90)
Altès	1869–93	Artaud	1990–
Taffanel	1894–1908	Marion (Rampal's	
Hennebains	1909–14	assistant from 1974)	1977–98
Lafleurance	1915–19	Cherrier	1998–
Gaubert	1920–31		

permanency. Adolphe Hennebains (1862–1914) succeeded Taffanel as solo flute of the Opéra orchestra in 1891, and after deputizing frequently from 1905 to 1908 at the Conservatoire, was elected Professor in 1909. One of the earliest French flutists to record, Hennebains left accounts of the Beethoven *Serenade* op. 25 (*c*1907), a number of works with orchestral accompaniment (1908), and some of Taffanel's Chopin arrangements with piano accompaniment (*c*1913). His pupils included Gaston Blanquart, Georges Delangle, Marcel Moyse, Georges Laurent, Aimable Valin, Joseph Rampal, and René Le Roy, most of whom themselves became influential teachers.

Philippe Gaubert (1879–1941; Conservatoire 1894) gained his First Prize at the age of fifteen after four years as Taffanel's pupil. Gaubert, who maintained a strong artistic relationship with Ravel, played the premiere of the *Introduction et allegro* in 1907, and became Professor of Flute in 1919, succeeding Léopold Lafleurance (1865–1951) who served as Acting Professor from 1915 to 1919 during the war and after the death of Hennebains. Marcel Moyse took postgraduate lessons with Gaubert for four years, imitating and trying to analyse his instinctive playing.

After the war Gaubert completed the flute method for which Taffanel had left extensive notes, and the Taffanel-Gaubert *Méthode Complète* was published in 1923. The method, modelled like Altès's on Baillot's Conservatoire violin method, attempted to cover all aspects of technique and remains a standard today. It retained little of the basic theory or principles of music from earlier Conservatoire flute methods, but presented exhaustive daily exercises, progressing from the simple articulation and joining of notes to elaborate scale and arpeggio studies, and focusing on phrasing, breathing, style, finger technique, and tone. Taffanel's notes for a projected reference book on the flute became the basis of an article of 1926 in Albert Lavignac's *Conservatoire Encyclopaedia* (*c*1913–31) by Fleury, who contributed several other articles on music and flute-playing to musical journals.[43] Fleury's own interest in earlier repertoire led him to edit much unknown or forgotten eighteenth-century music and to found the Société des Concerts d'Autrefois (Concert society of olden times, not to be confused with an ensemble of the same name founded by Geneviève Thibault in 1926) to explore the music and instruments of the seventeenth and eighteenth centuries.

The Taffanel-Gaubert *Méthode* and Fleury's encyclopaedia article, the principal writings on Taffanel's playing and teaching, were thus compiled after his death by pupils, a provenance some contemporaries felt made them inadequate documents of his style. Georges Barrère wrote to Emil Medicus in 1923 that the Taffanel-Gaubert method 'deviated from the subject and became commercial' rather than encapsulating Taffanel's precepts. He noted that while Taffanel's pupils had played studies by Joachim Andersen, those mentioned in the *Méthode* were Gariboldi's, which were never used in the class but happened to be published by the same firm as the method.[44] Claude Dorgeuille too wrote that he felt Gaubert had worked 'quickly and rather carelessly' on the method due to his other commitments. But however imperfectly the two sources may express the fine nuances of Taffanel's taste and practice, they provide concrete enough detail to establish that concepts of the flute's tone, repertoire, pedagogy, and even the instrument, continued to shift with the changing conditions of musical life and with the personalities of his various pupils.

The generation of Taffanel's pupils lived at a time when musical performance and education were rapidly becoming more common, and an enormous increase in the Conservatoire flute class's productivity helped extend their influence. Under Dorus and Altès, the graduation rate had averaged slightly less than one a year, about the same as the Dresden school, so that thirty-five flutists won first prizes in the forty years 1860–99. The next forty-year period, 1900–39, saw the rate more than double to eighty-six, with an unprecedented five students finishing in the same year (1920) immediately after World War I. The rate increased even more rapidly during the 1940s, when forty-eight first prizes were awarded to graduates of two flute classes, one taught by Gaston Crunelle and the other by Marcel Moyse. Thus in the forty years after Taffanel's tenure, the class produced nearly four times as many first prizewinners (188 from 1909 to 1950) as Dorus, Altès, and Taffanel combined had taught over the previous forty-eight years (fifty-one between 1860 and 1908). The overwhelming majority of the graduates were male and French. Foreigners, 90 of whom had been enrolled out of the Conservatoire's 630 students in the 1880s, were limited to two per class thereafter.[45] Non-French flutists could study privately with Conservatoire teachers, however: Frederick Griffiths, later Professor of Flute at the Royal Academy of Music in London, was one who took lessons with Taffanel in *c*1887–8.[46]

While the Conservatoire was producing more and more skilled flutists, work opportunities multiplied, so that between 1906 and the late 1920s, though solo wind recitals remained uncommon, the number of concerts in Paris more than doubled to as many as 1880 in a single year.[47] By about 1930 the Conservatoire, already the world's most influential musical institution, had become the apex of a highly centralized national pyramid of music education that included 23 branch academies, 21 'national' schools and 20 municipal schools.

For a number of reasons, those of Taffanel's pupils who spread the Conservatoire's influence most widely as teachers, Georges Barrère, René Le Roy, and Marcel Moyse, operated largely in the United States. This perhaps explains why the idea of a French Flute School, inasmuch as flutists believe it persists today, attaches not to the Conservatoire itself so much as to the personalities of a few famous players, particularly those most influential in America.

Moyse entered the Conservatoire in 1905, studied with Hennebains, Gaubert, and Taffanel, and graduated at the age of seventeen (he himself said sixteen). Far from slavishly imitating his teachers, he strove to imitate the range of sonority other instrumentalists and singers such as Pablo Casals (cello), Georges Enesco, Jacques Thibaud, and Fritz Kreisler (violin), and Enrico Caruso (tenor) could achieve. All these artists used a continuous vibrato to produce tones of lightness, sweetness, and brilliance rather than emphasis or strength. Moyse later wrote that his teachers and colleagues warned him to reduce a type of vibrato they considered 'excessive', but on another occasion he claimed to have invented the technique on purpose at an early recording session (see p. 232). His early career included notable premieres, among them Ravel's *Daphnis et Chloé* (1912) and Stravinsky's *Petrushka* and *Rite of Spring* (1913), but during World War 1, when food was rationed and music a low priority, he suffered such poor health that he was unable to play. He wrote out his daily regimen of practice, using small melodic fragments in predictable permutations, in his *Études et exercices techniques* (Studies and technical exercises), which he sold to the publisher Leduc in 1921.[48] His somewhat later *Enseignement Complet* (Complete instruction) contained a massive series of exercises intended to supplement, rather than to replace, one of the stock methods, such as Altès or Taffanel-Gaubert.

Moyse's exercise books illustrate a teaching style that seems to have been much more prescriptive than any before him. Beginning with simple studies for a beautiful tone, the series progresses to patterns written out over and over again in every key and every possible combination. Nothing is left to the student's discretion: 480 scales and arpeggios turn page after page black with notes. An exhortation to practise slowly contains a justification of this onerous programme: '… the reason has time to overcome the instinct[,] to guide and not suppress the temperament[,] and it is in my opinion on this happy balance that a fine interpretation should be based'. When Moyse succeeded Gaubert in 1932 after assisting at the Conservatoire for ten years, his teaching was noted as particularly authoritarian: René Rateau (Conservatoire 1928) recalled that Moyse expected his students to perform exactly as he did: 'He didn't like it if you didn't play his interpretation.'[49]

On his return to Paris after spending World War 2 in his home town of St Amour, Moyse found himself an outsider despite his earlier prominence: many of his posts, including his chair at the Conservatoire, had been awarded to younger rivals in his absence, and Jean-Pierre Rampal (1922–2000), a pupil of Gaston Crunelle, had become the new star flutist of Paris. After two years of negotiation, a second flute class was created for Moyse, but he soon left France in disillusionment. In his subsequent teaching in America and Europe (chapter 12), his prime concern remained beauty of sound, with an emphasis on homogeneity, variation, and nuance. His exercise book *De la Sonorité* (On sonority) was dedicated entirely to tone production, a matter he made the focal point of lessons he gave even to pupils who had already reached the highest levels of musical accomplishment. Michel Debost has recounted such an occasion that illustrates both Moyse's enduring concern for tone and his trust in his own instincts as the touchstone of traditional authority:

> He was sure that what he was teaching me was Taffanel's own words, but what he taught me that day in 1982 was very different from what he taught on the same G minor scale twenty years before. He showed me how E natural was to be played and how F♯ was to be played, and when you come from F♯ to the E♭, how the interval should sound and so on. Not one word about pitch but about the colour – about how the colour of B♭ should be in G minor.[50]

In personality and in ideas, Moyse could scarcely have been more different from his younger contemporary René Le Roy (1898–1985; Conservatoire 1918), who gained his First Prize at the relatively advanced age of twenty after studies with Hennebains and Lafleurance, and went on to study with Gaubert. As part of a distinguished career including premieres of numerous new works by Robert Casadesus, Jean Chartan, Vincent d'Indy, Gabriel Pierné, Guy Ropartz, and works already mentioned by Honegger, Martinů, and Rivier, Le Roy began his recording career two years after Moyse in 1929, the year in which he began making regular tours to the United States. From 1940 to 1950 he made his residence across the Atlantic, teaching at the Montreal Conservatoire beginning in 1943 and revisiting France in the summers after the war. Claude Dorgeuille collaborated with Le Roy a decade after his retirement from public performance on a *Traité de la Flûte* (Treatise on the flute, 1966) that rejected a pedagogy reliant on the 'automatic repetition of stereotyped exercises' – clearly a criticism of methods by Taffanel-Gaubert and Moyse – preferring a statement of principles that allowed practice material to be devised appropriately to each individual.

Dorgeuille devoted a chapter of his study of the French Flute School (1983) to Le Roy, depicting him as the summit of the school's achievements. Moyse too has been nominated Taffanel's spiritual successor by English flutists on whom he exerted the most influence, while a writer from Georges Barrère's adopted city of New York has called that flutist 'Taffanel's successor as the leader of the so-called "French school" of fluteplaying'.[51] These conflicting claims alone would seem to make any attempt to trace a single transmission of the French flute-playing heritage futile, even if flute-playing in Paris itself had not continued to follow its own direction. Conservatoire professors since 1950 have included Jean-Pierre Rampal and Michel Debost, while three of the most recent, Alain Marion (1938–98), Pierre-Yves Artaud (1946– ; Conservatoire 1970), and Sophie Cherrier (1959– ; Conservatoire 1979) have embraced new music and led full performing careers at the forefront of experimentation, including work with Pierre Boulez's Ensemble Intercontemporain and IRCAM. Indeed, by the 1970s the basic ideas of tone, instrument, repertoire, and pedagogy which Taffanel's French Flute School brought to flute-playing had merged with other influences into a new International style of flute and flute-playing, to be explored in chapter 14.

Chapter 12

The flute in the age of recording

The rise of mechanically-reproduced sound around the turn of the twentieth century utterly transformed the production and consumption of music in the historical twinkling of an eye. The new technology altered musicians' employment prospects almost immediately by displacing music-hall and silent cinema, but by turning musical performance from a fleeting event into something permanent, it eventually had an even more profound effect on playing styles and instruments. Within a few decades of the first high-fidelity recordings, previously distinct national fashions of playing had dramatically altered and begun to merge together into a new, recognizably modern shape (see pp. 227–8). Once memory of the nineteenth century's instrumental and tonal variety had vanished by about 1960, all but a handful of flutists in western Europe, North America, and Japan played a metal French-style Boehm flute – the only model by then available from the companies that had come to dominate flute production – with a relatively uniform technique and concept of style.

Few instrumentalists made recordings in the early years of acoustic recording (the late 1880s to 1890), when sounds played into a horn were directly engraved on a cylinder or disc, a process less unflattering to the piccolo than to the flute or violin. But by 1890 the catalogue of Edison's North American Phonograph Co. listed over a hundred solos and ensemble works with flute or piccolo. Typical repertoire was the kind George Schweinfest (1862–1949) recorded on both instruments in 1889: *The Wren-Polka, Skylark Polka, Waltz-Birds' Festival*, and *Turtle-Dove Polka*. Albert Fransella recorded similar bird-imitation pieces as well as Scottish songs and a work of his own, *Remembranza Napolitane*, for the Gramophone Company (London, 1898), while his quartet of flutes later recorded selections from *The Mikado*, a *Song Without Words* of Mendelssohn, and other light classics. Staple opera obbligati, such as Donizetti's 'Mad Scene' from *Lucia di Lammermoor* and Bishop's 'Lo, Here the Gentle Lark', provided another opportunity for flutists to record, as on London discs Gaubert (1904) and Fransella (1905) made with the soprano Nellie Melba (1861–1931).

Most flutists, particularly those beyond the recording industry centres of London, Paris, Berlin, and the U.S., left no recordings at all in the acoustic era, while the style of those who did record was markedly individual, even among French players. The French branch of Emile Berliner's Gramophone Company recorded piccolo duets and solos by flutists of the Garde Républicaine in Paris in 1899, and Georges Barrère began recording there in 1903, continuing at irregular intervals in America until 1941. In 1907 Adolphe Hennebains recorded chamber works with the Société de Musique de Chambre, including parts of Beethoven's *Serenade* op. 25, with Doppler's *Fantaisie*

51. Jean-Pierre Rampal in an HMV recording studio, c1950.

pastorale hongroise and transcriptions of Chopin waltzes and nocturnes in the following year. Styles of playing in England before 1910 are captured on discs by Fransella and by the famous music-hall player, London Symphony Orchestra principal, and piccolo soloist Eli Hudson (1877–1919), who recorded Boehm's *Variations* op. 22 for HMV in London in 1908. Major companies in America employed their own studio flutists, mostly drawn from the ranks of Sousa's and other bands, among whom Clement Barone Sr (1876–1934), Marshall Lufsky (1878–1948), Darius Lyons (*b* 1870), and Charles North (1866–?1935) dominated the catalogues. Three recordings by Frank Badollet and his well-blended and vibrato-free trio of flutes (1902) were among several he made beginning in 1899.

Flute solos, mostly of the bird-imitation variety, decreased after 1910 as the recorded repertoire began to include the flute in salon music ensembles and even in classical pieces. The ten titles Australian John Lemmone (1861–1949) recorded on his Radcliff flute while touring America with Melba were the only ones in the Victor Talking Machine Co. catalogue from 1910 to 1925. Among them was the first movement of Mozart's flute and harp concerto with Ada Sassoli, one of the earliest recordings of Mozart's flute music. John Amadio (1884–1964) of New Zealand, who also played a Radcliff flute, worked with famous singers including Melba, and played with a highly modulated but light vibrato, made many recordings displaying his blazing rapidity and technical facility in the usual *Carnival of Venice* and *Witches' Dance* as well as Chaminade's *Concertino*, Hoffman's *Konzertstück*, and a 'breakneck' finale from Mozart's D major concerto, in which he managed to fit six minutes of music onto a four-minute disc.[1] Another exceedingly fast early performance of a popular classic was Ary van Leeuwen's of Chopin's *Minute Waltz* (Vienna, 1905), which despite its rapidity lasted about a minute and fifty seconds.

Besides their enormous influence on listeners of their own time, early recorded performances are of great value to us by providing access to a sound-world totally different from our own. These documents serve as an often surprising reminder that our ears are fitted with filters we are not aware of, revealing that contemporary listeners had unfamiliar ways of hearing rhythm, vibrato, portamento, and other key aspects of musical performance. It comes as something of a shock at first to find how many of these qualities even the most critical listener takes for granted: the exercise tells us just as much about our own assumptions and tastes as it does about those of the musicians in whose steps we believe ourselves to be following. Robert Philip (1992) summarizes the main differences succinctly:

> The performances of the early twentieth century … are volatile, energetic, flexible, vigorously projected in broad outline but rhythmically informal in detail. Modern performances are, by comparison, accurate, orderly, restrained, deliberate, and even in emphasis.

The spread of recording, as well as increasingly regular orchestra personnel and longer rehearsal times, eventually led to profound changes in the character of concert performances, as musicians became accustomed to trust mechanical feedback in place of live audience response. The recordings of the early twentieth century, in Philip's view, retain characteristics of the world before recording existed, in that their style is fitted for performance before human beings rather than machines.

> If pre-war recordings are remarkably like live performances, many late twentieth-century live performances are remarkably like recordings. Detailed clarity and control have become the priority in modern performance, in the concert-hall as well as in the studio.

For musicians of the early twentieth century, Philip concludes, a piece could be given no immutable 'correct' performance. Composers approved of different orchestras with quite diverse playing styles, while multiple accounts of the same piece with various ensembles, such as Stravinsky's five of the *Rite of Spring*, 'demonstrate … that composers' views evolve as performance practice evolves'. To this evolution have been added changes in recording style and technology, from the live, warm sense of space in analogue recordings made at Abbey Road studios and Queensway Hall, to the heavily mixed and edited, metallic-sounding, and relatively lifeless products of digital editing and reproduction today.

RHYTHM

Tempo is more flexible in early twentieth-century playing than we expect, often seeming rhythmically uncontrolled, slapdash, even incompetent at first hearing, especially in loud or virtuosic passages, where hurrying was usual. In the early part of the century musicians often exaggerated dotted rhythms and rushed groups of short notes. Tempo was often flexible within movements, so that a movement's second subject could be given a quite different tempo from its first. Melody and accompaniment coexist in a relaxed relationship, and performers use rubato in individual and sometimes extremely skilful ways, generally reminiscent of rhetoric or dramatic speech. The best orchestras under great conductors often played with as close and flexible a sense of ensemble as a chamber group, but inaccurate chording is also often encountered, particularly in studio bands and at the beginning of a piece.

VIBRATO

Notices, principally in the form of complaints, of the increasing use of vibrato by violinists and singers appeared in music criticism from the 1890s onward, and its use in early recordings varied greatly. Against the objections of musicians and critics, a 'tiresome, irritating, and absurd' continuous vibrato, as one writer characterized it in 1912, had become widespread before World War 1 as an acceptable way of enhancing tone, rather than a device to be employed in the service of the music. France, America, Britain, Italy, Germany and Austria, and other European countries successively adopted vibrato in woodwind

continued overleaf

playing, except on the clarinet, where it never made an impact. According to Robert Philip's study of orchestral recordings, the flutists of the Berlin and Vienna Philharmonic Orchestras, and those of Prague, Budapest, and Milan, used little or no vibrato in the 1920s and 30s, while that of the Accademia di Santa Cecilia played with absolutely none in the late 1940s. In contrast, the Dresden State Opera's flutist in the late 1930s used a conspicuous and continuous vibrato, while Amsterdam's Concertgebouw Orchestra was closest to the French style, with a definite, fairly fast, flexible vibrato.

PHRASING

Recordings document a shift in phrasing from the phlegmatic British and Germanic style of phrasing common before World War 1 to one that was more histrionic, or 'expressive', in the late twentieth-century sense of the word. Philip writes, 'Styles of phrasing on all woodwind instruments tended to become more assertive, with more detailed nuances and a wider dynamic range used to shape melodic lines.'

INTONATION

Standards of playing in tune, especially in studio bands, were often low; indeed, most musicians seem to have considered approximately correct intonation close enough. French flutists of the early twentieth century were no exception: even their most ardent supporters agree that they played out of tune, but their 'expressive' tone and phrasing was clearly considered more important.

To compete with the Boston Symphony's wholesale importation of French woodwind players in the late nineteenth century, Walter Damrosch travelled to Paris in 1905 to recruit a set of Conservatoire-trained woodwind principals for his New York Symphony. Taffanel nominated Georges Barrère, an ambitious and energetic pupil of Altès and himself, to Damrosch's position. Barrère had commissioned more than sixty new works for the Société Moderne d'Instruments à Vent, a revival of Taffanel's group of 1889–93, had been one of the first French flutists to make recordings, and at the age of eighteen had played the premiere of Debussy's *Prélude à l'après-midi d'un faune*. He secured a year's leave from his positions in the Paris Opéra and the Colonne orchestra and signed a renewable exclusive one-year contract with Damrosch as 'Flute and teacher of flute' with guaranteed minimum annual earnings of $2000 ($8 per concert, $30 per week for out-of-town summer engagements). The following year he made a supplementary agreement with the Institute of Musical Art to teach at $3 per hour, which led to a further contract worth $1400 on the college's merger with the Juilliard Graduate School (1926). In America Barrère maintained his intensely active and entrepreneurial style, commissioning many new works from American composers at a time when foreign-born musicians and conductors preferred European ones. He organized the New York Symphony Wind Instruments Club, the thirteen-member Barrère Little Symphony, the Barrère Ensemble of Woodwind Instruments, and a trio with the harpist Carlos Salzedo. As a frequent soloist with New York Symphony and in recitals, he quickly earned accolades, not only as a musician but in particular as a flutist. A newspaper wrote in 1910:

> During five years in New York, Mr Barrère has won friends for that abused instrument, the flute; has shown that its repertory includes music of the masters

instead of second-class 'show pieces,' and that its players are really interpretative artists.[2]

Barrère's teaching schedule was no less dynamic, encompassing Juilliard, where he introduced Conservatoire-style teaching methods and repertoire and founded the woodwind ensemble programme, as well as summer schools in Woodstock and Chautauqua.

In 1907 another busy promoter of the flute, Emil Medicus (1882–1980), returned to the U.S. after studies in London with A. P. Vivian, Daniel S. Wood, and Albert Fransella. Medicus settled briefly in Brownsville, Tenn., playing solo engagements, teaching, writing, repairing flutes, and re-selling used wooden instruments for the William S. Haynes Co. Moving permanently to Asheville, N.C., after peripatetic teaching with his Medicus School of Flute Playing, Medicus convened a national panel of flute experts, 'The Big Six', to reinstate the flute as the leading solo instrument. With his magazine *The Flutist* (1920–9) Medicus stimulated a wave of enthusiasm for the instrument, which had already seen the establishment of flute clubs in Los Angeles (1916) and New York (by Barrère, 1919). The magazine's twenty-five or more pages, supported by advertisements and subscriptions, covered pedagogy, biographical sketches, question-and-answer columns, and reviews, and encouraged flute clubs, the sale of flutes, and composition for the instrument. It carried many articles about the French flute school, Barrère, Laurent, and their New York and Boston flute societies, helping to standardize flute-playing in the U.S. as players became aware of brands and styles of instrument, and learned what solo pieces were being played across the country.[3]

52. Georges Barrère and William S. Haynes, mid-1930s

By the 1920s the William S. Haynes Co. was considered the principal flute-maker in the United States, having established a mutually beneficial promotional relationship with Barrère, who had bought his first Haynes flute in 1913, and with a West Coast dealer, the Baxter-Northup Co.[4] The company's catalogues contained photographs and endorsements from flutists, giving special prominence to Barrère, as well as material on the history of the flute and details of the latest Haynes activities. Rudall Carte followed suit by filling its catalogues with photographs of players and testimonials to its own instruments, but these were priced out of the U.S. market after World War 1 by a federal tariff of forty per cent, so that an English flute cost $300 against a comparable Haynes at $200.[5] By 1924 Haynes had discontinued wood flutes in favour of silver, while Cundy-Bettoney produced 90 per cent metal instruments, 5 per cent wood, and 5 per cent ebonite in the following year.[6] The Boston makers' market dominance and the exclusion of international competition emboldened Haynes to state in his 1925 catalogue, '[t]he wooden flute has gone and gone forever'.

The Haynes name itself had become a valuable property by 1920, when the William S. Haynes Co. filed suit to deny Haynes's son the right to use the trademark 'The Haynes Flute'. In the same year George Bundy, on behalf of the Selmer company, bought the name and services of George W. Haynes for $6000. The relationship between George Haynes and Selmer collapsed after two years, but when Haynes left to work for his brother, Selmer sued the William S. Haynes Co. for mentioning George's name in its 1923 catalogue, and he was enjoined from signing his own name on business letterhead.[7] The William S. Haynes Co. registered trademarks for the name 'Haynes' in that year, and began advertising as the 'Original W. S. Haynes Co. of Boston, Established 1888' in response to similar claims made under George's name.[8]

In 1922 the William S. Haynes Co. added new 'French' model flutes with perforated keys. The 'handmade French' version was built on a thinner silver tube (0.013 inch), thought to be more responsive, and like those of Lot it had soldered toneholes with keys set in line and pointed arms connecting them with the rods, while the 'regular French' model, made of thicker tube, had an offset G mechanism. Haynes promoted the new open-hole flute as superior to his earlier type: 'Undoubtedly the players who take the trouble to adapt themselves to the French model flute become better musicians. As for the instrument itself, it is characterized by a greater clarity and brilliance of tone than that of the covered hole flute.'[9]

While Haynes introduced more expensive handmade instruments, other flute-makers took the more usual competitive course of improving production efficiency, price, and distribution. In 1924 Haynes wrote to Medicus about the efforts of one competitor, George Bundy, to buy the Haynes Co. on behalf of Selmer:

> He informed us that after installing $40,000 worth of machinery they were now prepared to grind out flutes like sausages. Even the embouchures are to be machine cut. In short, there is to be no hand work where a machine can be employed. He mentioned that while they had run at a loss ever since their flute factory was established they were prepared to do so for two years more. At the expiration of that time they expected to have their advertising and distributing machine in such perfect order that the rest of us will be sitting up begging for a customer.[10]

When Haynes rebuffed the takeover attempt, Selmer changed its focus to meeting the demands of the burgeoning school band industry with less expensive flutes. In 1927 the company ceased using George Haynes's name and moved its operations from Boston to Elkhart, which Conn and others had built up into a manufacturing centre for band instruments, particularly after 1915 when the C. G. Conn Co. was sold, renamed C. G. Conn Ltd., and retooled for assembly-line production.[11] Aware of the significance of the public school band business for his firm, Conn's new owner, Carl Greenleaf, founded the Conn National School of Music in Chicago (1923) to train school band directors, and gave generous financial and promotional support to several related organizations and associations.[12] After Selmer's move to Elkhart, Bundy brought Kurt Gemeinhardt from Markneukirchen to work with Philip H. Marcil in its flute-making division, which copied the de facto standard metal flutes by Louis Lot, with perforated or closed keys and open or closed G♯ key. George Bundy put his own name on a new line of inexpensive flutes before 1933; a year or so later these were withdrawn and a 'Marcil' student model added. The 'Bundy' trademark was reintroduced after World War 2, by which time Selmer had phased out high-grade flutes.

Haynes met more serious competition in the quality flute market from his associate, Verne Q. Powell (1879–1968), than from the band instrument makers. Powell had first heard Barrère play at the Chicago World's Fair in 1910, while he was working as a jeweller and engraver in Fort Scott, Ks. The performance inspired Powell, himself an accomplished flutist, to build himself an instrument out of scrap silver including spoons, watch cases, and coins from his brother's jewellery store. On the strength of this instrument, Haynes hired Powell as foreman of his flute workshop in 1913. During his thirteen years designing and making flutes and piccolos with Haynes, Powell rose to become general manager, before leaving in 1926 to start his own shop. Though talking pictures were putting many flutists out of work and the Depression was threatening, his firm was rumoured on its incorporation in 1927 to have been set up with capital of $10,000, and he managed to secure workmen and parts from Selmer at the time of its move from Boston to Elkhart. Powell, like all the other American flute-makers, took a Louis Lot flute as his pattern, but adjusted the scale to A=440, 442 and 444.[13] His first ten customers included John Wummer (Detroit Symphony), William Siebold (Baltimore Symphony), and William Kincaid (Philadelphia Orchestra and Curtis Institute).[14] Rather than use dealers, Powell sold most of his flutes direct, with a backlog of up to seven years, refusing to expand his business to meet the demand. When wartime caused a slack in business and cork and steel became restricted substances, Powell travelled to Washington to obtain government contracts, mostly for D♭ instruments, that would allow him to obtain his essential materials.[15]

The advent of electric microphones for recording and broadcasting in 1925 brought 'high fidelity' to recorded sound and allowed larger-scale works including the standard symphonic and chamber repertory to be heard on record and the radio for the first time. During the early electrical era (1925–35) a handful of prominent and enterprising flutists began to make recording an integral part of their careers. Two Frenchmen, Marcel Moyse and René Le Roy, were ideally placed to take the first initiatives in recording the major works.

Moyse, already a renowned flutist when the electrical recording process emerged, made by far the largest contribution of any flutist of the time to the recorded repertoire in Paris and London both as a soloist and as a member of numerous ensembles. He recalled in 1949 his determination to use mechanical reproduction, on radio as well as record, to promote the flute. 'The flute sounds very well over the radio because the sound engineers can amplify the lower register', he wrote.

> The question is to have the flute heard as often as possible in orchestra and in radio broadcasts. If the public understood the flute better, the conductors would give it more importance and predominance.... but it is our task alone to see that our [i.e. woodwind] instruments be considered the equal of the stringed instruments.[16]

The new recording and reproduction technology reproduced the flute's tone more faithfully than the acoustic method, but according to his own not entirely trustworthy account, Moyse felt the medium demanded another adjustment:

> I played for the first performance on His Master's Voice. ... We recorded, just us wind players – and it was awful! My tone had no life. What to do? Somebody suggested waving the tone. But no, I refuse. Better to go to a farm and imitate the noise of sheep. But what I developed was the vibrato. I was the first man to introduce vibrato, not only in a flute, but in a woodwind![17]

In fact, while Moyse may indeed have consciously employed vibrato to enrich his recorded sound and while it was still generally held in low regard in England, all the French flutists of the early twentieth century who recorded used some vibrato (see p. 220).[18]

Moyse made his debut recording in March 1927 with four pieces for flute and piano, one of which, Genin's *Carnaval de Venise*, immediately sold thousands of copies in Paris department stores, at least according to Moyse's own report. His first orchestral recording (with the Orchestre Symphonique de Paris, 1927) contained excerpts from Saint-Saëns's *Le carnaval des animaux*, and three years later he made the first French recording of Mozart's D major concerto, which won the *Grand Prix du Disque* two years later and introduced flutists all over Europe to the French style.[19]

Moyse's only competitor as a recording artist in Paris was René Le Roy, ten years his junior at the Conservatoire and associated with fewer recording ensembles. Like Moyse, Le Roy recorded from the 1920s until after the war, while other prominent French flutists of the period – Georges Laurent, Gaston Blanquart, and Gaston Crunelle – did so only sporadically. He made what were probably his first solo discs (1929) of Honegger's *Danse de la chèvre* (written for him in 1919) and the third movement of Bach's E♭ major sonata, later featuring baroque, classical, and modern repertory, including a premiere recording of Varèse's unaccompanied *Density 21.5*, written for Barrère.

Barrère himself recommenced recording in America in 1933 after an eleven-year hiatus. With various chamber groups he recorded contemporary works by Cowell, Riegger, Piston, and Salzedo, and in 1937 he recorded for RCA Victor on its prestigious Red Seal label, playing Rameau and Debussy transcriptions and three Bach sonatas with Yella Pessl, probably the first recordings of Bach's flute sonatas to employ harpsichord instead of piano.

Emil Prill recorded works by Quantz and other early composers little known outside Germany in the early 1920s, as did Heinz Breiden and Georg Müller, who used a baroque flute for at least one session. However, recordings of German flute-players were even more uncommon than those of French, English, Australasian, or American. Even though by about 1928 Karl Bartuzat had changed to the Boehm flute, his Mozart Divertimento with the Leipzig Gewandhaus Wind Quintet is an extremely rare document of the touching and traditional sound German players prized, as well as their unique sense of rhythm, with less *rubato* but more Quantzian overdotting than other styles.[20]

Other far-reaching changes in music came from jazz, beginning with the emergence of ragtime before World War I. Jazz players created a sense of vigour and energy by deliberately playing outside the 'proper' limits of pitch and tone, as well as by freely improvising their music. Their impact was, to use a contemporary term, sensational:

> All the so-called highbrow musicians are jealous, jealous of the immense popularity of our jazz leaders; jealous of their financial reward, but jealous above all of their ability and versatility.[21]

In contrast to the clarinet and saxophone, the flute was not initially thought of as a jazz instrument, though the New Orleans marching bands that prefigured jazz styles often used a piccolo. But the instrument occasionally made an appearance in early jazz music. Italian-born Clement Barone, who played piccolo and later solo flute in the Philadelphia Orchestra and recorded with the soprano Amelita Galli-Curci, played in Arthur Pryor's band in the teens.[22] Like the two flutists of the Sauter-Finnegan band in the 1930s and 40s, Barone probably played from a written part rather than improvising, though Cuban-born Alberto Socarras (Clarence Williams band) and the classically trained Wayman Carver (Chick Webb band) likely improvised. Carver became the first true jazz flutist by specializing in the instrument in 1932, making flute solo appearances on *Devil's Holiday* (1933, Col. 2898D), and later with Webb's band on *I got rhythm* (1937, Decca 1759) and other albums.

These early appearances were relatively obscure, and the flute remained a novelty in jazz as long as its tone was thought to lack the intensity needed for solos while its high register stood out as too distinct to blend with the rest of the band. But the enormous influence of Lester Young's light, elegant saxophone playing, the interest West Coast jazz composers and arrangers began to show in orchestral and chamber music textures, and the spread of new amplification technology gave the flute a place of its own during the 1950s. At the same time Latin music, with its own thriving flute tradition, began to exert an influence on the style.

Frank Wess, a saxophonist in Count Basie's band from 1953 to 1964 as well as a proficient flutist, brought the flute a more prominent role as a solo instrument in one of the world's most popular bands. On the West Coast Bud Shank played with

Howard Rumsey's band and Stan Kenton's Orchestra, and Buddy Collette, followed by Paul Horn and later Eric Dolphy, appeared with Chico Hamilton. Collette became the first to record on piccolo, flute, alto, and bass flutes on *Buddy Collette's Swinging Shepherds* (1958, EmA 36133), while Horn, Dolphy, and James Moody adopted a French-influenced orchestral tone, in contrast to the unfocused and vibrato-free sound of Jeremy Steig and many other post-war jazz flutists, most often saxophone doublers.

In 1956 the American jazz magazine *Down Beat* took the flute out of the 'Miscellaneous' category and gave it its own 'Reader's Poll' section, as the spread of live electronics and the waning of big bands made smaller ensembles of solo instruments and rhythm section more common. Hollywood's film industry, always seeking exotic sounds, began to require saxophonists to double on flute: even jazz saxophone legend John Coltrane attempted the flute briefly. As one wind-player recalled:

> [I]f you wanted to make money in this business, you had to learn how to play flute at one point. Originally it was tenor [saxophone] and clarinet. Then in the 40s and 50s it became flute. And suddenly, in the 60s, if you didn't play flute on dates, for example, you just wouldn't get called.[23]

Jazz musicians in search of new sonorities turned to the piccolo, the alto flute, and non-western and home-made flutes of different materials in the late 1950s. Sam Most and Sahib Shihab were among the first to produce a more African sound by singing or humming into the flute while playing. Yusef Lateef used voiced syllables to achieve unusual articulations, while Roland Kirk spoke through the flute to create a rasping vocal timbre.

The most prominent jazz flutists of the 1950s were the Belgian Bobby Jaspar and Herbie Mann, probably the first jazz musician to make a career on flute, doubling on saxophone instead of vice versa. Flutist-composer Henry Mancini scored for four unison bass flutes in a jazzy television soundtrack of the late 50s, and the flute of Jim Horn was sometimes heard in pop music of the early 60s by Carol King, Elton John, Neil Sedaka, and Sonny and Cher. Latin American jazz players had traditionally used the flute more than those of New Orleans or Chicago: Latin bands of the mid-1960s often featured a flutist, one of whom, Hubert Laws, also substituted at the Metropolitan Opera and New York Philharmonic, and recorded Chick Corea's trio for flute, bassoon, and piano on *Laws' Cause* (1968, Atl. 1509), as well as jazz adaptations of music by Bach, Stravinsky, and other composers. Laws continued, and continues, to play a flute with open G♯.

Jazz and highbrow contemporary music alike were notoriously considered degenerate by national socialist elements in early twentieth-century Germany, but the Nazis' cultural isolation grew not only from their political ideology but also from a long-term focus on exclusively Germanic traditions. Thus in editions of his book on flute-playing (1910 and 1923) Maximilian Schwedler had omitted any mention of new French repertoire by Stravinsky, Debussy, Ravel, Lalo, and Saint-Saëns, while even in England the 1927 edition of *Grove's Dictionary of Music and Musicians* listed Austrians and Germans Mozart, Spohr, Weber, Beethoven, Haydn, Kuhlau, Reicha, and Schubert as the major composers for the flute, but entirely excluded contemporary French names. Fleury's encyclopaedia entry of the same period, on the other hand, covered modern French music as well as the Germanic classics: Gluck, Mozart, Haydn, Beethoven, Mendelssohn, and Schumann.[24]

Not all German players resisted outside influences, however, and Gustav Scheck became a pioneer of the French style in his country during the 1930s. Scheck had taken up the conical six-keyed flute at the age of twelve, but five years later had begun Boehm flute studies with Richard Röhler, who played a silver instrument, as well as learning recorder and performance practice with Willibald Gurlitt, a protégé of Hugo Riemann, founder of the modern collegium movement (Leipzig, 1908). Hearing Roger Cortet (1903–50) and Marcel Moyse inspired Scheck to change his playing style, sound, and technique, so that in 1928 he switched from a grenadilla flute by Otto Mönnig of Leipzig to a silver Louis Lot. His attempted synthesis of German and French ideals led him to oppose Schwedler's Reform embouchure as well as the 'reform' embouchure of Mönnig. An article on vibrato he wrote in 1936, two years after Paul Hindemith appointed him flute instructor at the Berlin Hochschule as successor to Prill, recommended using it constantly rather than for special effect. This position stirred a controversy with Schwedler, who despite his advocacy of the technique at moments of high emotion held out against continuous vibrato in Leipzig, until his pupil Erich List, who had to play Reform flute in his lessons but Boehm flute in his nightly job playing for silent films, introduced a version slower than its French counterpart.[25] Vibrato had spread as far as Australia by the 1930s when Richard Chugg introduced the 'French singing vibrato' he had learned in Paris.[26] Yet even as late as 1954, in the aftermath of World War 2, with German national pride shattered and French flute-playing made familiar everywhere by recordings, Georg Müller thought continuous vibrato inappropriate to his own country's tradition:

> Despite the fact that constant vibrato more commonly appears in the Romance countries, we Germans possess our own way of playing, resting on a great tradition which begins with Quantz and has been constantly developed by the great German virtuosi, of which even today we need not be ashamed.[27]

Though certainly Müller was fighting a rearguard action by this time, Germanic players largely succeeded in keeping their focus on the flute's traditional sound and repertoire, resisting vibrato until after World War 2, despite the influence of Prill and Scheck in Berlin, of Kukala and van Leeuwen in Vienna, and of the recording industry.[28] Still, the Meyer and Reform flutes, though the latter lingered in German orchestras until 1950, had largely disappeared after World War 1, when the demands placed on orchestral flutists made them turn to the Boehm cylinder flute for its technical advantages.[29] Once again the Berlin Philharmonic became the first German orchestra to embrace a foreign style when it appointed the Paris-trained Swiss Aurèle Nicolet (1926– ; Conservatoire 1947, under Moyse) as principal flute in 1950.

French-style vibrato was still almost entirely absent in British flute-playing in 1931 when Henry Welsh expressed the opinion that '[w]ind instruments should be played with a tone that is steady as a rock and as pure as crystal'.[30] The British sound was linked to a particular type of flute: in England at the beginning of the twentieth century practically all symphony and band players used wooden cylindrical instruments with one fingering system or another. The market was dominated by Rudall Carte, whose Boehm-system and Carte 1867 instruments were the most widely used, furthering the tonal ideal that characterized British playing until after World War 2: a dense, firmly centred sound, with little or no vibrato, and a strong awareness of intonation and ensemble blend within the woodwind section. Another hallmark of British and Empire players on record was their astounding technique. Notable British recording artists of the period included Eli Hudson and Robert Murchie (1884–1949), the leading London flutist between the two World Wars. Good employment prospects gave English flutists no reason to seek new instruments or musical influences: in London, as in Paris, demand exceeded the supply of excellent musicians, so that young players who graduated from music college could expect to find work in theatre, recording, and symphony orchestras without the formality of an audition. The deputy system, in which a musician could send a substitute to play whenever he was offered more lucrative work, persisted despite efforts by Sir Thomas Beecham and other conductors to discourage it. Only Beecham's London Philharmonic and the BBC orchestras paid a salary, while other ensembles contracted on a freelance basis. Nonetheless, Sir Thomas could not promise players in his orchestra full-time employment: its piccolo player, Gervase Markham, became a taxi driver, a sideline he kept for his whole career.[31]

During the early electrical recording era the nature of orchestral sound as a whole was altering from a concept that prized rich tone and harmonic balance to one in which the brilliance of individual instruments became prominent. In this climate Geoffrey Gilbert (1914–89) played a key role in the breach in English resistance to the French flute sound. After serving as third flute in the Hallé Orchestra in 1930–3 Gilbert briefly became principal in 1934, before leaving with Beecham at the age of nineteen to become principal of the newly-formed London Philharmonic, where he remained until the outbreak of war in 1939. During the inter-war years continental wind-playing made a strong impression, most frequently an unfavourable one, on London musicians. Fleury, Gaubert, and Le Roy toured England in the early twentieth century, while broadcasts, recordings, and tours were making a large international public aware of their smooth, brilliant, vibrato-laden sound. Despite the strangeness of the style, Gilbert noted that London recording companies imported French flutists for solo and concerto recordings, and learned from HMV's recording manager 'that the reason was that my sort of playing[,] and English flute playing generally, was not acceptable to the gramophone company'. The conductor Eugene Goossens told him, 'if you want to be regarded as an international artist you'll have to change your style of playing; you'll have to change your instrument and you will have to learn to play the same as everybody else [i.e. in the French and American recording industry] does'.[32] Through Goossens, Gilbert arranged to have lessons with Le Roy on his visits to London. Over the next three years he altered his embouchure and articulation, learned to use vibrato, and bought a Louis Lot silver flute.

Established English flutists, Robert Murchie (BBC Symphony Orchestra), Gordon Walker (London Symphony Orchestra), Gerald Jackson (Royal Philharmonic), and

Gareth Morris (Philharmonia), disliked the French players' sound and scorned their poor intonation. On the other hand, a recording of Andersen's *Fantaisie Caractéristique* (1930), made by the female flutist Edith Penville even before Gilbert changed his style, displays a distinctly French-influenced tone and vibrato.[33] Though Miss Penville appeared at Sir Henry Wood's Promenade Concerts and toured as an accompanist to the coloratura soprano Luisa Tetrazzini and as a music-hall soloist, orchestral positions remained out of reach to her, as to all women flutists. The supposed health benefits of flute-playing had been regularly recommended to women from about 1880 until World War 1, with enough success that over a hundred 'Lady Flautists of Europe and America' received individual notice in one survey.[34] But if orchestras barred women, the recording industry set them no such obstacle: Erika Stolz (Erika von Klösterlein), a female flutist about whom little is known, recorded an orchestrated arrangement of Gounod's *Faustwalzer-Fantaisie brillante* in Berlin as early as 1906.[35] Other female soloists and recitalists in England included Erroll Stanhope, a flute teacher's daughter, Elgar (Winifred) Hudson, sister of flute and piccolo virtuoso Eli Hudson, and Cora Cardigan, 'The Queen of Flute-players'.[36] America had May Lyle Smith (*b* 1873) of New York, and Marguerite de Forest Andersen, who gave a Queen's Hall recital including the *Concertino* by female composer Cécile Chaminade in London in 1905.[37] Excluded from prestigious paid positions by men, women formed their own orchestra in the Chicago area in 1925,[38] the same year in which the British Women's Symphony Orchestra appeared at the Queen's Hall in a programme that included Susan Spain Dunk's *Sketch for Flute Solo and Strings 'The Water Lily Pool'* (see panel below). Frances Blaisdell became the first woman wind-player at New York's Institute of Musical Art as a pupil of Barrère's from 1928 to 1934.

BRITISH WOMEN'S SYMPHONY ORCHESTRA QUEEN'S HALL CONCERT, 22 MAY 1925

8 p.m.
Tickets: 8s 6d and 5s 9d reserved, 3s and 2s 4d unreserved.
Source: Poster, DCM.

Conductor: Dr Malcolm Sargent
Wilma Berkeley, vocal soloist
Flute soloist not identified

Overture, *Ruy Blas*	Mendelssohn
Aria 'Ah! fors è lui'	Verdi
Symphony no. 5	Tschaikovsky
Idylle élégiaque in C sharp minor for string orchestra	
Sketch for flute solo and strings 'The Water Lily Pool' (premieres)	Susan Spain Dunk
Aria Palatia 'Ah! Pour ce soir' (Mignon)	Ambroise Thomas
Overture *Meistersingers*	Wagner

Men dominated in orchestral positions at least in part because advanced instrumental education remained a privilege of institutions that were exclusively male (the military) or almost so (the music colleges). Connections with these institutions enabled some of the leading London orchestra and jazz musicians, including Gareth Morris, to spend the war in Air Force ensembles that left them free to fulfil London engagements in the evenings.[39] By this time the repertoire of the military-style bands as well as their organization and musical training had altered. Between 1900 and 1905, John Philip Sousa's band toured England several times, playing programmes that included orchestral works such as Mendelssohn's Violin Concerto. On Empire Day 1924 and the week following, six hundred bandsmen performed two concerts daily at Wembley Stadium, playing music of Holst, Vaughan Williams, Bach, and Wagner, 'utterly different from what a military band would have played a generation ago', according to the *Musical Times*.

Military and brass bands of less gargantuan size had long ago displaced flute bands almost everywhere, but in Northern Ireland and Scotland the earlier type continued to develop. Second and third B♭ flutes and sometimes a piccolo in D♭ joined the melody flute band as it became more popular, while early twentieth-century four-part harmony flute bands used six-keyed flutes of various sizes as transposing instruments – that is, all the parts were written as though for a C instrument (with a six-finger note of D), but played on flutes in flat keys. A typical early twentieth-century civilian band was disposed like the larger military ones of the period: six or more B♭ flutes playing in three parts, an E♭ piccolo, F flutes, and one or two B♭ basses.

Civilian flute bands in Ireland, Scotland, England, and Wales gradually adopted Boehm-system flutes and began to play concert performances and contests. Some bands had sets of instruments specially made: the Ravenhill Temperance Flute Band ordered instruments with metal heads and wood bodies. Other changes were due to the general shift from high (A=452) to low pitch (A=440) after about 1950. The new low-pitch flute band, pioneered by the Motherwell Flute Band in Scotland and soon followed by the progressive Ulster bands, used a C/G key system rather than a B♭/E♭ one. Since manufacturers already offered C flutes and piccolos, G alto flutes, and C bass flutes for use in school bands, the flute bands changed their entire instrumentation and scoring to match the new standard keys, adding G treble flutes, unknown in the classical flute market. The first bass flutes, which as yet made no appearance in flute bands, were made in post-war America by Telejoe Freeman (in E♭, to low D) and Thomas Ogilvie (in C), and used in film scores of the 1950s.[40]

Crossing the ocean became even more attractive to European musicians in the 1930s, remaining so until after World War 2, when as late as 1948 Arthur Gleghorn, who had been principal flute of the Philharmonia Orchestra, emigrated to Hollywood and exchanged his wooden Rudall Carte flute for a silver instrument on which he recorded new music such as Stockhausen's *Zeitmasze* and Boulez's *Le Marteau sans Maître*.[41] The Depression distressed flute-makers and players on both sides of the Atlantic. Marcel Moyse worked hard, often from 9 am until midnight, to maintain his supremacy as Paris's top flutist in these years, recording frequently, teaching exhaustively, and often sending deputies to his orchestral engagements. Yet even the annual salary of a

53. Artisans in the assembly, padding, and finishing department of the William S. Haynes Co., Boston, *c*1949.

Conservatoire professor was less than a second flutist could earn in a single month's work in an American sound studio.[42]

The Haynes Co. operated on a two- or three-day week during the Depression, selling cheap French and German instruments at the same time as competing with these imports by offering a new, low-cost model for school bands. 'By placing such a flute on the market,' the brochure of 1930 announced, 'it is hoped Public School Supervisors will be protected against the purchase of cheap foreign flutes scarcely worthy of the name. Why not American flutes for Americans where there is proof positive that our home made products are in every way superior to the best made abroad.'[43] Flutes with a range to low B became standard equipment in the U.S. in the 1930s as American flutists imitated Molé, Barrère, and his pupil William Kincaid (Philadelphia Orchestra, 1921–60) who used them.

Rudall Carte kept its work force busy by transplanting the mechanism of instruments previously built at high pitch onto a new body at A=440, adding an extra digit to the serial number to indicate the year of modification. In about 1933 the company introduced the 'New Metal' Boehm flute, endorsed by Gordon Walker and Gilbert Barton of the London Symphony and Covent Garden orchestras as 'much easier to play' than wooden flutes, as well as less expensive, but with the same sonority.[44] The nickel alloy in question had also been used to line wooden headjoints for some years.

Despite the extremely high cost of platinum and the severe economic climate of the times, Rudall Carte took its first order for a flute in this material in November 1933, and by the summer of 1935 had made a total of three. The Haynes Co. made the first American platinum flute for Barrère in July 1935, using annealed iridium-platinum, at the enormous cost of $2600. Spectrograph tests by the International Nickel Company in the Bell Telephone Laboratories showed that the platinum flute produced stronger odd-numbered harmonics in the low register and even-numbered harmonics in the middle register than 14-karat gold and sterling silver instruments.

The company stated that Barrère preferred the volume and quality of tone of his platinum flute, but Barrère wrote in 1941 that in fact 'platinum is not any better than silver. This is confidential, of course.'[45] Barrère asked Edgard Varèse, whose music he had programmed for many years, to compose a piece for the new platinum flute. The result was *Density 21.5* – though in reality the density of the alloy in the flute was 21.6. Barrère premiered Varèse's piece, the first to call for audible key noises, on 16 February 1936.

Jean-Pierre Rampal took over Marcel Moyse's position as the favourite flutist of Paris during the war years, which he had begun as a medical student in his home city of Marseilles and ended as a graduate of the Conservatoire after only five months' study under Gaston Crunelle, conducted while in hiding from the Nazi occupation forces. After the liberation of Paris Rampal became first flute at the Paris Opéra, and quickly gained recognition as a soloist, making his first broadcast in 1945 with Ibert's Concerto, and his first recording, Mozart's Flute Quartet in D, in the following year.

Rampal's popularity in Paris coincided with two events that fuelled a boom in the recording industry: the end of the war, and the advent of editable magnetic recording tape and long-playing records, which all studios had adopted by the end of 1950.[46] 'It seemed, those early days of recording in Paris,' Rampal wrote, 'as if I just finished one session only to start another for a different label in a different location in the city.'[47] In around four hundred original recordings he became the most recorded flutist, and one of the three or four most recorded musicians, of all time. Having already used libraries to find neglected repertoire while still his father's pupil in pre-war Marseilles, the younger Rampal began to record enormous quantities of hitherto unknown baroque and early classical flute music, including premiere recordings of Vivaldi's complete op. 10 concertos and others by Benda, Blavet, Buffardin, Pergolesi, Richter, and Stamitz, as well as anthologies of sonatas by Frederick the Great, Hasse, Leclair, Quantz, and Telemann, to name only a few. His editions of many of these pieces made them widely available for the first time since they had been composed. Rampal also transcribed works for other instruments: Schubert's *Arpeggione* sonata, and pieces for keyboard or violin, most famously Khachaturian's concerto for that instrument, which he played on a flute with a C-foot, even though his own transcription required a low B (one witness reported that to play that passage, Rampal pulled out his flute's headjoint to lower its pitch and transposed up a semitone).[48] Towards the end of the 1960s Rampal began to devote himself to the romantic repertoire, as well as contemporary works, many of which he inspired himself, by Poulenc, Boulez, Jolivet, Rivier, Bernstein, Penderecki, and others, though he left avant-garde music (chapter 14) to other interpreters including Aurèle Nicolet, Severino Gazzelloni, Pierre-Yves Artaud, and Robert Aitken. Rampal made his first international tour to Indonesia in 1953, and five years later, in defiance of the Opéra orchestra which denied him leave to tour the U.S., he made his American debut at the Library of Congress.[49] He was the natural choice to take over the Conservatoire flute class when Gaston Crunelle retired in 1969.

The new market for long-playing records respected national borders much less rigidly than the market for books, instruments, or performing skills. Exposure to

European wind-playing increased after the war in Britain, and particularly in London, as orchestras began to compete for international recognition, and for audiences for their records, by making foreign tours. Transatlantic exchanges had also become fairly frequent events by the LP era, after the London Symphony Orchestra had sailed on the Queen Mary to the U.S. with Nikisch in 1912 and Eugene Ormandy had brought the Philadelphia Orchestra to England after the war. Since American flutists had learned from Haynes's advertising that wooden flutes were 'gone, and gone forever', the English players' wooden instruments attracted comment. But the Britons retorted that 'when they made metal ones as good as those we already had we'd be very happy to use them'.[50] While the soloistic playing, harsh tone, and piercing upper register of some Continental orchestral flutists earned criticism in Britain, other qualities the English valued, such as blend, 'firmly centred tone', and 'well controlled vibrato', won praise.[51]

Taxes and assay laws made it difficult for French and American instruments to penetrate the British market, just as France protected local industry by outlawing foreign recipes for gold and silver. By importing a Powell flute from America, Geoffrey Gilbert raised the ire of flute-maker Albert Cooper, who protested that the instrument was not hallmarked according to British law. Postwar Britain levied a 25 per cent luxury tax on goods priced at or above £100, so that Cooper was obliged to price his flutes at £99.[52] Yet despite such obstacles to outside influence, British woodwind playing had altered permanently by 1961:

> Few of the leading players today, on any of the [woodwind] instruments, play with either style or tone in the least like those of thirty years ago. It is the new soloist who is most sought after, and interest in ensemble ceases once intonation, attack, and elementary balance have been secured.[53]

Gareth Morris (1920–) succeeded his teacher Robert Murchie as the principal exponent of the English flute-playing style after World War 2. Morris took a prominent part in London chamber music, and as a soloist, a professor at the Royal Academy of Music (1945–85), and principal in the Philharmonia Orchestra (1948–72). Though he played Murchie's wooden Rudall Carte flute throughout his career, his playing was less severe and more 'expressively' and elegantly phrased than his teacher's. Yet Morris continued in the 1990s to hold that '[a] perpetual vibrato is to be discouraged, because its cultivation is at the expense of interpretation and destroys the true sound of the flute'.[54]

John Wummer and William Kincaid, probably the first prominent American flute virtuosi to record consistently important repertory, illustrate how the French taste had become naturalized in the United States in a similar incomplete way. Kincaid, who played a platinum flute with a tone often described as 'virile', passed on a distinctively American tradition to his pupils including Julius Baker (1915–), who after holding orchestral posts in Cleveland, Pittsburgh, New York, and Chicago taught at Juilliard, Curtis, and Carnegie Mellon University with a non-prescriptive method that emphasized solid technique and stylistic flexibility.

54. The team: principal wind players of the Philharmonia Orchestra, London, *c*1950. (*left to right*) Sidney (Jock) Sutcliffe (oboe), Gareth Morris (flute), Dennis Brain (horn), Cecil James (bassoon), Harold Jackson (trumpet), Frederick (Jack) Thurston (clarinet).

Yet the 'virility' of the American style and the 'firmness' of the English seemed poles apart. After Sir Thomas Beecham brought the Royal Philharmonic Orchestra to the U.S. on its first American tour in 1950, New York flutists learned that their English counterparts played wooden instruments not out of ignorance, but because their instruments suited their 'entirely different ideal of flute-tone'.

> They find our silver-flute tone thin, lacking in fullness and richness, yet too penetrating for their pleasure. Conversely, we find their wooden-flute tone 'tubby', lacking in brilliance … undoubtedly the wooden flute lends itself more easily to … tone-blending.[55]

Less than a decade later, however, one of those New York flutists, Julius Baker, noted that orchestral flute-playing had already become more uniform world-wide. He looked back on his impressions of the flute-playing in foreign orchestras:

> If the tone of the flutist was heavy, we were reasonably sure it was a German orchestra; if the flutists had a very fast vibrato, it was an Italian orchestra; if the flutist's tone was dull, it was certain to be an English orchestra; if brilliant, it was sure to be French. The playing styles of each nation's players were so distinct…. What has been responsible for the tremendous change in the short period of twenty-odd years? Undoubtedly, the pupils of Marcel Moyse played an important part, especially in Europe. But the most important single factor, in my opinion, was the development of good sound reproducing equipment and the long-playing record.[56]

In suggesting that recording had played the most important part in the change, Baker, a radio and electronics enthusiast, perhaps possessed an especially keen appreciation for its role, since he had produced six discs in 1946–51 for his own company, Oxford Recording Co. But the other influential factor he mentioned, Moyse's influence in America, was still relatively slight. Moyse had taught several Americans, including Frances Blaisdell, Harry Moskovitz, Arthur Kitty, Robert Cavally, and James Pappoutsakis, at his home in St Amour during the 1920s and 30s, and his reputation was such that he had been invited to U.S. in 1938 by Koussevitsky in Boston and Toscanini in New York. At the Boston Symphony's fifth Tanglewood summer season, Moyse stood in for Laurent, playing his Couesnon flute as he had since the 1920s, but struggling to match the orchestra's pitch of A=442, to which Laurent's Powell was tuned. Koussevitsky offered Moyse's son Louis the second flute position for 1939–40, but the outbreak of war prevented his taking up the post.

In summer 1949, after his eclipse by Rampal in Paris and an abortive move to Switzerland, Moyse accepted Rudolf Serkin's invitation to Marlboro College near Brattleboro, Vt., where he taught until 1957. Moyse announced to a giddy interviewer his ambition to establish an American school of woodwind playing that would 'challenge the best anywhere in the world'.[57] He started private studios in several cities: New York, Boston, Montreal, and Hartford, Conn., and gave three weeks of masterclasses in Chicago in 1951. In the 1950s he participated in the Marlboro Music School and Festival, where his magnetism as well as his bad temper and insults became legendary. He was featured eight times in *Woodwind Magazine* 1949–52, on the cover of the October 1950 issue in a relaxed pose that contrasted with American flutists' formal portraits. Now 'mostly a historical figure' in France, Moyse became a U.S. citizen in 1959.[58] Marlboro students convened a woodwind seminar in 1961 that became an annual event later named the Marcel Moyse School of Wind Playing, with a peak enrolment in 1975–82. One first-year student was Paula Robison (1941–), who also studied at Moyse's studio in New York without telling Julius Baker, her Juilliard teacher. Moyse became still more visible in America when Robison made a successful New York debut in 1961, and won the Geneva International Competition in 1966, earning a solo performance with the Suisse Romande Orchestra and other opportunities. Moyse's *Tone Development Through Interpretation*, published in 1962 with a cover image of the *Maître* (teacher) wearing a beret and smoking his pipe, helped publicize him further.[59]

In 1964, a few months after his seventy-fifth birthday, Moyse was invited to teach for two weeks at an Artists' Home in Boswil, Switzerland, an event repeated annually until 1976. In the second year, James Galway (1939–), William Bennett (1936–), and Trevor Wye (1935–) attended, and in 1969 Wye founded the International Summer School in Canterbury 'for the purpose of bringing Moyse to the British'.[60] Moyse resigned from Marlboro in 1966 after feeling slighted by Serkin, but made connections with Japan at about the same time. Forty Japanese students came to Boswil in 1972, and Moyse travelled to their country in 1973 and 1977.[61] The first French flutist to come to Marlboro, Michel Debost, had been 'transformed' by Moyse at Boswil, and a reconciliation with French flutists was attempted when Moyse met Alain Marion, the new Conservatoire professor, who arranged a week of public masterclasses in Paris in 1977.[62]

The flute-making industry had for the first time become completely homogenized between the Depression and the post-war years, by which period all the flutes in regular production by firms with world-wide distribution, allowing for superficial variations from the standard, were metal Lot-style Boehm instruments with a closed G♯ key. Koichi Muramatsu (1899–1960) of Japan began to make silver Haynes- and Powell-type flutes in Japan in the 1930s, while the Elkhart companies Armstrong, Artley, and Gemeinhardt, as well as Altus, Miyazawa, Yamaha, and Sankyo in Japan, built instruments to compete not only with the American budget models but even with the high-priced professional flutes. Boosey and Hawkes Ltd bought the moribund Rudall Carte company in 1944, moving its workshop to north London shortly before the company was wound up in 1961, at which point a group of its craftsmen including Harry Seeley and Roger Harris put their wooden-flute making skills to use in a new company, Flute Makers' Guild, established with the help of City of London guild authorities to help preserve 'traditional British craftsmanship'.

The flute's popularity as a school band instrument received a further boost when a new type of flute method book appeared after the war, directed to American high school teachers 'who have not had the opportunity nor the time to become familiar with the flute' before teaching their band students. Methods by Hetzel (1940), followed by Gekeler (1951) and Voxman/Gower (1954), used photographs of the flute to demonstrate how to hold, blow, and finger the instrument, a style adopted by Herfurth and Stuart's popular *A Tune A Day* (1953). Frederick Wilkins (1957) included a chapter on the 'psychology of practice' and aimed to help those outside large cities 'where adequate teaching is meagre or non-existent'. Another work that attempted to reduce to writing what had traditionally been communicated by a teacher was F. B. Chapman's *Flute Technique* (1936), which dedicated twenty-seven pages to discussions of breath, lip, finger and tongue control, with a view to 'put the acquirement [*sic*] of a good technique on [a] scientific basis' and excluding the elements of music along with most of the artistic aspects. New periodicals for wind teachers, such as *The Instrumentalist* and *Woodwind World*, contained short articles on all aspects of teaching flute technique, as well as product news from manufacturers and publishers.

Despite the uniformity of the instrument and the standardization and increasing technical focus of teaching, the flute's repertoire had become somewhat more diverse, thanks to the recording industry's stimulus of interest in little-known music both new and old. 'Certainly the tyrannical monopoly of the standard repertory has been seriously weakened', wrote the New York early music pioneer Noah Greenberg, looking back on the recording industry's role in raising public understanding of early music's unfamiliar sounds in the 1920s.[63] This was nowhere more true than of the flute's eighteenth-century repertoire, which despite its long tradition in Germany and more recent attention in France had remained marginal until Rampal brought baroque music to a large public in his recordings of the 1950s.

Nonetheless, by the 1950s and 60s the flute's repertoire, the recording and manufacturing industries, and the ideas that prevailed in pedagogy and orchestral playing, had merged into a kind of world-wide orthodoxy for the first time in the instrument's history. As Moyse's pupil Raymond Meylan (1924–) observed in 1974:

Until about 1960 there were flautists in Italy and Germany who cultivated their own national style. However, these instrumental traditions, which differ from the French school of between the two World Wars, are gradually disappearing. I am not sure that this is a good thing.... Today flute-playing is in danger of becoming the same everywhere. Records and rapid travel have helped to ensure the prevalence of a certain view, that of the post-war French school, which is dominated by Jean-Pierre Rampal.[64]

Chapter 13

The flute in the early music revival

New attention began to focus towards the end of the nineteenth century on music in a style completely foreign to most musicians and listeners: the compositions of J. S. Bach. Despite revivals of large-scale works for choir and orchestra in Berlin (1829), London (1838), Boston (1850s), and the American Midwest (1860s), Bach's music, and i   d all repertoires earlier than the symphonies of Haydn, Mozart, and Beethoven, remained unfamiliar to most concert audiences. One British commentator of about 1850 recorded that many people thought the music incomprehensible, and suitable only for snobs:

> To confess any admiration of the works of the master was looked upon as affectation and cunning – as a mere device to exhibit an uncommon taste, and to appear more knowing than your neighbours.[1]

Yet many in Germany and England held Bach in high regard. Once his flute son?   s had been published for the first time (Leipzig: Peters, *c*1855) by Ferdinand David (1810–73) and Friedrich Hermann (1828–1907), they appeared as examination pieces for Moritz Fürstenau's pupils at the Dresden and Leipzig conservatories as early as the 1860s. Saxon flutists, with their vivid sense of tradition, also led a move to bring the sonatas to the concert platform (see p. 197): a premiere of the B minor sonata took place at the Dresden Tonkünstler-Verein in 1859–60, and of the E major in 1872, while Maximilian Schwedler performed Bach's Sonata in E♭ as a rare instrumental solo at a Gewandhaus Orchestra concert in 1882.[2] In 1857–8 the Dresden society first heard the B minor Suite for flute and strings, which by the end of the century had become a popular filler at orchestral concerts in England as well as Germany. The sonatas came to wider notice in the Bach-Gesellschaft edition (Leipzig, 46 vols, 1851–99), the first set of 'complete works' to publish a composer's notation without deliberate editorial tampering, to include almost every composition, and to provide a critical apparatus. Sonatas for flute and obbligato keyboard came in vol. 9 (1860), while the three continuo sonatas appeared in vol. 43 (1894).

Critics of the day often noted problems of balance in performances of Bach's music. At least three reviews of Brandenburg Concerto no. 4, given at the Gewandhaus several times in 1901 with flutes in place of recorders, complained that the accompaniment was 'much too strongly scored or played in comparison to the obbligato [i.e. concertino] instruments'.[3] One reviewer made a similar complaint of the

55. César Charles Snoek as a student with the beginnings of his collection of early instruments. *Die Woche,* 16 June 1902.

'massive string body' in a B minor suite of 1903, even though another found it 'extremely clear and transparent'.[4] When Jean Firmin Brossa gave the first Manchester performance of the B minor suite with the Hallé Orchestra (19 January 1899), the orchestra solved problems of balance with the solo flute by reducing the size of its string section to single players. The *Manchester Evening News* called the resulting performance 'a most delicate and dainty one', while the *Manchester Guardian* found it an unprecedented revelation:

> The effect of the tone colouring thus produced was quite different from anything we have heard before in the Free Trade Hall, and seemed … to transport one back to the age when music was made 'apt for voices or viols', and noisy display had not yet become a feature of the art.[5]

A later Manchester performance in 1923 reverted to 'noisy display', but addressed the balance problem by using Richter's arrangement for three flutes.[6]

On hearing a German Bach festival in 1884 one English writer, prefiguring Shaw's comment about Fransella quoted in chapter 10, suggested that contemporary instruments themselves were unsuited to perform earlier repertoire:

> [T]he deficiencies in Bach's music, as we commonly hear it, are due, in fact, not to the author, but to the imperfection, in several remarkable respects, of our vaunted modern orchestra.[7]

Performances of Bach's music called into question not only instrumentation but also the accepted performance style. A review of Emil Prill's performance in the *Musical Offering* trio-sonata (flute, violin, and continuo) in 1893 noted that modern musicians had become alienated from earlier repertoire:

> The right style must first be sought out again to perform works such as this Bach sonata, since after a gap of a century we are completely separated from it and a tradition unfortunately no longer exists.[8]

French players too, once they rediscovered the flute's early repertoire, found that it required adjustments from the style they had developed for modern music. Gaubert spelled out the sense of restraint he thought proper in early music:

> With Bach, as with all the great classical masters, the player must observe the utmost simplicity of style. There should be no vibrato or quavering of the sound – an artifice best left to mediocre instrumentalists and inferior musicians.[9]

The early-instrument pioneer Arnold Dolmetsch (1858–1940), who gave concerts of seventeenth- and eighteenth-century music featuring lutes, viols, and recorders, took this 'simplicity and dignity' to extremes: the deliberately anti-romantic playing style he adopted struck some listeners as 'absolutely devoid of musical expression and dynamic light and shade'.[10] Dolmetsch led a rebellion against the musical establishment, including the German-dominated musicological profession. *'Les musicologues?* BAH!' he once expostulated, 'I know how it goes. It is here, in my head.'[11] He insisted on drawing his own conclusions directly from original treatises, manuscripts, and instruments.

While interest in baroque music grew, the study of early instruments changed from a hobby for amateur enthusiasts into a more serious institutional undertaking. Music colleges in Paris (Conservatoire, 1864), Brussels (Musée Instrumental du Conservatoire, 1877) and Berlin (Hochschule, 1888) established the first permanent exhibitions of early instruments, basing them on private collections acquired by purchase. Similar displays of 'obsolete instruments' appeared before the general public at the 1885 International Inventions Exhibition in London, and four years later at the Exposition Universelle in Paris, where the historical artefacts on show included 'the first example of the Boehm Flute that arrived in France, made by Greeve [*sic*] of Munich', clearly the instrument Camus had owned.[12] Paul Taffanel gave one of his 'historic concerts' at the exhibition, using his Boehm flute but modifying its tone 'to give the impression of the old recorders'.[13] (According to Tula Giannini (1993), Taffanel's flute, no. 600 by Louis Lot, originally the property of Dorus, possesses 'a sweeter tone, very resonant and sonorous, and retains more of the qualities of the wood flute' than Lot's instruments made in the later nineteenth century.) At about the same time an exotic-looking three-piece transverse flute stamped HOTTETERRE attracted notice in the French woodwind-instrument making town of La Couture-Boussey in Eure, Normandy, home to the families who led the craft in France: Buffet, Chédeville, Godfroy, Hotteterre, Leblanc, Lot, Noblet, and Thibouville. The specimen, which in fact was not authentic but a recent copy of an original instrument, became the nucleus of a museum of historical instruments founded at la Couture in 1888.[14]

Musicians first turned to antique flutes such as the Hotteterre specimen to solve the problems of playing baroque music during the same few years after about 1880. According to Bernard Shaw a M. Dumon (about whom nothing further is known) performed in London in 1885 on 'an old ivory one-keyed specimen that Frederick the Great may (or may not) have performed upon',[15] and he appeared again at the Brussels Museum two years later playing an 'eighteenth-century flute'.[16] Schwedler, like most nineteenth-century flutists, began his early training on an obsolete type, when his mother bought a two-keyed flute in an estate sale along with a bound copy of the music examples from Quantz's *Essay*.[17] In 1893 he played in a concert of baroque music for the king of Saxony, using a one-keyed flute by Thomas Riszler of Hamburg most likely borrowed from his colleague Paul de Wit and dating from about 1800.[18] At the International Exposition for Music and Theatre in Vienna he performed a concerto by Frederick the Great on a one-keyed flute, accompanied by de Wit (viola da gamba) and others on period instruments.

While Bach had long been a favourite in Saxony, Frederick the Great's musical circle began to receive attention in the early twentieth-century climate of German nationalism. In Berlin, Georg Müller published a book on Frederick's flutes and flute-playing in 1932, the same year as de Wit's *Zeitschrift für Instrumentenbau* (Instrument-making magazine) carried an article by Müller on the makers of flutes in the King's collection. In the same year Müller recorded selections from Frederick the Great's concerti, on an instrument the monarch had owned.[19] He also gave many concerts using original flutes at Frederick's Potsdam seat, Sanssouci. Müller's own flute collection and library were destroyed in World War 2.

The individuality of these German players was reflected in the editions they made of early music. Schwedler published transcriptions and adaptations of Rameau, Couperin, Marais, Schubert, Kuhlau, Vivaldi, Bach, Haydn, Spohr, and Fürstenau,[20] while his edition of Bach's Partita (1918), discovered by Karl Straube in the previous year, added tempo indications, accents and slurs in abundance, as well as a piano accompaniment by the Thomaskirche organist, Gustav Schreck, along the lines of those Schumann had supplied for the Bach cello suites.[21] Schwedler's editions of the Bach and Handel sonatas (1910–23), his Mozart flute quartets (1924), a Bach edition (c1925) by his Gewandhaus colleague Wilhelm Barge (1836–1925), and many similar publications, were thickly annotated with expression marks in the manner of the time.

Early repertoire first attracted notice in France when Taffanel turned his attention to the previous century – that is, the eighteenth – as part of a thorough revision of the instrument's repertoire at the Conservatoire beginning in 1894 (chapter 11). Until then French musicians had ignored the Bach revival that had been taking place in Germany, Austria, and England, while the Conservatoire had been preoccupied with orthodox works by French composers. Alfredo Casella (1883–1947), who studied Bach in Italy before coming to Paris at the turn of the century, noted that none of his Conservatoire classmates knew the great composer's music.[22] But Taffanel, who had toured widely and even performed Mozart concertos at the Gewandhaus, was clearly ahead of his compatriots in his awareness of baroque repertoire. His colleague Louis Fleury (1878–1926) made the first French editions of baroque music, which, like the German versions, were supplied with 'missing' expression marks. He wrote in 1922 of Taffanel's advocacy:

> Bach's sonatas, those wonders, long buried in the dust of libraries, awakened to find a real interpreter [in Taffanel]. He was the first, at any rate in France, to find out the meaning of these works, which his colleagues thought dull and badly written for the instrument.... It is a fact, though hardly credible, that down to 1895 Bach sonatas were not taught in the flute class (under Altès) at the Conservatoire.[23]

Fleury's Bach editions of 1925 came at a time when audiences and musicians all over Europe and America, accustomed only to the tone-painting of late romantic works, were beginning to hear merit in the harmony and counterpoint of Bach's music. Still, a traditional scorn persisted for what was seen as the composer's lack of passion. One English commentator wrote in 1932:

> I do not know what value scientists put upon their mathematical calculations, but from an artistic point of view I put very little upon the logical demonstrations in sound worked out by John Sebastian Bach. I do not consider them, from a musical point of view, to be any superior to the mathematical demonstrations made by a good professor at any European University.[24]

Several movements in Germany between the World Wars brought the recorder and other historical instruments to amateur music-makers, prompting the first regular attempts to replicate early woodwinds; though at first these efforts focused on the recorder, they paved the way for later developments in the flute. Peter Harlan copied Dolmetsch recorders in 1926, changing the fingering, and making the 'German' recorder the trademark of the Youth Movement. Two enterprises, Bärenreiter (1924) and Moeck (1930), were established to publish early music and method books for use in the domestic music or *Hausmusik* movement.

Radio and recording first brought pre-classical music to a mass audience in the 1930s, when chamber orchestras playing baroque and contemporary neoclassical works multiplied. New early music groups in America in the 1920s and 30s formed when several well-known instrument collections arrived in Boston, New Haven, New York, and Washington, D.C. For the most part, European-born musicians led the

American Society of Ancient Instruments (Philadelphia), the Society of Ancient Instruments (Boston Symphony players, including Georges Laurent on baroque flute), and other ensembles.[25] The U.S. benefited from an influx of war refugees that included all the prominent German musicologists including Curt Sachs, as well as learned interpreters such as Wanda Landowska, Nadia Boulanger, Erwin Bodky, Alfred Einstein, and Yella Pessl, a harpsichordist who recorded Bach sonatas with Georges Barrère in 1937.[26]

In Switzerland in 1933, August Wenzinger and Paul Sacher founded the Schola Cantorum Basiliensis, an early music study centre 'conceived as a kind of half-way house between the ivory tower of the university and the seminarian atmosphere of the conservatory'.[27] The Schola shunned elitism, dilettantes, and 'lifeless scholarship' in favour of a robust and practical engagement with performing early music. Wenzinger (viola da gamba) later joined Gustav Scheck, an early exponent of the baroque flute and recorder, and the harpsichordist Fritz Neumeyer in a highly-regarded chamber ensemble, and in the Scheck-Wenzinger Kammerorchester, which performed on historical instruments.

Until historical musicology came of age in inter-war Germany, not much attention had been paid to the details of what early composers wrote: the Bach editions by Barge (c1925), Fleury (1925), and Schwedler (1936) had sold on the basis of their editors' markings just as much as for Bach's notes. But by now music scholars, following the lead of literary studies, felt it important to know exactly what the composer had written, and to avoid outside influences on the text that changed the effectiveness and emotional impact of the work. Their studies were showing how difficult and specialized the task of reconstructing an authoritative copy could often be. The first performing edition of the Bach sonatas to describe itself as an *Urtext*, or original text, issued by Peters in New York, London, and Frankfurt in 1936, started a revolution in the way flutists interpreted baroque music. Edited by Kurt Soldan and with a continuo realization by Waldemar Woehl, this edition made the entirely new claim that it was 'edited from the autographs and contemporary manuscripts'. When it reached London after the war, it came as a revelation to Gareth Morris, then the most prominent flutist working in a climate of intense interest in Bach's music under the conductor Otto Klemperer and in chamber groups such as Boyd Neel's orchestra. As Morris recalled, 'I was *staggered*, when I got it, to compare it with the old Peters edition [by Barge] I'd been using, which was *heavily* edited.'[28] The new text led Morris to interpret Bach's markings of slurs and dynamics in a new way, not as a complete and literal prescription for performance, but as a minimal set of instructions to be applied to the piece as a whole. By this time listeners had acquired a taste for difficult contrapuntal music to the extent that the first complete recording of Bach's *Musical Offering*, with Frances Blaisdell playing the flute, appeared in 1940.[29] Several other editions of Bach's flute sonatas, by Ernst Roth (1945), Henry Ernest Geehl and Charles Stainer (1947), and John Francis and Millicent Silver (1955), originated in post-war London, attesting to the era's fascination with Bach, while editions by Barrère (1944) and Rampal (1964) added to their status as standards.

While Gareth Morris relied on his musical training and intuition to make a new interpretation of Bach's text, curriculum changes at both conservatories and universities after 1945 brought a more formal historical perspective to music teaching. Musicology became established as an academic discipline in the U.S. and Europe, with France following only in 1969.

Amateurs were now taking up baroque and even renaissance instruments in larger numbers. While collectors such as Günter Hart and scholars led by Curt Sachs maintained an intense interest in original instruments, an industry of replica-manufacturing blossomed in small post-war German workshops. In 1949 Moeck opened a recorder factory, and an article of 1950 introduced the baroque transverse flute to German amateur recorder-players.[30] Meanwhile the American educator Leo Traynor instigated the mandatory teaching of recorder in Japanese primary schools, a stimulus that provided a market for the Aulos line of plastic recorders and, eventually, plastic baroque flutes.

The 1950s saw a boom still more vigorous than that of the pre-war years in records and concerts of baroque music. Most prolific were Jean-Pierre Rampal's recordings of the baroque pieces he had rediscovered (chapter 12). At the same time several performers made recordings using original historic flutes, if not always specimens of a particularly appropriate period. With Isolde Ahlgrimm at the harpsichord, Ludwig von Pfersmann recorded the Bach sonatas, the *Musical Offering*, and a Vivaldi concerto on a wooden ring-key flute by J. M. Bürger of Strasbourg. Gustav Scheck recorded on a one-keyed Kirst flute, his releases including a Leopold Hoffmann Concerto (1952) and Bach's B minor suite (1954). Hans-Martin Linde (1930–) used a flute by Martin Metzler in the Leclair concerto (1956), Bach's *Partita*, and works from Telemann's *Tafelmusik*. Leopold Stastny of Nikolaus Harnoncourt's influential Viennese ensemble Concentus Musicus played a boxwood C. A. Grenser flute in recordings of works by Bach, Handel, Hotteterre, Marais, Quantz, Telemann, and Vivaldi.

In 1948 Frans Vester (1922–87), later a leading teacher, editor, and scholar, broadcast the Bach *Partita* on Dutch radio using a baroque flute. Vester's extraordinary theoretical and practical musical education had begun at the age of eleven with private tuition from the musician and critic Jos de Klerk. He entered the Amsterdam Conservatory at the age of fifteen and premiered the Ibert concerto there at nineteen, but by the time he left in 1941 felt his time at the institution had been wasted and lost interest in the flute. He took it up again seriously on hearing Moyse after the war, and began teaching, holding a succession of orchestral posts, and copying music from libraries. His Danzi Quintet performed on early woodwind instruments, sometimes in the same concert as modern ones, on which it gave the premiere (1958) of Schönberg's wind Quintet op. 26, a piece previously considered unplayable. Vester's recordings and tours with Frans Brüggen, Gustav Leonhardt (harpsichord), Anner Bijlsma (cello), and Jaap Schröder (violin), including a recording of the Mozart concertos with Brüggen conducting (1973), were among the most influential made on original instruments. As a teacher at the Royal Conservatory in The Hague he made his ideas felt in the modern- and early-instrument spheres, through students including Jane Bowers, Eric Dequeker, Barthold Kuijken, Peter van Munster, Marten Root, Stephen Schultz, and Janet See. Players of Vester's Dutch school coined the name *traverso* for the baroque flute.

Disapproving voices, which had been raised against Arnold Dolmetsch in the 1890s, grew more urgent once historical instruments began to make regular appearances in the concert hall. The leading objector in the flute world was Hans-Peter Schmitz, who wrote much on the baroque flute and its music for a German amateur readership in the 1950s, as well as quasi-philosophical articles later on.[31] Schmitz recognized the longing for simplicity and truth that underlay the post-war love for baroque repertoire, a search for something felt to be missing from contemporary compositions. But however much he believed that the music could satisfy this longing, he thought long-term cultural changes made attempts to understand earlier instruments and practices futile. He argued that, since tonal and aesthetic ideals had changed, modern listeners had different expectations from early ones and so modern players could not interpret pieces as contemporaries did. Early music needed updating, like theatrical revivals, he felt, rather than museum-like reconstruction.

Schmitz quite accurately stated some of the challenges of playing old music on old instruments to modern audiences, but his argument failed to note that most of the problems he raised applied with equal or greater force to playing old music on modern instruments. He made no attempt to justify the disregarding of historical sensibilities or the reliance on anachronistic performance practices he seemed to advocate. Modern taste, in his view, had taken a permanent and immutable form, but in fact the neo-baroque style's rapid acceptance had demonstrated that it was actually as fickle as at any time in the past, if not more so. Schmitz continued for another thirty years to argue against the use of historical flutes, though, paradoxically, he urged flutists to 'use all means at our disposal to produce living music for living, feeling, people'.[32] Though in his later essays he no longer made as much of the defectiveness of early instruments, his most emphatically repeated point was that striving for a single 'correct' or 'authentic' interpretation was a mistake.[33] He apparently failed to appreciate that, by ruling out experimentation with historical information and insisting on an orthodox modern instrument and style, that was exactly what he was doing himself.

By the late 1950s no such protest could prevent the growing economic phenomenon of the early music revival, which was growing rapidly in partnership with the recording industry. Linde and Scheck were the flutists most frequently heard on German radio and records, while in America Shelley Gruskin took up the baroque flute in 1958, and together with Colin Sterne became one of the first professional baroque flutists there. Vester's playing awoke interest far beyond the Netherlands, while Johannes Brinckman was active in Sweden, and P. E. Olsen in Denmark. The pioneering French recorder and baroque flute player Roger Cotte demonstrated the baroque flute on two discs in the 1960s.[34] New record labels dedicated to early music, such as Telefunken's *Das Alte Werk* and EMI's *Reflexe*, responded to increasing interest in the genre. Deutsche Grammophon's *Archiv* series, which in the 1950s had carried baroque flute discs by Bopp, Linde, and Scheck, now produced larger and more influential anthologies. These included Bach Passions by Nikolaus Harnoncourt's Concentus Musicus of Vienna, and a monumental cantata series begun by Harnoncourt and Leonhardt in 1972. New ensembles were created especially to record, among them Capella Coloniensis (1954),

Collegium Aureum (1960s) for Harmonia Mundi, and later Christopher Hogwood's Academy of Ancient Music (1980s) for L'Oiseau-Lyre. These ensembles provided work, and a corresponding professional legitimacy, for baroque flutists Leopold Stastny, Günter Höller, and a growing number of others.

The recording industry made Frans Brüggen (1934–) the first star of the modern early music movement. Though he was principally a recorder player, Brüggen's career brought the baroque flute its greatest exposure hitherto, and changed the playing and teaching of all the baroque woodwinds from an eccentric sideline into a respectable profession, at least for a few musicians. Brüggen began learning with the eldest of his eight siblings on a German factory recorder at the age of six during the Nazi occupation of the Netherlands.[35] As a teenager he made the unprecedented decision to become professional recorderist, entering the Amsterdam Conservatory as a fifteen-year-old flute student while taking recorder lessons with Kees Otten (1924–). Brüggen, the first Dutchman to earn a recorder diploma (1952), began a performing career that earned him effusive praise for the unprecedented skill and expressiveness of his playing. In the sphere of early music Brüggen became a cult figure, and even the world at large began to appreciate the potential of early woodwind instruments. Few players of any wind instrument could expect a career as soloist or teacher of notable new knowledge at that time. Yet in 1962 Telefunken (now Teldec) began recording Brüggen, and in about 1965 took the decision to make him a star, issuing over fifty remarkable recorder and baroque flute recordings on its *Das Alte Werk* label. Another company, RCA, put Brüggen's recordings on its Stars label next to Domingo, Galway, Horowitz, and Rubinstein. Telefunken's astute marketing campaign used pictures and repetitive motifs, showing Brüggen with large or rare recorders, in light clothing and with a sporty, relaxed image. Many of his LP covers were textless except for his name, and one contained a brooding pinup poster 60cm square. None of this was exceptional promotion for a world-class performer, but it was the first time a player of any early instrument had inspired such treatment.

Brüggen, who had become professor of recorder at the Royal Conservatory, The Hague, in 1962, was swamped with talented pupils from the U.S., Brazil, Japan, Europe, and Australia in the mid-60s, their studies made possible by stipends from the Dutch government. By 1973 fifty full-time recorder pupils were studying at the conservatory, personal lessons with the professor were no longer possible, and a pecking order of secondary teachers had sprung up. Within a few years the Conservatory had established a full-scale Early Music Department to train professional early musicians. The department featured teachers of voice and all the principal early melody, keyboard, and plucked instruments, as well as courses in bibliography and historical documentation.

We have devoted some attention to the recorder revival because amateur baroque flute playing began to flourish in the 1960s as an outgrowth of this movement in England, the Netherlands, Japan, and especially in Germany, where the Moeck company organized summer workshops in recorder and flute with Gustav Scheck and Johannes Brinckman. These courses, as well as private study opportunities, attracted overseas students including Betty Bang Mather from the University of Iowa and David Lasocki

56. Dayton C. Miller's collection at his home in Cleveland in *c*1928, when it had reached about half its final size. The photograph shows only the instruments, not their associated cases, nor Miller's extensive collection of books, music, pictures, and other materials.

from England.[36] J. M. Thomson, editor of *Recorder and Music Magazine*, worked to solidify Brüggen's influence among recorder players before founding in 1973 the new journal *Early Music*, an organ now needed to provide 'a link between the finest scholarship of our day and the amateur and professional listener and performer'. Three years later Moeck's publishing arm responded to this need by creating a German-language forum for discussion of early woodwind instruments, music, and related topics with its quarterly journal, *Tibia*. Lasocki wrote on the baroque flute in Thomson's recorder magazine in 1967, addressing its 'natural as opposed to tempered intonation', articulation, ornaments, softness of tone, and fingering. He noted that original flutes could be obtained from the London antique instrument dealer Tony Bingham, and replicas from Rudolf Eras, Günter Körber, Hermann Moeck, Conrad Mollenhauer, Ernst Stieber, and Friedrich von Huene, all but the last in Germany. 'But,' Lasocki wrote, 'no copy I have tried is as good as an original, particularly in intonation.'[37]

By the 1970s demand for antique instruments at the London sales of auction houses such as Sotheby's had driven up prices so much that replica makers began to attempt copies of original instruments suitable for professional performance. Friedrich von Huene (1929–), who had emigrated to the U.S. in 1948 and apprenticed to Verne Q. Powell in 1956, set up his own shop in 1960 to make recorders and flutes after historic specimens. Von Huene initially shared a building with Frank Hubbard, who in 1949 had returned to Boston from a pilgrimage to Haslemere and a research tour of Europe to open a harpsichord workshop with the aim of copying historic instruments exactly, down to the finest detail. Von Huene, on the other hand, was obliged to alter most of his instruments from their original state to play at A=440, since no other pitch standard existed in modern performance. But when Gustav Leonhardt and Frans Brüggen urged that A=415, an equal-tempered semitone below modern concert pitch, be adopted for period-instrument performances of baroque music, the new pitch rapidly became established as a worldwide standard. Though Brüggen and others later made a few recordings at still lower historic pitches of A=410 or A=392, many 'replicas' of historic instruments were altered from their original dimensions to play at A=415.[38] Von Huene based his first baroque flute on a late-eighteenth-century instrument by Kirst, while other makers who began to operate around 1970 chose Stanesby, Grenser, or late-eighteenth-century English examples to copy.

The exuberant performances and recordings of another early music star, David Munrow (1942–76), with his Early Music Consort of London, brought the renaissance repertoire, formerly considered the domain of scholars, to mainstream audiences for the first time in 1967. Munrow's experience of South American folk music, played on the descendants of seventeenth-century instruments, informed his playing of nearly all the renaissance woodwind instruments, particularly recorders and flutes. His suicide at the age of thirty-three prematurely ended one of the most influential musical careers of his generation.

Meanwhile Stephen Preston (1945–), a student of John Francis and Geoffrey Gilbert, formed the Galliard Harpsichord Trio with Trevor Pinnock and the cellist Anthony Pleeth, using modern instruments. A chance encounter with an eighteenth-century flute stimulated his interest in its tonal potential, and he began to study similar instruments in the Adam Carse Collection at the Horniman Museum, trying out contemporary techniques and making a series of recordings for the BBC Sound Archives. After bringing the baroque flute into modern flute recitals, an effort he judged unsuccessful, Preston was invited to take part in concerts that accompanied an exhibition of eighteenth-century instruments from London and Paris museums. A year's paid work touring with the exhibition enabled him to give up the modern flute and become the first professional baroque flutist in England. Increasingly frequent concerts and recording work, principally with Christopher Hogwood's Academy of Ancient Music and Trevor Pinnock's English Concert, provided Preston and his regular second flutist Nicholas McGegan (1950–) with the opportunity to learn on the job as part of the core group of London freelance players that supplied musicians for Hogwood, Pinnock, Andrew Parrott, and later Roger Norrington, John Eliot Gardiner, and others.

The early flute revival came of age in the mid-1970s in a flurry of new recordings of standard repertoire on baroque instruments. Frans Brüggen (recorder and flute) and others recorded a complete set of Handel's woodwind solos in 1974.[39] In the following year Stephen Preston's complete Bach flute sonatas appeared, with Pinnock and viola da gambist Jordi Savall, while Linde released an incomplete Bach set with Colin Tilney and Josef Ulsamer on harpsichord and viola da gamba.[40] Two more Bach sonata sets appeared in 1976, by Stastny with Herbert Tachezi and Harnoncourt, and by Brüggen with Leonhardt and Anner Bijlsma.[41] By the late 1970s the discography of the baroque flute had expanded to cover repertoire by Quantz and Frederick the

Great, with Vivaldi, C. P. E. and J. C. Bach, Handel, Telemann, Hotteterre, and a few others represented. Recording artists included McGegan, Anton Winkler, Alexander Murray, Stastny, Linde, Vester, Barthold Kuijken, Joseph Bopp, Scheck, Robert Willoughby, Preston, Gottfried Hechtl, Brüggen, and Wolfgang Schultz.[42]

Knowledge of historical woodwind-making technique accumulated gradually along with attempts to replicate the playing qualities of the finest early specimens. Australian recorder-maker Fred Morgan (1940–99) began building hand-made instruments in 1970, after visiting workshops and instrument collections in Europe and the U.S. with the assistance of a Winston Churchill Memorial Fellowship. In an *Early Music* article of 1982 that holds enduring value, Morgan laid out the challenges of copying fine old woodwind instruments. Most historical woodwind players were already aware, as he put it, that 'it is possible to copy well or badly, loosely or closely', but his article made clear to what lengths a good instrument-maker had to go, and why it was worth the trouble. Old recorders, he noted, were completely different from modern ones, and those who aimed to copy them needed to learn the skills of the old makers to reproduce their work properly, including the 'dash and skill' that could not be supplanted by untrained carefulness or by machines.[43] The superb quality of Morgan's own instruments, as well as their appearance in the hands and on the record sleeves of Frans Brüggen and other virtuosi, lent weight to his point of view.

Though Morgan built only recorders himself, his observations of course applied with equal weight to flutes and other woodwinds. The first challenge he identified in building good replicas was choosing a model to copy. Early steps in this direction had already been taken by von Huene, who had studied original flutes as well as recorders in American and European collections on a Guggenheim Fellowship in 1966. But makers in Europe faced an urgent demand to produce playable flutes before much knowledge or experience of historically significant specimens by Hotteterre, Denner, Lot, Tromlitz, and others had accumulated. Instead, the first to gain wide notice, Andreas Glatt (Brussels), Rudolf Tutz (Innsbruck), and later Alain Weemaels (Brussels), built versions of a G. A. Rottenburgh flute (*c*1770 or later) that belonged to Belgian baroque flutist Barthold Kuijken (1949–), whose adept and stylish playing served as a persuasive advertisement for the instrument's qualities.

After building Rottenburgh and Hotteterre-type flutes for Kuijken, Preston, and others during the 1970s, Glatt abandoned instrument-making to found the Accent recording label. The new company, focusing on Belgian, Dutch, and Swiss early-instrument artists, released its first LP in 1978, and recorded its third, Kuijken's Telemann *Fantaisies*, in the same year.[44] The debut solo disc quickly established Kuijken as one of the world's most proficient and influential baroque flutists. Having studied at the conservatories of Bruges, Brussels, and The Hague, where his teachers included Vester (flute) and Brüggen (recorder), Kuijken was the natural choice to teach baroque flute when conservatories of The Hague and Brussels established early music departments in the early 1970s. Jean-François Beaudin, a Canadian pupil of Kuijken and Morgan, helped establish Kuijken's Rottenburgh as an ad hoc standard 'baroque' flute by freely distributing a detailed measured drawing of the instrument (1979) for other budding makers to replicate. With Canadian government assistance, Beaudin went on to study a series of ninety-six historic flutes by 1992. In the meantime, however, the younger generation of baroque flute enthusiasts that gathered around Kuijken began to ignore makers, including von Huene, who did not offer a Kuijken Rottenburgh model which, with its sweet, classical tone and small finger stretch, remained the most popular 'baroque' flute until the early 1990s.

Work opportunities for baroque flutists were multiplying fast in the mid-1970s. When Konrad Hünteler (1947–), a pupil of Günter Höller, Aurèle Nicolet, and Hans-Martin Linde, returned to Germany in 1975 after three years in South Africa, he found that the 'market situation' encouraged him to specialize in historical flute-playing. In 1987 he recalled:

> … after all, flutists were like the sands of the sea, but professional traverso players twelve years ago could practically be counted on one hand. So I was very quickly able to get a foot in the door of professional activity.[45]

By now the baroque orchestra had become a regular part of concert, opera, and chamber music life, indeed one of its most prominent and prestigious features. Hünteler, who played an original flute by Kirst, became active as a historical flutist with Collegium Aureum and other ensembles, and later principal flute of Brüggen's Orchestra of the Eighteenth Century. Other orchestras began to provide steady work for early-flute specialists during the late 1970s in London (Preston, Lisa Beznosiuk, and later Janet See, Hünteler, and Marten Root), as well as Ann Arbor, Mich. (Michael Lynn), Amsterdam (Wilbert Hazelzet, Masahiro Arita, Ricardo Kanji, and Hünteler), Boston (Nancy Roth, Christopher Krueger), Brussels (Kuijken, Robert Claire), Cologne (Hazelzet, Michael Schneider, Karl Kaiser), Paris (Claire, Pierre Séchet, Philippe Suzanne), New York (Sandra Miller, David Hart), Toronto (Claire Guimond), and Vienna (Leopold Stastny, David Reichenberg) – just to name those most frequently employed (always as freelancers) by the well-known recording ensembles.

The new style of baroque flute playing became established at educational institutions as more and more music colleges and conservatories, notably in London, Salzburg, and The Hague, appointed active local performers as professors of baroque instruments. The Oberlin Baroque Performance Institute, the first regular summer school for early instrumentalists and singers, began in 1972 with a visit from August Wenzinger and with Robert Willoughby (1920–) of the Oberlin (Oh.) College Conservatory teaching baroque flute. Impressed by recordings of Brüggen, Vester, and Leonhardt, Willoughby had studied baroque flute with Vester and recorder with Brüggen during a sabbatical in Europe in 1970. In his long teaching career at Oberlin, Peabody Conservatory (Baltimore), and the Longy School of Music (Boston), he passed on an interest in the baroque instrument to many students, including two who later became prominent exponents in Europe, Janet See and Jed Wentz. Music in American universities was changing at the same time: in the 1960s scholars raised the profile of ethnomusicology, emphasizing the study of music in performance, culture, and society rather than in an abstract theoretical sphere. Increasingly formal links between conservatories and universities began to heal 'the breach between making and doing and knowing … epitomized in the division between music colleges (places that do) and universities (places that know)'.[46] The baroque flute became part of the university curriculum when Betty Bang Mather (University of Iowa), Charles Delaney (Florida State University), and Alexander Murray (University of Illinois) encouraged students to gain experience with it as part of their work towards a degree in flute-playing.

The early music revival gained its first international competition when the Flanders Festival in Bruges, Belgium, began an annual presentation of early music performance in 1964, to coincide with a competition that in three-year cycles attracted organists, harpsichordists, and, from 1975, players of other baroque instruments. Masahiro Arita and Wilbert Hazelzet took prizes in a baroque flute competition in that year.

By about 1975 the tenets of the early music movement had brought profound changes in musical performance, education, and criticism. The British-American music critic Andrew Porter was one of the most influential to profess the new creed:

> I believe that, with very few exceptions, the music of any age speaks to listeners most clearly, most directly, with the tones and accents and in the forms that its creator intended. Hence the emphasis on accuracy and integrity of editions, on the aptness of instruments, acoustics, and performing style, on the circumstances of the original performances, on documents of all kinds (including phonograph records) that can shed light on a composer's intentions. Hence the concern with the performing history of a composition, with what past as well as present performances can tell us about it. Hence the repeated assertion that the discoveries of musicology become valuable only when they are put into practice.[47]

The new ideas had so altered public perceptions of what baroque music should sound like that those who played it in a routine manner on modern instruments now sometimes attracted criticism for unstylishness, or worse. Occasionally the same reasons were cited as in the previous century: Roger Rostron (1937–), principal flutist of the Hallé orchestra, gave a performance of Bach's Brandenburg Concerto no. 5 in Manchester as early as 1969 that critics censured on grounds of the unsuitable size of the ensemble and the hall.[48] In a misguided attempt to ward off such criticism by espousing 'authenticity' some modern instrumentalists now added an undue fixation with ornaments (trills and the like, rather than the free-style *coloratura* of the period) to their preoccupation with tone.

Frans Vester made strenuous efforts to bridge the gap between those who had absorbed the ideas of historical performance and those aware only of superficial mannerisms picked up from recordings. He tried to make players aware of those traits and concepts in the 'popular' style of performance that – as he believed – had survived from nineteenth-century music, and to explain that all compositions must undergo a process of 'translation', in which the musician uses a more or less trained personal judgement and feeling to turn marks on paper into a performance. Even if no single universally valid expression of a composition can exist, he wrote, it is important to concentrate on the achievable and try to answer the composer's intention as far as possible. Anyone unwilling to learn about the ideas and conventions of earlier times had better not play their music.[49]

Vester felt strongly that scholarly editions provided the essential tool 'to enable everyone to form an independent basis for interpretation'.[50] He advocated an 'ideal edition' (the scare quotes are his own), the work of careful editors who knew their historical sources, to be printed in modern type rather than in facsimiles of original notation that employed unfamiliar styles and conventions. The goal of such work was to strip away generations of accretion and error, to produce an *Urtext*, a 'correct edition, one which reproduces the text as it was originally handed down'. At the same time he set about reprinting in facsimile form some of the most important writings on flute-playing of the two previous centuries, as general editor of *The Flute Library* series for the publisher Frits Knuf.

The demand for access to reliable texts of eighteenth-century music in the mid-1970s, however, far outstripped the supply of such ideal editions. Despite the efforts of the London firm Musica Rara and others to provide scholarly performing editions of baroque wind repertoire, that demand was satisfied at first by photocopies of original prints or manuscripts passed from hand to hand and from teacher to student. Indeed, it would be difficult to overestimate the contribution the plain-paper xerographic process (1960) made to the revival of interest in reading music from original sources. As students gained experience reading these documents, the objections Vester raised to facsimile editions of baroque music – that the continuo parts were cryptic, the typefaces hard to read, and the clefs sometimes unfamiliar – melted away. The reward of reading baroque and classical music from facsimiles, performers soon learned, was that the text conveyed precisely the degree of information contemporary musicians needed to make a convincing interpretation – no more and no less. Stripping the text of editorial hints on performance forced them to search for appropriate directions in contemporary tutors, or within themselves. And in cases where the composer notated only a sketch, such as in figured bass parts and *adagio* movements, decisions as to what notes to play fell once more on the performer, as intended. Thus the way was clear for a proliferation of facsimile publishing to begin in the late 1970s. Mark Meadow's *Musica Musica* series produced inexpensive, spiral-bound editions of much of the most popular instrumental repertoire of the early eighteenth century, while his motto, 'be authentic – play from facsimiles', cheerfully announced the apparently simple connection between text and performance practice. Higher-quality facsimile editions of baroque music and tutors began to appear from the publisher Minkoff in Geneva, and the early eighteenth-century repertoire of the flute became a particular focus of Studio per Edizioni Scelte (Select Editions Workshop, or SPES) of Florence in 1978. The great majority of the SPES output of fine and luxurious editions, nearly 100 titles to date, consists of music for transverse flute, including the classics of eighteenth-century French flute music and a series of completely unknown transverse flute works by Italian composers, which it brought to the attention of an early music revival still narrowly focused on Bach and French composers.[51]

While for some flutists Vester and the facsimile publishers ushered in an exhilarating new freedom from stifling authority, some of those who had wielded that authority were less pleased. The British flutist Peter Lloyd recalled Marcel Moyse's furious rejection of 'clean' editions:

> I remember a lesson I had with Moyse when all this [*Urtext* editions] was just beginning to break forth, and I had the temerity to bring the [J. S. Bach] B-Minor Sonata to him. He looked at my Bärenreiter part and he said, 'Where are the marks?' He was very, very angry, and he proceeded to scrawl all over my music. 'Crescendo! Diminuendo! Mezzo-Forte! Forte!' He was sort of punishing them out at me – he was very angry.[52]

If Moyse's furious outbursts sometimes puzzled his students, the reason for this one seems rather clear. For him, the goal of playing a Bach sonata – at least in a masterclass setting – was to give a correct interpretation according to his own view of the music, which he held to be a traditional one. The purpose of notation, for Moyse, was to transmit this interpretation, not to allow the player freedom to depart from it. Moyse's own publications embodied this idea: when asked about his own Leduc edition of the Bach *Partita*, he replied, 'I did nothing. I just printed everything I learned from Hennebains.'[53] The arrival of *Urtext* editions, in challenging the right Moyse felt he possessed to dictate matters of musical interpretation to his pupils, struck at the authority of the tradition itself. Moyse was correct, though, if he foresaw that many students accustomed to an authoritarian teaching style would find the absence of expression marks disorienting and fall back on textbook rules rather than on a judgement they had never cultivated. Thus for many unprepared modern flutists baroque music has come to inspire fear of failure rather than freedom to play meaningfully, a fear intensified by misguided warnings that 'the modern-instrument player is as obligated as is his original-instrument counterpart to execute embellishments and rhythmic alterations within the customs of the time and place in which a piece was written', that a wide vibrato is 'categorically out of place', and that failing to observe these rules will result in a performance that is somehow 'less valid'.[54]

Flutists more familiar with the lessons of historical performance presented an altogether more positive view. Describing his work as a teacher in 1986, Konrad Hünteler spoke of conveying to students the idea that playing a piece of music did not consist in choosing between right and wrong, but in trying to recognize the musical content that really stood behind the 'shorthand' of musical notation and to identify with it personally. Pre-romantic music, Hünteler argued, provided even more scope for individual readings than later repertoire with its relatively fixed traditions of interpretation.[55] Hünteler called playing historical flutes 'a priceless enrichment of everything connected with flute-playing', capturing a sense of how playing early instruments changed not only the music's sound, but the way players and listeners felt about it. Within a short time, he found, the activity had stirred up the somewhat torpid state of modern flutists and forced them on the defensive. He countered Hans-Peter Schmitz's argument that a modern sound-ideal ought to apply to all music by calling attention to specific cases, such as C. P. E. Bach's A minor solo, with its speaking articulation and tonal irregularity. The piece, he wrote, was much more expressive, audacious, and 'modern' on a historically appropriate instrument, as were Beethoven's symphonies played by an excellent period orchestra. And Hünteler held the entire repertoire of early eighteenth-century French flute music to be unplayable on the Boehm flute without sounding unwieldy, inappropriate, and banal (probably he had not heard Vester's most talented modern flute students play it). Moving on to repertoire modern flutists considered their own, he cited Schubert's *Trockne Blumen* variations as a piece that expressed a degree of longing and melancholy that the brilliant Boehm flute could hardly achieve compared with the type of instrument for which the piece was conceived. Hünteler's method of interpreting music fitted neatly with Frans Vester's, and even with Louis Fleury's prescription (1925) for good performance:

> I consider that a secure technique, a rich and varied sonority, and the exact observance of the composer's wishes will produce the ideal interpretation: one in which the instrument serves the music, rather than the music serving the virtuoso player. But obviously these principles demand skill and artistry from the performer, rather than reckless fancy.[56]

Pioneering recordings of Haydn, Mozart, Beethoven, Schubert, and Mendelssohn during the 1980s brought the historical performance ideals to repertoire that need no reviving, at least not from the dead, while Brahms, Elgar, Gershwin, Rachmaninoff, Rossini, and others received the treatment in the 1990s. This infiltration of the orchestra's standard repertoire by historical-performance ideas intensified what Richard Taruskin, in a critique that prompted a much-needed self-examination on both sides, called a 'War of the Buffoons' between historicists and traditionalists, referring to a quarrel waged in Paris 1752–4 over the respective merits of French and Italian opera.

At the same time the general concept of what baroque flutes sounded like was changing. Throughout the 1980s a growing number of makers including von Huene, Roderick Cameron (San Francisco and Mendocino), and Folkers & Powell (Massachusetts and New York) began to study and produce a wider range of early eighteenth-century replicas, including some that originally played at non-standard pitches and others at the neo-baroque pitch of A=415. Models after P. J. Bressan and Thomas Lot gave players a hint of the strong tone obtainable from earlier baroque flutes, though both these types demanded excellent control of intonation. At the end of 1991 a rare and important early eighteenth-century flute by Jacob Denner came to light in a seventeenth-century house due for demolition near Nuremberg. The instrument, well preserved in its original case, possessed qualities of tone and intonation that by now had come to seem ideal for baroque music. At the urging of Konrad Hünteler, who was able to use it for performances and recordings, the Fund for Art and Culture of the Province of North Rhine-Westphalia acquired the flute at the unprecedented price of DM350,000 ($200,000, £110,000, or €180,000).[57] The sensational news drew more attention to the flute than earlier Denner copies by Robert Claire and others had been able to attract, and within a decade many leading players who had used Rottenburghs had switched to Denner models. With the waning of the Rottenburgh standard, other designs more or less closely following originals by Bressan, Lot, Palanca, Grenser, and even Quantz began to appear more frequently in concerts and recordings.

By the mid-1990s anyone who still believed historical-instrument performances of early music could be 'definitive' had not been paying attention to the debate. Yet despite the growing awareness of how diverse early instruments could be, steady jobs and teaching positions had cooled the revolutionary ardour of many performers and teachers and a certain standardized manner of performing baroque music had replaced the earlier experimental spirit all over Europe and America. As one commentator explained its components, 'the orthodoxy mediates between historical verisimilitude, current taste, and modern institutional demands', with the requirements of the marketplace often carrying the most weight.[58] Stephen Preston had sensed this encroaching institutionalization in 1985, in an interview in which he expressed the curiosity that motivated his early experience with historical flutes:

> One of the things that I think is useful about studying old instruments is that you can still be fairly open-minded and original in your ideas. The longer we can stave off a 'school of thought' about it, the better, the more useful it is. There should be grounds for experimenting. If we let it develop into fixed ideas of 'this is the way it should be' (which historically is absurd) then we are going to make it just another aspect of modern instrumental playing.[59]

Thus after more than a decade as London's leading solo and orchestral baroque flutist, Preston eventually abandoned the established scene to become a pioneer in a later period. 'Nineteenth-century flutes, if you can play them well, give you all the colour that you need for Romanticism but you never get on the modern flute,' he explained. But he noted that the modified 'baroque' flutes commonly used to play nineteenth-century repertoire are 'not like the instruments of the period at all'. In a jeremiad on the mainstreaming of the early music movement a decade later Barthold Kuijken echoed Preston's criticism of modern replicas and noted that the hardening of attitudes he warned against had come to pass.[60] While Kuijken believed, perhaps over-optimistically, that independent thought and historical perspective were playing a greater role, he felt that students tended to neglect the study of original sources, which in any case were now presented at second hand, in pursuit of quick professional success. He reported the emergence of a monotonous technique and undifferentiated taste, with a corresponding pressure on instrument-makers to alter instruments to make them more convenient for all-purpose use. Kuijken criticized his students' generation for holding a belief historical-instrument pioneers of his own age had fought against: 'that the reigning tradition is correct and better than the tradition of yesterday'. But now the reigning tradition, ironically, was one he had played a major role in creating.

Chapter 14

The postmodern age

Time magazine, announcing in 1966 that the world was 'now entering the golden age of the flute', noted that the number of American amateur players had more than tripled over the past decade, while the repertoire had grown with new compositions and the revival of older music. The magazine cited thirty 'first-rate' flutists in the U.S. and Europe, boasting Julius Baker, Jean-Pierre Rampal, Aurèle Nicolet, and Severino Gazzelloni as 'among the great flute players of all time'.[1] Such hyperbole aside, the number of flutists, the general level of their technical ability, and the breadth of the instrument's repertoire had indeed grown rapidly as an international mainstream of teaching, performing style, manufacturing, and recording emerged after World War 2 (chapter 12). With the growth came yet more changes in flute construction, sound, and musical interpretation.

American education had first embraced instrumental music as universities began to form orchestras half a century earlier, when the University of Kansas offered the first flute major (1891), Indiana University added reed, woodwind, and string instruction (1909), and Notre Dame University began to offer training specifically addressed to orchestra and band musicians. The school band movement and the manufacturers who supplied and encouraged it (chapter 12) placed instruments within the reach of nearly all American children, providing employment for music teachers, as well as for a growing army of players and stars who offered clinics and masterclasses for technically advanced students, while periodicals sprang up to inform and advertise to teachers. The Education Act of 1945 brought a less highly organized form of instrumental music to schools in Britain, where university music courses remained theoretical and most wind players still received their training in the music colleges and the military.[2] In Europe and America as a whole the educational industry grew steadily until, in the 1990s, at least 220 American colleges and universities employed flute professors, counting only those with their own web pages.[3]

As instrumental teaching became more organized, the content of lessons became more technical, so that for the first time flute teachers began to instruct their pupils in the physical aspects of embouchure, breathing, and sound production. Hans-Peter Schmitz set the tone for a number of distinguished German writings aimed at flute teachers with his *Flötenlehre* (1955), uniting history, criticism, musical analysis, and technique in a quasi-scientific approach. He gave physiology unprecedented attention, illustrating the torso with X-ray photographs, and the embouchure with diagrams annotated with angles indicated by Greek letters. Three later works, by Gustav Scheck

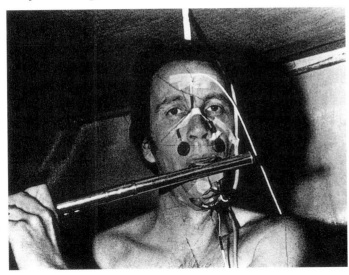

57. A scientific attempt to investigate what Moyse called the 'unsolvable problem' of vibrato.

(1975), Werner Richter (1986), and Hans Wurz (1988), reflected their intensive study of the flute and its technique as an end in itself. Wurz's and Richter's extremely rigorous plan indulged freely in diagrams, graphs, full citations of learned books and articles, and scientific language. Scheck gave a more approachable view of the history, science, music, and playing style of the flute, in which the level of his attention to detail can be gauged by the inclusion of complete measurements, to the nearest 0.1 mm, of historical instruments by Bressan and Hotteterre.

The Japanese violinist Shinichi Suzuki (1898–1998) developed an almost contrary method of teaching children as young as three in the early 1940s. In his system children learned to play music before learning to read it, memorizing each piece. The goal of Suzuki teaching was not to train professional musicians, but rather to give children the means to acquire hope and happiness, creativity, sensitivity, and understanding in a period of defeat and austerity in which these qualities seemed rare. The flutist Toshio Takahashi (1938–) studied with Suzuki, and later with William Kincaid and Marcel Moyse in America, returning to Japan to establish the Suzuki Flute School alongside the founder's violin school.[4]

In 1957 Gerald Jackson, principal of London's Royal Philharmonic Orchestra, echoing the words of J. G. Tromlitz a century and a half earlier, had written, 'sound is a personal matter.... It is simply a matter of taste.'[5] Yet however true Jackson's axiom may have been for his own, senior generation, more and more young English players were trying to make a French sound by learning the 'relaxed embouchure', and German flutists the *Stülpansatz* or 'snub-nosed embouchure'.

In fact far from being open to choice, events of the 1970s began to suggest that tonal variety had, at least for the moment, become a thing of the past. Along with new fashions in teaching beginners and advanced students came a new requirement, as it was then perceived, for flutists to acquire the final polish on their preparation for a professional career through masterclasses with one of a handful of famous player/teachers including Moyse, Kincaid, and Rampal. As distinctive orchestral sounds and playing styles in England and Germany disappeared, metal flutes and continuous vibrato became all but universal among young players with professional aspirations. Perhaps the most dramatic sign of change occurred in 1972, when Gareth Morris, one of London's most distinguished instrumentalists and a man considered the leading exponent of English flute-playing, was asked to resign after twenty-four years as principal flutist of London's New Philharmonia Orchestra on account of his tone, which his colleagues considered too 'assertive'. A London newspaper explained to any readers who might have found the charge somewhat nebulous that '[m]ost of Mr Morris's colleagues have already plunged into a kind of musical Common Market [forerunner of the European Community] and play *continental*. More vibrato! Mr Morris plays British – a bit firmer.'[6] Setting his ideal of the flute's character apart from the lighter, more brilliant French-influenced style, Morris told the reporter: 'Some people think of the flute as a bird-like instrument – but to me it is *heroic!*' While others had altered with the times, his own tone, he said, was 'as natural to me as my speaking voice'.[7]

Morris had played throughout his career on his teacher Robert Murchie's wooden Rudall Carte flute, but now that French-style tone and vibrato had become a rigid requirement for orchestral professionals in most of Western Europe and America, open-holed silver instruments, promoted by most influential French players and by American advertising as the only legitimate professional flutes, displaced nearly all remaining instruments by Rudall Carte, Hammig, and others in the orchestras of those continents. Only a few held out: after playing Gerald Jackson's wooden Rudall Carte flute in the Hallé Orchestra for twenty years, Roger Rostron switched to a gold Powell in the late 1980s.[8]

Many who adopted French-model flutes, however, found them difficult to play in tune. Louis Lot and others had built their instruments at the earlier Continental pitch of A=435, whereas by the 1960s all orchestras played at A=440 or above. In England, where orchestral and band pitches as high as A=452 had made the discrepancy impossible to ignore, Rudall Carte had long ago re-scaled its flutes to pitches including A=440 (perhaps by shortening a scale originally designed for A=435), while in America Haynes had been making A=440-scale flutes since 1911–12, and Powell had adjusted Lot's scale to the higher pitch on forming his own company in 1926.[9] All these, however, were closed-hole models marketed only to students, while the American open-hole models for professionals achieved the higher pitch by shortening the headjoint without re-positioning their toneholes, an alteration that left notes towards the top of the scale sharp in relation to those at the bottom. As a result players using shortened headjoints on old-scale flutes could no longer employ the French School's relatively effortless method of sound production. In France, players covered the embouchure and blew harder, while American flutists such as Joseph Mariano and Julius Baker left the headjoint in its A=435 position so that the flute was in tune with itself, but uncovered the embouchure and blew more forcefully to bring the pitch up to the newer standard.[10]

Working with Albert Cooper (1924–), an apprentice and employee at Rudall Carte from 1938 to 1958, London players including Elmer Cole, Christopher Taylor, and William Bennett took steps to overcome the intonation problems of the shortened

58. Metal flutes remained unfamiliar enough in 1922 to be the subject of humorous comment.

scale during the 1960s. Because these players offered Cooper far from unanimous advice, he first collected measurements from several flutes and devised an empirical design that, according to his own account, he intended to be playable in tune by all his advisers. After building about ten examples, Cooper abandoned the design in favour of a mathematically calculated scale, which he used for several years before further adjusting it in the light of criticism from players. Realizing the limitations of his one-man shop, and having, as he put it, 'reached the end of the road, scale-wise', Cooper approached U.S. makers in the 1970s with offers to license his A=440 scale for wider distribution. At first he found an unsympathetic reception. American flutes were selling well: by 1960 Verne Q. Powell, Inc., the smaller of the two prestigious Boston firms, was producing about 140 flutes a year with a workforce of four or five. But in 1961 Powell sold his company to Edward Almeida, Richard W. Jerome, Edmond K. Machon, and Elmer W. Waterhouse, who had apprenticed with him on the post-war G.I. bill, and in 1975, six years after Powell's death, these successors adopted the Cooper A=440, 442 and 444 scales. Still, the company applied the Cooper scale only to a downmarket model with drawn toneholes, retaining Powell's own A=440 scale for its handmade instruments.[11] The Haynes company, considering that it had been making modern-scale flutes since 1910, saw no reason to adopt the new scale. But modern flute scales had become the flute world's major talking point by the late 1970s, and in response to the demand Haynes's president Lewis Deveau devised a new scale that began production in 1981 and became standard in mid-1982.

Noticing that players who bought his experimental flutes fitted them with headjoints by other makers, Cooper discovered that, at a time when all orchestral instruments were striving to play louder, his instruments were considered lacking in volume. As a result, he introduced a slightly larger embouchure hole, as well as extreme undercutting and overcutting of its side walls, replacing the straight surfaces Boehm and Lot had used with a curved, convex wall. Apparently this idea was not new: during Marcel Moyse's most influential period as a teacher he had played a closed-hole flute by Couesnon (after signing a promotional contract with the manufacturer in the late 1930s) with a headjoint probably by Lebret that he had altered himself by overcutting the sides and rounding the side shoulders of the embouchure hole.[12] In any case, Cooper's new embouchure style completed the revision he and his flute-playing colleagues made in the flute's sound and their break with the aesthetic aspects of nineteenth-century flute-playing. He spent much of the 1980s rebuilding numerous original flutes by Louis Lot for English professionals to meet the new ideals, removing the toneholes, patching the tubes, replacing the holes in new positions, and altering the embouchures.[13]

The new Cooper-style flute, with its revised scale and headjoint and its enhanced volume and overtones, was soon taken up by the world's other industrialized flute makers, in Japan. Koichi Muramatsu had established the Muramatsu Company in Tokyo in 1923 to build Japan's first Boehm flutes, based on Haynes's French model, and though the factory closed during World War 2 the company reported making its 10,000th flute in 1957. In 1974 Muramatsu began exporting its instruments to the U.S., making enough inroads into the market to attract the attention of the *Wall Street Journal* three years later.[14] Muramatsu's company was followed by several others that soon became leading players in the world-wide flute industry. After experience at Muramatsu, Masashi Miyazawa established Miyazawa Flutes (1969), experimenting with new alloys for flute-making, and, like Muramatsu, successfully targeting the huge American market. Kikuo Hisakura established the Sankyo Flute Manufacturing Company in Sayama-city in 1968 to produce high-quality flutes. These featured a range of headjoint patterns, including the 'Raised Shoulder' design, based on the Schwedler Reform embouchure, and the 'High Wave', based on Mönnig's misnamed 'Reform' embouchure. The Nippon Gakki Co. Ltd, a manufacturer of reed organs founded by Torakusu Yamaha in 1887, spent much of the next century as the Yamaha Corporation adding audio-visual products, semiconductors, sporting goods, home appliances, furniture, speciality metals, machine tools, industrial robots, and eventually musical instruments to its products. In 1960, it branched out as the Yamaha Corporation of America, later Yamaha International Corporation, and in 1965 the company began to make wind instruments, including the best-selling student flute of the 1970s and 80s. After experience with Muramatsu, Miyazawa, and other companies, Shuichi Tanaka designed his Altus flutes in collaboration with William Bennett to imitate Louis Lot's instruments. Some Altus models employed embouchures without Cooper-style over- and undercutting, sometimes combined with a seamed tube, all in an attempt to capture the Lot sound Bennett and other English players prized. In 1969 the Pearl Company began making a full range of more modernized flutes from student model to hand-made, all featuring a 'pinless' mechanism to increase strength, reduce corrosion, and allow easier maintenance.

The uniformity that afflicted the flute and flute-playing in the late twentieth century was not a new phenomenon, only one that some observers felt had reached alarming proportions. In a chapter in his *Essay* of 1752 on 'How a Musician and a Musical Composition are to be Judged', J. J. Quantz warned against conformity of taste and encouraged his readers to develop personal judgement:

> The agreeableness of music lies not in uniformity or similarity, but in diversity. If it were possible for all musical artists to play with the same proficiency, and with the same taste, we would miss the greatest part of our pleasure in music, because of the lack of an agreeable variety.
>
> Rarely do we follow that surest of guides, our feelings; instead we seek eagerly to learn which singer or player is the ablest, as though it were possible immediately to survey and weigh the skills of different persons, just as one judges other things whose price and quality are determined by a pair of scales. Then we listen only to the person who passes for the strongest. (Quantz, *Essay*, XVIII, 2–3)

This expectation for performers to conform to predictable patterns seems to have intensified during the brief period (c1925–70) when 78 RPM and LP records had spread far and wide, but remained few and highly influential. The tendency seems to have reversed as recordings in music of different genres became more common.

Once all the world's manufacturers were building Boehm-Lot-Cooper flutes and the distinctive national styles of playing had been banished from symphony orchestras, the new International style quickly gained a stranglehold on flute-playing world-wide. In 1976, two years after Raymond Meylan pointed out that 'flute-playing is in danger of becoming the same everywhere' (p. 245), Peter Riedemeister criticized the new style in detail for its 'big' tone, loud low register, continuous vibrato, tone-colour control chiefly by means of the throat, and aggressiveness in tone and musicality. Between the International style and its equally new polar alternative, the neo-baroque style, Riedemeister proposed a revival of the ring-key flute for nineteenth-century music.[15]

Frans Vester articulated a withering critique of the International style, the dictatorship of the symphony orchestra, and the wretched acoustics of modern concert halls at the National Flute Association's eighth annual convention in Boston in 1980, at the first Finnish Flute Week at Tampere five years later, and in several published articles. He censured the monotony of modern breathing technique, with its exclusive focus on 'long line playing', as inappropriate for most of the flute's repertoire, particularly that of the baroque and classical periods, when Italian *bel canto* singing had been the archetype of expression and technique on the flute. In the older technique, Vester wrote, 'the voice rests on the column of air; the breath supports the voice principally from the chest region, without the active use of the diaphragm. The productivity [i.e. penetrating ability or carrying power] of the sound depends more on intensity than volume.'[16] By now *bel canto* singing had almost vanished, while the dominant Franco-American flute-playing style and the instruments it had spawned had created a new sound that Vester called 'smoother, more empty, and less full of character', using a stereotyped vibrato to conceal its lack of inner life. Vester saw the new technical uniformity as a symptom of a still graver disease: an increasing focus on the technical aspects of flute-playing at the cost of musical content. He noted that never before in history had all flutists played the same pieces – mainly from a tradition that demanded variety of feeling and emotion – in the same monotonous way. Warning that such a situation was an artistic dead end, he urged flutists to break out of the 'trained canary' mentality he saw as afflicting many.

Claude Dorgeuille made similar observations on modern flute-playing from a quite different perspective in 1983. He too lamented the 'monotonous sound' of the period, noting that earlier exponents of the 'French Flute School' displayed a tone with 'quite personal aspects of timbre, like a singer'. Like so many others, he decried the appearance of a 'throaty wobble [that] attempts to revive a lifeless sound', lack of coherent articulation, and 'insanely fast tempi' in place of music that sings.[17]

These critics confined their remarks to the flute establishment, the orchestral and teaching professions. Yet outside this privileged world lay a wider culture of experimentation in new musical styles, instruments, and the adapting of historical ideas. Paradoxically, many if not most of the individuals who participated in these movements also held positions as teachers or players within the mainstream world.

In 1948 Alexander Murray, solo flutist of the British Royal Air Force Band, began a series of experiments on the flute in collaboration with Elmer Cole and Albert Cooper. Convinced of the superiority of the open G♯ over the closed, Murray also developed an open D♯ key, a new F♯ lever, and other mechanical alterations, as well as acoustical innovations such as separate functions for the C♯ hole and D vent. Around 1961 Cooper built a model that became known as Murray's Mark I. While teaching at Michigan State University in 1967, Murray began collaborating with Jack Moore at Armstrong on a Mark II, and eventually around 1972 Armstrong built fifty Murray flutes and six piccolos. Later the Murray 'Multiple Option' flute was devised to allow open holes. Philip Bate predicted in 1969 that the Murray flute might 'possibly become the final Boehm flute', but it eventually became clear that its combination of novelty, mechanical complexity, and unfamiliar fingering made it unsuited to large-scale commercial production.[18]

Other still more radical experiments led to instruments that were never intended to be built in large numbers. In 1972 Greta Vermeulen invented a slide flute, which had no toneholes but a trombone-like telescoping tube. Three years later the Viennese flutist Thomas Pinschof invented the *Pinschofon*, a sub-bass flute, built by Werner Wetzel, with a range to G an octave below the alto flute. New types of low flutes became more popular with increasing use in flute choirs, jazz, and film scores, where amplification and electronic manipulation could take advantage of their relatively soft but colourful tone. In Germany in 1981 Christian Jaeger made a *Grossbass* (double-bass, i.e. two octaves below the concert flute) for Max Hieber, while makers of low flutes in France included Michel Parmenon, Jack Leff, who built a double-bass flute in C with a B foot in collaboration with flutist Pierre-Yves Artaud in 1983, and Jean-Yves Roosen, who made a similar flute with a range extending one tone lower. Kotato & Fukushima (Japan) developed a range of flutes from a soprano in F down to a double-bass with a range to C. The Dutchman Jelle

PAN 102 STEREO

The Sound of a New Instrument ...**the**

MURRAY FLUTE

KARL CZERNY
Duo-Concertante
For Flute and Piano
Opus 129

J.S. BACH
Partita For Flute and Harpsichord

Alexander Murray, Flute
Martha Goldstein, Keyboard

59. In this recording of 1974 Alexander Murray demonstrated Murray flutes by Albert Cooper and W. T. Armstrong. The sleeve photo placed the Murray flute in a sequence of mechanical development leading from the primitive keyless 'renaissance' flute, considering the Murray flute as 'the final development of the Boehm flute'. *The Murray Flute*, Alexander Murray (flute), Martha Goldstein (keyboard), Pandora Records PAN 102.

Hogenhuis built cheap but effective wide-bore altos and basses for amateur use from PVC (plastic) tubes.[19]

Another Dutch maker, Eva Kingma, the first female flute-maker to reach international prominence, trained with Dirk Kuiper of the Concertgebouw Orchestra, who began building wooden flutes in the 1950s. Kingma worked with the Dutch flutist Jos Zwaanenburg on an open-hole alto flute, later applying the concept to bass flutes. She also developed revolutionary quarter-tone flutes of various sizes that were enthusiastically taken up by Robert Dick, Matthias Ziegler, and other innovative flutist-composer/improvisers.

Brannen Brothers Inc., established by Bickford and Bob Brannen in 1978 after working at Powell, adopted Albert Cooper's scale and headjoint designs, as well as innovations made by the Danish flute-maker Johan Brögger. The strong market presence of the company's Brannen-Cooper flutes encouraged dealers and repair staff to accept an unfamiliar mechanism, and the company later adopted the even more radical innovations of Eva Kingma in its Brannen-Kingma quarter-tone flute. On the other hand, the wooden ring-key flute the company was building when Peter Riedemeister advocated the instrument in 1976 was soon discontinued.

In the interest of mechanical reliability or ease of production countless other innovations in flute-making, many of them proprietary or patent-protected, have been made since the 1970s. The most radical is the 'Matit' flute, a carbon-fibre tube with a mechanism operated by magnets instead of springs, by Finnish industrial designer Matti Kähönen and flutist Matti Helin. But these innovations are principally of technical interest, whereas the developments that principally concern us here are those that extended the flute's sound, range, or capability in new music.

French works drawing on the Pan myth, including Debussy's *Prélude à l'après-midi d'un faune* (1895), *Chansons de Bilitis* (1900), Trio for flute, viola, and harp (1915), and *Syrinx* (1913), might well be said to have begun a fundamental revision of the flute's character that combined a late-romantic tonal and dynamic variety with its traditional melodic role. While Debussy's concept of the flute was rooted in the instrument's mythical past, he used a revolutionary musical language drawing on oriental styles, pentatonic and whole-tone scales, and other influences beyond the pale of official recognition. The flute cut a less traditional figure in the instrumental ensemble that accompanied a notated speaking voice (*Sprechstimme*) in Arnold Schönberg's atonal *Pierrot Lunaire* (1912). Schönberg exploited the flute's registral contrasts, articulation range, and dynamics in unprecedented ways, particularly in the dialogue of flute and voice in the work's seventh section, *Der kranke Mond* (The Sick Moon).[20] Varèse's *Density 21.5* (1936) struck out in another new, non-melodic, direction, prescribing key noises as well as extreme dynamics.

Post-war composition increasingly explored such new expressive possibilities and demanded specially-developed techniques as the period's prevailing neoclassicism gave way in the 1950s and 60s to an experimental spirit that came to be called avant-garde, or progressive. The style of Heitor Villa-Lobos combined Brazilian folk influences with the historicism of the Parisian Schola Cantorum, a music academy that provided an antiquarian and musicological counterbalance to the Conservatoire. His *Assobio a jato* (Jet Whistle, 1950) had the flutist blow directly into the embouchure to create the whistle sound.[21] Pierre Boulez dedicated his *Sonatine* (1945–6), with its rhythmic complexity, giant leaps, flutter tonguing, dynamic contrasts, and fiercely percussive piano part, to Jean-Pierre Rampal, who found the piece too 'extreme' to perform. Almost a decade after a premiere in Brussels in 1947 it won enthusiastic acceptance in a performance by Severino Gazzelloni (1915–) and pianist David Tudor at the International Summer Course for New Music in Darmstadt in 1956.[22] Luciano Berio wrote his *Sequenza I per flauto solo* (1958), in collaboration with Gazzelloni, in John Cage's 'space notation', in which the duration of a sound was denoted by vertical stokes indicating the passage of time measured by metronome beats, so that intense rhythmic complexity was made simple to read. *Sequenza I* contained the earliest notated multiphonic sound for the flute.[23]

Other pioneering compositions included Olivier Messiaen's *Le Merle Noir* (1951), André Jolivet's *Cinq Incantations* and *Suite en Concert* (1965), and Bruno Maderna's *Musica su due dimensioni* (1952) for flute and tape. Among Cage's own innovative works for flute were *Three Pieces for Flute Duet* (1935), *Atlas Eclipticalis* (1961), *Ryoanji* for flute and taped flute (1983), *Music for – – –* (1984), and *Two* (1987). Brian Ferneyhough produced *Unity capsule* (1976), Boulez *... explosante-fixe ...* (1991–4), and Yoritsune Matsudaira *Sonatine* (1936), based on traditional Japanese court music. Roman Haubenstock-Ramati, Franco Evangelisti, Stefan Wolpe, Bernd Alois Zimmermann, and Morton Feldman wrote for the flute in other avant-garde works, while flutists who played a major part in enlarging their own repertoire included Gazzelloni, Aurèle Nicolet, Istvan Matuz (1947–), Pierre-Yves Artaud, and Robert Dick (1950–). Karlheinz Stockhausen, once the *enfant terrible* of the avant-garde movement, composed several of his theatrical pieces during the 1990s for the Dutch flutist Kathinka Pasveer, at the time still a pupil of Frans Vester.

The avant-garde repertoire made use of new sound effects such as microtones and multiphonics, whistle-tones and whisper-tones, humming, and slap-tones, unpitched air noises, and electronically manipulated sound, demands which brought a need for specialist tutors to deal with these 'extended' techniques. Bruno Bartolozzi's *New Sounds for Woodwind* (1967), a handbook for flute, oboe, clarinet and bassoon, detailed microtones, timbric transformations of sound, and multiphonics for the flute, giving a quarter-tone scale from D1 to C$\sharp$3, lacking three notes.[24] Thomas Howell's *Avant-Garde Flute* (1974) and Robert Dick's *The Other Flute* (1975) each explained in almost identical language its 'attempt to define the full range of the flute's potential as a sound generator'. Howell examined such differences as he could find between instruments of various national makes, giving over 1800 listings of special fingerings, with a further hundred pages of remarks. Dick's work included complete quarter-tone scales from D1 to E4 for closed- and open-hole flutes, prescriptions for all imaginable sounds from the instrument itself, and information on amplification and electronic modification. Martin Gümbel's *Neue Spieltechniken* (1974) provided a similarly exhaustive compendium. James J. Pellerite's 1964 work on fingerings applied some of these principles in advanced prescriptions for mainstream music, as well as quarter tones including trills, and multiphonics.

Robert Dick explained the urge the new flutist-composers felt to extend the flute's capabilities, contrasting this with the International school's monotony:

> The difference between Eric Clapton, George Harrison, and Jimi Hendrix is much greater than the difference between Julius Baker and Jean-Pierre Rampal. The guitar players are endlessly inventing new sounds and new tone qualities. Why can't the flute have this much range?[25]

In the three decades beginning with his *Afterlight* (1973), Dick composed seventy pieces for flute, piccolo, bass flutes in F and C, A♭ piccolo, and alto flute, providing them with ensemble partners including vibraphone, vibraharp, electric guitar, other orchestral and ethnic woodwinds, drums, and live electronics. Unlike the composers of the academic avant-garde, Dick's career was guided by his dependence on commissions, fellowships, concert fees, and income from his own Multiple Breath Music company, which published his *Tone Development through Extended Techniques* (1986) and *Circular Breathing for the Flutist* (1987). After a period in New York during which he held a Solo Recitalist Grant from the National Endowment for the Arts (1983), as well as the same agency's Composer's Fellowship (1988 and 1992), Dick moved to Lucerne, Switzerland, in 1992, and was awarded a Guggenheim Foundation Fellowship in 1994.[26] In 1997 he expressed the rewards, artistic as well as financial, of following his own path:

> Why play the whispertones? Because they are incredibly beautiful and have an absolutely magical effect in concert. My New Age musician friends speak of whispertones as a 'healing' sound. Maybe that[']s overstating the case, but whispertones make me and the audience feel good, and they earn me money, too.[27]

A detailed survey of new flute music since the 1970s that does justice to the immense breadth and inventiveness of the new repertoire forms the topic for a book that remains to be written. Here there is space only to recognize the notable contributions made by women in all areas. To give just a handful of examples, Anne La Berge's electronically-enhanced improvisations use the Brannen-Kingma quarter-tone flute, the first major innovation in flute design at the hands of a female maker; Elizabeth Brown composes microtonal pieces of transcendent beauty that can be played on ordinary modern instruments; and the three women of the Scottish Flute Trio continue to commission new music (*Circe*, 1996) from Thea Musgrave, a pioneering female composer and herself a Scottish native who wrote a serial-style *Trio* for flute, oboe, and piano as long ago as 1960.

The flutists of contemporary music shared their excitement over new techniques and musical ideas with the jazz sphere: indeed some flutists inhabited both worlds. Herbie Mann, Eric Dolphy, Roland Kirk and others used unpitched air noises, simultaneous singing and playing, and buzzing, a technique in which the embouchure is blown like a trumpet that produces a pitch a sixth or a seventh below the fingered note and allows effective jazz sounds such as scoops, smears, and lip glissandos.[28] Modern jazz often used the flute in new combinations of instruments. Herbie Mann created a commercially successful sound in Latin music with flute, guitar, vibraphone, bass, and drums. Paul Horn specialized in solo improvisation, while saxophonist Bud Shank (Stan Kenton Orchestra) appeared in a quintet that placed alto flute alongside cor anglais.[29] Claude Bolling's *Suite for flute and jazz piano trio No. 2* (1973) remained on the *Billboard* chart of top-selling albums for ten consecutive years in Jean-Pierre Rampal's recording of 1975, a popularity achieved only once previously, by Pink Floyd's *Dark Side of the Moon*.[30] Jim Walker and his band Free Flight (1980) and Steve Kujala with his 'fretless flute' also used the flute in new jazz sounds. More recently Matthias Ziegler worked with the jazz/new age harpist Andreas Vollenweider and blazed new trails in electronic manipulation: digital delay, octave dividing, reverberation, and amplifying the sounds and noises produced by his instruments, often large sizes.

The guitar took over from the saxophone as the jazz instrument of the moment in the 1970s, when all at once electric instruments were everywhere. Jazz and rock styles mixed with the innovations of guitar legend Jimi Hendrix to influence many flutists, including Jeremy Steig, Robert Dick, Dave Valentin, and James Newton in America. Others forged individual musical personalities out of the mix: Mike Mower in England, Emil Mangelsdorff, Gerd Dudek, Michael Heupe, Lenny McDowell (Friedemann Leinert), and other Czech, Polish, Dutch, and Austrian players. Ian Anderson and the British band Jethro Tull (1968) brought the flute to rock music in 'Locomotive Breath' and other pieces, creating a distinctive new sound with unconventional blowing and articulation techniques. Rhonda Larson, after coming to prominence in New York's Paul Winter Consort, became the first female star of the flute to bring her polished classical training to a popular fusion of jazz, Celtic, ethnic, and sacred music.

Though jazz studies have been established at conservatories in Amsterdam, The Hague, Helsinki, Linz among others and at American institutions such as the University of Northern Iowa (early 1950s), jazz flute classes remain a rarer route to learning than 'play-along' CDs. Jazz musicians rely heavily on old-fashioned technical facility, oral tradition, and live experience; the precise tone, vibrato, and tempo feeling of particular players does not lend itself to codification or precise imitation. The work environment too is less formal: jazz flutists, often also working as composers and arrangers, frequently act as their own managers, agents, and record producers, activities many mainstream flutists still consider beneath their dignity.

Flute-playing since 1970 has been transformed not only by jazz and new music, but also by old. Frans Vester probably more than any other flutist of the late twentieth century led the call for greater attention to the flute's heritage. In his teaching and lecturing he urged flutists to develop listening habits, musical knowledge, and good taste, to understand and show respect for the composer's work, and attentively to keep vibrato under control.[31] His energetic scholarship, including numerous editions, beginning with the works of Blavet in 1953, two valuable repertoire catalogues, and a series of facsimiles of early flute methods, were all aimed at reviving inspiration-driven playing while counterbalancing what he called 'a capricious and subjective approach to interpretation'.[32] At the same time his influential playing and recordings showed that he could practise what he preached.

However, now that original-instrument baroque music had itself become part of the established musical scene, independence proved a more elusive goal than uniformity. By the mid-1970s early music departments had been established at several leading music colleges, particularly in Austria, Belgium, England, the Netherlands, and one or two North American cities – that is, in places where such performance could provide a viable career path (chapter 13). Yet as Barthold Kuijken complained in 1994, this official recognition allowed many students to trade the opportunity of study and development for mere job training in the style of playing required to win one of the few available performing or teaching posts. Ransom Wilson had already demonstrated by about 1980 that the neo-baroque style, a mixture of inherited and revived historical traits with invented ones, was not necessarily the province of original instruments, but could cross over into mainstream performance even on their modern counterparts.[33] Wilson's baroque style was radical and experimental because he adapted it to the modern flute at a time when similar performances on original instruments were in danger of becoming routine.

The standard mainstream repertoire, on the other hand, was rarely handled in the same experimental spirit until original-instrument recordings of orchestral works by Haydn, Mozart, Beethoven, Schubert, and Mendelssohn appeared during the 1980s. The treatment of these familiar pieces in a new manner showed that relying on traditional criteria for performing old scores now posed something of a problem for all musicians. In 1994 Jaap Frank tackled the question Schmitz had left unaddressed (p. 253) of what the interpretation of old flute music in a deliberately anachronistic style could mean. He argued that without special reconstructive insight, matters of articulation, phrasing, tempo, agogics, attack, ornamentation, dynamics, tone, and everything that communicated musical feeling could not be 'translated' (a term he borrowed from Vester) for modern performance.[34]

Frank noted that pre-1940 Boehm flutes, no longer meeting modern needs, had moved from professional use to amateurs or collections, while almost all European and American professionals now played a 'French model' flute, with in-line, perforated keys, B-foot, Cooper embouchure and Cooper scale, often wholly or partially in gold. Only east Europeans such as Czechs, Hungarians, Baltics, and Russians, who had missed the post-60s boom, had an identifiably old-fashioned sound, and played on old, un-Coopered flutes. Since the Boehm flute of the nineteenth and early twentieth centuries had thus become an obsolete instrument along with its own repertoire and sound character, it now called for the same special study as any other such relic.[35] Accordingly Frank vigorously decried the destruction of fine original flutes by Louis Lot, Bonneville, and their contemporaries by moving the toneholes, altering the mouth-hole or lip-plate, 'and other acts of pure vandalism' against the 'cultural, musical, and artistic value of these instruments'.[36] He did not propose that all music not composed in modern times must be played on original instruments, and still less that all old instruments belonged in museums. More important, he wrote, was the careful study of original notation, performance directions, and contemporary instruments and practice, with the aim of conveying the composer's intention, even if the means, usage, and playing technique of performance were those adapted to modern instruments. He advocated a truly modern flute sound, an instrument that employed modern materials and technology, and the clear understanding of the differences between modern and earlier instruments and practices.[37]

Frank presented a new view of the International style as a 'traditional' performance practice, a view that grew just as much from a new understanding of different folk and world music traditions as from a historical sense of perspective. One American flutist, Lamar Stringfield (1897–1959), showed an early interest in folk music: he organized the University of North Carolina's institute of folk music (1932) and used traditional Appalachian material in his flute compositions *Indian Sketches* (1922), *Mountain Dawn* (1945), and *To a Star* (1948).[38] The wider folk revival of the 1960s brought an enormous surge of vigour to Western musical life – but for many decades it left the official flute world largely untouched.

Perhaps the most influential flutist to break the boundaries between mainstream, folk, jazz, early, and pop music beginning in the 1970s was James Galway, who began the flute as a boy in an Irish flute band. With distinguished orchestral service (London and Berlin, 1961–75) behind him and a stellar solo career under way in concertos, chamber, and contemporary music, Galway stepped into a role as the flute's cultural ambassador, appearing in a wide range of repertoires on recordings, on television, and at high-profile events. His popoularity, skill, and unaffected personal charm led to many honours, including an OBE (1977), Musical America's Musician of the Year (1997), an honorary doctorate (St Andrews, 1998), and a knighthood (2001).

Meanwhile the flute grew in popularity outside the mainstream. Traditional musicians in Ireland had taken up the flute as cheap instruments became available, first from Germany in the late nineteenth century, and later from England once eight-keyed instruments by Rudall & Rose arrived in the second-hand market.[39] The flute had become common in the West of Ireland by about 1900, to be carried to Chicago and other destinations for Irish emigrants thereafter. One such transplant, John McKenna (1880–1947) from Co. Leitrim, joined a strong Irish-American music scene in the 1920s and 30s that coincided with the early days of commercial recordings, of which he made over sixty. His breathy and rhythmic style of playing, typical of the province of Connaught and commonly referred to as the 'Sligo Style', was adopted by many flutists, and later modified by Matt Molloy (1947–), the son, grandson, and father of County Roscommon flutists, who added borrowings from fiddling and uilleann piping.

The folk revival of the 1960s and the rise to stardom of the Chieftains and other Irish bands spread the style even farther, providing the impetus for the first Irish-made flutes. These were based on the English keyed flutes now established as traditional, but sometimes re-scaled to play at A=440 and supplied without keys, which were unused in traditional music in any case. By the 1980s these modified designs were being produced in Ireland by Hammy Hamilton, Sam Murray, Brendan McMahon and others, and in England, the U.S., and Australia by numerous makers among the most widely-known of whom were Chris Wilkes, Patrick Olwell, Ralph Sweet, and Michael Grinter.

After the harpist and bombarde player Alan Stivell of Brittany brought his region's music to wide notice in the 1970s, another Breton musician, Jean-Michel Veillon (1959–), took up the 'Irish' flute and forged a new Irish-Breton flute style. In North America Chris Norman (1963–), a native of Nova Scotia, won a place on *Billboard's* crossover charts with his solo CD of Scottish and Nova Scotia tunes played on an eight-keyed Rudall Carte flute. The recording's title, *The Man with the Wooden Flute*, cast a sideways glance at the status of James Galway, Prill's successor as 'The Man with the Golden Flute', who was now challenging Rampal's position as the most recorded flutist in music of many genres including pop, jazz, easy listening, baroque, and classical.

The important function of finger ornaments such as cuts, taps, and rolls in Irish traditional music make the modern flute too awkward in comparison to the less mechanized types. Other flute-playing traditions, however, adopted the modern flute more readily. In Prague in the 1640s bands of Jewish musicians known as *klezmer* had played on strings, flutes (*fleytn*), drums, and dulcimer, adding the clarinet in the early nineteenth century and brass later on as military bands had done. The flutists of the nineteenth-century *klezmer* bands, often using Viennese-style instruments commonest in central and eastern Europe, played their part an octave higher to make it audible in the often raucous ensemble. Jewish migrations to the U.S. from 1880 to 1924 came at a time when vaudeville, catering halls in Manhattan and Brooklyn, the Catskill resorts, and eventually the recording industry provided employment for musicians, though the majority of the more than 700 *klezmer* records made between 1894 and 1942 focused on a handful of prolific performers. As in classical music, recording caused styles to homogenize. Once audiences from Poland, Belorussia, and America learned each other's styles, '[p]atrons would demand of their local *klezmer* that they "play it like on the record" establishing a "right" and "wrong" version'.[40] A single phonograph in a town served effectively to de-regionalize its style, while radio had an even greater impact in the 1920s because its music was free. The folk revival saw re-issues of many *klezmer* recordings in the late 1970s and 80s, along with exposure in Hollywood films and new recordings. New bands sprang up in New York, Seattle, Washington, New Mexico, New Orleans, Boulder, Portland, and Montpelier Vt., and a summer camp was established in 1985.

Traditional flute-playing in other cultures has achieved less public notice, even if in some countries such as Sweden and New Zealand traces have remained to attract the attention of researchers.[41] Other traditional flute styles have managed to survive by radical adaptation. In the early twentieth century Cuban *danzón* orchestras created an offshoot called *charanga* or *charanga francesa*, a term that referred both to the classic French trio of violin, flute, and piano and to the music's popularity with the *francesas* or high-class brothel owners of Havana.[42] As the style reached its peak of popularity from the 1930s to 50s, the *charanga* musicians of Havana and Miami continued to use nineteenth-century French five-keyed wooden flutes, their embouchure holes enlarged for playing in the extreme high register. Flutist and band leader Eddie Zervigon and his Orquesta Broadway became a fixture at clubs in New York, while in the 1940s and 50s Afro-Cuban sounds returned to Africa on records and radio and became the rage in the Ivory Coast, Benin, Senegal and the Congo, where violin and flute melodies often reappeared on the ubiquitous guitar. Latin dance and jazz music, often using traditional material, has perhaps made the greatest impact on the flute mainstream. James Galway recorded a CD entitled *Tango del Fuego* with Mike Mower and his band in 1998,[43] while the Orquesta Nacional de Flautas of Venezuela galvanized the National Flute Association's 25th and 26th annual Conventions in Chicago and Atlanta (1997–8) with its lively tradition of memorized dance music, presented at impromptu evening clubs in hotel lobbies rather than in formal concerts.

Indian classical music has influenced new composition for the modern flute even though it uses a quite different instrument, an improvised compositional structure, and a fundamentally incompatible musical theory. The flute, the harp, and the drum were the three major instruments mentioned in the Vedic literature of the first millennium B.C.E., but the bamboo flute returned to Indian music only with Pannalal Ghosh (1911–60) after a period of neglect that had lasted since the twelfth century. No separate tradition of instrument-making exists, but instead part of the extremely rigorous training of an

Indian flutist, along with intensive study of tuning, memorization, and improvisation, consists of learning by experience to make *bansuri*. The most famous and influential modern player, Hariprasad Chaurasia (1938–), studied Indian music with Prasnana Bolanath of All India Radio in Allahabad, and with the *surbhar* player Annapurna Devi, who taught him by singing rather than playing. Chaurasia worked for the radio in Cuttack and Bombay from 1956 to 1963, and as a composer and musician for films. He is artistic director of Indian music in the prestigious World Music department (1990) at the Rotterdam Conservatory in the Netherlands.[44]

Traditional flute ensembles have provided other paths for the flute to make new, or new-old, sounds. While many of the northern Irish flute bands (chapter 12) migrated from their traditional band flutes to the Boehm instrument after World War 2, around 2500 fife and drum bands were formed in the U.S. and Canada, using reproductions of eighteenth-century fifes and rope-tensioned wooden field drums with gut snares, and usually appearing in period or Civil War uniforms.[45] A Company of Fifers and Drummers devoted to the preservation and promotion of martial music was founded in 1965, establishing a museum, archive, and library in Ivoryton, Conn.

Drawing on a similar military pedigree, the 'Basel piccolo' has become the vehicle for a popular annual three-day celebration known as *Fasnacht* (Shrovetide) in the Swiss city, beginning at 4 am on a February or March morning when companies of piccolos and drums assemble in elaborate costumes and masks to march through the streets. The *Guggenmusiken*, traditional musical ensembles assembled for the occasion, began to add fifes to their drums in the late nineteenth century, at first playing in unison until three-part playing began in the early twentieth century.[46] Once Erwin Oesch improved the Basel piccolo's intonation in the 1950s, three-part playing became universal.[47] The movement has grown rapidly from seven bands in 1946 to ten times that many in 1995.[48] The instrument, not a true piccolo but rather a high-pitched six-keyed flute, has a wood body and a metal headjoint with a plastic 'Reform' embouchure. Bands memorize their repertoire of jazz, marches, and popular tunes, while new influences on the Basel corps have come from visiting Scottish and American fife and drum bands.

Another ensemble of flutes made its way into the official flute world when Leonardo De Lorenzo introduced the flute ensemble to the curriculum at the Eastman School of Music in the 1930s.[49] One of the first pieces specifically written for such a grouping, Henry Brant's concerto for eleven flutes, *Angels and Devils* (1931 R/1956), included a massed flutter-tongued passage.[50] Since then, and with the development of lower flutes for playing inner and bass parts, local and university flute choirs have flourished, particularly in the U.S. and Japan.

Many of the new influences on flute-playing have come with increasing contact between flutists, teachers, and makers with the growth of flute clubs, specialized magazines, and the internet. From today's perspective it seems clear that although the flute societies acted at first as an echo chamber for the views and playing styles of a few famous players and makers, the most important role they played was to open up and diversify the information sources and range of musical stimulation available to flutists. Experience of jazz, folk, baroque, contemporary, and ethnic musics, performance styles, and instruments effectively leavened mainstream tastes and practices as more and more individual flutists became acquainted with them.

After flute clubs in Manchester and London had flourished during previous centuries, flutists established local organizations in Los Angeles (1916), New York (1919), and Boston (1921), followed by new American groups encouraged by Medicus's magazine *The Flutist* (chapter 12) in Pittsburgh, Long Island, Tucson, Washington, D.C., and elsewhere. The earliest moves toward a national association of flutists were made in the U.S. in 1971. The group's first attempted meeting, planned for 24–27 January 1973 by James Pellerite, Professor of Flute at Indiana University, failed to materialize owing to financial concerns, and the charge passed from the academic to the commercial sphere when Mark Thomas, Vice-President of W. T. Armstrong Co. of Elkhart, arranged a convention to coincide with the 1973 Southwestern Music Festival at Anaheim, Calif. Thomas personally underwrote the initial expenses of the convention, which he planned together with Walfrid Kujala and Philip Swanson, incorporating the society as a not-for-profit organization. *The School Musician* and *The Instrumentalist*, two periodicals widely read by American flute teachers, provided publicity, and on 10 August 1973, 169 flutists, many from the west coast, as well as fifteen flute-makers and music publishers, arrived in Anaheim to participate in the convention. In order to expand and balance the new society's membership, its officers decided that future conventions would take place in a different U.S. city each year, rotating as far as possible between the east, west, midwest, and south. At the third convention, in Milwaukee (1975), the Association organized its first competition, to select participants in a masterclass taught by Kujala. New competitions for Young Artist, High School Flute Choir, Newly-Published Music, and Masterclass Performers were inaugurated the following year in Atlanta, while competitions for Chamber Music, Piccolo Artist, Baroque Flute Artist, High School Soloist, and six other masterclasses were added in the 1980s. In March 1976 the NFA issued its first newsletter, transformed in 1984 into the *Flutist Quarterly*, and Betty Bang Mather (1927–) became the association's first woman president in 1988. The conventions presented an opportunity for flute-makers to exhibit alongside each other, dealing directly with players rather than store managers or other intermediaries. At its first thirteen conventions (1973–86), the Association's Exhibits Chair, Ross Prestia, 'guided the whole industry, the custom flute makers and the mass producers, through a whole new phase of marketing practices'.[51]

In 1983 Trevor Wye called a meeting of British flutists to form a similar national society, initially served by Christopher Hyde-Smith as chairman and John Francis as secretary, with James Galway as president and Albert Cooper as vice-president.[52] The British Flute Society enrolled a thousand members in its first year.[53] Germany, Italy, Spain, France, and Finland followed, though a planned Association of Societies to hold European conventions never materialized. By 1997 the NFA's membership had reached 5750, 4161 of whom, along with 103 exhibitors, attended its 25th annual convention in Chicago.

The internet, and particularly the explosive growth of the World Wide Web that began in 1994, took the interconnectedness of flutists to a new level. In March 1996 Canadian flutist Larry Krantz began his FLUTE e-mail list, whose 2193 subscribers from

44 countries had posted 60,755 messages by November 2000.[54] Another Canadian, Les Green, founded an 'Earlyflute' list in May 1998, since when countless groups with a narrower focus or more restricted access have sprung up. The sphere of the flute reflects the wider world in the proliferation of home pages for performers and teachers, online catalogues for music dealers, flute-makers, and others, and more recently the promise of direct music distribution.

It would be unwise to conclude that the flute's mechanical development for musical purposes seems essentially to have ceased, since changes in the flute and flute-playing since the 1970s have been at least as profound as in any thirty-year period in the past. A rich recorded legacy illustrates the many ways in which tone and interpretation have altered, but other changes, even more surprising, have come in employment and the variety of instruments available. Three decades ago, though girls were taking up the flute in unprecedented numbers, women flutists who held prominent positions in orchestras or as soloists were few: Doriot Anthony Dwyer (principal flutist of the Boston Symphony as early as 1952), Lois Schaefer, Patricia Lynden, Susan Milan, Paula Robison, and Carol Wincenc were among the best known. In a count made in January 2001, 429 women held posts as flutists or piccoloists in 998 orchestras in 35 countries, as compared with 569 men. Though men still outnumbered women as principals in the most prestigious orchestras, particularly in Italy, 193 women held first-flute positions in the ensembles surveyed.[55]

A strange and wonderful interaction of tradition and fashion continues to drive changes in the instrument itself. Makers now offer a wide variety of modern flute models, most with a wide choice of embouchure cuts drawing on Lot, Cooper, and still more advanced ideals of tone as well as dozens of slightly different modern scales. Even in the past two decades, makers of wooden flutes – Harry Seeley, Robert Bigio, Chris Abell, and the historical replica makers – were few, along with only a handful of prominent professional players outside eastern Europe: Roger Rostron (Hallé Orchestra), Colin Chambers (Royal Liverpool Philharmonic), David Butt (BBC Symphony), Felix Skowronek (Puerto Rico and St Louis Symphonies, Seattle Opera), Jacques Zoon (Concertgebouw and Boston Symphony), and a few others in Minneapolis, Nashville, and Victoria, B.C. Today the Haynes company, in a reversal of its catalogue boast of about 1925 that 'the wooden flute has gone and gone forever', has revived a wooden model, while Verne Q. Powell Flutes Inc. has built its first ever in response to 'some internationally acclaimed flutists, such as András Adorján, who find that they prefer to perform or are being required to perform certain music on a wooden flute'.[56] Even William Bennett, who claims to be 'the natural heir to the legacy of Marcel Moyse' and serves as an icon to those who look to the silver Louis Lot as the ideal flute, now appears in publicity photographs with a wooden instrument.[57]

As for the future, we can at least predict that the sphere of the flute will continue to reflect the world at large, as it always has. But quite how it will change next, history does not prompt us to foretell.

Abbreviations

a	*ante* (before)
AmZ	*Allgemeine musikalische Zeitung* (Leipzig: 1798–1848)
DCM	Dayton C. Miller Collection, Music Division, Library of Congress, Washington, D.C.
EM	*Early Music* (London: 1973–)
fl	*floruit* (flourished)
FoMRHIQ	*Fellowship of Makers and Researchers of Historical Instruments Quarterly* (Oxford: 1978–)
FQ	*The Flutist Quarterly* (1975–)
HBQF	ed. Gabriele Busch-Salmen and Adelheid Krause-Pichler, *Handbuch Querflöte: Instrument, Lehrwerke, Aufführungspraxis, Musik, Ausbildung, Beruf* (Kassel: Bärenreiter, 1999). Where an author's name and a chapter title are given in the notes, the essay in question is particularly recommended for further reading.
JAMS	*Journal of the American Musicological Society* (1947–)
JAMIS	*Journal of the American Musical Instrument Society* (1975–)
MGG	ed. Friedrich Blume, *Die Musik in Geschichte und Gegenwart* (Kassel: Bärenreiter-Verlag, 1949–79); new edition ed. Ludwig Finscher (Kassel: New York: Bärenreiter and Stuttgart: Metzler, *c*1994–)
NGD2	*New Grove Dictionary of Music and Musicians, Second edition* (London: Macmillan, 2001 and in an online edition at www.grovemusic.com)
NLI	William Waterhouse, *The New Langwill Index* (London: Tony Bingham, 1993)
p	*post* (after)
Recherches	'Recherches' sur la musique française classique: La vie musicale en France sous les Bourbons (Paris: A. et J. Picard, 1960–)
RidIM	Research Center for Musical Iconography, City University of New York
Rudall Carte	Rudall, Carte & Co.
SIFTS	ed. Gianni Lazzari, *Bollettino della Società Italiana del Flauto Traverso Storico* (Bologna: 1996–)
SPES	Studio per Edizioni Scelte
TKF	Ardal Powell, trans. and ed., *The Keyed Flute by Johann George Tromlitz* (Oxford: Clarendon Press, 1996)
VFP	Ardal Powell, trans. and ed., *The Virtuoso Flute-player by Johann George Tromlitz* (Cambridge and New York: Cambridge University Press, 1991)

References and notes

The following bibliographic essays discuss a selection of the documents I consulted in writing this book, with the dual aim of acknowledging my sources and suggesting further reading. I have tried to make clear the sources of quotations and my authority for any surprising or radically new conclusions either in the notes or in the text itself, but when a book or an article has provided my entire basis for a paragraph or a section, the debt is acknowledged once in the relevant essay rather than repeatedly in the notes. To make full details of frequently-cited writings easier to find, the index lists principal references to authors' names that appear in the essays.

Omission from these essays should not necessarily be taken to indicate disapproval, since today the mark of a useful bibliography, except in an academic dissertation, is its selectiveness rather than a pedantic supererogation. The most recent attempt to compile a general bibliography of the flute was Dayton C. Miller's, in a self-published catalogue of his books and papers of 1935, before the torrent of words in which the subject is now awash had begun. Miller's catalogue has not lost its power to astonish anyone who studies it, not only by virtue of its comprehensiveness, but because its author owned a copy of every document he listed and knew its contents in detail. In the meantime the task he undertook has become all but impossible to achieve, even with computer indexing. Much of the new information incorporated into this book was first announced in short articles on a single subject often only indirectly related to the flute or flute-playing, many in a language other than English. With the growth in research and writing since World War 2 such writings have increased in number (as well as, largely, in quality), providing a rich new field for primary research in the future.

By the same token, inclusion of a book or article in this section should not be taken as approval of everything it contains. Older sources – and even some quite recent ones – often mix valuable information with egregious factual errors, selective and biased accounts, conclusions later disputed or overturned, and other traps that will lead today's reader astray unless he or she is endowed with scholarly caution and an uncommon store of patience. To catalogue errors in my sources or points of difference with them is obviously out of the question, but I judged it essential, particularly for the benefit of younger readers, to call attention in a more general way to some of these dangers.

Reference, General works

The most useful and balanced survey of the flute's history, construction, and repertoire to date is in German, in the compilation ed. Gabriele Busch-Salmen and Adelheid Krause-Pichler, *Handbuch Querflöte: Instrument, Lehrwerke, Aufführungspraxis, Musik, Ausbildung, Beruf* (Kassel: Bärenreiter, 1999), which contains chapters and essays by twenty experts including Konrad Hünteler, Dieter Krickeberg, Peter Spohr, and Manfredo Zimmerman. I have also used for reference R. S. Rockstro's *Treatise* (1890) and Nancy Toff's *Development of the Modern Flute* (1979), noted below under History and Criticism, as well as historical material by Howard

Mayer Brown, Jeremy Montagu, Jaap Frank, and myself in the article 'Flute' in *NGD2*. Dayton C. Miller's bibliography of literature on the flute, mentioned above, is his still extremely valuable *Catalogue of Books and Literary Material Relating to the Flute* (Cleveland: Author, 1935). As a measure of the literature's growth, the Miller catalogue contains about 1200 items, while David Lasocki's 'Historical Flute Bibliography, 1989–89' in Ardal Powell, ed., *Traverso, Historical Flute Newsletter: Volumes 1–10, 1989–89* (Hudson, N.Y.: Folkers & Powell, 1999), 161–90, lists no fewer than 549 books, articles, and dissertations published in that decade alone.

For the periodical literature, particularly since about 1970, I have relied heavily on *RILM Abstracts of Music Literature*, available online through Biblioline at www.nisc.com. RILM covers the journals of organology, such as the *Galpin Society Journal* and the *Journal of the American Musical Instrument Society*, as well as more specialized publications such as *Tibia* and *Traverso*. Most of the periodicals specifically relating to the flute are unfortunately not indexed by RILM or even by their own publishers, however, and so my use of publications such as *The Flutist* (Asheville, N.C.: Emil Medicus, 1920–9) and the numerous national flute society magazines has been limited, despite their occasional relevance, by the lack of a catalogue. A list of articles in *Flöte Aktuell* from 1986 to 1998 recently became available at http://home.foni.net/~dgffloete/fl_im.htm, and I hope that up-to-date indices of *Pan*, the *Flutist Quarterly*, *Bollettino della SIFTS*, and Denis Verroust's most valuable *Traversières* will in time appear to make the path of future researchers, particularly into the twentieth century, somewhat smoother.

The American Musicological Society lists dissertations in the field of musicology in its *Doctoral Dissertations in Musicology*, now online at www.music.indiana.edu/ddm, and a similar service is provided for German-language dissertations by the *Dissertationsmeldestelle der Gesellschaft für Musikforschung* at http://musikwiss.uni-muenster.de. Dissertations in English with a particular focus on the flute have been listed in an occasional series of articles by Nancy Toff in the *Flutist Quarterly*. Most are available from Dissertation Express at University Microfilms International (www.umi.com).

William Waterhouse's *The New Langwill Index* (London: Tony Bingham, 1993) is the starting point for research on flute-makers and their work. All but the most recent catalogues of the public musical instrument collections are listed in James Coover, *Musical Instrument Collections: Catalogs and Cognate Literature*, Detroit Studies in Music Bibliography, no. 47 (Detroit: Information Coordinators, 1981), while addresses of public institutions are in Jean Jenkins, *International Directory of Musical Instrument Collections* (Buren: Frits Knuf, 1977). Still, many of the most significant flute collections remain in private hands. Peter Spohr's *Kunsthandwerk im Dienste der Musik* (Frankfurt: Author, 1991) contains photographs and brief descriptions of a comprehensive exhibition of historic flutes from private collections which Spohr and associates mounted in Frankfurt and Munich in 1991.

Histories of music and of instruments have for the most part been written as though composers, musicians and, to a lesser extent, instrument-makers, lived in a 'a sphere of self-sufficient abstract expession', as Walter Salmen has put it, in which only their art matters and the mundane concerns of every day play little or no part. Economists first examined the social and economic status of musicians in the early twentieth century, since when a handful of scholars, particularly in Germany, have tried to learn about the working lives of musicians in times past. Walter Salmen, ed. *The Social Status of the Professional Musician from the Middle Ages to the Nineteenth Century, Sociology of Music No. 1* (New York: Pendragon Press, 1983), an expanded version, trans. Herbert Kaufman and Barbara Reisner, of *Sozialstatus des Berufmusikers vom 17. bis 19. Jahrhundert* (Kassel, 1971), contains thoughtful and informative essays by Salmen, Heinrich W. Schwab, Dieter Krickeberg, Werner Braun, Richard Petzoldt, Klaus Hortschansky, and Christoph-Hellmut Mahling, on the lives of ordinary professional musicians in town bands, court ensembles, military bands, and as itinerants, from the Middle Ages until the nineteenth century. One of the first writers in English to recognize the importance of economic history was Michael Chanan, whose *Musica Practica: The Social Practice of Western Music from Gregorian Chant to Postmodernism* (London and New York: Verso, 1994), despite an inadequate index and occasional evidence of hasty editing, is a wide-ranging and thoroughly persuasive survey that takes full account of many of the factors most often overlooked. Chanan's account of how the recording industry transformed musical performance and the music business is noted below in the bibliography for chapter 12.

Space forbids a listing of the works on musical and non-musical history and traditions I have found helpful. But Arnold Pacey's *Technology in World Civilization* (Cambridge, Mass.: MIT Press, 1991) is especially important because the way in which different types of flute have been transferred from one place to another so closely mirrors the way in which other tools and techniques cross cultures. Pacey portrays the transfer of technology as a complex 'dialogue' in which one society takes inventions from another and adapts them to suit its special requirements, a much more convincing view than the still widespread notion that mechanical progress is something simple and linear.

Old instruments and written instructions for playing them are our most important links to the way the flute sounded before gramophone recording was invented. Consequently the instrumental tutors of the past, along with collections of instruments, constitute the chief basis for studying historical performance practice. We can recover a surprising number of essential details of the constant flux in practice and taste by comparing and contrasting many approximately contemporary sources, each with a separate viewpoint, in conjunction with their appropriate instruments, music, and accounts of performances. Since the 1970s many tutors from the fifteenth to the eighteenth centuries have become widely accessible in editions and reprints, serving and stimulating the enormous growth of interest in the music of those eras, though the nineteenth and twentieth centuries remain less well served. The *Flute Library* series under Frans Vester's general editorship (Buren: Frits Knuf, 1973–97) presented, among others, works by Tromlitz (1791, 1800), Hugot & Wunderlich (1804), Fürstenau (1844), Rockstro (1890), and flute-related content in the *AmZ* (noted below under chapter 7). I maintain a bibliography of flute method books at www.flutehistory.com. That list grew from my chapter, 'Flute Tutors: Records of the Methods, Taste and Practice of Earlier Times', written in 1992 for the *Cambridge Companion to the Flute* and still forthcoming from Cambridge University Press. I published another survey and a list in 'Les méthodes pour flûte des XVIIIe, XIXe et XXe siècles', *Traversières* 18/52 (January 1996), 22–36, and covered a shorter period in 'Flute Methods, 1511–1832: A Bibliography', *Traverso* 8.2 (1996), 1–3.

History and criticism of the flute

Many histories of the flute still offer much of enduring value even though the state of knowledge has moved on since they were written: the best among them are great achievements of synthesis, while even the prejudice and myth to be found in some illustrate better than any factual or statistical reporting how people of earlier times thought and felt about their own music-making and its heritage. Obviously none can be unreservedly recommended to modern readers, otherwise there would be no need for this book. But the alert reader in this large field will find plenty to enlighten, or at least amuse.

In 1826 the twenty-five-year-old William Nelson James, who possessed the era's self-satisfaction in abundance, announced the recurring theme of flute histories. According to this view, the flute had recently been transformed from an 'infancy … passed in ignorance and barbarism' to a state of definitive and final perfection:

> [T]he flutes of the present day are so differently constructed from those made fifty years ago, that it at once presents to the mind the immense progress that has taken place since that period…. The perfect mechanism of our present flutes could not even have been contemplated at that time, and the admirable compositions which we now invariably meet with, however easy to the experienced amateur of the present day, would, fifty years ago, have bewildered a first-rate master.

James's 'perfect' mechanism was that of the eight-keyed flute, not that of Boehm's conical or cylinder flute, or a hybrid type. Yet the same claim to ultimate perfection continued to be made by British and American advocates of all these designs throughout the nineteenth century. These authors wrote about the flute's history not because they saw any inherent interest in earlier types of flute or their music, but because drawing a line of 'progress' from primitive early types to sophisticated modern ones helped them argue that their particular favourite was superior in an absolute sense. Thus Richard Carte, in his *Sketch of the Successive Improvements Made in the Flute* (London: Rudall, Rose & Carte, 1851), described a sequence of advances culminating in his own design of that year. Carte made a good case for his flute as mechanically superior, but distinctly weaker arguments that musical theory had become more rational, and that the abilities of musicians had improved. He thought earlier ideas on intonation tenable only by incompetents:

> [Quantz] was also a manufacturer of Flutes. He added another D sharp or E flat key ... but it has puzzled the critics to divine what could possibly have been the object of this additional key, which [was] said at the time to have corrected 'all the imperfections of this instrument, in terms of bad notes and false tuning.' They could not suppose it intended to make the enharmonic difference between D sharp and E flat. This would have been attributing a refinement of perception to Quanz [*sic*] utterly inconsistent with the obtuseness of ear, which could endure the extreme imperfection, not only of the chromatic, but of the diatonic intervals of his instrument...

If Carte's prejudice seems plain to us now, he was one of only a few writers on the topic to use rational argument at all. Charles T. Howe, in *All About the Flute: Containing a History of the Flute from Ancient Times to the Present* (Columbus: Author, 1892), simply poured scorn on any who had not seen the benefits of progress:

> Although the old-system flute has been abandoned by all self-respecting musicians, it is surprising how many amateurs still cling to the old relic, especially those who frequently hear the wondrous effects of Boehm's invention as produced by the best professional artists. An occasional genius like Fursteman [A. B. Fürstenau?] has succeeded in overcoming the defects of the old system to a surprising degree; but nature has endowed such men with powers beyond the ordinary mortal; and he who expects to produce good musical effects with a defective instrument will labor in vain.

Because most nineteenth-century histories in English deliberately set out to disparage earlier instruments and practices in this way, their coverage of times before their own generally serves as a poor source of historical material for us. On the other hand personal accounts of the authors' experiences in developing and building instruments are valuable as primary material. For example, one of the earliest histories, Cornelius Ward's *The Flute Explained* (London: Author, 1844), begins with a brief and trivial history of the instrument's development, but later gives unique details of the crucial period in which its author collaborated with Gordon on his London flute of 1831.

The first serious attempt to cover the subject as a whole was made by Richard Shepherd Rockstro, in *A Treatise on the History, Construction and Practice of the Flute*, 4 vols in 3 (London: Rudall Carte, 1890, R/London: Musica Rara, 1967, and Buren: Frits Knuf, 1986). Rockstro too viewed his own flute designs as the final phase of a long development, while his agenda included casting discredit on Boehm (see p. 174) and making a case for equal temperament. In the most substantial part of his treatise, Part II, on 'the Construction of the Flute and the History of its Development', he described pre-Victorian instruments as 'barbaric', 'primitive', and only 'quasi-musical' (§399). On the other hand he made unprecedentedly vigorous efforts to discover the facts about changes in flute construction rather than merely repeating unverified stories, and in contrast to Carte's disparagement, he credited Quantz with an 'indubitable refinement of ear' (§445). To emphasize the contrast between English-language and continental handling of these matters, the first Italian history of the flute appeared in the same year as Rockstro's treatise, but favoured the old flute ('Ziegler system') over those of Boehm and Briccialdi.

Christopher Welch's *History of the Boehm Flute* (London: Rudall Carte, 1883) contained a rare unprejudiced account of the Boehm-Gordon controversy. The work's third edition, published in 1896 as a rebuttal of Rockstro's biased commentary on the Boehm flute, contained the completest documentation until that time of the new flute's development and, with the inclusion of Schafhäutl's mostly reliable 'Life of Boehm', of the inventor's work. Another flutist, Henry Clay Wysham, took such umbrage at Rockstro's treatment of the inventor that he castigated Rudall Carte for publishing Rockstro's book, even though the company also published Welch's rejoinder. But again Wysham's own book, *The Evolution of the Boehm Flute* (Elkhart: C. G. Conn, 1898), was a thinly-disguised marketing tool, though an uncommonly entertaining one, for the Conn 'Wonder' flute.

A number of works of the early twentieth century tried to treat the flute's technical development more dispassionately. These included T. Lea Southgate, 'The Evolution of the Flute', Proceedings of the *Royal Musical Association* 34 (June 16, 1908), 155–175, and Paul Wetzger, *Die Flöte: ihre Entstehung und Entwicklung bis zur Jetztzeit in akustischer, technischer und musikalischer Beziehung* (Heilbronn: C. F. Schmidt, 1905). Later efforts addressed to flutists broadened the topic, addressing the flute's music and players as well as technical matters. H. Macaulay Fitzgibbon's *The Story of the Flute, being a History of the Flute and Everything Connected with it* (London: William Reeves, 2/1929) was an engagingly-written anecdotal monograph on the instrument and its music, in which Fitzgibbon's wide reading of the literature and experience of the repertoire are evident, though he rarely identifies his sources and new information he provides often cannot be verified. Leonardo De Lorenzo's *My Complete Story of the Flute: The Instrument, the Performer, the Music* (New York: Citadel Press, 1951, R/Lubbock, Tex.: Texas Tech University Press, 1992) is a less readable and less reliable mosaic of reminiscences and factoids reflecting its author's wide experience of flutes and flute-playing in Europe and America.

After the study of musical instruments emerged as a separate discipline in Germany in the late nineteenth century, British scholars of the following generation first explicitly noted the important connections between early instruments and their music. Adam Carse, who had authored pioneering studies of the history of the orchestra, published *Musical Wind Instruments* (London: Macmillan, 1939 R/New York, 1965), covering the mechanical development of the flute together with the other winds. James A. Macgillivray's wise and brilliant chapter, 'The Woodwind', in Anthony Baines, ed., *Musical Instruments through the Ages* (Harmondsworth and Baltimore: Penguin Books, 1961), 237–76, was one of the first efforts to explain to the general reader why the history of woodwind instruments mattered to musicians and audiences. In it Macgillivray brought to bear not only his extensive knowledge of woodwind history, but also his familiarity with all the main characteristic styles of playing of his own age, at a time when they were fast disappearing. Noting changes in instruments, performance style, and attitudes to musical heritage, Macgillivray accurately foresaw their extent and influence. The volume in which his chapter appeared, though it will soon be half a century old and is inevitably out of date on some small matters of fact, is still highly recommended for the intelligent essays it contains by leading authorities on all the instruments except mechanical and electronic ones.

Baines's book drew on the combined expertise of members of the Galpin Society, an association of collectors and scholars interested in early instruments, named for the pioneering English collector Canon Francis Galpin (1858–1945). Philip Bate (1909–99) was one enthusiastic and lifelong collector of antique woodwinds who helped found the Galpin Society in 1946 and gave his collection of more than 300 instruments to the Music Faculty at the University of Oxford in 1968. His monograph *The Flute: A Study of its History, Development and Construction* (London: Ernest Benn and New York: W. W. Norton, 1969) took a broad view of the flute that involved not only the history of its mechanics, but acoustics, ethnic and ancient flutes, flute-making, and a brief treatment of playing technique. Bate covered the Boehm flute well, though many of the documents of its early history were not available when he wrote, and the same factor renders his coverage of the flute's earlier history relatively weak. He was the first to argue explicitly that the baroque flute had been invented by the Hotteterres (p. 80), though he also wrote that '[t]his attribution will not, of course, stand up to scrutiny' (p. 166).

Raymond Meylan's *The Flute* (Portland: Amadeus Press, 1988), a translation from the German edition of 1974 and originally written in French as *La flûte: les grandes lignes de son développement de la préhistoire à nos jours* (Lausanne: Payot, [1974]), was a nuanced, thoughtful, and richly illustrated account of the flute's history, concentrating more on early times and on non-written sources than most writers to date. Quite free from the bonds of the English 'mechanical development' thesis, the work contains inspiring, lively, and attractive ideas if not thorough documentation or invariably sound commentary. Like a good concert, Meylan's book leaves the reader feeling it was too short. Hans-Peter Schmitz treated history along with criticism, musical analysis, and technique in more severe fashion with his *Flötenlehre* (Kassel: Bärenreiter, 1955), as well as in several works on using eighteenth-century information in modern flute performance cited in the bibliography for chapter 13 below. Another German work, Gustav Scheck's *Die Flöte und ihre Musik* (Mainz: Schott, 1975), also integrated history into a general background presentation for teachers. Scheck's view of history seems strangely polarized today: he presented measured technical drawings of early instruments, but considered the Boehm flute as the culmination of the flute's development and omitted all mention of other nineteenth-century keyed types including Viennese and Schwedler flutes. On the other hand he gave informed stylistic analyses of selected works from different eras, insisting that 'the time is past when an "interpreter" stamped with the nineteenth-century style may simply transfer his virtuosic habit of treating music arbitrarily to the music of earlier epochs', and that 'today the performer is required to come to terms directly with the sources of older music and the results of musicological research' (p. 107). Busch-Salmen and Krause-Pichler's *Handbuch Querflöte* brings this attitude up to date with recently-won historical insights, adding information about career orientation for flutists in Germany.

Despite the growth of this stylistic awareness in Europe, the notion of scientific progress that sees modern concerns, practices, and instruments as superior to those of the past has remained until now the governing theme in writings on the flute in English. Even recent works have stressed the supposed technical defects of early flutes in comparison with the modern instrument, though it has for some time been widely understood how well adapted earlier types were to their own music and playing styles. Nancy Toff's highly detailed mechanical study, *The Development of the Modern Flute* (New York: Taplinger, 1979), largely succeeded in its goal of providing exhaustive coverage of its topic. But whereas the idea of mechanical development suited a discussion of the nineteenth century well, it could be made to fit earlier periods only by seriously misrepresenting their instruments and music. A few examples of its harmful misconceptions were that renaissance flutes were built to play in D major (p. 11), that Quantz was unable to play in tune on the flute he designed (p. 22), and that the vigorous diversity of nineteenth-century flute-making was nothing but a symptom of 'confusion' (pp. 122–3). Toff's work was the product of energetic research on its central topic and the book's middle three chapters remain by far the most detailed writing on the flute's mechanical evolution, but a better-balanced overview of the flute's physical development as a whole may be found in *The Flute* (Buckinghamshire (UK): Shire Publications, 1990) by Jeremy Montagu, one of the world's leading experts on historical musical instruments.

Nevertheless, another work by Nancy Toff, *The Flute Book* (New York and Oxford: Oxford University Press, 1985, R/1996), is more widely cited as an authority in matters of the flute's history. This general manual gives much useful detail on the flute and its music, particularly in the twentieth century, and includes helpful repertoire lists and information on performance for beginning flute-players. But its historical sections, highly compressed from material in the *Development*, contain an alarming number of new and inherited errors of fact and analysis, even in a revised second edition. This is most unfortunate in view of the book's wide appeal and distribution.

Introduction

The myth of Pan and Syrinx appeared in the works of classical authors including Ovid, Virgil, and Homer. Christopher Welch surveyed the legend's manifestations in literature and art in *Six Lectures on the Recorder* (London: H. Frowde, 1911), 201–18 and 261–303. Previous histories of the flute are covered above under 'History and Criticism of the Flute', and the beginnings of organology in chapter 13. Changing attitudes towards the development of musical instruments were explored by Laurence Libin in 'Progress, Adaptation, and the Evolution of Musical Instruments', *JAMIS* 29 (2000), 187–213.

1. *Webster's Third New International Dictionary* (1961), s.v. 'Evolution', quoted in Libin, 'Progress, Adaptation, and the Evolution of Musical Instruments', 194.
2. Ernst Gombrich, *The Story of Art*, 16th edition (London: Phaidon Press, 1995), 44.
3. Fétis, quoted in Robert Wangermée, 'Les Premiers Concerts Historiques à Paris', in *Mélanges Ernest Closson* (Brussels: Société belge de musicologie, 1948), 188, and in Harry Haskell, *The Early Music Revival: A History* (London: Thames and Hudson, 1988), 19.
4. Henry Fountain, 'After 9,000 Years, Oldest Playable Flute is Heard Again', *The New York Times*, 28 September 1999, D2.
5. Bate, *The Flute*, xi.
6. Julius O. Smith III (Stanford University), quoted in William J. Broad, 'Ancient Instruments Yielding Secrets of their Music', *The New York Times*, 19 January 1999, D1, D10.
7. Trevor Wye, 'Perspective: The Munich International Flute Competition', *FQ* 26.2 (Winter 2001), 69–72, 71.

Chapter 1 Shepherds, monks, and soldiers

Very little has been written on the subject of the medieval transverse flute, for the simple reason that almost none of the scant evidence for medieval musical performance refers directly to our instrument. Of the great progress that has been made in the past thirty years or so in the study of medieval instruments and music, only one article focuses directly on the flute. This is by Jane Bowers, a scholar at the University of Wisconsin, Milwaukee, whose research has taught us much of what we know of the early flute: '"Flaüste traverseinne"and "Flûte d'Allemagne": The Flute in France from the Late Middle Ages up through 1702', *'Recherches'* 19 (1979), 7–49. Bowers's scholarship is exemplary and her contribution, though available only through research libraries, is essential reading. I have relied heavily in chapters 1–5 on the same author's most valuable dissertation 'The French Flute School from 1700 to 1760' (Ph.D. diss., University of California, Berkeley, 1971), but where identical material appears in both publications have cited the 1979 article in the first three chapters of this book as being perhaps more easily found in libraries.

The medieval iconography of the flute has likewise received little attention. The most notable contribution is by Liane Ehlich, 'Zur Ikonographie der Querflöte im Mittelalter', *Basler Jahrbuch für Historische Musikpraxis* 8 (1984), 197–212. Edmund A. Bowles gives an iconographical survey of medieval music in performance, with a useful Introduction on the interpretation of iconographical sources in *La pratique musicale au moyen âge / Musical Performance in the Late Middle Ages* ([Paris]: Minkoff & Lattés, 1983). Emanuel Winternitz, curator at New York's Metropolitan Museum of Art and a great collector in his own right, covers similar ground in his lively and readable prose in *Musical Instruments and their Symbolism in Western Art* (London: Faber and Faber, 1967). Raymond Meylan's *The Flute* (1988), mentioned under History and Criticism above, focuses on early times and reproduces several medieval illustrations.

Of the scholars from whose work on other medieval instruments besides the flute we can learn the most, Christopher Page, a Cambridge scholar who has perhaps contributed most in our times to the study of medieval instrumental music, deserves first mention. Well-known for his work with the English *a cappella* ensemble Gothic Voices, his articles in *Early Music* from the 1970s onward are collected in a thorough and wide-ranging discussion of songs, instruments, and performance practice: *Music and Instruments of the Middle Ages: Studies on Texts and Performance* (Brookfield, Vt: Ashgate, 1997). Page focused on French practice in *Voices and Instruments of the Middle Ages: Instrumental Practice and Songs in France, 1100–1300* (Berkeley: University of California Press, 1986). Though most performances of medieval music in the early music revival of the 1970s combined voices and instruments, Page's work has persuaded nearly everyone that this was not a common practice in the Middle Ages, and unaccompanied voices are now more commonly heard.

An introduction to the instruments of the Middle Ages and Renaissance can be found in Jeremy Montagu's *The World of Medieval and Renaissance Musical Instruments* (Newton Abbot: David & Charles, *c*1976). Another helpful survey, though now hard to obtain, was provided by David Munrow's recording *Instruments of the Middle Ages and Renaissance* (2 LPs, EMI SAN. 392, 1976) which came with an illustrated 96-page book of the same title. Joscelyn Godwin's '"Main divers acors": Some Instrument Collections of the Ars Nova Period', *EM* 5 (1977), 148–59, discusses lists of instruments in literary and other sources. A handbook containing a collection of essays by experts on aspects of performing early music, Howard Mayer Brown and Stanley Sadie, eds., *Performance Practice: Music Before 1600* (New York and London: Norton, 1989) provides perspective for the flutist by almost never mentioning the instrument. Brown, the late professor at the University of Chicago and one of the world's most prolific and respected figures in modern historical musicology, lays out the nature of the inquiry in his Introduction, where he writes: 'Scholars studying the performance practices of the distant past must cast their nets wide, learning from wherever they can and gradually forming a composite picture of the nature of life in the Middle Ages from as large a pool of information as they can gather.' Now that it is generally agreed that the French chansons were not performed with accompaniment, and so his study has nothing to do with the flute, Hendrik van der Werf's Introduction to his *The Chansons of the Troubadors and Trouvères* (Utrecht: A. Oosthoek's Uitgaversmaatschappij, 1972) is still worth reading for its clear discussion of many of the questions that beset everyone interested in performing medieval music.

Thomas Binkley writes with authority and good sense on how to think about performing medieval music – indeed any music – in 'The Work is not the Performance', *Companion to Medieval and Renaissance Music*, ed. Tess Knighton and David Fallows (New York: Schirmer, 1992), 36–43. Binkley explains how modern musicology, following the example of literary studies, expects sources and texts to provide a basis for analysing the 'work', but that this is not appropriate for cases in which a written version is no more than a sketch to be fleshed out in different performances, all equally valid. Binkley links the decreasing input of the performer and the increasing control of the composer with a change in that individual's title, from 'trobador' to 'composer' (a point illustrated in lavish detail with reference to a later period by Rob C. Wegman in 'From Maker to Composer: Improvisation and Musical Authorship in the Low Countries, 1450–1500', *JAMS* 49 (1996), 409–79). Only recently have scholars taken up the challenge of these ideas, notably in an issue of *Early Music* devoted to 'Listening Practice' (25.4, November 1997).

Other useful essays in the Schirmer *Companion* include Rob C. Wegman on 'Musica Ficta' (265–74), Rogers Covey-Crump's 'Pythagoras at the Forge: Tuning in Early Music' (317–26), and Reinhard Strohm on 'Centre and Periphery: Mainstream and Provincial Music' (55–59). Covey-Crump's essay on tuning requires a previous knowledge of tuning systems and is not recommended to the faint of heart, but is informed by the author's practical experience of the topic.

Wulf Arlt, in 'The "Reconstruction" of Instrumental Music: the Interpretation of the Earliest Practical Sources', *Studies in the Performance of Late medieval Music*, ed. Stanley Boorman (Cambridge: CUP, 1983), 75–100, makes the point that while playing medieval music as written is a clearly unhistorical manner of performing it, attempting to realize the texts in the light of any unwritten practice calls for the interaction of historical knowledge and practical experience. 'In any case,' Art writes, 'it is an adventure.'

For those interested in the adventure of adding parts extemporaneously to monophonic music, a study of thirteenth- and fourteenth-century writings about improvising polyphonic music using the interval of the fifth and contrary motion can be found in Sarah Fuller, 'Discant and the Theory of Fifthing', *Acta Musicologica* 50 (1978), 241–75.

1. Page, *Voices and Instruments*, 77.
2. Athanaeus IV, 1760, cited in Meylan, *The Flute*, 38.
3. Volumnii catacombs no. 13, from one of 38 chamber graves in Il Palazzone near Perugia.
4. Florence: Museo Nazionale del Bargello, no. 26.
5. London: Victoria and Albert Museum, no. 216–1865.
6. Herrad's manuscript was destroyed by a fire at the municipal library in Strasbourg in 1870, but fortunately a study of it, including copies of the illustrations, was already under way and was published by Albert Marignan as *Étude sur le manuscrit de l'Hortus deliciarum* (Strasbourg: J. H. E. Heitz, 1910). A reprint of that work appeared in 1977, and a more detailed reconstruction of the lost original was attempted in Rosalie Green, ed., *Hortus deliciarum / Herrad of Hohenbourg* (London: Warburg Institute, University of London, and Leiden: E. J. Brill, 1979).
7. Leiden: University Library Codex B.P.L. 136 B, f. 7.
8. Munich: Universitätsbibliothek Codex 24, Cim. 15 f. 2.
9. *Musica* 1979 calendar (Kassel: Bärenreiter, [1979]), January.
10. Munich: Bayerische Staatsbibliothek Cgm 6404, f. 211r. See Gianni Lazzari, 'Una immagine inedita del flauto medievale', *SIFTS* 2.1 (June 1997), 25–31.
11. Munich: Bayerische Staatsbibliothek, Cgm 193/V, f. 10v.
12. Bowers, 'Flaüste traverseinne', 8.
13. Lines 7247–61, quoted in Bowers, 'Flaüste traverseinne'. My trans. follows suggestions in Godwin, 'Main divers acors', 157–8.
14. Pierre Belon du Mans, *Les observations de plusieurs singularitez* (Paris: Cavellat, 1555), quoted in Meylan, *The Flute*, 11.
15. Oxford: Bodleian Library, Flemish MS 264, f. 118v (Bowers, 'Flaüste traverseinne', 10–11).
16. New York: Metropolitan Museum of Art, f. 174.
17. Winternitz, *Musical Instruments and their Symbolism*, 131.
18. *Imago Musicae*, 1984–8.
19. Christopher Page, 'German Musicians and their Instruments: A 14th-century account by Konrad of Mengenberg', *EM* 10 (1982), 192–200, reprinted in *Voices and Instruments*, 192–9.
20. Bowers, 'Flaüste traverseinne', 11–12.
21. Godwin, 'Main divers acors', 157, my trans. following Godwin's suggestions.
22. Machaut, *Le Remède de Fortune*, lines 1174–6, quoted in Bowers, 'Flaüste traverseinne'.
23. Eustache Deschamps, *L'Art de Dictier et de Fere Chançons* (1392); see Christopher Page, 'Machaut's Pupil Deschamps on the Performance of Music', *EM* 5 (1977), 484–91, reprinted in *Voices and Instruments*, 484–91 [*sic*].
24. Page, *Voices and Instruments*, 489.
25. Godwin, 'Main divers acors', 153–6. A rubbing of the brass is reproduced on p. 155.
26. Page, *Voices and Instruments*, 118.

TERMINOLOGY
1. Page, *Voices and Instruments*, 140.
2. Godwin, 'Main divers acors', 158.

Chapter 2 The flute at war and at home

CONTEMPORARY SOURCES

Virdung, Sebastian, *Musica getutscht*, Basel: Michael Furter, 1511
    Facsimile ed. Klaus Wolfgang Niemöller, Documenta musicologica 1st series, 31 (Kassel:
    Bärenreiter, 1970)
    Translation: Beth Bullard, *Musica Getutscht: A Treatise on Musical Instruments (1511) by Sebastian
    Virdung* (Cambridge and New York: Cambridge University Press, 1993)
Martin Agricola, *Musica instrumentalis deudsch* (Wittenberg: Georg Rhau, 1529 and 1545)
    Facsimile (Hildesheim: Georg Olms Verlag, 1969)
    Translation: William E. Hettrick, *The 'Musica instrumentalis deudsch' of Martin Agricola*
    (Cambridge and New York, Cambridge University Press, 1994)
Sylvestro Ganassi, *Opera Intitulata Fontegara*, Venice: Author, 1635
    Translation: ed. Hildemarie Peter (Berlin-Lichterfelde: Robert Lienau, 1956)
Philibert Jambe de Fer, *L'Epitome musicale de Tons, Sons et Accords, des Voix humaines, Fleustes
    d'Alleman, Fleustes a Neuf trous, Violes, et Violons* (Lyons: Michael du Bois, 1556)
    Facsimile: François Lesure, "L'Épitome Musical' de Philibert Jambe de Fer (1556)', *Annales
    musicologiques, Moyen-âge et renaissance* 6 (1958–63), 341–86
Thoinot Arbeau (pseudonym for Jehan Tabourot, 1520–95), *Orchesographie* (1589)
    Translation: Mary Stewart Evans, *Orchesography: Thoinot Arbeau* (New York: Dover, 1968)

MODERN SOURCES

Italian scholars have led efforts to learn more about flutes of the Renaissance. Luca Verzulli, a musician and researcher who has devoted his energies to investigating the renaissance flute in Italian sources, has published articles on military flutes in *Bollettino della SIFTS* including 'Le musiche militari per flauto e tamburo' (*SIFTS* 4.2 (1999), 3–11), and 'Lo stile del flauto militare nelle "Battaglie" in musica' (*SIFTS* 4.3 (1999), 3–10). A brief article in English is Verzulli's 'The Pope's Flutes: The Military Transverse Flute in Rome from the Sixteenth Century to the Eighteenth', *Traverso* 11.2 (1999), 5–7, which appeared in earlier Italian versions in *SIFTS* and the Italian Flute Society magazine *Syrinx*. Marcello Castellani brought revealing documents to light in 'I Flauti nell'Inventario di Lorenzo il Magnifico (1492)', in Nikolaus Delius, ed., *Sine musica nulla vita: Festschrift Hermann Moeck, zum 75. Geburtstag am 16. September 1997* (Celle: Moeck, 1997), 185–91, while other articles on iconography by Verzulli and by Gianni Lazzari have appeared in the *SIFTS* Bulletin. A page entitled 'Testimonianze' on Verzulli's web site http://digilander.iol.it/~verzulli/rinasc/testim.htm (in Italian) is a useful compendium of references to the flute in Italian literature and documentary sources, though at the time of writing source references have not yet been provided. Howard Mayer Brown's study *Sixteenth-century Instrumentation: The Music for the Florentine Intermedii* (n.p.: American Institute of Musicology, 1973) describes in detail the ways in which flutes and other instruments were used in those theatrical entertainments.

    Georg Duthaler's books *Trommeln und Pfeifen in Basel* (Basel: Meiran, 1985) and *Vom Trommeln und Pfeifen* (Basel: Riannon, 1986) detail the history and culture of the Swiss fife and drum tradition. The illustration of Anthony and his fifers comes from Hans Burgkmair, *The Triumph of Maximilian I*, trans. and ed. Stanley Appelbaum (New York: Dover, 1964), a facsimile of all the plates, together with Maximilian's instructions, and a brief Introduction to this fascinating document. Print 33 of Burgkmair's *Der Weisskunig*, ed. Alwin Schultz, *Jahrbuch der Kunsthistorischen Sammlungen des Allerhöchsten Kaiserhauses* 6 (Vienna, 1888), is discussed in Christine K. Mather, 'Maximilian I and his Instruments', *EM* 3.1 (Jan 1975, 42–6).

    The Italian engineer and flute-maker Filadelfio Puglisi has contributed most to our understanding of the renaissance consort flute. His article 'The Renaissance Flutes of the Biblioteca Capitolare of Verona: The Structure of a "Pifaro"', *GSJ* 32 (1979), 24–9, describes a seventeenth-century collection of these instruments in lucid detail. 'A Survey of Renaissance

Flutes', *GSJ* 41 (1988), 67–82, is 'an attempt to provide a comprehensive view of the information which can be obtained from the surviving museum specimens', and is the most useful of his writings for general readers. His book *I flauti traversi rinascimentali in Italia* (Florence: SPES, 1995) expands on this theme by providing detailed measurements of the specimens preserved in Italian collections and comparing their pitches and sounding lengths. Puglisi's brief description of the Assisi flute, *GSJ* 37 (1984), 6–9, is supplemented by a fuller discussion by Vincenzo De Gregorio in *Il flauto dolce* 10/11 (Jan–Jun 1984), 48–51.

The surest way of dating museum instruments that lack a documented provenance is to match any makers' marks with archival documents of those makers' activities. Herbert Heyde's essay 'Makers' Marks on Wind Instruments' in William Waterhouse's *The New Langwill Index* gives an overview of some of the difficulties and rewards of interpreting makers' signatures. A richly illustrated catalogue of a Vancouver exhibition that assembled some of the most famous instruments, and drew attention to undeservedly obscure ones, is Phillip T. Young's *The Look of Music: Rare Musical Instruments 1500–1900* (Vancouver: Vancouver Museums & Planetarium Association, 1980). David Lasocki's study *The Bassanos: Venetian Musicians and Instrument Makers in England, 1531–1665* (Aldershot: Scolar Press, 1995) covers the Bassano marks as well as providing a wealth of evidence on the lives and work of this important musical family, while Frank P. Bär's article '"...Faict de la main de Raffy Lyonnois...": Folgerung aus einem Sigmaringer Instrumentenfund', *Musik in Baden-Württemberg* 2 (1995), 75–108, discusses those of the Rafis.

Philippe Allain-Dupré, a Frenchman who combines the talents of a performing musician, an instrument-maker, and a scholar, has written about the history, description, dimensions, attribution, and aesthetics of the Rafi flutes in *Les flûtes de Claude Rafi, fleustier lyonnais au XVIe siècle* (Courlay: Éditions J. M. Fuzeau, 2000), a quadrilingual publication in French, English, German, and Japanese, of which only the French is complete. I am also indebted to that author for answering my many questions in a private correspondence over several years. A brief notice by Maurice Byrne on the catalogues of Settala's collection appeared in *GSJ* 18 (1965), 126–7.

Joscelyn Godwin's article 'The Renaissance Flute', *The Consort* 28 (1972), 71–81, one of the earliest attempts to assemble and collate the literature on the subject, refers to printed theoretical sources on the flute in the sixteenth and seventeenth centuries and contains a comparative fingering chart. The article is well designed but contains some mistakes, and has now been superseded by Anne Smith's excellent and highly detailed article in German, 'Die Renaissancequerflöte und ihre Musik', in *Basler Jahrbuch für historische Musikpraxis* 2 (1978), 9–76. Although Smith contributed a perhaps excessively abbreviated English summary of this article in the form of a chapter, 'The Renaissance Flute', to John Solum's *The Early Flute* (Oxford: Clarendon Press, 1992), 11–33, her German essay remains the most thorough survey of flute pedagogy and repertoire in the sixteenth and seventeenth centuries. Bernard Thomas, in 'The Renaissance Flute', *EM* 3 (1975), 2–10, complained that the renaissance flute 'copies' of that date bore little relation to original instruments, but in his determination to find a consort of flutes with pitch-relationships that would permit the group to play all renaissance music without transposing, he misinterpreted some of the written sources and reached some unsound conclusions, as Anne Smith observed in 1978. Howard Mayer Brown, 'Notes (and Transposing Notes) on the Transverse Flute in the Early Sixteenth Century', *JAMIS* 12 (1986), 5–39, provided some details of previously unknown sources, though it too furthered a slight confusion of a similar kind. A chapter, 'The Transverse Flute in the Middle Ages and Renaissance', in *Cambridge Companion to the Flute* (Cambridge: Cambridge University Press, forthcoming), by Nancy Fenholt Hadden, an American musician resident in London who has made a speciality of playing renaissance flutes as well as writing about them, presents a more recent and more personal interpretation of the evidence.

Mary Rasmussen's 'The case of the flutes in Holbein's "The Ambassadors"', *EM* 23 (1995), 115–23, demonstrates that sixteenth-century imagery needs at least as much interpretation as that of earlier times before modern eyes can see what the artist intended, and that the flute's renaissance iconography provides a great deal of scope for further investigation.

Understanding music and performance in the sixteenth century requires us to know, among other things, how musicians learned their craft, found their posts, and made their living. One group of wind players has received ample attention from David Lasocki, in 'Professional Recorder Players in England, 1540–1740', 2 vols (Ph.D. diss., University of Iowa, 1983), and another in Andrew Ashbee and David Lasocki's *A Biographical Dictionary of English Court Musicians, 1485–1714*, 2 vols (Aldershot, Hampshire, and Brookfield, Vt: Ashgate, 1998), which contains a complete chart of the wind posts at Court. For general information on music and musicians in this period, Keith Polk gives an excellent survey in *German Instrumental Music of the Late Middle Ages: Players, Patrons and Performance Practice* (Cambridge: Cambridge University Press, 1992). Other helpful general essays can be found in Iain Fenlon, ed., *The Renaissance* (Man & Music series) (London: Macmillan, 1989). One of the most interesting for flutists is Frank Dobbins, 'Lyons: Commercial and Cultural Metropolis' (pp. 197–215), which provides a concise yet detailed survey of the musical life of this city, arguing for its key position in renaissance culture and commerce. His larger work, *Music in Renaissance Lyons* (Oxford: Clarendon Press, 1992), is recommended to anyone with a deeper interest in Lyonnais activities.

A lucid and highly recommended explanation of Renaissance music theory is given in Sarah Mead's chapter, 'Renaissance Theory', in Jeffery T. Kite-Powell, ed., *A Performer's Guide to Renaissance Music* (New York: Schirmer Books, 1994). Some of the material in the sidebars on modes and hexachords is reworked from my article 'The Hexachords and the Renaissance Flute', *Traverso* 11.1 (1999), 1–3. More detail on theory and practice appears in excellent essays in Tess Knighton and David Fallows, eds., *Companion to Medieval and Renaissance Music* (New York: Schirmer Books, 1992), especially those on wind ensembles (Lorenz Welker), pitch (Kenneth Kreitner), mode (Liane Curtis), tuning (Rogers Covey-Crump), and *musica ficta* (Rob C. Wegman).

1. Bowers, 'Flaüste traverseinne', 16.
2. Verzulli, 'The Pope's Flutes'. See also Douglas Miller and G. A. Embleton, *The Swiss at War, 1300–1500* (London: Osprey, 1979).
3. Miller and Embleton, *The Swiss at War*, 31.
4. Details on France in this paragraph come from Bowers, 'Flaüste traverseinne', 17–18.
5. Verzulli, 'The Pope's Flutes'.
6. Castellani, 'I Flauti nell'Inventario di Lorenzo il Magnifico', 189, 186.
7. Trans. by Stanley Appelbaum, from Hans Burgkmair, *The Triumph of Maximilian I*, trans. and ed. Stanley Appelbaum (New York: Dover, 1964), which does not supply the original German found in the manuscript.
8. Jane Bowers wrote of this description that Arbeau 'was obviously unacquainted with the large sizes of fifes that had been in use earlier in the century' ('Flaüste traverseinne', 19).
9. Arbeau, *Orchesographie*, 40.
10. Romanesca, *Biber Violin Sonatas* (2 CDs), Harmonia Mundi France 907134.35, CD1, track 16.
11. R. W. Hylands, *Development of the Flute and Flute Bands* (typescript, n.p., n.d.). Hylands cites the 'wyfflers' as though they were players of some kind of wind instrument, but the word could perhaps mean 'archers'.
12. Agricola, *Musica*, ed. Hettrick, 12. See also the same ed., p. 86, for a parallel passage in the 1545 edition.
13. Hadden, 'The Transverse Flute in the Middle Ages'.
14. Margaret Paine Hasselman and David McGown suggest in 'Mimesis and woodwind articulation in the fourteenth century', *Studies in the Performance of Late Medieval Music*, Stanley Boorman, ed. (Cambridge: Cambridge University Press, 1983), 101–7, that some of Ganassi's syllables may have been in use a century before he published *Fontegara*.
15. Hettrick, *The 'Musica instrumentalis deudsch' of Martin Agricola*, 114, comments by the editor.
16. Florence: Uffizi, Gabinetti dei disegni, Stampe sciolte 27.
17. Verzulli, 'Testimonianze'.

18. Ibid.
19. Brown, *The Florentine Intermedii*, 59.
20. Details of the 1548 events are from Dobbins, 'Lyons'.
21. Jambe de Fer, *Epitome*, 51.
22. Part of this passage (Jambe de Fer, *Epitome*, 51) reads: '*& pour descendre, il la faut faindre de peu à peu selon l'assiete de la Musique…*'. In the first printing of this book I translated the key verb *faindre* as 'to feint'. Although it sometimes has this meaning, I now think the context indicates that Smith's reading ('The Reniassance Flute', 18) is correct.
23. Bowers, 'Flaüste traverseinne', 20.
24. Bowers, 'Flaüste traverseinne', 21.
25. Lasocki, 'Professional Recorder Players', I, 51.
26. Lasocki, *The Bassanos*, 173.
27. Bowers, 'Flaüste traverseinne', 21.
28. Lasocki, 'Professional Recorder Players', I, 21–2 and 107, Table 4.
29. Budapest: Museum of Fine Arts.
30. Location unknown (RidIM 0030).
31. Treviso: Museo Civico (RidIM 0211).
32. *In dissem Buechlyn fynt man LXXV hubscher Lieder myt Discant. Alt. Bas und Tenor. lustick zu syngen. Auch etlich zu fleiten, schwegelen und anderen musicalisch Instrumenten artlichen zu gebrauchen* (Cologne: Arnt von Aich c1519).
33. Hans Mielich, *The Bavarian Court Ensemble* (gouache illumination in a manuscript of Psalms by Lassus. Munich: Staatsbibliothek MS A11 f. 187, repr. in *HBQF*, 19).
34. Praetorius, *Syntagma Musicum*, III.153.
35. James Haar, 'Munich at the Time of Orlande de Lassus', in Iain Fenlon, ed., *The Renaissance* (Man & Music series) (London: Macmillan, 1989), 243–62, 251–6.
36. Bär, 'Faict de la main de Raffy Lyonnois', 83.
37. Maggie Lyndon-Jones, 'A Checklist of Woodwind Instruments marked !!', *GSJ* 52 (1999), 243–80.
38. Private communication.

Chapter 3 Consort and solo: the seventeenth century

CONTEMPORARY SOURCES

Aurelio Virgiliano, *Il Dolcimelo, libro terzo* (p1600; Bologna, Civico Museo bibliografico musicale, MS C.33), Archivum musicum 11 (Florence: SPES, 1979)
Michael Praetorius, *Syntagma musicum*, 4 vols, of which only three and a set of plates were published (Wolfenbüttel: Elias Holwein, 1614–19)
   Facsimile (Kassel: Bärenreiter, 1958)
   Vol. 2 (De Organographia): translation ed. Harold Blumenfel (Kassel: Bärenreiter, 1962 and New York, 1986); A better translation of vol. 2, ed. David Z. Crookes (Oxford: Clarendon Press, 1986). I also consulted a critical edition ed. Eduard Bernoulli (Leipzig: C. F. Kahnt Nachfolger, 1916)
Marin Mersenne, *Harmonie universelle* (Paris: Sebastien Cramoisy, 1636)
   Facsimile: ed. François Lesure (Paris: Edition du Centre National de la Recherche Scientifique, 1965)
   Unevenly accurate translation of the Books on Instruments: R. E. Chapman (The Hague: M. Nijhoff, 1957)
Pierre Trichet, *Traité des instruments de musique* (MS, c1638)
   Ed. François Lesure, 'Le traité des instruments de Pierre Trichet', *Annales musicologiques* 3 (1955), 283–7 and 4 (1956), 175–248
   Also ed. François Lesure, *Traité des instruments de musique (vers 1640)* (Neuilly-sur Seine: Société de musique d'autrefois, 1957)

MODERN SOURCES

The history of music and musical life in the seventeenth century makes a fascinating study in which the role of instruments has only recently begun to be appreciated. Among instruments, the winds have taken second place to the strings, whose impact on music has been seen as far greater, while the flute itself has perhaps received the least sustained attention of all this period's winds. Secondary sources for this chapter are therefore rather few.

Once again I have relied heavily on Jane Bowers's 1979 *Recherches* essay. The same author's article, 'New Light on the Development of the Transverse Flute between about 1650 and about 1770', *JAMIS* 3 (1977), 5–56, recognized and attempted to address the need for more information about changes in the construction of flutes in the late seventeenth and early to mid-eighteenth centuries. The article suffered from the difficulty in any iconographical study of distinguishing between the outer appearance of instruments in works of art and their 'design' as musical instruments, and consequently tended to date instruments on the basis of relatively unimportant decorative features such as the length of their end caps. But bearing these shortcomings in mind, it gave a thorough survey, made many important observations, and remains essential reading for serious students.

The Recorder in the Seventeenth Century: Proceedings of the International Recorder Symposium, Utrecht, 1993, ed. David Lasocki (Utrecht: STIMU, 1995) contains several useful essays in which recorder scholars forge ahead with studies of that instrument beyond the comfortable boundaries of French documentation. The volume contains much of relevance to the flute. Two articles on van Eyck's music are Ruth van Baak Griffioen's 'A Field Guide to the Flowers of the Fluyten Lust-hof: Notes on the Familiarity of the Tunes Van Eyck Chose' (159–75), and Thiemo Wind, 'Jacob van Eyck's Der Fluyten Lust-hof: Composition, Improvisation, or…? Consequences for Performance Practice' (177–95). Peter van Heyghen's article, 'The Recorder in Italian Music, 1600–1670' (3–63), thoroughly and intelligently discusses many questions of instrumentation, transposition, and cleffing that are relevant to the transverse flute. Other essays I drew on for the sidebar on this topic are Andrew Parrott, 'Transposition in Monteverdi's Vespers of 1610: An "Aberration" Defended', *EM* 12 (1984), 490–516, and Patrizio Barbieri's more theoretical discussion, '*Chiavette* and Modal Transposition in Italian Practice (*c*1500–1837)', *Ricercare* 3 (1991), 5–79. I am grateful to Boaz Berney for internet postings and patient private communications that helped me to understand more about clefs in flute consort music.

Studies of seventeenth-century flutes, like the instruments themselves, are extremely rare. Trevor Robinson's attempted reconstruction of Mersenne's flute in 'A Reconstruction of Mersenne's Flute', *GSJ* 26 (1973), 84–5, is described in the text. Robinson's very brief article fails to address most of the problems in Mersenne's text, providing a solution that consequently seems tenuous at best. Vincenzo De Gregorio evaluated the Assisi flute in 'Il traversiere di Assisi, con alcune osservazioni sulla prima fase del flauto traverso barrocco', *Il Flauto dolce* 10/11 (Jan–Jun 1984), 48–51, and Filadelfio Puglisi gave a brief notice that included a measured drawing in 'A Three-Piece Flute in Assisi', *GSJ* 37 (1984), 6–9. The Haka flute was first noted in print, with a photograph, by John Solum in *The Early Flute* (Oxford: Clarendon Press, 1992), 36–7.

Few studies have investigated the use of instruments in sixteenth- and seventeenth-century church music, though some of this extensive and interesting repertoire is beginning to be performed and recorded. For coverage of Italian music, Stephen Bonta's 'The use of instruments in sacred music in Italy 1560–1700', *EM* 18 (1990), 519–35, is useful.

On performance matters, Patricia Ranum argued for the importance of precisely following French articulation and phrasing instructions of the seventeenth century in 'Tu-Ru-Tu and Tu-Ru-Tu-Tu: Toward an Understanding of Hotteterre's Tonguing Syllables', in the Utrecht Recorder Symposium volume (217–54), and in 'French Articulations: A Mirror of French Song', *Traverso* 10.3 (July 1998), 1–3. As an example of the over-homogenized method she deplores, Ranum cites Bruce Haynes's 'Tu ru or not Tu ru: Paired Syllables and Unequal Tonguing Patterns on Woodwinds in the Seventeenth and Eighteenth Centuries', *Performance Practice Review* 10 (1997), 41–60.

Modern research on the Hotteterre family and its flute-makers has been published by Jane Bowers, as 'The Hotteterre family of woodwind instrument makers', in Rien de Reede, ed., *Concerning the Flute* (Amsterdam: Broekmans & Van Poppel, 1984), 33–54, and Tula Giannini, 'Jacques Hotteterre and his Father, Martin: A Re-examination based on Recently Found Documents', *EM* 21 (1993), 377–95. My essay 'The Hotteterre Flute: Six Replicas in Search of a Myth', *JAMS* 49 (1996), 225–63 gave details of early biographical studies and later assumptions, and examined the provenance, construction, and authenticity of two original instruments and six nineteenth-century copies. My 'More on the Hotteterre Flute', *Traverso* 10.2 (April 1998), 1–2, described a second authentic Hotteterre flute that came to light after my *JAMS* essay was published.

1. Praetorius, *Syntagma Musicum*, III.137.
2. Rubric to 'Herr Christ der einig Gottes Sohn', *Polyhymnia* XXXIX.
3. Van Heyghen, 'The Recorder in Italian Music'. Lasocki suggests that similar mixed consorts may have appeared in England as early as the 1570s, though the earliest event in which the flute was actually named as a member took place in 1591 ('Professional Recorder Players In England', I, 147–50).
4. Lasocki, 'Professional Recorder Players', II, 661–2.
5. Praetorius, *Syntagma Musicum*, III, iii, 7 (Bernoulli ed., 124).
6. Parrott, 'Transposition in Monteverdi's Vespers', 506.
7. Vincenzo Giustiniani, *Discorso sopra la musica de' suoi tempi*, cited in Verzulli, 'Testimonianze'.
8. Verzulli, 'Testimonianze'.
9. Ibid.
10. Puglisi, 'The Renaissance Flutes of the Biblioteca Capitolare of Verona'.
11. The relevant parts are transcribed and discussed in Bär, 'Faict de la main de Raffy Lyonnois'.
12. Bär, 'Faict de la main de Raffy Lyonnois'.
13. For details of pitch levels, see Bruce Haynes, 'Pitch Standards in the Baroque and Classical periods' (Ph.D. diss., University of Montreal, 1995).
14. Verzulli, 'Testimonianze'.
15. Wind, 'Jacob van Eyck's *Der Fluyten Lust-hof*'.
16. Meylan, *The Flute*, 94–6.
17. Robinson, 'A Reconstruction of Mersenne's Flute', 84–5.
18. Bowers, 'Flaüste traverseinne', 28.
19. Fitzgibbon, *Story*, 77, 78.
20. Bowers, 'Flaüste traverseinne', 28.
21. Marcelle Benoit, *Musique de cour: chapelle, chambre, écurie, 1661–1733* (Paris: A. et J. Picard, 1971).
22. Paul F. Rice, *The Performance Arts at Fontainebleau from Louis XIV to Louis XVI* (Ann Arbor: University Microfilms International, 1989).
23. 'Mémoire de M. de Labarre'. Bowers points out that Labarre's recollection was inaccurate, and that in fact the two flutists took over posts that already existed.
24. Bowers, 'Flaüste traverseinne', 35–6.
25. *Mercure de France*, 1 June 1725, 1081, cited in Bowers, 'Flaüste traverseinne', 38.
26. *Mercure de France*, 11 December 1728, 2896–7, cited in Bowers, 'Flaüste traverseinne', 38.
27. Sébastien de Brossard, *Dictionaire de musique* (1703), cited in Bowers, 'Flaüste traverseinne', 39.
28. John Anderies, 'Vocal Music for the Transverse Flute', *Traverso* 6.3 (July 1994), 1–3.
29. Quoted in Jed Wentz, 'Freedom of Expression: A Right to "Mutilate the Meter"', *Traverso* 12.2 (2000), 1–3.
30. Peter Spohr, *Kunsthandwerk im Dienste der Musik* (Frankfurt: Author, 1991), 13.
31. Vincenzo De Gregorio, 'Il traversiere di Assisi, con alcune osservazioni sulla prima fase

del flauto traverso barrocco', *Il flauto dolce* 10/11 (Jan–Jun 1984), 48–51.

32. Ardal Powell, 'The Hole in the Middle: Transverse Flute Bores in the Late Seventeenth and Early Eighteenth Centuries', paper read at the annual meeting of the American Musical Instrument Society, Elkhart, Indiana, 20 May 1994.
33. Bowers, 'Flaüste traverseinne', 30–3.
34. Bowers, 'Flaüste traverseinne', 47–8.
35. Bowers, 'Flaüste traverseinne', 45.
36. Marco Brolli, 'Il flauto traverso basso nel XVIII secolo', *Syrinx* 41 (July–September 1999), 30–5, 33.
37. Ernst Kubitschek, 'Die Querflöte als Soloinstrument in Deutschland', *HBQF*, 209–14, 210; see also Johann Sigismund Kusser, ed. Helmuth Osthoff, *Arien, Duette und Chöre aus Erindo oder Die unsträfliche Liebe*, Das Erbe deutscher Musik, Zweite Reihe: Landschaftsdenkmäle der Musik Schleswig-Holstein und Hansestädte, Band 3 (Braunschweig: Henry Litolff's Verlag, 1938), 20–1.
38. Bowers, 'Flaüste traverseinne', 40; see also Julie Anne Sadie, 'Charpentier and the early French ensemble sonata', *EM* 7 (1979), 330–5.
39. Bowers, 'Flaüste traverseinne', 40.
40. Bowers, 'Flaüste traverseinne', 43.
41. Anthony Baines, 'James Talbot's Manuscript [Christ Church Library Music MS 1187]. 1. Wind Instruments', *GSJ* 1 (1948), 9–26.
42. Constant Victor Désiré Pierre, *Les Facteurs d'Instruments de Musique, les Luthiers et la Facture Instrumentale* (Paris: E. Sagot, 1893), 72–4.
43. Giannini, 'Jacques Hotteterre and his Father, Martin', 380.
44. Powell, 'The Hotteterre Flute'.

THE HOTTETERRE FLUTE
1. Stephen Jay Gould, 'The Creation Myths of Cooperstown', in Joyce Carol Oates and Robert Atwan, eds, *The Best American Essays of the Century* (Boston and New York: Houghton Mifflin, 2000), 520–31, 522. First published in *Natural History*, 1989.
2. I examined the 'fascinating accumulation of inference and rumour' surrounding the Hotteterre flute in 'The Hotteterre Flute'.
3. Compare the first and second editions of Nancy Toff, *Flute Book*, 43–4. See also Solum, *The Early Flute*, p. 36 n. 5.
4. Bruce Haynes, 'Lully and the Rise of the Oboe as seen in Works of Art', *EM* 16 (1988), 324–38.
5. Rebecca Harris-Warrick, 'A Few Thoughts on Lully's *Hautbois*', *EM* 18 (1990), 97–106.
6. 'Mémoire de M. de Labarre', 244; my emphasis.

Chapter 4 The early eighteenth century: the 'baroque' flute's golden age

Again this chapter relies heavily on the work of Jane Bowers, this time in her dissertation already noted. Bowers later presented two most useful articles that expanded on some of that material: 'A Catalogue of French Works for the Transverse Flute, 1692–1761', *Recherches* 28 (1978), 89–125 (errata in *Recherches* 29, 50), and the iconographical study already mentioned, 'New Light on the Development of the Transverse Flute'. John Huskinson, '"Les Ordinaires de la Musique du Roi": Michel de Labarre, Marin Marais et les Hotteterre d'après un tableau du début du XVIIIe seiècle', *Recherches* 17 (1977), 15–30, written, despite its title, in English, discusses the dating of the famous painting in ill. 21, the identity of the musicians, and the possible function of two extra holes in the ivory flute in the foreground, which disappeared once the picture was cleaned. The most frequently-quoted testimony on the flute's transformation in France, 'Mémoire de M. de Labarre: Sur les musettes et hautbois &c.', appeared in J.-G. Prod'homme, ed., *Ecrits de musiciens* (Paris: Mercure de France, 1912), 244–5.

Its date of *c*1730 was estimated by Marcelle Benoît in *Versailles et les musiciens du roi, 1661–1733: Étude institutionnelle et sociale* (Paris: Paris, A. et J. Picard, 1971), 223.

Though the flute's repertoire is not our primary focus, it is especially important to understand the nature of music written for the flute during times of major change in instrument design and performance practice. The flute music of Bach and Handel has received plenty of attention for a century or more, and Telemann and Quantz have more recently come under scrutiny, but the flute music of their less famous contemporaries in Germany, Italy, France, and England has been little studied. Marcello Castellani, a recorder and baroque flute professor at the Verona Conservatory, is general editor of two series of facsimiles (1978–) of seventeenth- and eighteenth-century transverse flute works for SPES of Florence that have recently provided the means to change this imbalance. These valuable publications have made available not only the famous early French baroque works but also dozens of less famous but no less important German and Italian publications and manuscripts, including Mattheson's *Der brauchbare Virtuoso,* Blochwitz's *Sechzig Arien,* and all the surviving manuscripts of Bach's B minor sonata. An interview with Castellani in *Tibia* 14 (1989), 512–18 and a brief article in *Traverso* 11.3 (July 1999), 9–12, contain further details of the publication series.

Castellani wrote his article 'L'art de "transposer" sur la flûte traversière. La pratica della trasposizione secondo Jacques Hotteterre', *Il Flauto Dolce* 17 (April 1987), 26–31, in response to Christopher Addington's error-filled theories on flute pitch and transposition in 'In Search of the Baroque Flute', *EM* 12 (1984), 34–47, in a letter to the editor of that journal in vol. 13 (1985), 331–5, and in 'The Bach Flute', *Musical Quarterly* 71 (1985), 264–80. Addington's *bas dessus* theory proposed the far-fetched notion that all of Bach's flute chamber music was intended for the *flûte d'amour* pitched a major or a minor third below the ordinary flute, and that every flutist of Bach's time would have recognized this at a glance. Peter Riedemeister wrote a scathing dismissal of Addington's scholarship in '"Neueste Forschungen" auf dem Holzweg: Die "Bachflöte"', *Tibia* 11 (1986), 200–3, but serious students of the flute and of Bach's works have for the most part ignored Addington's writings.

Bach's flute sonatas have inspired a thicket of writing. Philipp Spitta's early work on Bach, published in an English translation by Clara Bell and J. A. Fuller Maitland in 1899, gave rise to the long unchallenged myth that Bach had composed all his chamber music during his happy time at Cöthen before he moved to Leipzig as *Thomaskantor* in 1724. Robert L. Marshall called the myth into question in a wide-ranging survey of Bach's flute works in 'The Compositions for Solo Flute: A Reconsideration of their Authenticity and Chronology', in *The Music of Johann Sebastian Bach: The Sources, the Style, the Significance* (New York: Schirmer Books, 1989), 201–25 (a revised version of 'J. S. Bach's Compositions for Solo Flute: A Reconsideration of their Authenticity and Chronology', *JAMS* 32 (1979), 463–98). Marshall characterized his own ideas as 'frankly, quite speculative', and Hans Eppstein in particular raised objections to Marshall's claims for the authenticity of the E♭ and C major sonatas in 'Zur Problematik von Johann Sebastian Bachs Flötensonaten', *Bach-Jahrbuch* 67 (1981), 77–90. On the other hand Christoph Wolff largely followed Marshall in 'Bach's Leipzig Chamber Music', *EM* 13 (1985), 166–7. Michael Marissen wrote 'A Critical Reappraisal of J. S. Bach's A-Major Flute Sonata', in *The Journal of Musicology* 6 (1988), 367–86. Marcello Castellani investigated the Solo BWV 1013 in 'Il *Solo pour la flûte traversière* di J. S. Bach: Cöthen o Lipsia?', *Il Flauto Dolce* 13 (October 1985), 15–21, and in German as 'J. S. Bachs "Solo pour la flûte traversière": Köthen oder Leipzig', *Tibia* 14 (1989), 567–73. Ralph Leavis made a brief remark on the copyist's handwriting in a letter to the editor in *Tibia* 17 (1990), 254–5, and Yoshitake Kobayashi weighed in with a fuller discussion of this point in 'Noch einmal zu J. S. Bachs "Solo pour la flûte traversière" BWV 1013', *Tibia* 16 (1991), 379–82. Ten years later I co-wrote a thumbnail sketch of the flutists and flute music in Bach's circle, together with a listing of instrument-makers who made flutes that survive, in Ardal Powell with David Lasocki, 'Bach and the Flute: The Players, the Instruments, the Music', *EM* 23 (1995), 9–29. In the same issue Jeanne Swack presented her study , 'Quantz and the Sonata in E♭ major for flute and cembalo', 31–53. Mary Oleskiewicz has expanded on the links between Quantz and late works by Bach in writings cited in the bibliography for chapter 5.

David Lasocki liberated Handel's flute sonatas from an accretion of error and misinterpretation in 'Händels Sonaten für Holzbläser in neuem Licht', *Tibia* 5 (1980), 166–76, and in English as 'New Light on Handel's Woodwind Sonatas', *The American Recorder* 21 (1981), 163–70 . However, Alison Patricia Deadman seems to have been unaware of Lasocki's work on Handel and his biographical studies in her dissertation, '"Augeletti che cantate": Handel, his woodwind players, and his London operas' (Ph.D. diss., UCLA, 1998), though the dissertation is useful for new material on the flutists Dahuron and Weidemann.

Two recent dissertations have enlarged our understanding of Telemann's instrumental compositions, publishing business, and musical connections: Jeanne Roberta Swack, 'The Solo Sonatas of George Philipp Telemann: A Study of the Sources and Musical Style' (Ph.D. diss., Yale University, 1988) and Steven David Zohn, 'The Ensemble Sonatas of George Philipp Telemann: Studies in Style, Genre, and Chronology' (Ph.D. diss., Cornell University, 1995). Sources on Dresden, Quantz, and Italian opera are listed in the bibliography for chapter 5.

Gregory Paul Dikmans, 'The Performance Practice of Early Eighteenth-Century French Flute Music: A Critical Translation of Jacques Hotteterre's "Principes de la flûte traversière", Commentary and Recording of Selected Works' (M.A. thesis, La Trobe University [Victoria, Australia], 1991), relates the writings, compositions, and instruments of a single flutist-composer to one another, providing an example for possible further studies of flutist-composers and their instruments.

In the meantime, modern performers commonly draw together information from many sources, historical or otherwise, to devise a style for the type of instrument they happen to play, whether it is a modern flute or an earlier type. The case has recently been made that these modern vernacular styles have adopted non-historical conventions or ignored important stylistic signposts. Besides Patricia M. Ranum's work on French declamation (chapter 3), Jed Wentz focused on tempo in Bach in 'Bach: Quick Tempi and Passionate Expression', *Traverso* 5.3 (July 1993), 1–3, and on rubato in French music in 'Freedom of Expression: a Right to Mutilate the Meter', *Traverso* 12.2 (April 2000), 5–7. Contributions on rhythmic inequality by Claire Fontijn and John Byrt appear in the bibliography for chapter 5.

Study of the early eighteenth-century flute has still not managed to overcome the incorrect impression earlier histories left that nothing changed between the supposed invention of the baroque flute and the addition of keys in the late eighteenth century. The first chapter of Nancy Toff's *The Development of the Modern Flute* is a case in point, and should be read only with the greatest caution. On the positive side, recent work on the period's flute makers includes articles by Marcelle Benoît, Jan Bouterse, Maurice Byrne, Norbert Dufourcq, Herbert Heyde, Phillip T. Young and others, mostly in specialist periodicals such as *GSJ*, *Recherches*, *JAMIS* and *FoMRHIQ*, and too numerous to list individually here. Johann Gabriel Doppelmayr's biographical note on Jacob Denner (1681–1735) is described in Martin Kirnbauer and Peter Thalheimer, 'Jacob Denner and the development of the flute in Germany', *EM* 23 (1995), 83–100, which also discusses three Denner flutes that came to light in the 1980s. Peter Thalheimer presented a survey of lower-voiced flutes in 'Flauto d'amore, B flat Tenor Flute und "tiefe Quartflöte"', *Tibia* 8 (1983), 334–42, while Marco Brolli has studied low flutes extensively for his thesis, 'I flauti traversi gravi tra il XVI ed il primo XIX secolo: storia, morfologia e repertorio' (Tesi di diploma, University of Pavia, 1996–7). Three of his articles draw on this work: on the bass flute in 'Il flauto traverso basso nel XVIII secolo', *Syrinx* 41 (July–September 1999), 30–5, on the *flûte d'amour* in 'Il flauto traverso d'amore nel XVIII secolo', *Syrinx* 43 (January–March 2000), 26–9, and on the 'bass' flute in 'La "traversa bassa": Parliamo ancora dei flauti gravi nel XVIII secolo: la "traversa bassa" e il flauto traverso contralto', *Syrinx* 44 (April–June 2000), 18–21.

1. Lasocki, 'Professional Recorder Players', II, 900, n. 164, and 'A New Look at the Life of John Loeillet (1680–1730)', de Reede, *Concerning the Flute*, 65–73, 66.
2. Lasocki, 'Professional Recorder Players', I, 318–24.
3. Baines, 'James Talbot's Manuscript'.

4. Tula Giannini, *Great Flute Makers of France: The Lot and Godfroy Families, 1650–1900* (London: Tony Bingham, 1993), 45–6.

5. Lasocki, 'Professional Recorder Players', I, 361; II, 870–1.

6. Lasocki, 'Professional Recorder Players', I, 434–5.

7. Pierre Louis d'Aquin de Chateau-Lyon, *Lettres sur les hommes célèbres dans les sciences la littérature et les beaux-arts sous le règne de Louis XV* (Amsterdam: Duchesne, 1752), quoted in Bowers, 'French Flute School', 40.

8. See Ranum, 'Tu-Ru-Tu and Tu-Ru-Tu-Tu'.

9. Eberhard Preußner, *Die musikalischen Reisen des Hern von Uffenbach* (Kassel: Bärenreiter, 1949), 128 (my trans.)

10. Bowers, 'Catalogue of French Works', 103.

11. Giannini, 'Jacques Hotteterre and his Father, Martin', 390.

12. Giannini, 'Jacques Hotteterre and his Father, Martin', 383, 395.

13. Powell, 'More on the Hotteterre Flute'.

14. Bowers, 'French Flute School', 13–14.

15. A chronology of the Naust workshop and an identification of the various makers and associations under which the stamp was used can be found in Giannini, *Great Flute Makers*, 12 and chapter 1, *passim*.

16. Bruce Haynes, 'Pitch Standards in the Baroque and Classical Periods' (Ph.D. diss., University of Montreal, 1995), 104–28.

17. Quantz, *Essay*, XVII. vii. 6–7.

18. Hotteterre, *Principes de la Flûte Traversière* (Paris: Christophe Ballard, 1707), unnumbered page in the Preface.

19. Joachim Christoph Nemeitz, *Séjoir a Paris, c'est-à-dire, instructions fidéles, pour les voyageurs de condition* (Leiden: J. van Abcoude, 1727), 49, first published in German in 1718, cited in Bowers, *French Flute School*.

20. Julie Anne Sadie, 'Paris and its Environs', *Companion to Baroque Music*, Julie Anne Sadie, ed. (New York: Schirmer Books, 1990), 99.

21. See Leta E. Miller, 'C. P. E. Bach and Friedrich Ludwig Dülon', *EM* 23 (1995), 65–80, p. 78 n. 15.

22. Jacques Hotteterre, *L'Art de Preluder sur la Flûte Traversière, sur la Flûte-a-bec, sur le Hautbois, et autres Instrumens de Deßus* (Paris: Author, 1719), 51.

23. Swack, 'The Solo Sonatas of George Philipp Telemann', 20.

24. Lasocki, ' Professional Recorder Players', I, p. 499 n. 44.

25. Marcello Castellani, preface to facsimile reprint, Monumenta Musicae Revocata 22 (Florence: SPES, 1997).

26. Giuliano Furlanetto, preface to the facsimile reprint, Monumenta Musicae Revocata 23 (Florence: SPES 1998).

27. Brussels Conservatoire MS Litt. XY 15.115. A facsimile of the MS appeared as *Manuscrit Allemand du XVIIe Siècle, Thesaurus Musicus, Nova Series* (Brussels: Editions Culture et Civilisation, 1979).

28. Marshall, 'The Compositions for Solo Flute', 212.

29. Castellani, 'Il Solo pour la flûte traversière di J. S. Bach'.

30. Swack, 'The Solo Sonatas of George Philipp Telemann', 54.

31. Lasocki, 'New Light on Handel's Woodwind Sonatas', 168.

32. Lasocki, ' Professional Recorder Players', I, 464–5, and table 7, p. 467.

33. Deadman, 'Augeletti che cantate', 40–58.

34. Mary Oleskiewicz, 'Quantz and the Flute at Dresden: His Instruments, his Repertory[,] and their Significance for the Versuch and the Bach Circle' (Ph.D. diss., Duke University, 1998), 345.

35. Ernst Kubitschek, 'Der italienische Stil', *HBQF*, 206–9, 206.

36. Giannini, *Great Flute Makers*, 9.

37. Johann Joachim Quantz, *Versuch einer Anweisung die Flöte traversiere zu spielen* (Berlin: Johann

Friedrich Voss, 1752), trans. and ed. Edward R. Reilly, *On Playing the Flute* (London: Faber, 1966, and 2nd ed., New York: Schirmer Books, 1985), I. 9.

38. Stiftung Kunst und Kultur des Landes Nordrhein-Westfalen; see Konrad Hünteler, 'Ein neuentdeckte Traversflöte von Jacob Denner', *Tibia* 18 (1993), 461–4.

39. Martin Kirnbauer and Peter Thalheimer, 'Jacob Denner and the Development of the Flute in Germany', *EM* 23 (February 1995), 82–100, 96.

40. D-Halle: Händelhaus MS-577. See Oleskiewicz, 'Quantz and the Flute at Dresden', 80.

41. Quantz, *Versuch*, 1.17, Reilly's trans. (p. 34) modified.

42. [Michel Corrette], *Methode Pour apprendre aisèment à joüer de la Flute Traversiere* (Paris: Boivin, c1740), 11.

43. Maurice Byrne, 'Pierre Jaillard, Peter Bressan', *GSJ* 36 (March 1983), 2–28, 13.

44. Friedrich von Huene, 'A *flûte allemande* in C and D by Jacob Denner of Nuremberg, *EM* 23 (1995), 102–12.

45. Johann George Tromlitz, 'Neuerfundene Vortheile zur bessern Einrichtung der Flöte', in Johann Georg Meusel, ed., *Miscellaneen artistischen Inhaltes* 26 (1785), 104–9.

46. David Lasocki, 'Betty and David', David Lasocki, ed., *Fluting and Dancing: Articles and Reminiscences for Betty Bang Mather on her 65th Birthday* (New York: McGinnis & Marx, 1992), 173–6; Frans Vester, *Flute Music of the Eighteenth Century* (Monteux: Musica Rara, 1985), entries C292 and Q632.

47. SBB Mus. Ms. Bach P 1008.

48. Bowers, 'French Flute School', 59.

49. D'Aquin, *Lettres*, cited in Bowers, 'French Flute School', 65.

50. Ancelet, *Observations sur la musique, les musiciens, et les instruments* (Amsterdam: Aux dépens de la compagnie, 1757), 28, cited in Bowers, 'French Flute School', 414.

51. Louis Vaissier, 'Michel Blavet, 1700–1768: Essai de biographie', *Recherches* 22 (1984), 131–59, 144.

52. Zohn, 'The Ensemble Sonatas of George Philipp Telemann', 37.

53. Bowers, 'French Flute School', 76.

54. Bowers, 'French Flute School', 83.

55. Bowers, 'French Flute School', 172.

56. Oleskiewicz, 'Quantz and the Flute at Dresden', 227.

57. Bowers, 'French Flute School', 173–4.

58. Bowers, 'French Flute School', 50.

59. Gerhard Braun, 'Arrangé pour deux flûtes. Opernbearbeitungen für Flöteninstrumente', *Tibia* 12 (1987), 566–72.

60. Achim Hofer, 'Von der Militärmusik zur Kunstmusik: Die Flöte in Bläserformationen vom 16. Jahrhundert bis heute', *HBQF*, 265–71, 267.

61. Swack, 'The Solo Sonatas of George Philipp Telemann', 80.

62. Bowers, 'French Flute School', 63.

63. Horst Augsbach, *Johann Joachim Quantz: Thematisches Verzeichnis der musikalischen Werke, Werkgruppen QV 2 und QV 3* (Dresden: Sächsische Landesbibliothek, 1984), QV 2: Anh.3.

64. Phillip T. Young, 'The Scherers of Butzbach', *GSJ* 39 (1986), 112–24.

TUNING SYSTEMS

An introduction to playing pure intervals can be found in a brief article by Catherine Folkers, 'Playing in Tune on a Baroque Flute', *Traverso* 10.1 (January 1998), 1–3, available at www.flutehistory.com. For an idea of the wide range of opinion found in contemporary sources, see Bruce Haynes, 'Beyond Temperament: Non-keyboard Intonation in the Seventeenth and Eighteenth Centuries', *EM* 19 (1991), 357–81. The article by Douglas Leedy (with Bruce Haynes) in *NGD2*, s.v. 'Intonation', gives a good survey of the whole topic.

1. Alexander J. Ellis, trans. and ed., *On the Sensations of Tone [by Hermann L.F. Helmholtz]* (London: Longmans & Co., 1885, R/New York, 1954), 319.

2. Georg Philipp Telemann, 'Letzte Beschäftigung G. Ph. Telemanns in 86. Lebensjahre,

bestehend aus einer musikalischen Klang- und Intervallen Tafel', *Unterhaltungen* 3 (Hamburg, 1767), quoted in W. Rackwitz, ed., *Georg Philipp Telemann: Singen ist das Fundament zur Musik in allen Dingen* (Wilhelmshaven: Heinrichshofen, *c*1981), 266–73, and Haynes, 'Beyond Temperament', 379.

Chapter 5 Quantz and the operatic style

The published version of Edward R. Reilly's mighty translation and study of Quantz's *Essay*, Johann Joachim Quantz, *On Playing the Flute* (London: Faber, 1966, and 2nd ed., New York: Schirmer Books, 1985), begins with a lucid and helpful 37-page Introduction setting the events of Quantz's career and his ideas on performance against the background of the period's musical life, illuminating both the man and his world. Reilly's Introduction, as well as Quantz's own, 'On the Qualities Required of Those Who Would Dedicate Themselves to Music', make essential reading for anyone interested in understanding the author's advice on performing – though these parts of both books are neglected today in the search for precise 'how-to' instructions. Reilly's translation was originally part of his doctoral dissertation, 'Quantz's Versuch einer Anweisung die Flöte Traversiere zu spielen: A Translation and Study' (2 vols, Ph.D. diss., University of Michigan, 1958), which he followed with *Quantz and his Versuch: Three Studies* (New York: American Musicological Society, 1971). *Early Music* 25 (1997) contained another valuable contribution by Reilly, 'Quantz and the transverse flute: Some Aspects of his Practice and Thought Regarding the Instrument' (428–38), together with Steven Zohn's 'New Light on Quantz's Advocacy of Telemann's Music' (441–61).

Mary Oleskiewicz, a professor at the University of Massachusetts, has recently published work on Quantz that contributes a great deal to our understanding of his compositions, performance, and instruments. Her article, 'The Flutes of Quantz: Their Construction and Performing Practice', *GSJ* 52 (2000), 201–20, argues that anyone wishing to make sense of Quantz's flutes must pay much more scrupulous attention to his instructions for performance than these have hitherto received, and vice versa.

Apart from a lack of experience with Quantz flutes, the chief difficulty in interpreting Quantz's *Essay* today is perhaps our unfamiliarity with early eighteenth-century Italian vocal style. Operas are expensive to produce, and only a few good recordings have been made (one example: Hasse's *Cleofide*, in a 1987 recording with Cappella Coloniensis under William Christie, 4-CD set, Capriccio 10 193/96). Thus modern readers who have never heard operas by Handel and his less famous contemporaries open the *Essay* seeking instructions for playing small-scale instrumental music, especially that of Bach, that sometimes seems like a byway in this unfamiliar sound-world. Oleskiewicz's dissertation 'Quantz and the Flute at Dresden: His Instruments, his Repertory[,] and their Significance for the Versuch and the Bach Circle' (Ph.D. diss., Duke University, 1998) makes many specific observations which show that the musical environment of Quantz's formative years in Dresden strongly influenced his flute-playing and composition, as well as that of Berlin, where it contributed traits to the works of C. P. E. Bach often thought to have originated with him and the ideal of *Empfindsamkeit*. The same author's article, 'The Trio Sonate in Bach's Musical Offering: A Salute to Frederick's Tastes and Quantz's Flutes?' in *Bach Perspectives, vol. 4: The Music of J. S. Bach, Analysis and Interpretation* (Lincoln: University of Nebraska Press, 1999), 79–110, uses the flute pieces Bach composed for Potsdam to drive home the point that here as in so many other cases, understanding instruments and performance conditions is an essential step in making sense of the music. Jean-Christophe Frisch pointed out some of the more general features of the Italian vocal style and the associated full and vigorous manner of continuo accompaniment in 'The Italian Genius', *Traverso* 5.1 (January 1993), 1–3.

For reasons summarized in the text, Quantz's own music has been unjustly neglected, and somehow only the least interesting pieces have been published. That began to change when a facsimile edition of twenty sonatas from a Berlin manuscript appeared: *XX Sonate a flauto traversiere solo e cembalo*, Monumenta Musicae Revocata 21 (Florence: SPES, 1997). The new catalogues of Quantz's works are by Horst Augsbach, *Johann Joachim Quantz: Thematisches Verzeichnis der musikalischen Werke, Werkgruppen QV 2 und QV3* (Dresden: Sächsische Landesbibliothek, 1984) and *Johann Joachim Quantz: Thematisch-systematisches Werkverzeichnis (QV)* (Stuttgart: Carus-Verlag, 1997). The Quantz *Solfeggi* have been published in modern notation in an edition by Winfried Michel and Hermien Teske as *Solfeggi Pour la Flute Traversiere* (Winterthur: Amadeus, 1978) and the Caprices in Horst Augsbach's edition as *Capricen, Fantasien und Anfangsstücke* (Winterthur: Amadeus, 1980). Several studies have discussed the dating and contents of the *Solfeggi*, including Claire Fontijn, 'Quantz's unegal: Implications for the Performance of Eighteenth-century Music', *EM* 23 (1995), 55–62; and John Byrt, 'Quantz's Solfeggi: A Unique Document', *Leading Notes: Journal of the National Early Music Association* 16 (Autumn 1998), 6–15.

Details about how musicians of Quantz's time learned their trade and made their living can be found in Salmen, *The Social Status of the Professional Musician*. Quantz's autobiography is a unique personal account of the education and employment of one of the first flute specialists in Germany. It was published as 'Herrn Johann Joachim Quantzens Lebenslauf, von ihm selbst entworfen', in F. W. Marpurg's *Historisch-kritisch Beyträge zur Aufnahme der Musik I* (1755), 197–250 (R/1972 by Buren: Frits Knuf). An English translation appeared in Paul Nettl, *Forgotten Musicians* (New York: Philosophical Library, 1951). Quantz's reply to Moldenit, 'Hrn. Johann Joachim Quantzens Antwort auf des Herrn von Moldenit' in *Historisch-kritisch Beyträge zur Aufnahme der Musik* 4 (1759), 153–91, translated in Reilly's dissertation of 1958, contains interesting details and is worth reading even only for its comical side.

Vaucanson's mechanical flute-player is described in *Le Mécanisme du fluteur automate* (Paris: Jacques Guerin, 1738), trans. as 'Beschreibung des mechanischen Flötenspielers', *Hamburgisches Magazin* (Hamburg: G. C. Grund), 2 (1747), 1–24. An English translation, *An Account of the Mechanism of an Automaton or Image Playing on the German Flute* (London: T. Parker, 1742), has been reprinted together with the French text with an introduction and notes by David Lasocki (Buren: Frits Knuf, 1979). The English text alone appears in David M. MacMillan, 'Delightful Machines', www.database.com/~lemur/dm-vaucanson-flute-english.html.

Nikolaus Delius's article 'Quantz' Schüler', *Tibia* 7 (1982), 176–84, describes a 'family' tree of Quantz's pupil-descendants stretching over some 200 years. Based on an unpublished manuscript of 1941 by Georg Müller, the study shows how the flute virtuosi of the Berlin Staatskapelle were recruited from this school.

1. Nicolai's *Anekdoten*, quoted in Oleskiewicz, 'Quantz and the Flute at Dresden', 93–4.
2. Reilly, 'Quantz and the Transverse Flute', 429.
3. For information about town musicians see Heinrich W. Schwab, 'The Social Status of the Town Musician', in Salmen, *The Social Status*.
4. Schwab, 'Social Status', 50.
5. Oleskiewicz, 'Quantz and the Flute at Dresden', 49.
6. Oleskiewicz, 'Quantz and the Flute at Dresden', 337.
7. Oleskiewicz, 'Quantz and the Flute at Dresden', 341 and music example 4.10, p. 342.
8. Oleskiewicz, 'Quantz and the Flute at Dresden', 287.
9. Oleskiewicz, 'Quantz and the Flute at Dresden', 331.
10. Oleskiewicz, 'Quantz and the Flute at Dresden', 332.
11. Haynes, 'Pitch Standards', 88. See also Haynes's entry in *NGD2*, s.v. 'Pitch', §1, 2(i).
12. Oleskiewicz, 'Quantz and the Flute at Dresden', 333–4.
13. Oleskiewicz, 'Quantz and the Flute at Dresden', 162, n.11
14. Mus. ms. 18020. Facsimile cited in rubric above.
15. Oleskiewicz, 'Quantz and the Flute at Dresden', p. 204 and n. 56.
16. Cosimo Rossi-Melocchi, 'Memorie antiche' (Fondo Rossi Cassigoli, MSS 192–3), quoted in English in Jean Grundy Fanelli, 'The Manfredini Family of Musicians of Pistoia, 1684–1803', *Studi musicali* 26.1 (1997), 187–232, 197.

17. Oleskiewicz, 'Quantz and the Flute at Dresden', 294.
18. Oleskiewicz, 'Quantz and the Flute at Dresden', 333.
19. Oleskiewicz, 'Quantz and the Flute at Dresden', 325.
20. Oleskiewicz, 'Quantz and the Flute at Dresden', 347–52.
21. Oleskiewicz, 'Quantz and the Flute at Dresden', 235.
22. Nicolai, *Anekdoten* vi.71, quoted in Reilly, 'Quantz and the Transverse Flute'.
23. Giannini, *Great Flute Makers,* 10.
24. Antoine Mahaut, *Nouvelle Méthode pour Aprendre en peu de tems a Joüer de la Flute Traversiere/Nieuwe Manier om binnen korte tyd op de Dwarsfluit te leeren speelen* (Paris: Lachevardiere [1759], and Amsterdam: Hummel [1759]), 2–3.
25. Mahaut, *Nieuwe Manier,* 1.
26. *Versuch* I.14, Reilly's trans. modified.
27. Oleskiewicz, 'Quantz and the Flute at Dresden', 140. Oleskiewicz gives consistently lower pitches than other researchers because she believes Quantz meant the tuning slide to be extended 6–7mm and the embouchure to be turned inward and covered more than is common today, both of which actions cause the flute to sound at a lower pitch. Her highest pitch is A=410–12 with middle joint ♯5, and her lowest A=385–7.
28. Quantz, *Versuch,* XVII.vii.7.
29. Quantz, *Versuch,* IV.3, Reilly's trans. modified. For details of voice types, see Oleskiewicz, 'Quantz and the Flute at Dresden', 127–8.
30. F. D. Castillon, article on the flute in the Supplement (1777) to Diderot and D'Alembert's *Encyclopédie*, quoted in Eric Halfpenny, 'A French Commentary on Quantz', *Music & Letters* 37 (1956), 61–6, and in Reilly, 'Quantz's Versuch', II, 719.
31. Quantz, *Versuch,* IV.25, Reilly's trans. modified.
32. 'Mr Johann Joachim Quantz's Reply to Mr v Moldenit's so-called Published Missive', Berlin, 30 November 1758, trans. in Reilly, 'Quantz's Versuch', II, Appendix IV.
33. Louis Vaissier, 'Michel Blavet, 1700–1768: Essai de biographie', *Recherches* 22 (1984), 131–59, 138.
34. Richard Petzoldt, 'The Economic Conditions of the 18th-Century Musician', in Salmen, *The Social Status,* 170–1.
35. Oleskiewicz, 'Quantz and the Flute at Dresden', 215.
36. Oleskiewicz, 'Quantz and the Flute at Dresden', 425.
37. Oleskiewicz, 'Quantz and the Flute at Dresden'; see also her 'The Trio Sonate in Bach's Musical Offering'.
38. John Solum, 'J. S. Bach's Trio Sonata from *The Musical Offering*: A Study in Trills?', in Lasocki, *Fluting and Dancing,* 29–31.
39. Oleskiewicz, 'Quantz and the Flute at Dresden', 438.
40. Frisch, 'The Italian Genius'; Wentz, 'Bach: Quick Tempi and Passionate Expression'; Reilly, 'Quantz's Versuch', II, 838.
41. 'Mr Johann Joachim Quantz's Reply', 841.
42. 'Mr Johann Joachim Quantz's Reply', 836–8.
43. 'Mr Johann Joachim Quantz's Reply', 849.
44. Quantz, *Sei duetti a due flauti traversi,* op. 2 (Berlin: Winter, 1759).
45. Horst Augsbach, ed., *Capricen, Fantasien und Anfangsstücke* (Winterthur: Amadeus, 1980). On the differing uses of the 'beginner's piece' and the difficult 'study piece', see Quantz, *Essay,* X.5 and 10.
46. Delius, 'Quantz' Schüler', 176.
47. Delius, 'Quantz' Schüler', 178.
48. Hermann Mendel, *Musikalisches Conversationslexicon* (Berlin, 1870), cited in Delius, 'Quantz' Schüler'.
49. Friedrich Wilhelm Dülon, *Dülons des blinden Flötenspielers Leben und Meynungen, von ihm selbst bearbeitet,* 2 vols (Zurich: C. M. Wieland, 1808), cited in Delius, 'Quantz' Schüler', 179.
50. Reilly, 'Quantz and the Transverse Flute', 435.

51. Dülon, *Leben und Meyningen*, I, 183.

52. Fitzgibbon, *Story*, 222.

53. Reilly, 'Quantz and the Transverse Flute', 430.

54. Johann Samuel Petri, *Anleitung zur praktischen Musik* (Leipzig: Johann Gottlob Immanuel Breitkopf, 1782); Johann George Tromlitz, *Ausführlicher und gründlicher Unterricht die Flöte zu spielen* (Leipzig: Adam Friedrich Böhme, 1791), trans. as *VFP*.

55. Mary Oleskiewicz, 'A Museum, a World War, and a Rediscovery: Flutes by Quantz and Others from the Hohenzollern Museum', *JAMIS* 24 (1998), 107–45, 113.

56. *Daily Telegraph*, 21 February 1931 (DCM).

Chapter 6 The Classical flute

Two recent books on musical life in eighteenth-century London give a colourful picture of the social and commercial background of music-making in a time and place in which so many of our modern forms came into being. They are William Weber's *The Rise of Musical Classics in Eighteenth-Century England* (Oxford: Clarendon Press, 1992) and Simon McVeigh's *Concert Life in London from Mozart to Haydn* (Cambridge: Cambridge University Press, 1993).

Much of the material on the construction, purpose, and use of the classical flute is taken from my own study in *The Keyed Flute by Johann George Tromlitz* (Oxford: Clarendon Press, 1996), the principal text of which is a translation of Tromlitz's *Über die Flöten mit mehrern Klappen* (Leipzig: Adam Friedrich Böhme, 1800). Its other apparatus discusses in detail the printed sources and the instruments of the period, tracing the rise of the bravura playing style, and the emergence of keyed flutes in England and their transmission to Germany. To avoid unnecessarily dense notes here I have suppressed references to original documents quoted in *The Keyed Flute* and given only page references to those quotations. I gave a briefer summary of some of the material on Tromlitz's flute-making and the early history of the keyed flute in 'The Tromlitz Flute', *JAMIS* 22 (1996), 89–109. Other work on instruments includes Amy Shaw Kreitzer, 'Transverse Flutes by London Makers, 1750–1900, in the Collections of the Shrine to Music Museum' (M.M. diss., University of South Dakota, 1993), and my own article 'A Fake Grenser Flute by J. G. Otto, Dated 1798', *Traverso* 9.1 (January 1997), 1–3, as well as other short articles in the same newsletter on the flutes of the Rottenburgh, Grenser, and Schuchart workshops. In his chapter 'The Classical Flute' in *The Early Flute*, John Solum focuses on the instrument's mechanical development.

The more musically important subject of changing tone received attention from Marcello Castellani in '"Über den schönen Ton auf der Flöte". Il bel suono del flauto traverso secondo Johann George Tromlitz', *Recercare* 2 (1990), 95–119, and in a shorter English version as 'Tone Quality on the Transverse Flute in the Writings of Johann George Tromlitz', *Traverso* 5.2 (April 1993), 1–2. Catherine Smith's 'Changing Use of the Flute and its Changing Construction, 1774–1795', *American Recorder* 20 (1979), 4–8, examines the tessitura and tonality of flute parts in a selection of classical symphonies, and Janet S. Becker's 'The Eighteenth[-]century Flute Concerto: A Study and Edition of Two Manuscripts from the Fürst Thurn und Taxis Hofbibliothek Regensburg with Reference to Contemporary Treatises' (D.M. diss., Northwestern University, 1993) presents two concertos, by Mahaut and Tromlitz, in the light of their composers' performance instructions and with a discussion of the flute-playing at the court. The dissertation also contains interesting details of the flute pieces in the court library.

Nikolaus Delius has done pioneering work on the Florentine court and its leading flutist, Niccolò Dôthel. His article 'Note sulla tecnica e la musica flautistica nel '700 in Italia', *SIFTS* 3.1 (April 1998), 6–14, gives an overview of the topic, and his 'Die Flötenkonzerte von Pietro Nardini', in de Reede, *Concerning the Flute*, 75–9, considers some concertos written for Dôthel. Among the most interesting publications in the consistently valuable SPES series 'Archivum Musicum Flauto traversiere' is no. 19 (Florence, 1990), containing Dôthel's *XXVIII Studi per flauto solo* (=*Studi per il flauto in Tutti I Tuoni è Modi*, Paris: Berault, n.d.) together with his *VI Sonate per flauto e violoncello* op. 11 (=*Sonates pour une Flûte traversiere et un Violoncelle*, Paris: Taillart l'Aîné, n.d.). More on preluding and improvisation can be found in Betty Bang Mather and David Lasocki's *Free Ornamentation in Woodwind Music, 1700–1775: An Anthology with Introduction* (New York: McGinnis & Marx, 1976).

Leta E. Miller provided a revealing discussion of Dülon's improvising, performing, and personality in 'C. P. E. Bach and Friedrich Ludwig Dülon', *EM* 23 (1995), 65–80. Dülon's autobiography was published as Friedrich Wilhelm Dülon, *Dülons des blinden Flötenspielers Leben und Meynungen, von ihm selbst bearbeitet*, 2 vols (Zurich: C. M. Wieland, 1808), of which unfortunately no English translation has been made. Other useful studies are John A. Rice, 'The Blind Dülon and his Magic Flute', *Music & Letters* 71 (1990), 25–51, and Karl Ventzke, 'F. L. Dulon [*sic*], der blinde Flötenspieler (1769–1826): Über "Leben und Meynungen" eines reisenden Virtuosen', in de Reede, *Concerning the Flute*, 90–106. Ribock's writings were published as J. J. H. R., *Bemerkungen über die Flöte und Versuch einer Anleitung zur besseren Einrichtung und Behandlung derselben* (Stendal: Franzen & Grosse, 1782, R/Buren: Frits Knuf, 1980) and 'Über Musik, an Flötenliebhaber insonderheit', ed. C. F. Cramer, *Magazin der Musik* I (1783), 681–736. Karl Ventzke discussed Ribock's contributions in 'Dr J. J. H. Ribock (1743–1785): ein Beitrag zur Entwicklungsgeschichte der Querflöte', *Tibia* 1 (1976), 65–71.

Edward R. Reilly and John Solum discussed the earliest use of quarter tones on the flute in 'De Lusse, Buffardin, and an Eighteenth-century Quarter[-]tone Piece', *Historical Performance* 5. 1 (1992), 12–33. Patrizio Barbieri's article 'G. B. Orazi's Enharmonic Flute and its Music (1797–1815)', *GSJ* 52 (2000), 281–304, examined a further, quite extraordinary, development of the idea. Orazi's 'Enharmonic' flute contained 24 notes to the octave, but unlike other such systems that divided the whole tone into nine commas with a major and a minor semitone, his 24 subsemitones were all equal-sized quarter tones, intended to enable the flute to play slides and glissandi like those of the voice and violin.

Jane Bowers contributed a valuable study relating Mozart's compositions for flute to the players, instruments, and tonal ideals of his times in 'Mozart and the Flute', *EM* 20 (1992), 31–42. I concentrated on Mozart's ideas about intonation, arguing that modern equal-temperament performances fail to convey the composer's deliberate melodic inflexions and feeling for harmony, in 'Mozart und die Tromlitz-Flöte', *Tibia* 26 (2001), 549–56. Other recent work on Mozart's flute music has included Wolf-Dieter Seiffert, 'Schrieb Mozart drei Flötenquartette für Dejean?', *Mozart-Jahrbuch* 1987/88, 267–75, Roger Lustig, 'On the Flute Quartet, K. Anh. 171 (285b)', *Mozart-Jahrbuch* 1997, 157–79, and Henrik Wiese on the concertos in 'Zur Entstehungsgeschichte der Flötenkonzerte', *Mozart-Jahrbuch* 1997, 149–56. Nikolaus Delius reported the discovery of a lost flute concerto by Leopold Mozart in *Tibia* 29 (1994), 209–11.

1. Bowers, 'French Flute School', ch. 5, and p. 67.
2. Bowers, 'French Flute School', 404–6.
3. *Remora -ae* f. (Latin: delay, hindrance; i.e. an obstacle or hurdle).
4. Review of 'Lettre de M l'Abbé *Carbasus* … sur le mode des instrumens de musique', quoted in *Mercure de France*, 11 June 1739, 1359–60 (Bowers, 'French Flute School', 405).
5. Jane Bowers, 'Mozart and the Flute', *EM* 20 (1992), 32, citing H. Abert, *W. A. Mozart: Neubearbeitete und erweiterte Ausgabe von Otto Jahns Mozart*, 2 vols (Leipzig, 7/1955–6), i, 473, who in turn cites Wolzogen, *Recensionen*, 1865, no. 6, 82. My trans.
6. W. N. James, *A Word or Two on the Flute* (Edinburgh: Charles Smith, 1826), 86.
7. On changing concert life in London and Paris, see Simon McVeigh, *Concert Life in London*, and Bowers, 'French Flute School', 350.
8. Alan and Anne Gore, *English Interiors* (New York: Thames & Hudson, 1991), ch. 4.
9. Luke Heron, *A Treatise on the German Flute* (London: W. Griffin, 1771), 43.
10. McVeigh, *Concert Life*, 86–87.
11. [Thurston Dart], 'An Eighteenth-Century Directory of London Musicians Reprinted from

Mortimer's *London Universal Directory* (1763)', *GSJ* 2 (March 1949), 27–31.

12. Stuart Scott, *Hallé Flutes: Flautists of the Hallé Orchestra, 1858–[19]93* (Altrincham, Cheshire: S. J. Scott, 1998), 1; David William Eagle, 'A Constant Passion and a Constant Pursuit: A Social History of Flute-playing in England from 1800 to 1851' (Ph.D. diss., University of Minnesota, 1977), 5.

13. Amy Shaw Kreitzer, 'Transverse Flutes by London Makers, 1750–1900, in the Collections of the Shrine to Music Museum' (M.M. diss., University of South Dakota, 1993), 1–12.

14. Lewis Christian Austin Granom, *Plain and Easy Instructions for Playing on the German-Flute*, 3rd ed. (London: T. Bennett, 1766).

15. J. J. H. Ribock, 'Über Musik, an Flötenliebhaber insonderheit'. The myth of Dôthel playing without using his tongue reappeared in writings by Gerber in 1790 (*VFP*, p. 150, n. 1) and later by Mendel, Reissmann, and others. See Rockstro, *Treatise*, §846, s.v. 'Dothel (Nicholas)', citing Ribock's article.

16. McVeigh, *Concert Life*, 91.

17. Fitzgibbon, *Story*, 225.

18. The Company of Fifers and Drummers web site, www.fifedrum.com/thecompany/tcfdamer.html.

19. *Casselische Polizey- und Commercien-Zeitung*, October 1763, 407, cited in Werner Braun, 'The "Hautboist;" an Outline of Evolving Careers and Functions', in Salmen, *The Social Status*, 138.

20. Braun, 'The Hautboist', in Salmen, *The Social Status*, 153–4.

21. Braun, 'The Hautboist', 157–8.

22. Achim Hofer, '"… ich dien auf beede recht in Krieg und Friedens Zeit": Zu den Märschen des 18. Jahrhunderts unter besonderer Berücksichtigung ihrer Besetzung', *Tibia* 17 (1992), 182–91, 188–9.

23. Klaus Hortschansky, 'The Musician as Music Dealer in the Second Half of the 18th Century', in Salmen, *The Social Status*.

24. Ricarda Bröhl, 'Die Flötensonaten Wolfgang Amadeus Mozarts', *Tibia* 5 (1979), 369–77.

25. Willy Hess, 'Beethovens Werke für die Flöte', *Tibia* 10 (1985), 241–4, 241.

26. Hess, 'Beethovens Werke für die Flöte', 243–4.

27. *HBQF*, 223.

28. Patricia Joan Ahmad, 'The Flute Professors of the Paris Conservatoire from Devienne to Taffanel, 1795–1908' (M.A. diss., North Texas State University, 1980), 42, citing Millard Myron Laing, 'Anton Reicha's Quintets for Flute, Oboe, Clarinet, Horn, and Bassoon' (Ph.D. diss., University of Michigan, 1952), 48.

29. W. A. Mozart to Leopold Mozart, 10 Dec 1777. He described the commission differently in subsequent letters.

30. Mozart wrote: 'dann bin ich auch, wie sie wissen, gleich stuff wenn ich immer für ein instrument | das ich nicht leiden kan: | schreiben soll.' An alternative translation would be: 'And furthermore I'm completely dumb, as you know, when I have to write for one and the same instrument all the time – I can't stand that.'

31. Andrew Porter, 'Flute', *The New Yorker*, 4 August 1980, 58, cited in Toff, *Flute Book*, 236.

32. Roger Lustig, 'On the Flute Quartet, K. Anh. 171 (285b)', *Mozart-Jahrbuch* 1997, 157–79, 158.

33. Bowers, 'Mozart and the Flute', 33.

34. Diary of Joachim Ferdinand von Siedenhofen, quoted in Henrik Wiese, 'Zur Entstehungsgeschichte der Flötenkonzerte', *Mozart-Jahrbuch* 1997, 149–56, 155.

35. Bowers, 'Mozart and the Flute', 38.

36. Becker, 'The Eighteenth-century Flute Concerto', 9.

37. Becker, 'The Eighteenth-century Flute Concerto', 19.

38. Delius, 'Note sulla tecnica e la musica flautistica nel '700 in Italia'.

39. Smith, 'Changing Use', 4.

40. Neal Zaslaw, 'Mozart's Orchestral Flutes and Oboes', in Cliff Eisen, ed., *Mozart Studies* (Oxford: Clarendon Press, 1991), 201–11.

41. *HBQF*, 268.

42. Smith, 'Changing Use', 6.

43. John S. Sainsbury's *Dictionary of Musicians* (London, 1825), quoted or paraphrased by Rockstro et al. See p. 130 below. According to David Lasocki's article on Ashe in *NGD2*, the Brussels flutist Ashe replaced was Vanhamme rather than Vanhall.

44. Smith, 'Changing Use', 6; see also Rockstro, *Treatise*, §860.

45. The *Oracle*, 10 March 1792, quoted in H. C. Robbins Landon, *Haydn: Chronicle and Works* (Bloomington: Indiana University Press, 1976–80) and in Smith, 'Changing Use', 6.

46. Fitzgibbon, *Story*, 132.

47. A chronology of Tromlitz's announcements is given in *TKF*, 46–7.

48. Johann George Tromlitz, *Ausführlicher und gründlicher Unterricht die Flöte zu spielen* (Leipzig: Adam Friedrich Böhme, 1791), trans. as *VFP*.

49. Tromlitz, *Über die Flöten mit mehrern Klappen* (Leipzig: Adam Friedrich Böhme, 1800), trans. as *TKF*.

50. Since my study of the Tromlitz flute appeared in *TKF* (1996) a seventh Tromlitz flute has come to light, in a German private collection.

51. Carl Spazier, ed., *Berlinische Musikalische Zeitung* (Berlin: Neue Musikhandlung, 1794), 2–3.

52. Giovanni Battista Orazi, *Saggio per costruire, e suonare un flauto traverso enarmonico che ha I tuoni bassi del violino* (Rome: Michele Puccinelli, 1797). See Barbieri, 'G. B. Orazi's Enharmonic Flute and its Music'.

53. *TKF*, 199–200.

54. Powell, 'A Fake Grenser Flute by J. G. Otto'.

55. Dülon's report in his autobiography is translated in Miller, 'C. P. E. Bach and Friedrich Ludwig Dülon', 66.

56. Miller, 'C. P. E. Bach and Friedrich Ludwig Dülon'.

57. Reilly and Solum, 'De Lusse, Buffardin, and an Eighteenth-century Quarter Tone Piece'.

58. Péraut, *Méthode pour la flûte* (Paris: Author, c1800) and Devienne, *Nouvelle Méthode Théorique et Pratique pour la Flûte* (Paris: Imbault, 1794). See Miller, 'C. P. E. Bach and Friedrich Ludwig Dülon', n. 15, p. 78.

59. Becker, 'The Eighteenth-century Flute Concerto', 187; examples on pp. 189–200.

60. *TKF*, 35–36.

61. Jules Gallay, ed., *Un inventaire sous la Terreur* (Paris: G. Chamerot, c1890). For details of the flutes see *TKF*, 36.

62. 'Nachricht über das Ableben von Tromlitz', *AmZ* 7 (1805), 337–8.

63. Dülon, *Leben und Meynungen*, I.187.

64. *TKF*, 39.

THE KEYED FLUTE

1. *TKF*, 13.
2. *TKF*, 6–7, 11, 182.

GUILDS AND CAPITALISTS

1. Constant Pierre, *Les Facteurs d'instruments de Musique, les luthiers et la facture instrumentale: précis historique* (Paris: E. Sagot, 1893), 40–60.
2. Roland Champness, *The Worshipful Company of Turners of London* (London: Turners' Company, 1966), 22.
3. Hortschansky, 'The Musician as Music Dealer', 215–16.

Chapter 7 Travelling virtuosi, concert showpieces and a new mass audience

Since nearly all professional flutists travelled during the late eighteenth and early nineteenth centuries, but only a few attracted particular notice at the time or since, source material on their activities is quite abundant, though widely scattered. For this chapter I have selected a few figures whose lives are relatively well documented, using their biographies, writings, and reported performances to link a discussion of the period's most important themes.

Musical periodicals, which sprang up in large numbers in the late eighteenth and early nineteenth centuries, provide first-hand information about the period's flute-playing, particularly in reports of concerts by visiting artists. But the very quantity of the material makes access to it difficult. Bernhard Schultze's anthology *Querflöten der Renaissance und des Barock* I (Munich: Author [Unertlstrasse 33, D-80803 Munich, Germany], 1987), a 667-page bound xerox reproduction of many of the most important writings in German and French from the sixteenth to the nineteenth centuries, provided the first easy access to a selection of the classical era's periodical literature. Flute-related contributions to the most important publication, the *Allgemeine musikalische Zeitung*, have since been collected in an extremely valuable edition by Rien de Reede, *Die Flöte in der 'Allgemeine Musikalische Zeitung' (1798–1848)* (Amsterdam: Broekmans and Van Poppel, 1997), complete with indexes of authors, review subjects, persons, places, and topics. Rineke Smilde searched the *Amsterdamsche Courant* from 1740 to 1760 for flute references, publishing her findings in facsimile in de Reede's *Concerning the Flute*, 115–19. Many similar sources for the nineteenth century are not as well served, however, leaving the contents of *The Musical World, Caecilia, Harmonicon, The Flutist's Magazine*, and *La France Musicale*, among others, more difficult to navigate.

General works on the lives and work of late-eighteenth century flutists are few, despite, or perhaps because of, the plethora of material. David William Eagle's dissertation, 'A Constant Passion and a Constant Pursuit: A Social History of Flute-playing in England from 1800 to 1851' (Ph.D. diss., University of Minnesota, 1977), relies on many of the primary sources presented by Rockstro, Fitzgibbon, and others. It contains a useful overview of its subject and many good insights.

Many more biographies of particular players could usefully be undertaken to supplement the accounts and correct the errors of nineteenth-century writers, among whom François-Joseph Fétis (*Biographie universelle des musiciens*, Paris: Firmin Didot, 1860–6) is among the least and Rockstro among the most reliable. Studies of Dülon's career are mentioned in the bibliography for chapter 6, but much remains to be written on his musical style and its relations to contemporary flute-playing. The performance practice of other travelling virtuosi likewise provides scope for study, though as yet it has hardly been explored at all. Janice Dockendorff Boland wrote about one characteristic piece in 'Charles Nicholson's ornaments for *Roslin Castle*', in *Traverso* 8.1 (January 1996), 1–3, and B. Eldred Spell studied 'Selected Aspects of Flute Performance Practice as Evidenced in the Flute Tutors of Charles Nicholson (1816 through 1836)' (Ph.D. diss., Michigan State University, 1990), which unfortunately was not available to me. Janet Houston discussed some of Fürstenau's ornamentation practices in her article, 'A. B. Fürstenau's *The Art of Flute-Playing*', *Traverso* 7.4 (October 1995), 1–2, a brief summary drawn from her translation (a doctoral document for the Juilliard School in 1994) of his *Die Kunst des Flötenspiels, Op. 138* (Leipzig: Breitkopf & Härtel, c1844, R/Buren, The Netherlands: Frits Knuf, 1991). Theobald Boehm's travels are described in 'Schafhäutl's Life of Boehm', an English version of a largely trustworthy biography that originally appeared in German in the *AmZ* of 1882, the year after Boehm's death. The English is in Welch, *History of the Boehm Flute*, 3rd edition.

Other than Boehm, few nineteenth-century flute-makers and their work have been studied. Those few will be discussed in the bibliography for chapter 8.

1. Becker, 'The Eighteenth-century Flute Concerto', 16.
2. Bowers, *French Flute School*, 83.
3. *HBQF*, 224 (my trans.).
4. *VFP*, 14.
5. I am grateful to Christopher Hogwood for this detail from Hässler's autobiography.
6. *VFP*, 14.
7. *HBQF*, 224.

8. Rice, 'The Blind Dülon', 25, 32–4.
9. *Journal des Luxus und der Moden* (September 1805), 634–5, quoted in Ventzke, 'F. L. Dulon'.
10. *Journal des Luxus und der Moden* (June 1806), 355–7, quoted in Ventzke, 'F. L. Dulon'.
11. The essay is trans. in *TKF*, Appendix V.
12. Thomas Lindsay, *The Elements of Flute-Playing* (London: Author, 1828), 100–1.
13. Louis Drouët, *Méthode pour la Flute* (Antwerp: A. Schott, 1827), 69, quoted in Lindsay, *Elements*, 100.
14. Robin Stowell, *Violin Technique and Performance Practice in the Late Eighteenth and Early Nineteenth Centuries* (Cambridge and New York: Cambridge University Press, 1985), 247–8.
15. Stowell, *Violin Technique*, 18–23.
16. 'Schafhäutl's Life of Boehm', in Welch's *History of the Boehm Flute*, 406.
17. *Quarterly Musical Magazine* III (1818), 348, quoted in Eagle, 'A Constant Passion', 81.
18. Ibid.
19. Eagle, 'A Constant Passion', 124.
20. Rockstro, *Treatise*, §909.
21. *Athenaeum*, June 1828, 506, quoted in Eagle, 'A Constant Passion', 93.
22. Charles Nicholson, *A School for the Flute* (London and New York: W. Hall & Son, 1836), 3.
23. Nicholson, *School*, 4.
24. Nicholson, *School*, 5–6.
25. Ibid.
26. W. N. James, *A Word or Two on the Flute* (Edinburgh: Charles Smith and Cocks & Co., 1826 R/London: Tony Bingham, 1982), 131.
27. Nicholson, *'A Word or Two' to Mr W. N. James* (London: Clementi, Collard & Collard, 1829), 2.
28. Nicholson, *'A Word or Two'*, 3.
29. James, *A Word or Two*, 161.
30. Nicholson, *'A Word or Two'*, 1.
31. William Annand, *A Few Words on the Flute* (London: Author, 1843), 16.
32. 'Imitation Flutes in London', *Flutist's Magazine* I (1827), 177–80, quoted in Eagle, 'A Constant Passion', 193–4.
33. Eagle, 'A Constant Passion', 196.
34. *Athenaeum* 7 (1829), 478, cited in Eagle, 'A Constant Passion', 196–7.
35. Tulou's letter of 23 June 1829 printed in *Harmonicon* [7] (1829), 160; James's retort in *Harmonicon* 7 (1829), 191–2; both quoted in Eagle, 'A Constant Passion', 197–9.
36. James, *A Word or Two*, 176.
37. Fürstenau, *Kunst*, 89.
38. Charles Nicholson, *Nicholson's Complete Preceptor, for the German Flute* (London: Preston, 1816), 11, quoted in Richard Erig, 'Improvisation im 19. Jahrhundert', *HBQF*, 193.
39. T. Berbiguier, *Nouvelle Méthode pour la Flûte* (Paris: Janet et Cotelle, c1818), 21, quoted in Erig, 'Improvisation'.
40. Drouët, *Méthode*, 65.
41. Fitzgibbon, *Story*, 197.
42. Quoted in Rockstro, *Treatise*, §890.
43. Eagle, 'A Constant Passion', 114.
44. *Musical Memoirs* (London, 1830), 132, quoted in Eagle, 'A Constant Passion', 113.
45. George Hogarth, 'The Flute', *Musical World* 3 (November 1836), 114, quoted in Eagle, 'A Constant Passion', 116.
46. Fitzgibbon, *Story*, 198.
47. *Quarterly Musical Magazine* 5 (1823), 84, quoted in Rockstro, *Treatise*, §900 and Eagle, 'A Constant Passion', 112–13.
48. *AmZ*, December 1820, cols 845–7.

49. Nikolaus Delius, Introduction to Anton Bernhard Fürstenau, *Die Kunst des Flötenspiels Op. 138* (reprint of Leipzig: Breitkopf & Härtel, 1844, by Buren: Frits Knuf, 1991), x.

50. *The Flutist's Magazine* (1827), quoted in Rockstro, *Treatise*, §898.

51. Vera Funk, 'Beispielhafte Flöten-Metamorphosen beliebter Werke', *HBQF*, 227–36.

52. Preface to *Musical Library*, 1834, cited in Eagle, 'A Constant Passion', 160.

53. *Quarterly Musical Magazine* 2 (1820), 358, cited in Eagle, 'A Constant Passion', 158.

54. Maurizio Bignardelli, 'Die italienischen Flötisten des 19. Jahrhunderts und der *Carnevale di Venezia*', *Tibia* 22 (2000), 269–77, 269.

55. Arndt Mehring presents a useful study of Kuhlau's life and works in *Friedrich Kuhlau im Spiegel seiner Flötenwerke* (Frankfurt: Zimmerman, c1992).

56. Douglas Johnson/Scott G. Burnham in *NGD2*, s.v. 'Beethoven, Ludwig van: Works – folksong arrangements'.

Chapter 8 Flute mania

Except for David Eagle's dissertation mentioned in the bibliography for chapter 7, most writers have seen the early nineteenth century merely as a background for the mechanical development and acceptance of the Boehm flute. Thus chapter 3 of Nancy Toff's *The Development of the Modern Flute* manages to mention most of the important designs for flutes manufactured or proposed during the period, but treats them as the result of 'confusion' (pp. 122–3), concluding that 'such variety…was ultimately negative from a musical standpoint' (p. 124). In fact the aesthetic divisions between various musical styles, instruments, and traditions are extremely revealing, and provide rich scope for further exploration.

Studies of this period's instruments would hardly be possible at all without the Dayton C. Miller Collection, which gives public access to specimens and documentation of most of the important types. Another indispensable tool, Waterhouse's *New Langwill Index*, lists patents, inventions, and interrelationships between makers and inventors, and helps determine the origins and dates of extant instruments. But the sheer number of these items, and the lack of indexes or studies such as Phillip T. Young's *4900 Historical Woodwind Instruments* (which, however selective, imposes some order on the smaller number of surviving eighteenth-century flutes) makes comprehensive, detailed work a distant prospect at best. Flute-related British patents are summarized in *Patents for Inventions: Abridgements of Specifications relating to Music and Musical Instruments, A.D. 1694–1866* (London: Commissioners of Patents for Inventions, 1871). The few general studies that exist have differing priorities. The clear diagrams in Jerry L. Vorhees's valuable *The Classification of Flute Fingering Systems of the Nineteenth and Twentieth Centuries* (Buren: Frits Knuf, c1980) often show better than words or photographs how these complicated systems work. Amy Shaw Kreitzer's dissertation, mentioned above, gives some details of instruments by about 120 makers, inventors, and distributors, and contains a catalogue of extant flutes by the London firm of Monzani & Hill. Tula Giannini's study of the Lot and Godfroy families, *Great Flute Makers of France: The Lot and Godfroy Families, 1650–1900* (London: Tony Bingham, 1993), focuses on inventories and business documents. Though rendered less effective by inaccurate translations and poor editing, these documents together with copious photographs provide a broad sense of the changes in flute-making and in ideas about the instrument's sound and character. My own 'Science, Technology and the Art of Flutemaking in the Eighteenth Century', *FQ* 29.3 (Spring 1994), 33–42 (also available at www.flutehistory.com), surveyed technical developments and the study of acoustics as they affected early flute building.

A few studies have focused on particular flutes or flute-types. Boehm's flutes have received attention in works listed for chapter 9. Karl Ventzke wrote on Laurent's flutes in 'Kristallglasflöten im 19. Jahrhundert', *Tibia* 4 (1979), 397–9. But instruments without a representative in the Miller Collection have fared poorly: inventions such as Holtzapffel's chromatic flute of 1806 and Henry Potter's split-key flute of 1845, of which Miller managed to collect no specimen, have hitherto escaped mention in the literature. Nothing has been written on Viennese flutes, which are still relatively common in the antique trade, or on Liebel's, which are very rare: Miller collected a Liebel piccolo (DCM 789), but no flute. Andreas Masel made up for much of the neglect of Pentenrieder, whose inventive work also escaped inclusion in the Miller Collection, in his exhaustive study 'Der Münchener Holzblasinstrumentenmacher Benedikt Pentenrieder (1809–1849)' (M.A. thesis, Ludwig-Maximilian University, Munich, 1985/86). Similar studies of the 'Nicholson' flutes, the Viennese flutes, the Liebel flute, and Tulou's *flûte perfectionnée* would help to bring these historically important types into focus, and help us to realize that the variety in flute construction matched a real and healthy diversity of taste and opinion about the flute's tone and character.

Many of the early nineteenth-century tutors for instruments and polemics advocating one type of flute or another (see *Methods* above) provide useful details and insights, though they must obviously be read with caution and balanced against other competing claims. John Clinton's *Treatise upon the Mechanism and General Principles of the Flute* (London: H. Potter, [1852]) advocates a new flute, the result of his own experiments, in preference to the Boehm flute. He described this 'Equisonant' flute in his *A Few Practical Hints to Flute Players upon the Subject of Modern Flutes* (London: Clinton & Co. [1855]), and in *A Code of Instructions for the Fingering of the Equisonant Flute by the Inventor & Patentee* (London: Clinton & Co., c1860). A facsimile reprint (Buren: Frits Knuf, 1990) of the latter work contains a valuable preface by Karl Ventzke. Clinton also produced a tutor for the Boehm flute, designed for the American market, as *A Complete School, or Practical Instruction Book for the Boehm Flute (shut or open G♯), as Manufactured by A. G. Badger* (New York: A. G. Badger, c1860). Works in this class that contain histories of the flute, including Ward's *The Flute Explained* and Carte's *Sketch of the Successive Improvements*, are discussed above under 'History and Criticism of the Flute'.

The history of British military bands was given in a lecture at the Queen's Hall by Lieut. J. Mackenzie Rogan (1855–1932), Senior Director of Music to the Brigade of Guards, reported in *Musical Times*, January 1913, and extracted, with other sources, in Scholes, *Mirror*, 498–501. Details on the flute in particular are provided in R. W. Hylands, *History of the Flute and Flute Bands* (typescript, n.p., n.d.), a document of mysterious origins, knowledge of which I owe to Robert Bigio. American fife-making was lovingly documented in Lloyd P. Farrar, 'The American Fife and its Makers: An Historical Examination', *The Woodwind Quarterly* no. 11 (n.d), 84–96.

Once again periodicals, musical and general, provide some of the most useful information on the period of flute mania. Christopher Welch made good use of the *Musical World* in his contribution to the Boehm-Gordon controversy (chapter 9), and again Rien de Reede's edition of extracts from the *AmZ* (1798–1848) is of valuable service.

1. Toff, *Flute Book*, 49, see also Meylan, *The Flute*, 112.
2. [A. André], 'Beschiedene Anfrage an die modernsten Komponisten und Virtuosen', *AmZ* 1.9 (1798), cols 141–4, trans. in *TKF* appendix V.
3. *TKF*, 171.
4. William Close, 'Experiments and Observations on the properties of Wind Instruments, Consisting of a Single Pipe or Channel; With Improvements', in William Nicholson, ed., *A Journal of Natural Philosophy, Chemistry and the Arts*, 5 (1801), 212–23.
5. [H. W. T. Pottgiesser], 'Ueber die Fehler der bisherigen Flöten', *AmZ* 5 (1802–3), cols 609–16, 625–38, 644–54, 673–82, col. 680.
6. Patent no. 236 of 21 November 1806.
7. *Journal des Luxus und der Moden* (Weimar), June 1806, 385–6, cited in Ventzke, 'Kristallglasflöten'.
8. *AmZ* 1824, p. 402, cited in Ventzke, 'Kristallglasflöten'.
9. Rien de Reede, 'Nederlandische Flötisten und Flötisten in den Niederlanden 1700–1900', *Tibia* 24 (1999), 345–54, 433–41, 433.
10. A family tradition held that the flute was a gift from the Marquis de Lafayette, but a letter establishes that Laurent was the donor. See 'High notes', *FQ* 26.2 (Winter 2001), 8.

11. Ventzke, 'Kristallglasflöten im 19. Jahrhundert'. Value comparison from Giannini, *Great Flute Makers*, 135.

12. Patent no. 248 of 18 November 1806 (DCM). A specimen survives in a private collection, Frankfurt.

13. *VFP*, 234.

14. *AmZ* 30 May 1811, cols 377–9; November, col. 775; March 1812, Intelligenz-Blatt III, 9.

15. *AmZ* November 1813, col. 759.

16. Gustav Schilling, ed., *Encyclopädie der gesammten musikalischen Wissenschaften, oder, Universal-Lexicon der Tonkunst* (Stuttgart: F. H. Köhler, 1835–8), s.v. 'Panaulon'.

17. I am grateful to Gianni Lazzari for this information from his forthcoming book (in Italian) on the flute.

18. Bayr, *1ter Theil der Schule für Doppeltöne auf der Flöte* (Vienna: Author, n.d.).

19. Amy Sue Hamilton, 'The Relationship of Flute Construction to the Symphonic Role of the Flute and Orchestral Performance Practice in the Nineteenth Century' (D.M.A. diss., Northwestern University, 1984), 92, 101–2.

20. Hamilton, 'The Relationship', 101–2.

21. Hamilton, 'The Relationship', 93.

22. Toff, *Development*, 39.

23. Hamilton, 'The Relationship', 94.

24. Hamilton, 'The Relationship', 150–1.

25. Hamilton, 'The Relationship', 178.

26. John Robert Bailey, 'Maximilian Schwedler's *Flute and Flute-Playing*: Translation and Study of Late Nineteenth-century German Performance Practice' (D.M. diss., Northwestern University, 1987), 19.

27. Fitzgibbon, *Story*, 143; Bate, *The Flute*, 176.

28. Hamilton, 'The Relationship', 184.

29. Hamilton, 'The Relationship', 205.

30. Hamilton, 'The Relationship', 185–6.

31. Hamilton, 'The Relationship', 195, 199–200.

32. Hamilton, 'The Relationship', 311.

33. Jaap Frank, in *NGD2*, s.v. 'Flute'.

34. Gorm Busk, *NGD2*, s.v. 'Kuhlau'.

35. Frank, in *NGD2*, s.v. 'Flute'.

36. Rockstro, *Treatise*, §§919, 925.

37. Annand, *A Few Words on the Flute*, 32–3.

38. Fitzgibbon, *Story*, 178.

39. Johann Heinrich Lambert, 'Observations sur les Flûtes', *Nouveaux Mémoires de L'Académie Royale* (Berlin: C. F. Voss, 1777).

40. Johann Heinrich Liebeskind, 'Bruchstücke aus einem noch ungedruckten philosophisch-praktischen Versuche über die Natur und das Tonspiel der deutschen Flöte', *AmZ* November 1807, cols 97–105, 113–20, 129–38, 145–53.

41. Johann Heinrich Liebeskind, 'Versuch einer Akustik der deutschen Flöte. Als Beytrag zu einer philosophischen Theorie des Flötenspielens', *AmZ* November 1806, col 81–90, 97–107.

42. Gottfried Weber, 'Versuch einer praktischen Akustik der Blasinstrumente', *AmZ* January 1816, cols 33–44, 49–60, 65–74, 87–90.

43. 'Nachtrag zu der Abhandlung: "'Ueber die Fehler der Flöte, nebst einem Vorschlage etc.'", *AmZ* April 1824, cols 265–75.

44. William Bainbridge, *Observations on the Cause of Imperfections in Wind Instruments, Particularly in German Flutes* (London: Innes, 1823), 10.

45. Carl [August] Grenser, 'Für Flötenspieler bemerkenswerthe Stellen aus dem Buche: *A Word or Two on the Flute*', *AmZ* February 1828, cols 97–103, 113–19, 133–9, 154–60.

46. Hamilton, 'The Relationship', 97–8. More extensive particulars on orchestral forces are

given by Daniel J. Koury in *Orchestral Performance Practices in the Nineteenth Century: Size, Proportions, and Seating* (Ann Arbor, UMI Research Press, 1986).

47. Giannini, *Great Flute Makers*, 72.

48. Giannini, *Great Flute Makers*, 67–8.

49. Jaap Frank, in *NGD2*, s.v. 'Flute'.

50. Rockstro, *Treatise*, §932.

51. A. B. Fürstenau, 'Historisch-kritische Untersuchung der Konstruktion unserer jetzigen Flöte', *AmZ* October 1838, col 694–5, 706–8, 730–3.

52. Fürstenau, 'Historisch-kritische Untersuchung', 706.

53. [Jean Louis] Tulou, *Méthode de Flûte Progressive et Raisonnée adopteé par le Comité d'Enseignement du Conservatoire, Op. 100* (Paris: Chabal, [1835]), 1.

54. Giannini, *Great Flute Makers*, 119–20, p. 130 n. 25.

55. Tulou, *Méthode*, 1.

56. M[arie] B[oehm], 'Zur Erinnerung an Theobald Boehm' (Munich: privately printed, 1898), MS trans. Dayton C. Miller, 1908 (DCM).

57. Abstract of Patent 10553, 13 March 1845.

58. Pratten's dates from Rockstro, *Treatise*, §§935–7, given in other sources as 1814–62.

59. Frank, in *NGD2*, s.v. 'Flute'.

60. Hamilton, 'The Relationship', 405; Bailey, 'Maximilian Schwedler', 150.

61. John Clinton, *A School or Practical Instruction Book for the Boehm Flute* (London: Cramer, Beale & Co., 1846), 51.

62. Ibid., 'From a letter, dated Munich, March 1843'.

63. Clinton, *A School*, 45.

64. Clinton, *A School*, 24.

65. Adam Carse, *Musical Wind Instruments* (London: Macmillan, 1939 R/New York, 1965), 100, quoted in Toff, *Development*, 115.

EQUAL TEMPERAMENT

1. Quoted in Alexander J. Ellis, trans. and ed., *On the Sensations of Tone [by Hermann L.F. Helmholtz]* (London: Longmans & Co., 1885, R/New York: Dover, 1954), 548. See also Rockstro, *Treatise*, §282, and *NGD2*, s.v 'Intonation'.

2. Helmholtz, *On the Sensations of Tone*, 548–9.

3. Allan W. Atlas, *The Wheatstone English Concertina in Victorian England* (Oxford: Clarendon Press, 1996), 39–42.

4. Georg Andreas Sorge, 'Anmerkung über Herrn Quantzens … dis und es-Klappe auf der Querflöte', in F. W. Marpurg, ed., *Historisch-kritische Beyträge* 4 (1758), 1–7.

5. Karl [August] Grenser, 'Eine Stimme über den Nachtrag des Hrn. Dr. Pottgiesser in no. 17 dieses Jahrganges, zu den Abhandlung "Ueber die Fehler der Flöte, nebst einem Vorschlage u.s.w." im Jahrgange 1803. no. 37–39. dieser Zeitung', *AmZ* June 1824 cols 381–86, col. 385.

6. '*die rein temperirte Stimmung wird jedes gebildete Ohr befriedigen*' (§382). The term *rein temperirte Stimmung*, as I noted in *VFP* 119, n. 6, is self-contradictory if one takes *rein* to mean, literally, 'pure' and *temperirt* 'tempered'.

7. Quoted in Welch, *History of the Boehm Flute*, 334–8.

8. Giannini, *Great Flute Makers*, 126.

9. *Potter's Design for a Chromatic Flute Invented by W. J. Monzani* (London: Henry Potter, [1845]; Registered Design, London: Public Record Office, by courtesy of Tony Bingham). A specimen of the flute is in a private collection, Frankfurt.

10. Richard Carte, *The Boehm Flute Explained* (London: Addison and Hodson, 1846), 12.

11. Theobald Boehm, *Die Flöte und das Flötenspiel* (Munich: J. Aibl, 1871), trans. Dayton C. Miller (New York: Dover Publications, 1964), 74, cited in Hamilton, 'The Relationship', 365.

12. Helmholtz, *On the Sensations of Tone*, 325–7.

13. Rockstro, *Treatise*, §§265–90.

14. Rockstro, *Treatise*, §701.

MECHANICAL INNOVATIONS IN THE FLUTE MANIA PERIOD

1. Except where noted, patent numbers and dates are given in Bate, *The Flute* and/or Toff, *Development*.
2. Tula Giannini (*Great Flute Makers*, 80) claims that keys mounted on posts appeared in Hugot & Wunderlich's Conservatoire method of 1804, predating Laurent's patent by two years. The illustrations in question, on the keyed flute fingering charts before p. 1, show mounts on saddles that probably anchor brackets, not posts. Giannini's reading of Plate VIII of Diderot and D'Alembert's *Lutherie* (1762) is also incorrect: the one-keyed *dessus de flûte traversière* (not a piccolo) that is shown there has its key mounted on blocks rather than posts.
3. French Patent no. 248, 18 November 1806. A specimen exists in a private collection, Frankfurt.
4. Patent 3074, 19 October 1807.
5. Patent 3314, 12 March 1810.
6. Patent 3349, 19 June 1910.
7. *AmZ* November 1813, col 759.
8. *AmZ* April 1815, col 256.
9. *AmZ* May 1822, col 293–5.
10. Patent 6338, 27 November 1832.
11. Letter of 7 November 1843 to the *Musical World* from Cornelius Ward. See chapter 9.
12. The dates of Card's activities as a maker are uncertain. He was a flutist reported as active between 1825 and 1861 (Bate, *The Flute*, 136; see also *NLI*, s.v. 'Card, William').
13. Masel, 'Benedikt Pentenrieder', 120–46.
14. *NLI*, s.v. 'Siccama, Abel'.
15. Rockstro, *Treatise*, §659; Lazzari, forthcoming.

Chapter 9 The Boehm flute

The flute Boehm developed in the workshops of Gerock and Wolf in London in 1831 was described and illustrated, with a fingering chart, in *Scale and Description of Boehm's Newly-invented Patent Flute, Manufactured and Sold by the Patentees Only, Gerock and Wolf* (London: Dean and Munday, [1831]). Boehm's own prospectus for the ring-key flute of 1832 appeared as *Theobald Boehm's neu construirte Flöte* (Munich: Falter & Sohn, 1843). He described the cylinder flute in his essay *Über den Flötenbau und die neuesten Verbesserungen desselben* (Mainz: Schott, 1847), in French as *De la fabrication et des derniers perfectionnements des flûtes* (Paris: Godefroy, 1848), in an Italian version by Antonio Jóry entitled *Della Costruzione dei Flauti e de' più recenti Miglioramenti della Medesima* (Milano: Ricordi, 1851), and finally in an English edition by W. S. Broadwood of Boehm's own translation, as *An Essay On the Construction of Flutes* (London: Rudall Carte, 1882), reprinted with an introduction by Karl Ventzke as *On the Construction of Flutes* (Buren: Frits Knuf, 1982).

Boehm's *Die Flöte und das Flötenspiel* (*The Flute and Flute-playing*, Munich: J. Aibl, 1871) was first trans. by J. Passmore Triggs as 'The Flute and Flute-Playing in its Artistic, Technical, and Acoustical Relationships', *St Cecelia Magazine* nos 15 (March 1883)–22 (October 1883). A subsequent 'revised and enlarged' edition was published privately by Dayton C. Miller in c1908 and 1922, and by New York: Dover Publications, 1964.

Gordon's biography was first investigated by Percival R. Kirby in 'Captain Gordon, the Flute Maker', *Music & Letters* 38 (1957), 250–9. The Boehm-Gordon controversy produced a large volume of literature throughout the nineteenth century on the origins of the Boehm flute: though the dispute gave many uninformed participants the opportunity to publish opinions of no relevance to the question, it also produced some of the most valuable and interesting documents in the history of the flute. Many of these were reproduced, subject to varying interpretations and commentaries, in two late nineteenth-century studies. Rockstro's *Treatise*, despite its other merits, provided an account so heedlessly partisan that it referred even to Boehm's 1847 cylinder flute as 'Gordon's flute'. Christopher Welch responded to Rockstro in great detail in his *History of the Boehm Flute*, 3rd edition, to which the reader is referred for a thorough and lively treatment of the entire episode as well as references to the writings of Victor Coche and other participants in the dispute. Coche's pamphlet *Examen Critique de la Flûte Ordinaire comparée à la Flûte de Böhm, présenté a MM Les Membres de l'Institut (Académie Royale des Beaux-Arts, Section de Musique)* (Paris: Author, 1838) addressed the Academy commission, whose report he reproduced in his subsequent publications, *Méthode pour servir à l'enseignement de la nouvelle Flûte Inventée par Gordon, modifiée par Boehm et perfectionnée par V. Coche et Buffet, Jne.* (Paris: Schonenberger, 1838), and his polemic, *Mémoire adressé a Son Excellence M le Ministre d'État, a M Le Directeur du Conservatoire, et a M Le Général Mellinet, Président de la commission militaire au Conservatoire; par M V. Coche, Professeur adjoint au Conservatoire impérial de musique, pour établir ses droits a la place de professeur en titre que laissera vacante la retraite de M Tulou* (Paris: Thunot, 1859). The other two early Boehm flute tutors are [Paul Hippolyte] Camus, *Méthode pour la nouvelle flûte Boehm* (Paris: E. Gérard, 1839), and Louis Dorus, *L'Etude de la nouvelle flûte, méthode progressive arrangée d'après Devienne* (Paris: Schoenenberger, c1840). John Clinton's *A Theoretical and Practical Essay on the Boehm Flute, as Manufactured by Messrs. Rudall & Rose* (London: R. Cocks & Co., 1843) contains his evaluation of the ring-key flute. A second work by Clinton, *A School or Practical Instruction Book for the Boehm Flute, with the Open or Shut G♯ Key* (London: Cramer, Beale & Co., 1846), was intended for players changing from the ordinary keyed flute. Other works by Clinton can be found in the bibliography for chapter 8.

Carl von Schafhäutl, Boehm's friend and collaborator both in acoustics and in the development of the Bavarian steel industry, published early accounts of Boehm's work on the flute, using the pen name Pellisov. One appeared in *AmZ* 1843, January no. 5, cols 71–80, trans. in Rockstro, *Treatise*, §§596–7. Schafhäutl also published an article on 'Theobald Böhm, and the flute called after him' in *The Musical World* of 18 February 1882, reprinted in Welch's *History of the Boehm Flute*. Schafhäutl's testimony is not always quite accurate with respect to dates, and sometimes conflicts with that of others. One of these is Farrenc, whose important witness concerning the chonology of the ring-key flute in Paris appears in A[ristide] Farrenc, 'Flute Boehm', *Revue et Gazette Musicale* 5 no. 36 (Paris, 9 November 1838) 364–5.

Karl Ventzke's scholarship has contributed most to modern knowledge of Boehm's work. His monograph *Die Boehmflöte: Wedergang eines Musikinstruments*, Fachbuchreihe Das Musikinstrument vol. 15 (Frankfurt: Das Musikinstrument, 1966) was the first thorough documentary study of the Boehm flute since Welch's and presented important new documents. This exemplary history has unfortunately not appeared in an English translation. Ventzke and Karl Lenski co-authored the visually lavish study of instruments *Das goldene Zeitalter der Flöte. Die Boehmflöte in Frankreich, 1832–1932* (Celle: Moeck Verlag, 1992). Andreas Masel expanded the documentary record to include material from the Munich archives in '"Th. Boehm et Grevé": Zur Geschichte der ersten Flötenbau-Werkstatt Theobald Böhms', *Tibia* 18 (1993), 602–10, a summary of a more detailed article in *Musik in Bayern* 43 (1991), 5–29. Ventzke briefly discussed the ideas of various German flutists of the period on the Boehm flute in 'Über das ambivalente Verhältnis der Fürstenaus zur Böhmflöte', *Tibia* 17 (1992), 48–9. Ventzke and Peter Spohr summarized recently-discovered details, added new material, and discussed some instruments, in 'Die Patente der Boehmflöte von 1847 und Instrumente der Frühzeit. Zum 200. Geburtstag von Theobald Boehm am 9. April 1994', *Tibia* 19 (1994), 89–97.

Philip Bate's *The Flute* contains an excellent chapter on 'The Work of Theobald Boehm' and a summary of the Boehm-Gordon controversy. Tula Giannini's *Great Flute Makers of France* provides exceptionally valuable and detailed documentation of the Conservatoire commission of 1838 in chapter 4, though too much reliance on Schafhäutl and other dubious witnesses sometimes leads her astray in minor matters. As well as previously unknown documentary material, Giannini reports on the account by Le Comte A. D. de Pontécoulant, 'Conservatoire de Musique Comité d'Enseignement', *La France musicale* (January and February 1840, beginning 19 January 1840, 29). Giannini's verbatim account demonstrates that Coche's efforts to have the ring-key flute approved at the Conservatoire in 1837 came to nothing. In 'An Old Key for a New Flute: The Boehm Flute with Closed G♯: Historical Perspectives', *FQ* 10 (1984), 15–20, Giannini argued that the modern-style ('independent') closed G♯ key first replaced the Dorus G♯ in Lot's workshop in the early 1860s.

Susan Marie Beagle Berdahl described the transmission of the Boehm flute to America in 'The First Hundred Years of the Boehm Flute in the United States, 1845–1945: A Biographical Dictionary of American Boehm Flutemakers', 3 vols, (Ph.D. dissertation, University of Minnesota, 1985). The principal primary source for that subtopic in chapter 9 is A. G. Badger, *An Illustrated History of the Flute:* (New York: A. G. Badger, 1853).

1. Most endnote references to documents cited in the principal modern studies, Ventzke, *Boehmflöte* and Welch, *Boehm Flute* (see bibliography), have been suppressed in the assumption that the interested reader will consult those important monographs at first hand.

2. Ventzke, *Boehmflöte*, 20.

3. Karl Grenser, 'Eine Stimmung über den Nachtrag des Hrn. Dr. Pottgiesser', *AmZ* 26 no. 24 (10 July 1824), 385.

4. Masel, 'Th. Boehm et Grevé'.

5. *AmZ* 1824, 265–75.

6. Cornelius Ward, *The Flute Explained*, 9.

7. TB to WSB, August 1871, quoted in Boehm, *An Essay on the Construction of Flutes*, 59.

8. Spohr, *Kunsthandwerk*, item A37, p. 29, is a Boehm 1831 flute marked [unicorn's head]/C. GEROCK/79/CORNHILL/LONDON/PATENT. The instrument also appeared as item 75 in Manfred Hermann Schmid, *Theobald Boehm, 1794–1881: die Revolution der Flöte: Katalog der Ausstellung zum 100. Todestag von Boehm* (Tutzing: Schneider, 1981), and is now in Munich: Stadtmuseum, Musikinstrumentensammlung.

9. Pamela Weston, *Clarinet Virtuosi of the Past* (London: Hale, 1971), 65. Welch's account in *History of the Boehm Flute*, 3rd ed., 44, appears to refer to the same contact. Buffet exhibited a *clarinette à anneaux mobiles* in Paris in 1839, and patented it in 1844. Instrument-makers in Munich (Pentenrieder) and Brussels (Sax) patented arrangements including ring-keys by 1840.

10. Ventzke, *Boehmflöte*, 32.

11. *Bazar für München und Bayern* no. 97, 25 April 1833, 391.

12. *Tablature de la Flûte Diatonique* (n.p., n.d.)

13. Giannini, *Great Flute Makers*, 109.

14. Welch, *History of the Boehm Flute*, 49–51, appears to have assumed that Camus 'brought a Boehm flute to Paris' at some unspecified time in 1837. But in light of Camus's own testimony that Boehm himself brought several in the spring, the assumption is unnecessary.

15. Giannini, *Great Flute Makers*, 101–6.

16. The illustration in Coche, *Examen critique* and *Méthode* of 1838 (reproduced in Toff, *Development*, 63), and the one in Buffet's patent application of 1838 (reproduced in Giannini, 'An Old Key') .

17. Giannini, *Great Flute Makers*, 110.

18. Ventzke, *Boehmflöte*, 28 (my trans.)

19. Giannini, *Great Flute Makers*, 115.

20. Giannini, *Great Flute Makers*, 126.

21. Ventzke, *Boehmflöte*, 33 (my trans.). No Viennese-made Boehm flutes of this early date have yet been identified.

22. See Maurizio Bignardelli, 'Die italienischen Flötisten des 19. Jahrhunderts und der *Carnevale di Venezia*', *Tibia* 22 (2000), 269–77, 272.

23. Eagle, 'A Constant Passion', 103.

24. Rockstro, *Treatise*, §917.

25. John Clinton, *A Theoretical & Practical Essay, on the Boehm Flute* (London: R. Cocks & Co., 1843), 57.
26. Masel, 'Th. Boehm et Grevé'.
27. Rockstro, *Treatise*, §917.
28. Macgillivray, 'Woodwind', 255.
29. Berdahl, 'The First Hundred Years', 46.
30. A ring-key flute by Larrabee is item A40 in Spohr, *Kunsthandwerk*.
31. Badger, *An Illustrated History of the Flute*, iii–iv.
32. Berdahl, 'The First Hundred Years', 47–8, 623.
33. Berdahl, 'The First Hundred Years', 57, 692.
34. Clinton, *Code*, Introduction.
35. Masel, 'Th. Boehm et Grevé'.
36. Clinton, *Code*, Introduction.
37. Facsimile in Lenski and Ventzke, *Das goldene Zeitalter*, 44–7.
38. Giannini, *Great Flute Makers*, 134–7.
39. Ventzke and Spohr, 'Die Patente der Boehmflöte von 1847', 91–2. I am grateful to Ludwig Böhm and Peter Spohr for a transcript of the letter in the original English.
40. Adrien Girard, *Histoire et richesses de la flûte* (Paris: Librairie Gründ, 1953), 64, cited in Ventzke, *Boehmflöte*, 43. Girard's source is probably Rockstro, *Treatise*, §929.
41. Giannini, *Great Flute Makers*, 209.
42. *Echo Musical*, Brussels, Jan. 1883, reprinted in Welch, *History of the Boehm Flute*.

THE RING-KEY FLUTE IN PARIS

1. Letter of 2 June 1838 to Coche, cited in Boehm, *Über den Flötenbau*.
2. According to Welch (*History*, 49) it would have been the fourth, after visits in 1833, 1834, and 1836.
3. [Jacques Hippolyte] A[ristide] Farrenc, 'Flute Boehm', *Revue et Gazette Musicale* 5 no. 36 (Paris, 9 November 1838), 364–5.
4. Camus, *Méthode*, p. 5 n. 2.
5. Schafhäutl's testimony cannot be viewed as above question in this matter, since he also wrote (Broadwood's trans., p. 77), 'In 1837 the Boehm flute was introduced into the Paris Conservatoire, after a committee – of which Savant [*sic*], Prony, and Dulong were members – had borne the highest testimony to its merits.' As the narrative makes clear, a Committee of the Paris Academy of Sciences did examine the Coche-Buffet-Boehm flute (in 1838, not 1837) but it had no standing at the Conservatoire, and though a commission of that institution examined the ring-key flute in 1839–40, it firmly rejected the new instrument. Boehm's manuscript of his essay *On the Construction of Flutes* (now in Karl Ventzke's collection) states that the examination of the Academy of Sciences 'led to its acceptance at the Conservatoire de Musique', but the printed version was corrected to omit these words. Nonetheless, Schafhäutl's error has passed into flute folklore, repeated as recently as 1996 (Toff, *The Flute Book*, 54, where the date is given as 1838).
6. Coche, *Mémoire*, 12.

Chapter 10 Nineteenth-century eclecticism

The diversity of late nineteenth-century flute-playing and the tendency of flutists to move around frequently has made this the most difficult chapter to write. The extant studies that contribute most to a coherent view of its forbidding complexity are those that focus on a particular orchestra, school of playing, or body of repertoire. Stuart Scott's *Hallé Flutes: Flautists of the Hallé Orchestra, 1858–[19]93* (Altrincham, Cheshire: S. J. Scott, 1998) is a fascinating historical survey of the oldest English orchestra's flutists, their repertoire, and instruments. Similar studies of the flute-playing in other long-established orchestras would doubtless provide further insights. Robert Bigio's eagerly-awaited study of Rudall Carte (forthcoming from London: Tony Bingham) will surely shed much light on the players of the British Empire, as Susan Berdahl's has done for American players and makers and Mary Jean Simpson's did for one pioneering maker in 'Alfred G. Badger (1815–1892), Nineteenth[-]Century Flutemaker: His Art, Innovations, and Influence on Flute Construction, Performance and Composition, 1845–1895' (D.M.A. diss., University of Maryland, 1982).

    John Robert Bailey's excellent study, 'Maximilian Schwedler's *Flute and Flute-Playing*: Translation and study of late nineteenth-century German performance practice' (D.M. diss., Northwestern University, 1987) provides the most comprehensive international survey of nineteenth-century flutes and flute-playing yet attempted. Bailey surveys Schwedler's activities in flute design, comparing them to flutists and flute-making in major centres of flute-playing in Europe, and to Schwedler's own experiences during his career as orchestral player and teacher. He relates Schwedler's aesthetic of flute-playing to those of Quantz, Tromlitz, and Fürstenau, to the French school, to German Boehm flutists, and to English players of the time. The dissertation contains a complete critical English text of the third (1923) edition of *Flöte und Flötenspiel*, and gives useful insight into the performance of flute parts in works for orchestra by Brahms, Bruckner, Mahler, Strauss, and Wagner. Though it ranges widely, Bailey displays an impressive command of important details. Yet as he notes, '[m]uch further scholarship needs yet to be done on this critical period of flute-playing' and many questions remain unanswered.

    A detailed examination of the flutes used in German orchestras in the nineteenth century appears in a second excellent dissertation on the period's orchestral flutes, Amy Sue Hamilton's 'The Relationship of Flute Construction to the Symphonic Role of the Flute and Orchestral Performance Practice in the Nineteenth Century' (D.M.A. diss., Northwestern University, 1984). Hamilton's dissertation lacks authoritative source material in its treatment of the eighteenth century, but intelligently considers the sound quality and balance of later ensembles, providing well-substantiated reasons for many of the idiosyncrasies of nineteenth-century woodwind orchestration. Further details on the nineteenth-century orchestra can be found in Adam Carse, *The Orchestra from Beethoven to Berlioz* (Cambridge: Heffer, 1948) and Daniel J. Koury, *Orchestral Performance Practices in the Nineteenth Century: Size, Proportions, and Seating* (Ann Arbor: UMI Research Press, 1986). With so much attention focused on the orchestra, information about bands is exceedingly rare; material here on flute bands comes from R. W. Hylands, *History of the Flute and Flute Bands*. Likewise the period's solo and chamber music repertoire has suffered neglect, largely because of the shift in taste in the 1890s: Gian-Luca Petrucci has led a re-examination with his article on Italian virtuoso studies, 'Entdecken wir unsere Meister wieder! Betrachtungen zu hundert Jahren italienischer Flötendidaktik', *Tibia* 20 (1994), 98–103, which first appeared as 'Riscopriamo i nostri maestri', *Syrinx* 2.5 (April–June 1990), 14–17.

    Biographical studies of flutists and makers would seem to promise rewards for further study. The Berlin amateur flutist Adolph Goldberg privately published a collection of photographs and short biographies in *Biographieen zur Porträts-Sammlung hervorragender Flöten-Virtuosen. Dilettanten und Komponisten* in c1906, reissued with an introduction by Karl Ventzke (Celle: Moeck Verlag, c1987). Leonardo De Lorenzo's *My Complete Story of the Flute* (noted above under 'History and Criticism') is a work of anecdotal rather than scholarly interest that contains colourful if not completely reliable biographical information on European and American flutists, as does Fitzgibbon's *Story of the Flute*. Bailey summarizes much of the important information from Goldberg and De Lorenzo, among others. A few good short studies of individual players have appeared, such as Robert Bigio's 'Albert Fransella: The Paganini of the Flute', *Pan* 12.2 (June 1994), 19–25, and Gernot Stepper's 'Die Gebrüder Franz und Karl Doppler', *Tibia* 7 (1982), 88–95, while a regrettably unpublished manuscript on Edward de Jong by Sarah Bull (Trevor Wye collection) helped me understand the unexpected richness of one Dutch-English flutist's musical life. Gianni Lazzari presented an interesting study of six pictures of Briccialdi in 'Ritratti di flautisti Italiani dell'Ottocento: Giulio Briccialdi', *SIFTS* 4.1 (April 1999), 17–37. Susan Berdahl's 'Haynes, Haynes, and Haynes', *Woodwind Quarterly* 1 (May

1993), 103–19, summarized material from her dissertation to describe succinctly the activities of the brothers William and George Haynes, as well as John C. Haynes.

Useful periodicals of the late nineteenth century include Paul de Wit's *Zeitschrift für Instrumentenbau*, available only on microfilm in a few research libraries as it awaits the comprehensive study it deserves. Percy A. Scholes, *The Mirror of Music, 1844–1944* (London: Novello and Oxford University Press, 1947) gives a detailed yet admirably coherent view of British musical life through the lens of *The Musical Times*.

1. Hylands, 'History of the Flute and Flute Bands'.
2. Shaw, 'Instruments and Pitch' (also titled in some Shaw editions 'Wanted – a flute that is a flute'), article dated 7 March 1894, quoted from the Pelican *G. B. S. On Music* by courtesy of Robert Bigio.
3. C. G. Conn's *Trumpet Notes* 15.4 (April 1888), quoted in Laurence Libin, *Our Tuneful Heritage: American Instruments from the Metropolitan Museum of Art* (Provo, Utah: Museum of Art, Brigham Young University, 1994), 33.
4. Scott, *Hallé Flutes*, 19.
5. Adam Carse, *The Orchestra from Beethoven to Berlioz* (Cambridge: W. Heffer & Sons, 1948), 99–100.
6. Gerald Jackson, *First Flute* (London: Dent, 1968), 25, 31.
7. Hamilton, 'The Relationship', 267–71, 318.
8. Jaap Frank, *NGD2*, s.v. 'Flute', and private communication, 20 October 2000.
9. Giannini, 'An Old Key', 16, and *Great Flute Makers*, 180.
10. TB to WSB, 23 September 1868, quoted in Boehm, *An Essay on the Construction of Flutes*, ed. Broadwood, 53.
11. Ibid.
12. Letter of 3 January 1846, cited in Ventzke, 'Über das ambivalente Verhältnis'.
13. Hamilton, 'The Relationship', 372–3. See also Welch, *History*, 473.
14. TB to WSB, August 1871, quoted in Boehm, *An Essay on the Construction of Flutes*, 59.
15. Bailey, 'Maximilian Schwedler', 155 (Bailey's trans. modified), from Wagner, 'On Conducting' 'Über das Dirigiren', ed. Wolfgang Golther, *Gesammelte Schriften und Dichtungen*, 10 vols (Berlin: Deutsches Verlagshaus Bong, 1913), 8.283. My trans. of Wagner's '*Gewaltrohr*' as 'mighty shawm' in place of the more customary 'power tube' is based on *Muret-Sanders Encyclopedic English-German and German-English Dictionary* (Berlin: Langenscheidtsche Verlagsbuchhandlung, and London: H. Grevel & Co., 1900), s.v. Rohr: 5 [musical] '(*cylindrisches Blase-instrument, bfd. Schalmei*) shawm, shalm'.
16. *Musikalisches Wochenblatt*, Leipzig, 26 November 1880, 578–9, quoted in Ventzke, 'Über das ambivalente Verhältnis', 49.
17. Schwedler, *Flöte und Flötenspiel*, 15, quoted in Bailey's trans., 'Maximilian Schwedler', 147.
18. Tillmetz, *Anleitung zur Erlernung der Theobald Böhm'schen Cylinder- und Ringklappen-Flöte mit konischer Bohrung Op. 30* (Leipzig: Kistner [1890]), v–vi.
19. Jaap Frank, *NGD2*, s.v. 'Flute'.
20. *Caecilia*, 1853, see Rien de Reede, 'Nederlandische Flötisten und Flötisten in den Niederlanden 1700–1900', *Tibia* 24 (1999), 345–54, 24.2, 433–41, 433.
21. James Browne in *Monthly Musical Record*, 1910, cited in Toff, *Development*, 124.
22. James in *Flutonicon* 5 (1846), cited in Eagle, 'A Constant Passion', 205.
23. 'Edward de Jong', unpublished MS by Sarah Bull (Trevor Wye collection), Appendix A, ff. 35–40, gives De Jong's repertoire in the period 1858–1909.
24. Lazzari, forthcoming.
25. Petrucci, 'Entdecken wir unsere Meister wieder!', 101. See also Benoît Tranquille Berbiguier, *30 Préludes ou points d'orgue Op. 134* (Paris, c1830), Joseph Fahrbach, *30 Préludes Op. 6* (Leipzig, n.d.), Giuseppe Gariboldi, *L'Art de préluder du flûtiste Op. 149* (Paris, 1882), and Leonardo De Lorenzo, *Die moderne Kunst des Präludiums* (Leipzig: W. Zimmerman, c1920). A good list is given in *HBQF*, 194.

26. Petrucci, 'Entdecken wir unsere Meister wieder!', 102.
27. Leonardo de Lorenzo, 'European Impressions of a Flute Player', *The Flutist* 8 (1927), 166, quoted in Bailey, 'Maximilian Schwedler', 104. See also Alwin Wollinger, *Die Flötenkompositionen von Sigfrid Karg-Elert (1877–1933)* (Frankfurt: Haag & Herchen, c1991). The information on Bartuzat's switch to the Boehm flute came from John Bailey in a private communication.
28. *Studies on Taste and Style composed expressly for the Boehm Flute and dedicated to Philip Ernst* (New York: C. Breusing, 1854), ii.
29. TB to WSB, May 1870.
30. Berdahl, 'The First Hundred Years', 59.
31. Bailey, 'Maximilian Schwedler', 44.
32. Müller, 'Berlin Flötenvirtuosen', 2, cited in Bailey 'Maximilian Schwedler', 20.
33. Kyle J. Dzapo, *Joachim Andersen: A Bio-bibliography* (Westport, Conn.: Greenwood Press, 1999); Jaap Frank, *NGD2*, s.v. 'Flute'.
34. Goldberg, *Biographieen*, 287–8.
35. Giannini, 'An Old Key', 19.
36. Emil Prill, *Schule für die Böhm-Flöte* (Leipzig: Wilhelm Zimmerman, 1927), 12, quoted in Bailey, 'Maximilian Schwedler', 163.
37. Georg Müller, 'Professor Emil Prill … Ein Gedenkblatt zu Emil Prills 60. Geburtstag', *Deutsche Militär-Musiker-Zeitung* (Berlin), 23 July 1927 (Trevor Wye collection).
38. Hamilton, 'The Relationship', 277–8.
39. Hamilton, 'The Relationship', 414 citing Rockstro, *Treatise*, pp. 624–6.
40. Bailey, 'Maximilian Schwedler', 35.
41. De Reede, 'Nederlandische Flötisten'.
42. Bailey, 'Maximilian Schwedler', 35.
43. John R. Bailey, 'Towards a History of the Dresden Flute Tradition, 1850 to the Present', paper read at the NFA National Convention, Boston, 21 August 1993.
44. Bull, 'Edward De Jong'.
45. See Bailey, 'Maximilian Schwedler', n. 72 p. 222, on dates.
46. Bailey, 'Maximilian Schwedler', 101.
47. Bailey, 'Maximilian Schwedler', 100.
48. Bailey, 'Maximilian Schwedler', 51–80.
49. According to Bailey ('Maximilian Schwedler', 80, 83) Bate and Toff mistakenly associated the 'Reform' embouchure with Schwedler. See also Reinhold Quandt, 'Zur "Reform"-Ansatz bei Querflöten', *Tibia* 8 (1983) 249–57, and a response by Gustav Scheck, 'Bemerkungen zu Reinhold Quandts Artikel "Zum 'Reform'-Ansatz bei Querflöten"', *Tibia* 8 (1983), 394–6; Bate, *The Flute*, 15.
50. Bailey, 'Maximilian Schwedler', 84.
51. Hamilton, 'The Relationship', 434–53.
52. Hamilton, 'The Relationship', 389, 538–9.
53. Bailey, 'Maximilian Schwedler', 90–1.
54. Letter of February 1886, quoted in Bailey, 'Maximilian Schwedler', 57.
55. Fitzgibbon, *Story*, 176.
56. Kreitzer, 'Transverse Flutes by London Makers'.
57. *AmZ*, 1 October 1800, 21.
58. Theodor Berthold and Moritz Fürstenau, *Die Fabrikation musikalischer Instrumente … im Königl. Sächsischen Vogtlande* (Leipzig: Breitkopf und Härtel, 1876).
59. Eagle, 'A Constant Passion', 188 and n. 15 (*Harmonicon*, 1832); see also Rockstro, *Treatise*, §559.
60. Rockstro, *Treatise*, §921.
61. Fitzgibbon, *Story*, 205.
62. Scott, *Hallé Flutes*, 9–15.
63. Fitzgibbon, *Story*, 42 and 192–3, note.

64. Fitzgibbon, *Story*, 213.
65. Berdahl, 'The First Hundred Years', 63.
66. Haynes catalogue, 1925; see also Toff, *Development*, 187, note.
67. Berdahl, 'The First Hundred Years', 90, 506, 513.
68. Berdahl, 'The First Hundred Years', 71.
69. Henry Clay Wysham, *The Evolution of the Boehm Flute* (Elkhart: C. G. Conn, 1898).
70. Berdahl, 'The First Hundred Years', 135 (Bate, *The Flute*, plate 8D).
71. Berdahl, 'The First Hundred Years', 94–5.
72. Berdahl, 'The First Hundred Years', 196.
73. Berdahl, 'The First Hundred Years', 177.
74. Shaw, 'Instruments and Pitch'.
75. Communication from Robert Bigio from his forthcoming study of Rudall Carte.
76. Giannini, *Great Flute Makers*, 209–11.
77. Berdahl, 'The First Hundred Years', 131; Giannini, 'An Old Key'.
78. Fransella to H. D. Seale, 4 October 1904 (Trevor Wye collection).
79. Berdahl, 'The First Hundred Years', 131; on p. 741 Berdahl has the date as 1894.
80. *Allgemeine Zeitung* (Chemnitz), May 1927; *Neues Pommersches Tageblatt* (Stargard), 8 May 1927; *Berliner Tageblatt*, 9 May 1937 (Trevor Wye collection). The instrument was item A86 in Spohr, *Kunsthandwerk*.
81. P. S. Alexejew, 'Flöte und Flötenspiel', *Neue Zeitschrift für Instrumentenbau* 38.31 (August 1918), 319, quoted in Bailey, 'Maximilian Schwedler', 158.

FURTHER INNOVATIONS IN THE ECLECTIC PERIOD

1. Except where noted, patent numbers and dates are given in Bate, *The Flute*, and/or Toff, *Development*.
2. Rockstro, *Treatise*, §§668–70, 673, 679–83, 791.
3. Gianni Lazzari, 'Ritratti di flautisti Italiani dell'Ottocento: Giulio Briccialdi', *SIFTS* 4.1 (April 1999), 17–37, 27.
4. Ibid.
5. Francesco Carreras, 'I flauti a doppia camera', *SIFTS* 3 (1999), 29–37.
6. Berdahl, 'The First Hundred Years', 59.
7. Mechanism registered patent no. 37441.
8. Patent no. 105527.
9. Patent no. 219649.
10. Patent no. 787509.

Chapter 11 The French Flute School

The two chief documents of Taffanel's teaching are [Claude-Paul] Taffanel and [Philippe] Gaubert, *Méthode Complète de Flûte* (Paris: Alphonse Leduc, 1923), and Louis Fleury's article on the flute in *Encyclopédie de la musique et dictionnaire du Conservatoire*, 11 vols (Paris: C. Delagrave [c1913]–31), part 2, vol. 3, 1523–25. Another useful article by Fleury is his 'The Flute and its Powers of Expression', *Music & Letters* 3 (1922), 383–93.

Claude Dorgeuille has written the only published study of the Taffanel school in *L'Ecole française de flûte* (Paris: Editions Codberg, 1983, rev. 1994), trans. and rev. Edward Blakeman with discography by Christopher Steward, *The French Flute School, 1860–1950 by Claude Dorgeuille* (London: Tony Bingham, 1986). The discography is a particularly useful guide for anyone seriously interested in investigating early twentieth-century French flute-playing, and the book contains helpful appendices such as a list of set pieces at Conservatoire examinations from 1860 to 1950 and a list of graduates (surnames only) for the same period. Dorgeuille collaborated with René Le Roy on *Traité de la flûte: Historique, technique et pédagogique* (Paris: Éditions musicales transatlantiques [1966]). Among unpublished material, Patricia Joan

Ahmad's 'The Flute Professors of the Paris Conservatoire from Devienne to Taffanel, 1795–1908' (M.A. diss., North Texas State University, 1980) contains some good background detail, while other British, Canadian, and American dissertations by Edward Blakeman, Mary C. J. Byrne, and Tula Giannini show how much interest the subject has attracted but were not available to me. The panel, 'Professors at the Paris Conservatoire' (p. 221), was compiled from Dorgeuille's *The French Flute School*, Adrien Girard's *Histoire et richesses de la flûte* (Paris: Librairie Gründ, 1953), and a private communication from Michel Debost.

Studies of Devienne and his tutor began with William Layton Montgomery's *Life and Works of François Devienne, 1759–1803* (Ph.D. diss., Catholic University of America, 1975). Jane Bowers, 'The Long and Curious History of the Devienne Method for the Flute', in *Music in Performance and Society: Essays in Honor of Roland Jackson*, ed. Malcolm Cole and John Koegel (Warren, Mich.: Harmonie Park Press, 1997), 205–27, gave an interesting discussion of the method's publication history. This was expanded in Bowers's exhaustive bibliographic study, *François Devienne's 'Nouvelle Méthode Théorique et Pratique pour la Flute'* (Aldershot and Brookfield, Vt: Ashgate, 1999), which presented a facsimile of the original edition, with an introduction, an annotated catalogue of later editions, and a translation with commentary. Apart from a facsimile, ed. David Jenkins, *A. Hugot & J. G. Wunderlich: Méthode de flûte, 1804* (Buren: Frits Knuf, 1975), no further studies of the Conservatoire flute texts have been published. An English translation of Tulou's tutor in an edition of 1853 has appeared in Janice Dockendorff Boland and Martha F. Cannon's translation, *Jean-Louis Tulou: A Method for the Flute* (Bloomington: Indiana University Press, 1995). Unfortunately what seems to have been the only extant copy of the method's first edition (1835) has gone missing from the Library of Congress. Tula Giannini's *Great Flute Makers of France* contains much valuable information on the flute at the Paris Conservatoire.

The literature on Marcel Moyse is extensive, but of uneven quality. Perhaps the clearest expressions of his ideals can be found in the rubrics to his *Enseignement Complet de la Flûte* (Paris: Alphonse Leduc, n.d.). Moyse's *How I Stayed in Shape*, trans. Paul M. Douglas (West Brattelboro, Vt: Marcel Moyse, [1974]), contains an interesting discussion of tone and vibrato. His 1949 article, trans. Maud la Charme, 'Marcel Moyse on Flute Playing', provides another perspective on, once again, tone. Originally in *Symphony* in June 1949, the essay is reprinted in Edward Blakeman's English edition of Dorgeuille's *French Flute School* (101–6). Quotations of Moyse's own words must be read with great caution, since he often spoke for effect and frequently contradicted himself. Trevor Wye's *Marcel Moyse: An Extraordinary Man* (Cedar Falls: Winzer Press, 1993) represents an intensely personal effort by an observant follower to explain Moyse's musical personality. Wye observes that Moyse did nothing to discourage accounts that contained inflated and exaggerated stories about him, and that recollections in his own portrait 'might be embellished with fantasy and wishful thinking'. Nonetheless, Ann McCutchan's *Marcel Moyse: Voice of the Flute* (Portland: Amadeus Press, 1994), which also provided much material for chapter 12, manages to present a clear, thoroughly-researched, and balanced account of the famous teacher's career and influence. McCutchan's study vividly conveys Moyse's view of Taffanel, Gaubert, Hennebains, and others, as well as the opinions and sentiments younger players such as Rampal expressed of him. Her own excellent scholarship is matched in an admirably thorough and exceptionally useful discography of 77 pages by Susan Nelson and William Shaman.

1. Moyse, quoted in McCutchan, *Marcel Moyse*, 46.
2. Macgillivray, 'Woodwind', 270.
3. Karl Kraber's notes, quoted in McCutchan, *Marcel Moyse*, 204.
4. Dorgeuille, *French Flute School*, 11, 40.
5. Wye, *Marcel Moyse*, 82.
6. Debost, quoted in Wye, *Marcel Moyse*, 11.
7. Wye, *Marcel Moyse*, 107.
8. See for example Toff, *Flute Book*, 101.

9. The German creation myth made what seems to have been its first appearance in Christian Friedrich Daniel Schubart, *Ideen zu einer Aesthetik der Tonkunst* (Vienna: J. V. Degen, 1806 R/Leipzig *c*1924), a work written in 1784–5.

10. Antoine Hugot and Johann Georges Wunderlich, *Méthode de Flûte du Conservatoire* (Paris: Conservatoire de Musique, 1804, R/Buren, The Netherlands, 1975), 7.

11. Bowers, *Devienne's 'Nouvelle Méthode'*, 7.

12. Cynthia M. Gessele, in *NGD2*, s.v. 'Conservatories', §III: 1790–1945.

13. Liebeskind, 'Versuch einer Akustik', n. 8 p. 231, trans. in *TKF*.

14. Bowers, *Devienne's 'Nouvelle Méthode'*.

15. As Nancy Toff wrote in 1979, 'In short, all musical elements join to extend the range of available tone colors; melody, harmony, rhythm, and dynamics, rather than maintaining their traditionally equal or superior status in relation to tone color, have … become subordinate to it' (*Development*, 205).

16. Hugot & Wunderlich, *Méthode de Flûte du Conservatoire*, 7.

17. See Rockstro, *Treatise*, §§553, 878.

18. Ahmad, 'The Flute Professors of the Paris Conservatoire', Appendix II, 132, quoting Pierre, *Le Conservatoire national de Musique*, 624.

19. Giannini, *Great Flute Makers*, 139.

20. Giannini, *Great Flute Makers*, 172, where Brossa's first name is given as Emil.

21. Welch, *History*, p. 193, n. 27.

22. French patent #250955; see *NLI*, 73, s.v. 'Couesnon'.

23. Dorgeuille, *French Flute School*, Appendix A.

24. Ahmad, 'The Flute Professors of the Paris Conservatoire', 76–7.

25. Jean-Philippe Rameau, *Œuvres complètes, publiées sous la direction de C. Saint-Saëns* (Paris: A. Durand et fils, 1895–1913).

26. Hamilton, 'The Relationship', 518; Bailey, 'Maximilian Schwedler', 107.

27. Gustav Doret, *Temps et Contretemps* (Freiburg, 1942), 94, quoted in Dorgeuille, *French Flute School*, 35.

28. Barrère, 'Address at the Annual Dinner of the New York Flute Club, March 25, 1923', quoted in Nancy Toff, *Georges Barrère and the Flute in America* ([New York]: New York Flute Club, 1994), 75.

29. Georges Barrère, 'Violin of the Woodwind Instruments', *Musical America*, 6 November 1909.

30. Taffanel & Gaubert, *Méthode*, 186.

31. *Encyclopédie de la musique et dictionnaire du Conservatoire*, Blakeman's trans.

32. Quoted by Paul de Wit, *Zeitschrift für Instrumentenbau* 17.32 (August 1897), 820, and in Bailey, 'Maximilian Schwedler', 156.

33. *Encyclopédie de la musique et dictionnaire du Conservatoire*, Blakeman's trans..

34. Taffanel & Gaubert, *Méthode*, 186.

35. *Encyclopédie de la musique et dictionnaire du Conservatoire*, 180.

36. Quoted in Marcel Moyse, 'The Unsolvable Problem: Considerations on Flute Vibrato', *Woodwind Magazine* 2.7 (1950), 4, quoted in Toff, *Flute Book*, 111.

37. Stowell, *Violin Technique*, 40.

38. Joseph Joachim to Franz von Vecsey, 20 November 1904, quoted in August Leopold Sass, *The secrets of violin technic. A guide to the more rapid attainment of a good technic. Practical hints for violinists … Appendix: The rules of violin-playing by Joseph Joachim. Translated from the German original (Thirteenth edition) by Jeffrey Pulver* (London: Bosworth [n.d.]), 36.

39. Philip, *Early Recordings*, 234; see p. 326 below.

40. Philip, *Early Recordings*, 212.

41. Jochen Gärtner, *Das Vibrato unter besonderer Berücksichtigung der Verhältnisse bei Flötisten* (Regensburg: Bosse, 1974 R/1980), 39, cited in Bailey, 'Maximilian Schwedler', 179. See also chapter 12 below.

42. Moyse, 'Marcel Moyse on Flute Playing'.

43. See rubric above.
44. Nancy Toff, *Georges Barrère*, 10.
45. Ehrlich, *The Music Profession*, 83–4.
46. Interview, Edward Blakeman, 3 March 2000.
47. McCutchan, *Marcel Moyse*, 72.
48. McCutchan, *Marcel Moyse*, 94.
49. McCutchan, *Marcel Moyse*, 116.
50. Wye, *Marcel Moyse*, 24.
51. Toff, *Development*, 125.

Chapter 12 The flute in the age of recording

Only a few works (see bibliography for chapter 10) have contributed much to our knowledge of early twentieth-century flute-playing, but recordings provide a rich area to learn more. Robert Philip has covered the orchestral repertoire in his fascinating and detailed *Early Recordings and Musical Style: Changing Tastes in Instrumental Performance, 1900–1950* (Cambridge and New York: Cambridge University Press, 1992), showing the ways in which performance styles altered in the early recording era and how modern tastes developed. Philip argues that the greatest value of getting to know early recordings 'is that it forces us to question unspoken assumptions about modern taste, and about the ways in which we use it to justify our interpretation of earlier performance practice'. Also highly recommended, though it appeared too late for me to profit from in this book, is Timothy Day's *A Century of Recorded Music* (New Haven and London: Yale University Press, 2000), especially Chapters 3, 'Changes in Performing Styles Recorded' and 4, 'Listening to Recordings'. Susan Nelson's studies of early flute recordings, along with re-issues on CD of a number of notable early issues (listed at http://recordings.flutehistory.com), have begun to bring the recorded legacy to the attention of flutists. A highly recommended general introduction can be found in Nelson's 'The Flute on Record to 1940', in David Lasocki, ed., *Fluting and Dancing: Articles and Reminiscences for Betty Bang Mather on her 65th Birthday* (New York: McGinnis & Marx, 1992), 61–73. Her excellent discography with William Shaman in Ann McMcCutchan's *Marcel Moyse: Voice of the Flute* has already been noted. 'The chronicle of performance practice we witness in these recordings is invaluable', she writes. 'It might serve as a more vivid, not to mention more accurate, source of illustration than the scores of written accounts that have enjoyed almost exclusive legitimacy for decades. This recorded legacy demands rediscovery and serious contemplation.' Michael Chanan's *Repeated Takes: A Short History of Recording and its Effects on Music* (London and New York: Verso, 1995) selects and elaborates on material in his *Musica Practica*.

Jochen Gärtner has given one aspect of performance practice a thorough treatment in his book *Das Vibrato unter besonderer Berücksichtigung der Verhältnisse bei Flötisten* (Regensburg: Bosse, 1974, R/1980), translated as *The Vibrato, with Particular Consideration Given to the Situation of the Flutist* (Regensburg: Bosse, 1981). At the opposite extreme, most of the literature on famous French flutists of the twentieth century loses its focus in an excess of reverence for its subjects and an inability to compare and contrast them with others (the exceptions have been noted in the bibliography for chapter 11). Similar drawbacks attend much of the anecdotal and interview material to be found in periodicals.

In contrast a level and lucid account of jazz flutists and their work is given by Jim Walker in 'The Flute in Jazz: An Historical Overview', *The Flutist's Handbook: A Pedagogy Anthology* (Santa Clarita Calif.: National Flute Association, 1998), 129–33, and in Heinrich von Kalnein's 'Jazz Talk – Die Flöte in Jazz und Populärmusik', *HBQF* 292–9, which gives a reading list and discography for jazz flute. Lewis Porter's entry on the flute in the *New Grove Dictionary of Jazz* (London: Macmillan, 1988) also provides a clear perspective, to which Peter Guidi adds somewhat more detail in *The Jazz Flute*, 2 vols ([NL–] Wormerveer: Molenaar Edition B.V., 1997). English flute-playing too has been the topic of some useful writing. James A.

Macgillivray's 'The Woodwind' presents an historically-aware evaluation of the postwar scene, and Kenneth Bell gives a broad view of the English style in 'Flute Playing in Britain: Stylistic Origins and Developments', *Pan* 7.4 (Dec 1989), 12–19. Valuable works of a more general nature include Cyril Ehrlich, *The Music Profession in Britain since the Eighteenth Century: A Social History* (Oxford: Clarendon Press, 1985), a thorough and revealing study based on census records, directories, biographies of musicians, labour relations, and the history of institutions such as the Royal Schools of Music. Some of the same territory is covered with perception and wit by Robert Stradling and Meirion Hughes, *The English Musical Renaissance, 1860–1940: Construction and Deconstruction* (London and New York: Routledge, 1993).

Personal reminiscences by flutists are rare, and all the more valuable for that. They include Gerald Jackson's *First Flute* (London: Dent, 1968), and Jean-Pierre Rampal with Deborah Wise, *Music My Love: An Autobiography* (New York: Random House, 1989). Nancy Toff, *Georges Barrère and the Flute in America: An Exhibit in the Music Division, New York Public Library for the Performing Arts, November 12, 1994–February 4, 1995* ([New York:] New York Flute Club, Inc., 1994) is a panegyric to the founder of the New York Flute Club and the man Toff credits with bringing the modern French Flute School to America. The catalogue documents many interesting and crucial details of Barrère's move to America, his employment in New York, and his life and work in general.

The most helpful studies of instruments and their makers have again been those of John Bailey and Susan Berdahl. Hannah Lang, 'Verne Q. Powell Flutes, Inc., Celebrates its 70th Birthday', *Pan* 17.2 (June 1998), 20–4, is a history of the flute-manufacturing company. Robert Bigio kindly provided unpublished details based on his knowledge of the stock books of the Rudall Carte Company. William Maynard's 'Dayton C. Miller: His Life, Work, and Contributions as a Scientist and Organologist' (Thesis, Long Island University, 1971) is available on the Library of Congress web site at http://lcweb2.loc.gov/ammem/dcmhtml/mayo.html.

1. Ann Cecil-Sherman, 'John Amadio – Virtuoso Flutist', *New York Flute Club Newsletter* (April 2000), 4–7, 6.
2. *New York Sun* (1910), quoted in Toff, *Georges Barrère*, 7.
3. Berdahl, 'The First Hundred Years', 5–14.
4. Berdahl, 'The First Hundred Years', 490, 493.
5. Rudall Carte catalogue for 1926 (DCM); Berdahl, 'The First Hundred Years', 73.
6. Berdahl, 'The First Hundred Years', 96.
7. Berdahl, 'The First Hundred Years', 500–1, 707.
8. Berdahl, 'The First Hundred Years', 477.
9. Haynes catalogue for 1930, 20; Berdahl, 'The First Hundred Years', 516.
10. W. S. Haynes to Medicus, 12 February 1924, quoted in Berdahl, 'The First Hundred Years', 713.
11. Berdahl, 'The First Hundred Years'. On p. 355 Berdahl has the date of Conn's sale as 1928; Margaret Downie Banks gives it as 1915 on her Conn web pages at www.usd.edu/~mbanks/CONTENT.html.
12. Berdahl, 'The First Hundred Years', 355–6.
13. Berdahl, 'The First Hundred Years', citing Powell's brochure of 1928.
14. Berdahl, 'The First Hundred Years', 600, 648–9.
15. Berdahl, 'The First Hundred Years', 650.
16. Dorgeuille, *French Flute School*, 105.
17. Jack Hiemenz, 'Marcel Moyse, Master Flutist: "I Imitate Caruso"', *High Fidelity/Musical America* 25.1 (January 1975), 14, quoted in Bailey, 'Maximilian Schwedler', 180. See also p. 227 above.
18. For example, Hennebains's 1908 recording of the Doppler *Fantaisie* op. 26 (Gramophone 39192/39184).
19. McCutchan, *Marcel Moyse*, 115.

20. Polydor 95166.
21. A correspondent in the *Sunday Referee* quoted in the *Musical Times* of August 1933 (Scholes, *Mirror*).
22. Note in CD liner, The Susan Milan Collection, Flute Archive Series 2.
23. An interviewee in *Down Beat*, 1974, quoted in *HBQF*, 294.
24. Bailey, 'Maximilian Schwedler', 205.
25. Bailey, 'Maximilian Schwedler', 92, 39–40, 185.
26. Cecil-Sterman, 'Amadio', 7.
27. Georg Müller, *Die Kunst des Flötenspiels* (Leipzig and Berlin: Pro-Musica-Verlag, 1954), I.79, quoted in Bailey, 'Maximilian Schwedler', 184–5.
28. Philip, *Early Recordings and Musical Style*, 118.
29. Hamilton, 'The Relationship', 502; Bailey, 'Maximilian Schwedler', 90.
30. Henry Welsh, 'Orchestral Reform', *Music & Letters* 12.2 (1931), 25, quoted in Toff, *Flute Book*, where the date is given in the text (p. 112) as 1951.
31. Interview with Andy Thomson, 10 November 1999.
32. Angeleita Floyd, *The Gilbert Legacy: Methods, Exercises and Techniques for the Flutist* (Cedar Falls, Ia.: Winzer Press, 1990), 8, and Wye, *Marcel Moyse*, 59–60, report Gilbert's accounts of these conversations, for which no dates are given.
33. WA 11003–2, Columbia DB398, December 1930.
34. William and Sidney Powell, *The Flautist's Guide* (MS, DCM), ff. 35–9.
35. G&T 49157 29186.
36. Fitzgibbon, *Story*, 223.
37. Fitzgibbon, *Story*, 244.
38. Jane Bowers and Judith Tick, eds, *Women Making Music: The Western Art Tradition, 1150–1950* (Urbana: University of Illinois Press, 1987), 354.
39. Interview, Gareth Morris, 12 November 1999.
40. Berdahl, 'The First Hundred Years', 208–9.
41. Christopher Steward, 'The Recording Legacies of John Francis and Arthur Gleghorn', *Pan* 19.3 (September 2000), 30–1.
42. McCutchan, *Marcel Moyse*, 138–9.
43. Haynes catalogue for 1930, 28, cited in Berdahl, 'The First Hundred Years', 514.
44. Endorsements dated April and June 1931 in an undated Rudall Carte brochure annotated 'Current August 1933' by Dayton C. Miller (DCM).
45. Barrère to Everett Timm, 29 November 1941, quoted in Toff, *Georges Barrère*, 30.
46. [Denis Verroust], 'Discographie' and 'A propos des enregistrements de Jean-Pierre Rampal ...', *Traversières* 24/58–25/59 [c1997], 76–109, 91.
47. Rampal, *Music My Love*, 63.
48. Evan G. Bauman, post to internet FLUTE list, 25 May 2000.
49. Rampal, *Music My Love*, 99, 104.
50. Gerald Jackson, *First Flute*, 112.
51. Scott, *Hallé Flutes*, 93.
52. Interview, Andy Thomson.
53. Macgillivray, 'Woodwind', 264.
54. Gareth Morris, *Flute Technique* (Oxford: Oxford University Press, 1991), 48. See also 47, 52.
55. Laurence Taylor, 'The Englishmen's Wooden Flutes', *The Instrumentalist* (March–April 1951), repr. in *Woodwind Anthology* (Evanston, Ill.: Instrumentalist, [1972]), 8.
56. Julius Baker, 'Flute Playing in the United States', *Woodwind World* 3.5 (December 1959), 7.
57. *Woodwind Magazine* (January 1950).
58. McCutchan, *Marcel Moyse*, 168–91.
59. McCutchan, *Marcel Moyse*, 198–9.
60. McCutchan, *Marcel Moyse*, 200.
61. McCutchan, *Marcel Moyse*, 207.
62. McCutchan, *Marcel Moyse*, 210.

63. Noah Greenberg, 'Early Music Performance Today', in Jan LaRue, ed., *Aspects of Medieval and Renaissance Music* (New York: W. W. Norton, 1966), 315, quoted in Haskell, *Early Music Revival*, 112.

64. Meylan, *The Flute*, 123–4.

Chapter 13 The flute in the early music revival

Harry Haskell's *The Early Music Revival: A History* (London: Thames and Hudson, 1988), together with the same author's entry 'Early music' in *NGD2*, provide an excellent overview of the ideas and events central to the rise of historicism and the early music movement. Though Haskell's book contains only a few details directly related to the flute, it is highly recommended for background reading.

I studied the publication and performance history of Bach's flute works for a presentation I gave at the NFA's 2000 Convention in Columbus, Oh., entitled 'Interpreting Bach's Flute Sonatas in the 20th Century, and the 21st'. Afterwards, John Bailey kindly shared with me details of his study of Dresden and Leipzig flute-playing (sidebar, 'Dresden repertoire 1854–1929', chapter 10), which disabused me of the conventional view I had just repeated that French players had rediscovered the pieces.

John Solum's *The Early Flute* (Oxford: Clarendon Press, 1992), as well as the articles cited in the notes, provided information about early recordings using historical flutes. Much of my information about baroque flute-playing and -making since the 1970s comes from my own personal experience, which is inevitably incomplete. I apologize to anyone who feels their own historic contributions have been inadequately recognized, and encourage them to publish recollections that may help future writers document this interesting period in the history of flute-playing. Stephen Preston, my first baroque flute teacher from about 1977, provided details of his early experiences with the baroque flute, as well as background on professional flute-playing in London during the 1970s and 80s, in an interview in November 1999. Further information on his career is in 'Profiles 4: Stephen Preston in conversation with Edward Blakeman', *Pan* 3.3 (Sept 1985), 8–13. Information on Konrad Hünteler came from Annette Struck's interview, 'Das Porträt: Konrad Hünteler', *Tibia* 12 (1987), 499–504, and from Konrad Hünteler, 'Traversflöte heute: Gedenken aus der Praxis des Traversospiels', *Tibia* 11 (1986) 248–56. Hünteler wrote on the new Denner flute in 'Eine neuentdeckte Traversflöte von Jacob Denner', *Tibia* 18 (1993), 461–4, also covered in a news item in *Traverso* 5.2 (April 1993), 2. Barthold Kuijken has written somewhat unfocused general criticisms of the modern performance of early music, one of which is his '"Auf Originalinstrumenten"… "historisch getreu"?', *Tibia* 17 (1994), 280–3. Regrettably few others prominent early in the baroque flute revival have written about their ideas or experiences at all. Robert Ehrlich's interesting article on Brüggen and the recording industry, 'Frans Brüggen, oder: Die Vermarktung eines Star-Musikers', *Tibia* 19 (1993), 449–53, provides a highly recommended second-hand account.

The most productive writer on the topic of this chapter has been Frans Vester, who fostered debate on historicism in lectures and articles cited in the bibliography for chapter 14, and in 'Acht Statements und eine Coda zur Wiedergabe der Music des 18. Jahrhunderts', a paper he read at the first Finnish Flute Week at Tampere, August 1985, *Tibia* 12 (1987) 487–90. Vester wrote on editions in 'Publishers, Editors, Editions and Urtexts' in de Reede, *Concerning the Flute*, 121–8. Some of the material on Studio per Edizioni Scelte appeared in Ardal Powell, 'Select Music Facsimiles from Italy', *Traverso* 11.3 (July 1999), 9–12.

Hans-Peter Schmitz's *Querflöte und Querflötenspiel in Deutschland während des Barockzeitalters* (Kassel: Bärenreiter [1952]) was the first book-length treatment since Quantz (1752) of how to play baroque music on the flute. His writings on using historical flutes in that repertoire include 'Über die Verwendung von Querflöten des 18. Jahrhunderts in unserer Zeit', in Walther Vetter, ed., *Festschrift Max Schneider zum achtzigsten Geburtstage* (Leipzig: Deutscher Verlag für Musik,

1955), 277–84, and 'Von Wohl und Wehe des Historismus in der Musik und ihrer Wiedergabe', *Tibia* 9 (1984), 81–99.

Modern evaluations of historical flutes have for the most part deliberately ignored the instruments' historical context and musical purpose and thus tended to obscure rather than reveal their subject. John W. Coltman cited specimens of early flutes in several papers dealing with the acoustics of flutes, including 'The Intonation of Antique Flutes', *Woodwind Quarterly* 2 (Aug 1993), 76–91. His method reflects the desire of a postindustrial engineer to 'observe some of the impediments to correct intonation faced by the makers and the degree of success with which they were able to overcome them'. Coltman labels historical examples as 'good' and 'bad' depending on their adherence to this unexamined ideal of 'correctness', attributing deviations to their makers' incompetence and lack of modern measuring equipment rather than to their utterly different tastes and ideas. A number of other quasi-scientific works in German on the tone, embouchure, and acoustical proportions of the baroque flute have appeared in *Tibia*. Anne Chatoney Shreffler wrote with a musician's more penetrating insight in her analysis of the sonic and spectral differences between baroque and modern flutes, 'Baroque Flutes and Modern: Sound Spectra and Performance Results', *GSJ* 36 (1983), 88–96. In a performance of Bach's *Partita* on the early type, she concluded that 'music and instrument reveal an absolutely organic relationship to each other', particularly in register shifts from octave to octave that help define musical structure. On the modern flute, low notes and high ones alike activate the same region of upper partials, so that these spectral transformations are missing.

1. Article reprinted from *Fraser's Magazine* in London's *Musical Times* in 1851 (Scholes, *Mirror*).
2. On Leipzig, see Bailey, 'Maximilian Schwedler', 109–11.
3. Review of 10 January 1901, quoted in Bailey, 'Maximilian Schwedler', 114.
4. Bailey, 'Maximilian Schwedler', 115.
5. Scott, *Hallé Flutes*, 23.
6. Scott, *Hallé Flutes*, 51.
7. 'The Bach Festival at Eisenach', *Monthly Musical Record* 14 (1884), 248–9, cited in Haskell, *Early Music Revival*, 25.
8. *Post* (Berlin), 14 December 1893 (Trevor Wye collection).
9. Taffanel & Gaubert, *Méthode*, 186.
10. 'Some Old-Time Music', in *The Year's Music, 1896* (London: J. S. Virtue, 1896), 24, cited in Haskell, *Early Music Revival*, 33.
11. Anselm Hughes, *Septuagesima* (London: Plainsong & Mediaeval Music Society, 1959), 56, quoted in Haskell, *Early Music Revival*, 34.
12. Masel, 'Th. Boehm et Grevé', 603, citing Constant Pierre, *La facture instrumentale à l'Exposition Universelle de 1889* (Paris: Librairie de l'Art indépendant, 1890), 364.
13. Haskell, *Early Music Revival*, 44.
14. Powell, 'The Hotteterre Flute', 234–40.
15. Dan H. Lawrence, ed., *The Bodley Head Bernard Shaw: Shaw's Music* (Oxford: Bodley Head, n.d.), vol. 1, 301–2.
16. Powell, 'The Hotteterre Flute', n. 39 p. 243.
17. Bailey, 'Maximilian Schwedler', 93–4.
18. Bailey, 'Maximilian Schwedler', 95, 98, 116. On Riszler see *NLI*, s.v. 'Riszler, Thomas Hinrich'.
19. Nelson, 'The Flute on Record', 70.
20. Bailey, 'Maximilian Schwedler', 127. Table 6 has a partial listing of publications.
21. Bailey, 'Maximilian Schwedler', 128.
22. McCutchan, *Marcel Moyse*, 53.
23. Fleury, 'The Flute and its Powers of Expression', p. 385 and note.
24. W. J. Turner in the *Radio Times* in 1932, quoted in *Musical Times*, December 1932, and in Scholes, *Mirror*.
25. Haskell, *Early Music Revival*, 102; Ahmad, 'Paris Conservatoire Professors', 115.
26. HMV D.B.3407/8, re-issued on Susan Milan Collection, Flute Archive Series 1, [c1998].

27. Haskell, *Early Music Revival*, 62–3.
28. Interview with Gareth Morris, 12 November 1999.
29. Victor M709=17460/65 ; Martin Elste, *Meilsteine der Bach-Interpretation, 1750–2000* (Stuttgart: Metzler, Kassel: Bärenreiter, 2000), 311–12.
30. R[olf] Ermeler, 'Über die barocke Traversflöte', *Hausmusik* 14 (1950), 39.
31. See rubric above.
32. Schmitz, 'Über die Verwendung von Querflöten des 18. Jahrhunderts', 279–80. See also Schmitz, 'Von Wohl und Wehe des Historismus'.
33. Ibid.
34. David Lasocki, 'The Baroque Flute and its Role Today', *Recorder & Music Magazine* 2.4 (February 1967), 96–104.
35. Ehrlich, 'Frans Brüggen, oder: Die Vermarktung eines Star-Musikers'.
36. Betty Bang Mather, 'A Summer in Germany with a One-Keyed Flute', *The American Music Teacher* 15.5 (April/May 1966), 20–1; David Lasocki, 'Betty and David', Lasocki, *Fluting and Dancing*, 173–6.
37. David Lasocki, 'The Baroque Flute and its Role Today', *Recorder & Music Magazine* 2.4 (February 1967), 96–104.
38. Bruce Haynes, 'Generic 415', *Traverso* 1.4 (October 1990, 1–2), a reprint of an article that appeared in *FoMRHI Quarterly* 53 (October 1988) .
39. Philips Seon 6747 096.
40. Linde: EMI Electrola C 065–28984. Preston: CRD 1014/15; see Elste, *Meilsteine der Bach-Interpretation*, 311–12.
41. Sastny: Tel 6.35339. Brüggen: ABC Classics AB–67015/2.
42. Dale Higbee, 'Baroque Flute Discography', *EM* 7 (1979), 250–3.
43. Fred Morgan, 'Making Recorders based on Historical Models', *EM* 10 (1982), 14–21.
44. ACC 7803, reissued on CD as ACC 57803 D.
45. Struck, 'Das Porträt: Konrad Hünteler', 500.
46. Wilfrid Mellers, 'Music in a Modern University: a Question of Priorities', *Musical Times* 104 (1973), 245–9.
47. Andrew Porter, *Music of Three Seasons, 1974–1977* (New York: Farrar Straus Giroux, 1978), xvi.
48. Scott, *Hallé Flutes*, 110–11.
49. Vester, 'Acht Statements'.
50. Vester, 'Publishers, Editors, Editions and Urtexts', 127.
51. Marcello Castellani, *Tibia* 14.3 (1989), 512–18, also Ardal Powell, 'Select Music Facsimiles from Italy'.
52. Peter Lloyd Masterclass 1995, dissertation by Suzanne Lord at the following web site: http://-users.uniserve.ca/~lwk/pindex.htm.
53. McCutchan, *Marcel Moyse*, 53.
54. Toff, *Flute Book*, 158–9.
55. Struck, 'Das Porträt: Konrad Hünteler'; Hünteler, 'Traversflöte heute'.
56. Fleury, *Encyclopédie de la musique et dictionnaire du Conservatoire*.
57. Hünteler, 'Eine neuentdeckte Traversflöte von Jacob Denner'. See also news item in *Traverso* 5.2 (April 1993), 2.
58. Stephen Rose, 'Bach Cantatas in Abundance', *EM* 28 (2000), 671–6, 671.
59. 'Profiles 4: Stephen Preston in conversation with Edward Blakeman'.
60. Kuijken, '"Auf Originalinstrumenten"… "historisch getreu"?'.

Chapter 14 The postmodern age

Just as the performance of nineteenth-century music only recently began to receive intensive scholarly attention and the foregoing chapter is the first account of the historical flute revival, little has yet been written on the flute and flute-playing of the last two generations. To the reminiscences by Gerald Jackson and Jean-Pierre Rampal noted in chapter 12 we can add De Lorenzo's *My Complete Story of the Flute* and James Galway's *An Autobiography* (London: Chappell, 1978), but personal reminiscences by flutists who witnessed the changes of the late twentieth century are unfortunately all too few. English writers seem to be awakening to the challenge first: Kenneth Bell, in addition to the article mentioned in the bibliography for chapter 12, broadly considered this period's passing as it affected Britain in 'Traditions and Fashions: Are we Neglecting our Flute-playing Heritage, and What can we Learn from it?', *Pan* 14.1 (Spring 1996), 8–19, Judith Fitton published 'Interview: Gareth Morris', *Pan* 9.3 (September 1991), 11–16, while Robert Bigio has contributed 'Richard Adeney at Eighty', with a discography by Christopher Steward, *Pan* 19.1 (2000), 14–20, and 'Gareth Morris at Eighty', *Pan* 19.4 (December 2000), 26–33.

Frans Vester's writings on the uniformity of the 1970s are still worth reading, even if the 'trained canary' mentality he warned of has become less acute, but unfortunately only one of his articles was in English. His brief introduction, 'Die Flötenspielpraxis zur Zeit der AMZ (1798–1848) und heute', to de Reede, *Die Flöte in der 'Allgemeine Musikalische Zeitung'* summarized his point of view. Fuller arguments came in 'On the Performance of Mozart's Music', *FQ* 6.1 (Fall 1980), 18–20, in German as 'Anmerkung zur Wiedergabe der Flötenmusik W. A. Mozarts', *Tibia* 11 (1986) 242–8, and in 'Acht Statements', noted in chapter 13.

Nancy Toff's *Flute Book* and *NGD2*, as well as a chapter by Gabriele Busch-Salmen in *HBQF*, 283–7, supplied background information on the avant-garde flute and other topics. I also relied on my own recollection, and look forward to the fuller account of new flute composition I hoped for in the text.

Two attempts have been made to analyse the intonation changes made in modern flute scales. In 'Theobald Boehm and the scale of the modern flute', *JAMIS* 9 (1983), 89–111, John W. Coltman traces differences between Boehm's own instruments and modern ones, once again anachronistically criticizing Boehm for his 'departures from the best modern practice', though at least now recognizing that changes in playing style play a part in these discrepancies. Another such exercise comes in Karyn Ann Berger's 'Flute Intonation: A Comparison of Modern and Theobald Boehm Flutes [*sic*] Scales' (D.M.A. diss., University of Cincinnati, 1999).

The growth of flute-playing in Irish traditional music has been documented by S. C. (Hammy) Hamilton in his book *The Irish Flute Player's Handbook* (n.p.: Breac Publications, 1990) and in 'The Reinvention of the Simple System Flute', *Woodwind Quarterly* 8 (February 1995), 40–4. Traditional music in general is well represented on the World Wide Web, and I used a number of documents mentioned in the notes. For klezmer music I relied on Henry Sapoznik, *The Compleat Klezmer* (Cedarhurst N.Y.: Tara Publications, 1989).

Walfrid Kujala, 'Music, Growth and Change', is one of several articles in *The Flutist Quarterly*, 23.2 (Winter 1997–98), a 25th Anniversary Issue that contains details of the organization's genesis and growth. Statistics are given on pp. 150–1. Information on the British Flute Society came in an interview with Trevor Wye on 5 March 2000.

1. *Time*, 11 March 1966, 49.
2. Toff, *Development*, 195.
3. http://www.harpsong.org/music-schools.html.
4. Janne Frost, 'Mr Toshio Takahashi, Founder of the Suzuki Flute School', www.sydneyfluteschool.com/aboutsuzukiflute.htm. Comments from teachers who have used the method can be found at http://www.usmo.com/~kstaff/prarchives6.html. See also Stephanie Jeanne Rea, 'The Suzuki Flute Method: A History and Description' (D.M. diss., Florida State University, 1999).
5. Gerald Jackson, 'A Talk for Flautists (and Others!)', *Woodwind Book, 1957–8* (London: Boosey & Hawkes, [1957]), 48–53, 50. See also *VFP*, 111.
6. Peter Lennon, 'Profile: The Tragic Flute – Or an Ill Wind that Blew Mr Morris no Good' (clipping from an unidentified and undated London newspaper, *c*1972, Trevor Wye collection).

7. Ibid.

8. Scott, *Hallé Flutes*, 108.

9. Powell brochure, 1928, cited in Berdahl, 'The First Hundred Years', 660.

10. 'Headjoint placement', 'Robert Dick Flute Corner', http://users.uniserve.com/~lwk/rdick.htm and 'Why I Love the Cooper Scale', http://users.uniserve.com/~lwk/rdick2.htm.

11. Berdahl, 'The First Hundred Years', 652.

12. Wye, *Marcel Moyse*, 44.

13. See [Jaap Frank, Michael Cox, and Hélène La Rue], 'The Louis Lot Debate: Should Old French Flutes be Modernised?', *Pan* 14.3 (September 1996), 31–6.

14. Toff, *Flute Book*, 13.

15. Peter Riedemeister, 'Zwischen Silberflöte und Traverso. Die konische Ringklappenflöte, mögliche Bereicherung einer einförmigen Scenerie?', *Tibia* 1 (1976), 129–36.

16. Vester, 'Acht Statements'.

17. Dorgeuille, *French Flute School*, 49. See also Kenneth Bell, 'Traditions and Fashions'.

18. Bate, *The Flute*, 151, cited in Toff, *Development*, 158.

19. Frank in *NGD2*, s.v. 'Flute'.

20. Gabriele Busch-Salmen, 'Werke der 1. Hälfte des 20. Jahrhunderts', *HBQF*, 284.

21. Toff, *Flute Book*, 259.

22. *HBQF*, 285.

23. Toff, *Flute Book*, 276.

24. Toff, *Development*, 205.

25. www.users.globalnet.co.uk/~jnrayw/flweb/rdick.htm.

26. Ardal Powell, *NGD2*, s.v. 'Dick, Robert'.

27. Robert Dick, 'Re: Fourth Octave G natural', post to internet FLUTE list, 18 December 1997.

28. Toff, *Development*, 218.

29. Heinrich von Kalnein, 'Jazz Talk – Die Flöte in Jazz und Popularmusik', *HBQF*, 292–99.

30. Anthony Tommasini, 'Jean-Pierre Rampal Dies; Popular Flutist Was 78', *New York Times*, 22 May 2000.

31. Vester, 'Acht Statements', 490.

32. Ibid.

33. Ransom Wilson, Flutist and Director, with Los Angeles Chamber Orchestra, *Baroque Concertos for Flute* (EMI Angel Digital DS-37338, 1982), programme note.

34. Jaap Frank, 'Alter Wein in neuen Schlauchen', *Tibia* 19 (1994), 283–6.

35. Jaap Frank, 'Wie "authentisch" ist die Boehmflöte?', *Tibia* 17 (1992), 271–8.

36. Frank, 'Alter Wein'. See also note 13 above.

37. Ibid.

38. Toff, *Flute Book*, 269.

39. Hamilton, 'Reinvention'; see also Gordon Turnbull, 'The Flow', www.oblique-design.demon.co.uk/flow/sligo.html.

40. Sapoznik, *Compleat Klezmer*, 9.

41. Henrik Norbeck's excellent study of folk flute-playing in Sweden appears as 'Woody Folk Notes', an English summary of an essay written for the course 'Folkmusik i Norden' at Högskolan Falun/Borlänge in June 1995, at http://home1.swipnet.se/~w-11382/traton/tratonen.htm. Richard Nunns appeared with the traditional Maori instruments of New Zealand, mostly flutes, at the NFA's 1999 Convention in Atlanta.

42. Simon Broughton and Mark Ellingham, ed., *World Music: The Rough Guide, Vol. 2: Latin and North America, Caribbean, India, Asia and Pacific* (London: Rough Guides, 2000), 388–9.

43. RCA Victor 09026–63422–2.

44. Jane Harvey, programme notes for *Hariprasad Chaurasia* (Nimbus NI 5469, 1996).

45. *HBQF*, 267.

46. Bernhard 'Beery' Batschelet, 'Musik an der Fasnacht: Volksmusik im Wandel', *Basler Zeitung* (27 February 1996), sec. iv, 37.

47. 'Vater des Piccolos: Erwin Oesch', *B wie Basel* (February 1996), 46–51.
48. Olly Klassen (GuGGenmusiGG LäGGerli-HaGGer), 'Die Guggenmusiken in Basel', www.gugge.ch/history.htm.
49. Toff, *Flute Book*, 77.
50. Toff, *Flute Book*, 270.
51. Bickford Brannen, quoted in Jan Spell Pritchard, 'Ross Prestia: A Biography and an Appreciation', *FQ* 26.2 (Winter 2001), 40–6, 44.
52. Interview, Trevor Wye, 5 March 2000.
53. Toff, *Flute Book*, 4.
54. Larry Krantz, 'The Flute World Expands' (post to internet FLUTE list, 18 March 1996), archived at http://users.uniserve.com/~lwk/fluteweb/history.htm, and 'FLUTE List Statistics' (post to FLUTE, 25 November 2000).
55. Larry Krantz, 'List Of Orchestra Flute Sections' (11 January 2001), http://users.uniserve.com/~lwk/sect.htm.
56. Verne Q. Powell Flutes Inc., 'Wooden flute', www.powellflutes.com/catalog/wood_flute.html.
57. William Bennett International Flute Summer School brochure, 2001.

Index

Page references to illustrations are in italic

Abell, Chris, 281
Academy of Sciences, French, 180–1, 177
Academy of Fine Arts, French, 171, 173–4, 177
Accademia Filarmonica, Verona, 47, 56
Accent, 257
acoustics of the flute, 5, 154–5, 180–1
Adam, Louis, 211
Adams, John Quincy, 137
Addington, Christopher, 299
Adorján, András, 281
Adson, John, 49
Agostinelli, Florante, 117–18
Agricola, Martin, 34–8, 292
Ahlgrimm, Isolde, 252
Ahmad, Patricia Joan, 323–4
air, column of, 212, 268
air de cour, 57, 62–3, 72, 107
Aitken, Robert, 240
Albert, Prince Consort, 200
Alberti, Nicholas, 189
Albisi, Abelardo, 204
Alborea, Francesco, see Franciscello
Alexander, James, 136
Alfonso X The Wise, 19
Allain-Dupré, Philippe, 47, 48, 52, 293
Almeida, Edward, 267
Altès, Joseph-Henri, 215–16, 221, 250, 187
  method, 223, 228
  works, 215
Altus see Tanaka, Shuichi
Amadio, John, 143
  recordings, 226
amateur flutists, 22, 42, 68, 72, 77–8, 80, 86, 104, 105, 110–11, 112, 115, 116, 117, 120, 125–6, 264
  in bands, 186–7, 238
America, 114, 158–9
  attraction of, 238–9
  Boehm flute in, 179–80, 193–5, 202–3, 204–5
  early music in, 253, 255–6, 258–9

education in, 264
flute clubs in, 279–80
flute-making in, 230–1, 239, 267, 270, 271
French Flute School in, 223, 228–9, 241, 243
Japanese flutes in, 268
jazz music in, 233–4, 274—5
recording industry in, 225–6
school bands in, 244
women flutists in, 237
Anciuti, Johannes Maria, 74, 80
Andersen, Karl Joachim, 141, 195, 196, 237
  works, 192, 193, 222
Andersen, Marguerite de Forest, 237
Andersen, Vigo, 195
Anderson, Ian, 275
André, A., 145
Annand, William, 153
Appelbaum, Stanley, 292
arab, see muslim
Arbeau, Thoinot, 30–1, 292
archaeology, 2–4
Aristotle, 22
Arita, Masahiro, 258, 259
Arlt, Wulf, 290
Armstrong, W. T., 244, 270, 271, 280
Arnold, Samuel, 120, 122
art, history of, 1–2
Artaud, Pierre-Yves, 221, 224, 240, 273
articulation, 26, 31–2, 36–8, 42, 72, 100–1, 113–14, 125
  double-tongue, 36, 101, 152, 153, 211
  French school, 211, 212
Artley Co., 244
Aschenbrenner, Friedrich, 104
Ashbee, Andrew, 294
Ashe, Andrew, 114, 119, 130, 135, 136
Astor, George, 134
Astor, John Jacob, 114
Athene, 3, 11
Attaingnant, Pierre, 45–6
Atterberg, Kurt, 204

Auber, Daniel-François-Esprit, 214
Augsbach, Horst, 89, 101, 304
Augustus II of Poland, 90, 98
aulos, 12
Aulos (trade name), 252
Aumont, Duke of, 75
Austria, 15–16, 115–17
  see also Viennese flute
avant-garde, 2, 272

Bach, Carl Philipp Emanuel, 98, 99, 110, 118, 123, 129, 130
  works, 197, 261
Bach, Johann Christian, 114
Bach, Johann Jakob, 86
Bach, Johann Sebastian, 49, 78, 81–2, 86, 90, 93, 94, 99
  band repertoire, 238
  recordings, 232, 233, 234
  revival, 192, 196–7, 199, 246–8, 249–51
Bach, Wilhelm Friedemann, 86–7, 102
Bacherelli, Vincenzo, 56
Baden-Württemburg, 43, 52, 109
Badger, Alfred G., 159, 179–80, 193, 194, 204
  method, 194, 318
Badollet, Frank, 204, 226
Bailey, John Robert, 197, 199, 320
Baillot, Pierre Marie François de Sales, 211, 216, 221
Baillot, Rode, and Kreutzer (violin method), 211
Bainbridge, William, 155
Baines, Anthony, 287
Baker, Julius, 241, 242–3, 264, 266, 273
Baldani, Vettorio, 56
Ballard, Christophe, 62
bands
  cinema, 188
  flute, see flute bands
  growth of, 200
  military, 114–15, 118, 186
Bannister, John, 70
bansuri, 1, 2, 11, 14, 26, 278–9
Bär, Frank P., 47, 56, 293
Barat, Emile, 215

Barbieri, Patrizio, 296, 307
Bärenreiter, 250
Barge, Wilhem, 191, 198, 249
Barnard, Ernest, 114
Barrère, Georges, 103, 204, 217,
    219, 222
  career in America, 228–9, 224
  editions, 251
  platinum flute, 239–40
  recordings, 225, 232–3
  relationship with Haynes, 229
Barone, Clement Sr, 226, 233
Barsanti, Francesco, 79
Bartels, Heinrich, 78
Bartolozzi, Bruno, 273
Bartuzat, Carl, 193, 233
Basie, Count, 233
Bassano
  Giovanni da, 55
  Jacomo da, 43
  Jacopo da, 39
  maker's mark, 47
  Santo da, 43
Bate, Philip, 112, *169*, 184, 185,
    210, 270, 287
Bauer, Johann Adam, 155
Bavaria, 15–16, 30–1, 46, 48,
    117–18
  see also Boehm, Theobald
Bayr, Georg, 150–1, 161, 196
Bayreuth, Margrave of, 98, 104,
    109
Beaudin, Jean-François, 257
Becker, Janet, 124
Beecham, Sir Thomas, 236
beer-fiddlers, 90
Beethoven, Ludwig van, 115, 118,
    136
  in repertoire, 192, 197, 214,
    234
  orchestral writing, 150–1
  recordings, 221, 225
  works, 116, 141, 142
Bell, Kenneth, 327, 332
Belon du Mans, Pierre, 19
Benda, Frantiszek, 240
Benedict, Sir Julius, 192
Bening, Simon, *41*
Bennett, William, 243, 266, 268,
    281
Benoît, Marcelle, 299
Beowulf, 14
Berbiguier, Benoît Tranquille, 131,
    135, 136, 151, 152, 153
  method, 193, 212–13
Berdahl, Susan Marie Beagle, 179,
    318, 320–1
Berger, Karyn Ann, 332
Berio, Luciano, 272
Berliner, Emile, *see* Gramophone
    Co.
Berlioz, Hector, 147, 160, 174, 193
Bernier, M, 85
Bernoulli, Daniel, 154
Bernstein, Leonard, 240

Berteling, Theodore, 189, 195, 204
Bertie, Willoughby, 111
Bettoney, Harry, 203
Beuker, Jan Barend, 74
Beukers, Willem Sr, 74
Beznosiuk, Lisa, 258
B-foot, *see* flute's range, low
    extensions of
Biber, Heinrich Ignaz Franz von,
    32, *33*
Biblioteca Capitolare, Florence,
    47, 56
Bigio, Robert, 281, 320, 332
Bijlsma, Anner, 252, 256
Bilse, Benjamin, 195
Bingham, Tony, 255
Binkley, Thomas, 290
Bishop, Sir Henry Rowley, 192,
    225
Bizey, Charles, 74, 113, 121
Blaisdell, Frances, 237, 243, 251
Blanquart, Gaston, 221, 232
Blavet, Michel, 62, 82–4, 86, 94,
    95, 101, 103, 107, 127
  revival, 240, 218, 275
Blève, 167
Blochwitz, Johann Martin, 77, 78,
    94, 102, 103
Blumer, 197
Bodky, Erwin, 251
Boehm flute
  alto, 185
  chronology, 177
  cylinder, 160, 161, *165*, 180–5
  in early music, 259, 261–2, 276
  mechanism, *168*
  objections to intonation, 149
  objections to tone, 158, 190–2
  official at Conservatoire,
    214–15
  piccolo, 185
  rejected by Conservatoire,
    174–6
  ring-key, 157–9, 161, *165*, 269
  schema, 185
Boehm & Greve, 161, *165*, 166,
    170, 176–7, 181–2
Boehm & Mendler, *165*
Boehm, Jakob, 166
Boehm, Theobald [Jr], 183
Boehm, Theobald, 106, 134, 141,
    142–3, 164–85, *181*
  early life, 164–7
  Essay, *168*, 206, 316
  iron and steel, 167, 170, 176,
    180
  noted by Grenser, 155
  works, 192, 214, 226
  see also Boehm & Greve
Boehm, Wilhelm, 183
Bogner, Ferdinand, 151, 196
Bohemia, 22–3
Boie, Johann Friedrich, 112, 122
Boismortier, Joseph Bodin de, 84
Boivin, François, 84

Bolanath, Prasana, 279
Boland, Janice Dockendorff, 310,
    324
Bolling, Claude, 274
Bonaparte, Louis, 147
Bonaparte, Napoleon, 137, 152
Bonnart, Nicolas, 64
Bonnart, Robert, *64*
Bonneville, Auguste, 202, 215
Bonnières de Souastre, Adrien-
    Louis, 117
Bononcini, Giovanni Battista, 70
Bonta, Stephen, 296
Boosey & Co., 160
Boosey & Hawkes Ltd., 244
Bopp, Joseph, 257
Borjon de Scellery, Pierre, 63
Borkens, Philip, 74
Boulanger, Nadia, 251
Boulez, Pierre, 244, 238, 240, 272
Bouys, André, *69*
Bowers, Jane, 20, 24, 27, 44, 61,
    210, 252, 289, 296, 297,
    298, 307, 324
Bowles, Edmund A., 289
Bracquemond, Marthe, 218
Brahms, Johannes, 193, 199, 220
Brain, Dennis, *242*
Brannen
  Bickford, 271
  Bob, 271
Brant, Henry, 279
Braun, Jean Daniel, 84
Breiden, Heinz, 233
Breitkopf, Johann Gottlob
    Immanuel, 115
Bressan, Pierre Jaillard, 63, 66, 70,
    74, 81, 113, 121, 262
Briccialdi, Giulio, 141, 162, 183,
    185, 189
  works, 192, 193, 215
Brinckman, Johannes, 253, 254
Britain, 19, 35, 43, 44, 47
  Adagio style, 110, 136, 138
  amateur flutists in, 110–12
  Bach in, 246–8, 251
  bands in, 186–7, 238
  baroque period, 68–70, 78–9
  Boehm flute in, 167, 177–8,
    183, 200–1
  classical period, 117, 119
  early music in, 256
  fife, 85–6
  flute making in, 81, *87*, 111–12,
    135–6, 159, 162–3, 2–3, 239,
    241, 266–7
  women flutists in, 237
Brix, 179
Broadwood, W. S., 167, 190, 215
Brögger, Johan, 271
Brolli, Marco, 300
Brooke, Arthur, 202
Broschi, Carlo, *see* Farinelli
Brossa, Jean Firmin, 187, 200, 215,
    247

Brown, Elizabeth, 274
Brown, Howard Mayer, 10, 20, 34, 39, 284, 290, 292, 293
Brown, John George, *194*
Brüggen, Frans, 252, 254–5, 256, 257, 258
Buffardin, Pierre-Gabriel, 78, 84, 86, 91, 93, 94, 95, 98, 101, 104, 107, 127
  and quarter-tones, 123
  recorded by Rampal, 240
Buffet, Auguste jeune, 156, 157, 161, 166, 167, 172–3, 176, 182, 200, 202
  patent, 174
  Boehm clarinet and oboe, 178
Bull, Sarah, 320
Bundy, George, 203, 230, 231
Bürger, Julius Max, 192, 252
Burghley, Dr R., 160, 161
Burgkmair, Hans, 30, *31*
Bürkly, Johann George, 147
Burmester brothers, 86
Burney, Charles, 88
Busch-Salmen, Gabriele, *see Handbuch Querflöte*
Butt, David, 281
Byrt, John, 102
Byzantine culture, flute in, *8*, 11, 12–13

cadenza, 124
Cage, John, 272, 273
Cahusac, Thomas the Elder, 87, 111–12, 113, 121, 122
Cameron, Roderick, 262
Campagnoli, Bartolomeo, 132
Campioni, Carlo Antonio, 118
Campra, André, 65, 70
Camus, Paul Hippolyte, 158, 159, 170–1, 175, 176, 177–8, 214, 249, 317
Cantigas de Santa María, 11, *18*, 19, 26
Capeller, Johann Nepomuk, 150, 161, 164
Card, William, 159, 161, 177, 189, 205
Cardano, Girolamo, 38
Cardigan, Cora, 237
Carse, Adam, 163, 287, 320
Carte, Richard
  1850, 1862, 1867 flutes, 162, 163, 192, *201*, 205
  and Boehm flute, 178
  history of the flute, 180, 286
  method, 174
  on equal temperament, 149
  patents, 189
Caruso, Enrico, 223
Carver, Wayman, 233
Casadesus, Robert, 224
Casals, Pablo, 223
Casella, Alfredo, 218, 250
Castel, 117

Castellani, Marcello, 292, 299, 306
Cavaillé-Coll, Aristide, 185
Cavally, Robert, 243
C-foot, *see* flute's range, low extensions of
Chaminade, Cécile, 192, 218, 226, 237
Champion, Max, 112
Chanan, Michael, 284, 326
Chapman, F. B., 244
charanga, 278
Charles II, 69
Charles VI, Holy Roman Emperor, 93
Charles X, Holy Roman Emperor, 180
Charpentier, Marc Antoine, 65, 70
Chartan, Jean, 224
Chaurasia, Hariprasad, 279
Chéron, André, 84
Cherrier, Sophie, 221, 224
Chambers, Colin, 281
Chevalier, 74
Chambille, Ernest, 215
Chambille, Gabrielle Pauline, 215
Cherubini, Luigi, 147, 174, 175, 178
chi, 11
Chopin, Frédéric François, 221, 226
chronology, 161–2, 176, 189
Chugg, Richard, 235
Ciardi, Cesare, 192, 193, 196
cinema orchestras, *see* bands
circus, Imperial Byzantine, 12
Claire, Robert, 258, 262
Clapton, Eric, 273
classical antiquity, 12
clefs, 52, 76, 296
  see also transposing
Clementi & Co., 135
Clinton, John, 161, 162–3, 200
  and Boehm cylinder flute, 1809, 182–3
  and ring-key flute, 159, *168*, 174, 178
  methods, 195, 313, 317
Close, William, 146, 161
Coche, Victor, 158, 159, *169*, 170–1, 173–4, 175, 177, 214, 317
Coldstream Guards, 114
Cole, Elmer, 266, 270
Collette, Buddy, 234
Collier, Thomas, 111, 113
Coltman, John W., 330, 332
Coltrane, John, 234
column of air, *see* air, column of
comma, *see* enharmonics; pitch of flutes; tuning systems
competition, 5
concertina, 148, 192
Concert spirituel, 82
Conn, Charles Gerard, 203–4, 231

Connix, 175
consciousness, 5–6, 8–9
Conservatoire, Paris
  foundation, 124
  methods and flutes adopted, 147, 159
  and Boehm flute, 174–6, 214–5
consort
  of flutes, 32, 44–6, *51*, 54
  of flutes in inventories, 43, 47, 56
  of flutes, popularity in France, 44
  mixed, with flute, 40–1, 44, *45*, 46, 49, *54*
Cooper, Albert, 241, 266–8, 270, 271, 280
Coover, James, 284
Corea, Chick, 234
Cornet, Louis, 74
Corrette, Michel, 81, 84, 107, 18
Cortet, Roger, 221, 235
Cotte, Roger, 253
Couesnon, Amédée Auguste, 215, 243, 268
Couperin, François, 65, 75, 102
  revival, 218, 249
court flutists, 60–3, 68, 69, 75, 82, 127, 164, 181–2
Cowell, Henry, 232
Crookes, David Z., 52
Crozat, Pierre, 75
Crunelle, Gaston, 221, 222, 223, 240
  recording, 232
Cundy-Bettoney Co., 230
Czerny, Carl, 152

Daily Advertiser, 81, 111
Damiani, 185
Damperre, Gui de, 16
Damrosch, Walter, 202, 228
dancing, 23, 62–3
Daufresne, J., 215
David, Ferdinand, 246
David, King, 12, 15
Davis, W. J., 159
Day, Timothy, 326
Deadman, Alison Patricia, 300
de Bacilly, Benigne, 62
de Berry, Jean, 24
Debost, Michel, 210, 221, 224, 243
Debussy, Claude
  Prélude, 217, 228, 233, 234
  other works, 197, 217–8, 272
de Coutelier, Debonneetbeau, 215
D'Eissenberg, George, 114
De Gregorio, Vincenzo, 63, 293, 296
de Grise, Jehan, 20
de Guines, Comte de, *see* Bonnières de Souastre, Adrien-Louis
Dejean, Ferdinand, 116, 117
De Jong, Edward, 192, 198

de Klerk, Jos, 252
de Labarre, Michel de, *see* Labarre, Michel de
Delaney, Charles, 259
Delangle, Georges, 221
de la Not, Mathurin, 43
Delerablé, Antoine, 74
Delius, Nikolaus, 206, 304, 306, 307
De Lorenzo, Leonardo, 279, 287
  works, 193
Delusse, [Charles], 123, 211
de Lusse, Jacques, 121
de' Medici, *see* Medici
Demersseman, Jules, 141, 196, 216
Demeurs, Jules Antoine, 158
de Michelis, Vincenzo, 192, 193
Denner, Jacob, 74, 80, 81, 113, 210o, 262
Dequeker, Eric, 252
de Reede, Rien, 252, 310
Descoteaux, René Pignon, 61–2, 65, 67, 72, 130
d'Este, Ercole, 39
d'Este, Ippolito II, 40
Deutsche Grammophon, 253
Deveau, Lewis, 267
development, mechanical, of the flute, 4–5, 145–63, 157–8
  by Boehm, 166, 167, 169–71, 184–5
  by Buffet, 166, 167, 172, 174
  by Gordon, 166-7, *168–9*, 170
  chronology of, 161–2, 176
development, progressive, 1–3, 4, 144–5
Devi, Annapurna, 279
Devienne, François, 103, 221
  method, 124, 125, 153, 211–12, 210
de Vos, Marten, *54*
d'Evreux, Jeanne, 20
de Vroye, A., 160
de Wit, Paul, 249, 321
Diabelli, Anton, 141
Dick, Robert, 271, 273–4, 275
Dihan, Désiré, *187*
Dikmans, Gregory Paul, 300
d'Indy, Vincent, 224
di-zi, 1, 11
Dobbins, Frank, 39, 294
Döbbler, Heinrich, 77
Dodd, John, 132
Dolmetsch, Arnold, 248, 253
Dolphy, Eric, 234, 274
Doltzflöt, 51–2
Domingo, Placido, 254
Donizetti, Gaetano, 214, 225
Donjon, Johannes, 215
Doppler
  Franz, 196
  Karl, 141
  works, 197, 225
Dorgeuille, Claude, 209, 214, 222, 224, 270, 323

Dornstätt, Anthony of, 30, *31*
Dorus, Louis [Vincent Joseph van Steenkiste], 221
  and Boehm flute, 158, 159, 170–1, 174, 175, 176, 214–15, 317
  G♯ key, 161, 172–3, 185, 189
  playing of, 184, 190
d'Orvieto, Giulio Cesare, 55
Dôthel, Niccolò, 113, 118, 124, 306
Dotzauer, Juste Jean Frédéric, 152
Douglas, Sir Charles, 184
Dresden Hofkapelle, 90, 94
Dressler, Raphael, 151
Drouët, Louis, 136–8
  and Boehm flute, 193
  methods, 150, 153
Dubois, 147
Du Buc, 67
D'Ucé, Jean Baptiste, 91
duck, mechanical, 100
Dudek, Gerd, 275
Dülon, Friedrich Ludwig, 104, 105, 123, 125, *128*, 307
  tone of, 126
Dülon, Louis, 104, 129
Dumon, 249
Dumont, 67, 74
Dunk, Susan Spain, 237
Duthaler, Georg, 292
Duverger, Nicolas, 211
Dvořák, Antonin, 197
Dwyer, Doriot Anthony, 281

Eagle, David William, 134, 310
early music, 88, 246–63
  performance style for, 136, 219–20, 246–8, 259–62
  on modern flute, 275–6
  Schmitz and, 253, 261
  see also historical performance
Eccles, John, 70
Eerens, Frederick, 74
Ehlich, Liane, 11, 24, 289
Ehrlich, Cyril, 327
Ehrlich, David, 179
Ehrlich, Robert, 329
Eichentopf, Johann Henrich, 74
Eidgenossen, 27
Einstein, Alfred, 251
Eisel, Johann Philipp, 87
Eliason, 200
Ellis, Alexander J., 148
embouchure
  coverage of, 190, 260
  hole of flute, 97–8, 113, 268
  mass production of, 230
  'reform', 235, 268, 279
Ems, Rudolf von, 15
encyclopaedia, 10, 51, 57, 105, 222, 235
Enesco, Georges, 223
England, *see* Britain

enharmonics, 38, 72, 83, 95–6, 120–1
  and equal temperament, 148–9, 212
  see also tuning systems
Eppstein, Hans, 299
equal temperament, *see* tuning systems
Eras, Rudolf, 255
Erdmann, Ludwig, 94
Ernst, Philip, 159, 179, 180, 184, 193, 204
Esterházy, Paul Anton, 118
Euler, Leonard, 154
Euler, Philip Otto, 150
Evangelistis, Franco, 273
extended techniques, 273–4

Fabre, Toussaint, 43
Fahrbach, Joseph, 193
false makers' marks, 123, 135–6, 200
fame, of flutists, 61, 72
  and gold flutes, 206
Fantin, Pierre, 43
Farinelli, 94
Farrar, Lloyd P., 313
Farrenc, Aristide, 171, 317
Fauré, Gabriel, 216
Fave, Antoine, 65
Fehling, Carl Heinrich, *89*
feints, 42, 295
Felchin, Caspar, 155
Feldman, Morton, 273
Female Half-Lengths, Master of, 44, *45*
Fenlon, Iain, 294
Fentum, Jonathan, 111
Ferneyhough, Brian, 273
Ferrabosco, Henry and Alfonso, 44
Festing, John, 79
fête galante, 75
Fétis, François-Joseph, 2, 171, 310
fiddle (medieval stringed instrument), 9, 10, 15, 21, 22, 24
fife, 28, 32, 34, 58–9, 85–6
  in America, 193, 279
  see also flute, military
Fischer, Carl, 195
Fischer, Johann Christian, 114
Fischer, Oskar, 199
Fitton, Judith, 332
Fitzgibbon, H. Macauley, 199, 287
Fleischhack, Johann Adolf, 90
Fleury, Louis, 216, 219, 262
  and early repertoire, 250
  encyclopedia entry, 222, 235, 323
  in U.K., 236
Florio, Pietro Grassi, 110, 111–12, 113, 122, 127
flute bands, 186, 238
flute, bass, 238

flute, body materials of
  Boehm and, 180
  carbon fibre, 272
  early, 16, 43
  ebonite, 194, 205
  gold, 205–6, 276
  gold plate, 203
  in England, 236–7
  in flute bands, 238
  in Lot workshop, 215
  platinum, 239–40
  silver, thickness of, 202
  wood vs. metal, 195, 202, 203,
    204, 205, 230, 238, *267*
flute choirs, 279
flute clubs, 229, 279–30
flute family, 1, 10, 14, 37
  see also sizes of flute
flute, military, 20, 21, 23, 27–39,
  51, 58–9, 114–15
  and Swiss mercenaries, 27–9
  cases of, *28*, *29*
  in Italy, 30, 38
  playing style and repertoire,
    31–2, *33*, 36
  special fingering of, 52
flute, structure of, 1, 5
  addition of keys, 111–12,
    119–21, 122–3
  classical, 112–14
  development, *see* development,
    mechanical
  early baroque, 63
  high baroque, 68, 74–5, 80
  medieval, 24
  military types, 30––1, 35
  Quantz type, 93, 94, 95–8
  renaissance types, 46–7, 58–9
  romantic, 150–2, 155
  Viennese, *see* Viennese flute
  see also experimental flutes;
    development, mechanical;
    Boehm, Theobald
flutes, experimental
  by Close, 146
  by Boehm, 181
  by Holtzapffel, 147
  by Tromlitz, 145
  keyless, 160
flute's range
  high extensions of, 101, 199
  low extensions of, 81–2, 101,
    194, 211, 239, 240, 276
  see also Viennese flute
Folkers, Catherine Eileen, 302
  see also Folkers & Powell
Folkers & Powell, 262
Folz, Ignazio, 177
Fontijn, Claire, 102, 304
Forkel, Johann Nikolaus, 129
Forni, Egidio, 162, 189
Förster, Christoph, 78
Forster, Georg, 46
Fortier, [Jean-Baptiste], 74
Fox, Paul, 202

France
  Bach in, 248, 250
  baroque, 71–4, 75–6, 82–5
  Boehm flute in, 170–6, 189–90
  classical, 107–8, 124
  consorts, 39–44, 45, 57–9
  fife in, 28, 31
  French Flute School in,
    208–23, 224, 235
  Louis XIV, 60–3, 64–7
  middle ages, 16, 19, 20, 23, 24
  romantic, 156, 158
Franceschini, Filippo, 193
Francis, John, 251, 256, 280
Franciscello, 94
Franck, César, 216
Frank, Jaap, 276, 284
Fransella, Albert, 143, 192, 196,
    204
  recordings, 225, 226
Frederick II of Prussia 'the Great',
    83, 88, 98, 99, 100, *102–3*,
    104, 110, 118, 154
  works, 249, 256–7
  recordings, 240
Frederick William I of Prussia,
    98
Freeman, Telejoe, 238
Frémont, Etienne, 67
French Flute School, 103–4, 207,
    208–24
  in America, 229
  in France, 208–23, 224, 235,
  in Germany
  see also tone of the flute;
    International style;
    Dorgeuille, Claude
Freytag, Johann Heinrich, 78
Friese, Christian Friedrich, 78
Frisch, Robert, 175, 200
Froment, *see* Frémont, Etienne
Fuller, Sarah, 291
Funk, Vera, 140
Furlanetto, Giuliano, 77
Fürstenau, Anton Bernhard,
    138–9, *140*, 141, 142, 190,
    286
  articulation, 152
  choice of instrument, 152
  fingering, 153
  opposition to Boehm flute,
    158
  works, 192, 196, 249
Fürstenau, Caspar, 138, *140*, 152
Fürstenau, Mortiz, 143, 159, 246
  and Boehm flute, 180, 190–1,
    196
Fux, Johann Joseph, 91, 93

Gabrieli, Andrea, 46
Gabrieli, Giovanni, 46, 54, 56
Gabrielski, Johann Wilhelm, 152
Gainsborough, Thomas, *108*
Galli, Raffaelo, 192
Galli-Curci, Amelita, 233

Galpin, Francis, 287
Galway, Sir James, 243, 254, 277,
    280, 332
gamut, 16–17, 35
Ganassi, Sylvestro, 38, 292
Gantenberg, Heinrich, 195
Gardiner, Sir John Eliot, 256
Gariboldi, Giuseppe, 193, 215,
    222
Gärtner, Jochen, 220, *265*, 326
Gasparini, Francesco, 93
Gaubert, Philippe, 143, 221–2,
    224, 225
  and classical style, 248
  in U.K., 236
  see also Taffanel-Gaubert
    method
Gautier, Pierre, 73
Gazzeloni, Severino, 240, 264,
    272, 273
Gedney, Caleb, 81, 112, 113
Geehl, Henry Ernest, 251
Gekeler, Kenneth, 244
Gemeinhardt, Kurt, 244
Genin, 232
genius, cult of, 22, 130–1
George III, 111
Gerber, Ernst Ludwig, 125
Gericke, Wilhelm, 202
'German' flute, 13, 20, 33, 44
Germany, 13, 20–3, 31–2, 127–9
  and Viennese flute, 152
  Bach in, 246, 248, 252
  baroque, 76–8
  Boehm flute in, 160, 190–2,
    195–6
  consorts in, 49–52
  cultural isolation of, 234–5
  flute-making in, 81
  French Flute School in, 235
  keyed flute in, 119–23, 188,
    200
  music publishing in, 115
  orchestral style in, 190–2, 198,
    206
  origin of flute, 23
  recorder movement in, 250–1
  tone in, 125
  see also Austria; Baden-
    Württemberg; Bavaria;
    Prussia; Saxony
Gerock & Wolf, 158, 160, 161,
    167, *168*, 177
Ghosh, Pannalal, 278
Giannini, Tula, 95, 156, 159, 173,
    176, 195, 249, 297, 312,
    317–8
Gilbert, Geoffrey, 214, 256
  and French style, 208, 236
Giorgi, Carlo T., 189
Girard, Adrien, 324
Giustiniani, Vincenzo, 55
Glareanus, 59
Glatt, Andreas, 257
Gleghorn, Arthur, 238

Gluck, Christoph Willibald, 118, 160
Godet, Peter, 114
Godfrey, Sir Dan, 187, 203
Godfroy, Clair aîné, 156
Godfroy, Vincent Hypolite, 172
  see also Godfroy & Lot
Godfroy & Lot, 147, 158, 172, 174, 176, 177
  license for cylinder flute, 183
  cylinder flutes in wood, 184
Godwin, Joscelyn, 14, 16, 23, 290, 293
Goldberg, Adolph, 206, 320
Goldstein, Martha, 271
Goodyear, Thomas, 194
Goossens, Eugene, 236
Gordon, James Carel Gerhard, 156–7, 158, 161, 166, 168–9, 170, 174, 205
  chronology, 177
Gorlier, Simon, 39
Gossec, François-Joseph, 147
Gould, Stephen Jay, 66
Gounod, Charles, 197, 237
Gradi, Pacol, 56
graduation rates, 222
Graf, Urs, *28*
Gramophone Co., 225
Granom, John Baptist, 79
Granom, Lewis Christian Austin, 113–14
Green, Les, 281
Greenberg, Noah, 244
Green Howards, 19th Yorkshire Regiment, 86
Gregory of Nazianzus, St, *8*, 12
Grenser
  August, 112–13, 122–3, 164, 252
  fake flutes by Otto, 123
  Heinrich, 123, 148, 150
  workshop, 112, 120, 122, 126, 130, 256, 262
Grenser, Karl, 148–9, 151, 156, 164, 198
Greve, Andreas, 166
Greve, Rodolphe, 159, 166, 178, 248
  see also Boehm & Greve
Griesling & Schlott, 155
Griffiths, Frederick, 222
Grinter, Michael, 277
Grove's Dictionary of Music and Musicians, 234
Gruskin, Shelley, 253
Gualdo, Giovanni, 114
Guards' Model, 188, *201*
Guidi, Peter, 326
guilds, 121
Guillemant, Benoît, 84
Guillou, Joseph, 116, 156, 213, 216, 221
Guimond, Claire, 258
guitar, diversity of, 14

Gümbel, Martin, 273
Gunn, John, 111, 126, 211
Gurlitt, Willibald, 235

Haake, Wilhelm, 151, 198
Habeneck, François-Antoine, 214
Hadden, Nancy Fenholt, 36, 293
Hadlaub, Johannes, 21
Haindl, Hans, 159, 180
Haka, Richard, 63, 65, 67
Hale, John, 111
Halévy, Fromental, 214
Hallé, Sir Charles, 187
Hamilton, Amy Sue, 150, 199, 320
Hamilton, Chico, 234
Hamilton, S. C. 'Hammy', 277, 332
Hammig, Friedrich, 122, 266
Handbuch Querflöte, 283, 288
Handel, George Frideric, 78–9, 85, 90, 91, 93, 94
  works, 192, 196, 197
  revival, 252
Handoville, J., 84
Harlan, Peter, 250
Harnoncourt, Nikolaus, 252, 253
harp, 10, 21, 24
  flute, voice, and, 15
  flute and, *194*, 218
Harrach, Franz, 122
Harris, Roger, 244
Harrison, George, 273
Harris-Warrick, Rebecca, 66
Hart, David, 258
Hart, Günter, 252
Hartmann, Christian Karl, 124, 130
Haskell, Harry, 329
Hasse, Johann Adolf, *92*, 94–5, 240
Hässler, Johann Wilhelm, 129
Haubenstock-Ramati, Roman, 273
Haydn, Joseph, 115, 118, 119, 122, 136
  orchestral writing, 150
  in repertoire, 214, 234, 249
Haynes, Bruce, 66, 75, 296, 302
Haynes, George Winifield, 189, 202, 230
Haynes, John C. & Co., 202, 204, 206
Haynes, William Sherman, 189, 194, 202–3, 204, 230–1, *239*, 281
  during depression, 239–40
  relationship with Barrère, *229*
  relationship with Medicus, *229*
  flute scales, 266–7
Hazelzet, Wilbert, 258, 259
Hechtl, Gottfried, 257
Heckel, Wilhelm Hermann, 198
Heidegger, Johan Jakob, 70
Heifetz, Jascha, 220
Heindl, Eduard Martin, 193, 202

Heinemeyer, C. or W., 196
Heinichen, Johann David, 91, 92–3, 94
Helin, Matti, 272
Hendrix, Jimi, 273, 275
Hennebains, Adolphe, *209*, 218, 220, 221, 261
  recordings, 225
Henrion, Charles and Jean Baptiste, 91
Henry II and Catherine de' Medici, wedding of, 39, 40
Henry VIII, 29, 32, 37, 43, 44, 49
Herfurth & Stuart method, 244
Hermann, Friedrich, 246
Héron, 67
Heron, Luke, 110, 112
Herrad von Landsberg, 15
Hettrick, William E., 34, 36
Hetzel, Jack, 244
Heupe, Michael, 275
hexachords, 35, 53
  see also mode
Hieber, Max, 270
Hi Henry's minstrel band, 203
Hindemith, Paul, 235
Hisakura, Kikuo, 268
His Master's Voice, 226, 232, 236
historical performance, 2, 4
  instruction in, 251, 254, 258–61
  see also early music
Hoffmann, Leopold, 252
Hoffmeister, Franz Anton, 115
Hogenhuis, Jelle, 270–1
Hogwood, Christopher, 254
Hohenzollern, Prince Friedrich Leopold the Younger, 105
Holborne, Anthony, 49
Höller, Günter, 254, 256
Holst, Gustav, 204, 238
Holtzapffel, Jean Daniel, 147, 155, 161
Honneger, Arthur, 218
Horn, Paul, 234, 274
Horowitz, Vladimir, 254
Hotteterre family, 65, 66, 67
Hotteterre flute, 63, 66–7, 74, 249, 257
Hotteterre, Jacques Martin 'le Romain', 62, 66, 72, 73, 74, 75
  works, 252
Hotteterre, Martin, 67, 74
Houston, Janet, 310
Howe, Charles T., 204, 286
Howell, Thomas, 273
Hubbard, Frank, 255
Hudson, Elgar (Winifred), 237
Hudson, Eli, 192, 236
  recordings, 226
Huë, Georges, 218
Hughes, Meirion, 327
Hugot, Antoine, 210, 211, 212, 221
Hugot & Wunderlich method, 132, 147, 153, 159, 210, 212, 216

Hulliger model (Haynes), 204
Hummel, Johann Nepomuk, 152, 192, 197, 214
Hünteler, Konrad, 258, 261–2, 329
Huskinson, John, 298
Hyde-Smith, Christopher, 280
Hylands, R. W., 313

Ibert, Jacques, 218, 252
Il Contadino, 56
improvisation
  in jazz music, 234, 274
  in monophonic music, 21
  Minnesänger and, 21
  on military flutes, 31–3
  troubadours and, 14–15
  see also prelude; cadenza
index foot, 95–7, *116*
Infante, manuel, 218
instruction books
  Agricola, 33–6
  Alexander, 136
  Altés, 216, 22
  Arnold, *120*
  avant-garde, 273
  Badger, 194
  Berbiguier, 212–13
  Carte, 174
  Clinton, 195
  Delusse, 123, 211
  Devienne, 124–5, 211–12
  Drouët, 150
  Eisel, 87
  Fürstenau, 152, *153*
  Granom, 113
  Gunn, 126, 211
  Heron, 110
  Hotteterre, 72–3
  Howe, 204
  Hugot & Wunderlich, 147, 210
  Italy, 192–3
  Jambe de Fer, 35, 39
  Le Roy, 224
  Lindsay, 132
  Majer, 87
  Moyse, 223, *223*
  Nicholson, 136
  Prelleur, 112
  Quantz, 80, 81, 88, 100–3
  school, 244
  Taffanel & Gaubert, 219–20, 221–2, 223, 224
  Tromlitz, 120
  Tulou, 159
  twentieth-century, 264–5
  Virdung, 33–6
  Virgiliano, 55
International style, 208, 268–70, 273
interpretation
  of music, 130–1
  of early music, *see* early music
  of history, 5–6, 7–11, 88–9
intonation, 82, 216, 266–7
  low standards, 205

in early recordings, 228
see also tuning systems; sensitive note
Ireland (flutist), 154
'Irish' flute, 2, 14
Italy, 19
  baroque, 79–80
  classical, 118
  consorts, 39, 46, 47, 49, 56
  nineteenth-century, 188
  military flute, 29–30, 38
  ricercate, 55

Jackson, Gerald, 188, 236, 265, 266, 327
Jackson, Harold, 242
Jaeger, Christian, 270
Jaeger, Henry, 206
Jambe de Fer, Philibert, 35, 39, 41–2, 53, 292
James, Cecil, *242*
James, William Nelson, 135–6, 192, 285
janissary band, 115
Japan, 244, 252, 268
Jaspar, Bobby, 234
jazz music, 233–4
Jenkins, David, 324
Jerome, Richard W., 267
Joachim, Joseph, 195, 220
John, Elton, 234
Jolivet, André, 240, 273
jongleur, *see* minstrel
Juillot, Djalma, 189
Julius II, Pope, 29
Jullien, Louis George Maurice Adolphe Roch Albert Abel Antonio Alexandre Noe Jean Lucien Daniel Eugène Joseph-le-brun Joseph-Barème Thomas Thomas Thomas-Thomas Pierre Arbon Pierre-Maurel Barthelemi Artus Alphonse Bertrand Dieudonne Emanuel Josué Vincent Luc Michel Jules-de-la-plane Jules-Bazin Julio César, 200, 204
just intonation, *see* tuning systems

Kähönen, Matti, 272
Kaiser, Karl, 258
Kaleve, Gustave, 192
Kalkbrenner, Friedrich, 152
Kanji, Ricardo, 258
Karl Theodor von der Pfaltz, *109*
Kastner, Georg, 118
Keiser, Reinhard, 70
Keller, Fortunato, 82
Keller, Karl, 150
Kempf, Françoise, 218
kena, 1
Kenton, Stan, 234, 274
Kiesewetter, Johann Friedrich, 90

Kincaid, William, 208, 231, 241, 265
King, Carol, 234
Kingma, Eva, 271–2
Kirby, Percival R., 316
Kirk, Roland, 234, 274
Kirnbauer, Martin, 300
Kirnberger, Johann Philipp, 129
Kirst, Friedrich Gabriel August, 105, 120, 130, 252, 256, 258
Kite-Powell, Jefferey T., 294
Kitty, Arthur, 243
Klemperer, Otto, 251
klezmer, 277–8
Klosé, Hyacinthe Eléonore, 187
Klughardt, August, 197
Kneller Hall, 186
knickers, 14
Knighton, Tess, 294
Knuf, Frits, 260
Kobayashi, Yoshitake, 299
Koch, Stephan Sr, 150, 155, 161, 188
Kodowski, Georg Wilhelm, 104
Koehler, Ernesto, 193
Kotato & Fukushima, 270
Körber, Günter, 255
Koury, Daniel J., 320
Koussevitsky, Serge, 202, 243
Krakamp, Emanuele, 192
Krantz, Larry, 280
Krause, Christian Gottlob, 104
Kreisler, Fritz, 220, 223
Kreitzer, Amy Shaw, 306
Kreutzer, Rodolphe, 193
Krishna, 11
Krueger, Christopher, 258
Krüger, Karl, 159
Kuhlau, Friedrich, 141, 150, 151–2, 170, 178, 205, 234, 249
  works, 192, 197, 199
Kuijken, Barthold, 252, 257, 263, 275, 329
Kuiper, Dirk, 271
Kujala, Steve, 274
Kujala, Walfrid, 280, 332
Kukala, Roman, 196, 235
Kummer, Friedrich August, 152
Kusser, Johann Sigismund, 65, 70
Kyle, John A., 179

Labarre, Michel de, 61, 65, 66, 71–2, 85, 108, 298
La Berge, Anne, 274
Lafleurance, Léopold, 218, 224
Lahou, Jean-François, 158
Lainez, Alexandre, 61
Lallemant, Mathieu, 60
Lalo, Edouard Victor Antoine, 234
Lambert, Johann Heinrich, 154
Landowska, Wanda, 251
Landsknechte, 27
Lang, Hannah, 327
Langer, 150
Lanier, Henry, 44, 49

Lanier, Sidney, 204
La Riche, François, 70
Larrabee, James D., 159, 161, 179
Larson, Rhonda, 275
Lasocki, David, 44, 47, 254–5,
    284, 293, 294, 296, 300,
    326
Lasso, Orlando di, 46
Lateef, Yusef, 234
La Tour, Peter, 70
Laurent, Claude, 147, 159, 161, 171
Laurent, Georges, 202, 220, 229,
    232, 243, 251
Lavignac, Albert, 222
Lavoix, Henri, 160
Laws, Hubert, 234
Lax, Frederick, 204
Lazzari, Gianni, 15–16, *54*, 292,
    320
Leavis, Ralph, 229
Lebret, Louis Léon Joseph, 215
Le Breton, 67
Leclair, Jean Marie, 84, 240, 252
Leclerc, Jean Nicolas, 74, 121
Leduc, Alphonse, 223
Lefèvre
    François, 167
    Martial, 215
Leff, Jack, 270
legal rights of musicians, 20
Le Jeune, Henri, 57
Lemmone, John, 192, 226
Leonhardt, Gustav, 252, 253, 256
le Roi, Adenet, 16
Le Roy, René, 209, 224, 236, 323
    recordings, 231
Levi, Hermann, 191
Libin, Laurence, 289
Liebel, Wilhelm, 152, 188
Liebeskind, Georg Gotthelf, 104
Liebeskind, Johann Heinrich, 154,
    211–2
Liège, Jacques de, 26
Life Dragoons, Hessian Regiment
    of, 114
Limbourg brothers, 24
Lind, Jenny, 143
Lindbauer, Joseph, 192
Linde, Hans-Martin, 252, 253, 258
Lindpaintner, Peter Josef von, 215
Lindsay, Thomas, 132, 136, 156
Lissieu, 63
List, Erich, 199, 235
Liszt, Franz, 193
literacy, musical, 13, 33–4, 55
Lloyd, Peter, 260–1
Loeillet, Jean Baptiste 'John
    Loeillet of London', 70, 78,
    79
Loeillet, Jacques [Jacob], 84
L'Oiseau-Lyre, 254
Lot, Gilles, 121
Lot, Isidor, 215
Lot, Louis, 195, 266
    customers, 215

flutes a marker of French style,
    202–3, 235, 236, 244
models, 189–90, 215, 249
rebuilding of flutes by, 268,
    276
Lot, Thomas, 74, 87, 113, 120, 121,
    262
Lotti, Antonio, *89*, 91
love, the flute and, 22, 64–5
Lucas, 82, 107, 127
Ludovic, 43
Lufsky, Marshall, 226
Lully, Jean-Baptiste, 60, 62, 65,
    66
Lustig, Roger, 307
Lynden, Patricia, 281
Lyndon-Jones, Maggie, 47
Lynn, Michael, 258
Lyon, 39–43

Macgillivray, James A., 178, 287
MacGregor, 161
Machaut, Guillaume de, 22–3
Machon, Edmond K., 267
Maderna, Bruno, 273
Madison, James, 147
Mahaut, Antoine, 95
Mahillon, & Co., 160
Mahler, Gustav, 199
Maintenon, Madame de, 60, 75
Majer, Joseph Christophe
    Friedrich Bernhard Caspar,
    81, 87
Mancini, Henry, 234
Mangelsdorff, Emil, 275
Mann, Herbie, 234, 274
Maquarre
    André, 202, 203
    Daniel, 202
Marais, Marin, 65, 72, 249, 252
Marcello, Benedetto, 218
Marcil, Philip H., 231
Maria of Hungary, 43
Mariano, Joseph, 266
Marion, Alain, 221, 224, 243
Markham, Gervase, 236
Marshall, Robert L., 299
Martinů, Bohuslav, 218
Masel, Andreas, 313, 317
Masnet, Guillaume, 43
Mason, John, 81
Massenet, Jules, 216
Mather, Betty Bang, 254, 259, 280
Matsudaira, Yortitsune, 273
Mattheson, Johann, 76
Matuz, Istvan, 274
Maximilian I, Holy Roman
    Emperor, 30
Maybrick, William, 155
Maynard, William, 327
McCutchan, Ann, 324
McDowell, Lenny, 275
McGegan, Nicholas, 256
McKenna, John, 277
McMahon, Brendan, 277

McVeigh, Simon, 117, 306
Mead, Sarah, 294
Meadow, Mark, 260
Mecklenburg-Strelitz, Duke of,
    105
Medici
    Catherine de', 39, 40
    Cosimo de', 39
    loans of flutes, 56
    Lorenzo 'il Magnifico' de', 30
    Piero di Cosimo de', 30
Medicus, Emil, 204, 222, 229,
    230, 280, 284
Mehul, Etienne-Nicolas, 147
Meinell, William R., 194, 206
Melba, Dame Nellie, 143, 225, 226
Melij, Pietro, 49
menali, 11
Mendelssohn Bartholdy, Felix,
    151, 220, 225
Mendler, Carl, *165*, 185
Menestrier, Claude, 59
Mengenberg, Konrad of, 20–1
Merry, Jan, 218
Mersenne, Marin, 57–9, 295, 296
Merulo, Claudio, 54
Messiaen, Olivier, 273
Metzler, Martin, 252
Metzler, Valentine, 155
Meyer, Heinrich Friedrich, 188,
    189
Meyer flute, 190, *194*, 199, 200,
    203, 206, 207, 235
    see also Meyer, Heinrich
    Friedrich
Meyerbeer, Giacomo, 214
Meylan, Raymond, 12, 58–9, 244,
    269, 288
Michel, Winfried, 101, 304
middle ages, 7–26
    classification of flute in, 23
    flute's repertoire in, 7, 10
MIDI, 148
Mielich, Hans, 46
Migot, Georges, 218
Milan, Susan, 281
Milhouse, William, 121, 135
Miller, Dayton Clarence, 166, *182*,
    206
    collection, 181, 184, 283, 284
Miller, George, 161, 180
Miller, Leta E., 123, 307
Miller, Sandra, 258
Minnesänger, *see* minstrel; impro-
    visation
minstrel, 10, 13, 20, 23
    see also troubadours
Miyazawa, 244, 268
mode, 17, 42, 47, 49–50, 53, 57,
    63
Moderne, Jacques, 44
Modulationsfähigkeit, 156, 190
Moeck, Hermann, 250, 252, 254,
    255
Moldenit, Joachim von, 98, 101

Molé, Charles, 195, 202, 239
Molique, Bernard, 143, 192
Mollenhauer
    Conrad, 255
    Konrad, 198
    Thomas, 185
Molloy, Matt, 277
Mönnig
    Moritz Max, 188, 198–9
    Otto, 188, 198, 235
    Wilhelm August, 200
Montagu, Jeremy, 284, 288, 290
Montéclair, Michel Pignolet de,
    62
Monteux, Pierre, 202
Monteverdi, Claudio, 54
Montgomery, William Layton, 324
Montgomery Ward, 195
Monzani
    Tebaldo, 135, 137, 153, 161
    Theobald P., 179
    W. J., 149
Moody, James, 234
Moore, Jack, 270
Moravia, Jerome of, 17, 24
Morell, Roger, 90
Morelli, Jacopo, 94
Morgan, Fred, 257
Morley, Thomas, 49
Morris, Gareth, 237, 238, 241, *242*,
    251, 266
Moskovitz, Harry, 243
Most, Sam, 234
Mower, Mike, 275, 278
Moyse, Marcel, 140, 143, 238,
    268, 281
    and vibrato, 220
    influence, 224, 235, 243, 244,
        252
    recordings, 231–2
    studies, 221, 223
    teaching, 222–4, 260–1, 265,
        324
Mozart, Wolfgang Amadeus,
    109–10, 115, 118–19, 136,
    307
    Die Zauberflöte, 126, 129, 131
    orchestral writing, 145, 150
    recordings, 226, 232, 233, 240
    supposed dislike of flute, 116–7
    works in repertoire, 196, 197,
        205, 214, 234, 249
Muffat, Georg, 102
Müller, August Eberhard, 131, 212
Müller, Georg, 104, 196, 206, 249
    on vibrato, 235
    recordings, on early flute, 233,
        249
multiphonics, 150
Munch, Charles, 202
Munrow, David, 256, 290
Muramatsu, Koichi, 244, 268
Murchie, Robert, 236, 241, 266
Murray, Alexander, 259, 270, *271*
Murray, Sam, 277

Musard, Philippe, 200
Musgrave, Thea, 274
Musical Times, see Scholes, Percy
music-hall, 187, 226
muslim, 19
myth, 3, 11
    Achilles, 13
    angels, 24, *25*, 60
    Hotteterre flute, 66
    King David, *see* David, King
    Odysseus, 15
    Potter and Gedney, 111–12
    Zeus, birth of, 12
    see also Pan

Naudot, Jacques-Christophe, 84,
    94, 107, 127
Naust, Pierre, 63, 67, 74, 80, 84
nay, 11
Nazis, 234, 254
Neel, Boyd, 251
Nelson, Susan, 326
Nemeitz, Joachim Christian, 75
Netherlands, The, 48, 56–7, 74,
    80, 252, 254, 270–1
Neuff, Augustin, 101, 104, 129
Neumeyer, Fritz, 251
Newton, James, 275
Nicholson, Charles [Jr], 103,
    133–5, 137
    and preludes, 136
    influence on Boehm, 167, 170
    methods, 153
    ornamentation, 136, *142*, 153,
        156
    successors, 177, 180, 190
    variations, 141
    works, 192
Nicholson, Charles Sr, 134, 161,
    178, 205
Nicolet, Aurèle, 235, 240, 258,
    264, 273
Niebelungenlied, 20
Nikisch, Arthur, 199, 241
Nippon Gakki Co., *see* Yamaha
Nolan, Frederick, 161, 166
Nonon, Jacques, 159, 213
Norman, Chris, 177
Norrington, Roger, 256
North, Charles, 226
notes sensibles *see* sensitive note
Nova Zembla, 48

Odysseus, 15
Oesch, Erwin, 279
Ogilvie, Thomas, 238
Oleskiewicz, Mary, 89, 93, 94, 97,
    98, 100, 299, 303
Olsen, P. E., 253
Olwell, Patrick, 277
Onslow, George, 197
opera
    in Dresden, 91–3, 95
    in Germany, 65
    in London, 70, 78–9, 94, 110

    in Paris, 65, 94, 215
Orazi, Giovanni Battista, 122, 150,
    307
orchestra, 206
    prestige of, 188, 192
    training, 198
    see also orchestral flute-playing
orchestral flute-playing, 135,
    144–5, 155–6, 188
    altered concepts of, 118–19,
        236–7, 241–3, 165–6
    distinct styles of, 188
    in Germany, 190–1
Orléans, Duke of, 75
Ormandy, Eugene, 241
Osiris, 11
Otten, Kees, 254
Otto, Johann Georg, 123
Ozi, Etienne, 147

Pacey, Arnold, 285
Paganini, Nicolò, 132, 143, 193
Page, Christopher, 7, 20, 24,
    289–30
Paisible, James, 70
Palanca, Carlo, 262
Pan, 11, 12, 13, 21, *209*, 272
Pandora Records, 271
Panon, 74
Pappoutsakis, James, 243
Paris de Montmartel, Mme, 84
Parke, W. T., 137
Parmenon, Michel, 270
Parrott, Andrew, 256, 296
Pask, John, 149
pastoral associations of the flute,
    11, 43
    see also Pan
Pasveer, Kathinka, 273
patents, 122, 161–2, 174, 179
    see also chronology
Patti, Adelina, 220
Paul, Jean, 131
Paulus, J. Friedrich, 200
Pearl, 268
Pellerite, James J., 273, 280
Pellisov, *see* Schafhäutl, Carl von
Penderecki, Krzysztof, 240
Pentenrieder, Benedikt, 161
Penville, Edith, 237
Pergolesi, Giovanni Battista, 240
Pessl, Yella, 233, 251
Petersen, Niels, 201
Petersen, P. N., 152, 155
Petri, Johann Samuel, 105
Petrucci, Gian-Luca, 320
Phalèse, Pierre, 44
Philbert, *see* Rebillé, Philbert
Philidor
    Anne Danican, 82, 84
    Pierre Danican, 75
Philip, Robert, 220, 227–8, 326
Philip II of Spain, 43
Phonograph Co., North American,
    225

photinx, 12
Picart, Bernard, 72, *73*
piccolo, 188, 226
piccolo, Basel, 279
Pierné, Gabriel, 218, 224
Pieroni, Leopoldo, 192
Piesche family, 65
Pillon, Jacques, 43
Pinder, Heinrich Franz Eduard, 198
Pinnock, Trevor, 25
Pinschof, Thomas, 270
Pisendel, Johann Georg, 98, 104
Piston, Walter, 232
pitch of flutes, 52, 57, 75, 80, 88, 93, 99
 adjustable, 150, 155
 change to 440, 204, 266–7
 early replicas, 255–6
 in bands, 238
 variable, 162–3
plagiaulos, 12
Playford, John, 62
Pleeth, Anthony, 256
Poerschmann, Johann, 74
Poeschl, Joseph, 192
poetry, the flute in, *3*, 16, 22, 30, 61, 84
Polk, Keith, 294
Pontécoulant, Comte A. D. de, 149, 175, 317
Popp, Wilhelm, 193, 199
Poppe, Theodor, 198
Porter, Andrew, 116, 259
Porter, Lewis, 326
Potter
 Henry, 162
 Richard, 112, 119, 121, 122, 123, 130
 William Henry, 147–8, 161
Pottgiesser, Heinrich Wilhelm Theodor, *144*, 146–7, 148, 155, 161, 166, 167
Poulenc, Françis, 218, 240
Powell, Ardal, 284, 285, 297, 299, 306, 307, 312, 329
 see also Folkers & Powell
Powell, Verne Q., 231, 255, 266, 267, 281
Pozzoserrato, Ludovico, 44
Praetorius, Michael, 46, 49, 50–2, 63, 295
Pratten, Robert Sydney, 160, 162, 163, 196
prehistory, 2–4, 11
 see also archaeology
prelude, 75–6, 123–4, 136, 307
Prestia, Ross, 280
Preston, Stephen, 256, 257, 263, 329
Prill, Emil, 195, 198, 199, 248
 gold flute, 206
 recordings, 233
 succeeded by Scheck, 235
progress

see development, progressive
Proser, 164
Prowse, Thomas, 178
Prussia, 98–100, 103–6, 249
Pryor, Arthur, 233
Pucelle, Jean, 20
Puglisi, Filadelfio, 47, 48, 292–3, 296
pulangoil, *see* menali
Pupeschi, M. Pupo, 198

Quantz, Johann Joachim, 38, 68, 77, 78, 79, 80, 81, 83, 84, 86, 88–106, *96*, 107, 114, 118, 120, 123, 124, 139
 biography, 90–101, 304
 composition style, 98–9
 design of flutes, 95–8, 99, 113
 influence, 103–6, 129, 304
 on intonation, 132, 146, 286, 287
 recordings, 233, 240, 252
 reputation of, 88–9
 study of flute, 91
 tradition cited, 195, 235
 -type flutes, 262
 Versuch, 88, 100, 249, 269
 works, 197, 256
Quantz, Justus, 90
Quatremère de Quincy, Antoine-Chrystostome, 173
Quentin, Jean Baptiste le jeune, 84

Rabaud, Henri, 202
Rabboni, Giuseppe, 150, 192
Rabelais, François, 39–40
Radcliff, John R., 189, 192, *201*, 205
Rafi
 Claude, 42–3
 Michaud, 42, 43
 flutes by, 48, 56
Rameau, Jean Philippe, 81, 85, 118
 revival, 216, 233, 249
Rampal, Jean-Pierre, 143, 205, 224, 264, 327
 dominates French school, 245
 editions, 251
 recordings, *226*, 244, 252, 274, 277
 repertoire, 218, 272
 supplants Moyse, 240, 223
 teaching, 265
Rampal, Joseph, 221
Rampone
 Agostino, 189, 203
 Teodoro Bonaventura, 188
Ranum, Patricia M., 62, 296
Rasmussen, Mary, 293
Rateau, René, 223
Rauch von Schrattenbach, Hans, 48
Ravel, Maurice, 204, 218, 223
RCA Victor, 232–3, 254
Rebel, Jean-Fery, 65

Rebillé, Philbert, 61–2, 65, 67, 72, 130
Rebour, Jacques, 84
recording, 225–8, 231–4, 236–7
 and increase of variety, 244
 and loss of variety, 225
 Rampal and, 240
 technology, 225, 231, 240
Redfern, E. Stanley, 203
Reform flute, 198–9, 235, 288
 see also Schwedler, Maximilian
Reger, Max, 197
Register, *see* index foot
Reicha, Anton, 116, 118, 152, 197
 quintets, 215, 234
Reichardt, Johann Friedrich, 88, 100, 129
Reichenberg, David, 258
Reichert, Matthieu André, 201
Reilly, Edward R., 88, 89, 98, 99, 104–5, 303, 307
Reinecke, Carl, 160, 197, 199
Reissiger, Carl Gottlieb, 215
Rémusat, Jean, 205
Renata of Lorraine, 46
repertoire of the flute
 air de cour, 57, 62, 63
 avant-garde, 272–4
 chamber ensemble, 85, 86, 115–15
 concerto, 84, 116–18
 consort, whole, 44–6, 50, 54, *57*
 consort, mixed, 49–50, *54*
 early, 196, 246–50, 256–7
 fantasy, 139–41
 in 19th-century France, 214
 in 20th-century France, 216–24
 in recordings, early, 225–6, 256–7
 in recordings, editable, 241, 244
 in recordings, electric, 231, 232–4
 jazz, 274–5
 middle ages, 5, 19
 military, 31–3
 poor quality, 154
 romantic, 150–4, 192–3
 solo sonata, 55, 93, 107, 110, 115
 solo suite, 71–2
 studies, 102–3, 192–3
 traditional, 276–9
 wind band, 114–15, 238
 see also voice, flute as accompaniment for; improvisation; opera; symphony
Ribock, Johann Justus Heinrich, 88, 113, 119–20, 125–6, 129, 130, 307
Rice, John A., 306
Richardson, Joseph, 160, 192, 200
Richter, Franz Xaver, 240
Richter, Hans, 248
Riedemeister, Peter, 269, 272, 299

Riegger, Wallingford, 232
Riemann, Hugo, 235
Rippert, Jean Jacques, 67, 70, 74, 84
Riszler, Thomas, 249
Rittershausen, Emil, 185, 192, 206
Rive, Claude, 215
Rivier, Jean, 240
Rizeffo, Giovanni Pietro, 43
Robinson, Trevor, 58, 296
Robison, Paula, 243, 281
Rockobaur, Mathias, 122
Rockstro, Richard Shepherd, 138, 139, 185, 200, 215
    on Boehm-Gordon, 174
    on equal temperament, 149
    patents, 189, 201, 205
    Treatise, 286, 310, 316–17
Rode, Jacques Pierre Joseph, 193
Rogan, J. Mackenzie, 313
Roger, Estienne, 71
Rognoni, Francesco, 55
Rohan master, 24
Röhler, Richard, 235
Romanino, Camillo, 193
Rönnberg, William
Roosen, Jean-Yves, 270
Root, Marten, 252, 258
Ropartz, Guy, 224
Rose, John Mitchell, 183, 189
Roset, 67
Rosseter, Philip, 49
Rossini, Gioacchino, 178, 214
Rostron, Roger, 259, 266, 281
Roth, Ernest, 251
Roth, Nancy Joyce, 258
Rottenburgh
    Godefroid Adrien, 257–8, 262
    Johann Hyacinth, 74
Rousseau, Jean-Jacques, 92
Roussel, Albert, 218
Rousselet, Jean, 67
royalty, the flute and, 23–4
    see also Frederick II of Prussia; George III
Rubinstein, Artur, 254
Rudall, Carte & Co. [Rudall Carte], 160, 189, 200, 266, 277
    in America, 202, 206, 230, 238
    in Britain, 236–7, 241
    platinum flute, 239–40
    see also Rudall & Rose; Rudall, Rose, Carte & Co.
Rudall, George, 178
Rudall & Rose, 143, 159, 161, 163, 166, 177, 178, 203, 205, 277
    licenses cylinder flute, 183
    see also Rudall, Carte & Co.; Rudall, Rose, Carte & Co.
Rudall, Rose, Carte & Co., 162, 205
    see also Rudall, Carte & Co.; Rudall & Rose
Ruge, Filipo, 124

Rumsey, Howard, 234
Rumslaut, Meister, 9

Sacchetti, Antoine, 181
Sacher, Paul, 251
Sachs, Curt, 11, 20, 251, 252
Sadeler, Johann, 54
Saint-Saëns, Camille, 160, 216, 232, 234
    works, 192, 197, 199
Salmen, Walter, 284
Salomon, Johann Peter, 119
Salzedo, Carlos, 228, 232
Sammartini, Giuseppe, 79
Sankyo, *see* Hisakura, Kikuo
Sapoznik, Henry, 332
Sassoli, Ada, 226
sausages, 230
Saust, Carl, 135
Sauvlet, Baptiste, 195
Savall, Jordi, 256
Savart, Félix, 170–1
Sax, Adolphe, 155, 205
Saxony, 88–98, 113, 196–9, 249
scale, 266–7
    quarter-tone, 123, 271
    see also intonation; gamut
Scarlatti, Alessandro, 70, 94
Scepeaux, François de, 43
Schaefer, Lois, 281
Schafhäutl, Karl Franz Emil von, 167, 171, 180, 317
Scheck, Gustav, 264–5, 288
    and early flutes, 251, 252, 253, 254, 257
    and French style, 198–9, 208, 235
Schein, Johann Herman, 49, 63
Schell, Johann, 74
Scherer workshop, 74, 87
Scherrer, Heinrich, 192
Schickhardt, Johann Christian, 76, 78
Schlegel, Christian, 74
Schmitz, Hans-Peter, 253, 2261, 264, 276, 288, 329–30
Schneider, Michael, 258
Schnietzhoeffer, Jacques, 211, 221
Schnitzer family, 47–8
Scholes, Percy, 321
Schönberg, Arnold, 252, 272
schools of flute-playing, 103–4
    English, 134, 136, *see also* Nicholson, Charles
    French, *see* French Flute School
    International, *see* International style
    Quantz, 103–6, 210
Schröder, Jaap, 252
Schubert, Franz, 141, 142, 234, 262
    in repertoire, 197, 249
    orchestral writing, 150, 151
    recordings, 240
Schultz, Stephen, 252

Schultz, Wolfgang, 273
Schultze, Bernhard, 310
Schulze, William G., 195
Schumann, Robert, 249
Schreck, Gustav, 249
Schröck, August, 151
Schuchart
    Charles, 81
    John Just, 81, 111–12, 113, 121
Schütz, Heinrich, 49, 50
Schwedler, Maximilian, 198, 246, 149
    on vibrato, 235
    patents, 189
    Germanic focus of, 234
    see also Reform flute
Schwedler & Kruspe, *see* Reform flute
Schweinfest, George, 225
scorn for the flute, 192, 228
Scott, Stuart, 319
Scott, Thomas, 161
Scottish Flute Trio, 274
screw-cork, 95–6
Sears Roebuck, 195
Séchet, Pierre, 258
Sedaka, Neal, 234
Sedlatzek, Johann, 151, 200
See, Janet, 252, 258
Seeley, Harry, 244, 281
Seffern, Ferdinand, 195
Seiffert, Wolf-Dieter, 307
Selmer
    Alexandre, 230–1
    Henri & Cie., 203
sensitive note, 131–2, 146–7, 213, 214, 216
Serkin, Rudolf, 243
Settala, Manfredo, 56
Shank, Bud, 233, 274
Shaw, George Bernard, 186, 205, 248, 249
Shihab, Sahib, 234
Shreffler, Anne Chattoney, 330
Siccama, Abel, 160, 161, 163
    patents 195, 200
Sieber, Ignazio, 79
Siebold, William, 231
Silbermann, Gottfried, 99
silver, flutes of, 16
    see also flute, body materials of
Silver, Millicent, 251
Simpson, Mary Jean, 320
sizes of flute, 21, 20, 24, 43, 56, 58, 80–1
Skousboe, Henning Andersen, 155
Skowronek, Felix, 281
Snickare, Lars, 29
Smilde, Rineke, 310
Smith, Anne, 53, 293
Smith, Catherine, 118, 306
Smith, May Lyle, 237
Socarra, Alberto, 233
Soldan, Kurt, 251

soldiers, *see* flute, military
Soler, Pedro Joachim Raymond, 178
Solum, John, 293
sonata, *see* repertoire of the flute
Song of Roland, 14
Sonny and Cher, 234
Sorge, Georg Andreas, 148
Sousa, John Philip, 203, 204, 226, 238
Soussmann, Heinrich, 130, 151
Southgate, T. Lea, 287
Spain, 19
    Philip II of, 43
Spell, B. Eldred, 310
Spitta, Philipp, 299
Spohr, Ludwig, 115, 132, 152, 154, 192, 197, 234, 249
Spohr, Peter, 284, 317
Spontini, Gaspare, 214
Stadler, John, 114
Stainer, Sir Charles, 251
Stamitz, Karl, 117, 240
Stanesby
    Thomas Jr, 74, 79, 112, 256
    Thomas Sr, 121
Stanhope, Erroll, 237
Sastny, Leopold, 2252, 254, 256, 258
Steffani, Agostino, 65, 70
Steig, Jeremy, 234, 275
Stepper, Gernt, 320
Sterne, Colin, 253
Stieber, Ernst, 255
Stimmer, Tobias, *3*, 44
Stivell, Alain, 277
Stockhausen, Karlheinz, 238, 273
Stolz, Erika [Erika von Klösterlein], 237
Stradling, Robert, 327
Strasser, Eustache, 202
Strasser-Marigaux Co., 215
Straube, Karl, 249
Strauss, Johann, 200
Strauss, Richard, 197, 199
Stravinsky, Igor, 223, 227, 234
Stricker, August Reinhard, 78
Stringfeld, Lamar, 276
Susato, Tielman, 44
Sutcliffe, Sidney 'Jock', 242
Suzanne, Philippe, 258
Suzuki, Shinichi, 265
Svendsen, Olaf, 201, 215
Swack, Jeanne Roberta, 299, 300
Swanson, Philip, 280
Sweet, Ralph, 277
Swiss Guard
    in Paris, 156, 166
    at Vatican, 29, 38
Switzerland, 27–9, 31, 35, 279
syagi, *see* tabla
symphony (compositon), 110, 116, 118–19, 130

see also works listed by composers' names
syrinx, 11

tabla, *29*
tablature, 33
Tacet, Joseph, 111-12, 113, 122, 127
Tachezi, Herbert, 256
Taffanel, Claude Paul, 103, 189
    and early repertoire, 196, 216–17, 249, 250
    and French Flute School, 208
    chamber music society, 196
    professor at Conservatoire, 216, 221
    promotes Barrère, 228
    students, 202
    works, 197
    see also Taffanel-Gaubert method
Taffanel-Gaubert method, 223, 323
Taillart, Pierre Evrart, 84, 127
Takahashi, Toshio, 265
Talbot, James, 70
Tanaka, Shuichi, 244, 268
Taruskin, Richard, 262
Tauber, Kaspar, 122
Taylor, Christopher, 266
Tchaikovsky, Pyotr Illych, 193, 199
Telefunken, 253, 254
Telemann, Georg Philipp, 38, 76, 86, 90, 101–2, 128
    recordings, 240, 252, 257
Terschak, Adolf, 143, 193, 200
Terton, Engelbert, 74
Tesi, Vittoria, 94
Teske, Hermien, 101
Tetrazzini, Luisa, 237
Thalheimer, Peter, 300
Thibaud, Jacques, 223
Thibouville-Lamy, J. & Cie., 189
Thomas, Mark, 280
Thomas, Theodore, 193, 195
Thomson, Andy, 328
Thomson, George,
Thomson, John Mansfield, 255
Thurn und Taxis, Carl Alexander von, 127
Thurston, Frederick 'Jack', 242
tibia, 12
Tibia, 255
Tieftrunk, Wilhelm, 199
Tilney, Colin, 256
Tillmetz, Rudolf, 191–2, 199
Tintoretto, 44
tonalities
    favoured by Nicholson, 135
    of Dresden works, 93
    of early repertoire, 53, 63, 65

of popular publications, 141
of studies, 123–4
tone of the flute
    and French school, 208, 212, 218–19, 223–4, 241–2, 270
    and International style 267–70
    and Italian vocal style, 97–8
    and Quantz school, 104
    classical, 112–13, 125–6
    in England, 134, 167, 236–7
    loudness of, 20, 134, 190, 245, 267–8
    negative comment on Boehm flute's 158, 204–5
    romantic, 131, 145
    silver?, 16
    variety of, 265–70, 273
    weakness of, 21, 98, 232
    see also Modulationsfähigkeit; vibrato
tonguing, *see* articulation
Toscanini, Arturo, 243
Tournier, Marcel, 218
Tourte, François, 132
Townley, Charles, 161
transposing, 17, 24–5, 34–6, 53, 76, 85
    flute by Close, 146
    see also clefs
traversa, 49, 55
Traverso, 248
Traynor, Leo, 252
Trichet, Pierre, 59, 295
Triébert, Georg Ludwig Wilhelm (Guillaume), 215
Tromlitz, Johann George, 38, 81, 88, 102, 105, 110, 111, 112, *116*, 119
    announcements, 166
    C key, 161, 170, 172, 184
    experimental flute, 145–6, 147, 148, 161
    methods 120–1, 123, 124
    on glide, 133, 150
    on intonation, 120–1, 132
    on touring, 128–9
    tone, 125, 265
troubadours, 14
Tudor, David, 272
Tulou, Jean-Louis, 132, 136, 137, 210, 213–15, 221
    flûte perfectionée, 161, 175, 214
    large tone, 190
    opposes Boehm flute, 149, 158–9, 174, 175, 214, 215
    works, 196, 216
tuning systems, 83
    equal temperament, 147, 148–9
    just intonation, 83
    Pythagorean, 25–6
    quarter-tone, 123, 211, 307
Türheim, Ulrich von, 15
Tutz, Rudolf, 257

Ulsamer, Josef, 256
uniformity, late 20th-century
    245, 253, 258, 263, 312–13
    see also International style
Urtext, 251, 260

Valentin, Dave, 275
Valin, Aimable, 221
van Aardenberg, Abraham, 74
van Aelst, Willem, 44
Vanderhagen, Amand, 124, 211
van der Werf, Hendrik, 290
van Eyck, Jacob, 56–7
Vanhall, Johann Baptist, 114
Vanhamme, 130
van Heerde, Jan Juriaenszoon, 74
van Leeuwen, Ary, 196, 199
    recordings, 226, 235
van Munster, Peter, 252
Vanotti, Luigi, 204
Varèse, Edgard, 232, 239–40, 272
Vaucanson, Jacques de, 100, 304
Vaughan Williams, Ralph, 238
Veillon, Jean-Michel, 277
Ventzke, Karl, 307, 312, 317, 320
Verdi, Giuseppe, 193
Vermeulen, Greta, 270
Vermeyen, Jan Cornelis, 44
Verroust, Denis, 284
Verzulli, Luca, 27, 32, 292
Vester, Frans, 212, 257, 258,
        259–60, 275, 276
    career, 252
writings, 285, 329, 332
vibrato, 36, 95, 98
    in Britain, 236, 241, 266
    in early repertoire, 248, 261
    in France, 219–20
    in Germany, 195, 198, 235
    on recording, 227–8, 232
Viennese flute, 150–2, 196, 200,
        278, 287, 288
Villa-Lobos, Heitor, 272
Villars, Paul, 121
Villette, H. D., 215
Vincent, Denis, 121
Virdung, Sebastian, 33–4, 292
Virgiliano, Aurelio, 55, 295
virtuosi, travelling, 127–43
Vivaldi, Antonio, 79, 84, 90, 240,
        249, 252
Vogt, Gustav, 116
voice, flute as accompaniment for,
        85, 143, 225, 226
Vollenweider, Andreas, 274
Volumier, Jean-Baptiste, 91
von Bülow, Hans, 195, 219
von Huene, Friedrich, 255–6,
        262

von Klösterlein, Erika, *see* Stolz,
    Erika
von Lascagno, Graf Peter Robert
    Taparelli, 93
von Pfersmann, Ludwig, 252
von Uffenbach, Johann Friedrich
    A., 73–4, 128
Vorhees, Jerry L., 312
Voxman/Gower method, 244

Wagner, Richard, 193, 196, 238
    and Boehm flute, 191
Walch, Georg, 74
Walker, Gordon, 236
Walker, Jim, 274, 326
Walsh, John the Elder, 70, 71, 76,
        79, 85, 93
war, *see* flute, military
Ward, Cornelius, 137, 159, 161,
        174, 177, 286
Waterhouse, Elmer W., 267
Waterhouse, William, 284, 293
Watteau, Antoine, 75
Webb, Chick, 233
Weber, Aloysia, 116
Weber, Carl Maria von, 138, 150,
        152, 196, 234
    orchestral writing, 150, 151
    works, 197, 214
Weber, Gottfried, 154–5, 161,
        170
Weber, William, 306
Weemaels, Alain, 257
Wegman, Rob C., 290
Wehner, Carl, 193, 202
Weichsell, Charles, 114
Weidemann, Carl Friedrich, 79
Weidner, 136
Weiss, Johann Sigismund, 78, 79
Weiss, Sylvius Leopold, 98
Welch, Christopher, *168*, 170, 172,
        215, 287, 289
    on Boehm-Gordon, 174, 317
Wells, Benjamin, 200
Welsh, Henry, 235
Wendling, Johann Baptist,
        109–10, 116, 117, 118, 127,
        130
Wentz, Jed, 258, 300
Wenzinger, August, 251, 258
Wess, Frank, 233
Wetzel, Werner, 270
Wetzger, Paul, 287
Wiener, Eugene, 193
Wiese, Henrik, 307
Wilhelm V, Duke of Bavaria, 46
Wilkes, Chris, 277
Wilkins, Frederick, 244
Wilkins, James S., 193

William and Mary, 69
Williams, Clarence, 233
Willoughby, Robert, 257, 258
Wilson, Ransom, 275
Wincenc, Carol, 281
Winkler, Anton, 257
Winter, Josef, 125, 129
Winternitz, Emanuel, 20, 24, 289
Woehl, Waldemar, 251
Wolff, Christian Michel, 102
Wolff, Christoph, 299
Wollaston, William, *108*
Wolpe, Stefan, 273
women, 195–6
    as flutists, *3, 45,* 50, 65, 84, 111-
        12, 281
    as flute makers, *see* Folkers,
        Catherine Eileen; Kingma,
        Eva
    as recording artists, 237–8
    excluded from paid positions,
        206
    in new music, 218, 274
Wood, James, 161
Wood, Sir Henry, 188, 237
Wummer, John, 231, 241
Wunderlich, Johann Georg, 147,
        211, 221
Wurlitzer, Edward H., 203
Wye, Trevor, 2009, 210, 243, 280
        324, 332
Wysham, Henry Clay, 203, 204,
        287

Yamaha, 244, 268
Young, Lester, 233
Young, Phillip T., 293, 312
Ysaye, Eugene, 220

Zacconi, Ludovico, 55
Zaslaw, Neal, 118
Zeisenis, Johann Georg, *109*
Zelenka, Jan Dismas, 91, 92,
        94–5, 99
Zervigon, Eddie, 278
Ziegler, Johann Joseph, 150, 188,
        190
Ziegler, Matthias, 271, 274
Zierer, Franz, 196
Zimmerman, Bernd Alois, 273
Zimmerman, Julius Heinrich, 192,
        198
Zimmerman, Wenceslao, 123, 139
Zohn, Steven, 102, 300, 303
Zoon, Jacques, 281
Zwaanenburg, Jacques, 271
Zwerchpfeiff, 33, *34,* 46, 47, 48
    see also flute, military
Zwerger, Michael, 151